ENCYCLOPEDIA OF SCIENCE

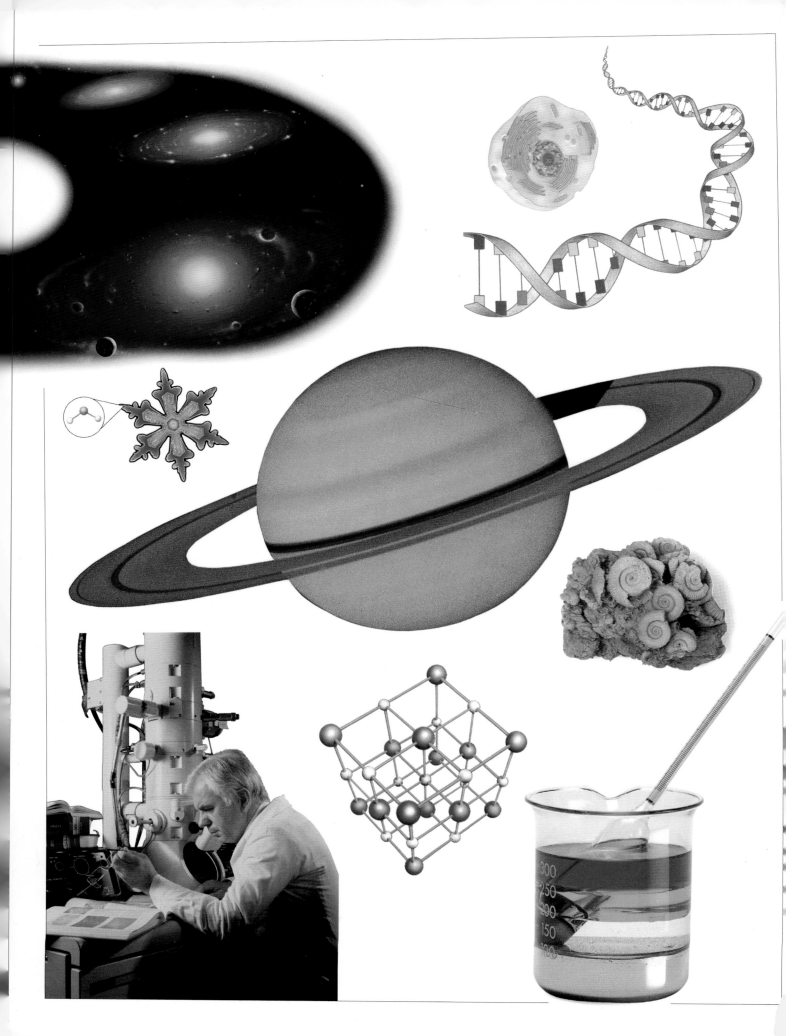

ENCYCLOPEDIA OF
SCIENCE

LONDON, NEW YORK,
MELBOURNE, MUNICH, AND DELHI

FIRST EDITION 1993
Senior Editor Susan McKeever
Senior Art Editor Martyn Foote
Editors Caroline Beattie, Helen Dowling, Linda Martin,
Mina Patria, Louise Pritchard, Jackie Wilson, Charles A. Wills (U.S.)
Art Editors Alexandra Brown, Wayne Holder, Marcus James, Rebecca Johns,
Carole Orbell, Tina Robinson, Simon Yeomans, Dominic Zwemmer
Managing Editor Sophie Mitchell
Managing Art Editor Miranda Kennedy
Picture Research Lorna Ainger, Caroline Brooke, Anne Lyons,
Catherine O'Rourke, Christine Rista
Production Louise Barratt, Ruth Cobb

THIRD EDITION 2006
Editors Jenny Finch, Rohan Sinha, Dipali Singh, Ankush Saikia,
Glenda Fernandes, Larissa Sayers, Shinjini Chatterjee
US Editor Margaret Parrish
Designers Kavita Dutta, Romi Chakraborty, Mini Dhawan, Enosh Francis
Managing Editor Linda Esposito
Managing Art Editor Diane Thistlethwaite
Publishing Manager Andrew Macintyre
Category Publisher Laura Buller
Picture Researcher Debra Weatherley
DK Picture Library Claire Bowers
Production Controller Seyhan Esen-Yagmurlu
DTP Designers Sunil Sharma, Balwant Singh, Pushpak Tyagi,
Harish Aggarwal, Govind Mittal, Pankaj Sharma
Jacket Designers Emy Manby, Johnny Pau
Jacket Editor Mariza O'Keeffe

Editorial Consultants
Heather Couper, BSc, FRAS, Hon. D. Litt; Nigel Henbest, BSc, MSc, FRAS

Contributors
David Burnie, BSc; Karen Davies, BSc PGCE; Dougal Dixon, BSc, PhD; David Glover, BSc, PhD; John Gribbin, MSc, PhD;
Mary Gribbin, BA; Ian Harrison, BSc, PhD, MBA; Robin Kerrod, FRAS; Peter Lafferty, BSc, MSc, PGCE;
Peter Riley, BSc, C. Biol, PGCE; Carole Stott, BA, FRAS; Barbara Taylor, BSc; Keith Wicks

Natural history consultant
Steve Parker BSc

Educational consultants
David Evans BSc, C. Biol, M. I. Biol; Kimi Hosoume BA

History of science consultant
Patricia Fara BSc, MSc

First American Edition, 1993
This revised edition published in the United States in 2006 by
DK Publishing
375 Hudson Street, New York, NY 10014

06 07 08 09 10 10 9 8 7 6 5 4 3 2 1
SD254 – 08/06

A catalog record for this book is
available from the Library of Congress

ISBN-13: 978-0-75662-220-6
ISBN-10: 0-7566-2220-4

Color reproduction by Colourscan, Singapore
Printed and bound by Toppan, China

Discover more at
www.dk.com

CONTENTS

145
ELECTRICITY AND MAGNETISM

177
SOUND AND LIGHT

209
EARTH

241
WEATHER

241
SPACE

305
LIVING THINGS

337
HOW LIVING THINGS WORK

369
ECOLOGY

401–425
FACT FINDER SECTION

426–433
GLOSSARY

434–445
INDEX

446
ACKNOWLEDGMENTS

HOW TO USE THIS BOOK

These pages show you how to use *The Dorling Kindersley Encyclopedia of Science*. The enyclopedia is divided into 12 thematic sections, such as Reactions and Living Things. Within each section are main entries on the subject, such as the Chemistry of Food or Reptiles. To find an entry, look on the Contents page, where the heading of each page is listed, or turn to the Index, which tells you which pages contain information on the subject you are looking up.

The index lists all the subjects in *The Encyclopedia of Science*, with the pages they appear on.

Each main entry is either one or two pages long.

The contents pages list each page subject under its thematic section head.

The 12-page index is at the back of *The Encyclopedia of Science*. The numbers refer to page numbers.

The page number in normal type gives general references within *The Encyclopedia of Science*.

The page number in **bold** type gives the main entry.

The page number in *italic* type gives pages in the *Fact Finder*.

SCIENCE THEMES
Information in the encyclopedia is arranged in a thematic way. Each entry gives detailed information on one topic, making it ideal for project work. Reading other pages in the same section enables you to explore and understand the subject fully. This page on Chemical Analysis is from the Reactions section. The words and pictures describe subjects such as Chromatography and Flame Tests in a clear and exciting way.

TIME CHARTS
There are four different time charts at the front of *The Encyclopedia of Science*. Each one has a theme: Matter, Energy, Earth and Space, and Living Things. The time charts trace the development of different branches of science, from the earliest times to the present day.

Atomic Structure tells you what atoms are made of.

Sources of Light explains why atoms give out light when heated—a method of identifying an element.

Genetics tells you how a chemical code in DNA makes each being unique.

Find out more

ATOMIC STRUCTURE P. 24
COMPOUNDS AND MIXTURES P. 58
SEPARATING MIXTURES P. 61
SOURCES OF LIGHT P. 193
GENETICS P. 364
FACT FINDER P. 404

FIND OUT MORE
There is a *Find out more* box in the bottom right-hand corner of each entry page. This box lists other pages in *The Encyclopedia of Science*, where you can find out more about your subject. For example, the *Find out more* box on the Chemical Analysis page lists six related entries and their page numbers.

The *Find out more* box on Sources of Light leads you to four related entries: Noble Gases, Chemical Reactions, Electricity Supply, and Color.

8

MAIN ENTRIES
The information on each page is presented in a way that makes it easy to understand what is going on. Start reading at the introduction, move on to the subentries, and then read the captions and annotations.

Introduction
Each main entry starts with an introduction that provides a clear explanation of the subject. After reading this, you should have a good idea of what the page is all about.

Subentry
A subentry is under the second-largest heading on the page. It examines aspects of the main entry in detail. For example, the subentries on Kinetic Theory are about diffusion and expansion, both important examples of kinetic theory.

Photographs
All the pages in *The Encyclopedia of Science* have photographs. This photograph of bromine diffusion was specially taken in a studio, so that you can see exactly what really happens.

Cutaway illustrations
Some pages have illustrations that reveal the insides of objects and living things. This illustration of a toadstool shows what it is made up of and how it works.

Special information boxes
On some pages, you will find information boxes that highlight particular aspects of a main entry. This box tells you about Brownian motion, which can be explained by kinetic theory.

Entry heading
This big heading at the top of the page describes a main entry.

Running head
This reminds you which section you are in. This entry on Kinetic Theory is in the Reactions section.

Maps
The maps in *The Encyclopedia of Science* give at-a-glance geographical information. For example, this map appears on a page about mountain ecosystems. It shows where the main mountain ranges of the world are.

Date boxes
Many pages have a date box. These give landmarks of achievement in date order. This date box appears on a page called Optical Instruments. It gives the dates of when the most important telescopes were built.

IMPORTANT TELESCOPES

1789 William Herschel telescope, England, 4 ft (1.23 m) diameter.

1845 Lord Rosse telescope, Ireland, 6 ft (1.83 m) diameter.

1917 Mount Wilson telescope, California, 8 ft (2.54 m) diameter.

1948 Hale Reflector, Palomar, California, 16 ft (5 m) diameter.

1976 Mount Semirodriki telescope, CIS, 19 ft 6 in (6 m) diameter.

1992 Keck telescope, Hawaii, 33 ft (10 m) diameter.

Captions and annotations
Every illustration has a caption. They often have annotations (in *italics*) as well. These point out important details within an illustration or photograph.

Illustrations
Most pages in *The Encyclopedia of Science* contain clear, detailed illustrations that help you to understand scientific concepts.

Biographies
Many pages contain biographical details of notable scientists and inventors. Biographies tell you about the life of the scientist or inventor, when they lived, and what they did.

FACT FINDER
The *Fact Finder* pages at the back of *The Encyclopedia of Science* are packed with useful charts, facts, and figures on all the topics in the encyclopedia. These pages are from the Reactions section.

A chart shows you the reactivity series and illustrates what happens to different metals when they are mixed with various substances.

The gas laws are clearly stated and illustrated.

The different laws for identifying gases are explained.

A table shows you what endings and prefixes of chemical names mean.

The chemical equipment you might use in a science laboratory is illustrated and explained.

ABBREVIATIONS
Some words are abbreviated (shortened) in *The Encyclopedia of Science*. The following list explains what the abbreviations stand for:

°C = degrees Celsius

°F = degrees Fahrenheit

mm = millimeter

cm = centimeter

m = meter

km = kilometer

sq km = square kilometer

km/h = kilometers per hour

g = gram

kg = kilogram

l = liter

in = inch

ft = foot

yd = yard

mph = miles per hour

oz = ounce

lb = pound

c. before a date = about

CE = common era

BCE = before common era

DISCOVERING MATTER

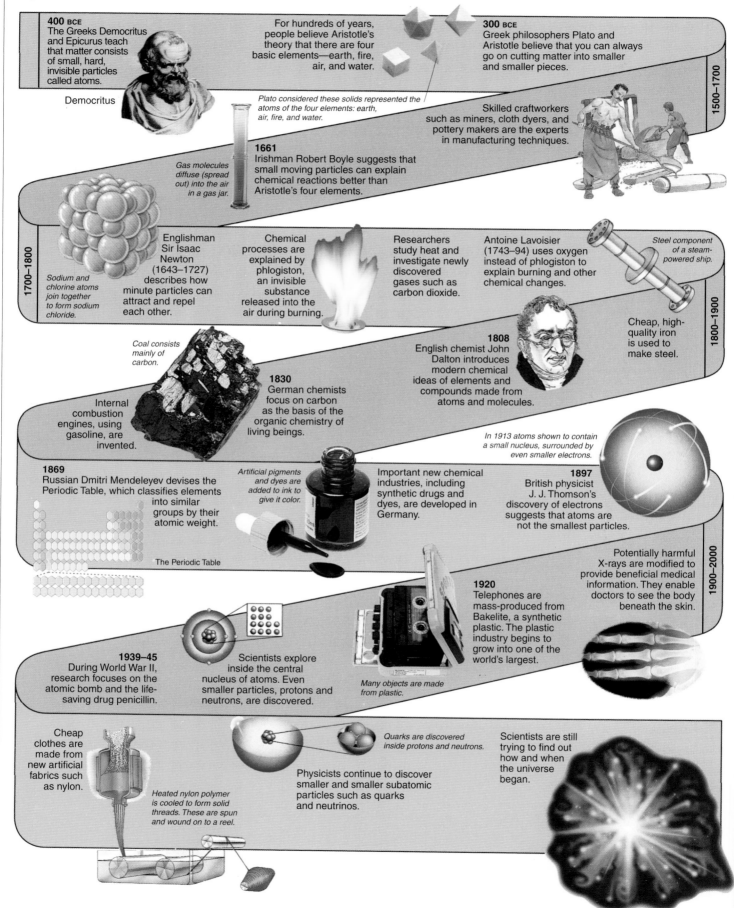

400 BCE
The Greeks Democritus and Epicurus teach that matter consists of small, hard, invisible particles called atoms.

Democritus

For hundreds of years, people believe Aristotle's theory that there are four basic elements—earth, fire, air, and water.

300 BCE
Greek philosophers Plato and Aristotle believe that you can always go on cutting matter into smaller and smaller pieces.

Plato considered these solids represented the atoms of the four elements: earth, air, fire, and water.

Skilled craftworkers such as miners, cloth dyers, and pottery makers are the experts in manufacturing techniques.

Gas molecules diffuse (spread out) into the air in a gas jar.

1661
Irishman Robert Boyle suggests that small moving particles can explain chemical reactions better than Aristotle's four elements.

Sodium and chlorine atoms join together to form sodium chloride.

Englishman Sir Isaac Newton (1643–1727) describes how minute particles can attract and repel each other.

Chemical processes are explained by phlogiston, an invisible substance released into the air during burning.

Researchers study heat and investigate newly discovered gases such as carbon dioxide.

Antoine Lavoisier (1743–94) uses oxygen instead of phlogiston to explain burning and other chemical changes.

Steel component of a steam-powered ship.

Cheap, high-quality iron is used to make steel.

Coal consists mainly of carbon.

Internal combustion engines, using gasoline, are invented.

1830
German chemists focus on carbon as the basis of the organic chemistry of living beings.

1808
English chemist John Dalton introduces modern chemical ideas of elements and compounds made from atoms and molecules.

In 1913 atoms shown to contain a small nucleus, surrounded by even smaller electrons.

1869
Russian Dmitri Mendeleyev devises the Periodic Table, which classifies elements into similar groups by their atomic weight.

Artificial pigments and dyes are added to ink to give it color.

Important new chemical industries, including synthetic drugs and dyes, are developed in Germany.

1897
British physicist J. J. Thomson's discovery of electrons suggests that atoms are not the smallest particles.

The Periodic Table

Potentially harmful X-rays are modified to provide beneficial medical information. They enable doctors to see the body beneath the skin.

1920
Telephones are mass-produced from Bakelite, a synthetic plastic. The plastic industry begins to grow into one of the world's largest.

1939–45
During World War II, research focuses on the atomic bomb and the life-saving drug penicillin.

Scientists explore inside the central nucleus of atoms. Even smaller particles, protons and neutrons, are discovered.

Many objects are made from plastic.

Cheap clothes are made from new artificial fabrics such as nylon.

Heated nylon polymer is cooled to form solid threads. These are spun and wound on to a reel.

Quarks are discovered inside protons and neutrons.

Physicists continue to discover smaller and smaller subatomic particles such as quarks and neutrinos.

Scientists are still trying to find out how and when the universe began.

Vertical markers: 1500–1700 · 1700–1800 · 1800–1900 · 1900–2000

DISCOVERING ENERGY

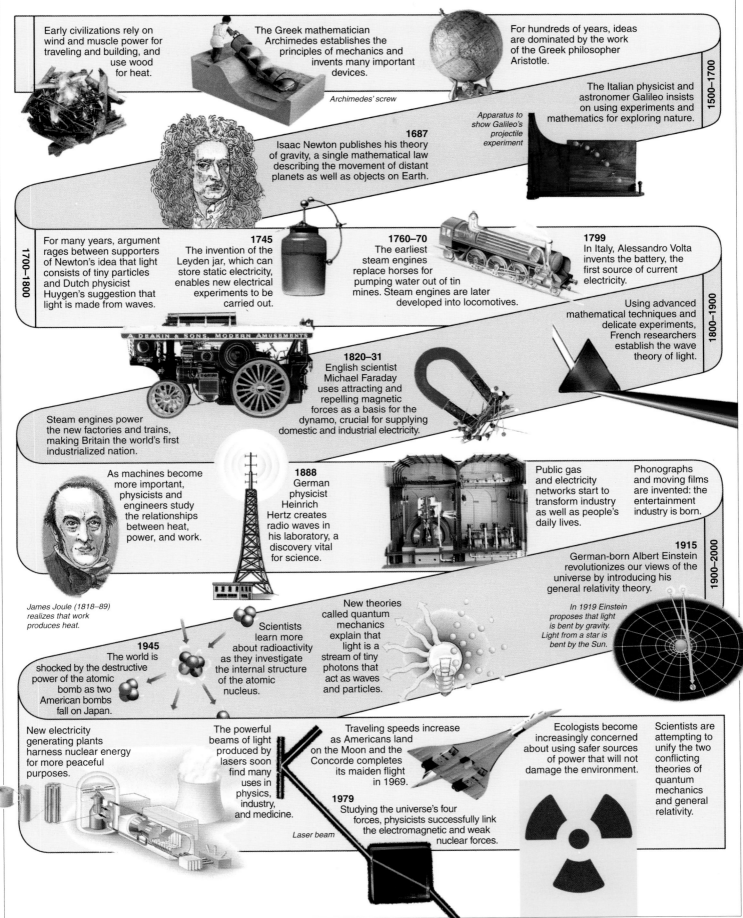

Early civilizations rely on wind and muscle power for traveling and building, and use wood for heat.

The Greek mathematician Archimedes establishes the principles of mechanics and invents many important devices.

Archimedes' screw

For hundreds of years, ideas are dominated by the work of the Greek philosopher Aristotle.

The Italian physicist and astronomer Galileo insists on using experiments and mathematics for exploring nature.

Apparatus to show Galileo's projectile experiment

1687
Isaac Newton publishes his theory of gravity, a single mathematical law describing the movement of distant planets as well as objects on Earth.

1500–1700

For many years, argument rages between supporters of Newton's idea that light consists of tiny particles and Dutch physicist Huygen's suggestion that light is made from waves.

1745
The invention of the Leyden jar, which can store static electricity, enables new electrical experiments to be carried out.

1760–70
The earliest steam engines replace horses for pumping water out of tin mines. Steam engines are later developed into locomotives.

1799
In Italy, Alessandro Volta invents the battery, the first source of current electricity.

Using advanced mathematical techniques and delicate experiments, French researchers establish the wave theory of light.

1700–1800

Steam engines power the new factories and trains, making Britain the world's first industrialized nation.

1820–31
English scientist Michael Faraday uses attracting and repelling magnetic forces as a basis for the dynamo, crucial for supplying domestic and industrial electricity.

1800–1900

As machines become more important, physicists and engineers study the relationships between heat, power, and work.

1888
German physicist Heinrich Hertz creates radio waves in his laboratory, a discovery vital for science.

Public gas and electricity networks start to transform industry as well as people's daily lives.

Phonographs and moving films are invented: the entertainment industry is born.

1915
German-born Albert Einstein revolutionizes our views of the universe by introducing his general relativity theory.

James Joule (1818–89) realizes that work produces heat.

Scientists learn more about radioactivity as they investigate the internal structure of the atomic nucleus.

New theories called quantum mechanics explain that light is a stream of tiny photons that act as waves and particles.

In 1919 Einstein proposes that light is bent by gravity. Light from a star is bent by the Sun.

1945
The world is shocked by the destructive power of the atomic bomb as two American bombs fall on Japan.

1900–2000

New electricity generating plants harness nuclear energy for more peaceful purposes.

The powerful beams of light produced by lasers soon find many uses in physics, industry, and medicine.

Laser beam

Traveling speeds increase as Americans land on the Moon and the Concorde completes its maiden flight in 1969.

1979
Studying the universe's four forces, physicists successfully link the electromagnetic and weak nuclear forces.

Ecologists become increasingly concerned about using safer sources of power that will not damage the environment.

Scientists are attempting to unify the two conflicting theories of quantum mechanics and general relativity.

DISCOVERING EARTH AND SPACE

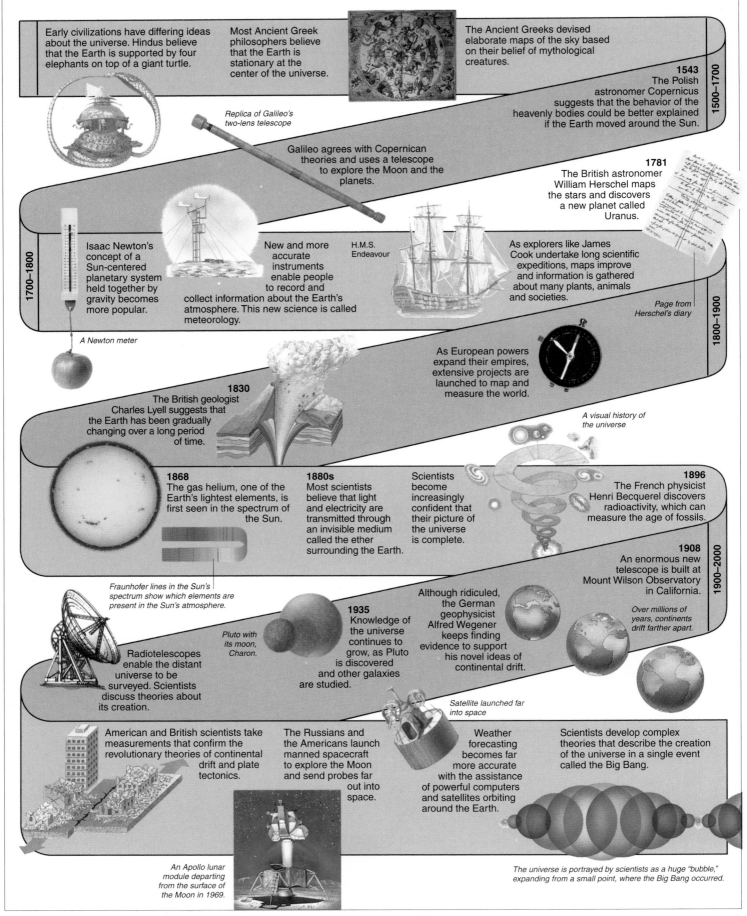

Early civilizations have differing ideas about the universe. Hindus believe that the Earth is supported by four elephants on top of a giant turtle.

Most Ancient Greek philosophers believe that the Earth is stationary at the center of the universe.

The Ancient Greeks devised elaborate maps of the sky based on their belief of mythological creatures.

1500–1700

1543
The Polish astronomer Copernicus suggests that the behavior of the heavenly bodies could be better explained if the Earth moved around the Sun.

Replica of Galileo's two-lens telescope

Galileo agrees with Copernican theories and uses a telescope to explore the Moon and the planets.

1781
The British astronomer William Herschel maps the stars and discovers a new planet called Uranus.

1700–1800

Isaac Newton's concept of a Sun-centered planetary system held together by gravity becomes more popular.

New and more accurate instruments enable people to record and collect information about the Earth's atmosphere. This new science is called meteorology.

H.M.S. Endeavour

As explorers like James Cook undertake long scientific expeditions, maps improve and information is gathered about many plants, animals and societies.

Page from Herschel's diary

1800–1900

A Newton meter

As European powers expand their empires, extensive projects are launched to map and measure the world.

A visual history of the universe

1830
The British geologist Charles Lyell suggests that the Earth has been gradually changing over a long period of time.

1868
The gas helium, one of the Earth's lightest elements, is first seen in the spectrum of the Sun.

1880s
Most scientists believe that light and electricity are transmitted through an invisible medium called the ether surrounding the Earth.

Scientists become increasingly confident that their picture of the universe is complete.

1896
The French physicist Henri Becquerel discovers radioactivity, which can measure the age of fossils.

1908
An enormous new telescope is built at Mount Wilson Observatory in California.

1900–2000

Fraunhofer lines in the Sun's spectrum show which elements are present in the Sun's atmosphere.

Over millions of years, continents drift farther apart.

Pluto with its moon, Charon.

1935
Knowledge of the universe continues to grow, as Pluto is discovered and other galaxies are studied.

Although ridiculed, the German geophysicist Alfred Wegener keeps finding evidence to support his novel ideas of continental drift.

Radiotelescopes enable the distant universe to be surveyed. Scientists discuss theories about its creation.

Satellite launched far into space

American and British scientists take measurements that confirm the revolutionary theories of continental drift and plate tectonics.

The Russians and the Americans launch manned spacecraft to explore the Moon and send probes far out into space.

Weather forecasting becomes far more accurate with the assistance of powerful computers and satellites orbiting around the Earth.

Scientists develop complex theories that describe the creation of the universe in a single event called the Big Bang.

An Apollo lunar module departing from the surface of the Moon in 1969.

The universe is portrayed by scientists as a huge "bubble," expanding from a small point, where the Big Bang occurred.

DISCOVERING LIVING THINGS

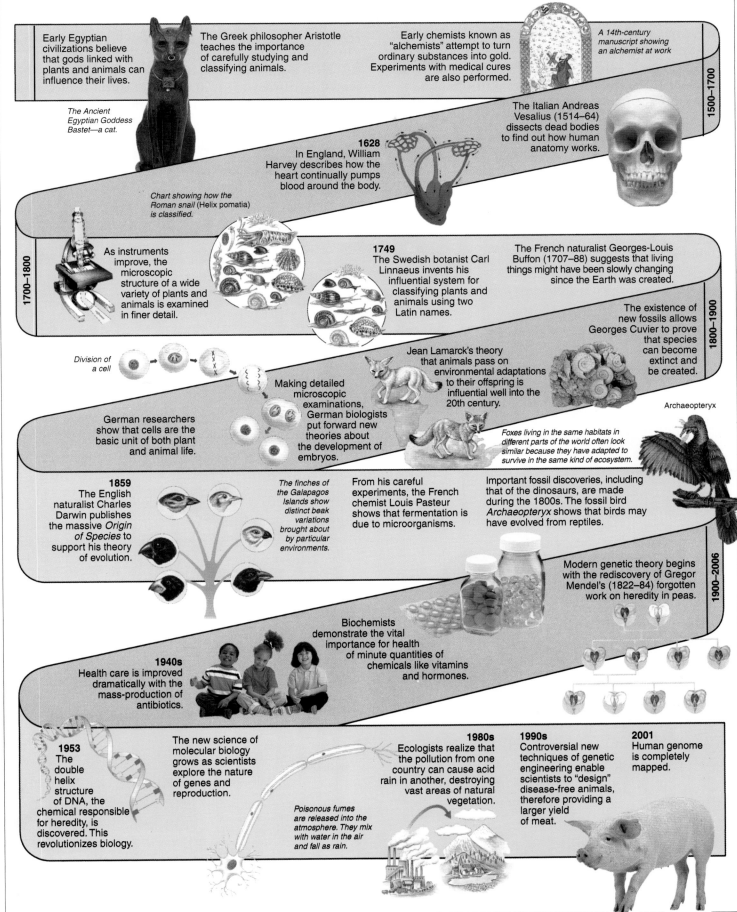

Early Egyptian civilizations believe that gods linked with plants and animals can influence their lives.

The Greek philosopher Aristotle teaches the importance of carefully studying and classifying animals.

Early chemists known as "alchemists" attempt to turn ordinary substances into gold. Experiments with medical cures are also performed.

A 14th-century manuscript showing an alchemist at work

The Ancient Egyptian Goddess Bastet—a cat.

The Italian Andreas Vesalius (1514–64) dissects dead bodies to find out how human anatomy works.

1628 In England, William Harvey describes how the heart continually pumps blood around the body.

Chart showing how the Roman snail (Helix pomatia) is classified.

1500–1700

As instruments improve, the microscopic structure of a wide variety of plants and animals is examined in finer detail.

1749 The Swedish botanist Carl Linnaeus invents his influential system for classifying plants and animals using two Latin names.

The French naturalist Georges-Louis Buffon (1707–88) suggests that living things might have been slowly changing since the Earth was created.

1700–1800

The existence of new fossils allows Georges Cuvier to prove that species can become extinct and be created.

Division of a cell

Jean Lamarck's theory that animals pass on environmental adaptations to their offspring is influential well into the 20th century.

German researchers show that cells are the basic unit of both plant and animal life.

Making detailed microscopic examinations, German biologists put forward new theories about the development of embryos.

1800–1900

Archaeopteryx

Foxes living in the same habitats in different parts of the world often look similar because they have adapted to survive in the same kind of ecosystem.

1859 The English naturalist Charles Darwin publishes the massive *Origin of Species* to support his theory of evolution.

The finches of the Galapagos Islands show distinct beak variations brought about by particular environments.

From his careful experiments, the French chemist Louis Pasteur shows that fermentation is due to microorganisms.

Important fossil discoveries, including that of the dinosaurs, are made during the 1800s. The fossil bird *Archaeopteryx* shows that birds may have evolved from reptiles.

Modern genetic theory begins with the rediscovery of Gregor Mendel's (1822–84) forgotten work on heredity in peas.

1900–2006

Biochemists demonstrate the vital importance for health of minute quantities of chemicals like vitamins and hormones.

1940s Health care is improved dramatically with the mass-production of antibiotics.

1953 The double helix structure of DNA, the chemical responsible for heredity, is discovered. This revolutionizes biology.

The new science of molecular biology grows as scientists explore the nature of genes and reproduction.

1980s Ecologists realize that the pollution from one country can cause acid rain in another, destroying vast areas of natural vegetation.

Poisonous fumes are released into the atmosphere. They mix with water in the air and fall as rain.

1990s Controversial new techniques of genetic engineering enable scientists to "design" disease-free animals, therefore providing a larger yield of meat.

2001 Human genome is completely mapped.

HOW SCIENTISTS WORK

Men and women leading very different lives and interested in a range of different topics describe themselves as scientists. The hospital technician examining blood samples, the mathematician thinking about the origins of the universe, the botanist collecting rare plant specimens, and the chemist developing a new type of food flavoring are all scientists who share a belief in studying the world to discover how it works and to find ways to improve our lives.

Surgeons performing plastic surgery

WHAT IS A SCIENTIST?
Modern scientists are professional men and women who earn their living by investigating the universe around us and inventing new ways of using its resources. A few scientists become famous by making spectacular discoveries, but millions more make important contributions to scientific knowledge by their careful and patient work.

Louis Pasteur (1822–95), who discovered a vaccine for rabies.

THE REWARDS OF SCIENCE
Scientists value their work because it is personally satisfying, and because scientific advances can benefit society.

Nuclear bomb test in the Nevada desert.

POSITIVE AND NEGATIVE
Our modern world depends on telephones, electricity, cars, and countless other scientific discoveries and inventions. Millions of lives have been saved by drugs such as penicillin and the smallpox vaccine. But some people hold science responsible for worldwide disasters like the atomic bomb, pollution, and the thinning of the ozone layer.

Nuclear plant in Sellafield, England

PERSONAL REWARDS
Many people choose science as a career because it offers them an exciting challenge. Making an outstanding scientific discovery can bring international fame, wealth, and important awards like the Nobel Prize.

Alfred Nobel (1833–96)

RESPONSIBILITY
Politicians, economists, scientists, and other social planners must jointly decide whether experiments such as setting up reactions in a nuclear reactor, or trying to correct a baby's inherited defects are going to harm or benefit society.

THE RESEARCH TEAM
Modern scientific experiments are so complex that people often work in teams. Each team member contributes his or her own particular knowledge and skills. Some scientists organize the team and their apparatus.

SCIENTIFIC EQUIPMENT
Helium-filled balloons like this carry instruments into the air to collect data on temperature, pressure, and wind speed at different heights.

This scientist is calculating the photosynthetic rate in a rapeseed field.

Scientist working on experiments in genetic engineering.

WORKING ENVIRONMENTS
We usually picture scientists working in a laboratory, but many scientific studies need to be conducted outside. Ecology (the study of plants and animals in their habitats), meteorology (the study of the weather), and horticulture (the study of crop growing) are all areas of science that require experimental work outside.

COMPUTERS
Scientific experiments often use computers to work out lengthy mathematical calculations quickly and accurately. They are also able to store and organize vast collections of data.

SCIENTIFIC EXPERIMENTS

Experiments are central to the success of science. By trying out what happens when they slightly alter the natural world, scientists can collect information that gives them ideas about how the world works. They can test and compare different theories to see which one is the most useful for describing the world's behavior, and can develop effective new equipment, chemicals, and techniques.

OBSERVATION

Some important discoveries—such as the invention of electric batteries which originated in 18th-century experiments on frogs—are the result of scientists observing an unusual event and appreciating its significance.

The bending of light from a star by the Sun.

Alessandro Volta with his early battery, 1799.

TESTING

New ideas must be tested to make sure that they work. Albert Einstein's relativity theory was tested during an eclipse of the Sun to see if the light from a distant star was curved—it was. Louis Pasteur tested his new rabies vaccine on a boy who had been bitten by a dog. Scientists also design experiments to show which of two competing theories is better at explaining the world.

COLLECTING INFORMATION

Working like detectives, scientists must carefully gather together and share detailed information on everything in the world around them. Scientific theories are based on interpreting and explaining this enormous collection of data. Computerized systems have helped to make the gathering of information and its analysis more efficient.

Sparks jumped when lightning flowed along the kite string to which Franklin had attached a key.

EXPLORATION

Whether they are investigating the effects of a new drug, the internal structure of an atom, the life of a dolphin, or the nature of the Sun, scientists use experiments to explore the nature of the world.

DEMONSTRATION

Experiments can be useful for convincing other people about a scientific theory. In a dangerous and dramatic experiment designed to demonstrate that lightning discharges are a form of electricity, Benjamin Franklin (1706–90) flew a kite during a thunderstorm to draw electricity down from the sky.

SCIENTIFIC TECHNIQUES

All scientific work is carried out systematically and methodically. Scientists have developed various ways of dealing with different types of information.

CLASSIFICATION

Scientists classify objects to give nature some kind of order. Plants and animals are grouped into families. In the chemical world, the periodic table puts the elements into groups to show the relationships between them.

Charles Darwin divided finches he saw on the Galapagos Islands into different species.

MEASUREMENT

Accurate measurement is crucial for modern science and engineering. Scientists must find ways of measuring enormous distances, such as those between stars, as carefully as measuring the size of tiny biological cells, and the tiny dimensions of atoms and molecules.

A transmission electron microscope (TEM) is used for studying microscopic cells.

Satellites are sophisticated robots that are sent into space.

EQUIPMENT

Sophisticated apparatus enables scientists to peer into tiny atoms, distant galaxies, and the hidden secrets of living nature.

MODELS AND THEORIES

Just as globes are used as miniature models of the Earth, scientists develop theories, construct laws of nature, and build mathematical models to describe how the universe works.

THEORIES

Scientists aim to produce theories that will not only successfully describe the information they have collected, but which will also explain how different events are related to each other, and that can predict the results of future experiments.

MATHEMATICAL MODELS

Isaac Newton's famous law of gravity is a mathematical model describing how the universe is held together.

Isaac Newton (1643–1727)

Molecular computer graphic of DNA model showing the double helix structure.

PHYSICAL MODELS

The double helix is a physical model of DNA. It shows the structure of the chemical that lies at the heart of heredity.

SAFETY CODES

We all come across dangerous and poisonous substances in our everyday lives, but they are not always obvious. To help us identify them, safety codes—a combination of pictures and words—are used as warning symbols. It is essential for your health and safety that you follow these at all times.

IN THE HOME

Many cleaning materials used in the home have safety codes printed on them to show that they are poisonous if swallowed, breathed in, or allowed to stay on the skin. You should always wash your hands after using chemicals. Sometimes protective clothing is necessary.

Poisonous substances

Wear protective clothes

Always ask an adult before using any substance at home. Cleaning fluids in particular can be extremely poisonous.

Harmful chemicals

Wear masks

Danger Dust hazard

IN THE SCHOOL LABORATORY

Care must be taken when conducting experiments in the school laboratory. Some laboratory chemicals are toxic. Heating others over a Bunsen burner can be dangerous if the correct procedures are not carried out. Many substances have very strong smells, and can cause unpleasant symptoms if inhaled.

Wear glasses

Always wear protective glasses, tie back long hair and be careful of loose clothes.

Wear gloves

Dangerous chemicals

Biological hazard

IN THE STREET

Look out for safety codes when you are out walking in the street. In particular, construction sites and gas stations can be dangerous. Safety codes help you to avoid accidents.

No smoking

Flammable liquid

Radiation risk

It is against the law for pedestrians to cross some roads, such as highways, since traffic speeds are high.

Wear ear protectors

Wear welding mask

Wear boots

No pedestrians

Danger Explosives

MATTER

EVERYTHING YOU CAN SEE, from the book that you are holding, to the chair that you are sitting on, to the water that you drink, is made up of matter. But matter is not just things that you can touch. It includes the air that you breathe. The planets in the universe, living things such as insects, and nonliving things such as rocks are also made of matter. All matter is made of tiny particles called atoms, which are themselves made up of even smaller particles, called subatomic particles. Chemistry involves studying what matter is made of, and how atoms join together to make different things.

CREATION OF MATTER

Most scientists believe that all the matter in the universe was created in an explosion called the Big Bang (left). Great heat and energy followed the explosion. Then, after just a few seconds, some bundles of the energy turned into tiny particles. The particles turned into the atoms that make up the universe that we live in today.

ORIGINS OF CHEMISTRY

Hundreds of years ago, before anyone knew about atoms, people called alchemists tried to find out what things were made of. They tried to turn metals such as lead into gold. They also searched for a medicine that would give eternal life. They tried without success. Some alchemists were women. One name for alchemy, *opus mulierum*, is Latin for women's work.

This page is from a 14th-century Arab manuscript.

These pictures show alchemists at work.

NONLIVING MATTER

Most matter in the universe is nonliving. This means that it does not grow, reproduce, or move itself about. A good example of nonliving matter is the rock that makes up the Earth that we live on.

LIVING MATTER

The Earth is home to many living things, including plants and animals of all kinds. Although a butterfly seems very different from a rock, they are both made out of atoms. The atoms just connect in a different way to create something else.

FOUNDERS OF CHEMISTRY

The French chemist Antoine Lavoisier (1743–94) is thought of as the founder of chemistry. Antoine showed that burned substances are heavier than unburned substances. He concluded that this was because the burned substances gained a gas, oxygen. Marie Lavoisier (1758–1836) worked with her husband by translating scientific works and campaigning for acceptance of their ideas.

PARTICLES OF MATTER

Scientists have used bubble chambers to identify many subatomic particles. The bubble chamber contains liquid hydrogen near its boiling point. Subatomic particles traveling through the liquid cause it to boil, leaving trails of bubbles. Although the particles are invisible, the trails that they leave can be seen, and are different for each type of particle.

STATES OF MATTER

IMAGINE A MOUNTAIN, a lake, and the air around them. These three things represent the three states in which matter occurs. Mountains are made of rock, which is solid. A lake is made of water, which is liquid. And the air that we breathe is made of gas. Solids have a definite volume and shape, and these can be changed by exerting forces on them. Most solids are hard. Liquids have a fixed volume but no definite shape, and they can flow. Gases have no definite volume or shape, and they can also flow. And you can't see most gases. Because they can flow, liquids and gases are called fluids. The three states of matter behave the way they do because the particles that make them up move in different ways.

THREE STATES
This picture of hot springs, in Waiotapu in New Zealand, shows the three states of matter, all together in one place. The rock is a solid, the water is a liquid, and the rising vapor is a gas.

LIQUID

Next time you have a drink, notice what is happening inside your glass. The liquid takes on the shape of the glass. But if you spill it, the shape of the liquid changes. If you pour the liquid into a different container, the shape of the liquid changes, but the volume remains the same.

SOLID

A solid object, such as a book, has a definite shape that is not easy to change. This is because the particles of a solid are packed close to one another to form a firm structure.

GAS

A gas quickly fills any space it is put in because its particles move fast. This means that a gas has no shape or volume of its own, but takes the shape of its container. For example, this balloon is filled up with the gas helium. Objects can pass through a gas easily because its particles are far apart. We can walk through air and not feel a thing.

Particles in gases are far apart and move at high speed. They have little effect on one another.

Particles in liquids have more energy than those in a solid, and are free to move past each other.

Particles in solids are tightly packed together. They are packed so close together that they cannot move around: they only vibrate.

PLASMA

There is a fourth state of matter, called plasma, but it is not often seen. It only exists at very high temperatures inside the Sun and other stars, or on Earth at low pressures. It consists of atoms split up by great heat or electricity. This ball contains a central electrode surrounded by gases at low pressure. Electricity discharges through the gas in long streaks of plasma, as the gas atoms are ripped apart by a high voltage on the electrode.

The particles that result from the split atoms are called ions and electrons.

USING STATES OF MATTER

Solids, liquids, and gases are all around you and are used in many ways. If you have a bicycle, you can see the three states of matter working together. Many parts of the bicycle are made of solids. Even the rubber of the tires is a solid, although it is flexible, and will change shape if you go over a bump. The tires are filled with air. And the oil on your bicycle chain is a liquid.

SOLIDS IN USE

A bicycle frame is solid, as are the rim and the spokes of the wheels. The frame has to be solid to keep the bicycle together. And the steel rim and spokes on the wheels ensure that they keep their circular shape, which is important if you want to cycle comfortably.

LIQUIDS IN USE

All liquids can flow, and some can flow more easily than others. A liquid's viscosity is a measure of how fast or slowly it flows. Water flows easily because it has low viscosity. Oils flow more slowly, and have higher viscosity. A viscous liquid such as an oil is used between metal parts to stop them from rubbing against each other. This is called lubrication.

You can reduce the volume of a gas by squeezing it into a smaller space. Or you can squeeze more and more gas into the same space. This is what happens when you pump up a bicycle tire.

Oil on a bicycle chain keeps all the parts moving easily and prevents them from wearing down.

Water striders are so light that the surface tension of water holds their weight. Their feet just cause little dents on the surface.

The piston transmits the pressure from the brake pedal.

Brake pads are forced against the wheel by liquid pressure.

GASES IN USE

Unlike solids and liquids, gases do not have a fixed volume. This means that you can compress them, or reduce their volume. Gases are compressible because there is plenty of space between gas particles. When you cycle over a bump, the air in your tire is compressed. So it absorbs the shock of the bump instead of passing it through the bicycle.

Pressure is applied to the brake pedal.

Pressure travels through the brake fluid.

HYDRAULIC BRAKES

Car brakes work because liquids are not easily compressed. This means that if you apply pressure to a liquid, the force will go right through it. When a driver presses the brake pedal down, the pressure goes through the piston to liquid in the brake pipes. This makes the brake pads grip the wheel disk, which in turn makes the wheels stop turning. Liquid pressure like this is known as hydraulic pressure.

Wheel disk

SURFACE TENSION

Particles in water attract each other—they pull toward each other equally in all directions. But particles on the surface can only be pulled into the water by particles underneath—there are no particles to pull in the opposite direction. This creates a stretchy skin around water, called surface tension, that is strong enough to support the weight of tiny insects.

Find out more
CHANGES OF STATE P. 20
PROPERTIES OF MATTER P. 22
BONDING P. 28
KINETIC THEORY P. 50
BEHAVIOR OF GASES P. 51
FORCES IN FLUIDS P. 128
SUN P. 284

CHANGES OF STATE

IF YOU TRY TO STIR hot cooking oil with a plastic spoon, the spoon will probably melt. Plastic is a solid. This means that it is usually solid at normal temperatures and pressures. But change the circumstances, and you can change the state of a substance. In the same way, if you put orange juice, normally a liquid, into a freezer, it will go solid. And if you breathe onto a cold windowpane, the water vapor in your breath (normally a gas) will condense into drops of liquid. If the Sun shines on them, the heat turns them back into a gas and they evaporate into the air again. Even the hardest rocks melt at the very high temperatures and pressures found underneath the Earth's crust. Most substances that we know will change state when the temperature or the pressure changes enough.

The safety valve allows excess steam to escape.

A weight ensures the pressure remains constant.

A seal around the lid enables the pressure to build up.

PRESSURE COOKING
The temperature at which a liquid boils (boiling point) depends on the pressure around it. A liquid boils when the pressure of its vapor is equal to the air pressure around it. When the air pressure goes down or up, the boiling point goes down or up too—because vapor pressures are less at lower temperatures and greater at higher temperatures. In pressure cookers, the increased pressure raises the water's boiling point. At the higher temperature, the food cooks more quickly.

FROM SOLID TO GAS
If you heat a solid to a temperature called the melting point, it will melt into liquid. If you heat it even more, it gets to a point when the liquid changes into a gas. This is the boiling point. At the boiling point, all the particles in a liquid get enough energy from the heat to break free from each other. Then bubbles of gas form in the liquid. Particles in liquids are always slowly escaping as gas, even below boiling point. This is called evaporation.

CONDENSATION
Cold glasses get little droplets of water on them because water vapor from the air turns back into water on the cold glass. Cold glass removes energy from particles and so turns them into liquid.

EVAPORATION
Why does wet ink dry? Because the liquid in it turns into vapor and evaporates into the air. Some of the liquid particles get enough energy to escape and form the gas.

SUBLIMATION
Sometimes a solid turns straight into a gas. This is called sublimation. It is what happens with dry ice, which is used to make dramatic-looking clouds on stage in a theater. Dry ice is really frozen carbon dioxide. It is called dry because it does not become liquid before turning into a gas.

GAS

The particles in a liquid move faster and split up to become a gas. Or the particles in a gas slow down to become a liquid.

The particles in a solid move fast enough to escape as a gas. Or the particles in a gas slow down to become a solid.

The particles in a solid vibrate faster and particles can move over one another to create a liquid. Or the bundles of particles in a liquid slow down to become a solid.

LIQUID

SOLID

MELTING
Particles in a solid are packed tightly together. But when heated, they vibrate more and more until they can break free of fixed positions and move freely past each other. The solid turns into a liquid. This is what happens when chocolate melts.

FREEZING
A dripping candle will soon freeze into a solid if you blow it out. This is because the particles, speeded up by the heat of the flame, slow down again when the heat is removed. When they slow down enough, they get locked into position again, forming a solid.

STATES OF WATER

Water is unusual because it can be found in all three states of matter in everyday life. In solid form it is ice, in liquid form, water, and in gaseous form, steam or water vapor. The properties of water in these three states are important to everything on Earth. For example, plants and animals need liquid water to survive.

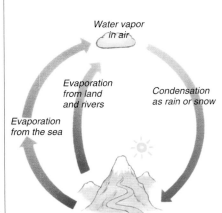

Water vapor in air

Evaporation from land and rivers

Condensation as rain or snow

Evaporation from the sea

WATER CYCLE
The never-ending cycle between the different states of water is essential to everything on Earth. Liquid water evaporates and solid snow sublimes into the air. Water vapor condenses into droplets to form clouds. Water droplets fall back to Earth as rain or snow.

Most solids are denser than their liquid form. But ice is less dense than water, and so floats on the top.

The water under the ice is warmer than the outside air, so the seal and other animals it feeds on can survive.

WATER VAPOR
When the temperature is high, water evaporates quickly. In the warm tropical forests of South America there is plenty of rain, and because the temperature is high, water evaporates all the time. The water vapor in the air makes it very humid, and means that some unusual plants that have no roots, such as some orchids, can thrive. They take all the moisture they need straight from the air, not from the ground.

The seal gives out water vapor as it breathes.

Pressure on the ice from the weight of the skater lowers the freezing point, which is why the ice melts.

STEAM POWER
When water boils, it turns into steam. Steam is water in gas form. Being a gas, it takes up much more space than the liquid it came from. It is full of energy and can be used to drive heat engines such as the steam turbine. It enters the turbine at high temperature and pressure, and drives the turbine wheels around.

Steam goes into the turbine under pressure.

The blades are forced around, and this movement is used to generate other types of energy, such as electricity.

CHANGES WITH PRESSURE
Pressure can bring about a change of state. Surprisingly, increasing the pressure on ice lowers its freezing point. So ice skaters actually move over ice on a thin layer of water. The skater's weight on the blade causes pressure, lowering the freezing point so that the ice melts.

The blade presses down on the ice.

The ice melts underneath the blade, allowing it to glide over the ice.

The ice makes the water refreeze behind the skate.

EXPANDING ICE
Have you noticed how pipes often burst in freezing weather? This is because the water inside them expands as it freezes into a solid.

Find out more
STATES OF MATTER P. 18
SOLUTIONS P. 60
CHEMISTRY OF WATER P. 75
WATER INDUSTRY P. 83
FORMATION OF THE EARTH P. 210
CYCLES IN THE BIOSPHERE P. 372

PROPERTIES OF MATTER

A SAUCEPAN IS MADE OF STEEL and plastic for a very good reason. The handle is plastic because plastic is an insulator and it stops the handle from getting too hot and burning your hand. The pan is steel because it is a conductor and lets the heat go through to the food. Insulation or conductivity is an example of a particular property of matter. Some properties, such as conductivity, can be measured. Others, such as the smell of an object, can only be described. Scientists measure the properties of many different materials. They do this at the same temperature and pressure so that they can make accurate comparisons between them.

You can describe an orange by its color and shape, how it feels to the touch, how it smells, and how it tastes.

NEUTRON STAR

The metal osmium is the densest substance on Earth. It is twice as dense as lead and over 22 times as dense as water. But the densest material in the universe is found in neutron stars. A pinhead of that matter would have a mass of a million tons.

Neutron star

A pinhead of a neutron star

A hydrometer is used to measure the density of a liquid. It floats in a container full of the pure liquid, and the reading is taken at the top of the liquid. The hydrometer floats high up in a dense liquid, but lower in a less dense liquid.

SENSING MATTER

In the everyday world, people do not usually describe objects in the same way as scientists do. We rely more on our senses than on measurements with instruments. But human senses are not consistent. They cannot measure how much something smells, or exactly what it tastes like, and one person may sense things in a different way from another.

DENSITY

Different materials have a different mass for the same volume. The mass (usually in kilograms, kg) of a particular volume of a material (usually a cubic meter, m^3) is its density (usually given as kg per m^3 or kgm^{-3}). Sometimes, densities are given as relative densities, a comparison to the density of liquid water.

WEIGHT, MASS, AND VOLUME

You can measure the amount of something in two ways: by its volume or by its mass. You buy gasoline by its volume (in gallons or liters)—that is the amount of space it occupies. But you buy potatoes by mass (in pounds or kilograms)—that is a measure of the amount of matter in the bag of potatoes. The volume of something can often be changed by compressing or heating it, but the mass stays constant. When gravity pulls on an object, it creates a force called weight, which depends on the mass of the object.

Water has a relative density of 1 (about 1,000 kgm^{-3}). Liquids with a lower density float on the water and those with a higher density sink below it.

The cube of lead is as heavy as a piece of wax with a volume 13 times greater, and a piece of balsa wood with a volume 56 times greater.

Gases always bubble to the surface of a liquid because they have such a low density. Air has a relative density of only 0.0012.

Methylated spirits: relative density 0.8

Corn oil: relative density 0.9

Water: relative density 1

Mercury: relative density 13.6

Lead: density 11.3 (11,340 kgm^{-3})

Wax: density 0.9 (900 kgm^{-3})

Balsa wood: density 0.2 (198 kgm^{-3})

STRENGTH

Most metals are strong when they are pulled, so they can be used to build structures such as this cable-stayed bridge. The road is held by cables made of steel, which do not break when they are pulled by the downward force of the road. The pillars that hold up the bridge are made of concrete because it is strong enough not to break up when it is squashed by the force of the bridge pushing it down.

A tower holds the cables in place.

PLASTICITY

If you press some materials, such as dough or putty, they change shape and stay that way. This property is called plasticity. There are different kinds of plasticity, called malleability and ductility. If a material can be beaten into thin sheets without breaking, it is malleable. If it can be drawn into a fine wire, it is ductile.

This silversmith is making a bowl by beating out the silver into the right shape. This means that silver is malleable.

Copper and some other metals can be drawn into wire finer than a human hair. This means that copper is ductile.

If you press pieces of wax onto the end of a metal spoon and a plastic spoon in hot water, the wax on the end of the metal spoon will start to melt first.

CONDUCTING HEAT

Metals conduct (pass on) heat well. They have high thermal (heat) conductivity because of their atomic structure. Materials such as plastic and wood have poor thermal conductivity, so they are good insulators. This makes them very useful for covering thermal conductors. This is why the handles of kitchen utensils and saucepans are usually plastic.

Water is a good thermal conductor. It transmits heat to the metal spoon.

A rubber balloon stretched out as far as possible

ELASTICITY

Rubber has an interesting property. When you pull it, it stretches. When you let go, it shrinks back to its original size. This property is called elasticity. Most materials, including metals, are elastic to a certain extent. All materials have an elastic limit, which means that they do not return to the original shape and size if they are stretched too far.

The balloon has returned to its original shape after being stretched.

CONDUCTING ELECTRICITY

Electricity can flow easily through metals, meaning that metals can conduct electricity. This is because metals have free-moving electrons in their atoms. Plastics, glass, wood, and most other solid materials, except for carbon, are very poor conductors. They are electrical insulators, which is why plastic is used to cover conductors such as the wire in a cable.

Copper wire

The plastic completely covers the copper wires.

Some substances are more soluble than others. Chalk hardly dissolves in cold water. But sugar dissolves easily, even in cold water.

BRITTLENESS

Rubber is elastic at normal temperatures. But this balloon was dipped in liquid nitrogen at a temperature of -385°F (-196°C). The balloon became brittle and shattered into pieces when tapped with a hammer. Some substances, such as glass, are brittle at normal temperatures. Other substances, such as clay, are normally plastic, but they become brittle after being baked in a kiln.

Chalk in cold water

Sugar in cold water

Chalk is not very soluble, even in hot water. But sugar is much more soluble in hot water. The hotter the water, the more soluble sugar becomes.

The boiling point: liquid turns into vapor, or vapor condenses into liquid. It is always higher than the melting point.

MELTING AND BOILING POINTS

Every pure substance has a constant melting point and boiling at normal air pressure. But if the substance is not pure, the melting and boiling points change. Salt on snow lowers the melting point, so it melts to water, and the weather has to be much colder before it freezes again.

Chalk in hot water

Sugar in hot water

SOLUBILITY

Many solids, liquids, and gases dissolve in water and other liquids to form a solution: they are soluble. Sugar dissolves in tea, and salt dissolves in water. The dissolving substances are called solutes, and the liquids that they dissolve in are called solvents. Water is often called the universal solvent because so many things dissolve in it. This property is vital to life. Water carries dissolved substances around in blood and sap. One such dissolved substance is the gas oxygen, enabling certain animals to live in water.

The melting (or freezing) point: solid melts into liquid, or liquid freezes into solid.

Find out more

ATOMIC STRUCTURE P. 24
TRANSITION METALS P. 36
CARBON P. 40
SOLUTIONS P. 60
CHEMICAL ANALYSIS P. 62
FLOATING AND SINKING P. 129
CURRENT ELECTRICITY P. 148
FACT FINDER P. 402

ATOMIC STRUCTURE

EVERY SINGLE THING you can see, hear, feel, smell, and taste is made from microscopic particles. These particles are called atoms, and it would take millions of them just to cover the period at the end of this sentence. An atom is itself made up of even smaller particles. In the center of each atom is a nucleus made up of protons and neutrons. Particles called electrons whiz around this nucleus in different shells (layers). Protons and neutrons are much heavier than the electrons, so the nucleus makes up most of an atom's mass. Some substances, such as water, are made up of molecules. These consist of several kinds of atom joined together in a group. Other substances, such as iron, have just one kind of atom.

MOLECULE PICTURE
This photograph shows 28 carbon monoxide molecules. They have been cleverly arranged into the shape of a person. More than 20,000 of these "people" would be needed to cross the width of a human hair.

Six protons   Nucleus

Six neutrons   Six electrons

Carbon atom sliced in half

The number of shells an atom has depends on the number of electrons it contains. A bromine atom has 35 electrons in four shells. Some atoms have as many as seven shells.

The first shell of a carbon atom contains two electrons. The other four electrons are in the second shell.

PROTONS, NEUTRONS, AND ELECTRONS

The nucleus of every atom contains two types of particle—protons and neutrons. The number of protons gives the atomic number. Protons have a positive electric charge, while neutrons have none. The electrons that spin around the nucleus, like planets orbiting the Sun, have a negative charge. But electrons are not solid balls; they are bundles of energy that move almost as fast as light. There are always the same number of electrons and protons in an atom.

CARBON-12 ATOM
This drawing shows a carbon-12 atom sliced in half. The nucleus of a carbon-12 atom is made up of six protons and six neutrons. The atom's six electrons are contained within two shells.

Carbon-14 has six protons and eight neutrons.

Protons, neutrons, and electrons are called subatomic particles.

The commonest isotope of carbon, carbon-12, has six protons and six neutrons in its nucleus.

ISOTOPES
All the atoms of an element have the same number of protons, but some have different numbers of neutrons. All of these are called isotopes. The normal isotope of carbon, called carbon-12, has six protons and six neutrons in its nucleus. The nucleus of another isotope, carbon-14, has an extra two neutrons. It is radioactive. Radioactive isotopes are called radioisotopes.

JOHN DALTON
A Greek philosopher, Democritus (c. 460–361 BCE), put forward the idea that the universe is made of tiny, indivisible particles he called atoms. His concept was discussed for hundreds of years. Then, in 1808, the English chemist John Dalton (1766–1844) suggested from his experimental work that each chemical element is made up of identical atoms, and that elements are different because they are each made of different atoms. This became known as Dalton's atomic theory.

Even in atoms with many particles, most of the atom is empty space.

HOW BIG IS AN ATOM?
Atoms are far tinier than anyone can imagine. It would take as many as 10 million of them side by side to measure one millimeter. Even though they are so small, atoms are mostly made of space, because the electrons are so far from the nucleus. If the nucleus were the size of a tennis ball, the whole atom would be as big as the Empire State Building in New York City.

ERNEST RUTHERFORD

The New Zealand-born physicist Ernest Rutherford (1871–1937) discovered in 1911 that atoms have a tiny, dense nucleus. Rutherford and his colleagues were shooting positively charged alpha particles at a very thin sheet of gold foil. Alpha particles consist of two protons and two neutrons and so have a positive charge. Most of the alpha particles went straight through, but some changed path and some even bounced back. This showed that the atom's positive charge is concentrated in a small nucleus, which was changing the paths of the alpha particles. Most of the atom is made up of empty space.

SUBATOMIC PARTICLES

The protons, neutrons, and electrons that make up an atom are just three of the hundreds of subatomic particles that are now known. Scientists are discovering new particles all the time. They use powerful machines called particle accelerators to smash atoms or subatomic particles together, at incredible speed, to make other subatomic particles. They give the particles weird and wonderful names such as kaon, upsilon, and charmed lambda.

INVENTORS

John Cockcroft (1897–1967) and Ernest Walton (1903–95) were the first to develop a particle accelerator, in 1932. For this they won the Nobel Prize for Physics in 1951. In the picture, Ernest Walton is seated inside the counting room, where the particles are detected. The long tube above it is the accelerating tube, and the hat-shaped part above that is where the particles start off.

PARTICLE ACCELERATOR

In accelerators such as a synchrotron (right), beams of subatomic particles are sent around in circles by powerful electromagnets, and speeded up by pulses of electricity. When the particles are traveling fast enough, they are extracted and made to smash into each other. Scientists can then analyze the particles produced.

Nucleus
Electron
Neutron
A neutron is made up of three quarks.
Quark
Gluons

INSIDE A NUCLEUS

We know that the nucleus of every atom contains protons and neutrons. And these in turn are made up of smaller particles, called quarks. The quarks are held together by other particles, aptly called gluons.

SUBATOMIC PARTICLES

1897 J. J. Thomson (1856–1940) discovers the electron.

1909 Robert Millikan (1868–1953) measures the negative charge on the electron.

1911 Ernest Rutherford (1871–1937) discovers that atoms have a nucleus.

1913 Niels Bohr (1885–1962) discovers electron shells.

1932 James Chadwick (1891–1974) discovers the neutron.

1963 Murray Gell-Mann (born 1929) suggests the existence of quarks.

Particle tracks in a bubble chamber

PARTICLE TRACKS

Scientists often use electronic detectors to pick up the tracks of particles created by collisions in particle accelerators. A computer processes the information and displays the tracks on a screen. From the tracks, scientists can work out the mass and electric charge of the particles that made them. For example, the green spiral is the track of a low-energy electron.

Find out more

RADIOACTIVITY P. 26
BONDING P. 28
ELEMENTS P. 31
CARBON P. 40
NUCLEAR ENERGY P. 136
LIGHT P. 190
FACT FINDER P. 402

RADIOACTIVITY

THE RADIATION THAT IS USED in hospitals to treat disease is caused by atomic nuclei (plural of nucleus) breaking up. Most atoms have stable nuclei—meaning that the number of neutrons and protons stays the same. But some nuclei are unstable and can split up: they are radioactive. These unstable nuclei have a different number of neutrons from stable nuclei, and are called radioisotopes. When they break up, the nuclei give out radiation. This process is known as radioactive decay. The larger the number of subatomic particles in an atom, the more likely it is to be radioactive. Uranium, for example, has 238 subatomic particles and is highly radioactive.

RADIOACTIVITY

1896 Antoine Becquerel (1852–1908) discovers radioactivity.

1898 Marie Curie (1867–1934) and Pierre Curie (1859–1906) discover radium and polonium.

1934 Pavel Cherenkov (1904–1990) discovers Cherenkov radiation.

1934 Irène Joliot-Curie (1897–1956), Marie and Pierre's daughter, and her husband, Frédéric (1900–1958), show that radioactivity can be produced artificially.

RADIATION GLOW

Radioactive materials are often stored in water. The water acts as a shield to absorb the radiation. As the particles travel through the water, they make it emit a bluish light. This is called Cherenkov radiation, after the Soviet physicist Pavel Cherenkov, who won a Nobel Prize for its discovery.

Fuel rods from a nuclear reactor

Water showing Cherenkov radiation

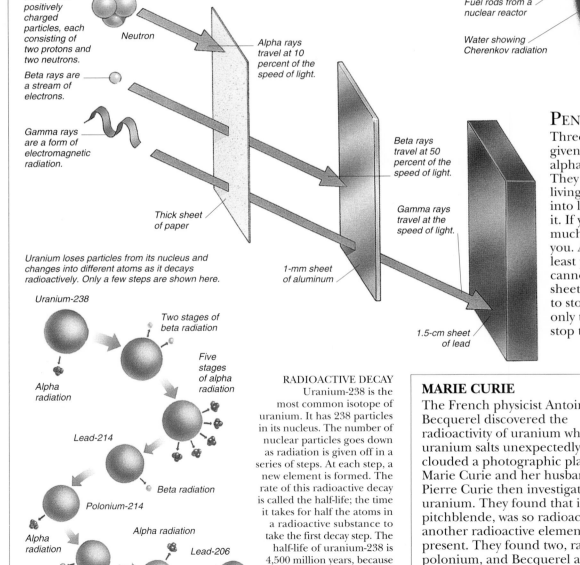

Alpha rays are a stream of positively charged particles, each consisting of two protons and two neutrons.

Proton

Neutron

Beta rays are a stream of electrons.

Gamma rays are a form of electromagnetic radiation.

Alpha rays travel at 10 percent of the speed of light.

Beta rays travel at 50 percent of the speed of light.

Gamma rays travel at the speed of light.

Thick sheet of paper

1-mm sheet of aluminum

1.5-cm sheet of lead

Uranium loses particles from its nucleus and changes into different atoms as it decays radioactively. Only a few steps are shown here.

Uranium-238

Two stages of beta radiation

Alpha radiation

Five stages of alpha radiation

Lead-214

Beta radiation

Polonium-214

Alpha radiation

Alpha radiation

Lead-206

Three stages of beta radiation

Polonium-210

PENETRATING POWER

Three types of radiation are given out by radioisotopes: alpha, beta, and gamma. They are all dangerous to living things. They can pass into living tissue and damage it. If you are exposed to too much radiation, it can kill you. Alpha radiation is the least penetrating. Its particles cannot even pass through a sheet of paper. Metal is needed to stop the beta particles. But only thick lead or concrete can stop the powerful gamma rays.

RADIOACTIVE DECAY

Uranium-238 is the most common isotope of uranium. It has 238 particles in its nucleus. The number of nuclear particles goes down as radiation is given off in a series of steps. At each step, a new element is formed. The rate of this radioactive decay is called the half-life; the time it takes for half the atoms in a radioactive substance to take the first decay step. The half-life of uranium-238 is 4,500 million years, because it takes 4,500 million years for half the atoms in any amount of uranium-238 to decay radioactively.

MARIE CURIE

The French physicist Antoine Becquerel discovered the radioactivity of uranium when uranium salts unexpectedly clouded a photographic plate. Marie Curie and her husband Pierre Curie then investigated uranium. They found that its ore, pitchblende, was so radioactive that another radioactive element must be present. They found two, radium and polonium, and Becquerel and the Curies shared the 1903 Nobel Prize for Physics for isolating radium. Marie Curie died of leukemia, probably caused by exposure to so much radiation.

USEFUL RADIATION

The radiation from radioactive materials can be deadly, so it always needs to be treated with care. But it can be put to good use. Some heart pacemakers contain nuclear batteries, because they last so much longer than ordinary batteries. Cancers are detected and destroyed using radioactivity.

Battery
Horn
Indicator light

This sensing chamber contains a radioactive substance that is used to detect the presence of smoke.

SMOKE ALARMS

Many smoke alarms have a weak radioactive source such as americium-241. Its rays split the atoms inside a chamber into ions, which makes them pass a slight electric current. If smoke enters this chamber, it disturbs the ions and reduces the current. A microchip senses this and triggers the alarm.

The worker is shielded from the radiation by leaded glass walls.

The hat and coat prevent radioactivity from clinging to clothes and hair.

GEIGER COUNTER

A Geiger counter detects and measures the intensity of radiation. It is named after Hans Geiger (1882–1945), the German physicist who perfected it. The detecting probe is filled with gas at low pressure. The radioactivity splits the gas into ions, which produce a pulse of electricity. The needle on the dial or the speed of the clicks produced indicate the amount of radioactivity.

Ions and electrons are created when radiation splits atoms in the Geiger counter tube. These then conduct electricity between the cathode and the anode and set off a counter or loudspeaker.

Ion

Radioactivity

Plastic window

Anode (positively charged wire)

Cathode (negatively charged cylinder)

HANDLING RADIOACTIVE SUBSTANCES

Radioactive materials must be handled with care. In the nuclear industry, the workers handle the materials through special gloves fitted into a cabinet. Sometimes people have to work outside a room with the deadly materials in it, so they use remote-handling instruments that mimic the action of their own hands. All nuclear workers wear a special badge called a dosimeter, which records the amount of radiation they receive over a certain period.

RADIOACTIVE FALLOUT

Nuclear power plants hold large quantities of radioactive material, usually quite safely. But one of the world's worst nuclear accidents was the explosion at the Chernobyl nuclear reactor in Ukraine in April 1986. Radioactive material thrown into the air eventually returned to the ground as fallout, contaminating large areas of Europe. This map shows the contamination 10 days after the explosion.

Chernobyl

CARBON DATING

Animals and plants have a known proportion of a radioisotope of carbon, carbon-14, in their tissues. When they die they stop taking carbon in, and the amount of carbon-14 goes down at a known rate (the half-life). Using the half-life, the age of ancient organic materials can be found by measuring the amount of carbon-14 that is left. This wooden mummy label is about 2,500 years old.

RADIOTHERAPY

Hospitals use radiotherapy to treat patients suffering from cancer. In this machine, gamma rays from a cobalt radioisotope are being focused on a cancer to kill the cells and prevent the cancer from spreading to other parts of the body. Gamma rays are also used to sterilize medical equipment.

RADIOISOTOPE LABELING

When certain radioisotopes are injected into the body, they collect in, or label, particular organs. This allows doctors to examine the organs more easily. The radiation that the isotopes give off may reveal damaged tissue. In this false-color image of a human heart, the damaged tissue is the horseshoe shape on the right of the picture.

Find out more

ATOMIC STRUCTURE P. 24
BONDING P. 28
ELEMENTS P. 31
HYDROGEN P. 47
NUCLEAR ENERGY P. 136
ELECTROMAGNETIC SPECTRUM P. 192
FACT FINDER P. 402

BONDING

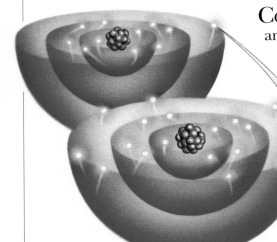

Sodium atom

One electron travels from the sodium atom to the chlorine atom.

Chlorine atom

COMMON SALT IS MADE OF sodium and chlorine. These substances aren't just mixed with each other; their particles are stuck together with a chemical "glue," known as a bond. All bonding involves the movement of electrons in the outermost shells of the atoms. But atoms use these electrons to bond in different ways. In salt, for example, atoms give away or take in electrons; this forms what is called an ionic bond. In a compound such as water, atoms share their electrons; this forms what is called a covalent bond. And in metals, the electrons flow around all the atoms; this is called a metallic bond. Different atoms stuck together with different bonds make up the millions of different substances found on Earth.

IONIC BONDS
An ionic bond happens when an atom loses or gains one or more electrons from its outer shell. Each atom becomes electrically charged in the process and is then called an ion. Ions are either cations or anions. The atom that has lost electrons is called the cation and has a positive charge. The atom that has gained electrons is called the anion and has a negative charge. These opposite electrical charges attract the ions to each other very strongly. So most ionic bonds are very difficult to break. Ionic compounds are usually solids and will only melt at a very high temperature. When sodium and chlorine atoms form an ionic bond together, they become the ionic compound sodium chloride (common salt).

The sodium atom has lost a negatively charged electron and thus becomes a positively charged ion, called a cation.

Sodium atom

Chlorine atom

The chlorine atom gains an electron and thus becomes a negatively charged ion, an anion.

VALENCY
The number of bonds an atom can form is called its valency. Atoms have a valency number that gives you this information. For example, a sodium atom has a valency of one. It has one electron in its outer shell, and eight in its second shell. It has to give away a single electron to leave a stable octet, so it bonds with one other atom (as in sodium chloride). A carbon atom has four electrons in its outer shell. It can bond with four other atoms to form a stable octet. It has a valency of four. Some atoms have a variable valency: iron can bond with two or three other atoms.

Atoms bond because it makes them more stable chemically. They are usually most stable when their outer shells have eight electrons. This is called a stable octet.

Salt crystals

LINUS PAULING
During the 1930s, the American chemist Linus Pauling (1901–1994) developed important theories of chemical bonding and molecular structure. He calculated energies needed to break bonds and angles of bonds, and measured distances between atoms. For this work he was awarded the 1954 Nobel Prize for Chemistry. He was also awarded the 1962 Nobel Prize for Peace for his efforts to stop the testing of nuclear bombs.

IONIC STRUCTURE
In the ionic compound sodium chloride, all the ions are arranged in a regular structure called a giant ionic lattice. The crystals of salt are cubes, because of the basic structure of the lattice. All ionic compounds form a lattice, but their ions may be arranged in a different way. This will give the lattice a different structure, and the crystal a different shape.

Ionic bond

Sodium cation

Chlorine anion

COVALENT BONDS

A lot of atoms do not easily lose or gain electrons to form ionic bonds. Instead, they share electrons between them. The electrons are shared in pairs called electron pairs. This type of bond is called a covalent bond. The smallest part of a compound with covalent bonds is called a molecule. While the bonds inside molecules are often strong, forces between molecules are usually weak. That is why so many covalent compounds are gases or liquids. They have low melting and boiling points because it does not take much energy to push the molecules apart.

Nitrogen has five electrons in its outer shell and bonds with three hydrogen atoms to make a stable octet.

Single bond

Hydrogen atom

COVALENT MOLECULES
This computer simulation shows the three-dimensional structure of the carbon compound butane (bottled gas). Butane is a typical covalent compound. Because its molecules are held together with weak forces, called Van der Waals' forces, liquid butane easily becomes a gas.

Hydrogen

Each carbon atom is bonded to other atoms.

Butane flame from bottled gas in a camping stove

DOUBLE BONDS
In covalent bonds, sometimes atoms share two pairs of electrons between them, instead of one. The oxygen that exists in the atmosphere consists of two atoms linked together by a double bond.

Double bond

Oxygen atoms

HYDROGEN BONDS

A molecule of water (H_2O) is made up of two hydrogen atoms linked to one oxygen atom by covalent bonds. The main forces holding water molecules together are called hydrogen bonds. These bonds occur because the hydrogen part of the water molecule is slightly positively charged, and the oxygen part is slightly negatively charged. This is because the oxygen atoms in the water molecule pull the electrons toward them, away from the hydrogen atoms.

Water has a high boiling point for a covalent substance because the molecules are linked by strong hydrogen bonds.

Hydrogen bond

Slightly negative oxygen atom

Slightly positive hydrogen atom

METALLIC BONDS

In the atoms that make up a metal, the electrons in the outer shell are only loosely attached. These electrons float around in a common pool, or "sea" of electrons. This is metallic bonding. The electrons in the sea can flow around easily. This explains why metals can conduct electricity so well. When heat or electricity is applied to one part of the metal, the electrons quickly carry it to all the other parts.

A false-color image of a gold lattice. Each yellow dot represents a gold atom.

Crystalline gold nugget

The outer electrons of metal atoms can move freely from one to another.

A metal bulb filament glows as electricity passes through it.

METAL STRUCTURE
Metal atoms are arranged in rows that fit neatly together, held by a sea of electrons in a giant metallic lattice. The atoms in a metal lattice are not bonded directly to their neighbors, so they can move around and still form part of a strong lattice structure. This is why metals are easily bent and hammered.

CRYSTALS

IF YOU LOOK at sugar under a magnifying glass, you will see tiny, glassy cubes. These are sugar crystals. Gems such as rubies and sapphires are also crystals. Most solids, including metals, are made up of lots of crystals. Sometimes you cannot see them because they are too small or stuck together, but you can often see them in rocks. Crystals in rocks often have no definite shape because they are packed together. But when they grow freely in rock cavities, they form beautiful, regular shapes. There are seven main crystal shapes, or systems. These shapes reflect the arrangement of the atoms or ions that the crystal is made of, called the crystal lattice. Scientists investigate this lattice with X-rays.

CRYSTAL COLOR

Some crystals, such as sulfur, are almost always the same color. But quartz (silicon dioxide) comes in different colors. This is because it gets colored by impurities. In its pure form, quartz is transparent and is called rock crystal. But it can be white (milky quartz), pink (rose quartz), or yellow (citrine). In this purple variety (amethyst), the color comes mainly from iron.

LIQUID CRYSTALS

The displays you see on digital watches and calculators consist of transparent liquid crystal held between two sheets of glass in a certain pattern. When electricity is passed through the liquid crystal, it appears darker in the segments needed to show the right number, while the other segments stay transparent. This type of display is called a liquid crystal display (LCD).

CLEAVAGE

When crystals break, they tend to cleave (split) along certain planes. The planes are related to the basic crystal lattice. Mica, for example, cleaves into thin sheets parallel to the base of the crystal.

PEGMATITE

The crystals in this rock, called pegmatite, are large because the rock cooled slowly. The crystal shapes are not regular because the crystals formed right next to each other, not in a free space.

Idocrase has tetragonal symmetry.

Gypsum has monoclinic symmetry.

Axinite has triclinic symmetry.

Quartz has trigonal symmetry.

Topaz (right) has rhombic symmetry.

Emerald has hexagonal symmetry.

Galena (lead ore) has cubic symmetry.

MAKING CRYSTALS

This pattern of different crystals was made from ammonium iron sulfate crystals (brown), cobalt chloride crystals (dark blue), and copper nitrate crystals (light blue). Crystals are easy to grow by hanging a string in water into which you have stirred a lot of sugar or bath crystals.

CRYSTAL SYSTEMS

The seven basic systems of crystals are shown above. Perfectly shaped crystals are rare, but whatever the shape of the crystal, its symmetry can be measured. This helps scientists to identify it.

WILLIAM BRAGG

X-ray crystallogram of a protein

William Henry Bragg (1862–1942) and his son William Lawrence Bragg (1890–1971) were the first to study the structure of crystals using X-rays. They won the Nobel Prize for Physics in 1915 for their work. If a beam of X-rays is passed through a crystal, it makes a pattern on a photographic plate. This pattern is called a crystallogram. It reveals the crystal's internal structure, which is the arrangement of the atoms. Each crystal has its own crystallogram.

Find out more

STATES OF MATTER P. 18
BONDING P. 28
SULFUR P. 45
SALTS P. 73
CHEMISTRY OF WATER P. 75
ROCKS AND MINERALS P. 221
FACT FINDER P. 402

ELEMENTS

A GOLD BAR is made of atoms of one kind only, gold atoms, which means that gold is an element. Most things in the universe consist of combinations of different elements, called compounds. Only a few elements can be found in the pure state, such as gold, copper, and silver. So far more than 112 elements are known, of which 90 occur naturally on Earth. About 10 of these were known before the 18th century, but most were discovered in the 18th and 19th centuries. It was then that chemists seriously began to investigate chemical elements and compounds. Today, many artificial elements have been created that do not exist in nature. All are radioactive. Some only exist for a few millionths of a second.

ANCIENT ELEMENTS

During the 4th century BCE, ancient Greek philosophers such as Aristotle believed that all forms of matter were made up of just four elements in different proportions. These were fire, air, water, and earth. Bone, for example, was thought to be made up of four parts fire, two parts water, and two parts earth. This illustration, from a 17th-century German poem on alchemy, shows four characters symbolizing earth (*Terra*), water (*Aqua*), air (*Aer*), and fire (*Ignis*).

ELEMENTS IN PREHISTORY

Iron was one of the elements familiar to ancient people from about 1500 BCE. The Hittites, in what is now central Turkey, found that they could obtain it by heating iron ores and extracting the iron. Their knowledge then spread across Europe. This iron reaping hook is over 2,000 years old.

Iron blade fitted into handle made from antler.

AGE OF THE ELEMENTS

In 1669 a German man named Hennig Brand was probably the first to extract an element when he discovered phosphorus. But it was nearly a century later before others followed him and heated substances to extract the elements from their compounds. Others separated elements by electrolysis, which means passing electricity through a substance.

LINEAR ACCELERATOR

Nuclear physicists can create a new element by bombarding an existing element with high-speed particles in a linear accelerator. By adding to the number of protons in the nucleus, a new element is made.

BIRTH OF THE ELEMENTS

The simplest element, hydrogen, was the first to form, shortly after the Big Bang, which created the universe billions of years ago. It was followed by helium. All the elements that now make up the Earth were created in the heart of giant stars. The elements were scattered through space when these stars exploded.

Exploding star

A 19th-century laboratory

COMMON ELEMENTS

In the universe as a whole, hydrogen and helium are by far the most common elements. They are the main elements in the stars, making up 98 percent of their matter. In the Earth's crust, there is more oxygen than any other element, followed by silicon. Together they account for nearly three-quarters of the crust. Carbon, hydrogen, and oxygen are the most common elements in the human body, because they make up the compounds in all the body cells.

Elements in the Earth's crust

- Rarer elements
- Potassium
- Magnesium
- Sodium
- Calcium
- Iron
- Aluminum
- Silicon
- Oxygen

In this carbon atom, the six electrons spin around, constantly ready to bond with other atoms.

ATOMS

All the atoms of an element have the same numbers of electrons in their shells and protons in the nucleus. This gives each element its unique chemistry.

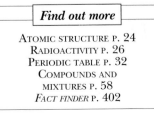

Find out more

ATOMIC STRUCTURE P. 24
RADIOACTIVITY P. 26
PERIODIC TABLE P. 32
COMPOUNDS AND MIXTURES P. 58
FACT FINDER P. 402

PERIODIC TABLE

THIS COMPLICATED-LOOKING TABLE is really an ordered list of all the elements. They are arranged in rows in order of increasing atomic number, or number of protons in the nucleus. During the 1860s, chemists noticed that certain groups of elements behaved in similar ways and tried to set the groups out clearly in a table. In 1869 Dimitri Mendeleyev published the best table, which is still used today. A chemist can tell a lot about an element just by looking at its position in the periodic table.

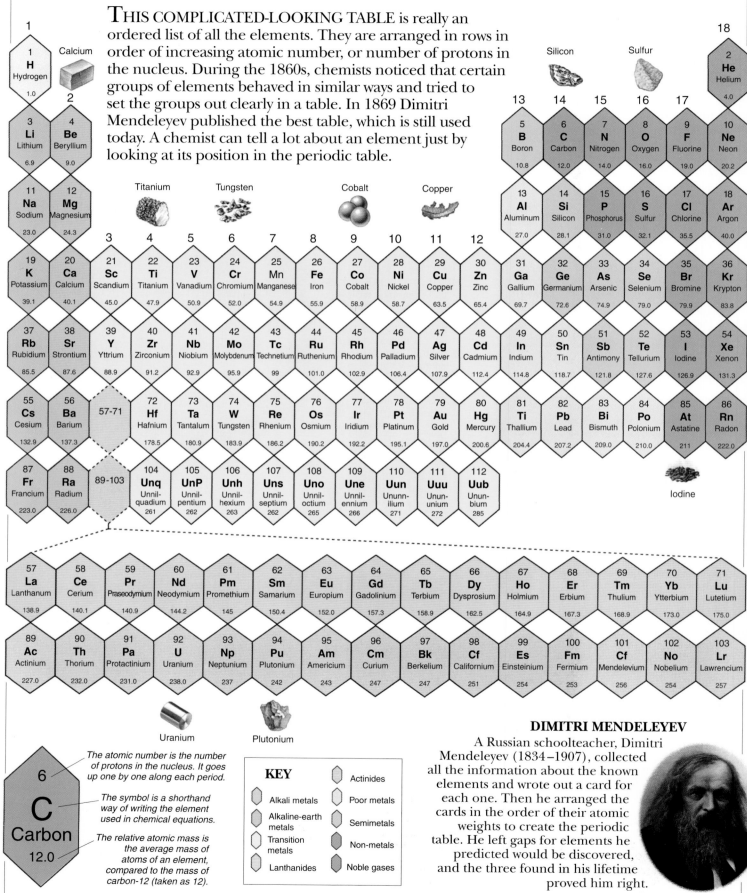

DIMITRI MENDELEYEV

A Russian schoolteacher, Dimitri Mendeleyev (1834–1907), collected all the information about the known elements and wrote out a card for each one. Then he arranged the cards in the order of their atomic weights to create the periodic table. He left gaps for elements he predicted would be discovered, and the three found in his lifetime proved him right.

The atomic number is the number of protons in the nucleus. It goes up one by one along each period.

The symbol is a shorthand way of writing the element used in chemical equations.

The relative atomic mass is the average mass of atoms of an element, compared to the mass of carbon-12 (taken as 12).

KEY

Alkali metals
Alkaline-earth metals
Transition metals
Lanthanides
Actinides
Poor metals
Semimetals
Non-metals
Noble gases

GROUPS AND PERIODS

How does the periodic table work? The known elements are arranged in horizontal rows, called periods. The atomic number goes up as you move across. The periods start with an alkali metal on the left and end with a noble gas on the right. The atoms of the elements on the left, at the beginning of each period, have only one electron in their outer shell. By the end of the period the outer shell is filled. The vertical columns, called groups, each contain elements that have the same valency and behave in a similar way chemically because of the number of electrons in their outer shells.

PERIODIC TABLE

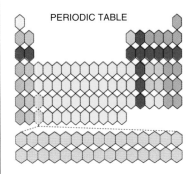

Group 14: carbon (C), silicon (Si), germanium (Ge), tin (Sn), lead (Pb)

Period 3: sodium (Na), magnesium (Mg), aluminum (Al), silicon (Si), phosphorus (P), sulfur (S), chlorine (Cl), argon (Ar)

METALS AND NONMETALS

Most of the chemical elements are metals. The nonmetals are in a triangle on the right of the periodic table. Between the two are the semimetals, which have some properties of metals and some of nonmetals. There are several big differences between metals and nonmetals. Metals are solid (the one exception is mercury, a liquid). They conduct heat and electricity well, and usually have high melting and boiling points. They form positive ions (cations) when they bond with other elements. Most nonmetals are gases, with low melting and boiling points. They are not good conductors, except for carbon. They form negative ions (anions) when they bond with other elements.

Carbon has two shells.

Silicon has three shells.

A

Germanium has four shells.

Tin has five shells.

Lead has six shells.

DOWN GROUP

In some groups, such as Group 1, the alkali metals, Group 2, the alkaline-earth metals, and Group 18, the noble gases, the group relationship is very obvious: the elements are similar in appearance and reactivity (ability to bond). In other groups, such as Group 14, the chemical properties remain similar, but the elements change from a nonmetal at the top to metals at the bottom. Carbon (C) is a nonmetal, silicon (Si) and germanium (Ge) are both semimetals, and tin (Sn) and lead (Pb) are both metals.

6	C Carbon 12.0
14	Si Silicon 28.1
32	Ge Germanium 72.6
50	Sn Tin 118.7
82	Pb Lead 207.2

Down a group, the number of shells increases by one with each element. An atom can have up to seven shells. The number of electrons in the outer shell is always the same as the other elements in the group.

The number of electrons for each element is the same as the atomic number.

Aluminum, from Group 13, has 13 electrons, with three in its outer shell.

Silicon, from Group 14, has 14 electrons, with four in its outer shell.

Phosphorus, from Group 15, has 15 electrons, with five in its outer shell.

Magnesium, from Group 2, has 12 electrons, with two in its outer shell.

Sulfur, from Group 16, has 16 electrons with six in its outer shell.

Chlorine, from Group 17, has 17 electrons, with seven in its outer shell.

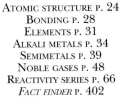

Argon, from Group 18, has 18 electrons, with eight in its outer shell.

DECREASING SIZE

The number of shells remains the same across a period, but as the number of electrons increases, the size of the atom decreases. This is because the extra protons in the nucleus pull the extra electrons closer to it.

ACROSS A PERIOD

Going across the period, the number of electrons increases by one with each element, and the chemical properties of the elements show a gradual change. In Period 3, the elements change from the metal sodium (Na), through the semimetal silicon (Si), to the nonmetal Argon (Ar). The elements change from forming cations to forming anions.

Sodium, from Group 1, has 11 electrons, with one in its outer shell.

11	12	13	14	15	16	17	18
Na Sodium 23.0	**Mg** Magnesium 24.3	**Al** Aluminum 27.0	**Si** Silicon 28.1	**P** Phosphorus 31.0	**S** Sulfur 32.1	**Cl** Chlorine 35.5	**Ar** Argon 40.0

Find out more

ATOMIC STRUCTURE P. 24
BONDING P. 28
ELEMENTS P. 31
ALKALI METALS P. 34
SEMIMETALS P. 39
NOBLE GASES P. 48
REACTIVITY SERIES P. 66
FACT FINDER P. 402

ALKALI METALS

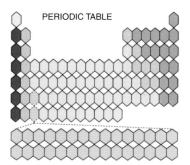

PERIODIC TABLE

Group 1: lithium (Li), sodium (Na), potassium (K), rubidium (Rb), cesium (Cs), and radioactive francium (Fr)

THE SALT THAT YOU EAT on your food is a compound of sodium, the most common element of Group 1 of the periodic table. All the members of this group are called the alkali metals, because they react with water to form alkaline solutions. Potassium, another member, is an ingredient in fertilizers, as potassium sulfate, or potassium nitrate (also called saltpeter). Doctors use compounds of lithium to treat manic depression, a mental illness. Also, lithium is mixed with aluminum to make a light but strong alloy (metal mixture) used in airplanes. All the alkali metals are a silvery-white color. Their reactivity increases going down the group. All have one electron in their outer shells.

Alkali metals are soft enough to cut with a knife.

Sodium reacts so quickly with oxygen in the air that a cut surface tarnishes within minutes. Alkali metals are stored in oil to prevent them from reacting.

Potassium reacts even faster than sodium with oxygen in the air.

SOAPMAKING
Sodium hydroxide and potassium hydroxide are boiled with fat to make hard soap and liquid soap. It is thought that soap was first made by the Ancient Egyptians.

SODIUM LAMPS
Street lamps glow a vivid orange-yellow because they contain sodium vapor. The color is produced when electricity passes through this vapor. Sodium compounds give a similar color when they are held in a flame.

REACTION WITH WATER
A piece of potassium metal reacts so vigorously with water that it zooms all over the surface, creating bubbles of gas. This gas is hydrogen, which burns with a pink-blue flame. The potassium and the water react to form potassium hydroxide, which makes an alkaline solution in water. When all the metal has reacted with the water, the water is warm because of the heat given out during the reaction. All the alkali metals react in a similar way with water. However, rubidium and cesium explode as they touch it.

Sodium chloride is fed in here.

Chlorine is given off.

Molten sodium is drawn off here.

Molten sodium chloride

Sodium is produced at the circular steel cathode.

Chlorine is produced at the graphite anode.

CESIUM ATOMIC CLOCK
Clocks keep time by "counting" some kind of rhythm, such as the swinging of a pendulum. Atomic clocks "count" the natural vibrations of cesium atoms. Scientists know that cesium atoms vibrate at 9,192,631,770 times per second, so fractions of a second can be measured very accurately using this clock. The vibrations are detected with the help of an electromagnetic field.

Cesium is heated so that it gives off atoms.

Atoms traveling through an electromagnetic field give a reading on the clock.

MAKING SODIUM
Sodium can be extracted from salt (sodium chloride), using a Down's cell. The salt is heated to 1,760°F (800°C) to make it melt. Electricity travels through the molten salt, via two rods called a cathode and an anode, to make it separate into sodium and chlorine. This process is called electrolysis and was first performed by Humphry Davy (1778–1829).

Find out more

BONDING P. 28
PERIODIC TABLE P. 32
ELECTROLYSIS P. 67
ALKALIS AND BASES P. 70
CHEMISTRY IN FARMING P. 91
ALKALI INDUSTRY P. 94
ELECTROMAGNETISM P. 156
FACT FINDER P. 402

ALKALINE-EARTH METALS

PERIODIC TABLE

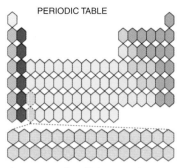

Group 2: beryllium (Be), magnesium (Mg), calcium (Ca), strontium (Sr), barium (Ba), and radioactive radium (Ra)

CALCIUM COMPOUNDS are found in chalk, milk, and your bones, so calcium is one of the most familiar elements in Group 2 of the periodic table. All these elements are called alkaline-earth metals because they react with water to produce alkaline solutions and their compounds occur widely in nature. For example, beryllium is found in the semiprecious gem beryl. Radium is the radioactive element discovered by Marie Curie. A radioisotope of strontium, strontium-90, is a dangerous part of nuclear fallout, but it is also used to treat skin cancers. In their pure form, alkaline-earth metals are silvery-white. They have a similar chemistry to the alkali metals, but they are less reactive. They all have two electrons in their outer shells.

FIREWORK COLORS

The vivid colors we see in fireworks are mainly produced by alkaline-earth metals. Magnesium metal is used in some fireworks to produce a brilliant white light. Strontium compounds are used to produce crimsons, and barium compounds are used to produce greens.

BARIUM MEAL
In hospitals, some patients have a "barium meal," which contains barium sulfate, before they have an X-ray. The barium sulfate blocks X-rays and makes the digestive system show up on X-ray photographs. Doctors can then see if there is anything wrong.

LIGHTWEIGHT ALLOYS
Magnesium is widely used in alloys for bicycle frames, which also contain such metals as aluminum and zinc. This makes them light but strong.

VITAL MAGNESIUM
The green pigment chlorophyll is essential for plants to be able to make food. Chlorophyll contains magnesium compounds, which help capture the energy in sunlight. This energy is used in the food-making process called photosynthesis.

Chlorophyll is the substance that makes plants green.

Chlorophyll is found in chloroplasts, tiny bodies in plant cells.

CHALKY FALLS
In hot springs, like Pammukale Falls in Turkey, warm water bubbles to the surface and cascades over the surrounding rocks. If it contains a lot of dissolved chalk (calcium carbonate), this will come out of solution as the water evaporates, and be deposited as chalky "icicles."

BONE CALCIUM
Calcium is a major ingredient of bone, where it is present as calcium phosphate. This makes bones hard, so that they can give structure and protection to other parts of the body.

Find out more
PERIODIC TABLE P. 32
COMPOUNDS AND MIXTURES P. 58
ALKALIS AND BASES P. 70
PHOTOSYNTHESIS P. 340
SKELETONS P. 352
FACT FINDER P. 402

TRANSITION METALS

IRON, NICKEL, SILVER, AND GOLD are typical metals. They are shiny, hard, and strong. They have high melting points and conduct heat and electricity well. In the periodic table, these and most of the other typical metals form part of a central block of elements called the transition metals. Each of the elements is very similar to those near it in the table. In addition to being typical metals, the transition elements have other things in common. Many have variable valencies, many are good catalysts, they form alloys with other metals, and many of their compounds are colored.

PERIODIC TABLE

There are a lot of transition metals. Some are very well-known, but some are very rare. The more familiar ones include iron (Fe), cobalt (Co), nickel (Ni), copper (Cu), zinc (Zn), silver (Ag), cadmium (Cd), tungsten (W), platinum (Pt), gold (Au), and mercury (Hg).

TRANSITION METALS IN CARS

A car is a good example of something that is made of many transition metals. The body shell is made of mild steel, which is iron with a little carbon. The steel also contains traces of manganese, to improve its quality and strength. Sometimes the steel shell is galvanized (coated with zinc), to protect the steel from rusting.

Lower electrode

Central electrode

SPARK PLUG
The main body and lower electrode of a spark plug are made of iron. The central electrode is usually made of a copper alloy.

Valve springs, which control the valves that regulate the flow of fuel mixture, are made of steel alloyed with chromium and vanadium, so that they can resist high temperatures and last for a long time.

Suspension springs are made of steel with a high percentage of carbon in it, hardened and heat-treated to give increased strength.

Most engine blocks (containing the cylinders, where the fuel mixture is fired) are made of cast iron, which contains a high percentage of carbon and other impurities. It is cheap and resists shock well.

The generator, the part of a car that produces electricity, contains coils of fine copper wire. Elsewhere, perhaps as much as 110 yards (100 m) of copper wire connect the car's electrical components.

The bearings in the gear box are layered, with an inner lining of relatively soft bearing alloy containing metals such as copper, tin, and lead, and an outer shell of steel.

Car paints are often made using transition metal compounds. White paint may contain titanium dioxide, and red and yellow paints may contain cadmium sulfides.

The headlight reflector is usually chromium plated. Chromium provides the final hard, shiny coating over base layers of nickel and copper.

The lightbulb contains tungsten in the coiled filament. It retains its strength when white hot, and is long-lasting.

Stainless steel, which is iron alloyed with chromium and nickel, is used for the trim in various places and sometimes for the exhaust system.

ZINC
Zinc is often used in batteries. In the type of battery you used in a flashlight, the zinc makes up the casing. In the pill-sized mercury battery, the zinc is inside.

An ordinary battery with the outside label stripped off to show the zinc casing.

This battery is the type you would find inside a watch.

IRON FOR LIFE
Compounds containing iron are essential to living things. In plants, iron compounds help to make chlorophyll, the green compound used by plants. In mammals iron is found in red blood cells in hemoglobin, which carries oxygen round the body.

Green cabbage

Red blood cells

MAGNETIC METALS
Iron, cobalt, and nickel are the only metals that can be made into strong magnets. Electromagnets have an iron core that becomes strongly magnetic when electricity is passed through surrounding coils. They are used to move waste iron in scrapyards. The electricity is switched on to pick up the iron, then switched off to drop it.

SILVER

The precious metal silver has been used to make jewelry for thousands of years. It is still also widely used in the photographic industry. This is because the compounds it forms with chlorine, bromine, and iodine are sensitive to light. They are the active ingredients on a photographic film. The silver compounds change chemically when light hits them. This change is made visible during the developing process, which turns the light-affected compounds to pure silver. Tiny grains of silver make up the dark areas on a photographic negative.

PLATINUM

Like gold and silver, platinum is a precious metal, used to make jewelry. It is precious because it is rare and attractive. It also never corrodes or wears away. This is also why it is used to make electrodes and electronic circuits—they would not work properly if their circuit metal tarnished. Platinum's main use in industry is as a catalyst, meaning it speeds up reactions such as the breakdown of oil products.

This small, square electrode is made of platinum. It is long-lasting and efficient because it does not corrode.

NICKEL ALLOYS

Silver-colored coins are made from cupronickel, an alloy of copper and nickel. Nickel is also used, along with two other transition metals, iron and chromium, to make stainless steel. Nickel is a shiny metal that does not corrode or tarnish, and it gives these properties to its alloys. Another interesting nickel alloy, with iron, is Invar. This is used in precision measuring instruments because it barely expands or contracts at all when the temperature changes.

These pellets are pure nickel.

NATIVE METALS

Most elements are not found native (in a pure state) in the Earth's crust, but a few of the transition metals are. The most important of these include copper, silver, gold, and platinum. Gold has been the most prized metal of all for centuries. It is one of the most chemically unreactive elements there is. These gold bars are almost 100 percent pure and will never lose their shine.

Each gold bar is numbered for security reasons.

Once in place, this titanium hip joint will not react chemically with the tissues around it.

Colored X-ray of a titanium hip joint in place.

INNER TRANSITION SERIES

Part of the transition metals, the inner transition series consists of two periods on the periodic table. The lanthanides in Period 6 are so called because of their first element, lanthanum. The actinides are in Period 7 and are named after their first element, actinium. Within each of these groups, the elements behave in a similar way chemically. The lanthanides are so similar that chemists had difficulty telling them apart. And besides having similar properties, the actinides are all radioactive.

CASSINI'S BATTERIES

The US space probe *Cassini*, now in orbit around Saturn, has nuclear batteries, called RTGs (radioisotope thermoelectric generators), which are powered by plutonium.

SAMARIUM IN MAGNETS

Magnets in a loudspeaker help to transmit the sound. Samarium, one of the lanthanides, and cobalt make powerful magnets, and so smaller loudspeakers can be made using magnets containing these metals.

Samarium magnet

TITANIUM

Titanium is a very strong, unreactive metal. This makes it useful for implants in the body, such as hip joints, and to repair or replace damaged bones.

Uranium

REFINED URANIUM

The best-known actinide, uranium, is the fuel used in nuclear reactors. It is extracted from the ore pitchblende. The mining of this ore is carefully controlled because it is so valuable.

Find out more

RADIOACTIVITY P. 26
CATALYSTS P. 56
IRON AND STEEL P. 84
ALLOYS P. 88
DYES AND PIGMENTS P. 102
NUCLEAR ENERGY P. 136
ELECTROMAGNETISM P. 156
PHOTOGRAPHY P. 206
FACT FINDER P. 402

POOR METALS

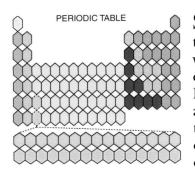

PERIODIC TABLE

Aluminum (Al), gallium (Ga), indium (In), thallium (Tl), tin (Sn), lead (Pb), bismuth (Bi), and polonium (Po)

SOME METALS ARE VERY soft and weak and melt easily. Although these are known as the poor metals, they are very useful. Tin and lead were two of the earliest metals used by people because they are easily extracted from their ores (minerals). They are especially useful in alloys. Bronze, a mixture of tin and copper, was the first alloy to be made, in about 3500 BCE. Pewter and solder are tin and lead alloys. Lead is one of the densest (heaviest) metals in common use. The Romans made drains out of lead, and their word for lead was *plumbum,* which is why we still call our drainage systems "plumbing." But lead is a serious health hazard because it gradually builds up in the body and is poisonous. Another poor metal, aluminum, is one of the least dense (lightest) of all metals.

The skin of an airplane is made of sheets of aluminum alloy riveted together. The aluminum quickly reacts with oxygen to form a protective coating of its own, so it does not need to be painted for protection as iron does.

The inside of an airplane wing is mostly empty, with a few "ribs" that hold the outer aluminum skin in place. This is to keep the airplane as light as possible.

HEAVY AS LEAD

Lead has a high density. For this reason it is a good barrier to radiation. This is put to use in the nuclear industry and hospital X-ray departments, where the staff wears lead aprons. These aprons are made by baking a mixture of fine lead powder and plastic to make a flexible sheet. This is then cut out to the right shape.

Lead shot can cause pollution in the wild. Birds that swallow it are gradually poisoned by it.

ALUMINUM ALLOYS

Aluminum is a soft and weak metal. It is the metal used to make aluminum foil. But when aluminum is alloyed with metals such as copper, it becomes hard and as strong as steel. Aluminum alloys are used to build airplanes because of their combination of lightness and strength.

ELECTRICAL USES

Aluminum is a good conductor of electricity. It is used for the transmission lines that carry electricity across the country on pylons. The lines have a core of steel to give them strength.

LEAD IN GLASS

The sparkle of crystal is the result of adding lead oxide to glass. The lead also makes crystal softer. This means that designs that will glitter can be cut into it.

TIN CANS

As the pure metal, tin is most used as a coating on steel, to make tinplate. The tin is applied by dipping or electrolysis. Ordinary tin cans are made of tinplate. Most soft drink cans are made out of aluminum.

TIN–LEAD ALLOYS

Pewter, an alloy of tin, is used to make tankards and ornaments. Solder is another tin-lead alloy, used to join metals in plumbing and electrical circuiting.

Tin has two forms, white and gray. The white form turns into the powdery gray form at low temperatures. Tin was one of the elements known to ancient civilizations, who combined it with copper to make bronze. Bronze was used to make jewelry and, later, tools.

Find out more

ATOMIC STRUCTURE P. 24
PERIODIC TABLE P. 32
REACTIVITY SERIES P. 66
ELECTROLYSIS P. 67
ALUMINUM P. 87
ALLOYS P. 88
FACT FINDER P. 402

SEMIMETALS

MOST OF THE CHEMICAL ELEMENTS have definite properties that identify them either as a metal or a nonmetal. But a few elements have properties that place them in between. These are the semimetals, or semiconductors. For example, arsenic looks metallic, but it is a poor conductor of heat and electricity. Like a nonmetal, it forms compounds with many metals. Several semimetals are used in alloys. Silicon forms part of steel, and antimony forms part of an alloy used to make ball bearings. But the most important use of semimetals is in electronics. They are used to make microchips and other electronic components (parts).

PERIODIC TABLE

Boron (B), silicon (Si), germanium (Ge), arsenic (As), antimony (Sb), selenium (Se), and tellurium (Te)

BORON AND SILICON
Glass is made from sand, which is one mineral form of silica or silicon dioxide. Quartz is another common silica mineral, often found as attractive crystals. Heatproof glass contains another semimetal, boron. The addition of the boron prevents the glass from expanding too much and cracking when it is heated. Borosilicate glass saucepans can be put directly onto a flame. Glassware in laboratories is also made of this type of glass.

SOLAR CELLS
Satellites are often designed to stay up in space for years. Ordinary batteries would not last long, so large panels of solar batteries are used instead. The solar panels contain thousands of tiny cells of silicon, which convert the energy of sunlight into electricity. The panels are positioned so that they always face the Sun, and as the satellite travels around the Earth, the maximum amount of sunlight can be used to provide energy.

These solar cells are cut from a cylinder of pure silicon.

SILICATES
Silicon is the most plentiful solid element on Earth. It is most commonly found in the form of compounds called silicates in clays and rocks. This crystal is a feldspar, a potassium aluminum silicate, one of the most common minerals on Earth.

Thousands of electronic components are crammed onto the microchips that form the circuits in electronic equipment.

Potentiometer

Fuse

Microchip

Capacitor

Transistor

SEMICONDUCTORS
Substances that conduct electricity only under certain circumstances are called semiconductors, and are very useful. Silicon and germanium are the most widely used semiconductors. Adding other elements to a semiconductor is called doping. There are two possible types of doped semiconductor, the p-type and the n-type. These are joined to form components such as diodes, transistors, and microchips, which are essential to modern electronic circuits.

Resistor

Capacitor

Microchips

Compact disc

Special lenses focus the laser.

The mirror reflects the laser beam onto the disc so that the laser can "read" the pits.

Atoms in the gallium arsenide are made to produce light. Some of it escapes in the form of a laser beam.

COMPACT DISC PLAYER
Music is recorded as pits on a compact disc, and these are "read" by a low-powered laser beam. The laser is a diode laser, made from a semiconductor compound called gallium arsenide. A diode is a device that has been doped to allow electricity to flow in one direction only. Diode lasers also transmit signals in fiberoptic telephone lines.

Find out more

CRYSTALS P. 30
PERIODIC TABLE P. 32
GLASS P. 110
MATERIAL DESIGN P. 111
CURRENT ELECTRICITY P. 148
ELECTRONIC COMPONENTS P. 168
ROCKS AND MINERALS P. 221
FACT FINDER P. 402

CARBON

WITHOUT CARBON, no living thing could survive. Our bodies are made of carbon compounds, and we take in carbon compounds in our food. The carbon atom can bond with as many as four other atoms from other elements, as well as other carbon atoms, so there are hundreds of thousands of different carbon compounds. Carbon is a nonmetal. In nature it occurs in its pure form as diamond and graphite. In compounds it occurs in carbonate rocks such as chalk, fossil fuels such as coal, and carbon dioxide in the air. When fuels burn, the carbon in them reacts with the oxygen in the air to form carbon dioxide. But too much carbon dioxide in the air traps heat like the glass of a greenhouse. This is called the greenhouse effect.

PERIODIC TABLE

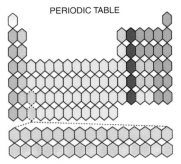

Group 14: carbon (C), silicon (Si), germanium (Ge), tin (Sn), and lead (Pb)

CARBONATED DRINKS
The fizz in drinks is carbon dioxide. The gas dissolves in the liquid under pressure, and bubbles come out when the pressure is released.

Diamond is the hardest mineral known.

Anthracite, the best coal, is 90 percent carbon.

In diamond, each carbon atom is attached to four other carbon atoms.

DIFFERENT FORMS OF CARBON
At first sight, diamond and graphite seem to have nothing in common. Diamond is hard and clear and graphite is soft and gray. But they are both forms (allotropes) of carbon. Carbon also makes up a large part of coal. When coal is heated out of contact with air, it turns to coke, a smokeless fuel. The charcoal used in barbeques is carbon made by partly burning wood or bones.

CARBON BUCKYBALLS
In 1990 scientists discovered a third allotrope of carbon, besides diamond and graphite. Its molecular structure looks like a soccer ball or the domed roof of the stadium developed by American engineer Buckminster Fuller. This form of carbon was therefore named buckminsterfullerene, and one molecule is sometimes called a "buckyball."

When you draw a line with a pencil, graphite is left as a mark because the sheets of carbon atoms are easily pulled apart.

In graphite, each carbon atom is attached to only three other carbon atoms in flat sheets that are weakly attracted to each other.

CARBON FIBERS
Organic textile fibers are heated to make silky threads of pure carbon. These fibers are combined with other materials such as plastic to make very strong and light composite materials. Carbon-fiber composites are useful for objects where lightness and strength are important, from tennis rackets to small airplanes.

Clean water flows back into the tank.

Activated charcoal traps dirt and impurities.

ELECTRIC CARBON
Carbon is unusual among nonmetals because it is a good conductor of electricity. In steelmaking, the electrodes in the electric arc furnace are graphite blocks. Electricity arcs (jumps) between the electrodes and the metal scrap. The heat produced melts the metal.

Carbon fibers are much thinner than human hair, but are eight times stronger than steel.

Tennis rackets made with a carbon-fiber frame can be lighter and stronger than wooden ones.

Dirty water from the tank flows into the filter canister.

ACTIVATED CHARCOAL
When specially treated, or activated, charcoal has great powers of adsorption, meaning it attracts materials to its surface. It can remove poisonous gases or unpleasant odors from the air. It forms part of gas masks, spacecraft ventilation systems, and extraction fans. It is also used to purify liquids, including the water in fish tanks. The water in the tank passes over the charcoal, which removes the dirt. The cleaned water then goes back into the tank.

Find out more
PERIODIC TABLE P. 32
ORGANIC CHEMISTRY P. 41
IRON AND STEEL P. 84
COAL PRODUCTS P. 96
MATERIAL DESIGN P. 111
CYCLES IN THE BIOSPHERE P. 372
FACT FINDER P. 402

ORGANIC CHEMISTRY

CARBON IS SO IMPORTANT that there is a whole area of science that studies it. This is organic chemistry. It is called "organic" because scientists used to believe that the complex carbon compounds occurred only in living organisms. But now we know that other, nonliving compounds contain carbon, the study of organic chemistry includes all compounds that contain carbon—except for simple "inorganic" compounds such as carbon dioxide. Carbon is different from all the other elements because it can form very stable bonds with itself. Because of this, there are long chains containing hundreds of thousands of carbon atoms. Organic compounds can be divided into families such as proteins, fats, and sugars.

Brightly colored fabrics that do not fade became possible with aniline dyes.

The benzene ring has six carbon atoms and six hydrogen atoms.

LIVING CHEMISTRY
Carbon compounds hold the key to plant and animal life on Earth. Life is only possible because of the extremely complex and varied chemistry of carbon that goes on in all living cells.

CARBON CYCLE
Carbon circulates through the air, animals, plants, and the soil all the time. This is called the carbon cycle.

Carbon dioxide in air

Organic compounds in animals turn into organic compounds and carbon dioxide as they breathe and decay.

Organic compounds in plants and fuels release carbon dioxide during burning.

Organic compounds in plants change into other organic compounds and carbon dioxide as they decay.

Animals

Animals get organic compounds from eating plants.

Plants make sugars from the carbon dioxide in the air.

ORGANIC CHEMISTRY

1808 The Swedish chemist Jöns Berzelius (1779–1848) uses the term organic chemistry to refer to the chemistry of living things.

1828 The German chemist Friedrich Wöhler (1800–82), succeeds in recreating a natural carbon compound in his laboratory. The meaning of organic chemistry now changes to refer to the chemistry of most carbon compounds, not just the natural ones.

1865 The German chemist Friedrich Kekulé von Stradonitz (1829–96) thinks up the idea of a ring structure for benzene after dreaming about a snake biting its tail.

AROMATICS AND ALIPHATICS
Benzene is an organic liquid with a powerful aroma. Organic compounds that contain the benzene ring structure are called the aromatics. The aromatic compound aniline, also called aminobenzene, is the starting point for a whole range of vivid dyes, called the aniline dyes. Organic compounds that are made up of chains of carbon atoms, with no rings, are called aliphatics.

ISOMERS
Some carbon compounds contain the same atoms, but have different properties. This is because the atoms are arranged in a different way. Such compounds are called isomers. Butane and 2-methyl propane are isomers of each other. Bottled gas always contains some 2-methyl propane as well as butane. They are both made up of four carbon atoms and 10 hydrogen atoms.

Butane

2-methyl propane

The molecular formula of ethene is C_2H_4. This gives the total number of carbon and hydrogen atoms. Its structural formula is $CH_2=CH_2$, which shows that two hydrogens are attached to each carbon. The carbons are linked by a double bond.

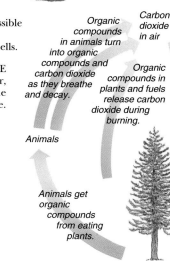

Molecules of ethene react together to create a long chain linked by single bonds. This makes the plastic polythene, with the formula $(CH_2)_n$. The "n" means that the unit of one carbon atom and two hydrogen atoms is repeated any number of times.

POLYMER PLASTICS
Molecules of carbon compounds such as ethene can combine to form huge chains that are typical of plastics. The single molecule is called a monomer, and the chain is called a polymer. Different plastics are made using different monomers.

OIL AND PLASTIC
Car lubricating oil and plastic don't seem very alike. But they have something in common. They are both organic materials, and are produced from the same source, crude oil.

Plastic is made by processing the lighter substances found in crude oil.

Car oil forms part of crude oil and is extracted from it by distillation.

Find out more

CHEMISTRY OF AIR P. 74
CHEMISTRY OF THE BODY P. 76
OIL PRODUCTS P. 98
POLYMERS P. 100
DYES AND PIGMENTS P. 102
MATERIAL DESIGN P. 111
CYCLES IN THE BIOSPHERE P. 372
FACT FINDER P. 406

NITROGEN

THERE IS AN ELEMENT that is vital to life, and forms almost 80 percent of the air around us. This element is nitrogen. It is a colorless gas with no taste or smell, and it forms part of the proteins in every living cell. A constant cycle keeps nitrogen in our lives. Plants get nitrogen from the soil. Animals get nitrogen by eating plants or other animals. When plants and animals die, they rot and return nitrogen to the soil. Nitrogen is also in the Earth as minerals such as sodium nitrate. Like oxygen, nitrogen in the air is made up of molecules with two atoms, which have the symbol N_2. Nitrogen forms several compounds with oxygen. These include the gases that come out of car exhausts and damage the environment.

PERIODIC TABLE

Group 15: nitrogen (N), phosphorus (P), arsenic (As), antimony (Sb), and bismuth (Bi)

NITROGEN EXPLOSIVES

Explosives are unstable substances that release a huge volume of gases quickly. The gases expand very rapidly and this produces a devastating shock wave. Most chemical explosives contain nitrogen, including nitroglycerine and trinitrotoluene (TNT). Nitroglycerine is an oily liquid that is highly unstable. It is made safer by being mixed with a sort of clay to make dynamite. Explosives are used to make bombs.

Explosives can be used in a very controlled way to bring down a building without damaging others nearby.

Nitrogen fertilizers help crops to grow.

NITROGEN FERTILIZERS

Farmers and gardeners apply fertilizers containing nitrogen to their soil, to put back the nitrogen that plants take out. In the past, rotted manure, which is rich in nitrogen, was used. Today, many people prefer to use artificial fertilizers such as nitrates and ammonium sulfate.

Nitrogen is fed in here.   Safety valve

Ethanol is pumped out here.

Ethanol is fed in here.

Ethanol storage tank

UNREACTIVE NITROGEN

Nitrogen is unreactive, so it is used to exclude oxygen, which is very reactive, from a range of containers. Ethanol (ordinary alcohol) is likely to catch fire if it comes into contact with oxygen, so nitrogen is used to exclude it from the storage tanks. Potato chip bags are filled with nitrogen. This excludes oxygen, which would react with fat in the chips and make them go stale.

NITROGEN CYCLE

There is a continuous exchange of nitrogen between the atmosphere, animals, and plants. This is called the nitrogen cycle.

Nitrogen in air   Nitrogen-fixing bacteria

Fertilizers

Death and decay

Death and decay

Nitrogen in plant proteins

Death and decay

Nitrogen in animal proteins

LIQUID NITROGEN

Food is quick-frozen using liquid nitrogen. Foods such as cheesecakes are loaded onto a conveyor belt in a tunnel freezer (left). As they move along, they are first cooled by nitrogen gas, then sprayed with liquid nitrogen, which freezes them.

ANESTHETIC NITROGEN

Dinitrogen oxide is a sweet-smelling gas used as an anesthetic. It is called "laughing gas" because it makes some patients laugh before and after they are unconscious. In the 19th century, demonstrations of the effects of laughing gas were given in private houses in London, England, just for fun. Later scientists realized how useful the gas could be as an anesthetic.

Find out more

BONDING P. 28
PERIODIC TABLE P. 32
CHEMISTRY OF AIR P. 74
AMMONIA P. 90
CHEMISTRY IN FARMING P. 91
RAIN P. 264
CYCLES IN THE BIOSPHERE P. 372
FACT FINDER P. 402

PHOSPHORUS

PERIODIC TABLE

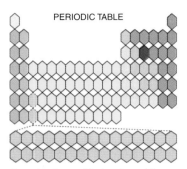

Group 15: nitrogen (N), phosphorus (P), arsenic (As), antimony (Sb), and bismuth (Bi)

HAVE YOU EVER WONDERED why cola has a sharp taste? The sharpness comes from phosphoric acid, a compound of phosphorus. In its common form, phosphorus is a yellowish, waxy, and slightly see-through solid. It glows in the dark, an effect called phosphorescence. Yellow phosphorus is so reactive that it must be kept under water to stop it from reacting with oxygen and catching fire. Phosphorus is important in living things. Plants extract phosphorus compounds from the soil. Animals get it from plants. In the Earth, phosphorus occurs mainly in mineral phosphates, most of which are made into fertilizers.

MINING PHOSPHORUS
In the Earth, phosphorus occurs in apatite (calcium phosphate), which exists in several forms. The main deposits are in North Africa. Phosphate rock is used in huge quantities in the chemical industry to make fertilizers. The rock is treated with sulfuric acid to make superphosphate, a fertilizer that is easily absorbed by plants.

PHOSPHORUS AND LIGHT
Red phosphorus is made by heating yellow phosphorus at high temperatures. It is then rolled into sheets. Red phosphorus is used in marine distress flares to create a very bright light. It is also an active ingredient in matches. A safety match will only strike on a surface containing red phosphorus. A strike-anywhere match has a phosphorus compound in the tip.

PHOSPHORUS ALLOTROPES
There are three main forms (allotropes) of the element phosphorus. Pictured left are sticks and chunks of yellow phosphorus. But they are slowly changing into red phosphorus because it is much more stable. You can see the dark patches on the sticks. Black phosphorus, the most stable form, can be made by heating the yellow under pressure.

Calcium phosphate is part of bones and teeth, but in nature it appears as crystals in a variety of colors and is called apatite.

PHOSPHATES
The washing powder or liquid used to wash clothes contains sodium tripolyphosphate. This softens the water. Phosphates from sewage, fertilizers, and detergents pollute rivers because they make a lot of algae grow. These then use up the oxygen in the water. Organic phosphates are used as pesticides.

PHOSPHORUS FOR LIFE
Bones and teeth are mainly made of calcium phosphate, which makes them hard. Phosphate groups form part of DNA (deoxyribonucleic acid) in the nucleus of cells, which controls each cell. A phosphate called ATP (adenosine triphosphate) provides energy in the body. When it breaks down to ADP (adenosine diphosphate), energy is released for doing something energetic or for body functions such as making muscle protein.

DISCOVERING PHOSPHORUS
A German alchemist named Hennig Brand (17th century) discovered phosphorus in 1669. He boiled down 50 buckets of urine and then heated up what was left. Brand chose the name phosphorus, which means light-bearer in Greek, because the element glows in the dark. Brand kept his method secret, but the Irish chemist Robert Boyle (1627–91) rediscovered phosphorus a few years later.

Find out more

PERIODIC TABLE P. 32
ALKALINE-EARTH METALS P. 35
NITROGEN P. 42
CHEMISTRY OF THE BODY P. 76
CHEMISTRY IN FARMING P. 91
SOAPS AND DETERGENTS P. 95
CELLS P.338
FACT FINDER P. 402

OXYGEN

THERE IS MORE OXYGEN on Earth than any other element. It is an invisible and odorless gas, and without it we would all die. We breathe it in all the time in air, where it is mixed with other gases. Oxygen is found in many things. In the oceans, it is dissolved in, and forms part of, water. In the rocks, it is found in most minerals. Ordinary oxygen gas is made up of molecules with two atoms, which have the symbol O_2. High in the atmosphere, a three-atom form called ozone is more common. A protective layer of ozone shields the Earth from dangerous radiation from space. Oxygen is very reactive. Burning, rusting, and respiration are just some of the chemical reactions that happen when substances combine with oxygen in the air.

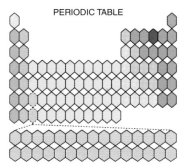

PERIODIC TABLE

Group 16: oxygen (O), sulfur (S), selenium (Se), tellurium (Te), and polonium (Po)

CUTTING WITH OXYGEN
Oxygen can be used to cut steel. In a special type of torch called an oxyacetylene torch, the gas acetylene is made to burn in pure oxygen to produce a temperature of over 8,600°F (3,000°C). This melts the steel underneath the flame and leaves a cut. Oxyacetylene torches are also used to weld steel. The two edges of the steel melt in the torch flame, and join up as they cool.

The reaction between the fuel and oxygen cannot take place without heat.

Oxygen combines with carbon in the fuel to make carbon dioxide.

The fuel must contain a substance which combines with oxygen from the air.

BURNING
The fire triangle shows what is needed to make a fire: heat, oxygen, and a fuel. If any one of these things is missing, the fire cannot start or will quickly go out. That is why covering a camp fire with sand or stones will make it go out. The sand or stones exclude oxygen, and so the fire cannot burn.

RED ROCKS
The atmosphere has not always contained oxygen. But we know when it first arrived because it reacted with the iron in these rocks and turned them red. The rocks are about two billion years old.

LIVING EARTH
The atmosphere contains about 21 percent oxygen. When animals breathe, they take oxygen from the atmosphere. Plants put it back again as they make their food by photosynthesis. Fish and many other aquatic creatures breathe the oxygen that is dissolved in water.

EMERGENCY OXYGEN
Patients with breathing problems or those who are very ill are given extra oxygen. Their lungs do not have to work so hard in order to keep the patient alive.

Carl Scheele   Joseph Priestley

DISCOVERING OXYGEN
The English chemist Joseph Priestley (1733–1804) announced his discovery of oxygen in 1774, not knowing that the Swedish chemist Carl Scheele (1742–86) had found it first one or two years earlier. They proved that air is not one element. But neither quite realized what he had discovered. It was the French chemist Antoine Lavoisier (1743–94) who showed, in 1775, what oxygen is.

RUST
Iron and steel left in the air and the wet soon become covered with an orange-brown deposit called rust. Rust is iron oxide, the result of a chemical reaction between iron, oxygen, and moisture.

Find out more

BONDING P. 28
PERIODIC TABLE P. 32
OXIDATION AND REDUCTION P. 64
CHEMISTRY OF AIR P. 74
CELLULAR RESPIRATION P. 346
CYCLES IN THE BIOSPHERE P. 372
FACT FINDER P. 402

SULFUR

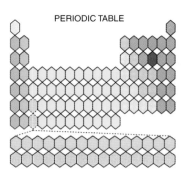

Group 16: oxygen (O), sulfur (S), selenium (Se), tellurium (Te), and polonium (Po)

WITHOUT SULFUR, substances such as paint and detergents could not exist. They are made by a process that uses sulfuric acid, a major industrial ingredient made from sulfur. Sulfur is a bright yellow solid. In the ground, sulfur minerals include sulfides such as galena (lead ore) and sulfates such as gypsum. Sulfur forms as many different compounds. It reacts with oxygen to form sulfur dioxide. This gas is given off in huge amounts by coal-burning power plants because coal contains sulfur. This causes pollution in the air. Sulfur is used to vulcanize (harden) rubber. This makes rubber hard enough to be made into tires.

PROTEIN SULFUR
Egg yolk contains sulfur, which moves out to the edge of the yolk to make a gray band if the egg is boiled for too long. Sulfur is a vital part of protein molecules. When these break down, they produce hydrogen sulfide, a poisonous gas that smells of rotten eggs.

Yellow sulfur crystals

Rhombic sulfur is made up of molecules with eight atoms. These molecules fit neatly together.

Monoclinic sulfur is made up of eight-atom molecules with more space between them than the rhombic form. It is only stable above about 205°F (96°C).

Compressed air is forced down the pipe. It mixes with the molten sulfur and makes it lighter.

Sulfur is forced out mixed with water and air.

Super-heated steam

The steam turns into very hot water and melts the sulfur.

The molten sulfur collects before being mixed with air.

SULFUR CRYSTALS
Fine crystals of sulfur are found among the rocks in volcanic regions of the world. These are the rhombic shape. Volcanic vents (cracks) are a major source of sulfur in countries such as Sicily, Java, and the United States. The sulfur comes from gases in the Earth's interior.

SULFUR ALLOTROPES
There are two main forms, or allotropes, of sulfur. The stable form at normal temperatures is the rhombic form. In both forms the sulfur atoms are arranged in rings of eight.

EXTRACTING SULFUR
Sulfur can be extracted from underground deposits by the Frasch process. Three pipes are forced down into the sulfur deposit. Superheated steam is pumped down the outside pipe, which melts the sulfur. Compressed air is then sent down the central pipe. It forces frothy liquid sulfur up to the surface.

SULFUR ON IO
Jupiter's large moon, Io, is one of the most colorful in the solar system. Its vivid yellow-orange color is caused by the flow of sulfur from erupting volcanoes. These were spotted by NASA's *Voyager* probes.

SULFUR BACTERIA
Some bacteria use sulfur instead of oxygen for energy, so they can only live on dissolved sulfur compounds. In the United States they are being used to release pure copper, and other transition metals, from their compounds with sulfur.

Find out more
CRYSTALS P. 30
PERIODIC TABLE P. 32
CHEMISTRY OF AIR P. 74
SULFURIC ACID P. 89
GAS PRODUCTS P. 97
INDUSTRIAL POLLUTION P. 112
RAIN P. 264
FACT FINDER P. 402

HALOGENS

PERIODIC TABLE

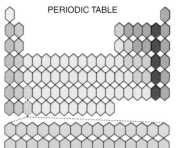

Group 17: fluorine (F), chlorine (Cl), bromine (Br), iodine (I), and radioactive astatine (At)

THE STRONG SMELL in swimming pools is caused by chlorine, one of the best-known elements in Group 17, the halogens. Chlorine also forms the compound sodium chloride (common salt). Fluorides, compounds of fluorine, help prevent tooth decay, so they are added to toothpaste and tap water. Organic chlorine and fluorine compounds (CFCs) were once heavily used as pesticides and in refrigerators, aerosols, and packaging. But they are harmful to the environment, so alternative chemicals have been found for these jobs. All the silver halides (halogen compounds) are light-sensitive, so they are used to make photographic film and paper. Silver bromide is the most commonly used. All the halogens are highly reactive. All have seven electrons in their outer shells.

CHLORINATING WATER

Chlorine can be extracted from concentrated brine (saltwater) using electrolysis. It is a strong bleach and disinfectant, killing harmful bacteria. For this reason it is used to treat water in swimming pools and at water supply plants. Chlorine is turned into a liquid for this purpose.

FLUORESCING FLUORITE

Fluorine occurs naturally in minerals such as calcium fluoride (known as fluorite or fluorspar). Fluorite forms cubic crystals in a variety of colors due to impurities. Many fluoresce (glow) in ultraviolet light.

CHLORINE

Chlorine is a yellow-green, poisonous gas. Like all the halogens, it readily combines with hydrogen and water. Together they make hydrochloric acid, a very strong acid.

SEAWEED IODINE

Traces of iodine occur in seawater and in seaweed. It is also important in the thyroid gland, which controls energy levels and growth in young mammals. People lacking iodides develop a swollen thyroid gland, called a goiter, on their necks.

BROMINE

Bromine is a dark red liquid that gives off a choking and poisonous red-brown vapor. Bromine is one of only two liquids in the periodic table. As well as being used in photography, bromine compounds are used as mild sedatives.

SLIPPERY PLASTIC

A fluorine compound, PTFE (polytetrafluoroethene), is used as the nonstick coating on pans because it is so slippery. Although it is a plastic, it is not affected by heat and is very unreactive. This makes it ideal for saucepans and ovenware.

IODINE

Iodine is a purple-black solid that turns to gas very easily, giving off a purple vapor. Iodine compounds, known as iodides, are used in dyes and as industrial catalysts. Iodine dissolved in water is used as a test for starch.

PTFE (also known as Teflon) works by actively repelling other chemicals. Even an egg cannot stick to a Teflon frying pan.

Clear evidence about the harmful effect of CFCs has led to alternative propellants being used in aerosol sprays.

An ozone "hole" now regularly appears in winter in the Antarctic over the South Pole.

THE OZONE HOLE

Compounds called CFCs (chlorofluorocarbons), once used in aerosol cans, encourage the breakdown of ozone in the atmosphere. The ozone layer protects the Earth and living things from dangerous ultraviolet radiation in the Sun's rays. The ozone layer is so thin around the South Pole that it is often said that there is a hole in it. For this reason, CFCs are hardly used today.

Find out more

BONDING P. 28
PERIODIC TABLE P. 32
OXYGEN P. 44
ALKALI INDUSTRY P. 94
INDUSTRIAL POLLUTION P. 112
PHOTOGRAPHY P. 206
CYCLES IN THE
BIOSPHERE P. 372
FACT FINDER P. 402

HYDROGEN

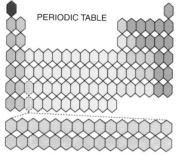

PERIODIC TABLE

Hydrogen (H)

IMAGINE A WORLD without sunlight or heat. This is what would happen if there were no hydrogen. You cannot see, taste, or smell hydrogen, yet it is the most plentiful element in the universe. It is a gas, with many uses. Much is made into ammonia, which is used to produce fertilizers and other chemicals. Hydrogenation (treatment with hydrogen) is used to harden vegetable oils and fats into margarine in the food industry. It also increases the amount of gasoline produced from crude oil. All acids owe their acidity to hydrogen ions.

IN THE SUN
Hydrogen makes the Sun shine. A huge amount of energy is given out when the nuclei of atoms of hydrogen join up, or fuse together, in the Sun's searingly hot interior. This process is called nuclear fusion. It is also used in the destructive hydrogen bomb.

IN THE UNIVERSE
Hydrogen is present not only in the stars but in the clouds, or nebulae, that exist in the space between them.

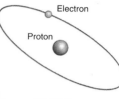

Electron

Proton

SIMPLE STRUCTURE
The most common isotope (form) of hydrogen has the simplest structure there is, with one proton, which forms the nucleus, and one electron.

Crab nebula

ON EARTH
There is a lot of hydrogen on Earth because it forms part of water (H_2O). It is the most common element, with carbon, in living things and fossil fuels.

HENRY CAVENDISH
The English scientist Henry Cavendish (1731–1810) found a gas he called inflammable air. But he did not identify it as the element hydrogen. He investigated the properties of the gas and showed that water is formed when it is burned in air. This proved that water is not, as had been thought, a separate element. Later, the gas was called hydrogen.

FUEL OF THE FUTURE
Cars that run on hydrogen are already being built. The fuel source is a hydrogen compound that is heated to release the hydrogen. The advantage of these cars is that they cause no pollution because hydrogen forms water when it burns.

BALLOONS AND AIRSHIPS
Hydrogen explosions were the cause of airship disasters in the 1930s, like that of the *Hindenburg* on May 6, 1937. Because it is so light, hydrogen should be ideal for filling balloons and airships. The drawback is that it forms an explosive mixture with air and easily bursts into flame.

Hydrogen-powered car

Find out more
ATOMIC STRUCTURE P. 24
PERIODIC TABLE P. 32
OXIDATION AND REDUCTION P. 64
MEASURING ACIDITY P. 72
AMMONIA P. 90
ENERGY SOURCES P. 134
NUCLEAR ENERGY P. 136
SUN P. 284
FACT FINDER P. 402

NOBLE GASES

BALLOONS THAT SOAR into the air when you let them go are filled with helium, one of the six gases that fill Group 18 of the periodic table. These are the noble gases, and they make up about one percent of the air. Neon, used in brightly colored neon lights, is another well-known noble gas. Radon is radioactive and is produced by the decay of radium. It makes up much of the background radiation that occurs in areas where there are granite rocks. Noble gases are also called the rare or inert gases because chemists have been able to make only a few compounds from them. They rarely react with anything because they are so stable: their outer shells are totally filled with electrons.

PERIODIC TABLE

Group 18: helium (He), neon (Ne), argon (Ar), krypton (Kr), xenon (Xe), and radioactive radon (Rn)

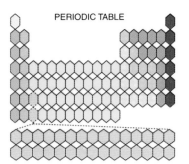

HELIUM
After hydrogen, helium is the lightest gas. It is lighter than air. That is why it is used to fill modern balloons and airships. It is safer than hydrogen because it does not burn. Only a faint trace of helium is present in the atmosphere. But some deposits of natural gas contain fairly large amounts, and these are the main commercial source of the gas.

Electron   Outer shell

COMPLETE SHELLS
A neon atom has eight electrons in its outer shell. With these, the shell is complete. The atom does not need to lose or gain electrons by bonding with other atoms. All noble gases have a complete outer shell. This is why they are so unreactive.

WILLIAM RAMSAY
In 1894, Lord Rayleigh (1842–1919) and William Ramsay (1852–1916) discovered the noble gas argon. Helium had already been found in the Sun, and in 1895 Ramsay found it existed on Earth. He went on to discover krypton, neon, and xenon in 1898. He prepared the last three by the distillation of liquid air. For this work he was awarded the 1904 Nobel Prize for Chemistry. In 1910, he discovered radon.

NEON LIGHTS
The colors of this neon rainbow are produced by passing electricity through the tubes, which contain a noble gas and other substances at low pressure. Each noble gas produces a different color, and other substances are added for more colors. Helium gives a yellow light, neon gives a brilliant red-orange light, argon gives a blue light, and krypton gives a violet light.

Lens
Xenon in bulb
Argon in bulb
Spotlight

GAS LIGHTS
Argon and xenon are used in electric lamps. Lamps filled with xenon produce an intense blue-white light. Lighthouses often use xenon arc-lamps, in which the light is produced by an electric arc, a sort of continuous spark. Argon, mixed with nitrogen, is used in ordinary electric lightbulbs. The inert mixture makes the white-hot tungsten filament inside a bulb last longer.

NUCLEAR BY-PRODUCT
Several radioisotopes of krypton are produced in the nuclear fission of uranium, including krypton-85. This gas escapes from nuclear power plants. During the Cold War, the United States was able to keep track of Soviet nuclear activity by measuring the amount of krypton-85 in the air.

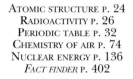

Novovoronezhskaya nuclear power plant in Russia

Find out more

ATOMIC STRUCTURE P. 24
RADIOACTIVITY P. 26
PERIODIC TABLE P. 32
CHEMISTRY OF AIR P. 74
NUCLEAR ENERGY P. 136
FACT FINDER P. 402

REACTIONS

EVERY MINUTE OF EVERY DAY, millions of chemical reactions are taking place around us. Some are natural processes, while others are the result of human activities. Inside our bodies, the food we eat is broken down in a complex series of reactions to provide us with energy. Plants are busy using the Sun's energy to convert carbon dioxide and water into carbohydrates and oxygen—a reaction called photosynthesis. Meanwhile, chemical reactions in power plants are used to burn fuels and provide us with electricity. In the laboratory, scientists use chemical reactions in many different ways: to make new drugs, to prevent food from rotting too quickly, to convert crude oil into gasoline, or to provide many of the materials that make our clothes and our homes.

Silver objects gradually become dull and blackened because hydrogen sulfide in the air reacts with the silver to produce a thin layer of silver sulfide.

A chemical in plants called chlorophyll uses sunlight to convert carbon dioxide and water into carbohydrates and oxygen.

When we wash dishes, the detergent in the dish-washing liquid removes dirt and grease by helping them to dissolve in the water.

The baked cake no longer resembles its ingredients of flour, eggs, butter, and sugar. They have been changed by a chemical reaction.

Baked cake

Melting ice pops

CHEMICAL CHANGE

Baking a cake is an example of a chemical change. Once cooked, the cake does not taste like its ingredients any more—it is chemically different. Most chemical changes are permanent or irreversible—you cannot turn the baked cake back into flour, butter, eggs, and sugar. However, some chemical changes are reversible.

PHYSICAL CHANGE

A melting ice pop is an example of a physical change. The ice pop has not changed chemically—it may look different, but it still tastes the same. Physical changes are not permanent, and they are reversible. The ice pop can be made solid again by cooling it down in a freezer.

FRANCIS BACON
Francis Bacon (1561–1626) was a lawyer, experimenter, and great English political figure. In 1620, he wrote a book called *New Method*, in which he said that theories about how matter works were only useful if they were supported by experiments.

Scientific equipment from the 18th century

2 vol.d'Hy

ROBERT BOYLE
The Irish chemist Robert Boyle (1627–91) was one of the first modern chemists. In 1661, he published a famous book, *The Sceptical Chymist*, in which he said that ideas should always be tested by experiment to see if they are really true. While experimenting with gases, he discovered a rule about how they behave, known as Boyle's law.

MODERN LABORATORY
Many scientific laboratories contain a range of equipment that scientists use to conduct different experiments. For example, some scientists might study the reactions involved in pollution so they can develop ways to prevent it. Other scientists may use chemistry to make new materials or to find treatments for diseases.

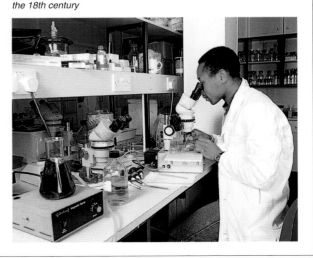

KINETIC THEORY

HAVE YOU EVER WONDERED why you can smell food cooking? The reason is that tiny gas molecules from hot food whirl through the air and some reach your nose. Although it is hard to believe, the atoms and molecules that make up everything we see are constantly moving. As the temperature rises, the particles move faster, and so they take up more space. This is the kinetic theory of matter. The word "kinetic" means moving. Not all particles can move in the same way. In solids, the particles are closely packed together and can only move by vibrating or shaking. In liquids, the particles are still close, but they can move more freely. In a gas, the particles are widely spaced and move very fast.

Air molecules inside a hot-air balloon are farther apart because they are moving so fast. This means that the air inside the balloon is lighter than the air outside. This is what makes the balloon rise.

Air
Barrier
Barrier removed
Bromine and air

Evenly mixed bromine and air particles

Heat causes particles of solids to vibrate faster than usual. This explains why the Eiffel Tower in Paris expands by 3 in (7.5 cm) every summer.

DIFFUSION
Because the molecules in a gas are moving so fast, gases will spread out and take up as much space as possible. The way in which gas molecules spread out is called diffusion, and it is the reason why smells travel so quickly. For example, when bread is baking in the oven, the smell of cooking soon diffuses through the whole house.

Gas jar

EXPANSION
If an object, like this thermometer, is heated, its particles start to move faster and take up extra space. It is said to expand. Liquids expand about 10 times more than solids, so the liquid in the thermometer rises because it expands more than the glass. Gases expand about 100 times more than liquids.

Mixed water and permanganate particles

Kinetic theory explains how a thermometer works. An increase in temperature causes the alcohol or mercury inside to expand and move up the scale.

Water

BROMINE DIFFUSION
When bromine is put into a gas jar, the gas molecules take up all of the available space. If a second gas jar is added, the gas soon diffuses into this as well.

DIFFUSION IN WATER
If potassium permanganate is put in water, its purple color soon spreads out. This is because molecules of water are bumping and pushing the permanganate particles. In the same way, tea left in a teapot will eventually flavor and color all of the water.

Potassium permanganate crystals

LUDWIG BOLTZMANN
In the 1860s, the Austrian scientist Ludwig Boltzmann (1844–1906) developed the kinetic theory of gases. Sadly, unhappy about the strong opposition from other scientists to his kinetic theory, he committed suicide.

BROWNIAN MOTION
In 1827, the Scottish botanist Robert Brown was surprised to see that some pollen grains in water were haphazardly bouncing around. The great scientist Albert Einstein explained this movement 80 years later by using the kinetic theory. The pollen grains are being constantly bombarded by tiny, unseen water molecules. This type of movement is now called Brownian motion.

Magnified view of sweet pea pollen grains in water

WATER BAGS
A solution of salt and sugar can cure children with severe sickness, but many of these children live in countries where clean water is not available. Special bags holding dry sugar and salt can help. If they are put into dirty water, water molecules, but not dirt, can diffuse through the tiny holes in the bag, making a sterile solution ready to drink.

Germ particle

Water molecules can diffuse through the holes.

Find out more
STATES OF MATTER P. 18
BEHAVIOR OF GASES P. 51
RATES OF REACTION P. 55
HEAT P. 140
TRANSPORT IN PLANTS P. 341
FACT FINDER P. 404

BEHAVIOR OF GASES

GAS PARTICLES MOVE around freely and very fast. This is why they can produce dramatic effects if their temperature, volume, or pressure are changed. For example, it may be dangerous to leave a spray can in a hot place. As they become hotter, the gas particles inside will move faster and so push harder against the sides of the can. They may even cause the can to explode. Heating the can has increased the pressure of the gas inside. Similar effects were observed in the 17th and 18th centuries by scientists. They devised laws that are still used to predict how a gas will behave.

Boyle's law explains why bubbles from a diver get bigger as they rise to the water surface.

BOYLE'S LAW

Have you noticed that bubbles of gas are smaller at the bottom and get bigger as they rise through a liquid? This is because there is more liquid pressing on the bubbles and making them smaller when they are at the bottom than when they are near the surface of the liquid. This is an example of Boyle's law in practice. It was discovered in 1662 by the Irish chemist Robert Boyle. The law states that, at constant temperature, the volume of a gas is inversely proportional to the pressure—if the pressure increases, the volume decreases.

Liquid nitrogen at a temperature of -385°F (-196°C)

The balloon deflates in the cold liquid.

CHARLES' LAW

A balloon full of air shrivels up when it is put in a container of liquid nitrogen. The very low temperature causes the air molecules inside the balloon to slow down. As a result, there are fewer collisions with the walls of the balloon and the balloon shrinks. This relationship between the temperature and volume of a gas was discovered by the French scientist Jacques Charles in 1787. His law says that, at constant pressure, the volume of a gas is proportional to the temperature—if the temperature is halved, then the volume is halved too.

REFRIGERATOR

Inside the pipes of a refrigerator, a fluid called a refrigerant continually flows around. When it passes through a narrow opening, it rapidly expands to a gas. To become a gas, the liquid molecules must take in heat from their surroundings (the inside of the refrigerator), which become cold. The gas then flows to a compressor, which forces it back to a liquid. This process gives out heat, which is why the back of a refrigerator feels warm.

Narrow opening

Compressor

The burst balloon holds very few air molecules and so is lighter than the full balloon.

Hydrogen gas   Oxygen gas   Water

HEAVY GASES

It is easy to think that as most gases are invisible, they weigh nothing. This is not true. All gases have some mass since they are made of particles. If two balloons full of air are balanced and then one is burst, the mass of the air in the remaining balloon pulls it down.

The balloon starts to expand as the gas molecules speed up in the warmer air.

AVOGADRO'S LAW

If a container is filled with chlorine and another identical one with oxygen, the two containers will contain the same number of molecules. This is true even though each chlorine molecule weighs twice as much as each oxygen molecule. This principle was discovered in 1811 by the Italian physicist Amedeo Avogadro. His law says that equal volumes of gases at the same temperature and pressure contain the same number of molecules.

Chlorine molecule   Oxygen molecule

GAY-LUSSAC'S LAW

In 1808, the French chemist Joseph Louis Gay-Lussac found that, when hydrogen and oxygen react to make water, two volumes of hydrogen always react with one of oxygen. He went on to discover that when any gases react together, the volumes in which they do so are in a ratio of simple whole numbers. This is known as Gay-Lussac's law.

BICYCLE PUMP

When you use a bicycle pump to inflate a tire, the pump becomes hot. This is because gases get warmer when you suddenly compress them.

The wall of the pump becomes warm as faster molecules bump against it.

Find out more

STATES OF MATTER P. 18
CHANGES OF STATE P. 20
KINETIC THEORY P. 50
CHEMISTRY OF AIR P.74
PRESSURE P. 127
FORCES IN FLUIDS P. 128
HEAT P. 140
FACT FINDER P. 404

CHEMICAL REACTIONS

WHAT IS A CHEMICAL REACTION? It is simply breaking substances apart and making new ones from the pieces. Whenever a reaction takes place, new substances, the products, are made. These have very different properties from the original starting materials, the reactants. For these new substances to be made, atoms and molecules must be rearranged. This requires the breaking and making of chemical bonds. For a bond to break, energy is needed, while making a bond releases energy. Both occur in every chemical reaction. The energy can be in the form of heat, light, or electricity. Reactions that release heat are said to be exothermic. Those in which heat is taken in are called endothermic.

Pressing a cold pack splits the inner bag. Ammonium nitrate dissolves in the water, making the solution very cold. Water | Ammonium nitrate

Methane and oxygen react to make carbon dioxide and water. This diagram shows how the bonds between atoms break and rejoin.

Hydrogen atom   Oxygen atom

Methane molecule

Carbon atom

Oxygen molecules

Carbon dioxide molecule

Water molecules

EXOTHERMIC REACTIONS
When wood burns, its chemical energy is released in the form of heat. The reaction involves bond-breaking and bond-making, but the amount of heat given off by making bonds is greater than that absorbed by bonds breaking. As a result, heat is given off and the surroundings become hotter. This is an example of an exothermic reaction.

ENDOTHERMIC REACTIONS
Cold packs are used by athletes to cool down injuries. The cold pack uses a reaction to take heat from the athlete's body. The heat absorbed by bond-breaking is greater than that given out by bond-making. This is an example of an endothermic reaction.

CHANGING BONDS
In every chemical reaction, bonds are broken so that new ones can be made. Methane, the main component of natural gas, has four hydrogen atoms bonded to one carbon. When burned, it reacts with oxygen in the air and all the bonds between the atoms are broken. New bonds form to make carbon dioxide and water. Since these new bonds have less stored energy than the original ones, the reaction gives out energy as heat.

The magnesium in a sparkler reacts with oxygen in the air to form magnesium oxide. This reaction gives out energy as light.

A book cover fades because light is taken in by the dye molecules and destroys some of the chemical bonds.

ACTIVATION ENERGY
Most reactions need a certain amount of energy to start. This is why a match will not light until it is activated by striking it. A candle will not burn until a match is held to it. The amount of energy needed to get a reaction started is called the activation energy.

The activation energy is like a hill that the reactants have to get over.

A lighted match starts the reaction between oxygen in the air and candle wax. Once started, the reaction continues without help.

This electric ray (Hypnos monoptergium) uses a reaction that gives out energy as electricity. This is used by the ray to stun its prey.

REACTIONS WITH LIGHT
When a chemical reaction gives out or takes in energy, it may do so as light. A burning sparkler gives out an intense white light. Posters and clothes fade in strong sunlight because a reaction occurs when light is taken in. Sunlight also sets off a reaction in our skin to form the pigment melanin. This is how people tan.

REACTIONS WITH ELECTRICITY
Some chemical reactions use electricity, others produce it. An electric ray, for example, can kill small fish with a 200-volt shock, through a reaction in its cells. Lightning is an electric spark. The energy it produces can cause reactions in the air. It causes nitrogen dioxide to be made from oxygen and nitrogen, and ozone from oxygen.

Lightning causes a reaction between nitrogen and oxygen to make nitrogen dioxide. This dissolves in water and falls to Earth as nitric acid, a component of acid rain.

Find out more
BONDING P. 28
DESCRIBING REACTIONS P. 53
RATES OF REACTION P. 55
CATALYSTS P. 56
ENERGY CONVERSION P. 138
FACT FINDER P. 404

DESCRIBING REACTIONS

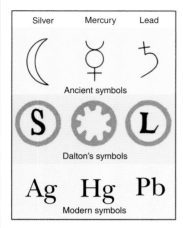

Silver   Mercury   Lead

Ancient symbols

S   L

Dalton's symbols

Ag   Hg   Pb

Modern symbols

CHEMICAL FORMULAE and chemical equations are the chemist's equivalent of shorthand writing. They are used to describe chemicals and their reactions. The chemical formula of a compound (combination of elements) shows which atoms it contains and in what proportions. A chemical equation is used to describe a chemical reaction. Like a cooking recipe, an equation gives a list of ingredients and the proportions in which they need to be mixed. It also shows what will be produced during the reaction. Chemical equations overcome problems of language. They are used by chemists to tell other scientists all over the world about what they have seen during their experiments.

The two clear solutions are mixed and a yellow solid, lead iodide, is formed.

SYMBOLS AND FORMULAE

In ancient times, seven elements were known, each of which was depicted by a different planet. Around 1800, the English chemist John Dalton devised a set of picture symbols for the known elements. In 1811, Swedish chemist Jöns Berzelius invented the system we now use, where letters represent elements. These letters can be put together to show a compound's chemical formula.

Calcium
Carbon *Oxygen*

FORMULAE EVERYWHERE

Every compound has a chemical name as well as a formula showing the elements it contains. For example, the chemical name of chalk is calcium carbonate. Its chemical formula is $CaCO_3$. This tells us that in chalk, for every atom of calcium (Ca), there will be one atom of carbon (C) and three atoms of oxygen (O).

This is an example of a double decomposition reaction in which two compounds in solution swap partners.

Solution of potassium iodide in water

Solution of lead nitrate in water

Word equation   potassium iodide + lead nitrate   lead iodide + potassium nitrate

Symbolic equation $2KI(aq)$ + $Pb(NO_3)_2(aq)$ $PbI_2(s)$ + $2KNO_3(aq)$

To make a balanced equation, the number of KI molecules (and the number of KNO_3 molecules) must be doubled.

Chemists use symbols that show what state the chemical is in: (s) means solid, (l) means liquid, (g) means gas, and (aq) means dissolved in water.

This 2 shows there are two nitrate groups joined to each lead atom.

MOLES

Because atoms and molecules are so tiny, chemists count them by mass. The mole is their counting unit. A mole of any substance contains 6×10^{23} particles, but each substance has a different mass (its molecular or atomic mass). Using the mole to count particles is just the same as a banker counting coins by weighing them.

One mole of lead tetraoxide contains 6×10^{23} molecules. It has a mass of 685 g.

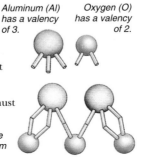

One mole of aluminum contains 6×10^{23} atoms. It has a mass of 27 g. 6×10^{23} is known as Avogadro's constant.

EQUATIONS

A reaction can be described in different ways. One way is to write an equation. This can be in words or with chemical formulae. If chemical formulae are used, the equation must balance; that is, it must have the same numbers of the same atoms on each side. Only a balanced equation can show the proportions in which the chemicals react together.

VALENCY

The number of chemical bonds an atom can make is called its valency. It is the number of electrons an atom gains, loses, or shares when it forms a bond. To form a compound, the total of the valencies of each element must add up to the same number.

When the compound aluminum oxide (Al_2O_3) is made, 2 atoms of aluminum combine with 3 of oxygen.

Aluminum (Al) has a valency of 3.

Oxygen (O) has a valency of 2.

LAW OF CONSERVATION OF MASS

When a chemical reaction occurs, nothing disappears, the atoms are just rearranged. An equation must therefore be balanced. The number of atoms on each side must be the same. This is the law of conservation of mass. It says that the total mass of the substances produced in a reaction equals the total mass of materials used.

Find out more

BONDING P. 28
PERIODIC TABLE P. 32
CHEMICAL REACTIONS P. 52
COMPOUNDS AND MIXTURES P. 58
FACT FINDER P. 404

REVERSIBLE REACTIONS

IMAGINE TRYING TO MAKE a log of wood from its smoke and ashes. Most chemical reactions, like burning, go only in one direction. Once they have happened, they cannot be reversed. They are irreversible. But not all chemical reactions are like this. Sometimes it is possible to reverse the change that has occurred. For example, when an alkali such as washing soda is added to red cabbage juice, the juice turns blue-green. If an acid, such as vinegar, is then added to this green juice, the juice is turned back to its red color. Such reactions are reversible. Reversible reactions have a forward reaction (red juice to green juice) and a backward reaction (green juice to red juice). In fact, both reactions are happening at the same time, but depending on the conditions, one may be stronger than the other.

Nitrogen dioxide gas ⇌ Nitrogen monoxide and oxygen gas

Scientists use this sign to show that a reaction is reversible.

EQUILIBRIUM

In a reversible reaction, after a time it will look as if nothing is happening. In fact, both the forward and backward reactions are continuing, but at the same speed. This is chemical equilibrium. In the same way, if you are using a treadmill, you will stay in the same position if you run at the same speed as the machine. If the machine speeds up, you will move backward. To reach equilibrium again, you need to speed up too.

Nitrogen atom

Oxygen atom

Nitrogen dioxide

Nitrogen monoxide and oxygen

NITROGEN DIOXIDE
If brown nitrogen dioxide gas is heated, the color becomes lighter and lighter until at 1,148°F (620°C), the gas is totally colorless. This is because it has broken down into nitrogen monoxide and oxygen, both of which are colorless gases. On cooling, the changes are reversed.

LE CHATELIER'S PRINCIPLE
A change in temperature, pressure, or concentration during a reversible reaction will change the speed of either the forward or backward reaction. If heated, for example, the reaction that takes in most heat will speed up, so as to reduce the effect of the heating. Such effects are summed up in Le Chatelier's principle. This says that if a change is made to a reaction in equilibrium, the reaction will adjust itself to counter the effects of that change.

The reaction is in equilibrium. The forward and backward reactions are continuing at the same speed.

If more of the products are added, the backward reaction will speed up so as to use up the extra ingredients.

If more of the reactants are added, the forward reaction will speed up, so that the extra reactants are used up.

HENRI LE CHATELIER
Born in Paris, Le Chatelier (1850–1936) worked for some years as a mining engineer before he took a teaching position at the University of Paris. He is remembered for his theory, Le Chatelier's principle.

IRREVERSIBLE CHANGE
When paper burns, carbon dioxide gas, water, and black carbon soot are produced. These cannot be turned back to paper again because burning paper is an irreversible reaction.

CHEMICAL CLOCKS
Some reversible reactions do not settle down to an equilibrium. Once started, they continue to oscillate backward and forward. Sometimes this produces amazing color changes. One moment a solution may be blue, and the next moment, red. Because these oscillations occur at regular intervals, these reactions have been called chemical clocks.

These photographs of two chemical clock reactions were taken at one-minute intervals. They show how waves of color move through the reaction.

RATES OF REACTION

EXPLOSIONS OCCUR very quickly. Other reactions occur more slowly—a bicycle might take several years to rust. In our lives, we often want to alter the rate (speed) of a reaction. When we put milk into the refrigerator, we are slowing down the rate at which it turns sour. Chemists also want to control the rate of reactions. Industrial chemists want to speed up reactions to lower costs. Environmental scientists want to slow down reactions that can damage the Earth. Many factors can affect the rate of a reaction. The important ones are temperature, pressure, concentration, surface area, and light.

COAL EXPLOSION
A large piece of coal will not react with air unless we light it. A mixture of coal dust and air, however, can react rapidly and explosively, as in a coal mine explosion. This is because coal dust has a larger amount of surface that can react.

Zinc mixed with a diluted mineral acid. The rate of reaction is slow.

Zinc mixed with a concentrated mineral acid. The rate of reaction is fast.

Lump of coal

Coal dust particle   *Oxygen molecule*

Oxygen molecules can only reach the surface coal particles.

In coal dust, there are many coal particles available to react with the oxygen molecules.

EFFECT OF SURFACE AREA
The surface area of a solid is the amount of surface on the outside. This can affect the rate of reaction. French fried potatoes have a large surface area compared to whole potatoes, so more of the potato can react with the hot oil.

EFFECT OF CONCENTRATION
The effect of concentration can be seen in the rate of reaction of zinc with a mineral acid, such as sulfuric acid. Zinc reacts with the hydrogen ions in the acid to release hydrogen gas (seen as bubbles in the test tubes above). Concentrated sulfuric acid has more hydrogen ions than diluted sulfuric acid. This means there are more hydrogen ions to collide with the surface of the zinc, and therefore the reaction rate is faster.

Ötze, a 5,000-year-old male body found in a glacier between Italy and Austria in 1991, was well preserved. His body would normally have been reduced to bones, but the low temperature slowed down his decomposition.

Potato is often cooked in a deep-fat fryer. The frying reaction occurs at the surface of the potato, so thin fries will react more completely than large chunks because of their larger surface area.

EFFECT OF TEMPERATURE
Most reactions go faster at higher temperatures. This is because the reacting particles have more energy and move faster. They are more likely to bump into one another with enough energy to cause a reaction. In the cold, all chemical reactions are slowed down. This is why a refrigerator is used to preserve food.

COLLISION THEORY
For a chemical reaction to happen, the reacting particles must bang into, or collide, with each other with enough force or energy (the activation energy) to break bonds. This is collision theory. If the particles do not have this energy, they will just harmlessly bounce off one another. It is like stock car racing, where two cars need to bump into each other with a lot of force in order to cause damage.

EFFECT OF PRESSURE
Particles in a gas are wide apart. But if the pressure is raised, they are brought closer together and are more likely to bump into and react with one another. In a machine called an autoclave, high pressure is used so that objects can be very quickly sterilized by steam.

EFFECT OF LIGHT
Biodegradable plastics will decompose more quickly in strong sunlight than in a kitchen cabinet. This is because some reactions are speeded up by light. Light gives the reacting molecules more energy to move.

If two particles meet, they may rebound with no reaction, but if they collide with enough force, a chemical reaction will occur.

CATALYSTS

THE MAGICIANS of the chemical world, catalysts can alter the speed of a reaction but are left unchanged once the reaction has finished. They work like an introduction agency, introducing the reactants to one another. Around 90 percent of all chemicals are made using a catalyst. Artificial catalysts are used in the manufacture of gasoline, plastics, fertilizers, medicines, and synthetic fibers for clothing. Enzymes are natural catalysts that control the way our bodies work. Usually, catalysts are used to speed up a reaction. But they can also be used to slow down a reaction, a process known as inhibition. For example, chemicals called antioxidants are added to food to keep it from rotting too quickly. The word catalyst was first used by the Swedish chemist Jöns Berzelius, and means "to break down."

Have you noticed the fizz that sugar makes when it is put into a carbonated drink? The sugar is acting as a catalyst for the dissolved carbon dioxide gas to come out of solution.

Reacting molecule trapped in the pore of a zeolite

Catalysts lower the activation energy of the reaction.

REACTION PATH
To speed up a reaction, catalysts provide an easier pathway for the reaction to follow. Imagine a cycle race in which one team struggles over the top of the mountain, while the other team freewheels down a lower path. The path over the mountain is like the normal route for the reaction. The lower path is the route the catalyst provides.

These holes control the size of the molecules that can enter. By altering the size of the holes, chemists can create a zeolite suitable for a certain reaction.

Zeolite structure

This is a selection of different catalysts. They come in all shapes and sizes, but they must always have a large surface area.

ZEOLITES
The zeolites are an amazing family of catalysts. These occur naturally in volcanic rocks, but they can be made artificially as well. They are usually made up of aluminum, silicon, and oxygen atoms joined together in a beautiful honeycomb structure which contains millions of holes or pores. During a reaction, the reacting molecules are trapped in these pores while they react with each other. The size of the pores is very important, as only molecules of a particular size can enter and undergo a chemical reaction.

Zeolites were named after the Greek words for boiling stone because when they are heated, water is driven out of the millions of channels that they contain, leaving a very effective catalyst.

METHANOL
Methanol is a clear liquid that can be stored in a bottle for a hundred years without changing. But if it is passed over a heated zeolite catalyst, it immediately undergoes a chemical reaction and is converted to gasoline. This remarkable reaction is used in New Zealand as part of a process for converting natural gas to gasoline.

Methanol

Zeolite catalyst

Gas

The holes in a spoonful of zeolite give a reaction area of two soccer fields.

SURFACE AREA
Most catalysts work by bringing the reactants close together. They do this by forming a temporary bond with one or both of the reactants. So it is important for a catalyst to have a large surface area, as this is where the reaction takes place. For instance, a spoonful of a zeolite has the same surface area as two soccer fields.

FUEL CELLS
Even astronauts rely on catalysts. To send people into space, you need a power supply for the spacecraft, and a supply of water for the crew. The fuel cell provides both of these. It uses a metal catalyst, usually platinum, to convert hydrogen and oxygen into water. This reaction produces electricity. In this way, a fuel cell can provide all the energy a spacecraft needs, as well as all the water needed for drinking, washing, and rehydrating dried food.

WILHELM OSTWALD

Born in Latvia, Wilhelm Ostwald (1853–1932) spent most of his life in Germany. He conducted research into catalysts at a time when the idea of a chemical that could drastically alter the speed of a reaction seemed ridiculous. Ostwald persevered and showed the world how extremely useful catalysts can be by developing a process for converting ammonia into nitric acid. In 1909, he was awarded the Nobel Prize for Chemistry.

ENZYMES

Nature produces remarkable catalysts called enzymes, without which the thousands of reactions in the human body would be so slow that life could not go on. Enzymes in our bodies catalyze the breakdown of our food and help to make important chemicals such as proteins. Today, enzymes are even used in industry to make detergents, medicines, and fruit juices.

Cloudy fruit juices are made clear by enzymes.

Enzymes in soap powders help to break down stains.

ENZYME DETERGENTS

Biological detergents contain enzyme catalysts that help to break down stains. Because enzymes are destroyed at high temperatures, biological detergents are not effective in very hot water.

Inside the convertor is a honeycomb structure, coated with a tiny amount of the metals platinum and rhodium. These metals are the catalysts.

Unlike other catalysts, an enzyme will only catalyze one type of reaction. Just as only the correct key will fit a lock, the reacting molecules must be exactly the right shape to fit the enzyme molecule.

CATALYTIC CONVERTOR

Most cars contain a catalyst called a catalytic convertor. This changes the toxic exhaust gases that would pollute the atmosphere into less harmful gases. It is made of a thin coating of two metals, platinum and rhodium, on a solid honeycomb support. Because lead can poison platinum and rhodium (it will stick to them and prevent any reactions from taking place), cars with catalytic convertors must use lead-free gasoline.

Ozone layer over the Arctic

Exhaust gases containing carbon monoxide, nitrogen oxides, hydrocarbons, and air enter the catalytic convertor at one end.

The exhaust gases form temporary bonds with the surface of the catalyst. This brings them into close contact and allows the reactions to occur.

In the convertor, carbon monoxide and the hydrocarbons are converted into carbon dioxide and water. The nitrogen oxides are converted to nitrogen. These less harmful gases are released into the air.

OZONE CATALYST

Chlorine from the decomposition of chlorofluorocarbons (CFCs) is the catalyst for the breakdown of ozone to oxygen in the upper atmosphere. As with all catalysts, the chlorine is left unchanged at the end of the reaction and so can go on to more ozone destruction. This is what is causing a hole in the ozone layer.

Mineral wool soaked in paraffin oil

Broken china

Bubbles of gas forming. Small gas molecules have been made from large oil molecules.

Heat

LABORATORY CRACKING

Broken china can be used as a catalyst to break down paraffin oil. This is known as a cracking reaction. If mineral wool soaked in paraffin oil is put in a test tube and heated so that the oil passes over the china, the bonds in the large oil molecules are broken. Smaller, lighter gas molecules are made and can be collected.

CATALYTIC CRACKING

Molecules with very long chains of carbon atoms are more useful if they are heated and broken down into smaller molecules, but this process requires very high temperatures. By using a catalyst such as a zeolite, this splitting, or "cracking" process is made much easier and quicker. In this way, large crude oil molecules can be turned into smaller, more useful ones, such as those that make up gasoline.

Find out more

CHEMICAL REACTIONS P. 52
RATES OF REACTION P. 55
COMPOUNDS AND MIXTURES P. 58
CHEMISTRY OF THE BODY P. 76
OIL PRODUCTS P. 98
DIGESTION P. 345

COMPOUNDS AND MIXTURES

ELEMENTS THAT EXIST on their own are rarely found in the natural world. Most substances are made up of two or more elements that bond in different ways to form compounds. In a compound, atoms of different elements bond in a chemical reaction. Once this reaction has taken place, it is very difficult to separate the different elements of the compound. Water is a good example of a compound. It is made up of two atoms of hydrogen combined with one of oxygen. Combining elements to form a compound is very different from just mixing them together. Mixtures are combinations of different elements or compounds. Seawater, for example, is a mixture of water with other compounds, such as salt. But unlike compounds, no chemical reaction takes place when the elements or compounds mix together. This means that it is usually possible to separate mixtures into their different parts.

BUILDING BLOCKS
Just as letters of the alphabet can be used in different combinations to make millions of words, the elements can be arranged to make countless different compounds. The elements are nature's building blocks. Like a handful of building blocks, they can be used to build many different chemical structures.

IRON AND SULFUR
A mixture of iron and sulfur contains separate iron and sulfur atoms. If this mixture is heated, a chemical reaction occurs and a new compound, iron sulfide, is made. Iron sulfide contains iron and sulfur atoms joined together and has very different properties from the mixture.

When iron filings are mixed with sulfur in a watch glass, you can still see the black iron specks in the yellow sulfur powder.

Sulfur atom   Iron atom

Heat source

The iron from the iron and sulfur mixture can be pulled away by a magnet. As the iron is in a mixture, it has kept its magnetic properties.

The iron from the iron sulfide cannot be pulled away by a magnet. As the iron is in a compound, it has not kept its magnetic properties.

Iron sulfide molecule

Iron sulfide is a black shiny compound with different properties from those of its elements.

In a mixture, iron filings can be separated from sulfur using a magnet.

Magnet

PROPERTIES OF COMPOUNDS AND MIXTURES
A compound, such as iron sulfide, is very different from its elements, but a mixture keeps the properties of the substances it contains. It is difficult to separate a compound into its elements, but a mixture can be separated quite easily. A mixture of iron and sulfur, for example, can be separated by removing the iron with a magnet. A compound always contains the same proportions of its elements. Iron sulfide (FeS) always contains one part of iron to one part of sulfur. The amounts of the different substances in a mixture can vary.

JOSEPH-LOUIS PROUST
French chemist Joseph-Louis Proust (1754–1826) liked to analyze the content of anything that came within his reach. He discovered that the proportions of elements in any compound was always the same. This went against the thinking of respected scientists, but Proust was proved right. He had discovered the law of constant composition.

LAW OF CONSTANT COMPOSITION
Salt (sodium chloride, NaCl) is a compound that is found in seawater, salt mines, or can be made in a laboratory. But it is always the same salt, containing one sodium atom to one chlorine atom. A pure compound always contains the same elements in the same proportions.

Plastics are compounds of mostly hydrogen and carbon.

There are compounds and mixtures everywhere in this city scene from Florida.

Glass is a compound of silicon and oxygen.

Car bodies are made using mixtures of metals, called alloys.

TYPES OF MIXTURE

Solids, liquids, and gases can all be mixed in different combinations. Liquid mixtures, for example, are found in several forms. Alcohol and water mix easily. They are miscible liquids. Immiscible liquids such as vinegar and oil separate into two parts. By adding a substance called an emulsifier, the oil droplets will float suspended in the vinegar to produce a mixture called an emulsion. Mayonnaise is an emulsion of oil in vinegar. The emulsifier used is egg yolk.

Incense smoke is a mixture of solid dust and the air.

Bread is a mixture of a solid and a gas.

Shaving cream is a mixture of a liquid and a gas.

Soda drinks have a gas, carbon dioxide, dissolved in the liquid.

In salad dressing, oil floats on top of vinegar. These two liquids will not mix. They are immiscible.

Whisky is a mixture of two miscible liquids, alcohol and water, which is why it does not separate into two parts.

Hair gel is a mixture of a solid, fat, and water. The fat traps the water and stops it from moving around.

When flour is mixed into water, it stays suspended in the water. Flour and water form a suspension. A colloid is a suspension in which the suspended particles are very tiny.

ALLOYS

Objects such as spacecraft must be made of light yet strong material. Pure metals are not tough enough and so mixtures of metals, called alloys, are used. Alloys are made by adding a small amount of one pure metal to another. Since the atoms of the second metal are different in shape, they change the formation of the original metal. This makes it tougher and more difficult to bend.

In an alloy, atoms of one metal stop those of another from sliding around.

This space shuttle is made of a titanium alloy.

SYNTHESIS AND DECOMPOSITION

Chemists often build bigger and more useful molecules from smaller ones. This is called synthesis. Sometimes it is necessary to do the opposite and break down the larger molecules into smaller ones. This is called decomposition.

Chlorine is a poisonous green gas.

Sodium is a highly reactive, silvery-gray metal.

When sodium and chlorine combine, they make sodium chloride, or common salt.

MAKING A COMPOUND

Compounds are very different from the elements that make them. Common salt is a compound of sodium and chlorine. Sodium is a metal that is stored in oil since it reacts dangerously with air or water. Chlorine, a reactive green gas, is poisonous in large quantities. When sodium and chlorine atoms join, they lose their dangerous and poisonous properties. They form a new compound, sodium chloride, which is the familiar salt that we use to flavor our food.

A sodium atom gives one electron to a chlorine atom so that each ends up with eight electrons in their outer shell.

Sodium atom   Electron   Chlorine atom

DIFFERENT COMPOUNDS

Copper and oxygen can make two different compounds. Copper (I) oxide, a red-brown powder, has two parts of copper to one part of oxygen. Copper (II) oxide has one part of copper to one part of oxygen and is gray-black.

Copper (I) oxide (Cu_2O)

Copper (II) oxide (CuO)

MOVING ELECTRONS

Atoms are made of a nucleus with electrons moving around in it in different levels or shells. An atom is generally most stable if it has a complete outer shell. If the outer shell is incomplete, the atom is reactive and may be dangerous. When sodium and chlorine combine, electrons move places so that both sodium and chlorine each have a stable outer shell of electrons and the compound they make, salt, is stable and unreactive.

PURITY

In chemical terms, pure substances contain only one type of atom or molecule. Pure gold is made up of gold atoms and nothing else. Some drinks are described as "pure juice," which means that nothing artificial has been added to them. To a chemist, however, the juice is not a pure substance since it is a mixture of compounds like water and sugar. Mixtures are not pure, unlike compounds, which contain only one kind of molecule.

Although freshly squeezed orange juice contains no additives, a chemist would not call it pure, since it is made of more than one kind of molecule.

Only 24-carat gold is pure gold. Lower carats of gold are mixtures of gold with other, cheaper metals.

9-carat gold contains only 37% gold.

24 carat
22 carat
18 carat
14 carat

9-carat gold ring

Find out more

SOLUTIONS

SEAWATER LOOKS CLEAR, but it contains many substances, such as salt and oxygen, which have dissolved in the water and become invisible. It is an example of a solution, a special type of mixture in which different molecules are evenly mixed. Solutions are often made by dissolving a solid into a liquid, such as when sugar is stirred into tea. Sugar is called the solute and tea is called the solvent. There are other kinds of solutions too. Gases, liquids, and solids can all be solutes or solvents. Concentrated solutions contain a large amount of solute in a solvent, while in dilute solutions there is only a little solute. Orange juice concentrate is a concentrated solution that is diluted by adding water.

A carbonated fruit drink is a solution of fruit juice, sugar, and carbon dioxide.

Tube of glue

Adhesive molecule

Solvent molecule

When glue dries, the solvent evaporates, leaving the reactive adhesive molecules to link up.

ATTRACTING MOLECULES

Whether a substance will dissolve depends on how much the molecules of solute and solvent are attracted to each other. Water is a good solvent because it has a slight electric charge and can form weak bonds with other charged particles. Certain compounds, such as salt, break down in water into two particles, one with a positive charge and one with a negative charge. These particles, called ions, can form weak bonds with the water molecules.

A positively charged ion is attracted to the negative end of a water molecule.

Water molecule

Water molecule

Fish use the small amounts of oxygen dissolved in water to stay alive. Unlike solids, gases dissolved in liquids come out of solution when the liquid is heated. This is one reason why fish cannot survive in very warm water.

NONLIQUID SOLUTIONS

Air is a solution of oxygen and other gases dissolved in nitrogen. Boats are made from alloys that are solid solutions of one metal dissolved in another metal.

Dissolved particles mix with water molecules.

DIFFERENT SOLVENTS

Some substances will not dissolve in water. Some types of glue, for example, have to be dissolved in another type of solvent called an organic solvent, such as acetone. When glue dries, the solvent evaporates, leaving behind the sticky solid that binds the surfaces together.

The air that deep-sea divers breathe dissolves in their blood to form a solution. If the diver surfaces too quickly, the air can come out of solution to form bubbles in the blood. This is a dangerous condition known as "the bends."

UNIVERSAL SOLVENT

Alchemists were early chemists. In the course of their experiments, they discovered ways to purify metals by dissolving them in solvents. The alchemists dedicated themselves to the search for a "universal solvent," a substance in which all things would dissolve. They never found it. If they had, what would they have kept it in?

SATURATED SOLUTION

The Dead Sea between Israel and Jordan contains a massive amount of salt. The water evaporates in the hot Sun, leaving the same amount of salt but less water. There is no longer any room for all the dissolved salt, and it forms solid crystals. When solutions cannot hold any more solute, they are said to have become saturated.

Find out more

INSOLUBLE SOLIDS

Substances that dissolve in water, such as salt, are said to be soluble in water. Insoluble substances, such as sand and oil, will not dissolve. This is because the water cannot overcome the forces holding the molecules of sand or oil together. These molecules prefer to stay bonded to each other, rather than separate and mix with the water molecules.

SEPARATING MIXTURES

ONE WAY TO COOK RICE uses a sieve to separate the rice from the water, a method known as filtration. Chemists use this and other familiar techniques to separate mixtures in a laboratory so that they can study one particular substance. The method they choose depends on the type of mixture and the different properties of the substances it contains. For example, since tea leaves do not dissolve in tea, you can use a strainer to filter them. If the tea leaves were fairly large, you might just leave them to settle before drinking the tea. This is another technique known as decanting.

DECANTING

To search for gold in rivers, huge pans were once used to scoop up a mixture of sand, gravel, and river water. The mixture was swirled around, and any heavy gold particles sank to the bottom. The unwanted muddy liquid could then be decanted (poured) off. Decanting separates two substances with different densities. Because cream is less dense than milk, for example, it can easily be decanted off.

FILTRATION

In a coffee maker, a filter is used to separate the ground beans from the liquid coffee. As the water runs over the grounds, the coffee dissolves in the liquid and passes through the tiny holes in the filter paper. The grounds are too large to pass through the filter, and so they are left behind. To separate a mixture by filtration, the different parts of the mixture must be present in different-sized pieces.

Only the water can fit through the holes in the filter paper. The coffee ground particles are too large.

Water particle

Coffee ground particle

DESICCATION

To keep substances dry in the laboratory, chemists might put them in a desiccator. This sealed dish contains a solid, such as silica gel, that absorbs the moisture in the air. Packets of silica gel are often put inside camera cases so that moisture will not ruin the lens. Desiccation is simply a separating technique that removes water from a solid.

Substance to be kept dry

Silica gel

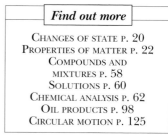
Centrifuge

CENTRIFUGING

A centrifuge is like a spin-dryer. It separates mixtures of liquids and solids by spinning them around at high speed. Dense substances sink to the bottom, while the less dense substances rise to the top. Test tubes of blood are centrifuged to separate the heavier blood cells from liquid plasma.

As the tubes are spun, the heavy particles sink to the bottom.

DISTILLATION

If you were marooned on a desert island, how would you obtain pure water to drink? If seawater is boiled, the water comes off as steam. If this is then cooled, pure liquid water can be collected. This is a separating method called distillation that is used whenever the liquid part of a mixture is needed. The method can also be used if a mixture of liquids needs to be separated. This is fractional distillation. By heating the mixture, the liquid with the lowest boiling point will come off first. The liquid fraction with the highest boiling point will come off last.

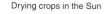
Drying crops in the Sun

EVAPORATION

Fruit such as grapes can be left outside to dry in the Sun. The heat turns the liquid water in grapes into water vapor which is lost to the air, leaving wrinkled raisins. This process of removing a liquid by heat is known as evaporation. Drying your hair with a hair drier is another example of evaporation.

Cooling water out

The heat turns a pure liquid component of the mixture into a gas.

Cooling water in

The mixture is heated in a flask.

When the gas is cooled, it turns to a liquid and is collected.

Find out more

CHANGES OF STATE P. 20
PROPERTIES OF MATTER P. 22
COMPOUNDS AND MIXTURES P. 58
SOLUTIONS P. 60
CHEMICAL ANALYSIS P. 62
OIL PRODUCTS P. 98
CIRCULAR MOTION P. 125

CHEMICAL ANALYSIS

CHEMISTS OFTEN WORK like detectives. They look for clues to reveal the true identity of a substance. Food chemists conduct experiments to find whether food contains poisons or bacteria. Medical chemists examine fluids such as blood and urine for signs of disease in our bodies. Environmental chemists measure the health of the environment by testing samples of air, water, and soil, so that they can record levels of pollution. Scientists can use a wide range of techniques to analyze substances. Identifying the ingredients of a substance is called qualitative analysis. Finding out exactly how much of each ingredient it contains is called quantitative analysis.

Solution of known concentration

The indicator added to the test solution turns from colorless to pink when it has all reacted.

TITRATION
To find out the concentration of a solution, chemists use a method called titration. They make the solution react with a chemical whose concentration is known. When all of the solution has reacted, a color change occurs. Its concentration can then be worked out by measuring how much of the chemical was used.

GAS CHROMATOGRAPHY
To separate a mixture of gases, chemists sometimes use a technique called gas chromatography. The mixture is made to travel through a solid, and because some parts of the mixture are more strongly held by the solid than others, the mixture is separated into its components.

The blue dye stays near to the center of the paper because it is more attracted to the paper than the other dyes.

The yellow dye travels on to the edge of the paper since it is more attracted to the water than the other dyes.

Scientists need weighing scales so that they can make accurate measurements of the substances they use in the laboratory. This is a type of quantitative analysis.

Everyone—except identical twins—has a DNA fingerprint that is unique to them.

CHROMATOGRAPHY
Black ink may be a mixture of different dyes. When you put a drop onto filter paper and then add water, the blot spreads out into different colored rings. Each separate ring contains a different dye. The dyes separate because some stick to the paper, and so remain near the center, while others stay dissolved in the water and are taken farther out. This is a technique known as chromatography. Chemists often use chromatography to test a substance for purity, and doctors use it to analyze urine samples for traces of sugar (which would indicate diabetes).

Fool's gold

When fool's gold is dragged across a white tile, it leaves a black trail. Real gold leaves no mark.

FORENSIC SCIENCE
Forensic scientists use many tests to solve crimes. One technique called DNA fingerprinting is used to find out if a sample of blood or other body tissue, found at the scene of a crime, came from a particular person. Tiny fragments of genetic material (DNA) from the sample of tissue are separated according to their mass, using electricity. The resulting pattern, which looks like a supermarket bar code, is called a DNA fingerprint. It is compared with a suspect's own DNA fingerprint, to help solve the crime.

126.34 g

DESTRUCTIVE TESTING
Real gold or fool's gold? Fool's gold is a compound of iron and sulfur that looks like gold. To test a sample, chemists can weigh it (fool's gold is lighter), drop acid onto it (fool's gold will dissolve), or drag it across a white tile (fool's gold leaves a black streak). The acid test and the white tile test damage the sample. They are destructive testing methods. Nondestructive testing, such as weighing, leaves the sample intact.

FRANCIS ASTON

English chemist Francis William Aston (1877–1945) invented the mass spectrometer in 1919. Aston worked as assistant to J. J. Thomson at the Cavendish Laboratory, Cambridge University, where he studied positively charged rays. The invention of the mass spectrometer led Aston to discover many new isotopes. This work won him the Nobel Prize for Chemistry in 1922.

MASS SPECTROMETER

Although the masses of atoms are too small to be measured, they can be compared. A very accurate piece of equipment that does just this is the mass spectrometer. It separates the atoms in a sample according to their mass and shows the amounts of the different atoms that are present. It does this by turning the atoms into ions and deflecting them in a magnetic field. The less mass an ion has, or the more electric charge, the more it will be deflected.

The sample is turned into a gas, and its atoms are converted into ions.

The stream of ions is speeded up by an electric field and then deflected (made to alter its direction) by a magnetic field.

Ions with a small mass are deflected too far to be picked up by the detector. Ions with a large mass are not deflected enough.

Only one type of ion is deflected by the right amount. By changing the strength of the magnetic field, different ions are recorded by the detector.

Detector

The height of the peak gives the number of each ion present.

The bottom scale gives the mass of each ion.

Reading from mass spectrometer

Atomic emission spectrum of the element helium

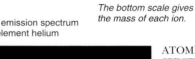

ATOMIC EMISSION SPECTRUM

The colored light given out, or emitted, by an atom during a flame test is only part of the story. The atom actually emits a whole range of different lights when it is heated, but only some light is visible to us. The other frequencies of light can be picked up by an instrument called a spectroscope to give the atomic emission spectrum. Each element has a different spectrum, and can therefore be identified.

Sodium compounds glow with an orange flame.

Lead compounds glow with a blue flame.

Copper compounds glow with a green-blue flame.

Barium compounds glow with a brown-green flame.

Potassium compounds glow with a lilac flame.

Lithium compounds glow with a red flame.

Environmental chemist testing the purity of a river

FLAME TESTS

When a metal compound is heated in a flame, it gives the flame a particular color. This happens because the heat of the flame makes the electrons in the atom move around, and as they do so they give off light. Different metals give different colors of light to the flame and so this color identifies the metal. Copper compounds, for example, always give a green-blue color to a flame. These characteristic colors of metal compounds are also responsible for the beautiful colors of fireworks.

WATER TESTING

Environmental scientists use chemical analysis to test the quality and safety of water. A river may be polluted with fertilizers, detergents, waste, sewage, or acid rain. A scientist can use titration methods, for example, to find out how much of a dissolved substance a sample of water contains.

ANALYZING NAPOLEON

After his death, chemists analyzed hair samples from the French emperor Napoleon Bonaparte (1769–1821) and found traces of arsenic, a poison. Murder was suspected. But recently it was discovered that the coloring in his wallpaper contained high levels of arsenic. Dampness and mold may have turned it into a deadly gas.

Find out more

ATOMIC STRUCTURE P. 24
COMPOUNDS AND MIXTURES P. 58
SEPARATING MIXTURES P. 61
SOURCES OF LIGHT P. 193
GENETICS P. 364
FACT FINDER P. 404

OXIDATION AND REDUCTION

Every time something burns, it combines with oxygen from the air. Burning is an oxidation reaction.

IF YOU FELT COLD ON THE MOON, you would never be able to light a fire to keep warm. This is because burning is a reaction in which a substance combines with oxygen—an oxidation reaction—and there is no oxygen around the Moon. Many important, everyday chemical reactions involve oxidation. It occurs when substances burn, when metals rust, and even when we breathe. The food that we eat is converted into energy by combining with the oxygen that we breathe in. Substances that combine with oxygen or that lose hydrogen are said to be oxidized. The process where a substance loses oxygen or gains hydrogen is called reduction, and it always happens at the same time as oxidation: when one substance gains oxygen, another must give it up.

REDUCTION
When a substance loses oxygen or gains hydrogen in a chemical reaction, it is reduced. This is caused by another substance removing oxygen or giving hydrogen. This other substance is known as a reducing agent. One example of this is the gas carbon monoxide given out by car exhausts. This will readily gobble up oxygen to form carbon dioxide.

This molecule is an oxidizing agent, as it is giving oxygen to another molecule.

This molecule is a reducing agent, as it is giving hydrogen to another molecule.

Oxygen atom *Hydrogen atom*

OXIDATION
When a substance gains oxygen or loses hydrogen in a chemical reaction, it is oxidized. Oxidizing agents are substances that give oxygen to, or accept hydrogen from, another substance. Familiar examples are the air and bleach—both have a high oxygen content.

This molecule has been reduced. It has gained a hydrogen atom.

This molecule has been oxidized. It has gained an oxygen atom.

RUSTING
If iron or steel are exposed to air and moisture, they will rust. Rusting is a destructive example of an oxidation reaction. The iron is oxidized to form iron oxide (rust). Once the top layer of metal has rusted, oxygen from the air can reach the inner layers. Rust will therefore quickly eat its way through the metal. Applying a coat of protective paint to a surface such as the hull of a ship prevents rust from forming, because the oxygen in the air cannot reach the iron.

OXIDATION IN KILNS
Potters may put a glaze on their pots that contains a metal—iron, for example. When the pot is baked in a kiln containing a lot of oxygen, the iron is oxidized to one form of iron oxide, Fe_2O_3, which is red. If the pot is baked in a kiln containing only a little oxygen, another form of iron oxide, FeO, is formed, which is black.

PHLOGISTON THEORY
Watching flames leaping from wood inspired a German doctor, Georg Stahl (1660–1734). He suggested that everything that burned gave out a substance called phlogiston. Later, Antoine Lavoisier (1743–94), a French chemist, dismissed this theory. He proved that when something burns, it combines with oxygen from the air.

OXIDES
When nonmetals combine with oxygen, they form oxides that make acid solutions in water. Nitrogen oxide and sulfur dioxide, for example, are nonmetal oxides produced by power plants. When these oxides dissolve in the moist air, they fall as acid rain, harming trees, lakes, and buildings. This is why power plants are now trying to control their emissions. Metals, on the other hand, combine with oxygen to form oxides that make alkaline solutions in water.

ELECTRON TRANSFER
During the oxidation and reduction processes, there is always a movement of electrons between the atoms. Atoms that gain electrons are said to be reduced. Atoms that lose electrons are said to be oxidized. Today, chemists call these processes oxidation and reduction, even when oxygen and hydrogen are not involved in the reaction.

Electron

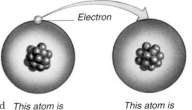

This atom is being oxidized.

This atom is being reduced.

MAKING MARGARINE

The margarine that you spread on your bread is made from liquid vegetable oils, such as sunflower oil. To turn these liquids into solid fats, the oil is combined with hydrogen. This process is called hydrogenation and is an example of a reduction reaction. By controlling the amount of hydrogen added to the oils, the margarine can be made as soft or as hard as needed.

Hydrogen atom

Molecule of hydrogen gas

Carbon atom

Portion of oil molecule

The liquid oil molecule has been reduced, because hydrogen has been added to it. This process turns the liquid oil into a solid.

Liquid oil

Solid fat

Portion of fat molecule

GUNPOWDER

Gunpowder was discovered accidentally by Chinese alchemists in the 7th century. Its main ingredients are saltpeter (potassium nitrate), sulfur, and carbon. Setting light to gunpowder is an example of an explosive oxidation reaction. While most substances burn by taking oxygen from the air, gunpowder burns by taking oxygen from the saltpeter. The chemical formula for saltpeter, KNO_3, shows it contains a lot of oxygen.

ANTIOXIDANTS

Food can go bad by reacting with oxygen in the air. To prevent this, chemicals called antioxidants are added to the food when it is made. It is these, rather than the food, that will react with the oxygen and so the food is kept fresh. Antioxidants are often found in fatty foods such as vegetable oils because fats are very quick to oxidize.

The gasoline and air are compressed and exploded by an electric spark. The hot gases that are produced force the piston down.

Internal combustion engine

Gas vapor and air are mixed together and sucked into the cylinder.

Exhaust gases

COMBUSTION

Combustion means burning. Inside the internal combustion engine of a car, gasoline is burned to release the energy that the car needs to move. Like all burning reactions, this is an example of an oxidation reaction. Gasoline combines with oxygen, and this reaction releases energy.

As the piston rises, the hot gases are pushed out of the cylinder and into the car exhaust. The cycle is then repeated over and over again.

Piston

The movement of the piston in the cylinder provides the power to make the car move.

FIREFIGHTING

To burn, a fire needs a fuel (the burning substance) and heat. Since burning is an oxidation reaction, a fire also needs a supply of oxygen to keep going and by taking this away, the fire can be stopped. This can be done either by smothering the flames with a blanket, or by covering them with foam or carbon dioxide from an extinguisher.

BREATHALYSER

Police officers often use an oxidation reaction to test for drunk drivers. When someone breathes into a breathalyser, any alcohol (ethanol) in their breath is oxidized to make ethanoic acid. This produces an electric current. The strength of the current shows the amount of alcohol present in the driver's breath.

Oxygen in the air

Plants release oxygen by photosynthesis

RESPIRATION AND PHOTOSYNTHESIS

Two life-giving reactions called respiration and photosynthesis are oxidation and reduction reactions. In respiration, the food we eat is oxidized. This releases the energy our bodies need. Plants use a reaction called photosynthesis to reduce carbon dioxide from the air to form sugars and starches.

Animals take in oxygen given out by plants and use it to oxidize the food they eat.

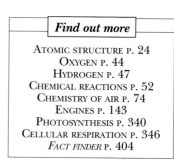

BLEACHING

Household bleaching fluids contain powerful oxidizing agents that oxidize the colored substances in cloth and make them colorless. Modern bleaches contain hydrogen peroxide, H_2O_2. Its formula shows that it contains a lot of oxygen.

Find out more

ATOMIC STRUCTURE P. 24
OXYGEN P. 44
HYDROGEN P. 47
CHEMICAL REACTIONS P. 52
CHEMISTRY OF AIR P. 74
ENGINES P. 143
PHOTOSYNTHESIS P. 340
CELLULAR RESPIRATION P. 346
FACT FINDER P. 404

REACTIVITY SERIES

POTASSIUM IS SO REACTIVE that it is rarely found on its own. It is usually tightly bonded to other elements. Silver, on the other hand, is such an unreactive element that it can be safely used for cutlery because it will not normally react with food. By comparing the way they react, a league table of metals can be drawn up. This is called the reactivity series. The metals at the top of the series are the most reactive; the metals at the bottom are the least reactive. The series is used to predict what will happen when different metals react together. For example, if potassium and silver were competing to react with chlorine, potassium would win and potassium chloride would be formed. A metal will win any competition between it and another metal lower in the series.

Copper metal

Silver metal collecting

Silver nitrate solution

Blue solution of copper nitrate forming

UNREACTIVE GOLD
Archeologists sometimes discover gold objects, such as jewelry or masks. These are often as good as new, even though they have been buried for thousands of years. Unlike most metals, which would have corroded, gold is an unreactive metal. This is why it is placed at the bottom of the reactivity series.

DISPLACEMENT

When copper is dropped into a solution of silver nitrate, the two metals compete for the nitrate ions. Because copper is higher in the reactivity series, it is able to "grab" the nitrate ions from the silver. The result is a blue solution of copper nitrate and needles of silver metal. This is called a displacement reaction, as the copper metal has displaced the silver from solution.

If aluminum's oxide layer is removed, the exposed aluminum reacts violently with air.

Cu

Copper metal

Ag

Silver metal

Ag+

Cu+

Silver in solution

The silver and the copper have swapped positions.

Copper in solution

ALUMINUM
Aluminum is an odd metal. It is high in the reactivity series, and yet aluminum saucepans are used to cook food. This is because it reacts with oxygen in the air to form a protective layer of aluminum oxide. But if this layer is broken down, for example, by rubbing aluminum foil with a chemical called mercury chloride, the exposed aluminum is extremely reactive.

HISTORY OF METALS

The use of metals came late in history. Early people used only bones, stone, and wood. Since copper, silver, and gold are at the bottom of the reactivity series, they were easily found and were the first metals ever used. By 2000 BCE, iron, a more reactive metal, could be extracted from its ores by heat. The Iron Age had begun. Aluminum is a common but very reactive metal that could not be extracted until the 19th century.

Iron tongs from the Iron Age

THE SERIES
This is the reactivity series. It shows the order of reactivity of different metals. Those at the top, such as sodium and potassium, react violently with air. Those at the bottom, such as silver and gold, are unaffected by air. Those in between, such as iron and zinc, react slowly. The way a metal is extracted from its ores (naturally occurring compounds) depends on its position in the reactivity series.

Potassium

Sodium

Calcium

Magnesium

Aluminum

Zinc

Iron

Lead

Copper

Mercury

Silver

Platinum

Gold

Sodium is high in the reactivity series and so forms very stable compounds. Sodium metal has to be obtained from molten sodium chloride by the powerful but expensive method of electrolysis.

Copper is lower down the reactivity series and so less energy is needed to extract it. Copper can be obtained by just heating its ores.

Gold, at the bottom of the reactivity series, is unreactive and can be found uncombined in nature.

GALVANIZING
Objects made of steel, which is mostly iron, can be protected against rusting by a coating of a more reactive metal, usually zinc. This process is called galvanizing. Oxygen in the air will react with the zinc rather than with the iron, even if the zinc layer is scratched. This is sometimes called sacrificial protection, since the zinc has been sacrificed to protect the iron.

Find out more

ALKALI METALS P. 34
TRANSITION METALS P. 36
SOLUTIONS P. 60
ELECTROLYSIS P. 67
IRON AND STEEL P. 84
COPPER P. 86
ALUMINUM P. 87
FACT FINDER P. 404

ELECTROLYSIS

TEARING A COMPOUND APART using electricity is a process called electrolysis. For this to work, the compound has to conduct electricity—it must be either molten or in solution, and it must contain electrically charged ions that are free to move. Two metal or carbon rods, the electrodes, are placed in the substance to be split (the electrolyte). When a battery is connected, electricity flows through the liquid. The positive ions of the compound move to the negatively charged electrode (the cathode). The negative ions move to the positively charged electrode (the anode). The compound is split into two parts.

ANODIZING
If electricity is passed through acid with aluminum as the anode, oxygen is formed at this anode and reacts with the aluminum to form a protective coating of aluminum oxide. This is called anodizing. Colored foils are made by dyeing this oxide layer.

MOVING IONS
When electricity is passed through a solution of potassium chloride (KCl) in water (H_2O), not only is the potassium chloride pulled apart, but also the water. The potassium ions and hydrogen ions, both positively charged, move to the cathode but because potassium "prefers" to stay as an ion, it stays in solution and only hydrogen gas is given off. Chloride ions and hydroxide ions, both negatively charged, move to the anode. The hydroxide ions stay in solution and only chlorine gas is given off.

Hydrogen ion

Potassium ion

Anode

Potassium hydroxide is left in the container.

Hydroxide ion

At the anode, negatively charged chloride ions give up their extra electrons to form chlorine atoms, which join up to make chlorine gas.

Chloride ion

Cathode

At the cathode, positively charged hydrogen ions take electrons to form hydrogen atoms, which join up to make hydrogen gas.

ELECTROREFINING
Electrolysis can be used to purify copper. This process is called electrorefining. Impure copper is the anode, a sheet of pure copper is the cathode, and the electrolyte is copper sulfate solution. When electricity is passed through the solution, pure copper is transferred from the impure to the pure sample. The impurities fall to the bottom of the solution.

Key before electroplating

Key after electroplating. It has been coated with copper.

Instead of using electricity to produce chemical reactions, chemical reactions can also generate electricity. This happens in a battery.

Pure copper metal

Copper sulfate solution

Battery

The key must be rotated so that it gets an even plating.

HUMPHRY DAVY
The English chemist Humphry Davy (1778–1829) is best known for his invention of the miner's safety lamp, but he was also one of the first to use electrolysis. He discovered sodium, potassium, calcium, and a number of other metals because he was able to separate them from their compounds by electrolysis. Davy appointed an assistant called Michael Faraday in 1813, who continued Davy's work and went on to become a very famous scientist himself.

ELECTROPLATING
Coating an object, like a key, with a thin layer of metal is a process called electroplating. The object is made the cathode. The anode is a pure piece of plating metal, such as copper. The electrolyte contains a compound of this metal (copper sulfate, for example). Metal ions move through the solution and coat the object. Tin cans are made by electroplating tin onto steel.

WATER
When electricity is passed through water (H_2O), hydrogen gas forms at the cathode and oxygen at the anode. Because water contains two hydrogen atoms for every oxygen atom, twice as much hydrogen as oxygen is produced.

Oxygen gas

Hydrogen gas

Water

Electrode

Battery

Find out more

BONDING P. 28
SOLUTIONS P. 60
REACTIVITY SERIES P. 66
COPPER P. 86
CELLS AND BATTERIES P. 150
FACT FINDER P. 404

ACIDS

Scientists use the pH scale to describe the strength of acids and alkalis. It runs from 1 to 14. The more hydrogen ions there are in a solution, the lower its pH. All acids have a pH of less than 7.

Acid half of the pH scale

1	2	3	4	5	6	7 (neutral)	

A LEMON TASTES SOUR because it contains an acid called citric acid. In fact, the word acid means "sour" in Latin. Acids are everywhere. They are found in ants (methanoic acid), grapes (tartaric acid), fizzy drinks (carbonic acid), car batteries (sulfuric acid), and even in our stomachs (hydrochloric acid). Strong acids such as sulfuric and nitric acids, which are used in laboratories, are dangerous and can attack clothes or skin. Some weak acids, such as those found in fruits, are safe to eat. All acids contain hydrogen and dissolve in water to form positively charged hydrogen ions. It is these ions that give acids their special properties. The number of hydrogen ions an acid can form in water is a measure of its strength, known as its pH.

HIGH pH
Citrus fruits such as lemons and oranges contain citric acid. This is a weak acid. It has a fairly high pH, but still under 7.

STRONG ACIDS
Some acids, such as nitric acid and sulfuric acid, are strong. Their molecules completely dissociate (split up) into hydrogen and other ions in water. The strength of an acid tells us what fraction of the molecules have split up to make hydrogen ions. Just as you dilute orange juice concentrate with water, you can dilute strong acids with water, so there are fewer hydrogen ions in solution. This lowers their acidity (increasing the pH).

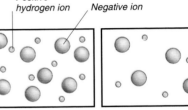

Positive hydrogen ion   Negative ion

Concentrated strong acid   Dilute strong acid

WEAK ACIDS
Some acids, such as the citric acid found in oranges and lemons, are weak acids. When dissolved in water, only a small number of their molecules will dissociate to form hydrogen ions. You can make concentrated or dilute solutions of a weak acid by either removing or adding water. A very concentrated solution of a weak acid and a very dilute solution of a strong acid may well have the same pH.

LOW pH
Acids found in the laboratory, such as sulfuric acid, are strong. They have a low pH. We have a strong acid, hydrochloric acid, in our stomachs to help digest our food.

Positive hydrogen ion

Negative ion

Concentrated weak acid   Dilute weak acid

Positive lead oxide electrode

ACID FROM ANTS
An acid called methanoic acid (formic acid) is produced naturally by both stinging ants and stinging nettles. Long ago, people made formic acid by boiling ants in a big pot. Today, it is made from other chemicals. It is used to preserve silage (crops stored for animal fodder) and to make paper and textiles.

Negative lead electrode

Sulfuric acid electrolyte

LEAD-ACID BATTERY
Strong acids make good electrolytes (liquids that conduct electricity). This is because in water they are almost completely split up into positive hydrogen ions and negative ions. These electrically charged ions can carry an electric current. Sulfuric acid is used as the electrolyte in the lead-acid batteries found in cars. Lead plates act as the electrodes. These batteries produce the energy to start the car.

A clam will die if the pH of its water falls below 6.

A salamander will die if the pH of its water falls below 5.

A brook trout will die if the pH of its water falls below 4.5.

A wood frog will die if the pH of its water falls below 4.

ACID WATER
Lakes and rivers can be polluted by acid rain. This increases the acidity, or lowers the pH of the water, and so may be harmful to fish and other aquatic life. Some animals are more sensitive to these pH changes than others. A clam, for example, cannot survive if the pH of its water falls below 6. Wood frogs, on the other hand, can survive in water with a pH as low as 4.

ACID ON PAPER

Concentrated sulfuric acid is very corrosive. It acts as a dehydrating agent, which means that it removes water from any substance it comes into contact with. Paper is made from cellulose, a plant material that contains carbon, hydrogen, and oxygen. When sulfuric acid reacts with paper, it removes the water (hydrogen and oxygen) and leaves the black carbon behind. This is why the paper looks burned.

The cork flies out of the bottle. It is pushed by the carbon dioxide gas created during the chemical reaction between the vinegar and the bicarbonate of soda.

YELLOWING PAGES

Have you noticed that the pages in new books look very white, while those in older books have turned yellow? Paper contains tiny amounts of an acid. Over years and years, this acid very slowly starts to break down the cellulose fibers in the paper. This changes the color of the paper from white to yellow. The reaction is speeded up by sunlight, and the paper may turn brown and become brittle.

ACID ON CARBONATE

If you add vinegar (ethanoic acid) to bicarbonate of soda (sodium hydrogen carbonate) in a corked bottle a fizzy reaction occurs. The acid breaks down the carbonate to make carbon dioxide gas. So much gas is produced that it fills up the bottle, and then forces the cork out like a cannonball. Acids will always break down carbonates to form carbon dioxide. This reaction is used in cooking. Baking powder is a mixture of cream of tartar (a form of tartaric acid) and bicarbonate of soda. In water, they make carbon dioxide, which is the gas that makes cakes rise.

A furious bubbling of hydrogen gas is given off.

Vinegar mixed with bicarbonate of soda

Hydrochloric acid

Chippings of zinc metal

A compound called sodium ethanoate is left behind in the bottle. This is a salt.

ACID ON METAL

You should never store vinegar in a metal bottle. It can create a slight fizzing of hydrogen gas. The hydrogen that all acids contain can be driven off when the acid meets a reactive metal. This is why acids are never kept in metal containers. When hydrochloric acid is poured on zinc (above) there is a fizzing of hydrogen gas. The zinc replaces the hydrogen in the acid to form zinc chloride.

WARNING SYMBOL

Although acids often look like water, strong acids are corrosive and cause severe burns. Because of this, the containers in which acids are transported carry a hazard warning sign. This has a code that identifies the acid and tells the fire brigade how to deal with a spillage.

PICKLING

Since acids are dangerous to living things, they can be used as preservatives to kill bacteria. Many foods, like onions and beets, are preserved by soaking in vinegar (ethanoic acid). This process is called pickling. The acid kills any microorganisms and stops the food from going bad. Pickling was widely used before the invention of refrigerators.

ACID DISCOVERIES

11th century Arabic chemists find out how to make sulfuric, nitric, and hydrochloric acids.

1675 Irish chemist Robert Boyle investigates the chemistry of acids and suggests that they might be made up of sharply pointed particles.

1770s French chemist Antoine Lavoisier suggests that all acids contain oxygen and are formed when oxygen compounds dissolve in water.

1887 Swedish chemist Svante Arrhenius puts forward the modern theory that all acids contain hydrogen ions and these give acids their special properties.

ACID IN RAIN

Rainwater has always been slightly acidic, as carbon dioxide in the air dissolves in rain to form carbonic acid. But the acidity of rain has increased since the world became industrialized. This is because fossil fuels such as coal release sulfur dioxide and nitrogen dioxide when they are burned. These gases react with the water in clouds to form sulfuric acid and nitric acid. Acid rain threatens many buildings, especially those made of limestone, which is calcium carbonate. This is because acids easily break down carbonates into carbon dioxide gas.

Find out more

BONDING P. 28
HYDROGEN P. 47
SOLUTIONS P. 60
ALKALIS AND BASES P. 70
MEASURING ACIDITY P. 72
SALTS P. 73
SULFURIC ACID P. 89
CELLS AND BATTERIES P. 150

ALKALIS AND BASES

WHEN YOU ARE STUNG by a nettle, the first thing you reach for is a dock leaf. The leaf contains a natural base that counteracts the acid in the nettle sting. Bases are substances that can cancel out acidity. They are said to neutralize acids. Alkalis are bases that can dissolve in water. Bases and alkalis are all around us—in oven cleaners, polish, baking powder, indigestion tablets, saliva, and chalk. Like acids, some alkalis are very dangerous and can cause burns if splashed onto the skin. All alkalis dissolve in water to form hydroxide ions (OH-). These ions react with the hydrogen ions (H+) in acids to cancel out acidity. The number of hydroxide ions an alkali can make in water is a measure of its strength. This is measured on the pH scale.

SOAP
Alkalis feel soapy when rubbed between the fingers. This is because they react with the oils in our skin and start to dissolve them. Soap is made by boiling animal fats or vegetable oils with the strong alkali sodium hydroxide (NaOH).

ALKALI FROM ASHES
The word alkali is Arabic and means the "ashes of a plant." Alkalis used to be made by burning wood and other plants—sodium carbonate from sea plants and potassium carbonate from land plants. Alkalis can now be made by electrolysis.

This is a type of alkaline battery you might find in a watch or a calculator.

Negative zinc electrode

Potassium hydroxide electrolyte

Positive mercury oxide electrode

ALKALI CONDUCTORS
Since alkalis break up in water to form ions, alkalis are good conductors of electricity. In an alkaline battery, the strong alkali potassium hydroxide is used to conduct electricity between two electrodes.

ALKALI ON METAL
When a solution of sodium hydroxide is poured onto some pieces of magnesium metal, there is a tremendous fizzing. This is hydrogen gas that has formed during the reaction. Magnesium hydroxide is left in the flask. This is the active ingredient in milk of magnesia, which people take to cure indigestion—it works by neutralizing excess acid in the stomach.

ALKALIS IN SPACE
Astronauts in the Apollo space missions used the alkali lithium hydroxide to neutralize the dangerous levels of carbon dioxide gas they were breathing out. This type of neutralization is also used to remove carbon dioxide from air-conditioned buildings.

WARNING SYMBOL
Concentrated solutions of alkali are corrosive and can cause severe burns. Because of this, the containers in which they are stored and transported always carry a hazard warning sign.

Sodium hydroxide mixed with magnesium pieces

CALCIUM CARBONATE
Seashells, coral, chalk, limestone, and marble are all made of the base calcium carbonate. It is a very important and useful compound in the chemical industry for making fertilizer, glass, cement, and steel. By heating calcium carbonate, calcium oxide (quicklime) is made. Just by adding water, this can be made into calcium hydroxide (slaked lime), which is used to neutralize acid in water supplies. Slaked lime can be mixed with sand and water to make mortar.

Limestone processing plant

The more hydroxide ions an alkali contains, the stronger it is, and the higher its pH. All alkalis have a pH greater than 7.

Alkali half of the pH scale

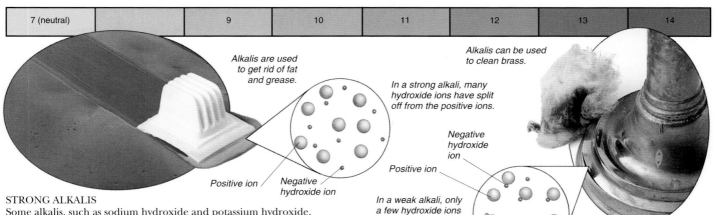

7 (neutral)		9	10	11	12	13	14

Alkalis are used to get rid of fat and grease.

Alkalis can be used to clean brass.

In a strong alkali, many hydroxide ions have split off from the positive ions.

Negative hydroxide ion

Positive ion

Positive ion

Negative hydroxide ion

In a weak alkali, only a few hydroxide ions have split off from the positive ions.

STRONG ALKALIS
Some alkalis, such as sodium hydroxide and potassium hydroxide, are called strong alkalis. When they dissolve in water, all their molecules dissociate (split up) into ions. This means they contain many hydroxide ions, and so have a high pH. Oven cleaners, for example, contain the strong, corrosive alkali sodium hydroxide. This reacts with the burned, fatty deposits that form on the oven walls during cooking.

WEAK ALKALIS
Some alkalis, such as ammonium hydroxide and bicarbonate of soda (sodium hydrogen carbonate), are weak alkalis. In solution, only a few molecules dissociate into ions. They therefore contain only a few hydroxide ions, and so have a lower pH. Brass cleaner is a weak alkaline solution. It works by breaking down the oxide layer that forms on the surface of the brass when brass is left exposed to the air.

A bee sting is very painful since it contains an acid. This can be neutralized by an alkali such as soap.

LIMING FIELDS AND LAKES
Acid rain increases the acidity of the lakes and soils on which it falls. This causes problems for plants growing in the soil. To fix this, farmers spread powdered lime (calcium hydroxide) on their fields. The lime is a base that neutralizes the acidity. Lime can also be added to lakes to reduce acidity. Adding lime to lakes and fields can relieve the damage caused by acid rain, but it does not stop the cause of the pollution.

Farmer liming field

Close-up view of the sting of a bee

NEUTRALIZATION
Every time a base meets an acid, neutralization occurs, and water and a compound called a salt are produced. This reaction can be used to treat some animal and plant stings. If you are stung by a wasp which has a basic sting, you can neutralize it with an acid such as lemon juice or vinegar. If you are stung by a bee or an ant, you can neutralize the acid sting with an alkali such as bicarbonate of soda. Nettles also give acidic stings which can be treated by rubbing with a dock leaf, which contains an alkali.

A wasp sting is very painful because it contains an alkali. This can be neutralized by an acid such as vinegar.

FIRE EXTINGUISHER
Some fire extinguishers used to work by using the neutralization reaction between an acid and a base. They contained sulfuric acid and bicarbonate of soda, which mixed when the extinguisher was turned upside down. This produced water and carbon dioxide gas. The pressure of this gas forced a foam of liquid and carbon dioxide bubbles out of the nozzle.

Bicarbonate of soda

Sulfuric acid

The fizzy reaction between the acid and the alkali forces out a foam, which can be used to put out fires.

ALKALI IN THE PLAGUE
Seventeenth-century London, England, was an unhealthy place to live and was continually ravaged by plague—the plague of 1665 killed 80,000 people. The bodies were buried in mass graves that were covered with a strong alkali called lime (a mixture of calcium compounds), which was thought to speed up the rate of decomposition (rotting).

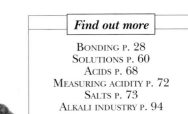

Find out more

BONDING P. 28
SOLUTIONS P. 60
ACIDS P. 68
MEASURING ACIDITY P. 72
SALTS P. 73
ALKALI INDUSTRY P. 94

MEASURING ACIDITY

HAVE YOU NOTICED how the color of tea changes slightly when you add a slice of lemon? The tea is acting as an indicator, showing that the lemon has increased the acidity. Some colored chemicals are used in the same way to show whether a solution is acid or alkaline. A measure of the acidity or alkalinity of a solution is called pH, short for "power of hydrogen." This is a scale that runs from 1 to 14. It is based on the number of hydrogen ions a solution contains. A pH of 1 shows the solution contains many hydrogen ions and is a strong acid. A pH of 14 indicates that the solution contains few hydrogen ions and is a strong alkali. Neutral solutions have a pH of 7.

Beet   Radish   Pear   Red cabbage

The inner circle is the universal indicator color scale. It is pink in strong acid (pH 1) and blue in strong alkali (pH 14). The outer circles show how the color of the juices of red cabbage, pear, radish, and beet change as the pH changes.

SOIL ACIDITY
Gardeners often have to worry about the pH of their soil. Some plants will only grow in a certain pH range. Soils in chalk and limestone regions are usually alkaline (pH 7 to 7.5). Soils in sandstone, clay, moorland, and peat areas are usually acidic (pH 6.5 to 7). Heather prefers to grow on acidic soils, and that is why it often covers open moorland.

Hydrangeas grown in alkaline soil produce red flowers.

INDICATORS
There are many different indicators that can tell us the acidity or alkalinity of a solution. A very useful indicator is a mixture of dyes known as universal indicator. This gives a range of color changes from red for pH 1 (very strong acid) to blue for pH 14 (very strong alkali). The dyes obtained from fruits and vegetables, such as pears, onions, and red cabbage, can also be used as indicators. They change color as the pH changes. The juice of a red cabbage, for example, turns from red in strong acid, through to pink, purple, blue, and green in strong alkali.

Phenolphthalein is deep pink above pH 9.5.

Phenolphthalein is colorless below pH 8.5.

Contact lens solutions and injections have to be buffered so the pH of your body fluids is not altered.

BUFFERS
Sometimes, we don't want the pH of a solution to change. In the body, for example, most reactions will only take place within a narrow range of pH. A change of just 0.5 in the pH of your blood could kill you. To prevent this from happening, the body produces substances (called buffers) that neutralize any changes in acidity or alkalinity and keep the pH of the blood constant. For the same reason, intravenous injections have to be carefully buffered.

Methyl orange is red below pH 3.

Methyl orange is yellow above pH 8.

LABORATORY INDICATORS
Scientists often use special laboratory indicators to help find when just enough acid has been added to neutralize all the alkali in a reaction. Two examples are methyl orange and phenolphthalein. These change color at a precise pH.

Methyl orange is orange between pH 4 and 8.

NATURAL INDICATORS
Some plants are natural indicators. The color of hydrangeas depends on whether the soil is acidic or alkaline. Litmus is an indicator obtained from a plant called a lichen. Litmus paper is made by soaking paper in litmus solution. It turns red in acid and blue in alkali.

Hydrangeas grown in acidic soil produce blue flowers.

Alkalis turn litmus paper blue.

Acids turn litmus paper red.

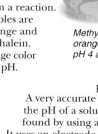

pH METER
A very accurate measure of the pH of a solution can be found by using a pH meter. It uses an electrode to measure the concentration of hydrogen ions in solution and displays the pH of the solution on a screen.

SALTS

Common salt is made up of sodium ions (Na⁺) and chloride ions (Cl⁻).

HAVE YOU WONDERED why the sea is salty? Salts are naturally occurring compounds that are often soluble in water. Rivers dissolve salts from the ground and carry them down to the sea. The salt we put on food is just one type of salt. But there are many others. In fact, salts are very common and useful chemicals. Plaster of Paris, gunpowder, chalk, paint pigments, garden insecticide, and fertilizers are all examples of salts. They are compounds of a metal and a nonmetal joined together by an ionic bond. A salt is made whenever an acid reacts with a metal or a base, and they usually form beautiful crystals.

IONS
All salts are made up of ions. It is because of these ions that salts are able to dissolve in water, and their solutions will conduct electricity. The strong ionic bond explains why salts usually have such high melting and boiling points.

BODY SALTS
The next time you sweat, see how salty the sweat tastes. Every time you sweat, you lose salt from your body. Because salt is vital to the healthy running of the body, this can lead to sickness and collapse. This is why doctors advise people to take salt tablets when they visit hot countries. This replaces the salt that is lost in sweat.

Nerve cell

NERVES
Messages in your body are carried as electrical signals along nerve fibers. These are produced by sodium and potassium ions flowing (or being pumped) in and out of the nerve cell. These vital ions come from the salts you eat.

Dilute sulfuric acid

Tiny blue crystals of the salt, copper sulfate, start to appear once the solution is heated.

When the acid mixes with the black copper oxide, a blue solution of copper sulfate is made.

MAKING A SALT
Every time an acid and a base are mixed, a salt is made. If black copper oxide (a base) is mixed with dilute sulfuric acid and heated, a blue solution is created. The base has neutralized the acid and a dissolved salt, copper sulfate, has been formed. The water from this solution can be boiled away, until the blue crystals of copper sulfate slowly start to appear.

Blue copper sulfate crystals

Tarnished copper

The copper is cleaned by a lemon. In doing so, a salt is made that dissolves in the lemon juice.

Bunsen burner

The heat from the bunsen burner drives off the water from the solution, leaving the salt behind.

SALT FAMILIES
In a salt, the metal (copper) comes from the base (copper oxide) and the nonmetal part (sulfate) comes from the acid (sulfuric acid). Each acid therefore has its own family of salts. Sulfuric acid makes sulfates, citric acid makes citrates, and so on. Each base also forms a family of salts. Copper oxide, for example, always makes copper salts.

COPPER SALT
Copper easily reacts with oxygen from the air to form a thin coating of copper oxide. Copper that has tarnished in this way can be cleaned with lemon juice. The acid in the lemon juice (citric acid) reacts with the copper oxide (a base) to form a salt (copper citrate) and water. This salt will dissolve in water, leaving the copper clean and shiny.

Salts often make beautiful crystals.

NATURAL SALTS
Many ores and minerals are made of salts. These include limestone (calcium carbonate), gypsum (calcium sulphate), and fluorite (calcium fluoride). If they grow in the right conditions, all salts will form beautiful crystals.

Fluorite crystal

CHEMISTRY OF AIR

Air contains many different colorless gases.

THE INVISIBLE BUT VITAL AIR surrounds us all the time. It is a mixture of different gases, mainly nitrogen and oxygen. We are constantly changing the composition of the air around us—just by breathing, we are reducing the amount of oxygen it contains. The air in the atmosphere is like a protective shield. It filters out the Sun's harmful ultraviolet rays but allows the visible and infrared rays, on which we depend for light and heat, to pass through. The air in the atmosphere also acts like an insulating blanket, preventing extremes of temperature. Without it, the Earth would be like the Moon—boiling hot by day, and freezing cold at night.

Nitrogen makes up 78% of the air.

Oxygen makes up 21% of the air.

Argon makes up 0.9% of the air.

Gasoline-driven cars cannot be used on the Moon. Astronauts must use electric cars.

Carbon dioxide makes up 0.03% of the air.

Small amounts of other gases make up the remaining 0.07% of the air.

LIFE-GIVING AIR
Nearly all life depends on air for its survival. We use the oxygen in air to convert food into energy, and we breathe out carbon dioxide. Plants use a reaction called photosynthesis to convert the carbon dioxide from the air into foods, such as sugars, which they need to grow.

On Earth, a car continually takes in air. The oxygen in the air is needed to burn gasoline— the energy released in the reaction drives the car.

ESSENTIAL AIR
It is easy to forget that we are surrounded by air. But without it, many of the things that we take for granted could not happen. For example, if you took a car to the Moon, it would not work because there is no air there. This is why astronauts have to use an electric car when they explore the Moon.

FRACTIONAL DISTILLATION OF AIR
Air contains some very useful gases. They can be separated by a process called fractional distillation. Air is made into a liquid by being cooled to a very low temperature. When it is left to warm up, the gases boil off the liquid at different times since they have different boiling points. The gases can therefore be collected separately.

Air   Liquid air

Oxygen boils at -361°F (-183°C). It is used for breathing apparatus.

Argon boils at -367°F (-186°C). It makes an unreactive filling for lightbulbs.

Nitrogen boils at -305°F (-196°C). It is used to make fertilizers and nitric acid.

AIR QUALITY
Human activities have caused changes in the composition of the air. For example, it wasn't necessary to clean silver until around 1600, when the levels of sulfur in the air started to rise. The biggest changes have occurred since the Industrial Revolution in the 19th century, when people started burning carbon fuels on a large scale. Carbon dioxide makes up a larger part of air today than it ever did before. We must control the levels of pollution released into the air to protect life on Earth.

DISCOVERIES

1754 Scottish doctor Joseph Black finds carbon dioxide in air.

1772 Scottish physician Daniel Rutherford finds nitrogen in air.

1774–79 Joseph Priestley (English) and Antoine Lavoisier (French) find oxygen in air.

1892–98 British scientists Sir William Ramsay and Lord Rayleigh find air contains inert gases.

Find out more

NITROGEN P. 42
OXYGEN P. 44
NOBLE GASES P. 48
BEHAVIOR OF GASES P. 51
COMPOUNDS AND MIXTURES P. 58
OXIDATION AND REDUCTION P. 64
INDUSTRIAL POLLUTION P. 112
ATMOSPHERE P. 248

CHEMISTRY OF WATER

DON'T BE FOOLED BY WATER. What appears to be just a colorless, odorless, and tasteless liquid, is actually a hard-working chemical whose reactions are vital to life. Water is a compound of hydrogen and oxygen. Its chemical formula, H_2O, shows that each molecule of water contains two atoms of hydrogen and one atom of oxygen. Water is not only all around us, in rain, clouds and the seas; it is inside us as well. Water carries nutrients to your cells and waste products from your body. Water is very good at dissolving substances. Because of this, it is hardly ever found in its pure form. The water from a faucet, for example, has been in contact with rocks, soil, and air before it reaches us and contains many dissolved chemicals.

The human body is around 65% water by weight.

Thin people may contain as much as 75% water; fat people may contain only 55% water.

A tomato contains 95% water.

Water covers over 70% of the surface of the Earth.

There are more molecules of water in just one drop than all the millions of stars we can see in the sky.

At room temperature, pure water is a colorless liquid. It boils at 212°F (100°C), freezes at 32°F (0°C), and has a neutral pH of 7.

Close-up of kettle scale

WATER EVERYWHERE
Water is the most common chemical compound, and covers over 70 percent of the Earth's surface. On average, the human body is about 65 percent water. Some foods are almost all water. A ripe tomato, for example, is 95 percent water. In all these places, the water is busy carrying out important chemical functions.

Adding water to white copper sulfate crystals turns them blue.

WATER OF CRYSTALLIZATION
Many compounds contain water molecules trapped in their crystals. This is the water of crystallization. It can be driven off by heating. If blue copper sulfate crystals are heated, they lose their water of crystallization and turn white. Adding water to these white crystals turns them blue again. Because only water can produce this color change, the process is used as a chemical test for water.

SOLID WATER
Unlike most other substances, water expands when it freezes. When water forms ice, each of the water molecules forms a weak bond (called a hydrogen bond) with four other molecules. This creates a tetrahedral shape, which has plenty of empty space inside it. This structure explains why ice is less dense than water.

Hydrogen atom

Water molecule

Oxygen atom

HARD WATER
Certain dissolved chemicals make water "hard." Hard water does not easily form a lather with soap. Instead, a white precipitate, scum, is formed. There are two types of hardness in water. Calcium and magnesium hydrogen carbonates cause temporary hardness, which can be removed by boiling. This makes a solid (calcium carbonate)—the scale found in kettles. Permanent hardness is caused by calcium and magnesium sulfates. These can be removed by passing the water through a water softener, which swaps the magnesium and calcium ions for sodium ions.

WATER IN AIR
On a humid day, the air contains a lot of water vapor. Humidity is a measure of the amount of water in the air. Dry air, such as that in a desert, contains very little water vapor.

Deserts contain too little water to support very much life.

Find out more

CHANGES OF STATE P. 20
BONDING P. 28
CRYSTALS P. 30
SOLUTIONS P. 60
WATER INDUSTRY P. 83
HUMIDITY P. 252
SNOW P. 266

CHEMISTRY OF THE BODY

YOUR BODY IS A MOBILE CHEMICAL FACTORY that processes raw materials, such as food, water, and oxygen. After being fed in, these raw materials go through a series of complicated chemical reactions, known as metabolism. This produces the energy the body needs to function. One series of reactions breaks down large molecules of food into smaller ones, such as glucose, that can pass into the bloodstream. This process is called digestion. The blood transports the glucose to the liver, where it is stored as the body's fuel. The cells release the energy in this fuel by a reaction called respiration. Waste products are taken for disposal to the end of the body's factory line.

SALIVA
The first site of chemical attack on the food that we eat is our mouth. Here, saliva pours out of the salivary glands and onto the food, which is being ripped apart by our teeth. The saliva is a watery mix that contains an enzyme called amylase. This enzyme starts to break down the starch in food. Since amylase will only work in alkaline conditions, saliva is very slightly alkaline.

STOMACH
Once the food has reached the stomach, it is swirled around with gastric juices, which have poured from the gastric glands. Gastric juices contain a strong acid called hydrochloric acid and several enzymes. The acid kills germs in the food and activates an enzyme called protease, which breaks down proteins.

Hydrochloric acid is made in the gastric glands by a chemical reaction involving carbon dioxide, water, and salt.

While the stomach enzymes are working, the contractions of the stomach wall work like a food processor, pounding the food into a fluid called chyme.

MAKING GLUCOSE
In the intestine, the food is bombarded by a mix of chemicals called bile. This is piped in from the liver, via the gall bladder. It contains bile salts that help to break down fats. Enzymes to complete the digestion of food come from the pancreas and the intestinal wall. Glucose, one of the products of all these reactions, is transported to the liver.

Gall bladder

The bile contains bicarbonate of soda (sodium hydrogen carbonate), which neutralizes the acid from the stomach.

Brain

Esophagus

Heart

Lungs

Stomach is behind liver

Liver

Intestine

CATABOLISM
Some chemical reactions in the body produce energy. Respiration, for example, releases energy by breaking down glucose into smaller molecules. This energy is not produced as a result of breaking the glucose bonds but is released when stronger bonds are formed in the smaller molecules. Energy-releasing reactions are called catabolic reactions, and the process itself is called catabolism.

The chyme from the stomach is piped into the small intestine.

Intestine

ANABOLISM
Chemical reactions in the body that involve building up structures are known as anabolic. They differ from catabolic reactions as they use up energy, rather than release it. They get this energy from all the catabolic reactions in the body. Making blood proteins involves building large, complex molecules from simple ones. It uses a great deal of energy and is an anabolic reaction. The process itself is called anabolism.

ENZYMES

Many chemical reactions in the body are speeded up by special catalysts called enzymes. Each enzyme helps with one particular reaction. They are cleverly able to distinguish between molecules that are very similar, so they will not speed up the wrong reaction. Enzymes are remarkably efficient and fast-working catalysts. Without them, our body reactions would be so slow that we would certainly die.

LIVER

The liver is the body's chemical powerhouse. It produces a green liquid, bile, that aids digestion, and it keeps a store of glucose, vitamins, and minerals. Poisons from drugs and alcohol are also removed from the blood by the liver. The reactions that occur in the liver are mostly exothermic, which means they give out heat. This heat is spread around the body by the blood to keep us warm.

BODY ELEMENTS

Your body is made up of many different chemical elements. Oxygen, carbon, and hydrogen are found in the fats, proteins, and carbohydrates that make up most of the body tissues. Nitrogen is found in proteins, and bones contain calcium. Trace elements in the body include iron, sodium, potassium, copper, zinc, magnesium, phosphorus, iodine, chlorine, silicon, and sulfur. These elements, although present in only minute amounts, are essential for keeping the body healthy.

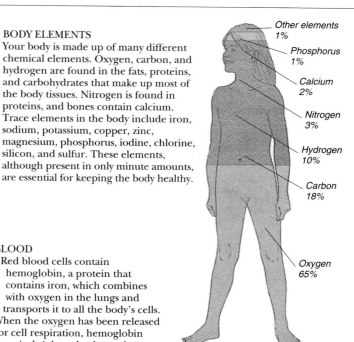

Other elements 1%
Phosphorus 1%
Calcium 2%
Nitrogen 3%
Hydrogen 10%
Carbon 18%
Oxygen 65%

BLOOD

Red blood cells contain hemoglobin, a protein that contains iron, which combines with oxygen in the lungs and transports it to all the body's cells. When the oxygen has been released for cell respiration, hemoglobin loses its bright red color and becomes purplish. Blood also carries away waste carbon dioxide produced by the cells and deposits it in the lungs so that it can be breathed out.

RESPIRATION

The energy contained in food is converted into energy we can use by a chemical reaction called respiration. This reaction is carried out in every single cell of our body and in nearly all living cells in the world. There are two kinds of respiration: aerobic and anaerobic. Aerobic respiration requires oxygen. It releases a great deal of energy.

Oxygen + glucose $\rightarrow$ carbon dioxide + water + ENERGY

A burning nut gives out heat and light energy. This reaction is very similar to aerobic respiration. In both cases, food combines with oxygen to give energy. But inside your body, the energy is not suddenly released as a flame, it is released more gradually in chemical form.

The liver stores vitamins, regulates the amount of glucose in the blood, purifies the blood, and gets rid of excess protein.

Liver

Glucose from the liver is given to the blood.

ANAEROBIC RESPIRATION

If you are running fast in a race, your muscles are using up oxygen faster than your lungs can take it in. The cells start to use anaerobic respiration to give you extra energy. This reaction does not require oxygen but produces less energy than aerobic respiration does.

Glucose $\rightarrow$ lactic acid + energy

Lactic acid causes muscle ache and cramp. This is why athletes take deep breaths at the end of a race, to replace oxygen supplies and to get rid of the lactic acid.

Blood is busy traveling to every cell of your body. On its journey, it picks up glucose from the liver and oxygen from the lungs. These two chemicals are needed by every cell for a reaction called respiration. This releases all the energy our body needs.

Solid waste is excreted.

The kidneys are in charge of the body's cleaning and waste disposal. Millions of small filters, called nephrons, remove poisons and waste substances from the blood.

Amazingly, the kidneys can filter all the body's blood in only five minutes. The dissolved waste, urine, flows into the bladder.

Find out more

CATALYSTS P. 56
CHEMISTRY OF FOOD P. 78
DIGESTION P. 345
CELLULAR RESPIRATION P. 346
BLOOD P. 348
INTERNAL ENVIRONMENT P. 350

CHEMISTRY OF FOOD

THERE ARE MORE CHEMICALS in the food you eat than you would ever find in a laboratory. Many of the chemicals contained in food are vital to life. Groups of chemicals called proteins, carbohydrates, fiber, fats, vitamins, minerals, and water are all needed for a healthy diet. Other chemicals may be responsible for the flavor, while still more may give the food color. Just the oil from orange peel contains around 50 different chemical compounds. Whenever food is cooked, reactions occur that change these chemicals. In fact, cooking and chemistry have a lot in common. Many of the processes they use, such as heating, mixing, and filtering, are very similar.

Carbon atom

Hydrogen atom

Oxygen atom

This is a molecule from the herb oregano. It has 10 carbon atoms, 14 hydrogen atoms, and 1 oxygen atom.

CHEMICAL PIZZA
A pizza is really just a plate of chemicals, and most of them are nutritious. The hundreds of different chemicals present have very complicated formulae. Just look at the chemical above, which gives the herb oregano its flavor.

PROTEIN TEST
Food scientists test a food for proteins by crushing up a sample with water. If dilute sodium hydroxide, followed by a few drops of copper sulfate solution are added, the color will change from pale blue to pale purple if protein is present in the food.

Fat is not present

FAT TEST
Fats are large molecules of carbon, hydrogen, and oxygen found in foods such as cheese, peanuts, and butter. A food sample can be tested for fat by shaking it in ethanol (a type of alcohol). Any fats in the food will dissolve to give a clear solution. This is then poured into a tube of water. Because fats are insoluble in water, tiny droplets of fat will cloud the water if fats are present in the food.

Fat is present

Protein is not present

The protein chains in a raw egg are neat spiraled chains.

As the egg is heated, the protein chains start to unravel.

Protein is present

When the chains are unraveled, they become tangled with each other and form a solid mesh.

PROTEINS
Life-building chemicals called proteins are found in foods such as eggs, meat, and nuts. They are made up of carbon, nitrogen, sulfur, oxygen, and hydrogen atoms. Some protein molecules are joined together in long, spiraled chains. As you cook an egg, the protein molecules first unravel (called denaturation) and then tangle up together to form a solid mesh. This is why the protein white of an egg becomes solid when cooked.

ONION CHEMICALS
Why does chopping up an onion make you cry? Onions contain a number of unusual sulfur compounds. When the onion is cut, these react with oxygen in the air to form strong-smelling chemicals that cause your eyes to water. Scientists have recently discovered that some of the sulfur compounds may be useful for treating asthma.

MINERALS
The tiny amounts of inorganic substances we need in our diet are known as minerals. Water dissolves these minerals, containing the elements calcium, iron, potassium, and magnesium, out of the soil. They are then taken up through the roots of the plants growing in the soil. By eating these plants, we also eat the minerals they contain.

VITAMINS

The vitamins are a mixed assortment of chemical compounds that the body cannot make itself. They are found in many foods, such as citrus fruits (vitamin C), green vegetables (vitamins A and K), carrots (vitamin A), wholemeal bread (vitamin B), and oily fish (vitamin D).

Vitamin C is not present

Vitamin C is present

LEMON PRESERVATIVE

Freshly cut fruits, such as apples and bananas, soon become brown when they are exposed to the air. This is a reaction between chemicals in the fruit and oxygen, speeded up by an enzyme in the fruit. Since enzymes are very sensitive to changes in acidity, the browning reaction is slowed down by adding an acid, such as lemon juice, to the freshly cut fruit.

VITAMIN C TEST

There is a blue dye, called DCPIP, which vitamin C can turn colorless. If this change happens when a sample of food (crushed in water) is added to the dye, it proves that the food contains vitamin C.

SUGARS

The sweetness of jams and cakes is due to a group of chemicals called sugars. These are compounds of carbon, hydrogen, and oxygen. One of the simplest sugars is glucose. Its chemical formula is $C_6H_{12}O_6$. Other simple sugars include lactose, which is found in milk, and fructose, which is found in fruits. Sugars are not confined to the kitchen any more. Industrial chemists have started to convert sugars into industrial chemicals, which are used to make paints and detergents.

Sugar is not present

CARAMELIZING SUGAR

When sugar is heated the sugar molecules start to break down, giving off water. If the heating is continued the sugar caramelizes, becoming dark brown and sticky. Caramel is used as a coloring for vinegar, gravies, and other foodstuffs.

Caramelized sugar

Sugar is present

SUGAR TEST

A food can be tested for sugar by crushing it with water and adding a special chemical called Benedict's solution. If an orange-brown precipitate (tiny solid particles) forms when this mixture is heated, it shows that sugar is in the food.

Sugary foods

PRESERVING FOOD

Fresh foods, such as fish, soon go bad if they are left in the open air, because harmful microbes start to grow on them and inside them. But food can be preserved by killing the microbes or by slowing down their growth. There are a number of common methods for doing this. Freezing, salting, smoking, and pickling all slow down, or even stop, the microbes from multiplying. Heating or passing radiation through the food are the only ways to kill all the microbes.

Fish are smoked by holding them over a wood fire. The heat from the fire and the chemicals in the smoke slow down the rate at which microbes grow. Smoking also adds flavor and changes the texture of food.

STARCH TEST

Starch can be detected by crushing up a food sample with water and adding a few drops of iodine solution. If this turns to a blue-black color, it shows that the food contains starch.

Starch is not present

Pasta, potatoes, and rice all contain starch.

Starch is present

Starch granules in water, magnified 60 times

STARCH

Starchy foods, such as bread, potatoes, rice, and pasta, are made up of sugar molecules joined together in long chains. Starch and sugar are sometimes called carbohydrates. The starch in flour is used to thicken sauces like gravy. When starch granules are heated in water, some of the water gets inside them and forces the individual starch molecules inside the granules apart. This causes the granules to swell up until they burst, leaking the starch molecules into the surrounding liquid, and thickening the sauce.

FOOD POISONS

Some foods naturally contain tiny amounts of poisons, which in very large doses can make us sick. Bananas contain a chemical that can produce hallucinations. Green potatoes contain a poison, solanine, which causes a stomach ache. Cheeses can contain tyramine, a chemical related to the body hormone adrenaline. This affects our pulse rate and can cause nightmares.

Find out more

ORGANIC CHEMISTRY P. 41
CHEMICAL ANALYSIS P. 62
CHEMISTRY OF THE BODY P. 76
FERMENTATION P. 80
FOOD INDUSTRY P. 92
NUTRITION P. 342
FEEDING P. 343

FERMENTATION

Magnified view of yeast cells

FOR THOUSANDS OF YEARS, fermentation has been used to make bread, beer, and wine. Today, it is used to make foods such as bread and yogurt, alcoholic drinks such as wine, drugs such as penicillin, and chemicals such as methanol and citric acid. Fermentation is a chemical process. Tiny organisms called microbes grow by converting the sugars in foods, such as fruits and grain, into alcohol and carbon dioxide. Microbes can live almost anywhere. It is likely that fermentation was discovered by accident when fruits or grain were stored in containers. One safe and commonly used microbe is yeast. Not all microbes are safe to eat—many are harmful and poisonous.

Yeasts are tiny living organisms that are only visible through a microscope. Yeasts grow on the skins of fruits, such as grapes and apples, by feeding on sugars. Each yeast cell divides rapidly as it feeds.

The gas given off travels through this tube to the limewater.

Airtight stopper

Yeast converts the sugar into alcohol, which is left in the flask, and carbon dioxide gas.

Bubbles of gas forming

The clear limewater turns cloudy after mixing with the gas. This proves the gas is carbon dioxide.

Yeast mixed with warm water and sugar

When water is mixed with the flour and the dough is kneaded, some of the proteins in the flour combine to form a network of molecules that is strong and elastic.

MAKING BREAD
One of the ingredients of bread is yeast. After the dough has been kneaded, it is put in a warm place. The yeast respires with oxygen by feeding on the sugars and breaking them down into carbon dioxide and water. These gases cause the dough to rise. As you bake the dough, the yeast is killed, and the gases expand to give the bread a spongy texture. If dough without yeast is used, it will not rise. The bread it makes is called unleavened bread.

FIRST FERMENTATION
The Ancient Egyptians were the first to make leavened bread 5,000 years ago. They used to keep a store of sour fermented dough (called sourdough) that was added to each mix to make the bread rise. Sourdough was probably discovered when yeast spores were blown onto dough that had been mixed and put to one side before baking.

YEAST
If a mixture of yeast, sugar, and warm water is left to stand, bubbles of gas appear as the yeast ferments. If this gas is bubbled through limewater (a solution of calcium hydroxide in water), it turns the limewater cloudy. This result proves that the gas is carbon dioxide—the cloudiness in the limewater is the insoluble compound calcium carbonate suspended in the water. The yeast is respiring without oxygen. This means it feeds on the sugar, converting it to carbon dioxide and alcohol, which is left in the flask.

Lactobacillus bulgaricus bacteria, magnified

ALCOHOL
Microbes will normally produce carbon dioxide and water by respiration (as in breadmaking). However, if the microbes do not have a good supply of air, they make carbon dioxide and alcohol. This is why alcoholic drinks are made by carrying out the fermentation in sealed containers. When the solution contains around 14 percent alcohol, the microbes become poisoned, and fermentation stops. This is why alcoholic drinks with more than 14 percent alcohol cannot be made just by fermentation.

YOGURT
Yogurt is made by adding certain bacteria (lactobacilli) to milk and allowing this to ferment without oxygen. The bacteria multiply and cause the milk to thicken. They reduce the sugar content by converting the milk sugar, lactose, into lactic acid. This is why natural yogurt tastes sour.

BLUE CHEESES
A special type of penicillin mold is added to blue cheese to give it its color and taste. As the cheese matures, small holes are made in it with stainless-steel needles to ensure that the mold has enough oxygen to grow.

Find out more
CHEMISTRY OF THE BODY P. 76
CHEMISTRY OF FOOD P. 78
SINGLE-CELLED
ORGANISMS P. 314
FUNGI P. 315
ASEXUAL REPRODUCTION P. 366

MATERIALS

IMAGINE WHAT LIFE would be like if you wore concrete shoes and rode bicycles made of glass. These are just two of the many materials we use in our daily lives—but not for walking or cycling! Most of the materials around us have been changed from their natural state. The original materials come from substances in the ground, in water, or even in the air. Chemical processes change these raw materials into materials with special properties that we can use. For example, the materials in our clothes are made from fibers that are stretchy, soft, and strong. This makes our clothes comfortable and durable.

MATERIALS FOR TENNIS

All the materials used in a game of tennis are perfectly suited to their functions. Rackets are strong because they need to stop balls that are traveling very fast. Balls are made from materials that do not tear when they collide with the racket or the court. Tennis shoes and the court surface are both made of tough materials to withstand the wear and tear caused by players running all over the court.

A sports cap is made of cotton for keeping cool.

Sunglasses made from chemicals in oil are light and safe to wear.

Racket frame is made of plastic containing graphite, synthetic leather-cushioned grips, and synthetic strings.

Sports socks are made of natural fibers to keep feet cool.

Wood is a tough and hard natural material made from trees.

Sports clothes are made from strong, comfortable materials, such as polyester, cotton, and nylon.

Paper consists of natural fibers made from trees.

Tennis balls are made from rubber, nylon, and natural fibers.

Sports shoes are made from leather or canvas, with rubber soles for flexibility.

TERRA-COTTA
About 7,000 years ago, people found that if they heated clay it changed into a hard, brittle substance. By shaping the clay before baking, people could make bowls, cups, and urns to hold food and drink. They called this material terra-cotta, which means baked earth. This was one of the first manufactured materials.

EXTRACTING IRON
The Hittites of Turkey discovered how to extract iron 3,500 years ago. The secret was to heat rock containing iron with burning charcoal. This made the metal soft enough to hammer into weapons and tools.

FROM IRON TO STEEL
Early metalworkers knew that carbon could make iron harder. In 1742, an English inventor called Benjamin Huntsman found a way to control the amount of carbon, to produce the first true steel. Steel is now used to make a range of products, from needles to car bodies.

CLOTH STEAMS AHEAD
Since 8000 BCE people have been spinning natural fibers to make threads, and weaving or knitting them together to make cloth. In the late 18th century, Europeans invented machines that could spin and weave using steam power.

AGE OF PLASTICS
In the 1850s, Alexander Parkes, an English chemist, made the first plastic material. Today, plastics are made from the chemicals in oil. They are used to make toys, as well as many household products, such as trash cans and chairs.

CHEMICAL INDUSTRY

MATERIALS MADE IN THE CHEMICAL INDUSTRY are all around you and some are inside you, too. These materials range from the paint on cars to the food you eat. Each material is made in a factory called an industrial plant. Raw materials, such as minerals, oil, water, coal, and gas, enter the industrial plant where chemical reactions take place. These reactions change the raw materials into useful materials. The useful materials are then transported to be used by people all over the world. Industrial plants are very expensive to build and to run. They are one of the largest industries in the world, and their goal is to make materials at prices people can afford.

IN THE PIPELINE
Color-coded pipes transport cooling water, steam, liquid, and chemical gases around modern industrial plants.

Energy provides the power to run the plant.

Raw materials must be stored near the plant.

The industrial plant is conveniently located for raw materials, workers, and transportation.

People in nearby towns are employed to work in the plant.

Cows eat pellets made from harmless waste food materials.

Some waste materials are recycled to make other products.

Boat to transport materials

It is vital to have roads and rivers nearby to transport materials away quickly and efficiently.

THE SITE
An industrial plant needs raw materials, energy, and water. These must be close to the plant for it to work efficiently. Materials made in the plant must be cheaply transported away, and waste materials must be carefully disposed of. Some wastes are sold to make into other useful materials. This is recycling. Waste materials that cannot be sold are made as harmless as possible before being released into the environment.

KEEPING SAFE
Chemical reactions can produce poisonous fumes, start fires, and cause explosions. Industrial workers are protected from such hazards by safety equipment and warning systems in the plant. Special protective clothing is provided in case of such emergencies.

SMALL SCALE MODEL
Before building an industrial plant, a small scale model is built in a laboratory. Chemicals are passed through glass apparatus to make each stage of the process easy to see and check. When the scientists are sure the chemical reactions and equipment work safely, this model is scaled up.

SCALING UP
When the small scale model is running well, and ways have been investigated to make the material cheaply, the equipment and processes are scaled up to make a full-size plant.

Find out more
CHEMICAL REACTIONS P. 52
WATER INDUSTRY P. 83
INDUSTRIAL POLLUTION P. 112
ENERGY SOURCES P. 134
FACT FINDER P. 406

WATER INDUSTRY

A PERSON CAN LIVE for about six days without water, but most of industry would stop working right away. Industry needs large amounts of water to make almost all the materials we use. Every day, the world's industries use on average four times as much water as people use in their homes. Rain is the main source of all this water, but before we use it, it must be cleaned. When rain hits the ground, it rushes into streams and rivers, or sinks into rock beneath the ground. On its journey, the water picks up small particles of rock, bacteria from the soil, and dissolved chemicals from almost everything it flows over.

DESALINATION
In places where there is little rain, such as the Middle East, people obtain water from the sea. The seawater is heated, at low pressure. Only pure water evaporates, and is condensed in collecting trays. The salt is left as a concentrated solution.

Water is trapped behind a dam in a reservoir.

In the chemical filter, aluminum sulfate (alum), and calcium hydroxide (lime) are added. These form a sticky substance, aluminum hydroxide, which traps any suspended particles in the water.

The water travels through beds of sand and gravel, where dirt particles are trapped.

Water storage towers

Any bacteria that survive the filters are killed in the contact tank by chlorine gas which is bubbled through the water for about an hour.

Not all industries need very pure water. Some, such as power plants, can use the impure water straight from rivers or the sea.

To stop bacteria from reinfecting the water, low doses of chlorine are left in it when it is sent to our homes.

PURIFYING WATER
Rivers, lakes, and underground wells are nature's stores of water, but artificial reservoirs allow us to store large amounts of water near to factories and homes. As the water leaves the reservoir, it passes through a screen to remove objects such as garbage and twigs. Filters made from chemicals, sand, and gravel remove smaller particles that could scour (wear away) the inside of water pipes, damage industrial equipment, or make drinking water cloudy. Bacteria or viruses, which may cause disease and death, are dealt with by bubbling toxic gases, such as chlorine or ozone, through the water.

HOW INDUSTRY USES WATER
Industry uses large amounts of water. The water cools furnaces, where chemical reactions release heat, provides the heat to start a chemical reaction, or generates steam to drive a pump or electrical generator. Used as a solvent, water dissolves many substances, making the diluted solution easier to handle. Finally, water cleans materials, equipment, and the workplace.

Manufacturing a car involves a surprising amount of water.

Lemonade   Shower   Steel   Car

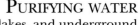

WATER FACTS
To make a car requires 8,000 gallons (30,000 liters) of water. To make 1 ton of steel requires 1,125 gallons (4,500 liters) of water, but a shower uses only 9 gallons (35 liters). A pitcher of lemonade uses 2 gallons (8 liters) of water.

IRON AND STEEL

WITHOUT IRON AND STEEL, what would we use for making cars, supporting tall buildings, or producing machines to make nearly every product there is? Iron is the cheapest and most important metal we use. Iron is extracted from a rocky material called iron ore, and most iron is then made into steel. Like many elements, iron is too reactive to exist on its own in the ground. Instead, it combines with other elements, especially oxygen, in ores. The chemical process for extracting a metal from its ore is called smelting. Iron ore is heated with limestone and coke, which is mostly made up of carbon. Coke and limestone remove the unwanted parts of the iron ore to leave almost pure iron, which still contains some carbon. Steel is made by removing more carbon and adding other metals.

CAST IRON
The dome of the Capitol, in Washington, D.C., contains 4,000 tons of cast iron. The different parts were made by being cast in a mold.

THE BLAST FURNACE

Iron is extracted from iron ore in blast furnaces. The biggest are 200 ft (60 m) high, produce 10,000 tons of iron a day, and work nonstop for 10 years. The furnace gets its name from the blast of hot air that heats up the raw materials. These are iron ore, limestone, and coke (a form of carbon). As carbon is more reactive than iron, it grabs the oxygen from the iron ore, leaving iron metal behind.

Safety valve

Waste gases are cleaned and used to heat the hot-air blast.

Raw materials enter through two bell valves. The valves prevent hot gases from escaping.

Iron ore

Limestone

Coke, made by heating coal without air present

Furnace lined with heat-resistant bricks

Bustle pipe around furnace delivers a blast of hot air. This gives the furnace its name.

Ladle for carrying molten iron

Outlet for molten slag

Outlet for molten iron

HENRY BESSEMER
Steel is the most useful form of iron, but removing the carbon from the iron used to be an expensive process. In 1856, a British inventor, Henry Bessemer (1813–98), devised a cheap way of removing most of the carbon. Air was blown through the molten metal in a furnace called a converter. The oxygen in the air removed the carbon.

INSIDE THE BLAST FURNACE
The chemical reactions begin when hot air is blasted into the furnace. As the coke burns, the carbon in it gets enough energy to react with oxygen from the air to form first carbon dioxide and then carbon monoxide. The carbon monoxide takes oxygen atoms from the iron oxide to leave carbon dioxide and iron metal. Temperatures inside the furnace reach 3,500°F (1,900°C), melting the iron which sinks to the bottom.

IRON IN CLOSE-UP
Cast iron can be made in a number of different forms. In the form shown here, magnified 200 times, tiny spheres of graphite (blue) make a hard but workable cast iron.

SLAG
Limestone is included in the furnace because it mixes and combines with sand, clay, and stones in the ore. They form a waste material, called slag, which floats on top of the molten metal.

IMPURITIES
Iron from a blast furnace is 90–95 percent pure. The main impurity is carbon, absorbed from the coke in the blast furnace. Carbon makes the iron hard but not very strong. Most iron is converted into steel, a form of iron that contains less than 1.7 percent of carbon.

Steel scissors contain about 1 percent carbon.

A steel anchor chain contains about 0.1 percent carbon.

Stainless steel in the laboratory

CONTINUOUS CASTING

Molten steel in reservoir

Water-cooled rollers

Molten steel is poured between water-cooled rollers that shape and cool the steel until it solidifies. The rollers form the metal into standard shapes, such as slabs or bars, known as billets.

DRAWING

A rod becomes wire if squeezed through a series of small holes.

A series of rollers shape a billet into rods, tubes, girders, or rails.

ROLLING

Steel billet

Rotor shaft of a turbine engine

A metal block presses the steel with a force of up to 10,000 tons.

FORGING

Steel slab

Steel is poured into a mold, and solidifies in the shape of the mold as it cools.

Train wheels

Molten steel

CASTING

MORE THAN ONE STEEL

There are carbon steels and alloy steels. Low-carbon steels are tough yet easy to shape. High-carbon steels are hard and brittle, but can be given sharp cutting edges. Alloy steels contain a range of metals, each giving the steel a special property. Chromium, nickel, and steel make stainless steel, which is hard-wearing and does not rust.

Molten iron poured into furnace

Oxygen is blown onto the molten metal.

The oxygen combines with carbon in the iron to make carbon monoxide. This reaction releases heat, and the iron stays molten.

Scrap steel forms up to a quarter of the molten metal used.

SHAPING STEEL

Steel can be shaped in a variety of ways. Rolling stretches and squeezes ingots of steel into sheets, tubes, or strips. In drawing, rolled steel is pulled through a hole to make a wire. In casting, it is left to cool in a mold. Forged steel is made by squeezing hot steel.

Lime removes impurities such as phosphorus. The lime reacts with the impurities to form a slag that floats on the steel.

Ingots of steel

When the process is complete, the furnace tilts to pour the steel into a ladle. Slag is removed by turning the furnace upside down.

AFTER THE FURNACE

The ladles of molten steel are poured into molds to make ingots, or a reservoir that serves a continuous casting process. Most steel is continuously cast because it is cheaper and better quality. These blocks of steel, called billets, can then be shaped by rolling, forging, or casting.

STEEL IN CLOSE-UP
This picture shows a low-carbon steel, containing 0.87 percent carbon. The structure of steel is varied with different amounts of carbon and by the way it cools.

BASIC OXYGEN FURNACE

Most iron is converted into steel in a basic oxygen furnace. A mixture of iron and steel scrap is poured into the furnace, and a jet of oxygen is blown over it. Oxygen combines with the carbon in the iron, carrying it away as carbon monoxide. It takes a basic oxygen furnace just 40 minutes to produce 350 tons of steel.

Find out more

TRANSITION METALS P. 36
CARBON P. 40
OXIDATION AND REDUCTION P. 64
REACTIVITY SERIES P. 66
COAL PRODUCTS P. 96
SEDIMENTARY ROCKS P. 223
FACT FINDER P. 406

COPPER

YOU MAY NOT BE ABLE TO SEE IT, but copper is all around you. The walls and ceilings of almost every room contain copper wire leading to light fixtures and electric sockets. These wires carry the electricity that provides light and power in our homes. In its natural form, copper occurs in the ground as copper ore, a mineral. But this ore contains only 0.5–1 percent of the metal. The rest is rock. The world produces nearly 10 million tons of copper a year. This means that more than a billion tons of ore have to be removed from the ground and the pure copper extracted.

Chalcopyrite is a sulfide ore—it contains copper, combined with iron and sulfur.

Sulfide ore

Hot air

Outlet for sulfur dioxide

Outlet for iron-silicate slag (waste)

Outlet for copper

Silica is added and reacts with iron oxide to make iron-silicate slag.

The molten copper is cast into flat slabs. Each slab of blister copper is about 3 ft (1 m) across and weighs 900 lb (400 kg).

EXTRACTING COPPER

Most copper is extracted from a compound of iron, sulfur, and copper called sulfide ore. Hot air is blown into a furnace to separate the copper from the iron and sulfur. The iron and sulfur react with the oxygen to form iron oxide and sulfur dioxide, leaving molten copper metal. This copper, known as blister copper, is about 98 percent pure. A process called electrolysis is needed to separate the remaining impurities.

LEACHING
In some ores, the copper is combined with oxygen. In a process called leaching, sulfuric acid is sprayed over these copper oxide ores, which dissolves the copper but not the rock. The copper and sulfuric acid form a solution of copper sulfate, which is purified by electrolysis.

CARRIE EVERSON
Ores contain a mixture of valuable metallic substances and worthless rock. An American schoolteacher, Carrie Everson, invented a way of separating the two in 1886. She ground up ore and mixed it with oil and acid. This produced a froth in which the metallic substances floated, while the rocky materials sank.

Carrie Everson

ELECTROLYSIS
A slab of blister copper can be transformed into pure copper by electrolysis. The slab is suspended in a solution of copper sulfate and sulfuric acid, where it acts as a positive electrode (anode). When electricity is passed through the solution, the copper in the anode is dissolved. The pure copper collects at the negative electrode (cathode) and the impurities fall below.

Electric coils in motor

Pure copper collects at cathode—the negative electrode.

Solution of copper sulfate and sulfuric acid

Blister copper acts as anode—the positive electrode.

Copper ions move toward the cathode

Pure copper

Impurities collect as slime

Atoms of copper stack together in a regular way as the metal forms to make crystals. The way the crystals interlock allows the metal to be easily pushed or pulled into shape.

Micrograph of copper

USES OF COPPER
Copper is a good conductor of heat and electricity. We use it to make cooking utensils and all sorts of pipes for carrying hot water, both in homes and in industry. We also use it to make different kinds of electrical devices, such as lightning conductors and the electric coils in motors. Copper does not rust easily, so it lasts a very long time.

Gold

Silver

Platinum

COPPER BY-PRODUCTS
Gold, silver, and platinum can be found in their pure state in the Earth's crust, so they do not have to be extracted from ores. However, useful amounts are found in the slimes that form during the electrolysis of copper.

Find out more

TRANSITION METALS P. 36
REACTIVITY SERIES P. 66
ELECTROLYSIS P. 67
ALLOYS P. 88
SULFURIC ACID P. 89
FACT FINDER P. 406

ALUMINUM

YOU'VE PROBABLY SEEN aluminum in the form of soft drink cans or thin sheets of foil. It is the most common metal on Earth. It occurs naturally in many different kinds of rock. But most of the aluminum we use is extracted from an ore called bauxite. Because aluminum easily combines with other elements, a great deal of energy is needed to separate it into its metallic (pure) form. Chemists discovered a cheap way of extracting aluminum in 1886. Before this, the metal was much more expensive than silver and gold.

The Emperor of France, Napoleon III (1808–1873), used aluminum plates to impress his most important guests. Today, we use aluminum foil to wrap food because it is so cheap.

Huge wheel extracts bauxite ore from the Earth's crust.

The bauxite ore is crushed into pieces.

CYCLE SUPPORT
Aluminum is easy to work and shape. As a tubular frame, it provides a very lightweight support for the racing cyclist.

The major aluminum ore, bauxite, is formed over long periods by the weathering of rocks containing aluminum silicates (aluminum, silicon, and oxygen).

Each cell (used for electrolysis) is up to 30 ft (9 m) long by 13 ft (4 m) wide. Carbon anodes hang in the molten cryolite.

EXTRACTING ALUMINUM

Aluminum is extracted from bauxite by the Bayer process and electrolysis. In the Bayer process, bauxite is mixed with caustic soda and heated. This produces sugarlike crystals of pure aluminum oxide. These are dissolved in molten sodium aluminum fluoride, called cryolite. Electrolysis is then used to split up the aluminum and oxygen.

Electric current passes through the liquid, driving the oxygen from the aluminum oxide to the anodes.

Sodium hydroxide is added to bauxite and pumped into a large tank called a digester.

Heat and high pressure help sodium hydroxide digest (break down) bauxite. Aluminum oxide from the ore dissolves, forming a solution of sodium aluminate. A filter removes the insoluble impurities.

Digester

Filter

Crystals of aluminum oxide form as the solution cools, leaving sodium hydroxide.

Heat drives water from crystals, to leave a fine powder.

Molten aluminum collects at the carbon cathode that lines the bottom and sides of the cell.

Aluminum is collected and used to make many products. It can also be easily recycled.

COINCIDENTAL CHEMISTS

In 1886, two chemists independently discovered how to extract aluminum using electricity. Their discovery reduced the price of aluminum to a fraction of the price of silver in four years. The two chemists were Charles Martin Hall (1863–1914), a student at Oberlin College in Ohio, and P. L. T. Heroult (1863–1914), a young chemist working in France. By coincidence, they were not only the same age when they made their discovery, but also died within eight months of each other.

C. M. Hall   P. L. T. Heroult

USING ALUMINUM
When the surface of aluminum reacts with oxygen in the air, a thick coating of aluminum oxide forms. This seals the metal from the air and stops it from corroding. Aluminum is also durable, light, and a good conductor of electricity. We use it to make parts for planes, cars, and trucks, and to make electric cables.

Find out more

POOR METALS P. 38
REACTIVITY SERIES P. 66
ELECTROLYSIS P. 67
CHEMICAL INDUSTRY P. 82
ALLOYS P. 88
FACT FINDER P. 406

ALLOYS

IF YOU HAD BEEN A SOLDIER in Ancient Greece you would have had to stop in battle to straighten your bronze sword. But bronze was a great improvement on copper, which bends even more easily. Most pure metals are weak and soft. But two soft metals mixed together make a harder metal called an alloy. Bronze is an alloy of copper and tin. By changing the amounts and combinations of the metals, the properties of an alloy can be altered. Most alloys consist of two or more metals, but some contain a nonmetal, such as carbon. The most widely used alloy of this type is steel.

THE FIRST ALLOY
About 6,000 years ago, people discovered that copper could be made harder if mixed with tin. This alloy is called bronze. It was so widely used for many years that this period of time became known as the Bronze Age.

Aluminum mixed with magnesium and copper provides a lightweight body that is strong enough to stand up to high-speed winds and the impact of landing.

HIGH TEMPERATURES
A drill bit cuts its way through hard material, spinning thousands of times a minute. A tungsten carbide alloy, with a melting point of over 5,250°F (2,900°C), provides the hardness and strength to do this.

In a jet engine, metal disks hold the turbine blades in place. Disks are made from a superalloy of 11 elements including nickel and titanium.

LOW TEMPERATURES
Solder, an alloy of tin and lead, is perfect for joining metal parts together. It has a lower melting point than either of its pure metals, so it does not damage any of the parts. It creates a bridge between the two metal parts.

ALLOYS IN AIRCRAFT
Jet aircraft need lightweight alloys for their bodies to make take off easier and to keep fuel consumption down. Their engines need special alloys designed to withstand very high temperatures. Rapidly spinning turbine blades at the front of the engine suck in air at temperatures of up to 1,100°F (600°C).

MAKING ALLOYS
Most alloys are made by melting metals and mixing them together. Care must be taken to make sure that one metal does not boil before the other melts. When making brass, for example, solid zinc is dropped into molten copper. If the zinc were heated to the same temperature as the copper, it would boil away into a vapor.

Metals in an alloy dissolve in each other. Their atoms mix freely and lock together to make strong crystals when they cool.

DENTAL ALLOY
You may have an alloy in your teeth. Dentists use amalgam—the alloy of mercury, silver, tin, zinc, and copper—to fill cavities. It forms a solid that can be shaped like putty to match the contours of the teeth before it hardens.

Find out more

BONDING P. 28
ALKALI METALS P. 34
TRANSITION METALS P. 36
POOR METALS P. 38
REACTIVITY SERIES P. 66
FACT FINDER P. 406

SULFURIC ACID

WHAT DO FERTILIZERS, PAINTS, explosives, and detergents have in common? They are all made with sulfuric acid. In fact, many of the items we use every day would not exist without it. Sulfuric acid does not occur naturally; it has to be manufactured. The chemical industry produces about 150 million tons of it each year. Fortunately, sulfuric acid is cheap to make because the waste heat from one stage of the process can be used to provide heat for the next stage.

Sulfur (a solid element) is the key raw material in sulfuric acid. But water and air are also needed.

The steam from a coiled pipe melts the sulfur, which is then sprayed into a furnace.

Heat exchanger

Dry air is blasted into the furnace. Oxygen in the air combines with sulfur to make sulfur dioxide gas.

In the converter, more oxygen is added to the sulfur dioxide to make sulfur trioxide.

Converter

In the heat exchanger, the sulfur dioxide passes over a pipe of water, heating the water as it cools. This heat is used to melt the sulfur and drive the fans that blow air into the furnace.

SULFUR TRIOXIDE
Without a catalyst, sulfur dioxide and oxygen are slow to react. Pellets of vanadium pentoxide act as a catalyst to speed things up. They provide a huge surface for the molecules to settle on. This draws the molecules close together, so that they start reacting.

Sulfur dioxide

Oxygen

Vanadium pentoxide

Sulfur trioxide forms at the surface

JEAN ANTOINE CHAPTAL
In the 18th century, factories used sulfuric acid for making plaster, dyes, and buttons. The French chemist Jean Antoine Chaptal (1756–1832) saw the need to make sulfuric acid on a large scale for these and other rapidly growing industries. In the 1780s, he set up the first commercial factory for making sulfuric acid in Montpellier, France.

Absorber

Sulfur trioxide passes through a spray of sulfuric acid, which absorbs the sulfur trioxide. This forms a concentrated fuming liquid called oleum.

Sulfur trioxide could be added directly to water to produce sulfuric acid. But the reaction would be too violent.

MAKING ACID
There are two stages in making sulfuric acid. First, air and sulfur are heated to make sulfur dioxide. In the second stage air and sulfur dioxide are mixed to produce sulfur trioxide, and this gas is dissolved in sulfuric acid to give oleum, a super concentrated form of sulfuric acid.

The oleum is diluted with water to make sulfuric acid of the right strength.

MAKING RAYON
A bath of sulfuric acid is essential for making rayon, a synthetic fiber. Strands of syrup, made from wood pulp, pass through 10,000 holes in this head. The acid in the bath hardens the strands into 10,000 solid threads of rayon.

Manufacturing chemicals 24%

26%

Other uses

Dyes and pigments

15%

13%

Fertilizers 10%

12%

Plastics and fibers

Detergents and soaps

USING SULFURIC ACID
Industrially, sulfuric acid is a very useful chemical because it reacts readily with other materials, removing metals, oxygen, water, and other unwanted substances. Aside from manufacturing other chemicals, sulfuric acid is also used in car batteries, oil refining, and for cleaning metals.

Find out more

SULFUR P. 45
CATALYSTS P. 56
OXIDATION
AND REDUCTION P. 64
ACIDS P. 68
AMMONIA P. 90

AMMONIA

IF YOU'VE EVER HAD a whiff of ammonia, then you know how strong the smell is. In the 19th century, ammonia (a compound of nitrogen and hydrogen) was used in smelling salts to revive people who had fainted. Today, ammonia is an important raw material for many chemical processes and products—especially fertilizer. Much of the 140 million tons of ammonia produced each year is used to make fertilizers. These give plants the nitrogen they need to grow. In fact, it was the shortage of nitrogen fertilizers that led to the development of a process for manufacturing ammonia on a large scale. Modern ammonia plants make hundreds of tons of this colorless, strong-smelling gas every day.

RAW MATERIALS
Hydrogen and nitrogen are the raw materials for ammonia. Hydrogen is made by reacting methane in natural gas with steam. Nitrogen is extracted from the air.

Nitrogen

Hydrogen

Fritz Haber

Carl Bosch

FRITZ HABER AND CARL BOSCH
In 1908, the German chemist Fritz Haber (1868–1934) used this apparatus (left) to produce ammonia. Making nitrogen and hydrogen react together was not easy, but Haber calculated how to make the reaction work. Five years later, Carl Bosch (1874–1940) had scaled the experimental apparatus up to industrial size. Bosch, a German industrial chemist, had to design large pieces of equipment that would endure the high pressures and temperatures needed to make ammonia.

Haber's apparatus for making ammonia

Modern ammonia plants are huge. This equipment removes carbon dioxide from hydrogen—just one stage in preparing one of the raw materials from methane.

MAKING AMMONIA
Today, ammonia is still made in plants that have Bosch's basic design. The process is very complicated. It involves several stages, including purifying the nitrogen and hydrogen. The most important stage, though, is converting nitrogen and hydrogen to ammonia. Bosch did 6,500 experiments to find that the best catalyst for speeding up the reaction was iron.

Pure hydrogen

Pure nitrogen

Less than a third of the hydrogen and nitrogen is converted to ammonia. The uncombined gases are recycled until they form ammonia too.

Catalyst chamber

The hot gases are pushed through a 65 ft (20 m) tall catalyst chamber.

Cooling chamber

Compressor

The gases are squeezed by a pressure 250 times greater than the air around you and heated to 850°F (450°C).

When the hot gases touch the catalyst (pellets of iron), they are drawn together and react to form ammonia.

The gases are cooled until ammonia liquefies and can be drained off.

USING AMMONIA
Ammonia has many uses aside from fertilizers. Large quantities of ammonia are converted into nitric acid. The acid is used to make nylon, explosives, varnishes, lacquers, and rocket propellants. Urea, made from ammonia and carbon dioxide, is used as a food supplement for farm animals and in plastics.

Fertilizers

80%

8%

7%

5%

Nylon

Nitric acid

Other uses

ACID TO FERTILIZER
Farmers use ammonium salts as a fertilizer. These are made by mixing ammonia gas with hot nitric acid and then spraying the solution into the top of a tower. The droplets fall into a rising current of cold air and form pellets.

Find out more
BONDING P. 28
NITROGEN P 42
HYDROGEN P. 47
CATALYSTS P. 56
FACT FINDER P. 406

CHEMISTRY IN FARMING

MUCH OF THE FOOD YOU EAT has been grown with the help of chemicals. In order to provide this food, farmers need the help of the chemical industry. This industry produces fertilizers that contain minerals for plants. Without minerals, plant growth is poor, and food production is low. Some chemicals control the ripening of fruit, so it doesn't go bad before you eat it. Chemical food supplements for farm animals help them grow faster and avoid disease. But many people are concerned about the amount of chemicals we use to produce food. Too much fertilizer can lead to water pollution, and some pesticides can kill harmless plants and animals, and can be dangerous to people's health.

CHEMICAL FOOD
In addition to their natural food, farm animals eat pellets of chemicals. These contain extra nitrogen to help build strength and speed up growth.

INSECT KILLERS
Insecticides kill in three different ways. If an insect touches contact insecticides, eats stomach poisons, or breathes in fumigants (poison gases), it will die.

Insects eat their way through crops of corn.

Fungus can destroy a whole crop of wheat.

ORGANIC FARMING

The crops and livestock on an organic farm do not receive any synthetic chemicals in fertilizers and food supplements. Organic farmers treat the soil with manure, to provide minerals for the crops. Every year, they grow a different crop in each field, so that all the plants can benefit from the range of minerals in the manure. This also disrupts the lives of pests and keeps their numbers low. Organic farm animals get supplements from natural chemicals found in seaweed.

Seaweed

Weeds deprive other plants of space and food.

FUNGUS KILLERS
Fungicides are organic chemicals that may contain zinc, manganese, and copper. Farmers spray them on to crops or put them in the soil. This stops the fungus from spreading and destroying the whole crop.

PEST KILLERS

Any living thing that disrupts the growth of crops or livestock is a pest. It may be a weed competing with crop plants for space, water, and minerals. It could also be a fungus sending out its feeding threads to destroy plant tissue, or an insect eating its way through leaves, fruits, and roots. Farmers reduce the number of pests by using pesticides—chemicals designed to stop one or more life-giving reactions in a pest's body.

WEED KILLERS
Herbicides kill weeds in a variety of ways. Some interfere with photosynthesis and stop the weed from making food. Others work by poisoning the growing cells at the tips of the roots and shoots.

CHEMICALS TO GROW CROPS
Fertilizers provide the range of minerals that plants need. Each mineral helps the plant to grow in a different way. To test the effects of a fertilizer, farmers grow two groups of plants and give fertilizer to one group. Then they compare the two groups at the end of the growing period.

Find out more
ALKALI METALS P. 34
NITROGEN P. 42
PHOSPHORUS P. 43
ALKALIS AND BASES P. 70
FACT FINDER P. 406

FOOD INDUSTRY

MOST OF THE FOOD in your last meal was probably harvested on a farm many weeks ago, but it still tasted good. The food industry processes much of our food with chemicals so that it remains edible and safe, and looks attractive, for a long time. Without these chemicals, microbes (bacteria and fungi) would get to your food before you had a chance to eat it. Many microbes produce compounds that taste and look unpleasant and may be toxic. Food processing began thousands of years ago to help people keep food through the lean winter months. Today, food processing allows food from other parts of the world to be transported to our local stores so that we can enjoy a great variety of things to eat all through the year.

FREEZE THEN DRY
Astronauts rely on freeze-dried food. In the freeze-drying process, the food is frozen and then the water is removed. You can keep freeze-dried food at room temperatures because bacteria cannot live without water.

IN THE CAN
Walk into any supermarket and you'll see lots of canned food. Canning is the most popular way of preserving food. Fresh foods are first boiled for a short time, to destroy their enzymes, and then put in cans and heated to kill bacteria. Finally, the cans are sealed to prevent air from bringing oxygen and bacteria to the food again.

QUICK FREEZING
Bacteria cannot feed and breed if the food is frozen. In fluidized freezing, small items of food, such as peas, pass over a blast of cold air (-29°F or -34°C) on a conveyor belt. The air makes the peas rise and move freely over one another like particles in a fluid. The peas freeze in minutes.

After cows are milked, a tanker transports their milk to the dairy.

The milk is heated to pasteurize it.

Special bacteria are added to the milk. They feed on lactose (milk sugar), making lactic acid in the process. The acid thickens the milk and makes it turn sour.

PASTEURIZATION
Boiling kills bacteria but also destroys nutrients. In the pasteurization process, liquids such as milk are heated to 160°F (70°C) for 15 seconds and then cooled quickly. The flavor is preserved while the bacteria are destroyed.

FROM MILK TO CHEESE

Milk is a watery solution of protein, sugar, vitamins, and minerals, with fat drops that make the milk white. But it also contains bacteria that feed, breed, and make the milk sour in a few days. Our ancestors discovered that they could preserve the nutrients in milk by turning it into cheese. Today, there are many varieties of cheese, but most of them share the basic stages of production.

The milk is warmed and rennet, which comes from calves' stomachs, is added. Rennet contains an enzyme called rennin that makes part of the milk thicken into solid lumps.

Salt is added to the curds, and they are pressed to remove any remaining whey. The curds are shaped into molds and stored on cool shelves and left to ripen into cheese.

The solid lumps are called curds. They are cut up to help the watery part of the milk (whey) drain away. The whey is made into food for farm animals.

ADDITIVES

It does not take long to collect the foods shown here for a snack. Snacks should only be eaten occasionally because of the high level of fats and sugar they contain. They also contain chemicals called additives. The food industry uses additives to stop food from going bad before we eat it. Additives also keep food looking attractive and tasting good. There are hundreds of different additives, some natural and some synthetic.

In bread rolls, a natural chemical such as vitamin C (ascorbic acid) stops oxygen from reacting with the fat in the bread.

EMULSIFIERS

Normally fat and water quickly separate. But emulsifiers, such as lecithin from egg yolk, keep them in place in yogurt, chocolate, and ice cream.

FLAVORINGS

Drinks such as cola contain natural flavoring chemicals. But if the chemicals break up, flavor is lost. So synthetic chemicals, which are stronger tasting and less likely to break up, copy the natural chemicals.

ANTIOXIDANTS

Fats react with oxygen to make acids, which turn the food rotten. Antioxidants prevent this from happening. For example, a synthetic chemical, butylated hydroxy-toluene (BHT), will stop the fat in chips from going bad.

In cookies, bases such as sodium and ammonium hydrogen carbonate improve flavor and prevent changes in acidity and color.

PRESERVATIVES

Salts and sugar can poison and kill bacteria and fungi. This is why sodium nitrite is added to salami and hot dogs, and potassium sorbate to chilli dip. These preservatives make your food last longer.

Sweets have synthetic colorings from dyes, which tempt us to eat them.

COLORINGS

Natural pigments may break up, leaving the food looking pale and unappetising. A stronger natural coloring, such as beta carotene from carrots, keeps your orange juice looking orange.

FOOD PROCESSING

4000 BCE Salt and chemicals in smoke are used to preserve food.

3000 BCE Yeast is used to make alcoholic drinks by fermentation.

CE 200 Bacteria is used to make yogurt by fermentation.

1804 Nicolas-François Appert (1752–1841) discovers a way of preserving food in sealed containers. Canning industry is developed from his discovery.

1860s Louis Pasteur (1822–95) invents a way of killing harmful microbes in wine and beer.

1920s Clarence Birdseye (1886–1956) develops a method for quick-freezing food.

IRRADIATION

Food irradiation uses radiation or high energy electron beams to preserve food. The radiation or electrons pass into the food, killing harmful microbes. But in fruits and vegetables, irradiation slows ripening and stops further growth. The technique also alters the molecules of the food itself and can destroy vitamins and other nutrients. Because of this, and because of fears about levels of radioactivity in treated food, irradiation remains a controversial technique.

Electron gun releases high-energy electrons.

Scan horn keeps the electron beam in a small area of the processing plant.

The scan chamber

In the food chamber, food passes through the electron beam at two different heights and distances to make sure that it is completely irradiated.

The conveyor belt moves food at the correct speed to receive the permitted dose of radiation.

Tiny yeast cells

HELPFUL MICROBES

Grape juice in these vats is being turned into wine by the action of millions of tiny yeast cells. This fungus has been used for thousands of years in making alcoholic drinks and bread. Today, the use of microbes to make materials for us is called biotechnology. Microbes can make useful materials from unlikely substances. Some microbes can turn methanol, made from natural gas and waste products from the paper-making industry, into food for farm animals.

Find out more

RADIOACTIVITY p. 26
OXIDATION AND REDUCTION p. 64
CHEMISTRY OF FOOD p. 78
FERMENTATION p. 80
FACT FINDER p. 406

ALKALI INDUSTRY

THE SALT WE SPRINKLE on our food can also be used to make the soap that we rub on our skin. Salt, also known as sodium chloride, can be made into two different alkalis: sodium hydroxide and sodium carbonate. These are used to make many products. Of all the alkalis produced in the industry, these two are the most important. Each year, chemical plants throughout the world produce about 35 million tons of each alkali. Sodium hydroxide is made by passing a current of electricity through a salt solution called brine. This also produces chlorine, which is why the alkali industry is also known as the chlor-alkali industry. Sodium carbonate can be made from brine and carbon dioxide.

Sodium hydroxide is made by passing electricity through brine in these cells.

SODIUM HYDROXIDE

Salt dissolved in water consists of four different ions (particles): sodium, chloride, hydrogen, and hydroxide. During electrolysis, a current of electricity draws the negative ions (chloride and hydroxide) to the anode, and the positive ions (sodium and hydrogen) to the cathode. When separated from the chloride, sodium reacts with the water to form sodium hydroxide.

Chloride ions form chlorine gas, which leaves the solution.

Hydrogen ions collect at the cathode and escape from the cell as hydrogen gas.

The strength of the sodium hydroxide can be increased by evaporating some of the water contained in the solution.

Solution of sodium hydroxide in water

Anode

A partition stops chlorine reaching the sodium hydroxide and reacting with it.

Cathode

Ammonia and brine

Waste gas

Carbon dioxide rises up through tower and dissolves.

Carbon dioxide

Carbon dioxide released from crystals is recycled.

Ammonia is extracted and recycled.

Rotary filter separates crystals from the solution.

Steam pipes heat the crystals to drive off carbon dioxide and water.

Sodium carbonate

SODIUM CARBONATE

Brine will absorb carbon dioxide to form sodium carbonate. In a process called the Solvay process, carbon dioxide is dissolved in brine and ammonia. This produces crystals of sodium hydrogen carbonate and ammonium hydroxide solution. The crystals are then heated to form sodium carbonate.

USING SODIUM CARBONATE

You've probably seen this alkali in the form of bath crystals or washing soda. But it is also used for making a wide range of products from ceramics and textiles to photographs and leather goods.

Glass containers 50%

Float glass and other glass 10%

Detergents 15%

Chemicals 25%

Miscellaneous 39%

Making chemicals 30%

Artificial fibers 16%

Paper making 5%

Neutralization 5%

Soaps 5%

USING SODIUM HYDROXIDE

Alkalis are well known for neutralizing acids. But in industry, sodium hydroxide has many other uses, including making bleaches, drugs, dyes, and oil products, as well as processing foods, metals, and rubber.

TRONA ORE

In parts of the United States and Africa, trona ore provides a source of sodium carbonate. Trona ore is sodium hydrogen carbonate, and is easily refined without using the Solvay process.

Find out more

BONDING P. 28
ALKALI METALS P. 34
HALOGENS P. 46
ELECTROLYSIS P. 67
ALKALIS AND BASES P. 70
FACT FINDER P. 406

SOAPS AND DETERGENTS

IMAGINE HOW DIRTY you would be without soap. Water can dissolve many dirty substances, but not grease. Certain salts of sodium, known as soap, can break up the grease so that the water can wash it away. Soap is made by reacting sodium hydroxide with animal and vegetable fats, or oils. Some kinds of water, however, contain chemicals that react with the soap to form a white insoluble powder, called scum. Detergents copy the action of soap without making scum. To make detergents, chemicals from crude oil are reacted with sulfuric acid.

Floor cleaner

Shampoo

Dishwashing liquid

Soap

Water molecules attract water-loving heads. Grease and detergent molecules are lifted into the water and washed away.

DIFFERENT CLEANERS
Cleaners help us in many different ways. Soap coats your skin in grease-removing molecules. Shampoo has extra chemicals that make the lather stay in place on your hair while attacking the grease. Floor cleaner has chemicals called builders that clear away gritty dirt, while dishwashing liquid has other chemicals to clear away greasy scraps of food.

Detergent molecules in water

Water-loving heads

Grease-loving tails

Lumps of grease on a dirty surface

The tails of the detergent molecules surround the grease and then sink into it. The water-loving heads stay on the outside.

Sodium hydroxide *Water*

At high pressure, fats and oils react with hot water to form fatty acids and glycerol.

When boiled, sodium hydroxide reacts with fatty acids to produce soap.

Brine

Soap curd forming

Brine dissolves the glycerine. The soap, which is insoluble in the salt solution, rises to the surface of the kettle as a curd.

Brine and glycerine

CLEANING FABRICS
The fibers of a cotton shirt are covered in grease (left). But when you wash the shirt, the soap and detergent molecules attack and remove the grease clinging to the fibers (right).

The kettle spins at a high speed to separate the soap from the brine and glycerol. These drain away, leaving pure soap behind.

Hard water contains calcium or magnesium. This reacts with the carbon head of a soap molecule to form scum.

CLEANING IN ACTION
When you mop a floor, the soap or detergent works as hard as you do. Soap and detergent molecules have a head that is attracted to water and a tail that is attracted to grease. When you mix soap or detergent with water, the water-loving heads dissolve, while the grease-loving tails attach themselves to grease and lift it away from any surface.

Soap

Sodium

Sulfur

Oxygen

Carbon

Detergent

MOLECULE HEADS
Unlike soap, a detergent doesn't form scum in water. This is due to its different molecular structure; the carbon atom (which is the "head") of a soap molecule is replaced by a sulfur atom (the head) to form a detergent molecule.

MAKING SOAP
To make soaps, fats or oils are heated to break them up into fatty acids and glycerol. The fatty acids will react with an alkali, such as sodium hydroxide, to produce soap. Brine removes the glycerol from the soap. Before the soap is made into blocks, flakes, or powders, chemicals are added to kill germs, add color and scent, and soften water. Manufacturing a bar of soap from raw materials takes just 15 minutes.

WHAT'S IN A DETERGENT?
Most detergents contain enzymes to break down the molecules in sweat and bloodstains. Dyes, called brighteners, make clothes look brighter. Builders stop dirt from settling back on cleaned clothes, soften the water, and keep the acidity constant for all the chemical reactions.

Find out more

PHOSPHORUS P. 43
COMPOUNDS AND MIXTURES P. 58
SOLUTIONS P. 60
ALKALIS AND BASES P. 70
CHEMISTRY OF WATER P. 75
FACT FINDER P. 406

COAL PRODUCTS

WHEN WE BURN COAL, we release energy and chemicals that were trapped for 250 million years. Back then, huge numbers of dying plants decomposed slowly to form coal. We use coal to provide the energy to spin electrical generators in power plants. Heating coal without air turns it into coke, which provides the energy in blast furnaces for making metals. When we process coke, it releases other chemicals—ammonia, a flammable gas, and tar. These can be changed into new chemicals to produce many different products, including dyes, paints, and medicine. In fact, more than 2,000 chemicals can be made from coal.

COAL IN THE MAKING
Swamp plants used the Sun's energy and chemicals in their surroundings to make chemical energy in their cells. When the plants died, their remains turned into coal.

Coal gas contains hydrogen, methane, and carbon monoxide. It was first used for lighting in 1792. In the 19th century, coal gas provided energy for both lighting and cooking in many towns.

Ammonia gas is dissolved in sulfuric acid, where it reacts to form crystals of ammonium sulfate. Until 1913, these crystals were the main source of fertilizers.

FROM COAL TO COKE
When coal is heated to a temperature of 1,650°–2,400°F (900°–1,300°C) in ovens, without any air, a mixture of gases and liquids escape from it. These are separated into coal gas, a watery solution of ammonia called ammoniacal liquor, and coal tar. The solid left behind is called coke. It contains more than 80 percent carbon.

Ammonia liquid

Coal gas

Different cokes are made by heating different kinds of coal at either a low or high temperature. The cokes produced provide fuel for heating in homes and industries.

COAL TAR CHEMICALS
Coal tar contains several useful chemicals. These are separated by distillation, because each has a different boiling point. Chemicals with high boiling points include pitch and creosote. Those with lower boiling points include benzene and carbolic acid.

Coal tar

Burning coal

Coke

Carbon

Hydrogen

Benzene is a ring compound of hydrogen and carbon atoms.

Spraying fruit trees with pesticides made from coal tar

USEFUL MOLECULES
The molecules in coal tar form the raw materials for making hundreds of new chemicals. By adding other chemicals to these molecules, thousands of useful products can be made. Creosote in its unrefined state is a wood preservative. If the different molecules in it are separated, they can be used for making pesticides and drugs.

Coal tar soap

Early dyes made from aniline—one of the compounds in coal tar.

COLORS AND KILLERS
In the 1850s, chemists made the first synthetic dyes from coal tar chemicals. They were brighter than most natural dyes and did not fade in light or easily wash out of fabrics. When carbolic acid (a coal tar chemical) was discovered to have antiseptic properties, it was added to soap to kill germs.

Pills made from coal tar

Find out more
CARBON P. 40
AMMONIA P. 90
GAS PRODUCTS P. 97
OIL PRODUCTS P. 98
DYES AND PIGMENTS P. 102
FACT FINDER P. 406

GAS PRODUCTS

Methane

Propane

Butane

Ethane

MIX OF GASES
There are four main gases in natural gas. The proportions vary, but a typical ratio is 80 percent methane, 7 percent ethane, 6 percent propane, and 2.5 percent butane.

THE FLAME BURNING on a gas cooker marks the end of a long journey for a chemical called methane. The trip began millions of years ago, when the remains of tiny marine plants and animals formed natural gas that became trapped in rock. Most of this gas is methane, but there are many other chemicals in it too. In the 1930s, natural gas was cleaned of any impurities, and we began to use it as a fuel. Chemists soon discovered that these impurities could be used as raw materials in other industrial plants. Methane itself is also used as a raw material to produce hundreds of different products, from fertilizers to detergents. It can even be used to make protein.

A mixture of gases and liquids is piped from the rig to the separation plant.

Methane is piped directly to towns to provide fuel.

In the extraction plant, methane is separated from other gases and any remaining liquids.

The pressure is reduced, so that the heavier hydrocarbons become liquid.

Liquids are trapped at the bottom of the "slug catcher."

GAS SEPARATION

Impurities are removed from natural gas in a variety of ways. When the pressure is reduced, some of the heavier hydrocarbons become liquid and separate from the gas. Alcohol removes water, while special chemicals absorb sulfur and carbon dioxide from the gas.

In this column, heat drives ethane to the top to be piped away. Other gases and liquids pass to the next column.

Propane is piped away after heat drives it to the top.

Heat drives butane to the top. The remaining liquid, natural gasoline, is piped away from the bottom.

Ships transport liquid methane to different countries.

Natural gasoline is used to make diesel fuel.

Freezer units

When ethane is heated, it loses two hydrogen atoms and turns into a molecule of ethene. The double bond between the carbon atoms makes ethene much more reactive than ethane. So ethene is a very useful raw material.

Butane is turned into a liquid and piped to a storage tank.

Propane is turned into a liquid and piped to a storage tank.

PLASTICS

The world's chemical industry produces about 40 million tons of ethene from natural gas and oil every year. Ethene reacts easily with other chemicals, or even with itself, to form a range of plastic materials.

Ethane is piped to a chemical plant for further processing.

LIQUID GASES
Butane and propane are pressurized to form a liquid. When the pressure is released, the liquid becomes a gas once more. Camping stoves, lanterns, and cigarette lighters rely on these liquefied gases.

Plastic ducks and ski boots are just two of the many plastic products formed from ethene.

USEFUL IMPURITIES
The chemicals removed as natural gas is purified have their uses too. Sulfur provides the raw material for making sulfuric acid. Hydrogen is used to make ammonia. And the uses of helium, a very light and unreactive gas, include filling balloons and controlling the pressure of rocket fuel.

Find out more

CARBON P. 40
BEHAVIOR OF GASES P. 51
SEPARATING MIXTURES P. 61
COAL PRODUCTS P. 96
OIL PRODUCTS P. 98
OIL AND GAS P. 239
FACT FINDER P. 406

OIL PRODUCTS

OIL DOES NOT JUST PROVIDE the power to turn the wheels of a car, but it covers the roads they run on too. Crude oil is a sticky, dark liquid that occurs naturally under the ground or the sea and has a pungent smell. Most of the substances found in crude oil are hydrocarbons: compounds of hydrogen and carbon atoms joined together in chains. They formed over 200 million years ago as the remains of marine plants and animals decayed. Early this century, chemists discovered that they could separate the different hydrocarbons in oil by heating them. Chemists now make thousands of products from crude oil.

Heavy, or long-chain, hydrocarbons are black, thick, and waxy.

Light, or short-chain, hydrocarbons are relatively pale and thin.

CRUDE OILS
Oil contains a mixture of hydrocarbons, each with a different number of carbon atoms in its chain. The proportion of hydrocarbons in oil varies from one place to another. Middle Eastern oil has more long molecules, which makes the oil thick. North Sea oil has fewer long molecules and is thinner.

GASOLINE
Between 70° and 160°F (20°—70°C) a thin, runny liquid runs out. This is called gasoline. The hydrocarbons in gas have between five and 10 carbon atoms. Gas is mostly used as an automobile fuel, but it also acts as a raw material for making plastics or chemicals such as detergents.

KEROSENE
A light oily liquid called kerosene condenses at temperatures between 320 and 480°F (160°—250°C). Kerosene, with between 10 and 16 carbon atoms, is made into aviation fuel for burning in jet engines. Paraffin is used for heating and lighting, and in solvents for paints.

The crude oil is heated in a furnace to about 750°F (400°C) and passes as gases into the fractional distillation column.

FRACTIONAL DISTILLATION
When crude oil is heated to a certain temperature, the hydrocarbons in it turn into different gases. Each gas condenses back into a liquid at a different temperature. In this way, oil can be separated into various parts, or fractions. The separating process is called fractional distillation. Hot crude oil is fed in near the base of the column. The heaviest hydrocarbons condense at once and fall into the level below. The other hydrocarbons, still gases, rise through the column until they cool off enough to condense back into a liquid (at a temperature just below their boiling point). They are then piped away for processing.

REFINERY GASES
At 68°F (20°C), only four hydrocarbons remain as gases. These are methane, ethane, propane, and butane. Some methane and ethane is used as a fuel to heat the oil for fractionating, but most is used for making chemicals. Propane and butane are bottled as fuel for portable gas stoves and lights.

NAPHTHA

This yellow liquid condenses at temperatures between 160° and 320°F (70°—160°C). With 8–12 carbon atoms, naphtha can be made into automobile fuel, plastics, and chemicals for drugs, pesticides, and fertilizers. It is also used as a solvent for processing rubber or extracting oil from seeds.

GAS OIL

At this level, which is kept at 480°—660°F (250°—350°C), gas oil condenses. It has between 14 and 20 carbon atoms. Gas oil is used to make diesel fuel and central heating oil. It also makes asphalt softer and easier to spread.

Gases pass up the column through bubble caps. If the temperature is cool enough, the gas condenses on the cap and runs off as a liquid.

Asphalt provides the surface for many of the world's roads.

RESIDUE
All hydrocarbons with more than 20 carbon atoms condense as soon as they enter the column. The mixture of heavy hydrocarbons is separated by heating to produce lubricating oil, petroleum jelly, candle wax, and bitumen.

BREAKING UP MOLECULES

Separating the hydrocarbons in oil by fractional distillation gives more long-chain molecules than we can use and not enough small ones such as naphtha and gasoline. Catalytic cracking splits, or cracks, the larger molecules into more useful, smaller ones. Cracking involves heating the heavy oil under pressure in a special cracking chamber. Some of the bonds between the carbon atoms break to leave a mixture of shorter chain hydrocarbons. By using a catalyst, the process is speeded up and cracking can take place at a lower temperature.

A 16-carbon hydrocarbon is sent to the catalytic cracker to be broken into a mixture of lighter hydrocarbons. After cracking, the mixture passes to a fractionating column to be separated.

Industrially, cracking is done on a large scale in big plants.

Polyethene toys

The catalyst is continuously cleaned and recycled.

Powdered catalyst mixes with the hydrocarbon in steam.

The catalyst becomes dirty as tar and coke form on it during cracking.

INSIDE THE CRACKER

The hydrocarbons, heated by steam, pass over the hot catalyst of powdered alumina-silica gel. The catalyst provides a huge surface on which the hydrocarbons break up into smaller, more useful hydrocarbons.

PLASTICS

Heat ethene under pressure, and groups of between 1,000 and 10,000 molecules join to make long-chain molecules of polyethene. In another form of polyethene, as many as 100,000 molecules join up. Polystyrene, used as packaging, is made from ethene and benzene, while PVC (polyvinyl chloride or polychlorethene) is made from ethene and chlorine.

A fragment of polyethene

Propene, three carbon atoms, used for plastics.

Heptane, seven carbon atoms, used for gasoline.

ETHENE'S MANY USES

After cracking, the compounds are separated by fractionation. One of them, ethene, is so reactive that it can easily join with many chemicals, and even other ethene molecules, to be converted into a wide range of useful liquids and solids.

Bromine is added after cracking.

Ethene

Water is added after cracking.

Ethene reacts with water to provide a solvent for paints and perfumes.

Dibromoethane

Ethanol

GASOLINE ADDITIVE

Adding bromine to ethene produces dibromoethane, which is used as an octane booster for automobile fuels. It prevents gasoline from igniting too quickly in the engine and causing "knocking," which reduces the engine's performance.

ETHANOL

Ethene and water combine to produce ethanol, a solvent used for manufacturing many paints, cosmetics, perfumes, soaps, and dyes. Adding oxygen to ethanol produces ethanoic acid, used in making synthetic fibers.

Find out more

ATOMIC STRUCTURE P. 24
BONDING P. 28
CRYSTALS P. 30
CATALYSTS P. 56
ROCKS AND MINERALS P. 221
FACT FINDER P. 406

POLYMERS

IS THAT A POLYMER GROWING out of your head? The fibers that make up your hair are made of long, strong, flexible molecules. They are polymers—long, winding chains made up of thousands of smaller molecules, called monomers, linked together. Polymers are common and useful molecules. Natural polymers not only make up hair, but also the cellulose in plants, and the wool of sheep. Polymers can also be made from chemicals. All plastics and many of the clothes we wear are made in this way. The first synthetic polymer, Parkesine, was made by English chemist Alexander Parkes in the 1850s. Today, chemicals are made into a wide range of polymers. They can be designed for particular jobs.

Table tennis balls are still made from celluloid.

CELLULOID
By changing the ingredients of Parkesine, an American chemist, John Hyatt, made celluloid. This was used for making eyeglass frames and photographic film, but other plastics have now replaced it.

This is chloroethene, the monomer that makes PVC. The double bond makes it very reactive.

One of the bonds from the double bond breaks in half. One half bonds with the chain. The other half will link with the next chloroethene molecule that comes along.

Chlorine atom

Carbon atom

Hydrogen atom

ADDITION
Have you heard of PVC? This is short for polyvinyl chloride, more properly called polychloroethene. You can tell from its name that the monomer that makes PVC is vinyl chloride, although this is now called chloroethene. In PVC, the monomers are linked up by a method called addition polymerization. This just means that one molecule is tacked onto the end of another one. Given the right conditions, thousands of chloroethene molecules will link up in this way to make one huge molecule of PVC.

This inflatable snake is made from PVC, a thermoplastic.

THERMOPLASTIC
The way that polymer chains are arranged affects the way a plastic behaves when it is heated. In a thermoplastic, the chains are arranged side by side, with no links between them. When heated, the chains slide over each other and the plastic melts. It sets again when the temperature falls.

The two monomers that make nylon approach each other.

A reaction occurs and some atoms of hydrogen and oxygen split off.

The words polymer and monomer come from Greek words. "Poly" means many, "mer" means part, and "mono" means one.

PLASTIC PELLETS
Most plastics are produced in the form of granules or pellets. Polystirene granules are white, polyethene granules are transparent. When these pellets are melted, they can be colored and made into whatever object is required.

The delicate electronic components of this personal stereo are protected in a case made from a thermoset.

THERMOSET
Polymers such as melamine and silicone are thermosets. Their polymer chains are linked together to form a strong network. When heated, the chains cannot move, and so the plastic does not melt.

The carbon atoms join up. The chain is growing.

The released atoms join to make a water molecule.

CONDENSATION
Another method of making a polymer is by condensation. With this method, a small molecule is thrown out when the monomers join up. Nylon, a polymer used to make clothing, is made in this way. It is made from the linking of two monomers. Every time one monomer joins onto the chain, a molecule of water is released.

BAKELITE
During an experiment, American chemist Leo Baekeland (1863–1944) found a sticky mess in the bottom of his apparatus. On heating, this softened and then set into a hard solid. He improved its properties to make a tough, resistant plastic that could be molded into different shapes. He called it Bakelite. It was used to make cameras, telephones, and plugs.

USING POLYMERS

Freshly made polymer granules have little use on their own. But if they are heated, they will fuse together to make a substance that can be easily shaped. The types of material that polymers make are very useful because they are very strong, and yet very light in weight.

Pellets are fed in here.

Extruding machine

The pellets of polymer are fed in at one end.

Molding machine

Turning screw takes pellets through heaters.

Heaters melt the pellets.

Ram pushes the plastic pellets through the machine.

Die shapes molten plastic into tube.

Heater

EXTRUSION

To make plastic into tubes or sheets, a method called extrusion is used. Plastic pellets are taken by a turning screw to heaters which melt them and turn them into a thick, sticky liquid. This is squeezed through a specially shaped hole called a die to form a tube or a sheet. When this passes through a cooler, it quickly hardens.

RUBBER

Rubber, a gum extracted from tropical trees, is a natural polymer. Its molecules have twists and loops in them that give rubber its elasticity. Raw rubber is weak because its molecules are not linked together. To make these links, it is heated with sulfur in a process called vulcanization. This toughened rubber allows tires to squash and stretch without breaking.

Many miles of tubing can be made by an extruding machine.

Vacuum forming machine

Heater

Plastic sheet warms under heater.

Mold

Mold for bicycle helmet

MOLDING

One way of turning plastic into special shapes is by a method called molding. A ram pushes the pellets through a machine where heaters melt them. The hot, liquid plastic is then forced into a mold. Water cools the mold and makes the plastic set.

Up to 90 bicycle helmets an hour can be made on one molding machine.

VACUUM FORMING

Intricate plastic shapes can be made from plastic sheets by a process called vacuum forming. A plastic sheet is put over a mold and a heater softens it. When air is sucked out of the mold by a vacuum pump, the softened plastic sheet is pushed into the mold by the air pressure above. When it is cooled, the plastic shape can be turned out of the mold.

Sheet is pushed into the mold by air pressure pushing from above.

This quick and simple process makes millions of plastic cups every day.

STEPHANIE KWOLEK

An American research chemist, Stephanie Kwolek (born 1923) has made many discoveries about polymers. She discovered a solvent that could make Kevlar aramid fiber. Its threads are stronger than steel, yet very light. It is used to build spacecraft and bullet-proof vests.

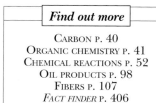

RECYCLING PLASTICS

Some plastics can be recycled. Polyethene terephthalate (PET), used for drink bottles, is collected into bales, cleaned, and then shredded into chips that can be used again. Biodegradable plastic bottles are made from a polymer of a sugar, glucose. Microbes on a garbage dump will break them down into carbon dioxide and water.

Find out more

CARBON P. 40
ORGANIC CHEMISTRY P. 41
CHEMICAL REACTIONS P. 52
OIL PRODUCTS P. 98
FIBERS P. 107
FACT FINDER P. 406

DYES AND PIGMENTS

It took 9,000 whelk shells to make just one gram of purple dye for a Roman Emperor's toga.

Shell of the murex whelk

WE LIVE IN A COLORFUL WORLD. Most of the objects around us have been colored by dyes or pigments. Dyes color the fibers in our clothes, in paper, leather, and even food. Dyes can dissolve in water so they can get into the nooks and crannies of a fiber. Here, they bond to the fabric in a chemical reaction. Pigments are colored particles that do not dissolve in water. This means they can only coat the surface of a material and they do not react chemically with it. They are used to make paints, printing inks, and for coloring plastics.

The cuttlefish is not a fish, but a mollusk, related to the octopus. Its ink contains a natural pigment.

The pigments in this ink are made from organic chemicals.

NATURAL OR SYNTHETIC

There are thousands of different dyes. Natural dyes are made from plants such as the woad or madder, or shellfish such as the murex whelk. Synthetic dyes are made by adding sulfur or chlorine to the colorless chemicals made by distilling petroleum or coal tar.

PIGMENTS

The cuttlefish escapes from its predators by squirting a cloud of black ink into their paths. The pigment in this ink was used to give photographs a brown tint in the 19th century. Today, however, most pigments are made from organic chemicals that produce bright colors and do not fade too quickly.

Mordant dyeing process

Metal salts are mixed with water to form a mordant solution. This solution is then heated.

The fabric is soaked in the mordant solution.

The mordant clings onto the fibers by chemical bonds.

The fabric is immersed in a solution of mordant dye.

A chemical bond forms between the mordant and dye that holds the dye to the fabric.

WILLIAM PERKIN

While trying to make synthetic quinine, William Perkin (1838–1907) accidentally discovered the first synthetic dye. He extracted a purple substance from the mixture he was working on and found it could dye silk. He called it mauve. Perkin went on to build a dye factory. This was the start of the dye industry.

DYE FAMILIES

Dyes work because their molecules join on to the material they are dyeing. Different families of dyes are suitable for different materials. Direct dyes work best on fabrics that are only washed occasionally, such as curtains. Vat dyes are ideal for fabrics that need frequent washes. Mordant dyes will not color a fabric on their own. In the mordant dyeing process, an extra chemical (a metal compound) fixes the dye molecules to the fabric.

The dye will hold fast, which means it will not fade when the fabric is washed.

Water-based paint

Gloss paint

Emulsion paint

PAINTS

All paints contain a pigment to give them color. But they also need a chemical called a binder to hold the pigment in place, and a solvent so the paint can flow easily. Some paints have water as their solvent. Gloss paints, however, have a white spirit solvent. This is why they have such a strong smell.

1. Pigment particles give the paint its color. Each particle in this powder may be as small as a millionth of a centimeter across.

DRYING PAINT

When a surface is painted and left to dry, the solvent in the paint evaporates into the air. This leaves the binder and the pigment close together. They react to form a tough weather-resistant film. Paint may also contain a white pigment. This scatters light back to our eyes so that we can clearly see the paint color.

2. The pigment is mixed with the binder so that the particles can spread out evenly.

Close-up view of surface being painted

3. The paint flows into tiny cavities on the surface and is trapped.

4. As the paint dries, the solvent evaporates, bringing the chemicals and pigments in the paint closer together.

5. The binder holds the pigment particles in place.

Find out more

BONDING P. 28
ORGANIC CHEMISTRY P. 41
SOLUTIONS P. 60
COAL PRODUCTS P. 96
COSMETICS P. 103
FACT FINDER P. 406

COSMETICS

AS LONG AGO as 5000 BCE, the Ancient Egyptians used cosmetics to change their looks. Their cosmetics were made from ground-up minerals. The cosmetics we use today are made from a mixture of chemicals. Many of these come from the petroleum industry. They are mixed with plants, oils, waxes, talcs, clays, and various metal compounds. When a new cosmetic is made, great care is taken to make sure the chemicals it contains do not harm the skin. There are tighter controls on makeup such as lipsticks, as these may accidentally get into the mouth. In the past, the chemicals were tested on animals, but today, more companies are finding new ways to test the chemicals.

ANCIENT COSMETICS
Fashionable Egyptian women wore kohl to blacken their hair, eyebrows, and eyelashes. They also used malachite powder as eye shadow. Kohl is made from naturally occurring lead sulfide, called galena. Malachite is made from ground copper carbonate.

Loose powder, made of white pigments, gives the skin a smooth surface.

Liquid cream holds other cosmetics to the skin.

Eyebrow shadow and pencil make the eyebrows more striking.

This eye shadow contains turquoise pigments to coat the upper eyelid.

BEFORE AND AFTER
Cosmetics were applied to one half of this model's face to show how they can change a person's appearance. The first step was to apply the foundation cream to help keep the makeup in place. Next, a mixture of peach, yellow, and white powders was applied to the skin. These cover marks on the skin such as blueness below the eyes or redness caused by blood vessels close to the surface of the skin.

Black eyeliner on the eyelids highlights the eyes.

The black pigment in mascara emphasizes the eye lashes.

Blusher contains brown and pink pigments to color the cheeks.

Lip pencil marks the outline of the lip, and the lipstick contains pigments that color the lips to complement skin and hair color.

ANCIENT TRADITIONS
For many years, people have colored their skins with substances from plants, animals, clays, and minerals. The reasons for doing this ranged from showing the rank of a person in society, to preparation for a special ceremony. Today, the people of New Guinea still keep these ancient traditions alive.

These are some of the cosmetics you'll see in any department store. Each one comes in a variety of shades to match your skin type.

Since nails are a fairly tough part of the body, nail polish contains chemicals that cannot be used elsewhere. It consists of a pigment in an organic solvent such as acetone.

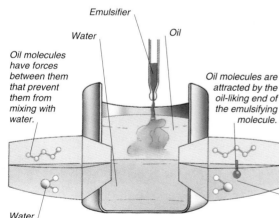

Emulsifier

Water

Oil

Oil molecules have forces between them that prevent them from mixing with water.

Oil molecules are attracted by the oil-liking end of the emulsifying molecule.

Water molecules are attracted by the water-liking end of the emulsifying molecule.

Water molecules have forces between them that stop them from mixing with oil.

Emulsifying molecules link the oil and water together. This forms an oil-in-water emulsion.

EMULSIONS
Cosmetics are often made from oil and water. These do not mix, but by adding an emulsifying agent such as soap, a creamy substance called an emulsion can be made. Liquid paraffin and petroleum jelly from petroleum, castor oil from beans, and lanolin from wool grease make up the oily part of an emulsion.

WHAT ARE COSMETICS MADE OF?
Every cosmetic contains a mix of chemicals. Nail polish has at least 11 chemicals. It usually contains resin, plasticizer, solvents, and pigments. Foundation cream contains up to 23 chemicals. It is an oil-in-water emulsion that contains a complex mixture of acids and alcohols.

CHEMISTRY IN MEDICINE

Over 200 years ago, a brew containing foxglove leaves was used to treat people with heart failure. Many years later, these leaves were found to contain the drug called digitoxin. Today, digitoxin is still used to treat heart failure.

Foxglove plant

Chunks of willow bark

YOUR BODY IS MADE from thousands of different chemicals. If these are not working correctly, you become sick. A doctor may treat you by giving you more chemicals in the form of medicines. This treatment of illness is not new. Over 2,000 years ago, the people of Ancient Mesopotamia used 250 different plants and 120 minerals to treat ailments. Many of these were still used in the 19th century, when the chemicals from plants were put into tablets. But some of these gave people a second illness, called a side effect. Today, scientists are able to make chemicals similar to the natural ones. By altering the molecules slightly, they can prevent side effects.

NATURAL DRUGS
The Greek doctor Hippocrates used willow bark as long ago as 400 BCE to relieve the pain of his patients. But it also caused stomach irritation. The bark contains a chemical called salicylic acid. In 1893, a German chemist, Felix Hoffman, made a very similar chemical from coal tar, which had fewer side effects. This drug is now known as aspirin. Over 100,000 million aspirin tablets are taken every year throughout the world.

PAUL EHRLICH
The German doctor Paul Ehrlich (1854–1915) sought a "magic bullet" that would kill disease-giving bacteria, but would leave human cells undamaged. He thought that dyes that could stain bacteria but not other cells might be a good starting point. The first synthetic drug he discovered was the dye trypan red for treating sleeping sickness. Ehrlich later found that a very similar chemical, salvarsan, could cure syphilis.

DEVELOPING A DRUG
A new drug is made to treat a specific illness. Up to 30 chemicals may be selected for the first set of drug tests. These may have been made from chemicals in plants, or chemicals from the laboratory. The chemicals are tested for poisonous effects. For example, they may break down to form harmful substances. The tests take three years and only very few chemicals will pass them.

TRACKING THE DRUG
The chemicals that pass the first drug tests are carefully tested on healthy humans to investigate any side effects they may give. Samples of each chemical are made slightly radioactive, so that their movement through the body can be tracked with an instrument called a Geiger counter.

DRUG TEST
After eight years of testing, one drug is selected. One group of patients is given tablets that contain the drug. A second group is given placebos (inactive drugs). The effectiveness of the drug can be assessed by comparing these two groups.

HOW DRUGS WORK
Every cell of your body has receptors on its surface. Some drugs are thought to work by their interaction with these receptors. Adrenaline is a chemical your body produces. It makes your heart beat faster in times of stress. A drug called salbutamol relaxes lung muscles by joining adrenaline on the receptors of lung muscle cells. But another drug called propranolol blocks off receptors on heart muscle cells. This prevents adrenaline from reaching the receptors. In this way, it prevents a heart from beating dangerously fast.

1. Body chemical   Receptor   Drug

Message that chemical sends to cell.

This drug is helping the body chemical. It is reinforcing the message sent to the cell.

2. Body chemical   Receptor   Drug

Message that chemical sends to cell.

This drug is blocking the body chemical. It prevents the message from being sent to the cell.

Chicken pox is a disease caused by a virus.

BACTERIA

Organisms called bacteria cause diseases such as tonsillitis. They can be killed by chemicals called antibiotics. Early antibiotics, such as one called penicillin, were all made from molds and fungi. Today, most are created from other chemicals. There are two main ways in which antibiotics work. One type prevents the bacteria from making its cell walls. Another type interferes with the chemical activities in the cells of bacteria.

Bacteria breaking down due to effect of antibiotic

Viruses cannot be killed by antibiotics. Antiviral drugs must be used.

VIRUSES

Microorganisms called viruses cause diseases such as chicken pox and colds. Because they inhabit body cells, it is difficult to create drugs that kill them, yet do not harm the person. Antiviral drugs work by blocking the chemicals the virus needs to reproduce. AIDS is caused by a very tough virus. It may take many years before a drug can control it.

BODY CHEMICALS

A healthy body makes many different chemicals that control the action of the different body systems. Some illnesses occur because the body produces too much or too little of one of these chemicals. Many drugs are chemicals designed to treat a particular illness. They work with the appropriate body chemical to bring the system back under control.

We feel pain because our nervous system sends messages from the injured part of our body to our brain. Anesthetic drugs are used to stop these messages and numb pain.

Extreme anxiety is sometimes eased with drugs. Chemicals called diazepam and nitrazepam work with chemicals in the brain. These drugs can be addictive.

High stress causes the body to release too much of the chemical adrenaline. This makes the heart beat faster, leading to high blood pressure. Drugs called beta-blockers stop adrenaline from reaching the heart muscles.

ANTISEPTICS

Wounds can become infected with harmful bacteria if an antiseptic is not applied to kill them. Antiseptics are able to kill bacteria in many ways. The alcohol rubbed onto your skin by a doctor before an injection kills bacteria by breaking up the protein that makes up their cells.

In an asthma attack, tiny muscles in the lungs squeeze the airways, making it difficult to breathe. When the drug salbutamol is inhaled, the muscles relax, and breathing becomes easier.

Stress can make the stomach produce large quantities of acid, which can result in an ulcer. Antacid tablets can reduce the acidity. Special drugs called H2 blockers can stop the production of the acid.

FIGHTING DISEASE

1796 English doctor Edward Jenner performs first vaccination against smallpox.

1867 English scientist Joseph Lister discovers first widely used antiseptic—carbolic acid.

1928 Scottish scientist Alexander Fleming discovers that penicillium kills bacteria. This leads to further developments on the antibiotic by Florey and Chain.

1932 German chemist Gerhard Domagk develops first synthetic drug to kill bacteria (sulfa drug).

1941 Australian doctor Howard Florey and German doctor Ernst Chain develop penicillin.

Body chemicals are controlled by glands, such as the pancreas. One chemical called insulin is used to keep a store of sugar in the liver. In a disease called diabetes, not enough insulin is produced. Extra insulin must be injected.

White blood cells are made by cell division in the lymphatic system. If they do not divide correctly, cancer cells develop that produce a disease called leukemia. This can be controlled by cytotoxic drugs that interfere with the way the cancer cells divide and grow.

A disease called arthritis occurs when the tissues in a joint become inflamed and painful. Anti-inflammatory drugs such as aspirin block off the body chemical that makes the joint swell.

Find out more

CHEMISTRY OF THE BODY P. 76
VIRUSES P. 312
BACTERIA P. 313
PRIMATES P. 336
CELLS P. 340
INTERNAL ENVIRONMENT P. 350
FACT FINDER P. 406

ADHESIVES

IMAGINE TRYING TO WALK in your shoes if you did not have adhesives holding them together. Adhesives have a wide variety of uses. They range from the sticky substances on the back of postage stamps and on the flaps of envelopes, to the substances that hold together the pages of this book, and that strengthen the joints in your chair. Many different materials are used as adhesives. The first adhesives came from plants and animals. In the 19th century, rubber was a major ingredient in adhesives. Today, polymers are widely used. Every adhesive sticks because its molecules form bonds with the objects it is joining together. These bonds can be as strong as those that hold together the molecules in a piece of rock.

RESIN AS GLUE
Liquid oozes from the cut branch of a pine tree. This contains a resin that has been used as a glue for hundreds of years.

The yellow car is stuck to the board with a strong epoxy resin.

Stabilizing molecules prevent polymerization and keep the glue in its liquid form.

EPOXY RESIN
Industries often use epoxy resin glues. Epoxy resins are chemically manufactured synthetic glues. They are popular because they stick a wide range of materials together, and can form very strong bonds that are resistant to both heat and weather.

Adhesive molecule

Joints are glued to the model.

Adhesive molecules begin to polymerize.

Moisture from the surface neutralizes the stabilizing molecules.

THERMOPLASTIC GLUE
This glue is used in model-making. It contains polystyrene molecules dissolved in a solvent such as acetone. The solvent evaporates when the glue is applied to a joint, and the polystyrene molecules combine to form a bond. If the joint is warmed, the molecules slide over each other as the glue melts, allowing the joint to be reshaped.

HOW ADHESIVES WORK
Acidic stabilizers prevent adhesive molecules from joining together in the tube. When you squirt the glue from the tube, it comes into contact with moisture in the air, and on the surface that it touches. The moisture neutralizes the stabilizer, leaving the adhesive molecules to join together. Polymers, which are chains of molecules, form strong, solid bonds between the surfaces in contact with the glue.

Strong bonds develop between the ends of the polymer and the surface.

A photograph of magnified molecules joining together in an adhesive

Resin

Catalyst

A TWO-PART GLUE
Some epoxy resins need a catalyst or a hardener to make them set. The resin and catalyst are kept in separate tubes and mixed together when needed. The mixture quickly forms a bond that will not melt when heated.

REUSABLE LABELS
The sticky strip on a reusable label has thousands of tiny adhesive bubbles. A few bubbles burst each time it is stuck to a surface, making it removable and reusable.

Find out more
CHANGES OF STATE P. 20
CATALYSTS P. 56
SEPARATING MIXTURES P. 61
POLYMERS P. 100
FACT FINDER P. 406

FIBERS

A wide range of petrochemicals are made into pellets and spun into fibers.

Making nylon

WHEN YOU GET DRESSED, you cover your body in clothes made of fibers. Natural fibers come from the seeds of a plant or from the fur of an animal. Other fibers are artificial. For example, nylon is made from chemicals found in oil. The first clothes were just animal skins. Then, five thousand years ago, people began to use natural fibers to make strong fabrics. They spun (twisted) cotton and wool fibers to make threads of yarn. The first process of interlocking the yarn into a fabric was weaving. This is still a major fabric-making process today. Later, the knitting process developed, producing warm, flexible clothes. During the 19th century, people became more aware of how natural fibers were formed, and soon chemicals were being used to make fibers too.

Chemicals from oil are the raw materials for nylon.

Wool is a loosely packed fiber, which makes this material a good insulator.

The liquid forced through tiny holes in the spinneret, a liquid dispenser, emerges as molten fibers of equal thickness.

Molten polymer is forced through the spinneret.

Raw materials are heated to make molten polymer.

The yarn is wound onto the reel.

Nylon fibers are strong and flexible.

NATURAL AND SYNTHETIC FIBERS
The original fibers used for clothing, such as wool, cotton, and silk, came from plants and animals. Today, people also use chemicals, known as petrochemicals, to make synthetic fibers. These include polyester, acrylic, and nylon, which are cheaper and stronger than natural materials.

Polyester fibers are durable. They are not very stretchy, but do keep their shape well.

The fibers solidify in a cooling bath.

The fibers form a cable.

MAKING NYLON
Nylon was the first synthetic fiber to be made entirely of chemicals. Nylon pellets are heated to 500°F (260°C) to form a molten polymer solution. This is forced through the spinneret: a process known as extrusion. As the polymer comes out of the tiny holes into the cool atmosphere, they begin to form solid threads of nylon. These are treated in a special cooling bath, spun into a long yarn, and wound onto the reel.

Closely woven fabric prevents rain drops passing through it.

Threads of rayon travel around rotating wheels to form the yarn.

The silicone resin bath coats the fabric.

The fabric is heated to help the resin to spread and cover all the fibers.

WATERPROOFING
Fibers in water-repellent clothes are coated in silicone resin. The fabric is passed through the resin with the aid of rollers. Heat is then applied to it to help the resin coat the fabric evenly. The resin prevents the fabric from absorbing water, making it an ideal material for raincoats and tents.

RAYON MANUFACTURE
Rayon is an artificial fiber made from cellulose in wood pulp. It is a reconstituted fiber because the original raw ingredient, cellulose, is broken down and then re-formed. This creates a superior form of the orginal material: it is stronger and easier to dye. There are different types of rayon. The most important is called viscose.

CHARDONNET
The French chemist, Count Hilaire Chardonnet (1839–1924), treated cotton fibers with chemicals and alcohol, then forced them through a spinneret. The alcohol evaporated, leaving shiny fibers that appeared to give out rays of light. These new fibers were called rayon or "Chardonnet silk" and became very popular at the beginning of the 20th century.

Find out more

CHANGES OF STATE P. 20
BONDING P. 28
SOLUTIONS P. 60
POLYMERS P. 100
DYES AND PIGMENTS P. 102
MATERIAL DESIGN P. 111

PAPER

EARLY PAPER
Making paper from wood began in China in about CE 105 using the fibers from the mulberry tree. But the idea is thought to have come from someone watching wasps building their nests from tiny wood chips.

Making paper

Most paper comes from forests of softwood trees such as spruce and pine.

NEARLY ONE-THIRD OF THE EARTH is covered in trees. Many of these trees supply us with paper. The lines you can see in a piece of wood are called the grain. They are made by thousands of tiny fibers that the tree produces as it grows. The tree uses these fibers to carry water through its trunk and to support the weight of its branches. In the papermaking industry the fibers are separated, then joined together in a crisscross pattern to make thin sheets like the one these words are printed on. Try tearing a sheet of paper—you will see tiny fibers that have been stuck together to make it. By replanting trees to replace those chopped down for paper, this supply of raw material should not run out.

The trees are cut into logs and transported to paper mills by road and rail, or by floating the logs down a river.

Each log is broken down into chips about 1 in (2 cm) long and 0.25 in (0.5 cm) thick.

Wood chips are cooked into pulp

Wood chips from spruce are heated with acid, and wood chips from hardwoods and pine are heated with alkalis to release the fibers.

Fibers are mixed with fillers, sizing, pigments, and dyes into a smooth pulp.

Paper is sent back to the paper making machine for recycling.

MAKING PAPER
Paper is made in a factory called a paper mill. Wood is broken into small pieces to help chemicals to attack it and release the fibers. The lignin, which gives the fibers their strength, is dissolved in hot chemical liquids. Then chemicals are added to the fibers to make the paper smooth, strong, and opaque. Sizing, made from rosin or wax, is added to make the paper water-resistant.

Water is removed from the liquid pulp by suction, and by pressing the paper between rollers.

RECYCLING PAPER
The number of trees, and the amount of chemicals and energy used in papermaking can be reduced by collecting newspapers from homes, notepaper from offices, and cardboard from factories. The fibers these contain are reused to make more paper products.

Tissue fibers are lifted by a knife as they roll off the machine to give tissue its soft texture.

Rollers remove excess water and compress the paper.

Card is made by a similar process to paper.

Stacks of rollers smooth the surface of the paper.

Pulp is drained on wire mesh.

Paper is sent back for recycling.

PAPER PRODUCTS
Types of paper vary because of the fibers they contain, the chemicals added, and the way the pulp is treated on the papermaking machine. There are two kinds of wood fiber. The first are cheap, ground wood fibers. The second are more expensive, chemically prepared fibers.

The wood finally emerges as a roll of paper.

A felt belt soaks up any remaining water in the paper.

A huge variety of paper exists, varying in size, strength, and uses. Dyes and pigments are added to paper to create an unlimited range of colors and patterns.

Find out more

CARBON P. 40
ACIDS P. 68
POLYMERS P. 100
DYES AND PIGMENTS P. 102
FIBERS P. 107
FACT FINDER P. 406

CERAMICS

YOU ARE SURROUNDED by ceramics. Many of the objects you handle every day are made out of a ceramic material. Ceramics have a range of uses from making the walls of your home, insulating cables on overhead power lines, to repairing broken teeth. Ceramics are divided into two groups. In the first group are materials that are molded into their shape before being heated. Pottery and bricks are examples of this first group. The second group consists of materials that are shaped after being treated by heat. These include glass and cement.

POTTER'S CLAY
Pottery clay is a mixture of two clays. Kaolin (china clay) gives pottery its smooth texture. Ball clay gives the pottery its strength.

USING CERAMICS
Ceramics are the hard, brittle substances made by firing clay. Clay has been used to make pottery for thousands of years. It was originally baked in an open oven, but it is now heated in a kiln or furnace until it hardens. New ceramics are being developed for use in car and aircraft engines. These last longer and are able to withstand very high temperatures.

Strong, weather-resistant bricks are ideal building materials.

The shiny glazes on clay beads are also made out of clay.

Water molecules in wet clay

Fired clay loses its water, forming a tighter, stronger structure.

INSIDE A KILN
Moist pottery clay is molded and then placed in a kiln until it hardens. Reactions take place in the clay in which chemicals separate and then join together again to form stronger substances.

Cement holds pieces of rock together in a concrete mixture.

Making cement

Clay, chalk, and water are the raw materials for cement.

The porous clay of a plant pot lets water evaporate from the soil and keeps the plant roots cool.

Raw materials are mixed to form a slurry.

The rotary kiln is up to 600 ft (180 m) long and heats the clay mixture.

The glazed surface of a tile is easy to clean.

Lumps of cement (clinkers) are cooled.

Gypsum is added to the clinkers.

Making concrete

A mixture of sand, gravel, and stones

Cement is added to the mixture.

Water is added, transforming cement particles into crystals.

Clinkers are ground with gypsum to stop the cement from setting too quickly.

Crockery holds your drink because it is watertight.

The end product: powdered cement

Glass is a hard, transparent material made from metal silicates. It is shaped from a molten state.

MAKING CONCRETE
Calcium silicate and aluminate form crystals when mixed with water. In concrete, the crystals grow in the spaces between the sand and gravel. As the crystals grow, they surround the sand and gravel, forming strong bonds to hold the cement together.

The concrete sets as the crystals bind the sand and gravel together.

MAKING CEMENT
Cement is also a ceramic. During the cement-making process, calcium oxide forms from the chalk as the slurry is heated. This joins with silicon and aluminum in the clay to form calcium silicate and aluminate. The clinkers are ground up with gypsum to stop the cement from setting too quickly for the construction workers to use.

Find out more

CHANGES OF STATE P. 20
BONDING P. 28
ORGANIC CHEMISTRY P. 41
MATERIALS P. 81
DYES AND PIGMENTS P. 102
FIBERS P. 107

GLASS

Calcium
carbonate

Waste
glass

Sand

Sodium
carbonate

HANDMADE GLASS
To make glass by hand, molten glass is collected onto the end of a hollow blowing iron and a small bubble is blown. The glass is then cooled by rolling it on an iron slab and it is shaped with tools. The glass is reheated during shaping, so it is easier to handle.

The raw ingredients of glass are fed into the furnace.

RAW MATERIALS
Sand usually melts at 3,090°F (1,700°C). But if it is mixed with sodium carbonate (soda), the melting point is reduced, saving energy. Calcium carbonate (limestone) is added to stop the glass from dissolving in water. Waste glass is also added, and melted down for reuse.

ONE OF THE OLDEST ARTIFICIAL MATERIALS, glass was first made around 5,000 years ago. Glass is actually cooled liquid sand. Like thick molasses, it is a liquid that has never set—an old sheet of glass is always slightly thicker at the bottom than at the top. Glass is very useful since it is easily shaped, rust-proof, and forms hard, transparent objects that are not affected by chemicals. It is also very cheap to make and can be recycled over and over again. Glass has a wide range of uses, from holding our drinks to helping us to see. Its properties can be changed by adding chemicals, by adding other materials such as wire, and by controlling the way glass cools down.

A gob is dropped into the mold.

Compressed air forces the glass into the shape of the mold.

The finished glass bottle is removed from its mold.

Molding process

BOTTLE MAKING
To make special shapes from molten glass, a mold has to be used. A bottle, for example, is made from a lump of molten glass called a gob. This is dropped into a mold and forced into the bottom of it by compressed air. The tough shape of the bottle is made by blowing air upward through the gob. This is then transferred to a second mold, where it is blown again to form the final shape of the bottle.

The furnace is heated up to 2,550°F (1,400°C) to melt the raw materials.

FLOAT GLASS
It is very difficult to make sheets of glass for windows. One method is to flatten the glass between rollers, but this produces an imperfect sheet. A very clever way to make perfectly smooth glass is by the float glass method. Molten glass is floated on top of a "river" of molten tin. The surface of the glass becomes as smooth as the surface of the molten metal. Rollers carry the glass to be cooled and hardened.

The molten tin is kept in an atmosphere that contains no oxygen. Otherwise, the tin would react with the oxygen and make the glass surface uneven.

Float glass process

Continuous sheet of cooled glass

Chemicals make glass colorful. Selenium sulfide makes it red, copper oxide makes it blue, phosphates and alumina make it milky.

Very thin glass fibers are used in heat and sound insulation, and for strengthening plastics.

CHANGING GLASS
The way glass is treated after it has emerged from the furnace changes its properties, making it suitable for a particular job. By rapidly cooling the glass with jets of air, toughened glass suitable for car windows can be made. The green tint in raw glass can be removed by adding cobalt and selenium oxide.

The glass is cooled slowly so it does not break.

Cooling unit

The glass is cut into lengths with a diamond-tipped cutter.

Boron oxide is added to the raw materials of glass to make borosilicate glass. This is used in oven dishes and laboratory glassware because it is able to resist temperature changes.

> **Find out more**
> CHANGES OF STATE p. 20
> SEMIMETALS p. 39
> FIBERS p. 107
> MATERIAL DESIGN p. 111
> REFLECTION p. 194
> *FACT FINDER p. 406*

MATERIAL DESIGN

IMAGINE WHAT YOUR HOME would look like if everything were made out of just one material, such as steel. A wide range of materials need to be used in the home. A window frame is made from wood for strength, while the window glass lets in light, but keeps out rain. Today, the wood may be replaced by plastic, and two panes of glass are often used to stop heat from escaping. People are always looking for new materials to make life easier and cheaper. This search may involve using an old material in a new way, joining different materials together, or experimenting with chemicals to make a completely new material. Every new material or new combination of materials must be thoroughly tested to check it can stand up to the job.

GLASS-REINFORCED PLASTICS
If glass fibers are embedded in plastic, they reinforce it, and give it extra strength. This glass-reinforced plastic, known as fiberglass, is used to build boats. It is an example of a composite material, in which the properties of two common materials are combined.

The body of the satellite is made from a core of a plastic or metal honeycomb structure. Strong adhesives join this on either side to thin sheets of plastic, reinforced with carbon fibers.

The covering plastic is stuck to this side of the adhesive film.

Film of adhesive

Metal or plastic honeycomb core

Because of composite materials, these large satellites can hurtle into space. Here, they can transmit signals to a precise point on Earth.

The many antennae work like mirrors, focusing any signals that reach them. In this way, they receive and transmit signals from Earth.

Antenna

SATELLITE MATERIAL
If you need to send something into the harsh conditions of space, it needs to be built out of a material much more resilient than wood or metal. Satellites are made from specially developed materials. These are light enough to be launched, but can withstand the stresses produced when the satellite is put into orbit.

SEEING STARS
Enormous telescopes are needed to explore the vastness of space. The light they collect must be reflected from a huge mirror to make an image that astronomers can see. The mirror is made from glass mixed with ceramics. This gives a material that is strong, so it does not break under its own weight, and does not change shape as the temperature changes.

LIFE-SAVING MATERIALS
Many damaged or diseased body parts can be replaced by synthetic materials. Metal alloys are used to make skull plates. Artificial hip joints are made from a combination of metal alloys and plastics. Blood vessels are made from fibers of fabrics. Today, even artificial hearts are made from a combination of plastic and aluminum.

HEAT-RESISTANT MATERIALS
Extratough materials called cermets can withstand incredible heat. They are made by mixing metal and ceramic particles. Cermets are shaped into jet turbine blades and rocket nozzles, which both get extremely hot in use. Over 30,000 cermet tiles protect the space shuttle from the frictional heat produced as it reenters the Earth's atmosphere.

Find out more
PROPERTIES OF MATTER P. 22
ALLOYS P. 88
FIBERS P. 107
PAPER P. 108
CERAMICS P. 109
GLASS P. 110
FACT FINDER P. 406

INDUSTRIAL POLLUTION

THE PRICE WE PAY for using so many different types of material is pollution. This occurs when we release substances into the environment that harm living things as well as structures. Up until about 200 years ago, there was very little pollution. The population was smaller and people used mostly natural materials. Their wastes could be broken down by microbes in the soil. Today, some of our machines, factories, and power plants disfigure the environment. Some of our wastes do not break up but pollute the land, the water, and the air. Industry is now trying to limit the pollution it creates.

COVERING EYESORES
Quarries near towns can be filled in with garbage. This is stored on polyethene sheets to control the drainage of water. The methane produced by the decaying garbage is collected in pipes and used as a fuel. When the quarry is full, the trash is covered with soil and appropriate plants to create new habitats for animals.

Solid particles in smoke can be removed in chimneys by an electrostatic filter. The particles collect on the chimney walls.

Many of the substances in waste water can be used as raw materials for other industrial processes.

OZONE LAYER
Chemicals called CFCs, once widely used in aerosols, destroy ozone when they escape into the atmosphere. Aerosols now use pressurized hydrocarbons and other gases that do not destroy ozone.

The amount of sulfur dioxide in smoke can be reduced by using fuel which has had sulfur removed from it or by spraying the smoke with water before it leaves the chimney.

Using lead-free gasoline reduces the amount of lead pollution in the environment.

MAKING POLLUTION
Industrial pollution takes many forms. Raw materials are extracted from the ground, destroying vegetation and animal habitats and leaving enormous holes. Unwanted solid wastes can form heaps the size of small hills. The smoke from factory chimneys produces acids in the clouds and mixes with exhaust gases from road traffic to produce smog over cities. The water released from factories can contain wastes that kill aquatic life. Oil slicks may be created when ships are involved in accidents.

RECYCLING MATERIALS
Fewer raw materials need to be used if materials are recycled. This conserves raw materials for the future, reduces pollution, and saves energy. Using recycled materials to make aluminum cans, for example, would give a 95 percent saving in energy and a 95 percent fall in pollution.

CONSERVING HEAT
If heat is wasted, more fuel has to be burned to replace it. This causes extra pollution. The loss of heat energy from a building or factory can be revealed by an infrared photograph. The regions losing the most heat, hot spots, show up as white. They can be treated with extra insulation to stop the heat from escaping.

False color image showing the heat lost from an office block

Find out more
SULFUR P. 45
CATALYSTS P. 56
CHEMISTRY OF AIR P. 74
CHEMICAL INDUSTRY P. 82
BIOSPHERE P. 370
FACT FINDER P. 406

FORCES AND ENERGY

ENERGY MAKES THINGS HAPPEN, from a bolt of lightning to tying a shoelace. Nothing could live or move without energy. Animals use energy to walk and run; plants use energy to grow. Winds use energy when they blow; waves use energy when they roll across the ocean. And when a car moves, it is using energy stored in its fuel. But none of these things would happen if there were no forces at work. Whenever energy is used, forces are involved. Forces are needed to start things moving, to change the way they move, and to stop them from moving. Forces are also responsible for breaking things and for holding things together. Without forces and energy, nothing would happen in the universe.

IN SPACE

Forces and energy act on a huge scale in space. The stars shine because they are producing energy in the form of heat and light. The atmosphere of a star is kept in place by the force of gravity—the same force that pulls objects toward the Earth.

NIGHT LIGHTS

Electricity is a form of energy. It can be generated in large power plants and transmitted long distances by cable to homes, offices, and factories. A flick of a switch easily changes it into heat and light energy, and mechanical power.

SUBATOMIC FORCES

Tiny particles are influenced by forces just as large objects are. The forces that act inside the nucleus, or center, of an atom are the strongest of all forces. Their energy is released in a nuclear bomb explosion.

Forces act on particles that can be seen only under a microscope.

USING THE WIND

Windsurfing involves the use of forces and energy. Windsurfers use their own energy to control the board and leap over the waves. The wind's energy creates the force that blows them along. But if there is too much force in one direction, the board will overturn. Windsurfers must therefore exert a force against the wind so that they can balance and keep the sail upright.

ENERGY FROM THE SUN

The Sun provides most of our energy in the form of sunlight. More energy reaches the Earth from the Sun in an hour than all of us use in a year. Plants like these sunflowers need the Sun's energy to grow. They store some of it in chemical form. An animal that eats a plant uses this stored energy.

FORCES IN BUILDINGS

Buildings must be made to withstand large forces or they would fall down. The roof of the terminal at Jeddah airport in Saudi Arabia is made of fiberglass, which is even stronger than steel. Forces stretch the roof into an unusual shape.

FORCES

THERE ARE FORCES all around us. A force is a push or a pull. It is something that acts on an object. The wind exerts a force when it blows; gravity is a force that pulls everything down toward the center of the Earth and gives objects their weight. Animals and machines make forces too. When a grasshopper leaps from a leaf, its legs exert a small force on the leaf. Machines are used to produce large forces. A jet engine can produce a force that is millions of times larger than the force produced by a leaping grasshopper.

FORCES IN FLIGHT
An airplane in flight has four forces acting on it. The engine produces a forward force called thrust, the wings produce an upward force called lift, and the force of gravity pulls the aircraft downward. A force called drag, caused as the aircraft pushes against the air, slows it down.

Forces can stretch an object.

Forces acting in pairs can twist materials.

Pairs of forces can bend an object.

Forces can stop a moving object or make it slow down.

Forces can tear things.

Forces can make a moving object swerve and change direction.

Forces can make an object move, and make a moving object go faster.

Forces can make a moving object bounce.

Forces can make an object sink or float in a liquid.

Forces can squash or deform an object.

Forces acting in pairs can make an object turn or spin.

EFFECTS OF FORCES

If a force pushes or pulls something, there are four main things that could happen. A stationary object might start to move, the speed of a moving object might change, the direction of a moving object might change, or the shape or size of an object might change. The greater the force, the greater the effect it has.

FORCE FIELDS
The region in which a force can be felt is called a force field. The strength of a force field is greatest close to its source, such as a magnet. Iron filings scattered on a piece of paper on top of a magnet will gather along the lines of force in the magnet's force field. The lines show how the force field spreads out around the magnet.

FORCES OF NATURE
Some weather conditions create strong forces. A tornado, a whirling spiral of wind, can cause a huge amount of damage. Large tornadoes toss anything in their paths—cars, buildings, trees—high into the air and then smash them down hundreds of yards away. The most destructive tornado on record occurred in the United States, in 1925. Hundreds of people were killed as it left a 1,000 ft- (300 m) wide trail of demolished buildings, uprooted trees, and overturned cars.

The heat and light energy released by the Sun comes from the nuclear forces of its atoms.

BASIC FORCES

The basic forces are gravity, electricity, magnetism, and two kinds of nuclear force called the weak and strong forces. All other forces come from them. In 1979, Sheldon Glashow, Steven Weinberg, and Abdus Salam received the Nobel Prize for Physics for proving that the magnetic, electric, and weak nuclear forces are really aspects of one force. They called this force the electroweak force. Scientists are now trying to prove the theory that gravity and the strong nuclear force are related to the electroweak force. This theory is called the Grand Unified Theory, or GUT.

The solar panels of a satellite produce electricity from the Sun's light.

Gravity is a long-distance force. The Earth's gravity reaches far into space and keeps satellites in orbit.

ABDUS SALAM

In 1979, the Pakistani scientist Abdus Salam (1926–96) became the first person from his country to receive a Nobel Prize. Salam had wanted to be a civil servant but changed his mind when he won a scholarship to study physics at Cambridge University, England. At Cambridge, he developed the theory of the electroweak force. His ideas were proved correct at CERN, the European research laborataory near Geneva, Switzerland, in 1973.

The Earth is a huge magnet. Its magnetic force makes compass needles point northward.

CONTACT AND NONCONTACT FORCES

Some forces are only produced when one object touches another. These are called contact forces. Other forces do not need contact to have an effect. For example, a magnet can pull a piece of iron toward it without touching it. These forces are called noncontact forces.

The more force used to hit the ball, the farther the ball will go.

Static electricity makes small pieces of tissue paper jump up and stick to the ruler.

The second ball starts to move only after a force has been applied by the first ball.

ELECTRIC FORCES

A plastic ruler can be given an electrical charge, called static electricity, by rubbing it against a T-shirt or a sweater. The static electricity will cause the ruler to attract small pieces of paper to it without touching them.

HITTING WITH FORCE

When a pool player hits the ball with the cue, a good contact is essential. The push of the cue applies a contact force to the ball. If the moving ball hits another stationary ball, the contact starts the second ball moving.

ELASTIC FORCE

In the pole vault, the athlete is helped over the bar by the elasticity of the pole. The athlete plants one end of the pole on the ground and bends the other end down. As the pole straightens it applies a force to the vaulter, lifting him upward. The vaulter and pole obviously need to be in contact with each other!

Find out more

FORCES AND MOTION P. 120
ENERGY SOURCES P. 134
NUCLEAR ENERGY P. 136
STATIC ELECTRICITY P. 146
MAGNETISM P. 154
STRUCTURE OF THE EARTH P. 212
TORNADOES P. 259

COMBINING FORCES

MANY OBJECTS ARE ACTED ON by more than one force. For example, a yacht's weight pulls it down but the water produces an equal upward force, which stops the boat from sinking. The wind blows on the sails to push the yacht through the water, but the water pushes back on the hull and slows the boat down. The overall result of two or more forces acting on an object is called the resultant force. The resultant of two forces is a single force, which has the same effect as the two forces combined. Forces are what are called vector quantities. A vector quantity has a direction and a size.

Wind

RESULTANT

To find the resultant of several forces, the direction of the forces must be taken into account, as well as their sizes. When two forces act at an angle to each other, the resultant lies between them.

Two teams of Ancient Egyptian workers hauling a block of stone produce two forces at an angle to each other.

Keel

PARALLELOGRAM OF FORCES

When two forces act on an object in different directions, with an angle between them, the resultant can be found by drawing a parallelogram. Sides A and B represent the size and direction of the forces; sides C and D are drawn parallel to A and B; then the line E indicates the size and direction of the resultant.

A   B

E

D   C

The resultant causes the block to be dragged forward.

FORCES IN SAILING

Sailors can make their boats go in any direction, no matter which way the wind is blowing. This is because two forces combine to produce a resultant that drives the boat in the required direction: the force on the sails, which depends upon the direction of the wind and the position of the sails; and the force produced by the keel, which stops the boat from being blown sideways.

When two magnets exert equal and opposite forces on steel ball bearings, the bearings stay still and do not move toward either magnet.

WEIGHTLIFTING

If two forces acting on an object in opposite directions are different sizes, the resultant will be in the direction of the larger force. A weightlifter strains to give an upward force to a bar. But the weight of the bar pulls it down. The upward force created by the weightlifter has to be larger than the downward pull if he is to lift the bar higher. If the weight of the bar is the larger force, the bar will fall back to the ground.

PULLING TOGETHER

When forces pull in the same direction, the resultant can be found by adding the forces together. Two train engines pulling together in the same direction combine their forces. The resultant force is double the force of a single engine.

EQUAL AND OPPOSITE FORCES

If two forces pull an object in opposite directions, the size of the resultant can be found by subtracting one force from the other. If the forces are equal, they balance each other. The resultant will be zero and the object will not move.

> ### *Find out more*
>
> FORCES P. 114
> FORCES IN FLUIDS P. 128
> FLOATING AND SINKING P. 129
> MAGNETISM P. 154
> *FACT FINDER* P. 408

BALANCED FORCES

IF NOTHING HAPPENS when a force acts on an object, it means that the force must be balanced by another force. For example, during a tug-of-war, the teams may both heave away but have no effect—the rope stays in the same position. This is because the teams are equally strong and are pulling in opposite directions with the same force. The forces cancel each other out and produce a zero resultant. The object is said to be in equilibrium. If you sit on a chair, you are pushing down on the chair with your weight. If the chair does not collapse, then it must be pushing upward with a force equal to your weight.

If one rope breaks, the balance is upset and the tent will collapse.

TUG OF WAR TENT
When a tent has been put up correctly with ropes pulled tight all the way around, the tent should not fall over. The ropes along one side of the tent pull in the opposite direction to the ropes on the other side, and the pulls balance each other.

In a simple bridge, the weight is supported through upward forces produced by the supports.

Beam bridge

Arch bridge

Suspension bridge

BUILDING BRIDGES
Bridges need to be built so that they support their own weight and the weight of heavy traffic without collapsing. These downward forces must therefore be balanced by upward forces. The simplest bridge is the beam bridge. It is supported at each end. In an arch bridge, the curve of the bridge structure transfers the weight to the supports at each end. In a suspension bridge, the weight is supported by upward forces from the cables as well as the towers.

If three forces are in equilibrium, a scale drawing of the forces forms a triangle. The sides of the triangle show the size and direction of the forces; the directions must all be clockwise or counterclockwise.

The towers pull some of the weight sideways as well as supporting it vertically.

Weight pushing down is supported by upward forces.

STRONG TRIANGLE
The triangle is the strongest shape to build with. It does not twist and collapse when under pressure. Many buildings and bridges are based on triangle shapes. The triangle sections in this radar dome allow the dome to be made of fiberglass. Unlike concrete, this is very light and transparent to radio waves.

CARRYING A LOAD
To carry a log, an elephant must lift it straight up with its trunk with an upward force exactly equal to the log's downward force, or weight. Two opposite forces cancel each other out if they are equal and in line.

FORCES IN BUILDINGS
Architects design buildings so that the forces on the walls and foundations are in equilibrium, otherwise the buildings would collapse. Many cathedrals have flying buttresses—structures that reach out from the outer walls and down to the ground. They help the walls to support the huge weight of the roof. The buttresses of Le Mans Cathedral in France are more complex than most!

Find out more

SPEED

WHEN WE SAY that a car is traveling at 30 miles (50 km) per hour we mean that the car will take one hour to travel 30 miles (50 km). This is true only if the car keeps going at a constant speed—the same speed all the time. During a real journey, a car will slow down sometimes and go faster at other times. It is therefore useful to calculate the average speed. If you traveled 120 miles (200 km) in two hours, your average speed would be 60 miles (100 km) per hour—distance traveled divided by time taken. In science, speed has no particular direction. It is known as a scalar quantity. Speed in a particular direction is called velocity. Velocity is a vector quantity.

RELATIVE SPEED
Two moving objects have a relative speed—the speed at which one seems to move when seen from the other. Two cars racing at the same speed have a relative speed of zero.

THE SPEEDOMETER
A speedometer in a car shows instantaneous speed—the speed at which the car is traveling at any instant. The speedometer is driven by a cable that is connected to the shaft that drives the wheels.

Spring turns the pointer back when the car slows.

Cable rotates with the wheel shaft at road speed.

Pointer

Magnet rotates with the cable.

Drag cup, rotated slowly by the magnet, turns the pointer.

Dial

Jet aircraft—2,192 mph (3,529 km/h)

Fastest high-speed train— 320 mph (515 km/h)

DIFFERENT SPEEDS
Light travels so fast—at 186,000 miles per second (300,000 km per second)—it is difficult to imagine it. A sloth, an animal from South America, moves so slowly— at about 7 ft (2 m) per minute—it is difficult to actually see it moving. Here is a selection of things that move at different speeds.

Thrust SSC—holder of the land speed record—763 mph (1,227 km/h)

Bird in level flight— 56 mph (90 km/h)

Racing speedboat— 165 km/h (103 mph)

Sports car— 200 mph (325 km/h)

Cheetah—60 mph (96 km/h)

FINISHING TIME
As athletes finish a race, they pass in front of a photo finish camera. The camera takes a picture of them against a computerized clock accurate to one-thousandth of a second. The developed picture shows who won the race and in what time. It is a picture of a small area taken over a period of time—the time it takes for all the competitors to finish.

Human—22 mph (36 km/h)

Rabbit— 25 mph (40 km/h)

Snail—0.03 mph (0.05 km/h)

ALBERT EINSTEIN
Born in Germany, Albert Einstein (1879– 1955) was one of the greatest scientists of all time. He developed the theory of relativity. He became Professor of Physics at the University of Berlin, and received the Nobel Prize for Physics in 1921. Einstein left Germany in 1933 and settled in the United States. He developed the special and the general theory of relativity—the basis for our ideas about the universe.

THEORY OF RELATIVITY
In 1905, Einstein published his theory of relativity, which described how time seems to run slowly on something moving at near light-speed, and nothing can move faster than light. A clock on a train moving at near light-speed would seem, to a person outside, to be running slow. Einstein also discovered that matter can be converted into energy. This is the source of energy in an atomic explosion and a nuclear reactor.

Find out more

COMBINING FORCES P. 116
ACCELERATION P. 119
NUCLEAR ENERGY P. 136
LIGHT P. 190
PHOTOGRAPHY P. 206
LIFE CYCLE OF STARS P. 280
MOVEMENT P. 356

GRAVITY

WHEN YOU DROP SOMETHING, it falls to the ground. The force that makes it do this is the Earth's gravity. Gravity is a force that pulls objects together. It is not just the Earth that has gravity. The Moon has gravity too. And the Sun's gravity attracts the Earth and planets and holds them in their orbits. The force of gravitational attraction between two objects depends upon the distance between them—the greater the distance, the smaller the force pulling them together. It also depends upon the masses of the objects—the greater the mass of the objects, the greater the force of gravity.

On the Moon   On Earth

MASS AND WEIGHT
Mass is not the same as weight. Mass is the amount of material in an object; weight is the force exerted on an object's mass by gravity. On the Moon, a pile of strawberries would weigh one-sixth as much as it does on Earth, but the mass would be the same. This is because the Moon's surface gravity is one-sixth as strong as the Earth's.

CENTER OF GRAVITY
The point at which the effect of gravity on an object seems to be concentrated is called the center of gravity. It is the point where the whole weight of the object seems to act. An object can be balanced if it is supported directly in line with its center of gravity. But balancing is easiest if the object has a low center of gravity.

1. Hang the object and the plumb line together from the same point. Draw a line where the plumb line falls.

Plumb line

Center of gravity

This cork is supported on the point of a needle. It is balancing because the heavy forks hanging underneath have put the weight of the whole object, and the center of gravity, lower down, directly under its support.

Jumping on the Moon

FINDING THE CENTER OF GRAVITY
It is easy to find the center of gravity of a flat object such as this kite. Hang the object and a plumb line together so that they can both swing freely. When they are still, the center of gravity will be directly below the point of suspension somewhere on the plumb line. Draw a line to show where the plumb line falls. Repeat this from a different point and the center of gravity will be where the two lines cross.

Center of gravity

2. Hang the object and plumb line from another point on the object and again mark where the plumb line falls.

THE MOON'S GRAVITY
Gravity on the Moon is less than that on the Earth because the Moon is much smaller and has less mass than the Earth. On the Moon, falling objects accelerate downward at one-sixth the rate they do on the Earth, and a person can jump six times as high on the Moon as on the Earth.

Jumping on the Earth

BOOMERANG
Some objects, such as a boomerang, have their center of gravity outside their bodies. Because of its shape, a boomerang cannot be balanced by supporting it at one point on its flat side. Edge-on, it will balance when supported at the point of the V.

TIDES
Gravity causes the tides. The ocean on the side of the Earth nearest the Moon is pulled outward by the Moon's gravity, creating a high tide. It is high tide on the far side of the Earth at the same time because the Earth is pulled toward the Moon more than the water on that side. The Sun has a small effect on tides. Twice a month, when Moon and Sun line up, their gravity combines to make a high spring tide.

Find out more

MEASURING FORCES P. 123
TURNING FORCES P. 124
CIRCULAR MOTION P. 125
WAVES, TIDES, AND CURRENTS P. 235
SOLAR SYSTEM P. 283
ROCKETS P. 299

FRICTION

IT IS HARD TO DRAG A HEAVY WEIGHT along a rough surface. This is because there is a force called friction, which slows down the movement of objects sliding over each other. Friction occurs because no surface is perfectly smooth. This means that when any two surfaces press together, the rough pieces, however tiny, catch on each other. The rougher the surfaces, the more friction there is. If there were no friction, it would be easy to drag large weights. But if there were no friction, everything would keep sliding. You would not be able to walk, since your shoes would not grip the ground; you would not be able to pick anything up because you would have no grip between your fingers and the object. Friction causes wear and tear, which is why even metal wears down.

AIR RESISTANCE
When an object moves through air, the air molecules bump against it, causing friction. This friction is called air resistance and it becomes greater the faster the object is moving. Friction makes things hot, so when a meteor hurtles through the Earth's atmosphere it becomes so hot it begins to break up.

The rider crouches low to make a streamlined shape that allows the air to slip past more easily.

The helmet is as streamlined as possible.

Handlebars are covered with rough material to increase friction between them and the hands for better grip.

Brake pads press against the rim of the wheel and friction slows the wheel.

Tires grip the road with friction. They have a pattern of grooves, called the tread, that allows water to escape from under the wheels. Otherwise, any water on the road would act as a lubricant and reduce the friction and the grip.

FRICTION EVERYWHERE
There are many places on a bicycle where friction acts. In some places, such as between the brake pads and the wheels, it is important to have friction. In other parts, such as the gears, you want as little friction as possible.

Oil flows into the "valleys" in the rough surfaces.

Pedals have a rough surface to increase friction and stop the cyclist's feet from slipping off.

Cogs, chain, and gears are lubricated with oil to reduce friction.

REDUCING FRICTION
Friction can cause machine parts to wear out, but it can be reduced by using ball bearings lubricated, or coated, with oil. The ball bearings work because they roll rather than drag across each other.

STREAMLINING IN NATURE
Objects experience friction moving through water too. This is called drag. A bird diving for a fish puts its wings back to make a streamlined shape. And most fish are streamlined so they can move through the water easily.

CHRISTOPHER COCKERELL
A British engineer, Christopher Cockerell (1910–99) invented the hovercraft in 1955. He thought up the idea of using a strong downward jet of air to push a boat up and away from the water, letting it move without friction. When Cockerell told the British government of his invention, they were so impressed that they placed the invention on the Top Secret list! He was eventually given permission to manufacture the new boat. The first large hovercraft was launched in 1969.

Air is drawn in and forced under the hovercraft. A "skirt" of flexible material around the hull stops air from leaking out. The hovercraft rides on this cushion of air which reduces friction between it and the water. Propellers drive the craft forward.

Find out more

ACCELERATION P. 119
MEASURING FORCES P. 123
MACHINES P. 130
ENGINES P. 143
COMETS AND METEORS P. 295

FORCES AND MOTION

ONCE AN OBJECT IS MOVING, it will keep moving until a force halts it. This is proved by spacecraft. They will travel forever through space at a constant speed until a force acts on them. It has taken people more than 2,000 years to understand this. The Ancient Greek thinker Aristotle thought that an object could only move if pushed by a force, and the movement stopped when the force was removed. But this did not explain why a ball continued to fly through the air after it had left a thrower's hand. A better theory was put forward in the 16th century by Italian experimenter Galileo. He recognized that no force was needed to keep an object moving, only to start, stop, or accelerate it. In 1687, Englishman Isaac Newton built upon Galileo's work. He put forward three laws of motion.

IN THE AIR
When you throw a ball, it moves in two ways at the same time: forward at a constant speed, and downward due to gravity. The resultant path it takes is caused by a combination of the two motions.

INERTIA
A bobsled team has to push hard to make the bob start to move. And they have to keep pushing to make it move faster. This tendency of the bobsled to resist having its state of motion changed is called inertia. All objects have inertia and the more mass they have, the greater their inertia.

The force that lifts the frog into the air is accompanied by an equal and opposite reaction force that drives the lily leaf backward.

The frog will stay still unless an unbalanced force acts on it.

The frog's leg muscles exert a force that pushes the frog into the air.

NEWTON'S FIRST LAW
A frog leaping from a lily pad illustrates Newton's Laws of Motion well. Newton's first law states that if an object is not being pushed or pulled by a force, it will either stay still or move in a straight line at a constant speed.

NEWTON'S SECOND LAW
Newton's second law states that when a force acts on an object the object will start to move, speed up, slow down, or change direction. The greater the force, the greater the change of movement.

NEWTON'S THIRD LAW
The third law states that if you push or pull an object, it will push or pull you to an equal extent. As Newton put it, "to every action there is an equal and opposite reaction."

ISAAC NEWTON

One of the greatest scientists of all time, Isaac Newton (1642–1727) was born in Lincolnshire, England. He was sent to study at Cambridge University in 1661. But during the years 1665–66, Newton returned home because Cambridge was struck by the plague. It was then that he made his most important discoveries. He formulated his laws of motion and invented a kind of mathematics, called calculus, to express them. He explained how gravity keeps the planets in orbit around the Sun. Newton was honored by being buried in Westminster Abbey in London, England.

MOMENTUM
A moving object has momentum—it will keep on moving until a force stops it. When you catch a ball, you must exert a force on it to remove its momentum and stop it form moving. But when your hand and the ball collide, the ball will exert a force on your hand so that the momentum of your hand will change. The momentum gained by your hand is equal to the momentum lost by the ball. The greater the mass and velocity of an object, the larger its momentum.

The best way to catch a ball is to recoil with it so that the collision lasts longer and the force is less.

Find out more

FORCES P. 114
ACCELERATION P. 119
GRAVITY P. 122
ENGINES P. 143
JUPITER P. 290
SOLAR SYSTEM P. 283
AMPHIBIANS P. 328

ACCELERATION

WHEN A CAR CHANGES SPEED it is said to be accelerating. When you are traveling in a car, you can feel if the car accelerates suddenly—you get "left behind." The car accelerates when the driver puts a foot on the accelerator. The farther the pedal is pushed down, the more the car accelerates. Acceleration is a measure of how quickly velocity increases. If velocity decreases, it is a negative acceleration called deceleration. Acceleration and deceleration happen when an unbalanced force acts on an object.

The ball rolls backward when the saucer is accelerated forward.

The ball rolls forward when the saucer is accelerated backward.

USING ACCELERATION
Pilots of modern aeroplanes have an autopilot to help them fly the plane. It contains an accelerometer, which senses if the plane's velocity—vertically or horizontally—has changed. If the plane accelerates in one direction, part of the accelerometer moves in the opposite direction—a bit like a ball on a saucer. A computer detects the movement and puts the plane back on course.

Terminal velocity for a skydiver falling in a flat position is about 120 mph (190 km/h).

30 ft (9 m)	46 ft (14 m)	76 ft (23 m)	At 30 mph (48 km/h)
49 ft (15 m)	125 ft (38 m)	174 ft (53 m)	At 50 mph (80 km/h)
69 ft (21 m)	246 ft (75 m)	315 ft (96 m)	At 70 mph (118 km/h)
Thinking distance	Braking distance	Total stopping distance	

STOPPING DISTANCES
Motor vehicles need to be able to accelerate and decelerate quickly to be safe. Good brakes are particularly necessary. The faster a car is going, and the heavier it is, the more difficult it is to stop. The shortest stopping distances for an average car in an emergency stop are shown here. Thinking distance is how far the vehicle travels before the driver reacts and uses the brakes. Braking distance is how far it travels while it slows. At 70 mph (118 km/h), the total shortest stopping distance is longer than a football field!

TERMINAL VELOCITY
A falling object, such as a skydiver, accelerates as it falls. Earth's gravity accelerates all falling objects downward at the same rate—32.2 ft (9.8 m) per second, per second. (They get faster by 32.2 ft [9.8 m] per second, every second.) But an object cannot really fall freely. Friction between it and the air, called air resistance, acts against the gravity. Air resistance increases as the object falls faster, and when it equals the force of gravity, the object stops accelerating and falls at a steady speed. This is called terminal velocity.

An open parachute increases the air resistance, which then equals gravity at a much slower speed.

DRAG RACING
Acceleration is calculated by dividing the increase in velocity by the time taken to reach that velocity. It is measured in units such as miles per hour per second. For example, in a drag race, a car can accelerate from 0 to 296 miles (476 km) per hour in 4.88 seconds (60.6 miles [97.5 km] per hour per second). The driver has to use a parachute to make the car decelerate and stop before it reaches the end of the track!

The ball bounces less high each time because it gradually loses energy.

At the top of the bounce, the velocity of the ball is zero.

The ball is bouncing from right to left.

BOUNCING BALL
A bouncing ball accelerates as it falls and decelerates as it rises. On the way down, the ball goes farther each tenth of a second; on the way up, it goes less far each tenth of a second. At the maximum height of each bounce, the ball is stationary for an instant.

Find out more

SPEED p. 118
FRICTION p. 121
GRAVITY p. 122
MEASURING FORCES p. 123
WORK AND ENERGY p. 132
ROCKETS p. 299

MEASURING FORCES

THE SIZE OF A FORCE is usually expressed in units called newtons, named after Sir Isaac Newton. On Earth, a mass of 1 kg (2.2 lb) weighs almost 10 newtons—9.8 newtons to be exact. A spring balance is often used to measure a force because springs are elastic—they stretch. The inventor Robert Hooke discovered that the amount an elastic body stretches out of shape is in direct proportion to the force acting on it. This is known as Hooke's law. As long as the force is not too large, stretching the spring past its limit of elasticity, the spring will go back to its original length when the force is removed.

Cavendish measured how much the beam moved to calculate the gravity between the balls.

MEASURING GRAVITY
Englishman Henry Cavendish (1731–1810) used this apparatus to calculate the Earth's mass. He hung two lead balls from the ends of a beam that turned horizontally. The balls were attracted by gravity to two larger lead balls nearby. As the small balls moved, they turned the beam. Cavendish calculated the gravity between the balls and, from that, the mass of the Earth.

THE NEWTONMETER
It is helpful when imagining a newton to know that 1 newton is about the force needed to lift a small apple. Forces up to about 100 newtons can be measured using a newtonmeter. As the spring inside is stretched, a marker moves down a scale along the side of the meter and indicates the size of the stretching force—in this case the weight of an apple.

COMPARING FORCES
Lifting a ball requires a force of about 4 newtons. A kick applies a force of about 10 newtons to the ball. Compare this with the force of a jet engine—100,000 newtons. On a small scale, an insect jumping into the air uses a force of about 0.001 newtons.

ROBERT HOOKE

Hooke's microscope

English inventor Robert Hooke (1635–1702) is best remembered for discovering how elastic objects stretch. He was a skilled instrument-maker and helped improve scientific instruments such as microscopes, telescopes, and barometers. He designed a telegraph system and a watch regulated by a vibrating spring, rather than a pendulum. In 1665, he published a book containing drawings of insects seen through the microscope.

The rough surface of sandpaper produces greater friction than a smooth surface.

Painted wood

MEASURING FRICTION
You can measure the drag produced by friction at home. Attach an iron mass to a block of wood with string and hang it over the edge of a table. See how much weight you need to make the wood move along different surfaces. Friction depends on the surfaces rubbing together and the weight of the sliding block. The area of the surfaces in contact does not matter.

A larger weight is needed to pull the block along the sandpaper.

Find out more

PROPERTIES OF MATTER P. 22
FRICTION P. 121
GRAVITY P. 122
VIBRATIONS P. 126

TURNING FORCES

WHEN YOU TURN THE HANDLEBARS of your bicycle, you pull on one side and push on the other. This pair of forces is an example of a couple, or pair of turning forces. The point around which an object turns is called the fulcrum, or pivot. A single force can make an object turn if it acts some distance away from a fixed fulcrum. When you open a door, you apply a single force to the door handle and the door turns as it swings open. The door hinge is the fulcrum around which the door turns. The turning effect of a force depends upon the size of the force and how far away from the fulcrum the force is acting. The farther away the force, the greater the turning effect.

MAXIMUM FORCE
In some countries, cattle are used to turn a wheel to raise water. They are harnessed to the end of a pole attached to the wheel. As they walk around, they turn the wheel. It is easier for them if the pole is as long as possible to make their turning force greater.

More weight presses down through the back wheel of a bike than through the front wheel. For the plank to balance, the back wheel of the bike must be closer to the log than the front wheel.

Fulcrum

Center of gravity

A tall bottle almost full of water is unstable because it has a high center of gravity. The center of gravity does not stay above the bottle's base when the bottle is tipped, so producing a turning force that topples it.

BALANCING THE FORCES
When an object is in equilibrium, or balanced, the turning force on one side of the fulcrum is equal to the turning force on the other side. A cyclist in trial riding uses this principle when he stops a plank from seesawing down over a log before he is ready.

Center of gravity

Fulcrum

Bar marked with scale

A steelyard used by the Ancient Romans

Hook for item to be weighed

Balancing bob

STABILITY
An object is said to be in stable equilibrium if, when pushed slightly, its center of gravity is still lying above its base. Gravity pulls the object back to its original position. If an object falls over when pushed slightly, it is in unstable equilibrium. Its center of gravity is no longer above its base and gravity pulls the object farther. An object is in neutral equilibrium if it remains in its new position when pushed slightly.

A bottle containing a small amount of water is stable as it has a low center of gravity. The center of gravity remains above the base of the bottle when it is tipped slightly, producing a turning force that returns the bottle to its original position.

WEIGHING SCALES
The Ancient Romans used turning forces to weigh things on a steelyard. Steelyards are still used today. You may get weighed on a steelyard at the doctor's. While you stand on the scales, a bob is moved along a bar until the bar balances. Your weight can then be read from a scale on the bar where the balancing weight stops.

VEHICLE TESTING
Tall vehicles are made safer by putting their wheels wide apart and their engines low down. This keeps their center of gravity low. This bus is being tested to see how far it will tip before it topples over.

Find out more

FORCES AND MOTION P. 120
GRAVITY P. 122
MEASURING FORCES P. 123
MACHINES P. 130

CIRCULAR MOTION

WHEELS, SPINNING TOPS, propellers, and merry-go-rounds all go around in circles. They are really changing direction all the time. Each part of the spinning object is trying to move forward in a straight line, but a force is pulling them in toward the center of the circle. This force is called centripetal force. It continually changes the direction of a turning object so that it goes around in a circle and not in a straight line. When an animal, running forward, makes a tight turn, its feet push into the ground. The ground pushes back and this provides a centripetal force. If the animal was running on ice and could not grip the ground, there would be no centripetal force and the animal would find it extremely difficult to make the turn!

SPINNING GYROSCOPE
Spinning objects have inertia, just as objects moving in a straight line have. They resist having their direction of movement changed. A gyroscope is a device that contains a spinning wheel. If the wheel is spinning fast enough, it resists gravity and it is then very difficult to push the gyroscope over. Electrically driven gyroscopes are used in navigation systems on airplanes and ships.

CENTRIFUGAL FORCE
A toy car racing around a loop-the-loop track does not fall off, even when it is upside-down. A force appears to be pushing it upward. This is sometimes called centrifugal force. But centrifugal force is really inertia trying to make the car go straight ahead.

As the bowl spins, the water rises up the walls.

CLIMBING WATER
If a bowl of water is spun quickly round and round, the water tries to fly out in a straight line. A force is needed to stop it. This is provided by the walls of the bowl. The faster the bowl spins, the more the water moves outward. A spin dryer uses this effect to remove water from clothes. The water moves toward the walls of the drum, and if it finds one of the holes it flies straight through.

The water is level when the bowl is not spinning.

Turntable spinning the bowl aound.

WEIGHTLESSNESS IN ORBIT

A space shuttle is held in orbit around the Earth because the Earth's gravity provides a centripetal force, which makes it move in a circle rather than fly off into space. Astronauts inside the shuttle are affected by gravity to the same extent. They feel weightless because they are continuously falling. But they are moving forward at such a speed that they are carried "over the horizon" in a circular path that never gets any nearer to the ground.

HAMMER THROW
A hammer thrower spins the hammer around as fast as he can before releasing it. The centripetal force needed to keep it spinning around is the pull on the wire. When the thrower lets go of the hammer, he removes the centripetal force and the hammer's inertia makes it fly off in a straight line.

The faster the thrower spins, the farther the hammer will fly when he lets go.

Find out more
FORCES AND MOTION P. 120
FRICTION P. 121
GRAVITY P. 122
ROCKETS P. 299

VIBRATIONS

I**F YOU HANG A MASS** from a piece of string, and push the mass to one side, it will swing from side to side in a regular way. These back and forth movements are called oscillations, or vibrations. The number of times an object vibrates in one second is called the frequency. Everything has a natural frequency. If you force an object to vibrate at its natural frequency, the oscillations get larger. In 1940, the wind made the Tacoma Narrows bridge in Washington State vibrate at a rate that matched its natural frequency. The vibrations became so violent that the bridge collapsed. But vibrations can also be useful. Pneumatic drills use vibrations to break up materials, and clocks measure time by counting regular vibrations.

The size of the movement or vibration is called the amplitude. The time taken for one vibration is called the period.

EARTHQUAKE VIBRATIONS
Vibrations caused by an earthquake can make buildings collapse. This special-effects photo symbolizes an earthquake in San Francisco. San Francisco lies on the San Andreas fault, one of the world's great fault lines. A fault line is where earthquakes are likely to happen.

PENDULUM
The swing of a pendulum is a vibration. The time taken for one swing depends only upon the length of the pendulum, provided the swings are small. The weight of the bob on the end does not matter. Italian experimenter Galileo suggested that a clock could be regulated by a pendulum. In a pendulum clock, the pendulum swings and turns a wheel at a regular rate. The wheel turns the hands of the clock.

Crest

Trough

WAVES
Vibrations cause waves. Some waves are obvious, as on the sea and on the surface of a pond. But some waves are not so easy to see, for example, sound waves, which are caused by something vibrating. Waves can be transverse or longitudinal.

WATER WAVES
Ripples on a pond or waves on the sea are transverse waves. As the wave passes, water particles vibrate up and down at right angles to the direction of the wave.

SOUND WAVES
When a musical instrument such as the cymbals vibrate, they cause sound waves in the air. In a sound wave, air particles vibrate back and forth in the same direction as the wave is traveling. They are longitudinal waves.

PIEZOELECTRICITY
Quartz has a special property—an electric charge changes its size. Because of this piezoelectric effect, a suitable electric current makes a crystal vibrate at a precise frequency. In a quartz watch, current from a battery makes a microthin slice of quartz crystal vibrate 32,768 times each second. A microchip reduces this rate to produce a signal once a second. This signal controls the motor that turns the hands or activates the digital display.

Quartz crystal

Find out more

CRYSTALS P. 30
SOUND P. 178
MEASURING SOUND P. 180
EARTHQUAKES P. 220
WAVES, TIDES, AND CURRENTS P. 235

PRESSURE

WHY DO CAMELS have large, flat feet? Why does a thumbtack have a sharp point? The reason is because if you spread a force over a large area, the pressure of the force will be reduced. And by concentrating a force into a small area the pressure will be greater. A camel does not sink into the sand because its weight is spread over a large area. But when you push a thumbtack into a bulletin board, the sharp point goes into the board easily because the force of your thumb is concentrated into a tiny area. Pressure is measured by the force acting on a single unit of area.

SPREADING THE LOAD
The jacana bird of South America has extremely long toes and claws. Its weight is therefore spread over a large area and it can walk on the floating lily pads without sinking.

SINKING IN
A watering can does not sink into soil because its weight is spread over its base. But a trowel is easy to push into soil because its weight is concentrated into the thin edge. A sharp knife cuts easily for the same reason: the force on the knife is concentrated into a small area along the cutting edge.

66,000 ft (20,000 m) high

Air pressure at 60,000 ft (20,000 m) is less than one-tenth that at sea level.

Airliners fly at a height where air pressure is less than pressure inside the body. It would be impossible for the body to take in air, so the inside of airliners is pressurized.

On mountain tops, the air is thin so climbers usually use breathing apparatus to give them more oxygen. Air pressure is half that at sea level.

At sea level, air pressure is roughly equal to the weight of a cow sitting on a large dinner plate.

Sea level

People cannot dive deeper than about 400 ft (120 m) since the water pressure would crush them.

Submarines can dive deep under water. They have thick hulls to withstand the great water pressure.

At a depth of 30,000 ft (10,000 m) under the ocean, the pressure of water is equivalent to seven elephants balanced on a small dinner plate!

33,000 ft (10,000 m) deep

UNDER PRESSURE
Liquids and gases, both called fluids, exert pressure on objects. Air exerts pressure on you. If it were not for the fact that the fluids inside your body exert as much pressure as the air outside, the pressure of air at ground level would crush you! Air pressure decreases the higher up you go because there is less and less air.

EVANGELISTA TORRICELLI

Air pressure is measured with a barometer. The mercury barometer was invented by Italian Evangelista Torricelli (1608–47) in 1643. He discovered that the height of mercury in a tube placed upside-down in a cup of mercury varies as air pressure changes. Torricelli learned from Galileo and eventually succeeded him as court mathematician to the Grand Duke of Tuscany. A unit of pressure, the torr, is named after him. One torr is the pressure that supports 1 mm (0.04 in) of mercury in a barometer.

Water squirts farthest through the lowest hole because pressure increases with depth.

PRESSURE IN LIQUIDS
The pressure in liquids acts in all directions. The water squirts through the holes in the side of this container because of horizontal pressure.

Find out more

FORCES IN FLUIDS

LIQUIDS AND GASES both flow when a force acts on them. They are known as fluids. Fluids have no definite shape and take the shape of their container. When fluids are squeezed by a force, the force is transmitted to all other parts of the fluid. This is called Pascal's Principle and it is used to drive some machinery. In the hydraulic brake of a car, for example, the force applied to the brake pedal is transmitted to the wheels by a liquid, called the brake fluid. Another useful property of fluids is that a fast-moving fluid has a lower pressure than a slow-moving one. This is known as Bernoulli's Principle. It enables lumbering airplanes to soar high into the sky.

A bird's wing is shaped like an aerofoil, giving it lift.

The extra pressure underneath pushes the wing upward.

AEROFOIL
The wing of an airplane is curved on top and nearly flat underneath. This special shape is called an aerofoil; it rises when air, which is a fluid, flows around it. This is because air flowing over the top of an aerofoil-shaped wing travels faster than air passing underneath. According to Bernoulli's Principle, this means that the pressure under the wing is greater than the pressure over the wing, creating lift. The faster the air flow, the greater the lift. This is why an aircraft must be traveling very fast to take off.

BIRD WINGS
A bird gets most of its lift by flapping its wings, which push the air downward, producing an upward reaction force. However, when the bird is just gliding, the wing itself produces some lift because of its shape.

Soapy bubbles can be stretched into strange shapes because soap weakens the surface tension of water.

SURFACE TENSION
A liquid behaves as if its surface was covered by an invisible stretched skin. This effect is called surface tension. It is caused by forces between molecules pulling those molecules at the surface inward. A bubble is normally a sphere because surface tension pulls it into this shape.

Molecules of water creep up the sides of the tube.

CAPILLARY ACTION
If a liquid is at the bottom of a very narrow tube, it may move up the tube. This is known as capillary action. It will happen if the force of attraction between the liquid molecules and the molecules of the tube is stronger than the attraction between the liquid molecules themselves.

BLAISE PASCAL
Frenchman Blaise Pascal (1623–62) was a brilliant mathematician and religious thinker. He made the first successful calculating machine at the age of 22. In 1646, he made a mercury barometer and later used it to measure air pressure. While studying liquids, he discovered the principle named after him. Pascal's Principle states that, in a liquid or gas, pressure applied to one point is transmitted equally to all parts of the fluid. Pascal's name is given to a unit of pressure. One pascal (Pa) is 1 newton per square meter.

Meniscus curves downward.

Mercury

COHESION AND ADHESION
The surface, or meniscus, of water in a tube is curved upward but that of mercury is curved downward. This is because the particles of mercury are strongly attracted to each other; they have strong cohesion (and a high surface tension). Cohesion is a force between particles of the same type. The water particles are more attracted to the glass particles of the tube. This force between two different materials is called adhesion. It is the reason why raindrops stick to a windowpane.

Meniscus curves upward.

Water

Find out more
PROPERTIES OF MATTER P. 22
BONDING P. 28
SOAPS AND DETERGENTS P. 95
ADHESIVES P. 106
PRESSURE P. 127
CALCULATORS P. 172
AIR PRESSURE P. 250
FACT FINDER P. 408

FLOATING AND SINKING

WHY DOES AN OBJECT seem to get lighter as you lower it into water? It is because the water pushes against it, supporting some of its weight. This supporting force is called the upthrust. Upthrust is equal to the weight of fluid an object displaces, or pushes away. This is Archimedes' Principle. An object will float if the upthrust is equal to its weight. It will sink if its weight is greater than the upthrust. Whether something floats depends on its density—a measure of how packed together its matter is. A wax candle floats on water because it has a low density and displaces enough water to provide a large upthrust. A stone is denser than water and sinks: the displaced water does not equal its weight. The stone pushes away with more force than that of the water pushing up.

GOING UP
Helium balloons rise in air because helium is less dense than air. The weight of air the balloons displace is greater than their weight.

FLOATING IN WATER
A peach floats in water because the weight of water it displaces is equal to its own weight. This means that the force of the upthrust exactly equals the force of the peach's weight pushing down.

Propellers drive the submarine forward.

When a submarine is on the surface, its ballast tanks are full of air that keeps it afloat.

To dive, water is pumped into the ballast tanks, making the submarine heavier.

To rise, air is pumped into the ballast tanks, making the submarine lighter.

SUBMARINES
Inside a submarine there are containers called ballast tanks. If these are full of air, the submarine will float. Even though it is made of steel, the average density of the submarine is less than that of water. By pumping water into the ballast tanks, the submarine can sink. This is because with its ballast tanks full of water, the submarine has a higher density than water.

ARCHIMEDES
It is said that Archimedes, a Greek inventor who lived in the third century BCE, discovered his Principle after noticing that his bath overflowed when he got into it. He ran through the streets naked, shouting "Eureka!" ("I've got it!"). With his Principle, he helped to prove that the King's goldsmith had tried to cheat him by putting silver into a gold crown. Archimedes made discoveries in hydrostatics (science of stationary fluids), geometry, and mechanics (science of machines).

Swim bladder

FISH
Some fish have a swim bladder like the ballast tanks of a submarine. Air can enter this bladder either via the fish's mouth, or from the bloodstream. This enables the fish to rise in the water.

Cork

Oil

Plastic block

Water

Grape

Syrup

HIGHER OR LOWER?
Oil floats on water because it is less dense than water. Water floats on syrup because it is less dense than syrup. A cork is less dense than all three liquids, and so floats on the surface of the oil. A plastic block has a density lower than water but higher than oil. This means it sinks through the oil, but floats on the water. A grape has a higher density than oil or water, but lower than syrup. So the grape floats on the syrup.

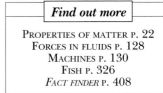

Find out more
PROPERTIES OF MATTER P. 22
FORCES IN FLUIDS P. 128
MACHINES P. 130
FISH P. 326
FACT FINDER P. 408

MACHINES

NOT ALL MACHINES are large and noisy. Many are small and they are used to do simple jobs. But whatever their size, all machines make a particular job easier to do. Some machines can change a small movement into a large one; some can change a small force into a large one; others can change the direction or position of a force, and apply it where it is most needed. The smaller the effort force, the greater distance it must move. This is called the Principle of the Machine. Unfortunately, all machines are less than 100 percent efficient. Some of the effort put in is not used to do the job, but to overcome friction between parts.

COMPLEX MACHINES

A combine harvester is a complex machine, but it is made up of lots of simple machines connected together in many ingenious ways: by gear trains, levers, moving belts, and hydraulic pipe systems. The result is a useful tool that combines the two parts of harvesting—cutting the crop and separating the grain—hence its name.

Threshing cylinder separates the grain from the heads.

Grain auger carries grain to the grain tank.

Auger unloads the grain.

Conveyor carries the stalks up to the threshing cylinder.

Auger carries corn to conveyor.

Reel feeds corn to cutting bar.

Cutter bar slices the stalks.

MAGNIFYING MOVEMENT

When rowers use their oars to move the boat, they are using machines that magnify movement. They move the inner end of the oars a small distance but the other end of the oars moves a larger distance, pulling the boat swiftly through the water.

MAGNIFYING FORCE

Archimedes, the Ancient Greek inventor, said, "Give me a lever long enough, and I could move the world." In theory, this statement is true because a lever magnifies force. For example, a claw hammer, a type of lever, can be used to remove a nail from a piece of wood.

If you pull gently down on the handle of the hammer, the claw at the other end will exert a large force on the nail.

INSIDE A PIANO

A pianist needs to play notes quickly to produce good music. Each key in a piano is linked to a complex system of levers that magnify movement. The pianist has to use only a small finger movement to make the hammer hit the piano wire strongly, and sound a note.

Damper to cut off the sound

Piano wire

Felt-tipped hammer

Piano key

AROUND AND AROUND

It is easier to walk up a mountain by taking the winding road than to try to walk straight up the side. The winding road is acting as a simple machine. It decreases the effort you use to reach the top of the mountain, but increases the distance you must move.

SIMPLE MACHINES

Slopes, wedges, screws, levers, wheels and axles, pulleys, and gears are all called simple machines. They can make a job easier to do because they allow a small force, the effort, to overcome a larger force, the load. Machines that increase force are said to give a mechanical advantage. Mechanical advantage can be calculated by dividing the load by the effort. In machines that are used to increase movement, the advantage, called the velocity ratio, is calculated by dividing the distance the load moves by the distance the effort moves.

WEDGE

The blade of an ax is a wedge—a machine that magnifies force. When the ax is swung into the wood, the force of the swing is transferred to the blade. The blade moves forward through the wood and forces it to split apart. The wood moves a smaller distance than the blade but with more force.

Effort

There are four strands of rope pulling up on the lower pulley and the load. This multiplies by four the load that can be lifted with a given effort.

Load

PULLEY

A pulley is useful for lifting things up vertically. It is simply a piece of rope wound around a wheel. One end of the rope is attached to the load, and force is applied at the other end to lift the load. A pulley magnifies force when more than one wheel is used. One wheel is attached to the load and the others to a support, such as a beam.

GEARS, AND WHEEL AND AXLE

An eggbeater contains two kinds of machine: gears, and wheels and axles. Gears are toothed wheels that are interlocked in pairs. They can magnify speed or force. Usually, one wheel is larger than the other. A wheel and axle magnifies force because the wheel is larger than the axle. The axle turns in a smaller circle but with greater force.

The handle turns a wheel, which itself turns a smaller wheel at greater speed.

The axle transmits the turning motion to the blades, which rotate at high speed.

Pliers are a class 1 lever—a force magnifier.

Nutcrackers are a class 2 lever—a force magnifier.

Tongs are a class 3 lever—a distance magnifier.

LEVER

A lever is a rod or bar that turns around a point called the fulcrum, or pivot, to move a load. There are three kinds of lever, with different arrangements of load, effort, and fulcrum. Some levers magnify force, others magnify movement. For a lever to be a force magnifier, the effort must be applied farther away from the fulcrum than the load. There are examples of levers in your body. For example, your arm is a class three lever. Your elbow is the fulcrum, the muscles in your arm provide the effort, and your hand is the load.

INCLINED PLANE

It is easier to push something up a slope, or inclined plane, than to lift it straight up. Movers use a ramp to load heavy items into a van. They have to move things farther than they would if they lifted them vertically, but they need to use less effort. An inclined plane is therefore a force magnifier.

The thread of a screw is like a slope wrapped around a cylinder.

Handle is turned to turn the screw.

Wooden tube cut away to show the screw.

Archimedes' screw

SCREW

The thread of a screw is really an inclined plane. A screw can produce a mechanical advantage because it turns around a greater distance than it moves forward. This means that it moves forward with a greater force than is used to turn it. Water is sometimes lifted, for example, from a river to irrigate a field, with a device called an Archimedes' screw. Each time the screw turns, it lifts water a little bit higher up inside a tube.

Find out more

FORCES AND MOTION p. 120
TURNING FORCES p. 124
FLOATING AND SINKING p. 129
MUSICAL SOUNDS p. 186
SKELETONS p. 352
FACT FINDER p. 408

WORK AND ENERGY

TO A SCIENTIST, work is done only when a force moves something. If you lift a heavy object, you do work because you exert a force that moves that object. Work cannot be done without energy. Energy is the ability to do work. When work is done, energy is used, or converted from one form to another. You get your energy from your food; it is called chemical energy. Some machines get their energy in chemical form—from fuels such as gasoline or diesel. And there are other forms of energy: heat, light, sound, nuclear, and electrical energy. To understand how and why things move we need to know what kind of energy they have, and how much.

When an apple that weighs 1 newton is lifted vertically by 1 m (3.3 ft), a joule of work is done.

MEASURING WORK
When a forklift lifts crates, it is working to overcome the force of gravity. The heavier the crates, and the farther the forklift raises them, the more work is done.

NATURAL ENERGY
A dung beetle uses energy stored in its muscles to do work—in this case, to push a ball of dung up a slope. The heavier the ball is, and the higher it is pushed, the more work the beetle does, and the more energy it uses.

2 lb (1 kg) tomatoes

1 oz (25 g) milk chocolate

FOOD ENERGY
You would not be able to stay alive without the energy you get from food. But it can be just as bad for you to take in too much energy as too little. Different kinds of food contain different amounts of energy. For example, you would have to eat over 2 lb (1 kg) of fresh tomatoes to get as much energy as you would from just 1 oz (25 g) of milk chocolate.

JOULES
The joule is used as the unit for work as well as energy. One joule is the work done when a force of 1 newton moves something a distance of 1 m (3.3 ft) in the direction of the force.

JAMES JOULE
Englishman James Joule (1818–89) was one of the first to realize that work produces heat and that heat is a form of energy. He rotated paddles in a container of water and the water became warmer. The more work that was done to turn the paddles, the hotter the water became. Joule realized that work was changing movement energy into heat energy. Joule loved experimenting. He once found that the water at the base of a waterfall was hotter than the water at the top, proving that the energy of the falling water was being converted into heat.

ENERGY REQUIREMENTS
Energy is measured in units called joules, but the joule is a small unit. There are 1,000 joules in a kilojoule (kJ)—a unit used for measuring the amount of energy in our food. Kilocalories (kcal) are also used. One kilocalorie is equal to 4.2 kilojoules. Males and females, babies, teenagers, and adults, all use different amounts of energy every day, and it depends on what they are doing. A teenage boy needs about 3,000 kcal (12,600 kJ) of energy each day. A teenage girl needs about 2,500 kcal (10,500 kJ).

Baby—1,100 kcal (4,620 kJ)

Child—2,000 kcal (8,400 kJ)

Girl—2,500 kcal (10,500 kJ)

Boy—3,000 kcal (12,600 kJ)

Woman—2,200 kcal (9,200 kJ)

Man—3,000 kcal (12,600 kJ)

Man doing manual work—4,000 kcal (l16,800 kJ)

TYPES OF ENERGY

A moving object has energy, called kinetic energy. The energy of a moving car could demolish a brick wall. Where there are forces, there is also stored energy, called potential energy because it has the potential to turn into kinetic energy. Chemical energy is a form of stored energy. It is stored in the chemical makeup of some substances such as plants, oil, coal, and batteries. The most versatile form of energy is electricity. It can be easily converted into other forms of energy: light, sound, and heat.

A portable television has chemical energy stored in its battery. This is released when an electric current flows through the television to produce heat, light, and sound.

JAMES WATT

Scottish engineer James Watt (1736–1819) became Mathematical Instrument Maker at the University of Glasgow when he was 20. While repairing a model steam engine, he realized how the engine could be improved by having two cylinders. He made a full-scale improved engine that was much more powerful and economical than earlier engines. His engines were soon used in factories and mines all over the country and were exported to other parts of Europe and North America.

A kitten has chemical energy stored in its muscles. It uses some of this energy to climb up a tree. As it climbs, it increases its gravitational potential energy—the potential to fall off! When it falls, the kitten will have kinetic energy.

A plant has chemical energy stored in its leaves. This can be released if the chemical makeup of the plant is changed, for example, if it is eaten by an animal or burned to produce heat and light.

It takes two children to lift the weight as quickly as the man.

POWER LIFTING

Power is the rate at which work is done, or how quickly one form of energy is changed to another. A man is more powerful than a child. He can lift a load quickly, but children can only lift it slowly. The unit of power is the watt, which equals 1 joule per second.

POTENTIAL ENERGY

Potential energy is the energy that a body has because of its position or because of the state it is in. For example, a jack-in-the-box has potential energy when it is squashed into its box. Types of potential energy are: gravitational potential energy (of a raised object), elastic potential energy (of a stretched or squashed elastic material), electrical potential energy (of an object near an electric charge), and magnetic potential energy (of a piece of iron near a magnet).

KINETIC ENERGY

Windmills were originally used to drive a machine such as a millstone. When the sails turned, they moved the millstone, converting the kinetic energy of the wind into the movement of the millstone. The amount of kinetic energy that a moving object has increases with the mass and speed of the object. If the mass of a moving object is doubled, its kinetic energy is doubled. If the speed doubles, the kinetic energy increases four times.

A jack-in-the-box has elastic potential energy when it is squeezed into its box.

When the lid of the box is lifted, the jack-in-the-box has kinetic energy as it jumps up.

Find out more

ENERGY SOURCES P. 134
HEAT P. 140
ENGINES P. 143
ELECTRICITY SUPPLY P. 160
SOUND AND LIGHT P. 177
FACT FINDER P. 408

ENERGY SOURCES

THE AMOUNT OF ENERGY that the Earth gets from the Sun is huge. Sunshine falling on the roads in the United States in one year contains twice as much energy as all the coal and oil used in a year worldwide. The Sun's energy shows in different ways—as wind and waves, for example, as well as direct solar energy. The only forms of energy that do not come originally from the Sun are nuclear energy, the chemical energy in electric batteries, tidal energy, and geothermal energy. Some energy sources are known as renewable energy, since they will not run out. Other energy sources, such as oil and coal, are nonrenewable—they will eventually run out.

Solar panel

Photovoltaic cell

Silicon doped (made impure) with phosphorus, which produces free electrons.

Silicon doped with boron, which makes "holes" where electrons are missing.

When sunlight falls on the cell, electrons are driven from one layer to the other, creating an electric current.

BIOMASS ENERGY
Energy derived from plants, such as burning wood, is called biomass energy. Almost half the world's population uses some form of biomass energy for cooking, heating, and lighting. This man in India is using biogas for cooking. This gas is a mixture of methane and carbon dioxide produced from rotting waste or animal droppings.

SUNLIGHT INTO ENERGY
The Sun is an important nonpolluting and renewable energy source. The Sun's energy can be converted into electricity inside photovoltaic (solar) cells. Photovoltaic cells are found in solar-powered calculators, radio beacons and telephone links in remote areas, space satellites, and navigation buoys on the oceans.

A wind turbine usually has a propeller-type rotor mounted on a tall tower.

WIND POWER
Windmills have been used to grind corn and pump water since ancient times. Today, wind turbines are designed to generate electricity. A wind farm at San Gorgonia Pass in California has 4,000 windmills supplying electricity to the nearby Coachella Valley. The world's largest wind generator is in Germany. The wind turbine has blades 202 ft (61.5 m) long on top of a tower 400 ft (120 m) high.

Water from a reservoir falls down to a turbine.

WATER POWER
About one-fifth of the world's energy comes from hydroelectricity. In a hydroelectric power plant, the energy of falling water is used to drive a turbine, which in turn drives an electricity generator. Hydroelectric programs can generate large amounts of power. The Three Gorges plant on the Yangtze River in China has 26 turbines and a potential output of 18.2 million watts (as much as 16 atomic power plants).

Electricity generator

Turbine

TIDAL POWER
The world's first large tidal power plant was built across the estuary at La Rance in Brittany, France. It can produce 240 million watts of power—enough for a city of 300,000 people. As the tide falls, water is kept at high tide level inside the barrage. When the difference in water levels is about 10 ft (3 m), water is allowed to flow out of the barrage to the sea, flowing through 24 huge turbines that drive electricity generators. As the tide rises again, water is allowed to flow through the barrage to fill the estuary, until it is high tide and the process begins again.

A road runs along the top to allow traffic to cross the estuary.

Turbine

HOT ROCKS
Some rocks in the Earth's crust are as hot as 1,800°F (1,000°C), making the Earth a vast storehouse of heat energy, called geothermal energy. Some of this energy makes its way naturally to the surface as hot water springs or steam geysers. Sometimes water has to be pumped down into the Earth to be heated and then returned to the surface. About 20 countries use geothermal energy for heating or for generating electricity.

Cooling tower

Some heat escapes through the chimney.

INSIDE A POWER PLANT

A coal- or oil-fired power plant contains a furnace where the fuel is burned to heat water and make steam. The steam drives a turbine attached to an electricity generator. The electricity is sent to homes, offices, and factories through a network of cables called a grid. The steam is usually sent through three turbines, on at a time, until all its energy is extracted. The steam is turned back to water in the condenser.

Electricity generator

Coal is crushed in a mill and the powder is blown to the furnace, where it is burned.

Water from the condenser flows to the cooling towers where it is sprayed into the air to cool it.

Furnace

Condenser

Turbine

Transformer changes the voltage before it is supplied to homes and factories.

Gas reserves will last for about 60 years.

Coal reserves will last for about 250 years.

Oil reserves will last for about 40 years.

FOSSIL FUELS

Coal, natural gas, and oil are called fossil fuels because they are the remains of long-dead plants and animals. They are convenient, power-packed fuels, but when they are burned, they release carbon dioxide into the atmosphere, contributing to global warming. They are also limited and are being used up quickly. At the present rate of consumption, the world's total reserves of fossil fuels will run out in about 250 years.

ENERGY SOURCES

c. 100 Romans use coal as fuel.

c. 650 Windmills in use in Persia.

1859 First oil well drilled in Pennsylvania.

1880 First electricity generating plant built in London, England

1891 First hydroelectric power demonstrated, in Germany.

1951 First nuclear electricity generated, in United States.

1960 First solar thermal power plant built, in Turkmenistan, former Soviet Union.

1968 First tidal power plant opened in France.

ENERGY IN THE HOME

In one year, an average house uses five times the energy used by all the runners in the New York or London marathon. The main source of energy in homes is electricity, but coal, oil, gas, and wood are also used. A modern home may heat water with a solar heater—a glass-fronted box with black-painted pipes inside. Black absorbs the Sun's heat so that water flowing through the pipes is heated up.

NUCLEAR ENERGY

Neutron

Nucleus of
Uranium-235
atom

Neutron

Energy
expelled

Neutron

THE ATOM contains a huge amount of
energy—nuclear energy. This is due to the
strong forces that exist between particles in
the nucleus of an atom. Nuclear reactions
happen naturally: they power the Sun.
Humans have tried to harness nuclear energy,
but have managed only to obtain it from
certain atoms, such as those of uranium,
plutonium, and deuterium (a type of
hydrogen). Just over 2 pounds (1 kg)
of deuterium can produce as much energy
as 6.6 million lb (3 million kg) of coal.
There are two basic processes for releasing
nuclear energy: nuclear fission, when the
nucleus of an atom splits, and nuclear
fusion, when the nuclei of two or more
atoms fuse, or join together.

RADIATION
These workers are preparing to
replace a fuel rod in the reactor core.
The core is under 10.5 m (35 ft) of
water to protect the workers from
the radiation produced. The blue
glow is due to the fact that energetic
charged particles travel faster through
water than light.

FISSION

Normally, nothing can
penetrate an atom's nucleus
because it is surrounded by
circling electrons. But a
high-speed neutron can
blast through to be
absorbed by the nucleus.
If the nucleus is unstable,
it will split into two parts.
This is nuclear fission.
Two or three neutrons are
produced, which can go on
to blast more nuclei, setting
up a chain reaction.

Pellet of
uranium or
uranium
dioxide

Fuel rods
are made of
several pellets

The fuel rods are
embedded in a
material known as a
moderator, which
slows down the
neutrons produced.

The core is
surrounded by a
thick concrete
shield to absorb
radiation.

The heated fluid
is used to
produce steam.

NUCLEAR REACTOR

A nuclear reactor has a
core containing rods of
uranium (fuel rods). Among these
are boron rods (control rods)
which can absorb neutrons and
control the rate of reaction. As
nuclear fission occurs, heat is
produced that is used to convert
water into steam. The steam is used
to generate electricity.

In the reactor
core, there are
about 90,000
fuel rods.

A fluid circulates
through the reactor
core to carry away
the heat produced
by nuclear fission.

The steam is piped to
turbines that are linked
to electricity generators.

MASS INTO ENERGY

When a nuclear reaction
occurs, the mass of the
products is less than the
starting mass. Some
mass has vanished.
Albert Einstein showed
that this disappearing mass is
converted to energy. When a
mass, m, disappears, energy, E, is
released. $E=mc^2$, where c is the speed of light. Since c is a
very large number, a tiny loss of mass produces a huge
amount of energy. Just over 2 lb (1 kg) of matter could
produce as much energy as a major earthquake, which can
cause great damage, as shown here in Mexico City in 1985.

NUCLEAR WASTE
Up to 97 percent of the fuel in a nuclear
reactor can be recycled into fresh fuel and reused.
However, the remaining 3 percent is highly
radioactive and therefore dangerous.
Nuclear waste remains radioactive
even after 25,000 years, so must
be disposed of carefully. It can
be stored as a concentrated
liquid in stainless-steel
tanks that are surrounded
in concrete. The most
dangerous nuclear
waste can be turned
into glass blocks and
stored in deep
underground mines.

RADIOACTIVE

NUCLEAR WEAPONS

An atomic bomb uses uncontrolled nuclear fission. If a certain amount of uranium-235 or plutonium-239 is brought together, it will explode. A hydrogen bomb uses nuclear fusion. It is an atomic bomb surrounded by deuterium. When the atomic bomb explodes, the high temperature produced makes the deuterium nuclei fuse. This photo shows the city of Hiroshima in Japan after an atomic bomb was dropped on it in 1945.

Heavy hydrogen (Deuterium) nucleus

Hydrogen nuclei fuse

Neutron

Heavy hydrogen (Tritium) nucleus

Helium nucleus formed

Energy given off

Neutron expelled

FUSION

All the stars, including the Sun, gain their energy from nuclear fusion. This is when two or more nuclei stick, or fuse together. In the Sun, for example, hydrogen nuclei are fusing to form helium nuclei. In the process, some mass is lost and converted to energy.

HARNESSING FUSION

As yet, fusion is not a practical way to obtain energy on Earth. Most fusion research uses a machine called a tokamak. This holds a doughnut-shaped vessel containing the gas to be fused, called a plasma. The plasma must be heated to a temperature of millions of degrees before fusion occurs. No container could cope with such heat, so magnetic fields are used to keep the hot plasma away from the vessel walls.

The circular vessel containing the plasma to be fused is called the torus.

A powerful electric current flows through the plasma. This heats the plasma and produces a magnetic field that compresses the plasma and contains it in the center of the torus. The high temperature and pressure of the plasma causes fusion.

FUSION ACCELERATOR

Other efforts to produce controlled nuclear fusion are carried out in machines called particle beam accelerators. This powerful one is in Albuquerque, New Mexico. It directs a 100-trillion-watt pulse of electricity toward a pea-sized pellet of deuterium gas. The accelerator sits in a tank of water. As the beam is fired, electric sparks cross the surface. The gas is heated to millions of degrees for a few billionths of a second—not enough to start a fusion reaction, but research is continuing.

NUCLEAR ENERGY

1905 German physicist Albert Einstein shows that mass can be converted into energy.

1919 New Zealander Ernest Rutherford changes the nucleus of a nitrogen atom into an oxygen nucleus.

1939 German scientists Otto Hahn and Fritz Strassman announce the discovery of nuclear fission.

1942 First nuclear reactor built by Italian Enrico Fermi in a squash court at the University of Chicago.

1951 First nuclear electricity made by an experimental breeder reactor in Idaho.

1956 The first commercial nuclear power plant starts up in Calder Hall, England.

1986 An explosion in a reactor at Chernobyl, USSR (now Ukraine), releases clouds of radioactive material, which spread as far as Sweden.

1991 First controlled nuclear fusion in JET (Joint European Torus), in Oxford, England.

LISE MEITNER

Austrian-born Lise Meitner (1878–1968) worked in Berlin from 1907 with a German physicist, Otto Hahn. In 1938, she had to flee from the Nazis and went to Sweden. A few months later, Hahn told her of some puzzling results he and another German, Fritz Strassman, had found in an experiment. Meitner realized that Hahn had split the uranium nucleus. This was the discovery of nuclear fission. When Hahn reported the discovery, he gave little credit to Meitner for her insight. In 1944, Hahn was given the Nobel Prize for the discovery but Meitner did not share the prize she rightly deserved.

ENERGY CONVERSION

WHEN LIGHTNING STRIKES, electrical energy is spectacularly converted into light, sound, and heat energy. This is just one example of energy changing from one form to another. Energy conversions are continually happening around us. When you press a light switch, electrical energy is converted into light and heat energy. A glowworm converts the chemical energy from its food into light energy and, if it needs to move, into movement energy. Energy is converted whenever work is done. When you lift something heavy, chemical energy in your muscles is converted into the potential energy of the raised object. The more work that is done, the more energy that is converted.

Inside the Sun, nuclear energy is converted to heat and light energy.

The green leaves of this carrot convert light energy from the Sun into the chemical energy of sugar by a process called photosynthesis.

If you eat a carrot, the chemical energy it contains is transferred to your body. It is used for activities, such as breathing and moving. Winding up an alarm clock changes this chemical energy to elastic potential energy in the spring.

ENERGY CHANGES
A drawn bow has elastic potential energy. The bow is like a compressed spring. When the bow is released, the potential energy changes to kinetic energy of the moving arrow. When the arrow hits the target, we hear a "thud"; its kinetic energy has changed into sound energy, and a little heat energy. This Egyptian wall painting shows the pharaoh Rameses II.

The remainder of the rocket's chemical energy is released as light and sound energy as it explodes in the air.

In an alarm clock, the potential energy of the wound spring is converted to movement energy of its hands and sound energy of its ticks. The clock keeps working until the spring is unwound and has lost its potential energy.

ENERGY CHAIN

Did you realize that your alarm clock is really powered by the Sun? Energy is seldom changed directly from its starting form to its final form. It usually goes through a chain of energy conversions. The Sun's energy makes food grow. By eating this food, we create a store of chemical energy inside us. Among other things, we can use this energy to wind up an alarm clock. This gives the clock potential energy, which it is able to change into movement and sound energy.

When the rocket is shooting upward, it has kinetic and potential energy, as well as chemical energy. As it gets higher, the rocket gains more potential energy. But its store of chemical energy gets lower as the fuel is burned.

When a firework rocket is on the ground, it has a large amount of chemical energy but no potential energy. When ignited, a stream of hot gas shoots downward and this pushes the rocket up.

EXPLOSIVE ENERGY
Explosives are very powerful stores of chemical energy. They need not contain any more energy than other substances, but they must be able to release it very quickly. Fireworks contain explosives. When a rocket firework, for example, is lit, it soars into the air and explodes in a colorful display. The chemical energy of the explosive has been converted into kinetic, heat, sound, and light energy.

LORD KELVIN
The British physicist William Thomson (1824–1907) was born in Belfast, Northern Ireland. He entered Glasgow University when he was just 10 years old and became a professor at the age of 22. He helped to found the new science of thermodynamics, establishing clear relationships between heat, work, and energy. He also invented the absolute temperature scale—the Kelvin scale—and made important discoveries about electricity and magnetism. His title became Lord Kelvin after he was honored by Queen Victoria.

Newton's cradle

If the end ball is lifted and dropped, it hits the line of balls.

Energy is gradually lost as sound and heat energy; each time the balls collide, there is a clicking noise. Eventually all the kinetic energy is converted to sound and heat, and the balls stop moving.

The energy is transferred to the ball at the other end. The ball will lift and then swing back and hit the line of balls.

CONSERVATION OF ENERGY

Energy can be neither created nor destroyed; it can only be converted into other forms. When energy is converted, some waste heat is always produced, but if we take this into account, the total amount of energy is unchanged. This is called the Principle of Conservation of Energy. The principle is illustrated by a toy called Newton's cradle. Little energy is lost as sound or heat, so the balls at each end will keep swinging for some time.

A perpetual motion machine proposed in 1834. The weight of the balls moving along the arms was supposed to keep the wheel turning.

PERPETUAL MOTION

Many people have tried to design machines that will go on working forever without an energy source—a perpetual motion machine. This is an impossible dream; all real machines need a continuous source of energy. Not only this, but they also always need more energy than they can give out.

USEFUL ENERGY

A steam train produces waste heat from its funnel. It would be hard to use this heat energy to power anything else. Waste heat is not useful energy; it is low-quality energy. Electricity, on the other hand, is useful; it is high-quality energy. Whenever energy changes form, some high-quality energy is lost. This means the amount of useful energy in the universe is always decreasing.

A conventional stove uses valuable energy to heat the saucepan.

A microwave oven does not waste energy in heating the plate; it just heats the food.

Dry-cell batteries, such as those used in a flashlight, waste only 10 percent of the energy they contain.

ENERGY EFFICIENCY

When we use a form of energy to do work, some of the energy does not go where we want it to go; it is wasted, usually as heat. For example, a lightbulb converts only about 5 percent of the energy that it consumes into light; the rest is converted into waste heat. The efficiency of the lightbulb is said to be 5 percent. No energy converter can ever be 100 percent efficient.

A lightbulb in an electric lamp wastes 95 percent of the energy it consumes.

SAVING ENERGY

We must conserve high-quality energy sources, such as electricity, coal, natural gas, and oil since they are in short supply. Using a microwave oven is one way of saving energy because a microwave oven uses less energy to cook food than a conventional oven. A well-insulated house needs less fuel to heat it, and a machine that is kept in good condition is able to work at its maximum efficiency.

Find out more

CHEMICAL REACTIONS p. 52
WORK AND ENERGY p. 132
ENERGY SOURCES p. 134
NUCLEAR ENERGY p. 136
HEAT p. 140
CURRENT ELECTRICITY p. 148
THUNDER AND LIGHTNING p. 257
FACT FINDER p. 408

HEAT

HOW HOT IS IT TODAY? To answer this question exactly, you need a thermometer, a device that measures temperature. All thermometers are marked with a scale using two fixed points: the temperature at which pure ice melts, and the temperature at which pure water boils, at normal atmospheric pressure. There are three temperature scales: Celsius, Fahrenheit, and the absolute or Kelvin scale. On the Celsius scale, the temperature of melting ice is 0°C, and the temperature of boiling water is 100°C. On the Fahrenheit scale, the temperature of melting ice is 32°F and boiling water is 212°F. The Kelvin scale starts at the lowest possible temperature theoretically achievable, called absolute zero. It has degrees the same size as the Celsius scale.

NATURAL THERMOMETERS
Crocuses are natural thermometers. The flowers open and close as the temperature rises and falls. They are very accurate, reacting to temperature differences of as little as 0.9°F (0.5°C).

HEAT AND TEMPERATURE

There is a difference between heat and temperature. Temperature is a measure of how fast the molecules in an object are moving. Heat is the energy that the object has because its molecules are moving. There is more heat in an iceberg than in a cup of boiling water, even though the water has a higher temperature. This is because the iceberg, although colder, is much larger.

MELTED ROCK
The lava that erupts from a volcano is molten rock. It is about 1,100°F (600°C). This volcano is on the island of Hawaii in the Pacific Ocean.

Anders Celsius

GABRIEL FAHRENHEIT AND ANDERS CELSIUS

The Fahrenheit thermometer was invented by Gabriel Daniel Fahrenheit (1686–1736). He was a German physicist who settled in Amsterdam, the Netherlands, where he worked as an instrument maker. Anders Celsius (1701–44) invented the Celsius scale. He realized the value of using a thermometer with 100 degrees between the freezing and boiling points of water. He was a professor of astronomy in Uppsala, Sweden. His favorite subject was the aurora borealis, a display of lights seen in the sky around the North Pole.

Meter to measure temperature

Electric filament changes color to match the color of the hot object.

MEASURING HIGH TEMPERATURES
A pyrometer is used to measure very high temperatures such as those of lava flowing from a volcano or the inside of a glassmaking furnace. The word "pyrometer" means fire measurer. Things glow a different color according to how hot they are. A pyrometer contains an electric filament and compares the color of an object with the color of the filament. An electric current heats the filament until its color matches the glowing object. The temperature is then found by measuring the electric current.

PRESS-ON THERMOMETER
Liquid crystals have molecules arranged in rows like those in a crystal, but they flow like a liquid. Some change color according to temperature and are used in strip thermometers to take the temperature of small children and babies. Heat rearranges the molecules, making it easy for light to pass through the liquid. A different color then glows according to the temperature of the child.

EFFECTS OF HEAT

Most substances expand (become larger) as they get hotter and contract (become smaller) as they cool. A 4,600 ft- (1,400 m-) long bridge can be 18 inches (half a meter) longer in summer than in winter. When a substance is heated, the energy it absorbs makes its molecules move faster and farther, and they take up more room. Changing the temperature enough makes a substance change from one state to another. If a solid is heated to a high enough temperature, it will melt; if a liquid is heated to a high enough temperature, it will boil and become a gas or vapor.

Cork seals the flask so that air cannot escape.

Water rises up the tube when the flask has been heated in a pair of hands.

Glass tube goes through the cork into the water.

Boiling water will not get any hotter even if it is still being heated.

HIDDEN HEAT

When a liquid changes to a vapor, it absorbs heat without increasing its temperature. The heat energy is used to change the liquid into vapor and is stored in the vapor. It is called latent (hidden) heat. When the vapor condenses into liquid, the latent heat is released, warming the surroundings. Latent heat is also absorbed when a solid melts, and released when the liquid freezes.

EXPANDING GASES

Gases expand about 1,000 times more than solids and 10 to 100 times more than liquids. If the temperature of a gas doubles, then its volume doubles. This flask was half-filled with cold water, sealed, and heated gently in a pair of hands. The air inside the flask expanded and pushed the water up the tube.

Wire firmly secured in a wooden block.

Candle flames heat the wire.

Pointer moves on the dial.

Knitting needle turns the pointer as the expanding wire makes it roll around.

Weight holds the wire down.

Iron

Brass

When the contact breaks, the heating is turned off.

As the strip heats up, the brass expands more than the iron, and the strip has to bend.

Temperature regulator

Electric current to heater

EXPANSION METER

This expansion experiment shows how a thick wire expands when heated. Candles heat the wire at one end, and as the wire expands it rolls a knitting needle, which turns a pointer across a dial.

UNEQUAL EXPANSION

Metals expand at different rates and this fact is used to make a thermostat work. A thermostat keeps temperature at a steady level. It contains a bimetallic strip—a strip made of two different metals, often brass and iron. In a heating thermostat, the bimetallic strip bends as it gets hotter and breaks an electrical contact when the room has reached the required temperature.

PAIN RELIEF

This athlete is being treated with a pain-relief spray. The spray contains a substance that evaporates (turns to vapor) very quickly. The latent heat needed for it to evaporate is taken from the athlete's hand. The hand cools and the pain is reduced. Sweating makes you cooler in the same way. As the sweat evaporates, it absorbs heat from your body.

AIR CONDITIONER

An air conditioner works by evaporation. A liquid called a refrigerant is allowed to evaporate to form a gas inside cooling pipes. The evaporating liquid absorbs heat from air inside the building. The gas is then compressed and turned back into a liquid. This process, which takes place outside the building, releases the heat absorbed from the air. The cool air then returns to the room.

Compressor

Cool air blown into the room

Heat released outside

Cooling pipes

Inside   *Outside*

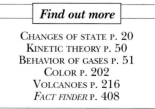

Find out more

CHANGES OF STATE p. 20
KINETIC THEORY p. 50
BEHAVIOR OF GASES p. 51
COLOR p. 202
VOLCANOES p. 216
FACT FINDER p. 408

HEAT TRANSFER

IF YOU STAND NEAR A FIRE, heat enters your body from your surroundings. If you are outside on a freezing day, heat escapes from your body into the cold air around you. Heat always travels from something hot to something cold, or from a hot part of something to a cold part. There are three ways that heat can travel: by convection, conduction, or radiation. Convection is how heat travels in moving currents through liquids and gases. Conduction is how heat travels through solids. When one part of a substance is heated, its molecules start to vibrate more violently. They knock against their neighbors and pass their energy on. Radiation is how heat travels through empty space by electromagnetic waves. This is how heat gets to the Earth from the Sun.

RADIATION
All objects emit heat radiation, also called infrared radiation. The hotter the object, the more radiation it emits. Infrared radiation travels at the same speed as light, but has a longer wavelength. Like light waves, infrared radiation is reflected by shiny surfaces and absorbed by dark surfaces. We cannot see infrared rays, but cameras with special film can take infrared photographs called thermographs. Different colors indicate different amounts of heat radiating out. The hottest part shows as white.

CONVECTION
When the land gets hot, it heats the air above it. The heated air rises because it expands and becomes less dense. Cooler air falls down to take its place. A continuous current of rising and falling air, called a convection current, is set up. Gliders and birds use convection currents called thermals to lift them up in the air.

RIGHT FOR THE CLIMATE
Many animals have shapes and colors to suit the climate in which they live. The fennec fox lives in the North African desert. During the day, the fox's pale fur does not absorb much heat radiation and its huge ears transfer heat to the air by convection. At night, when it is cold, the fox's fur traps air, which stops too much heat from escaping from its body by conduction.

Cavity wall filled with foam polystyrene

Fiberglass insulation in the roof and the attic

Air trapped in a space under the floorboards

Air trapped between two panes of glass in double-glazed window

Carpet on the floor

SAVING HEAT
It is easy for heat to escape from a building. Over one-third of the heat is lost through the walls, a quarter is lost through the roof, and the rest escapes through the floors and windows. To prevent these losses, buildings need to be well insulated.

Metal—a good conductor

Wood—a poor conductor

Marble—a good conductor

Plastic—a poor conductor

Poor conductors do not feel cold when you touch them because they do not take the heat from your hand quickly.

CONDUCTION
Different materials conduct heat by different amounts. Metals are the best conductors. Saucepans are made of metal so that they heat up quickly. Saucepan handles are made of wood or plastic which are poor conductors. Water is a poor conductor; cork and fiberglass are poor conductors because they are mainly air, and gases are the worst conductors of all.

Vacuum

VACUUM FLASK
The vacuum flask was invented by Scottish scientist James Dewar (1842–1923). It keeps hot drinks hot, or cold drinks cold, by stopping the transfer of heat. The flask consists of a glass bottle with double walls. A vacuum between the walls stops conduction and convection. Radiation is prevented by silvering the walls. The stopper is made of a good insulator such as cork or hollow plastic.

Find out more
HEAT P. 140
ELECTROMAGNETIC SPECTRUM P. 192
WINDS P. 254
FORMATION OF CLOUDS P. 262
DESERTS P. 390
FACT FINDER P. 408

ENGINES

Camshaft controls the opening and closing of valves.

Valves let fuel into the cylinder and exhaust out.

Belt drives a water pump.

Distributor feeds high-voltage electricity to the spark plugs.

Channels for cooling water

Clutch disconnects the engine when changing gear.

Crankshaft turns the wheels, via the clutch and gearbox. It is connected to the camshaft so that the valves open at the correct times.

Pistons and connecting rods drive the crankshaft.

THE ROCKET is the most powerful engine. It can lift a heavy spacecraft off the ground and send it into space. Aircraft, cars, boats, motorcycles, and many other machines are driven by a gas or diesel engine. Without engines, we would have to rely on our own strength and the strength of animals for transportation and industry. Every engine converts energy from some sort of fuel into movement. They work on the principle that a hot gas expands. Fuel is burned to heat gas and the expansion of the gas is harnessed to drive the machine. Some engines have pistons which move back and forth inside cylinders. They are called reciprocating engines. Other engines do not have pistons.

Fan belt drives a cooling fan.

Spark plug

1. Induction—Piston descends, sucking in fuel and air through the open inlet valve.

2. Compression—Piston ascends, compressing the fuel mixture. Both valves are closed.

3. Power—Spark plug ignites the mixture. The exploding fuel forces piston down.

4. Exhaust—Piston ascends, forcing the burned fuel out through the open exhaust valve.

Cylinder

Piston

Exhaust port

Transfer port

1. Piston rises, sucking fuel mixture into the lower part of the engine. The piston compresses the fuel already in the cylinder. A spark explodes the mixture when it is fully compressed.

2. Piston descends, pushing new fuel into the cylinder through the transfer port. The burned fuel is pushed out through the exhaust port.

INTERNAL COMBUSTION ENGINE
A car engine is called an internal combustion engine because the fuel is burned inside a cylinder ("combustion" meaning burning). Most cars have a four-stroke engine. They produce their power with four movements, or strokes, of the piston. Engines have between four and eight cylinders which move in sequence to produce a continuous output of power.

TWO-STROKE ENGINE
Motorcycles have two-stroke engines. These engines are small and powerful, but they are noisy. They have no valves. Instead, there are openings, called ports, in the side of the cylinder. The moving piston opens and closes the ports.

Water turned to steam in the boiler

High-pressure steam fed into the cylinder

Furnace

Cylinder

Piston

STEAM ENGINE
Because the fuel is burned outside the cylinder, in a furnace, a steam engine is called an external combustion engine. Hot gases produced by burning coal flow through a boiler and heat water, making steam. The steam is heated, until it is at high pressure and temperature, and fed to the cylinder. There it expands, forcing the piston along. In a locomotive, the moving piston turns the wheels.

GEORGE STEPHENSON
The first successsful steam locomotive was built by British engineer George Stephenson (1781–1848). He began his career caring for the engines and pumps in the mines near Newcastle, England. In 1825, he set up a locomotive factory where he designed and built the first locomotive to pull a passenger train, on the world's first public railroad between Darlington and Stockton. Stephenson's most famous locomotive was called the *Rocket*. In 1829, it won a competition, reaching a speed of 29 mph (46 km/h). It was then used on the Liverpool to Manchester line.

Continued on next page

ENGINE DEVELOPMENT

1712 Thomas Newcomen builds the first steam engine to use a cylinder and piston.

1765 James Watt builds a steam engine six times as powerful as the Newcomen engine.

1800 Richard Trevithick builds the first high-pressure steam engine.

1860 Etienne Lenoir designs the first internal combustion engine, using coal gas and air as fuel.

1877 Nikolaus Otto develops the four-stroke engine.

1883 Gottlieb Daimler builds the first gasoline engine.

1884 Charles Parsons builds the first steam turbine to generate electricity.

1926 Robert Goddard launches the first liquid-fuel-propelled rocket.

1930 Frank Whittle patents the jet engine.

Rocket speeds forward in reaction to the gases shooting out backward.

Liquid fuel

Oxidizer

Pump

Valves

Combustion chamber

ROCKET
The simplest type of engine is the rocket. It burns fuel in a combustion chamber. The hot gases produced expand and stream out from a nozzle at the bottom, thrusting the rocket upward at great speed. Some spacecraft are launched using solid-fuel booster rockets, which are like huge firework rockets. Other rockets use a liquid fuel, such as kerosene, which is burnt with a liquid called an oxidizer. The Space Shuttle has three liquid-fueled rocket engines. Together, they burn 98 tonnes of fuel in a minute.

Stationary blades are attached to the inner wall to direct the steam onto the blades of each wheel at exactly the right angle.

Steam in

The central blades, where the pressure is highest, are smaller than those at the ends.

Steam out

STEAM TURBINE
In its simplest form, a turbine is a wheel with blades mounted on an axle. It can be driven by gas, steam, or water. Steam turbines are used in power stations. Steam is driven at high pressure against the blades to turn the turbine that is connected to the electricity generator. Multistage turbines are most efficient, taking nearly all the energy from the steam.

Hot gases

Fans called compressors increase the pressure of the air and push it into the combustion chamber.

Air sucked in by spinning fan

Combustion chamber

Hot air and exhaust stream out over a turbine.

Some air bypasses the main part of the engine.

JET ENGINE
Most modern high-speed aircraft are powered by a jet engine. Fans at the front of a jet engine spin and suck air into the engine. Inside, more fans compress the air and force it at high pressure into the combustion chamber. Here, burning liquid fuel heats the air, which expands and rushes toward the tail of the engine. As the air streams out, it spins a turbine that drives the fans at the front. In a turbofan engine, shown here, some air flows through a duct around the main part of the engine. This means there is more air flowing through, giving the engine extra thrust.

JET PROPULSION
This toy car uses jet propulsion to speed along the floor. A balloon is attached to the car and filled with air. When a valve is opened, air rushes out backward through the neck of the balloon, thrusting the car forward.

FRANK WHITTLE
English test pilot and engineer Frank Whittle (1907–96) invented the jet engine in 1929. He tried to persuade the British Air Ministry that his engine would work, but his ideas were rejected. He set up his own company to make the new engine and, by 1937, the first engine had been built and tested on the ground. In 1941, an experimental aircraft with a Whittle engine made its first flight.

ELECTRICITY AND MAGNETISM

ALMOST ANYWHERE YOU GO, you will find electricity at work, and often magnetism too. Electricity and magnetism have completely changed our lives. Generators use magnetism to produce electricity from motion, so that light and heat are available at the flick of a switch. Electric motors use magnetism to change electricity into motion, so that machines can do tedious work for us, such as washing clothes. Other motorized machines, such as electric drills, help us to perform tasks quickly and with little effort. Electronics (the use of components, or parts, for controlling electricity in various ways) allows us to use electricity and magnetism in many ways, as in radio, radar, and computers.

ELECTRONICS THAT CARE
People who are very sick often need constant attention in hospitals. Instead of a nurse sitting at the bedside, electronic equipment monitors (constantly checks) their condition. If, for example, a patient's breathing or heartbeat changes, the equipment sounds an alarm to tell nurses and doctors that they are needed.

VERSATILE ENERGY
Electricity is easily generated, transmitted to where it is needed, and converted into other forms of energy. In an office, for example, a fan changes electricity into motion, and a bulb changes electricity into light. A telephone changes electricity into sounds, and also changes sounds into electricity. And a computer changes a steady supply of electricity into pulses to perform its tasks.

Since electric lightbulbs were first used in the late 1800s, they have become much more reliable and efficient.

Electricity helps to make our surroundings more comfortable. The motor in an electric fan makes the blades turn around to send out a stream of air.

LODESTONE
Found in the Earth, lodestone is a mineral that is naturally magnetized. It is a form of the mineral magnetite. Iron filings near it become magnetized and stick to it. Some early sailors used a piece of lodestone, suspended from a string, as a magnetic compass.

A modern telephone does more than let us talk to people. Its electronic memory can store different numbers so that we can call them by pressing a single button.

Until the mid-1970s, most people had never seen a computer. Now computers are almost everywhere. The principles of computing were set out more than 150 years ago, but electronic computers could only be made for everyone to buy when the complex circuits could be made small enough and cheap enough.

MODERN MAGNETS
Now that the nature of magnetism is understood, powerful magnets of various shapes can be made from steel. The best magnets are made from steel alloys (metal mixtures) specially designed to keep their magnetism.

Today's cheap pocket calculator would have amazed scientists in the early 1950s. Then, a whole room full of valves and other bulky components would have been necessary to make a calculator.

ANCIENT ELECTRICITY
Around 600 BCE, an Ancient Greek philosopher (thinker) called Thales of Miletus found that when he rubbed a piece of amber with a cloth, feathers, and other light objects stuck to it. We now know that the amber had become electrically charged by friction. The word "electricity" comes from the Greek for amber—elektron.

Steel pins can be temporarily magnetized, which allows them to be picked up with a magnet.

"ELECTRICS" AND "NONELECTRICS"
William Gilbert (1544–1603) did outstanding work in magnetism and electricity. He showed that the Earth must be like a magnet to affect compasses. He recognized the difference between electrical insulators and conductors, and called them "electrics" and "nonelectrics."

STATIC ELECTRICITY

A balloon can stick to a sweater because rubbing the two together gives each one an opposite charge.

THE CRACKLING NOISE you sometimes hear when you pull your sweater off over your head happens because of static electricity. If it's dark, you can see flashes of light as well. Static electricity is electricity that doesn't move. The crackles and flashes are the static electricity suddenly flowing away; this is discharging. You sometimes get an electric shock from touching a doorknob, because the static electricity that builds up in your body suddenly flows from your hand to the doorknob. Lightning is static electricity suddenly discharging between clouds or between clouds and the ground. Static electricity builds up with friction, when two different materials rub together.

ELECTROSTATIC INDUCTION

You can use a plastic spoon to make a stream of water from the faucet flow sideways by rubbing the spoon on your clothes. Negative charges on the spoon repel negative charges in the water to the far side and attract positive charges in the near side. The spoon induces these charged regions in the water, so the effect is called electrostatic induction.

The charges were built up on the spoon by friction.

CHARGING BY FRICTION

All objects are made of atoms. Each atom has equal numbers of electrons and protons. Electrons have a negative charge; protons have a positive charge. These charges balance each other exactly to make objects neutral (uncharged). But friction, like rubbing a balloon on your sweater, makes electrons rub off from your sweater onto the balloon. This charges the balloon with static electricity. It now has more electrons than protons, so it is negatively charged. And your sweater, with more protons than electrons, is positively charged.

These two balloons have been charged by being rubbed on a sweater.

REPULSION

Two charged balloons hang side by side on threads attached to the same point. They repel each other because they are both negatively charged. If they were both neutral, they would hang next to each other.

ATTRACTION

A balloon that has been charged by friction will attract small pieces of paper. Like charges repel each other, so the negative charges on the balloon force away the negative charges in the paper. The parts of the paper closest to the balloon become positively charged. They stick to the negatively charged balloon because opposite charges attract.

A comb, negatively charged by passing it through hair, repels negative charges to the leaves, making them deflect (alter their direction).

ELECTROSCOPE

The gold-leaf electroscope is an instrument that can show whether or not an object is charged. If you bring a charged object near the metal plate at the top, the gold leaves are both given the same charge by induction. Since like charges repel each other, the hinged leaves spread apart. Gold leaves are extremely thin and light. They are used to make the electroscope very sensitive.

Gold leaves

1. Toner is attracted to invisible charges on the drum.

2. Toner image transfers to charged paper.

3. Heated rollers bond toner image to paper.

PHOTOCOPIER

Photocopiers work using static electricity. A bright light shines an image of the original onto the drum inside the machine, making invisible positive charges. These attract particles of fine black powder, the toner, producing a visible image on the drum. The toner is then transferred to electrically charged paper as it passes round the drum. Heated rollers melt the toner, so that it sticks to the paper and forms a permanent image.

GIANT SPARKS

A fork of lightning flashing across the sky is a giant spark leaping between the ground and a cloud. In addition to giving out a very bright light, lightning is very hot. The air around it heats up and therefore expands so quickly that it explodes, causing thunder.

CHARGES
WITHIN A CLOUD

High in the air, in the clouds, swirling ice particles become charged with static electricity. The top of the cloud becomes positively charged, and the bottom of the cloud becomes negatively charged. Sometimes this electricity discharges as a flash of lightning inside the cloud to balance out the charges once more.

The lighter particles with positive charges are swept upward.

The larger, negatively charged particles cluster at the bottom of a cloud.

The top of the lightning conductor is pointed, and the lower end is connected by wire to the ground.

BENJAMIN FRANKLIN

American statesman, author, printer, and inventor Benjamin Franklin (1706–90) showed that lightning is caused by electricity by carrying out a very dangerous experiment. In 1752, he flew a kite in a thunderstorm. Electricity passed down the damp string to a key at the other end. When he put a finger near the key, a spark jumped between them. Franklin concluded that electricity in clouds caused the spark and that lightning is a kind of spark too. In 1753, he announced his invention of the lightning conductor.

The negative charge on the underside of a cloud induces a positive charge on the surface of the ground below.

Brass rod connected to chain, which contacts the inner foil.

Rubber stopper

Glass jar

Inner foil

Outer foil

HOW LIGHTNING STRIKES

If the charges in the cloud are strong enough, they force a path to the ground through the air and discharge as a lightning flash. Tall buildings, trees, and people on open ground are prime targets for lightning because they provide a convenient path for the discharge.

LIGHTNING CONDUCTOR

Most tall buildings have a metal rod called a lightning conductor on the roof. A wire connects the rod to the ground. The negative charges on the underside of the cloud attract positive charges from the ground. A stream of these positive charges flows up to the cloud, where they cancel out some of the negative charges. This may prevent lightning from striking, but if lightning does strike, the electricity flows harmlessly through the rod and wire.

Insulator

Metal foil plates

Connecting wires are welded to the plates.

CAPACITORS

Devices called capacitors are used to store an electric charge in electronic equipment such as televisions and computers. For example, electricity supplied as brief pulses is stored in a capacitor so that a steady current can be given out from it. Inside some capacitors, metal foil plates are separated by thin plastic, all rolled up and sealed.

LEYDEN JAR

Early experimenters sometimes stored electricity in a device called a Leyden jar. It was named after the Dutch city where the jar was first used, in 1745. One form consists of a glass jar with a coating of tin foil inside and outside. A metal rod connects to the inner foil. An electric charge can be stored on the tin foil plates. This Leyden jar was an early form of capacitor.

Find out more

CURRENT ELECTRICITY

ALMOST EVERYWHERE WE GO we can see current electricity at work. Bulbs change electricity into light, electric heaters change electricity into heat, and electric motors change electricity into motion. Electricity is a form of energy, and it has so many uses because it is easily changed into other forms of energy. Electricity is also very easy to use because it can flow along wires to wherever we need it. We call this flow an electric current. The flow is measured in units called amperes or amps. Most electric currents consist of a stream of electrons, but some currents consist of other kinds of charged particles, called ions.

Lights convert electricity into light.

The video screen converts electric signals received from the cameras into pictures.

A microphone converts sounds into electric signals and sends them to the amplifiers.

Speakers convert electric signals received from the amplifiers back into sound.

The pickup of the electric guitar changes string vibrations into electric signals and sends them to the amplifier.

The TV camera converts pictures into electric signals.

ELECTRICITY IN ACTION
At a rock concert, electrical equipment produces spectacular lighting effects and loud sounds. People a long way from the stage can watch the musicians on the huge screens around the stadium.

FREE ELECTRONS
Electricity can flow through a metal, such as copper, because the metal contains electrons that are free to move from one atom to another.

ROUND AND ROUND
Using marbles, you can demonstrate how an electric current flows. If you push a circle of touching marbles, they all move at once. The one at the other end moves as soon as you touch the first marble. A battery forces electrons along wires in a similar way to make an electric current flow.

CONDUCTORS AND INSULATORS
Copper wires in electrical cables are called conductors since they conduct electric current, or allow it to pass through. Around the wires is plastic, which does not conduct electricity, as it has no free electrons. It is called an insulator. It prevents electricity from flowing where it is not wanted.

In an insulator, all the electrons stay with their own atoms, so electricity cannot flow through it.

Positive terminal (+)

Negative terminal (−)

Conventional current

Electron flow

The bare overhead cables are supported using insulators.

The cables and the arms conduct electricity.

ELECTRON FLOW
People used to think electricity flowed around a circuit from a battery's positive terminal to its negative one. Many useful rules were figured out using this idea, so current is still shown like this. This is called conventional current. In fact, electrons flow from the negative terminal to the positive one.

OVERHEAD SUPPLIES
Some electric trains pick up electricity using arms that slide along cables above the track. These cables must be bare (uninsulated), so that the arms can make electrical contact with them. Current flows to the motor that drives the train. The overhead cables have to be supported using insulators. This prevents electricity from being wasted or dangerous. Conductors and insulators are used together to make electricity safe and efficient.

CHARLES AUGUSTIN COULOMB

Coulomb (1736–1806) was a French physicist, inventor, and engineer. His most important work involved friction, magnetism, and electricity. He devised sensitive instruments for measuring the forces between magnets and between electric charges. The unit for measuring an amount, or charge, of electricity is named after him. One coulomb (symbol C) is the amount of electricity that flows past any point when a current of one amp flows for one second.

A vacuum helps to keep the temperature down.

Liquid nitrogen runs around the three conductors.

Liquid nitrogen runs through the copper tube to keep the temperature of the wires at 77 K (-321°F, -196°C), the temperature at which the ceramic superconducts.

Paper insulation

These superconducting wires are made of a special ceramic covered in silver.

Outer coating and steel pipe protect all the wires inside.

SUPERCONDUCTING CABLES
A material that conducts electricity well has little resistance to the flow of current. In certain metals, such as tin and lead, and some ceramics, the resistance becomes almost zero when they are cooled to a very low temperature. In other words, they become superconductors (almost perfect conductors). Superconductors would be ideal as electricity supply cables, since they would waste hardly any power. But they need to be kept cool with liquid nitrogen or liquid helium, and this is expensive to install and run. Experiments are being done to find superconductors that work at higher temperatures.

ALEX MÜLLER
The main problem with superconductors is that they have to be kept at close to absolute zero. This is the lowest possible temperature, 0 K (-460°F, -273°C). But Swiss physicist Alex Müller (born 1927), helped by Georg Bednorz (born 1950), found that a copper oxide ceramic material containing barium and lanthanum can superconduct at 35 K (-396°F, -238°C). They won the Nobel Prize for Physics in 1987. By 1988, others had made a ceramic material superconduct at 123 K (-238°F, -150°C). But no one has yet made a superconductor that works at room temperature.

A crystal of pure silicon

Ions, which are positively charged, are attracted to the metal, which is negatively charged.

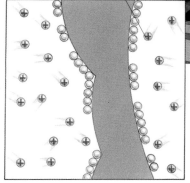

ELECTRICITY AND IONS
A current can flow through a solution not as electrons, but as charged particles called ions. Electroplating is a way of covering an object with a layer of metal using electricity. The object to be coated is connected to the negative side of the electricity supply, which makes it the negative electrode. It attracts positively charged ions (for example, silver, copper, or zinc ions) and therefore becomes coated (electroplated) with silver, copper, or zinc.

PURE SILICON
In pure silicon, there are four electrons for each of the silicon atoms. The charges of the electrons balance out four positive charges in each nucleus, so silicon is neutral.

Atom

P-TYPE SEMICONDUCTOR
Boron has only three electrons per atom. So if small amounts of boron are added to silicon, this leaves holes, which makes the material positive, and gives a p-type semiconductor.

N-TYPE SEMICONDUCTOR
Arsenic and phosphorus have five electrons per atom. So adding a trace of either to silicon introduces free electrons. This gives an n-type semiconductor.

SEMICONDUCTORS
Materials that do not conduct electricity very well are called semiconductors or semimetals. They are used to control current in electronic equipment. Silicon is the most common semiconductor. It is doped (made impure) with tiny amounts of arsenic, phosphorus, or boron to alter its electrical properties and make n-type (negative) or p-type (positive) semiconductors. In n-type semiconductors, electrons carry the current, and in p-type semiconductors holes carry the current. Semiconductors are used to make electronic devices such as silicon chips for computers.

ELECTROPLATING
These printed circuit boards have been dipped into a solution of copper sulfate. Electricity is run through the solution and the circuit boards. The boards form the anode in the circuit, so the copper ions are attracted to them and become attached to the board to make the copper tracks.

CELLS AND BATTERIES

HOW MANY BATTERY-OPERATED devices are there in your home? Radios, flashlights, toys, clocks, and watches are a few of the more common items that use batteries. Batteries come in many shapes and sizes. Some are little bigger than a pill, while others are too heavy for a person to lift. But most batteries have one thing in common: they store chemical energy and change it to electrical energy. A cell is the basic unit that produces electricity, and a battery has two or more cells. But we often use the word battery when talking about a single cell too, like a dry cell. The pill-sized battery in a watch is a cell. Cells act like pumps to force electrons to flow along conductors.

Actual size

MERCURY OXIDE CELL
Many electronic watches run on a single mercury oxide cell. This type provides a steady 1.35-volt supply over a long period.

INSIDE A CELL
A typical cell has three main parts. There is a negative electrode, a positive electrode, and between these is a chemical, or a mixture of chemicals, called the electrolyte. This is a moist paste or a liquid that conducts electricity because the chemicals in it split into charged groups of atoms called ions. Chemical reactions in the cell cause electrons to flow out of the negative electrode, through the device being powered and back via the positive electrode.

Actual size

NICKEL CADMIUM CELL
Unlike common cells, nickel cadmium cells can be recharged when they have run down. This makes running a battery-powered toy much cheaper.

Positive terminal (+)

Electrons flow from the negative terminal up to the positive terminal.

Electricity flows through the bulb and makes it glow.

Zinc casing, which acts as the negative electrode.

Carbon rod, which acts as the positive electrode.

Powdered carbon and manganese (IV) oxide

Ammonium chloride paste is the electrolyte.

Negative terminal (−)

Actual size

INSIDE A DRY CELL
The most common kind of cell is called a dry cell. It works like the cell invented by French engineer Georges Leclanché in 1865. His cell had a liquid electrolyte, but in the modern version the electrolyte is a moist paste. The electrolyte is the ammonium chloride paste. The powdered carbon and manganese (IV) oxide prevent hydrogen from forming on the carbon rod, which would stop the cell from working normally.

DRY CELLS
Ordinary dry cells are used in most flashlight batteries. Common dry cells use ammonium chloride as the electrolyte. Cells needed to supply heavier currents use zinc chloride. Alkaline cells, which last longer and can supply even heavier currents, use the alkali potassium hydroxide.

ELECTROMOTIVE FORCE
The electrical force of a cell or battery is called its electromotive force (e.m.f.). This force, which makes electrons flow around a circuit, is measured in units called volts (symbol V). Each kind of cell has a particular e.m.f. A dry cell, for example, has an e.m.f. of 1.5 volts.

A voltmeter connected across a cell will show its e.m.f. in volts.

ALESSANDRO VOLTA
An Italian count called Alessandro Volta (1745–1827) invented the first battery. Each cell had a copper disk and a zinc disk for the electrodes. Between them was a piece of cloth soaked in salt solution. This was the electrolyte. Each cell had a small e.m.f. But Volta found that a pile of these cells gave a large e.m.f. This, the first true battery, is known as Volta's pile, or a Voltaic pile. The volt, the unit for electromotive force, is named after him.

CELL SIZE

Most electric flashlights take two or more dry cells. As in Volta's pile, the cells are connected in series, or one after the other. This increases the total e.m.f. For example, two 1.5-volt cells in series have a total e.m.f. of 3 volts. A larger e.m.f. can force a larger current around a circuit. Large, powerful flashlights may take four or more cells. The size of a cell itself has no effect on its e.m.f. The chemicals in the cell determine its e.m.f. But large cells last longer than small cells of the same basic type.

These two flashlights use a 3-volt bulb because the batteries in each flashlight produce an e.m.f. of 3 volts.

Some small radios take a 9-volt dry battery. This contains six 1.5-volt dry cells, in a pile, like the cells in Volta's first battery.

LEMON CELL

You can make a simple cell by pushing objects made of two different metals into a lemon. The metals are the electrodes of the cell. The lemon juice, which is a weak acid, is the electrolyte. A piece of zinc and a piece of copper wire work well as electrodes. The e.m.f. produced lights up an LED (light-emitting diode).

Muscles used for swimming

Spinal cord

Muscles

The electric organs make up most of the fish's body.

Cross-section of an electric eel

ELECTRIC EEL

All animals have a bit of electricity in their nerves and muscles. Some animals, such as the electric eel *(Electrophorus electricus)* from South America, can produce a powerful blast of electricity, which they use to kill their prey. The organ that produces electricity takes up most of the eel's body, and is made of special muscles. Electricity is built up in the organ by the movement of ions, and then timed to discharge all at once to produce a voltage high enough to stun fish swimming nearby. In some electric eels this voltage can reach 650 volts—enough to stun a person.

SOLAR CELLS

Unlike ordinary cells, solar cells do not use chemical energy. Instead, they change light energy into electricity. Solar cells are also known as photovoltaic (light-voltage) cells. Small solar cells power some pocket calculators. In some places, such as Antarctica, where there is no electricity supply, big panels containing many solar cells are sometimes used instead. Most solar cells are devices called silicon diodes.

Light

When light hits the area where the two types of semiconductor join, electrons flow through the cell as an electric current.

N-type semiconductor

P-type semiconductor

ELECTRIC CAR

This car has a battery for use in towns and a gasoline engine to keep the battery powered up for longer journeys. Some prototype electric cars run on batteries only, but the batteries tend to be large and not last long enough. The batteries are recharged overnight on electrical outlets, making the most of a time when few people are using electricity. The great advantage of battery-powered cars is that they produce much less air pollution than those that use gas or diesel engines. So they are an important way of dealing with pollution problems.

Lead dioxide plate

Lead plate

Sulfuric acid

Electricity is produced in the reactions between the plates and the sulfuric acid.

CAR BATTERY

Most cars have a 12-volt battery containing six 2-volt lead-acid cells. Each cell consists of a lead plate, a lead dioxide plate, and sulfuric acid. Unlike dry cells, lead-acid cells can be recharged with electricity after use. So the battery does not have to be replaced unless it becomes faulty. Cells that cannot be recharged are called primary cells; cells that can be recharged are called secondary cells. The lead-acid battery powers the car's electrical system. It is recharged by a device in a car called the alternator.

Find out more

BONDING P. 28
TRANSITION METALS P. 36
SEMIMETALS P. 39
ELECTROLYSIS P. 67
ENERGY SOURCES P. 134
GENERATORS P. 159
LIGHT P. 190
MUSCLES P. 355
FACT FINDER P. 410

CIRCUITS

SWITCH ON A FLASHLIGHT: you have just completed a simple circuit. Electricity flows from the battery, through the switch and the bulb, and back to the battery. A circuit is the path electricity takes as it flows. All the parts of a simple circuit must conduct electricity and must be connected to each other. There are two main types of circuit: series and parallel. The flashlight is an example of a series circuit, where all the components are connected one after another. Parallel circuits have batteries or other components connected across one another. In both series and parallel circuits, voltages, resistances, or currents passing through can be calculated by using a formula called Ohm's law.

PRACTICAL CIRCUIT

In this circuit, three 4.5-volt batteries connected in series provide a 13.5-volt supply. If a fault causes too much current to flow, the fuse will blow and cut off the supply from the batteries. One of the multimeters is used as an ammeter to measure the current flowing through a single bulb. The other multimeter is used as a voltmeter to measure the voltage across another bulb.

The voltmeter is a moving coil meter with a high-value resistor in series. The resistor prevents the voltmeter from taking a large current and changing the circuit conditions.

The ammeter is a moving coil meter with a low-value resistor in parallel. The ammeter hardly reduces the current in the circuit when it is connected in series.

Three 4.5-volt batteries connected in series give an e.m.f. of 13.5 volts.

Fuse holder contains a cartridge fuse. A spare fuse is shown at the side. The metal in the fuse melts if a fault causes a large increase in the current flowing.

Multimeter switched to 250-milliamp range and connected in series with this branch of the circuit shows that the current flowing is 165 mA.

Switch controls current flow through entire circuit.

Bulb

Crocodile clip

Switch controls current flowing through this branch of the circuit.

Resistor causes voltage drop of 7.5 volts, so that remaining voltage (6 volts) is correct for the bulb in this part of the circuit.

Connection point

Multimeter switched to 10-volt range shows that the voltage across the bulb is 5 volts.

Bulb

Switch controls current flowing through this branch of the circuit.

Parallel-connected pairs of series-connected bulbs. All bulbs are identical, so the current flowing through each bulb is the same.

GEORG SIMON OHM

Ohm's law is named after the German physicist Georg Simon Ohm (1787–1854). The symbols used in Ohm's law are V for volts, R for resistance, measured in ohms (Ω), and I for the current, measured in amps. Ohm's law is used to calculate each of the above in electrical circuits. The form $V = IR$ is used to work out the voltage; $I = V/R$ is used to calculate the current; and $R = V/I$ the resistance.

CIRCUIT DIAGRAM

The components in a circuit are shown using a particular symbol for each one. This is so that the components and the connections can be shown in a very clear way. In this diagram, some of the wires have been rearranged to make the diagram simpler, but this would not affect the way the circuit works.

SERIES AND PARALLEL CIRCUITS

An electric current flows around a complete circuit without any gaps. This circuit may have sections or individual components connected in series or parallel. A circuit connected in series contains components attached to each other, like holding hands in a circle. Components connected in parallel are connected across each other.

The fairy lights are all connected to each other along half of the length of a wire. The rest of the wire doubles back to complete the circuit via the plug and supply.

PARALLEL CONNECTIONS
When resistors are connected in parallel, the total resistance is lowered. So the current that flows increases. Bumper cars at a fairground are connected in parallel. As the number of cars in use increases, their combined resistance decreases, and the total current taken from the supply increases. All the cars are independent, so if one fails, the others keep on working.

SERIES CONNECTIONS
When resistors are connected in series, the total resistance is increased. The current that flows when many resistors are connected across an electricity supply is lower than when just one of the resistors is used. Some sets of party lights have many bulbs connected in series. If one bulb fails, they all fail.

RESISTANCE
The greater the resistance in a circuit, the less current that flows. A variable resistor is able to control the amount of current that flows through a circuit. This lamp dimmer uses a variable resistor, made of graphite pencil lead, to alter the brightness of a bulb. A movable sliding contact alters the amount of carbon that the current has to flow through. Increasing the length of carbon in the circuit increases the resistance, reduces the current, and dims the bulb. Large variable resistors used in this way are called rheostats.

Battery

Bulb

Pencil lead

A large current flows when there is little resistance, so the bulb glows brightly.

Only a small current flows when the resistance is higher, so the bulb is dimmed.

You use the handset to vary the strength of the current that flows through the motor in the car via the metal strips in the track.

Connections to track

VOLUME CONTROL
The volume control in a typical radio is a variable resistor. It has a contact that slides over a carbon track when the control is adjusted. An electrical signal is applied across the resistor. By adjusting the setting, all or just a part of this signal can be used to make sound. This sort of variable resistor is called a potentiometer.

Carbon track *Contact*

Contact slides over resistor when trigger squeezed.

Resistor

Handheld speed control unit

ANDRE-MARIE AMPÈRE
The French mathematician and scientist André Ampère (1775–1836) carried out important experiments on electric currents. His work enabled people to measure the amount of electric current flowing through a circuit. In recognition of his contribution, the current is measured in units called amperes, or amps for short. One amp is a flow of about 6 quintillion (18 zeros) electrons per second.

SPEED CONTROL
Some electric model race car sets have a handheld unit to control the speed of each car. When you squeeze the trigger, a contact slides along a variable resistor that is connected in series with a power supply and one of the cars. As the resistance is lowered, the electric current through the car motor is increased, and so the car speeds up.

Find out more

CURRENT ELECTRICITY P. 148
ELECTROMAGNETISM P. 156
ELECTRICITY IN THE
HOME P. 161
FACT FINDER P. 410

MAGNETISM

A MAGNET IS NOT STICKY, and yet objects made of iron or steel cling to it. A magnet is surrounded by an invisible field of force (its magnetic field) that affects certain materials nearby. All magnets have a south pole and a north pole; north poles are always attracted to south poles. When you think of a magnet, you probably picture a permanent magnet (one that keeps its magnetic power). But an ordinary piece of iron becomes magnetized when it is near a magnet, gaining a north and south pole. The first use of magnetism was in the magnetic compass. Today, magnetism is used in many other ways.

Each individual iron filing has been turned into a tiny magnet. They align with the big magnet's field.

BAR MAGNET
Iron filings around a bar magnet always arrange themselves into the same kind of pattern. They make the magnetic field around the magnet show up. The lines show the direction in which a compass needle would point when placed near the magnet. The Earth's magnetic field has little effect on the compass, because it is so close to the bar magnet.

EARTH'S MAGNETISM
The region around any magnet, where its magnetism can be detected, is called a magnetic field. The Earth has a magnetic field, just as if a permanent bar magnet were inside it. The field is caused by the iron core at the center of the Earth.

MAGNETIC COMPASS
A pivoted magnet will line itself up in a north-south direction, because of the Earth's magnetic field. This effect is used in the magnetic compass. But navigators must allow for the fact that a compass will point to the Earth's magnetic north, which is not quite the same as the geographical north.

AURORA
The Earth's magnetic poles attract charged particles emitted by the Sun. When these particles strike gas particles in the atmosphere, colored light is radiated. In the Northern Hemisphere, the display of light, seen here in Alaska, is called aurora borealis, meaning "northern dawn." It is also called the northern lights.

POLES
Magnets show both attractive and repulsive forces. Every magnet has a north and a south pole, named according to which geographic pole of the Earth they are attracted toward; opposite poles attract and like poles repel. A north pole of a compass points north because the Northern Hemisphere has a south magnetic pole. Iron filings can reveal attractive and repulsive forces between magnets.

South pole North pole

North pole South pole

Iron filings reveal the repulsive forces between like poles.

South pole North pole *Iron filings reveal the attractive force between unlike poles.* South pole North pole

SOLAR PROMINENCE
Using special telescopes, astronomers can photograph glowing streams of hydrogen gas hundreds of thousands of miles above the Sun's surface. These are called prominences. The gas contains moving charged particles, which are affected by the Sun's powerful magnetism. The enormous prominence shown here is being held up by magnetic forces.

WHAT MAKES A MAGNET?

Inside a piece of steel are large numbers of tiny magnetized regions called domains. These are usually mixed up, so their effects cancel out, and the steel is not magnetized. If the domains point in the same direction, the steel becomes a magnet. The end that the north poles of the domains point toward becomes a north pole, and the other end is a south pole.

In unmagnetized steel, the magnetic domains are mixed up. Their north and south poles cancel each other out.

Stroking steel with a bar magnet magnetizes the steel. The magnet pulls the domains in the same direction.

Striking a magnet with a hammer shakes up the domains. Their like poles push apart and the steel loses its magnetism.

MAGNETIC CIRCUITS

A magnet gradually loses its magnetism if it is stored by itself. The domains may gradually shift position (especially if the magnet gets hot or is shaken), so they are no longer lined up. To stop this from happening, a piece of iron called a keeper is placed across the poles of a horseshoe magnet. Domains in the keeper are pulled into line by the magnet; domains in the magnet are kept in line by the keeper. This arrangement of domains is called a magnetic circuit; it prevents the magnet from losing its magnetism.

The domains in the magnet are lined up in relation to each other.

Keeper

REFRIGERATOR MAGNET

A refrigerator magnet can hold a piece of paper to a refrigerator door, showing that magnetism can act through a nonmagnetic solid. The fridge door acts like a keeper when a toy magnet clings to it. A magnetic circuit is set up between the refrigerator and the magnet; this preserves the magnetism of the magnet.

MAGNETIC TAPE

A cassette tape contains a plastic tape with a coating of iron oxide or chromium dioxide. Magnetic patterns can be applied to the tape by the head of a tape recorder. This changes electrical sound signals into a changing magnetic field, which induces patterns of magnetism on the tape. On replay, this magnetized tape causes or induces electrical signals in the head. These are reproduced as sound.

Recording arranges the domains into patterns. These match the patterns of the sound signal.

Information is stored on a disk as magnetic pulses that represent 1 (on) or 0 (off).

Sound signals

Sound signal

Twin-track electromagnetic record/playback head

Tape erased by high-frequency alternating magnetic field. The inaudible high-frequency signal replaces any previously recorded sound signals on the tape.

MAGNETIC DISKS

Computers store data on plastic disks that have a coating that can be magnetized. As in a tape recorder, the material to be recorded is in the form of electrical signals. The disk is spun, and a recording head passes over its surface. This head changes the electrical signals into magnetic pulses, leaving the information stored on the disk as magnetic patterns.

The hard disk drive unit contains a stack of hard (rigid) magnetic disks with their own read/write heads.

Electromagnetic read/write head, under computer control, moves to an unused part of the disk for writing (recording) information, or to a previously written section that is to be read (retrieved) from the disk.

BURGLAR ALARM

A permanent magnet is mounted on the door, and a reed switch is mounted on the frame. When the door is closed, the magnet makes the two upper magnetic iron strips cling together. When the door is opened, the magnet moves away and the center strip springs back. It touches the nonmagnetic contact below, completing the circuit and activating the alarm.

Reed switch with iron reed, unconnected iron contact (top), and nonmagnetic contact (bottom).

Permanent magnet on door makes iron reed stick to unconnected iron contact when door is closed.

Find out more

TRANSITION METALS P. 36
ELECTROMAGNETISM P. 156
ELECTRIC MOTORS P. 158
GENERATORS P. 159
STRUCTURE OF THE
EARTH P. 212
SUN P. 284
FACT FINDER P. 410

ELECTROMAGNETISM

MANY THINGS AROUND YOU, such as electric bells, motors, and loudspeakers, use electricity to make magnetism. An electric current will always produce a magnetic field. Magnetism made in this way is called electromagnetism; a magnet created in this way is called an electromagnet. Permanent magnets do not need electricity, so why would anyone want to use a magnet that works only when a current passes through it? In fact, electromagnets can do many things that permanent magnets cannot. You can switch an electromagnet on and off, so that it works only when you want it to. Also, changing the strength of the current alters the strength of the magnetism. This effect is used in loudspeakers.

Every electric current produces a magnetic field. If the current is moving away from you, the direction of the field is clockwise.

When a current flows through a coil (wire wound round and round), the magnetic field produced is like that of a bar magnet.

North   South

FIELD AROUND A WIRE
Around a wire carrying an electric current is a magnetic field. It can be detected using iron filings or a magnetic compass.

FIELD AROUND A COIL
The magnetic fields around the wires combine to form a stronger field. Like a bar magnet, the coil has a north pole and a south pole.

Before pressing the button to open an electromagnetic door latch, you first speak to the caller on an intercom to check who is there.

The latch is drawn into the coil when a current passes through it.

The amount of current passing through the electromagnets is automatically adjusted to keep the train hovering at the right height.

Attached to the sides of the track are rails containing electromagnets. The train's electromagnets pull toward them.

MAGNETIC LEVITATION
Magnetic levitation (maglev) trains give a very smooth and quiet ride. These do not run on rails but "float" above them by using electromagnetism. A current passes through electromagnets in the track and on the train. The magnetism produced lifts the train upward.

DOOR LATCH
You can unlatch your front door from elsewhere using an electromagnetic door latch. This has a coil called a solenoid. Pressing a switch inside the house makes a current flow through the solenoid. The magnetism produced pulls an iron latch into the solenoid so that a caller can open the door. A spring returns the latch afterward.

DOORBELL
One use of electromagnetism is in an electric doorbell. When a visitor rings, a current flows through the electromagnet. An iron bar linked to a hammer is attracted by the magnetic field, and the bell is struck. The circuit is now broken, the magnet is switched off, and the iron bar springs back. The whole process repeats rapidly to make a continuous ringing sound.

Bell

Hammer

Iron bar

Solenoid, which becomes magnetic when the current flows through.

HANS CHRISTIAN OERSTED
In 1820, Danish physics professor Hans Christian Oersted (1777–1851) was doing experiments with some electrical equipment. He saw that when he passed a strong electric current through a wire, a nearby compass needle deflected so that it no longer pointed to the north. Oersted realized the electric current was producing magnetism, and that this disturbed the needle. He had discovered electromagnetism.

A coil of fine, insulated copper wire wound on an iron nail

ELECTROMAGNET

Winding an electromagnet around an iron core increases the strength of the magnetic field produced. For example, if many turns of copper wire are wound around an iron nail, a strong electromagnet is made. The copper wire must be insulated so that the current cannot bypass any turns. When connected to a flashlight battery, this electromagnet will pick up small iron and steel objects.

While a battery is connected to the coil, the nail becomes magnetized and can pick up steel paper clips and thumbtacks.

VENDING MACHINE

In addition to electricity making magnetism, magnetism can make electricity too. This is used by vending machines to recognize coins. The coin passes through a magnetic field. This sets up an electric current in the coin, called an eddy current. This in turn produces a magnetic field, which slows the coin down. Genuine coins are slowed by just the right amount to fall into the next part of the machine. Other coins fall into a reject chute.

Coins inserted into machine

This electromagnet produces a high-frequency magnetic field.

Some coins of the wrong metal slow down too much and fall into reject chute.

Coins of correct metal slow just enough to pass over the reject chute into the next part of the coin-checking mechanism.

Nonmetallic objects are not slowed down, so they hit the upper plate and fall into reject chute.

This vending machine uses electromagnetism to recognize the right coins.

EYE SURGERY

A surgeon may use an electromagnet to remove a steel splinter from a person's eye. Once the electromagnet is in the right place, a current is passed through it. The powerful magnetism pulls the metal from the eye.

A doctor can remove a splinter much more cleanly using an electromagnet than he or she could by hand.

Coil of wire, through which a changing current flows

LOUDSPEAKER

A loudspeaker changes electrical signals into sound waves. The signals pass through a coil that is wound around the neck of a paper cone. This coil acts as an electromagnet. Nearby is a strong permanent magnet. When the current flows one way, the magnetic forces push the electromagnet and the cone outward. When the current flows the other way, the cone is pulled inward. The vibrations of the cone form sound waves.

The vibrations of the cone send sound signals through the air.

Powerful permanent magnet

CAR FUEL GAUGE

Electromagnetism can tell car drivers how much gasoline they have left. An electromagnet sits inside a permanent magnet. A current flows through the electromagnet, which then turns toward the permanent magnet. The amount it turns depends on the strength of the current. Inside the gasoline tank, a float moves a variable resistor to control the current flowing through the fuel meter. When the fuel level is high, a high current flows, causing a large deflection of the pointer.

METAL DETECTOR

In an airport, you may have to walk though a metal detecting arch on your way to the plane. Inside the arch are large coils of wire carrying an electric current. If a person goes through the arch with a gun concealed in their pocket, the metal in the gun alters the electromagnetism produced by the coils. This change can be detected and an alarm will sound.

Fuel tank

North pole

South pole

Permanent magnet

A float adjusts the setting of a variable resistor.

Battery

The current magnetizes the coil, causing the pointer to move.

Find out more
CURRENT ELECTRICITY P. 148
MAGNETISM P. 154
SOUND P. 178
FACT FINDER P. 410

ELECTRIC MOTORS

The thumb gives the direction of motion of the wire.

The first finger shows the direction of the magnetic field.

The second finger shows the direction of the conventional electric current.

LEFT-HAND RULE
You can work out which way a wire carrying a current will move through a magnetic field by using a rule called Fleming's left-hand rule. Hold your left hand as shown, with the two fingers and thumb all at right angles to each other.

MANY OF THE MACHINES that we use every day are powered by an electric motor. Such a motor changes electricity into movement. It makes use of the fact that a wire carrying a current produces a magnetic field and so will feel a force in another magnetic field. This force can produce movement. Electric motors are convenient sources of power because they are clean, fairly quiet, and very versatile. Washing machines, food mixers, video recorders, and record players have electric motors that make them work. Cars use electric motors to start up and to operate windshield wipers. But few cars run on electric motors because batteries of a reasonable size cannot store enough energy to power a modern car for long trips.

Magnetic field   Coil

South pole

Direction of rotation

Brush

Permanent magnet (north pole)

Commutator

Direction of current

Battery

1. Current flows through the coil, and the field of the permanent magnet forces the right side of the coil down and the left side up, in accordance with Fleming's left-hand rule.

2. The coil continues turning toward the vertical, and its inertia will carry it beyond this position.

JOSEPH HENRY
American physicist Joseph Henry (1797–1878) made many important discoveries about electromagnetism. He improved the design of electromagnets, and in 1829 he built the first useful electric motor. This used electromagnets to make a pivoted beam rock up and down.

SIMPLE MOTOR
In a simple electric motor, direct current is fed into a coil by carbon rods called brushes. The coil sits between the north and south poles of a permanent magnet. The magnetic fields of the coil and the permanent magnet interact, forcing the coil to turn. To keep up the rotation, the current is reversed every half-turn by an attachment called a commutator. The continuous turning motion of the coil drives the motor.

3. On passing the vertical, the commutator reverses the connections to the brushes and, therefore, also reverses the current in the coil. So the side that was moving up now moves down.

4. The coil continues spinning, and here its inertia is about to carry it past the vertical position again. The resultant reversal of current each half turn causes the coil to spin continuously.

Wheels of model locomotive pick up electricity supply from the rails.

MODEL TRAIN
An electric motor drives this model locomotive. It picks up electricity from the tracks through its wheels. Wires connect the wheels to the metal strips, which touch the motor's commutator. A control unit can vary the voltage supplied to the tracks. The higher the voltage, the stronger the magnetic field made by the coils in the motor. This means the motor turns faster, so the locomotive speeds up.

Low-voltage direct current supply to the rails

Metal strips (brushes) connect the electricity supply from the rails to the commutator of the motor.

The coils, wound on iron cores, act as electromagnets. They are connected to the commutator of the motor.

The commutator picks up electricity from the brushes. The commutator makes the coils carry on turning in the right direction.

MULTIPOLE MOTORS
In a simple motor, the turning force on a coil carrying a current is greatest when the windings are in line with the magnetic field, and weakest when the windings are at right angles to the field. Most electric motors have several coils to give a smoother turning force. Current is supplied to the coils by a commutator with many sections.

Permanent magnet produces the magnetic field in which the coils rotate.

> ### Find out more
> FORCES AND MOTION P. 120
> ENGINES P. 143
> CURRENT ELECTRICITY P. 148
> ELECTROMAGNETISM P. 156
> *FACT FINDER* P. 410

GENERATORS

EVERY DAY, WE USE ELECTRICITY made by powerful machines called generators. These work in the opposite way to electric motors; they turn movement into electricity. The principle they work on is called electromagnetic induction: electricity is produced in a wire when it moves in a magnetic field, or when a nearby magnetic field moves or changes in strength. Large generators are used in power stations to produce the mains supply that we take for granted in our homes. The movement is given by steam, moving water, or wind. Small generators called dynamos are used on bicycles to power the lights.

BICYCLE DYNAMO

One type of bicycle dynamo has a small wheel touching the rear tire of the bike. When the bike moves, the wheel turns; this movement makes a permanent magnet spin near a coil that is wound on an iron core. The wires in the coil experience a changing magnetic field from the spinning magnet, so electricity is generated in them. This effect is called electromagnetic induction— a voltage is induced in the coil.

The thumb shows the direction of motion.

The first finger shows the direction of the magnetic field.

The second finger gives the direction the conventional current will flow.

RIGHT-HAND RULE
A rule called Fleming's right-hand rule can show the direction in which current will flow in a wire when the wire moves in a magnetic field. Hold your right-hand thumb, first finger, and second finger at right-angles to one another.

Coil

Permanent magnet (south pole)

North pole

Commutator

DIRECT CURRENT GENERATOR
In this direct current generator, a coil of wire is turned between the poles of a permanent magnet. The direction of the current in the coil reverses every half-turn, because each side of the coil alternately passes up and down through the magnetic field. But the current that passes through the bulb flows in one direction only, because the commutator changes the connections every half turn.

ALTERNATOR
A generator that produces alternating current is called an alternator. In this simple version, a coil of wire is spun between the poles of a permanent magnet. This creates a current in the wire that is carried to the lamp by carbon rods called brushes. The current through the coil and bulb continually alternates (changes direction); the current through the bulb is alternating too.

Direct current is produced in pulses that flow in one direction only.

Alternating current is produced in waves that flow first in one direction, then in the opposite direction.

Coil

Magnet

Diaphragm

MOVING COIL MICROPHONE
A microphone generates electric signals from sounds. In a moving coil microphone, sound waves strike a diaphragm and vibrate a coil which is positioned between the poles of a permanent magnet. The voltage induced in the coil varies in strength and frequency in the same way as the sound waves.

MICHAEL FARADAY
Michael Faraday (1791–1867) was the son of an English blacksmith. He started work as a bookbinder. Inspired by the science books he bound, he took up physics and went on to make many discoveries. In 1821, he found that electricity could produce rotary motion; today's electric motors are based on this. In 1831, he showed that relative movement between a magnet and a coil of wire could induce electricity in the coil—an idea that gave birth to modern generators.

Find out more

NUCLEAR ENERGY P. 136
ENGINES P. 143
ELECTROMAGNETISM P. 156
MAKING AND HEARING
SOUND P. 182
ELECTROMAGNETIC
SPECTRUM P. 192

ELECTRICITY SUPPLY

HOW CAN THE WALL SOCKETS in your home supply you with electricity? Because they are connected to power plants. In a power plant, a turbine is driven by steam power (or water or wind power). The turbine then drives an electricity generator. So the generator converts kinetic energy (the movement of the turbine) into electrical energy. Most generators produce an alternating supply of electricity and are called alternators. Alternating current (AC) is more convenient than direct current (DC) because it can be changed to a higher or lower voltage by a device called a transformer. So the different voltages needed can be supplied to factories, offices, stores, and homes.

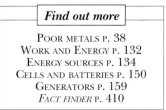

POWER PYLONS
The cheapest way to run cables across the country is to suspend them from towers called pylons. Insulators between the cables and the supports prevent the current from leaking away through the pylons. In towns, the cables are usually underground.

For heavy industry, the voltage is reduced from 132,000 volts to 33,000 volts.

At the power plant, steam turns a turbine linked to an electricity generator. The output of the generator is at 22,000 volts AC.

A step-up transformer changes the generator output of 22,000 volts to 400,000 volts for feeding the grid system.

The grid system carries the 400,000-volt supply around the country.

At a substation the voltage is reduced from 400,000 volts to 132,000 volts for local distribution.

For these electric railroad lines, 132,000 volts are reduced to 25,000 volts.

For use in homes, stores, and offices, the voltage is reduced from 11,000 volts to 240 volts.

The voltage is reduced from 11,000 volts to 415 volts for use by small workshops.

For light industries, the voltage is reduced from 33,000 volts to 11,000 volts.

POWER SUPPLY

Power plants send electricity through long cables to homes, offices, shops, railroads, farms, and factories. The same power can be sent at low voltage and high current, or at high voltage and low current. Resistance in the cables causes some power to be wasted as heat, but much less power is wasted at low current. So the electricity from a power plant is supplied at a high voltage, so that the current, and power, losses are reduced. Transformers reduce the voltage in stages to provide the supplies required by various consumers.

NIKOLA TESLA

In 1887, the American inventor Nikola Tesla (1856–1943) patented a generating and distribution system that transmitted alternating current. It won over his former boss Thomas Edison's direct current system. The two men were to have been awarded a joint Nobel Prize in 1912. But Tesla refused to have anything to do with Edison, and neither man received the prize.

Primary

Iron core

Secondary

A step-down transformer has fewer coils in the secondary coil.

Primary

Secondary

A step-up transformer has more coils in the secondary coil.

TRANSFORMERS
The high voltages from power cables need to be converted into levels that we can use in our homes. Transformers do this job. A simple transformer consists of two coils wound onto the same iron core. When an alternating voltage is applied to one coil (called the primary coil), it produces a changing magnetic field in the core. This induces an alternating voltage in the other coil (called the secondary coil).

Find out more

POOR METALS P. 38
WORK AND ENERGY P. 132
ENERGY SOURCES P. 134
CELLS AND BATTERIES P. 150
GENERATORS P. 159
FACT FINDER P. 410

ELECTRICITY IN THE HOME

WITH ELECTRICITY READILY AVAILABLE at the flick of a switch, it is easy to forget how much we depend on it. The electricity supply runs our homes. This electricity has traveled from far-away power plants. When there is a power failure, we realize how many devices in the home depend on this supply. The lights go out, and suddenly you have to search for candles. The television no longer works— you have to listen to a battery-operated radio instead. Electric heaters, stoves, dishwashers, washing machines, dryers, and many other appliances can no longer be used.

LIGHTBULB

Most electric lightbulbs have a thin tungsten wire called a filament, mounted in a sealed glass bulb. When a current flows through, the filament glows white hot. The wire takes some time to burn out because most of the oxygen (needed for burning) has been removed from the bulb.

DOMESTIC CIRCUITS

The electricity supply coming into our homes first passes through central fuses. It then reaches a meter that measures how much electricity we use. A consumer unit is connected to the other side of the meter. This contains fuses or circuit breakers to protect the house circuits.

All the ceiling lights are run from a circuit that runs between the ceiling fixtures.

The consumer unit contains fuses or circuit breakers that feed various circuits in the house. Units designed to take fuses only are called fuse boxes.

The electricity meter measures how much energy the consumer uses.

The incoming 110- or 220–240- electricity first passes through heavy-duty fuses.

An electric stove takes a lot of current, so it has its own circuit.

All the wall sockets on one floor of the house are connected across a looped circuit called a ring main.

Various appliances are plugged into the wall sockets.

PLUGS AND SOCKETS

Electrical appliances need to be connected to the electricity supply. This is usually done via plugs on the appliance that fit into sockets leading to the supply. Different countries use different wiring color codes.

The simplest electricity supply systems use two wires, and therefore need only two-pin plugs and sockets.

Many electricity supply systems have a third wire, the ground wire. It is connected to a metal rod in the ground and ensures that exposed metal parts never become live and cause shocks.

Ground wire

Some plugs have a fuse. If an appliance takes too much current, the fuse in the plug blows, rather than a fuse or a circuit breaker in the consumer unit. So power is still available at all the other sockets.

Fuse

CIRCUIT PROTECTION

Electricity can accidentally cause a fire by heating a wire so much that it becomes red hot. This usually happens when a fault causes too much current to flow. To prevent this from happening, domestic circuits are protected by devices called fuses and circuit breakers. Both cut off the current if it increases to a dangerous level.

POWER AND ENERGY

Power, the rate of using energy, is measured in watts. When electricity flows through a resistor, the power equals the voltage multiplied by the current. A 240-volt burner, taking a current of 4 amps, has a power of 960 watts. We can figure the total energy consumed by multiplying the power by the time that the burner is on; in two hours, the burner consumes $2 \times 960 = 1920$ watt-hours, or 1.92 kilowatt-hours (kWh) of electricity.

A circuit breaker is an electromagnetic switch that cuts off the current when it becomes too high.

This wire melts to break the circuit.

A fuse is an enclosed length of wire that forms the weakest link in a circuit. It burns out safely to cut off the current when this becomes too high. Fuses are available to withstand various currents.

Find out more

WORK AND ENERGY P. 132
CURRENT ELECTRICITY P. 148
CELLS AND BATTERIES P. 150
CIRCUITS P. 152
SOURCES OF LIGHT P. 193
FACT FINDER P. 410

TELECOMMUNICATIONS

THE WONDER OF TALKING to someone who is thousands of miles away is only possible because of electricity. Electronic equipment converts sounds and pictures into electricity, which then travels with lightning speed to somewhere else to be changed back into sounds and pictures by other electrically-powered equipment. A huge amount of information, from fax messages to telephone conversations, travels back and forth through telephone lines. Information can also be transmitted as light in fiberoptic cables or as radio waves, which are sent up to a satellite high up in space to be retransmitted to a receiving dish. Computers and other electronic machines can communicate with each other via telephone lines. All these forms of communication need three things: a transmitter to send out the information, something to carry the signals, and a receiver to convert signals back into a form that we can understand.

Inker

Morse key

TELEGRAPHIC RECEIVER
In the 1830s, Samuel Morse invented a printer to record messages sent on his electric telegraph. A strip of plain paper moved slowly through the machine. Each pulse of current received made an electromagnet move an inked wheel, so that the dots and dashes of the Morse code were printed on the paper strip. Operators used a switch called a Morse key to send signals. Pressing the key allowed electricity to flow, which activated the inker (or a clicker) at the other end. Messages were received as they were being sent.

Morse code is sent as a combination of dots, dashes, and spaces that represent numbers and letters of the alphabet. Here the numbers 4 and 2 have been printed out.

Four dots and a dash represent 4.

Two dots and three dashes represent 2.

TELEPHONE
When you dial or push buttons on a telephone, a series of dialing signals is sent out. These signals make automatic equipment connect your call. The bell or bleeper at the other end then sounds. When you speak, the microphone in the handset turns your speech into electrical signals, which are sent to the person at the other end of the line. Their receiver turns the incoming speech signals back into sounds.

VIDEO CALLS
Most telephone networks now use fiberoptic cables that can transmit information fast enough to carry video signals as well as voices. Telephones that allow callers to see each other are called videophones. Some people use small computer cameras known as webcams to make video calls over the Internet.

Electromagnet

Diaphragm

RECEIVER
The receiver in the handset turns the incoming electrical signal into sound. The signal passes through an electromagnet, which attracts a thin iron disk called a diaphragm. As the strength of the signal varies, so the pull on the disk varies, and this makes it vibrate. The vibrations pass through the air as sound waves, which you hear as speech.

Diaphragm

Carbon granules

MICROPHONE
Many telephones have a carbon microphone, also called a transmitter, which converts what you say into electric signals. Inside, there is a capsule containing granules of carbon. When you speak, the sound waves vibrate a plastic diaphragm. This pushes on the granules. Every time they are pushed together, their resistance decreases. So a current passed through them varies in the same way as the sounds causing the vibrations. This varying current forms the sound signal that travels to the receiver in another phone.

CELL PHONE
Cell phones work in the same way as fixed telephones, but they use radio waves to connect to the telephone network. Cells are becoming increasingly versatile. Many can now connect to the Internet, and can be used to send and receive pictures and video messages.

ALEXANDER GRAHAM BELL

In 1876, Scottish-born American inventor and teacher Alexander Graham Bell (1847–1922) invented the telephone. Bell gave music lessons, taught deaf people how to speak, and studied how sounds are emitted by vibrating objects. He invented a form of electric telegraph that sent signals as musical notes made by vibrating reeds. This idea led Bell to devise a way of sending and receiving the frequencies present in the human voice. The result was the telephone.

SATELLITES

Calls sent via communications satellites, which are in orbit around the Earth, are transmitted by radio from huge dish-shaped antennas on the ground. The satellite, powered by solar cells, beams the signals back to an antenna in another part of the world.

Communications satellite

Have you noticed a slight delay when talking to someone on an overseas call? This can be because the call is going via a satellite. Radio signals take a little time to travel to and from the satellite.

COMMUNICATIONS LINKS

When you make a call, the dialing pulses pass along wires to your local telephone exchange. Equipment there recognizes the codes in the pulses. For a local call, the local exchange connects you. For a different area, you are connected with the exchange in that area. Equipment there then makes the connection to the number you want. International calls are sent through international exchanges. The whole system of connecting links is called a network.

Sending and receiving dish

This dish receives radio waves from the satellite and sends the information on to the exchange.

International exchange

Local exchange

SATELLITE STATIONS

A satellite telecommunications station has a large dish-shaped antenna pointing at the satellite. Electronic equipment connected to the antenna amplifies the signals transmitted and received. Such stations are connected to local telephone exchanges.

Sending and receiving satellite communications dish

The wires from your telephone at home go, with similar wires from other homes, to the local exchange.

Local exchange

EXCHANGES

Exchanges covering different areas are linked together, by cables, microwave links, or satellite systems. Such links enable people in one area to contact people in other areas.

A fax machine both sends and receives letters and other documents.

Microwave transmitting and receiving antennas are placed on tall towers or buildings and carefully lined up with each other.

International exchange

MICROWAVE LINKS

Microwave links use radio waves called microwaves to carry telephone and other signals. Microwaves travel in a straight line from a dish-shaped transmitting antenna to a similar receiving antenna.

Microwave communications tower

FAX

Fax machines use the telephone network to send written or printed material. The sending machine changes the images on the document into a code of electrical signals and sends them down the telephone line. The receiving machine uses these to reproduce the original document.

Local exchange

A local exchange connects local calls, and routes other calls to other exchanges.

PORTABLE TELEPHONES

People on the move can talk to each other using portable telephones with built-in radio transmitters and receivers. A low-power transmitter in the telephone connects the call to permanent receiving equipment installed in the area, called a cell. From there, the call is connected into the telephone network. A local transmitter sends incoming signals to a radio receiver in the telephone. The whole system is called a cellular network.

Cellular communications exchange

Cell

Local transmitter

RADIO

Wavelength is longer at low frequencies. It can be measured from one peak to another.

Wavelength is shorter at high frequencies.

Long wave (low frequency) Medium wave Short wave VHF (very high frequency) UHF (ultra-high frequency)

WHEN YOU LISTEN TO THE RADIO, your set picks out the station you want from thousands that reach it. Radio signals travel as invisible waves through the air, other materials, and even empty space. Radio waves, like light waves, move at about 186,000 miles (300,000 km) per second. The main use of radio waves is for carrying sounds and pictures for broadcasting and for private communications. News that once would have taken months to reach distant parts of the world now gets there in less than a second by means of radio waves bounced from communications satellites in space. Radio waves are produced by a circuit carrying an electric current that rapidly oscillates (reverses its direction of flow). Radio waves are sent out most efficiently by putting the transmitting antenna on high ground, which is why many transmitters are on hills.

GUGLIELMO MARCONI

The first person to give a practical demonstration of radio was Sir Oliver Lodge. In 1894, he sent Morse code messages a distance of 180 ft (55 m). At about the same time, an Italian engineer named Guglielmo Marconi (1874–1937) managed to transmit a message over 1.25 miles (2 km). In 1896, Marconi came to England, where he established radio as an important and practical means of communication.

The carrier starts off with constant amplitude and constant frequency.

The sound signal varies in amplitude and frequency.

An AM radio signal. The strength of the carrier is varied (modulated), shown by the changing size of the wave.

An FM radio signal. Here, the frequency of the radio waves is varied (modulated).

MODULATION

Making radio waves carry sounds (or other signals) is called modulation. The sound signal makes a steady radio signal, called the carrier, vary in some way. In amplitude modulation (AM), the amplitude (strength) of the carrier changes. In frequency modulation (FM), the frequency of the carrier changes. FM transmissions suffer less from crackles and other interference.

Valve

Transistors

Coil and variable capacitor form tuned circuit to select the required station.

Wire antenna changes all received radio waves into electrical signals.

Crystal diode

Capacitor

Coil

Variable capacitor

Earth wire attached to pipe

The crystal diode and the capacitor detect the sound component of the transmitted signal.

Earphone reproduces the sound signal.

AMPLIFICATION

Some early radio sets had valves to amplify (strengthen) the received signals. Later, sets became much smaller when transistors replaced valves.

CRYSTAL SET

In the 1920s, many people listened to radio broadcasts using crystal sets. A common type of crystal set had a crystal of galena (lead sulfide) and a pointed wire contact (called the cat's whisker). Together these acted as a diode, which was used in the set's detector circuit. The detector extracted the sound component from the transmitted radio signal.

RADIO

1863 James Clerk Maxwell suggests a mathematical description of electromagnetic waves.

1888 Heinrich Hertz sends and receives radio waves in his laboratory.

1896 Guglielmo Marconi patents the first practical wireless telegraphy system.

1901 The first telegraph signal is sent across the Atlantic.

1906 Reginald Fessenden makes the first radio broadcast. This astonishes wireless telegraph operators, who hear music instead of the usual Morse code.

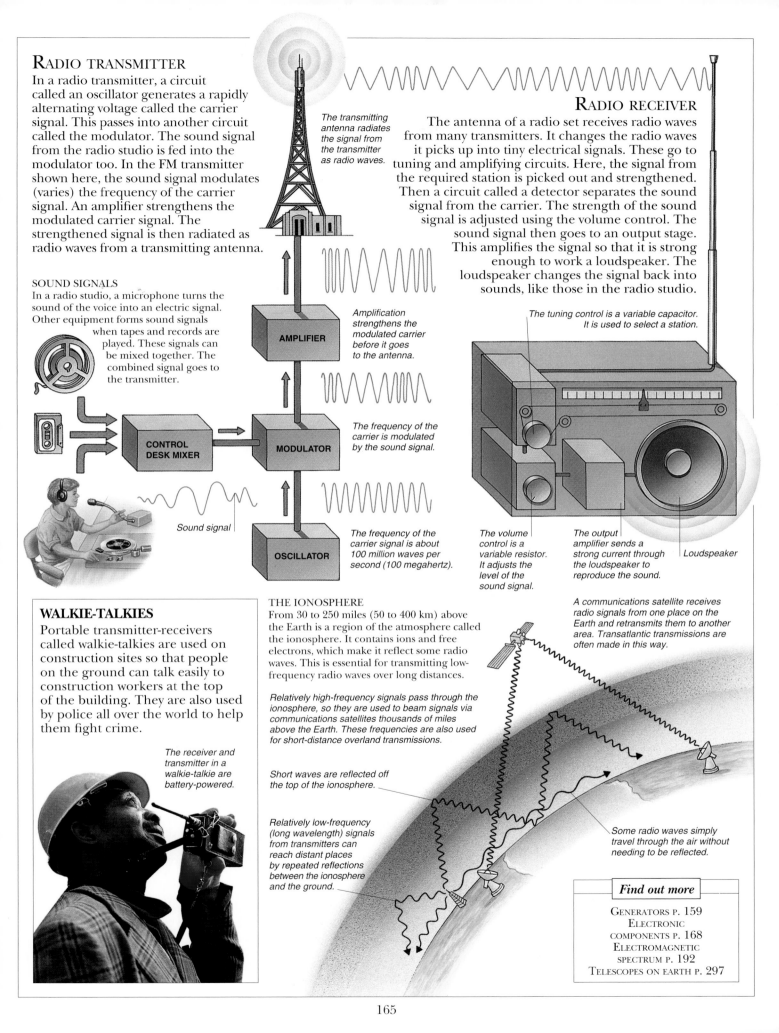

RADIO TRANSMITTER

In a radio transmitter, a circuit called an oscillator generates a rapidly alternating voltage called the carrier signal. This passes into another circuit called the modulator. The sound signal from the radio studio is fed into the modulator too. In the FM transmitter shown here, the sound signal modulates (varies) the frequency of the carrier signal. An amplifier strengthens the modulated carrier signal. The strengthened signal is then radiated as radio waves from a transmitting antenna.

SOUND SIGNALS

In a radio studio, a microphone turns the sound of the voice into an electric signal. Other equipment forms sound signals when tapes and records are played. These signals can be mixed together. The combined signal goes to the transmitter.

The transmitting antenna radiates the signal from the transmitter as radio waves.

Amplification strengthens the modulated carrier before it goes to the antenna.

The frequency of the carrier is modulated by the sound signal.

AMPLIFIER

CONTROL DESK MIXER

MODULATOR

Sound signal

OSCILLATOR

The frequency of the carrier signal is about 100 million waves per second (100 megahertz).

RADIO RECEIVER

The antenna of a radio set receives radio waves from many transmitters. It changes the radio waves it picks up into tiny electrical signals. These go to tuning and amplifying circuits. Here, the signal from the required station is picked out and strengthened. Then a circuit called a detector separates the sound signal from the carrier. The strength of the sound signal is adjusted using the volume control. The sound signal then goes to an output stage. This amplifies the signal so that it is strong enough to work a loudspeaker. The loudspeaker changes the signal back into sounds, like those in the radio studio.

The tuning control is a variable capacitor. It is used to select a station.

The volume control is a variable resistor. It adjusts the level of the sound signal.

The output amplifier sends a strong current through the loudspeaker to reproduce the sound.

Loudspeaker

WALKIE-TALKIES

Portable transmitter-receivers called walkie-talkies are used on construction sites so that people on the ground can talk easily to construction workers at the top of the building. They are also used by police all over the world to help them fight crime.

The receiver and transmitter in a walkie-talkie are battery-powered.

THE IONOSPHERE

From 30 to 250 miles (50 to 400 km) above the Earth is a region of the atmosphere called the ionosphere. It contains ions and free electrons, which make it reflect some radio waves. This is essential for transmitting low-frequency radio waves over long distances.

Relatively high-frequency signals pass through the ionosphere, so they are used to beam signals via communications satellites thousands of miles above the Earth. These frequencies are also used for short-distance overland transmissions.

Short waves are reflected off the top of the ionosphere.

Relatively low-frequency (long wavelength) signals from transmitters can reach distant places by repeated reflections between the ionosphere and the ground.

A communications satellite receives radio signals from one place on the Earth and retransmits them to another area. Transatlantic transmissions are often made in this way.

Some radio waves simply travel through the air without needing to be reflected.

Find out more

GENERATORS P. 159
ELECTRONIC COMPONENTS P. 168
ELECTROMAGNETIC SPECTRUM P. 192
TELESCOPES ON EARTH P. 297

TELEVISION

Transmitter

TELEVISION AFFECTS all our lives. We learn about places we shall never visit, we see important events as they take place; some programs we watch purely for entertainment. Television became popular in the 1950s, but ideas for sending pictures over long distances date back to the 19th century. Thanks mainly to inventions such as valves, transistors, and the cathode-ray tube, we now have high-quality television systems. In many countries, television pictures and sound are transmitted nationally using UHF (ultrahigh frequency) radio waves or electrical signals through cables. Television is also transmitted internationally via satellites. Closed-circuit television is used for security in banks and other buildings; the pictures travel straight from the camera to the screen.

TELEVISION STUDIO
Picture signals from the cameras and sound signals from the microphones go to a control room overlooking the studio. There, all the pictures are shown on screens. The program director decides which picture to use and when to change to another shot.

LIVE TELEVISION
When a program is broadcast live, a television camera changes light from the scene into electric signals. These are transmitted by radio and changed back into pictures by the television set.

The light enters the camera through the first lens.

Special mirrors split the light into three colors.

Red, blue, and green light fall on separate tubes.

TELEVISION CAMERA
In one type of color television camera, light from the scene passes through special mirrors that split the light into its primary color components—red, green, and blue. Images in these colors are formed on three camera tubes. The tubes scan the images, line by line. Each tube then puts out an electric signal that varies with the brightness along each line of the image.

An amplifier strengthens the modulated carrier signal. The strengthened signal is mixed with another carrier, which is frequency modulated with the sound signal.

AMPLIFIER

The vision signal amplitude modulates the carrier signal.

MODULATOR

A device called an oscillator generates a carrier signal, as in a radio transmitter.

OSCILLATOR

FILM AND TAPE
A movie film is run through a telecine machine, which forms electric signals from the sounds and pictures recorded on the film. Programs recorded on tape are played back on a videotape machine. The sound and vision signals from many sources go to the presentation suite. This is a control room with an adjoining announcers' studio.

PRESENTATION SUITE
Here, signals from live and recorded sources are selected and controlled. The pictures are displayed on screens called monitors. From the presentation suite, the sound signal, and a single vision signal containing all the color information, are sent to the television transmitter. The vision signal also contains timing information called synchronizing pulses. These enable the receiver to reconstruct the picture correctly.

Receiving aerial

JOHN LOGIE BAIRD

In 1926, Scottish television pioneer John Logie Baird (1888–1946) demonstrated the first television system. He used a rotating disk with holes in it to transform light from a scene into lines. A photoelectric cell changed brightness variations into electric signals. In Baird's receiver, the signals made a bulb vary in brightness. The viewer saw a faint, fuzzy image through holes in another spinning disk. The system was soon replaced by a higher quality, fully electronic system.

Baird's spinning disk was invented by Paul Nipkow (1860–1940) in 1884. This diagram shows how a nine-hole disk reproduces a picture when a vision signal makes the bulb flicker.

TELEVISION RECEIVERS

Signals from the television transmitter travel through the air at the speed of light. The antenna connected to a television set changes these radio waves back into electric signals. In the receiver, electronic circuits allow you to tune in to the television station you want. In a color television, other circuits sort out the three color components of the vision signal. The picture tube uses these to reproduce the picture in full color. A loudspeaker reproduces the sound signal.

Electrons pass as a beam through electrodes called anodes to the positively charged screen of the tube.

A small electric heater heats a surrounding metal cathode, driving off electrons.

Electron gun

COLOR PICTURES

Each electron beam varies in strength as it scans the screen, making the brightness of the phosphors (patches of chemicals) vary. The beams thus "paint" three color images on the screen. These give the impression of one image in full color.

ELECTRON GUNS

Devices called electron guns inside the cathode-ray tube fire beams of electrons at the screen. Color tubes have separate beams for each of the three primary colors. The beams vary in strength according to the brightness of the color components in the original scene.

Each electron gun produces one color— red, green, or blue.

These electromagnets guide the path of the electron beam across the screen.

PICTURE SIGNAL

The television antenna picks up the signal radiated by the transmitter and changes it into an electric signal. This passes down a cable to the receiver.

Synchronizing signals are fed to the scanning circuits. These determine the movement of the electron beams over the screen.

Circuits separate the three color signals. These control the strengths of the three electron beams.

A tuner selects the station. Other circuits separate and strengthen the vision, synchronizing (sync), and sound signals.

Screen covered in microscopic dots of phosphors

Shadow mask

SCREEN

Phosphors cover the television screen. These glow red, green, or blue when struck by an electron beam. Some color tubes have a perforated plate called a shadow mask just behind the screen. The holes in the mask ensure that each beam strikes only one kind of phosphor. So each beam forms an image of one color.

FLAT-SCREEN TV

Flat-screen televisions use new technologies that do not require a cathode-ray tube, yet provide much better picture quality. There are several different types of flat screen in development, but the most common use either plasma screen or LCD (Liquid Crystal Display) technology. Plasma screen televisions contain thousands of tiny lamps, which electricity causes to glow red, green, or blue. LCD screens use tiny colored filters in front of a white light the same size as the screen.

Flat-screen televisions are much less bulky than those that use cathode-ray tubes, yet can provide a sharper picture.

Find out more

ATOMIC STRUCTURE P. 24
RADIO P. 164
ELECTROMAGNETIC
SPECTRUM P. 192
COLOR P. 202
CINEMA P. 208

ELECTRONIC COMPONENTS

In a triode valve, the electrodes are in a glass tube that has had the air removed from it.

The cathode, heated by a glowing wire filament, sends out electrons.

The negative charge on the grid controls the flow of electrons to the anode.

The anode attracts electrons because it is positively charged and electrons are negatively charged.

ELECTRONICS AFFECTS OUR LIVES more than any other branch of technology. Radio and television sets, record players, and tape recorders were the first popular electronic devices to become available. They use parts called electronic components to control or change electric signals in some way. These parts include resistors, capacitors, transistors, and diodes. Today, many electronic components have been miniaturized (made tiny) so more and more devices can use them. Some watches, for example, contain complex electronic circuits that can tell us the time anywhere in the world. Electronic components in some cameras set the correct exposure and automatically focus the lens.

TRIODE VALVE

A component called a triode valve amplifies (strengthens) electric signals. It consists of a cathode and an anode with a wire grid between them. When a small signal is fed to the grid, the charge on the grid alters, which causes large changes in the electron flow to the anode. The signal to the anode is therefore an amplified version of the signal on the grid. Valves have been replaced in radios by transistors, which means that much smaller radios, called transistor radios, can be made.

Loudspeaker

Battery contact

Transformer

PORTABLE RADIO

A modern portable radio contains many different electronic components to carry out many different jobs. The antenna picks up the signals from the radio stations. You can select the station you want using a tuning circuit consisting of a coil and a variable capacitor. Components called transistors amplify these signals. The volume is controlled by a variable resistor that adjusts the level of sound signals fed to the final amplifier and the loudspeaker.

Variable capacitor (tuning control)

Waveband selector switch (MW/VHF)

Ferrite antenna rod (for medium waves)

Transistors are used to amplify the signals picked up by the antenna.

Printed circuit board

Telescopic antenna (for Very High Frequencies)

Diodes are used to change the alternating signals into pulses of direct current. This enables the sound signal to be re-formed.

Headphone socket

The capacitor changes pulses of direct current from the detector into a smooth sound signal by keeping hold of the charge between pulses.

Resistors are used to control the amount of current in the circuit. A resistor with a high resistance value passes a relatively small current.

Light-emitting diode (LED)

Variable resistor (volume control) with on/off switch

Shape of sound signal "carried" by the radio waves

Electrical copy of amplitude-modulated radio waves

RECEPTION
The signals sent out by an AM radio transmitter are radio waves that vary in amplitude. The antenna of a radio receiver changes all received radio waves into matching electrical signals. A tuning circuit then selects the signal required.

DETECTION
The signal selected by the tuning circuit passes to a diode. This changes the waves into pulses of electricity, which charge a capacitor. As it retains most of the charge between pulses, the signal across the capacitor is like the original sound signal.

VARIABLE CAPACITOR
When you tune into a station on a radio, you may use a device called a variable capacitor. This has one or more sets of fixed plates and movable plates that can cross over without touching. The capacitance (ability to store charge) is greatest when the plates are fully crossed over each other. Changing the capacitance makes the radio select different frequency signals.

Original sound signal

Signal pulses passed by diode

Signal across capacitor

MODERN COMPONENTS

Since the 1950s, many electronic components have been made much smaller, and new ones have been developed. They are now so small that miniature equipment is becoming more and more common. Tiny components called transistors, resistors, diodes, and capacitors are found in many common electronic gadgets. New technology has also produced more reliable components. For example, light-emitting diodes (LEDs) are often used instead of indicator bulbs because they hardly ever malfunction.

Light-dependent resistor

On the front of this night-light is a resistor that is sensitive to light. Its resistance increases when it gets dark. Electronic circuits detect this change and let the current through to switch the light on at night.

RESISTORS

CAPACITORS

The circuit in a flash unit includes a capacitor that can hold an electric charge. When this charge is released to a special tube, a bright flash is produced.

RESISTORS

The amount of current flowing in a circuit can be controlled by resistors: a resistor with a high resistance will only let a relatively small current flow. Variable resistors, made from carbon or wire, have a sliding contact so that the resistance can be varied. Light-dependent resistors (LDRs) decrease in resistance with more light. Most thermistors decrease in resistance when their temperatures rise.

CAPACITORS

Capacitors are devices that can store an electric charge and release it when needed. They are made from two layers of metal separated by a layer of nonconducting material, such as plastic. Special capacitors, called electrolytic capacitors, are made by depositing a layer of insulating material on to aluminum plates by electrolysis. Different value capacitors hold different amounts of charge when the same voltage is passed across their plates.

TRANSISTORS

DIODES

AMPLIFIER

An amplifier contains a circuit that makes a small electric signal bigger. Transistors feed the amplified (stronger) signal to the loudspeaker.

Emitter

Base

Collector

WHAT'S IN A TRANSISTOR

This transistor is made of a layer of p-type semiconductor sandwiched between two layers of n-type semiconductor. The middle layer is the base of the transistor and the outer layers are the emitter and the collector.

TRANSISTORS

Transistors are components that amplify electric current. They can also switch current on and off. Transistors vary in the frequency range of signals they can handle. Most transistors consume just a few milliamps from a supply of 12 volts or less. Transistors handling high power become hot and may have finned metal devices called heat sinks to help radiate the heat.

Base current

Collector current

HOW A TRANSISTOR WORKS

A small change in the current flowing into the base causes a larger change in the current flowing through the collector. So when a small signal is applied to the base, a larger signal appears at the collector. Strengthening a signal in this way is called amplification.

DIODES

Diodes will only let the current in an electronic circuit pass in one direction. This means they can change alternating current into pulses of direct current. Some diodes are designed to cope with weak currents; others can handle very high currents. Other diodes, called light-emitting diodes (LEDs), give off light.

Light given out as current passes through

Semiconductor junction

WHAT'S IN AN LED

Light-emitting diodes are made of a semiconductor junction encapsulated in plastic. It gives out light when a current passes through. LEDs hardly ever fail, and are used instead of bulbs.

LIGHT-EMITTING DIODES

Light-emitting diodes (LEDs) are used in some calculators for the numbers or as indicators on electronic panels. Columns of LEDs form the sound level indicators on some amplifiers. As the sound levels increase, more LEDs in a column light up.

Find out more

ELECTROLYSIS P. 67
CURRENT ELECTRICITY P. 148
CIRCUITS P. 152
RADIO P. 164
INTEGRATED CIRCUITS P. 170
CALCULATORS P. 172
FACT FINDER P. 410

INTEGRATED CIRCUITS

INSIDE AN ELECTRONIC GAME, one tiny part controls everything that the game can do: move characters around the screen, keep a record of the score, bleep when you win or lose. The tiny part is an integrated circuit (also called a silicon chip), which is a complete circuit in miniature; it is a few millimeters square. All the necessary electronic components are on the chip, and there are thousands of them on the one tiny slice of silicon. Integrated (all-in-one) circuits perform the same kinds of tasks as circuits made from separate electronic components. Chips are cheap to make, and are very reliable, so they have made electronic equipment cheaper, more efficient, and smaller.

ELECTRONIC TOY
Handheld electronic games are small computers with several chips inside. The chips detect the buttons you press and change the images on the display accordingly. The more powerful the chips, the faster and more complex the games you can play.

CIRCUITS IN MINIATURE
Many integrated circuits are formed at the same time on a silicon wafer, which is a slice from a crystal of pure silicon. After manufacture, each individual circuit is tested electronically. Those that pass all the tests are mounted in protective plastic or ceramic capsules.

DESIGNING A CIRCUIT
Before an integrated circuit can be made, a large plan of the whole circuit is drawn and checked for accuracy. Since integrated circuits are built up in layers, a plan for each layer is then designed and drawn up. A chip-sized version, called a mask, is made from these plans.

The silicon wafer is a p-type semiconductor.

Silicon dioxide layer for insulation

CIRCUIT BOARD
Some simple devices have one main chip and few other components. But more complex equipment, like a computer, may have many chips mounted on a printed circuit board, which has the connections between chips and other components "printed" on in copper.

MAKING CHIPS
The components in a chip are made by laying p-type and n-type semiconductors and other materials on the silicon base, using masks as guides. Heat and chemicals are used to shape the materials. The different combinations produce different components, such as transistors, diodes, resistors, and low-value capacitors. These are three of the many stages involved in producing just one component on the chip, in this case a special type of transistor with an insulated central electrode.

Polysilicon transistor electrode

Silicon dioxide

N-type semiconductor for outer electrodes

Chip in the center of a ceramic capsule

These connect the chip to the circuit board.

INSIDE A CHIP
This is part of the surface of a silicon chip (integrated circuit), magnified 40 times. Connections to other circuits are made through fine wires welded to pads around the edge of the chip.

The connections to electrodes are made of a conductor, aluminum.

P-type silicon

Silicon dioxide

This is a transistor, just one-thousandth of a millimeter wide.

CHIP IN A CAPSULE
A "chip" seen on a circuit board is actually a capsule that protects a chip inside. Connections from the chip to the circuit board are made with fine gold wires connected to the metal pins that stick out of the capsule. These are soldered to the circuit board or plugged into sockets.

Metal balls

A B C D E

+ Positive voltage

NOT gate

OR gate

USING INTEGRATED CIRCUITS

This pinball game uses a simple integrated circuit that contains several logic gates—each consisting of a few transistors and other components. A logic gate responds to the presence or absence of incoming signals and gives the appropriate output. The chip operates colored light-emitting diodes (LEDs) to show which slots the balls enter, and to indicate win or lose. To win, you must get at least one ball in a blue slot and at least one in a yellow slot, but none in the red slot. The green light comes on if you win. A red light means you lose.

As long as there is no ball in the red slot (C), there is no input to the NOT gate, so this normally gives an output signal to the AND gate.

The output from the red slot lights the red LED. You lose if this lights up.

OR gate

Light-emitting diode

AND gate

Resistor

PINBALL CIRCUIT

When a ball rolls down a slot, it connects the two metal contacts. One of each pair of contacts is connected to a small positive voltage. So when a ball goes into a slot, it causes this signal to be applied to one of the gates. The circuit is arranged so that an LED of the right color lights up when a ball is in a slot. The power supplies to the logic gates are not shown.

A ball in either blue slot sends a signal to the left-hand OR gate. This gives an output if there is an input signal at "A" OR "E" (OR both). This output lights the blue LED, and goes to the AND gate.

A ball in either yellow slot sends a signal to the right-hand OR gate. This gives an output if there is an input signal at "B" OR "D" (OR both). The output lights the yellow LED, and goes to the AND gate.

The three-input AND gate gives an output signal only when there is a signal at all three inputs. So the AND gate gives an output when you have a ball in one OR other of the blue slots, and in one OR other of the yellow slots, and NOT in the red slot. The output from the AND gate lights the green LED to show that you have won.

LOGIC GATES

Logic gates work with digital signals—usually the presence or absence of a small positive voltage. Truth tables show what happens when logic signals are applied to logic gates. In a truth table, the presence of a signal is written as 1, and no signal is written as 0.

THE "AND" GATE

A two-input AND gate gives an output when a signal is applied to one input AND to the other input.

Output

Input
A B

Input A	Input B	Output
0	0	0
1	0	0
0	1	0
1	1	1

THE "OR" GATE

A two-input OR gate gives an output when a signal is applied to one input OR to the other input OR to both.

Output

Input
A B

Input A	Input B	Output
0	0	0
1	0	1
0	1	1
1	1	1

THE "NOT" GATE

A NOT gate gives an output when a signal is NOT applied to its input. It gives no output signal when an input signal is present. A NOT gate is sometimes called an inverter.

Output

Input

Input	Output
0	1
1	0

ANALOG TO DIGITAL

Specially designed integrated circuits are used to convert analog signals, like a sound signal, to a digital form to be stored on a CD, for example. This gives a much better quality of sound because it doesn't get distorted when you amplify it, and it doesn't pick up noises like hiss from wear on a record. On reception or replay, digital signals are changed back into analog form. Analog signals are electrical copies of sound, vision, or other signals, so they vary continuously. Digital signals consist of simple pulses that are either on or off.

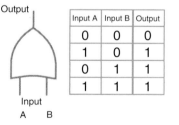

Loudness

Electric signal created by a sound wave

The analog signal is measured and converted into digital pulses at many points along the curve.

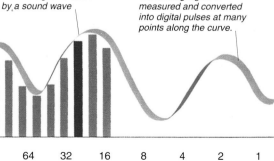

128	64	32	16	8	4	2	1
1	1	0	0	1	0	0	0

A digital signal is in binary form, which means that it is a sequence of on (1) and off (0).

The value of 200 is converted into the digital number 11001000, which represents 128 + 64 + 8.

MEASURING THE SIGNAL

To change an analog signal into a digital one, an integrated circuit measures the strength of the analog signal thousands of times each second. It then changes these measurements into the right pattern of digital signals.

CALCULATOR

A MODERN ELECTRONIC CALCULATOR is a miracle of miniaturization, and it has more computing power than a room full of early electronic computing equipment. An electronic calculator is a computer that does calculations only. These calculations are done so quickly that the result appears almost as soon as you press the last key. Calculators have the basic functions of add, subtract, multiply, and divide; they can also have function keys that perform complex calculations automatically. Some calculators can be programmed by the user to carry out specific calculations.

DIFFERENCE ENGINE
This early calculator was the first one designed by Charles Babbage. It had more than 2,000 moving parts.

POCKET CALCULATOR
This pocket calculator has an extra memory to store numbers needed later while other calculations are carried out. The calculator can also work out square roots of numbers.

NUMBER COMPUTER

Some people use their fingers to help when counting and doing calculations. This is why our system of counting and numbering is based on tens. This decimal counting system uses the 10 digits 0 to 9. Modern electronic calculators use the binary system, with two digits, 0 and 1, instead. This is because circuits designed to recognize just two signal levels, representing 0 and 1, are simpler and more reliable than circuits designed to recognize 10 signal levels.

Power socket

Resistor

Transistor

Capacitor

Numeral display

Integrated circuit

Ribbon connector connects the keypad to the circuit board.

Output (numeral display)

CPU (with memory)

Printed circuit board

Green insulating coating protects copper tracks that connect circuit components.

Switch contacts connect when buttons on keypad are pressed.

Input (keypad)

CHARLES BABBAGE

In the early 1830s, an English mathematician named Charles Babbage (1792–1871) designed a mechanical calculator called the Analytical Engine. It would have a store, or memory, to hold numbers. An arithmetic unit would do calculations according to instructions from a control unit. Instructions (programs) were to be fed into the machine in code, as patterns of holes on punched cards. In other words, it would have been programmable (unlike his Difference Engines); modern computers still operate on these basic ideas. Babbage devoted many years and much of his fortune to this machine, but it was never completed.

KEYPAD
Switches behind the keypad close briefly when you press the keys for numbers and instructions (such as +, −, ÷, or =). Electronic circuits detect what you key in and store it in binary form. Then other circuits perform the calculations.

CALCULATOR CHIP
Modern pocket calculators have just one chip containing all the complex circuits needed to carry out the calculations. Inside the chip, a central processing unit (CPU) controls operations and uses an electronic memory to store numbers used in calculations and the results that are displayed.

BINARY SYSTEM
The decimal number 25, for example, is 11001 in binary. This represents 1×16, plus 1×8, plus 0×4, plus 0×2, plus 1×1. This may seem complicated to us, but it is very easy for a calculator to represent, store, and recognize each 0 or 1 as the absence or presence of an electrical voltage. The binary number calculated is automatically converted into the decimal number shown on the display.

Find out more

HOW SCIENTISTS WORK P. 14
CELLS AND BATTERIES P. 150
ELECTRONIC
COMPONENTS P. 168
INTEGRATED CIRCUITS P. 170
COMPUTERS P. 173
FACT FINDER P. 410

COMPUTERS

COMPUTERS CAN HELP YOU write letters, draw pictures, play games, do calculations very quickly, and carry out many other tasks. For example, it would take hours to calculate and write down the 12 times table up to 3,000 times 12. But a computer can do this and produce a neatly printed and error-free table in minutes. Computers handle text by storing codes representing letters of the alphabet, spaces, and punctuation marks. Using a computer to write and edit text is called word processing. Computers also allow you to produce graphics (lines and pictures) without ever touching a pencil or paper. And in desktop publishing, words and pictures are combined using a computer to produce newspapers, books, and magazines. With a suitable program (set of instructions) and hardware (computer equipment), you can do all these things and more.

TABLET PC
Portable computers, such as laptops and tablet PCs, enable people to work while traveling. Most have built-in modems so people can connect to the internet away from the home and office.

HOME COMPUTER

A typical home computer system has input devices to put programs and data (information) into the computer. Electronic circuits inside the computer carry out the work and send the results to output devices. Programs from CD-ROMs or DVDs are fed into the computer, or can be downloaded from the internet. Many home computers now include special multimedia facilities including built-in microphones and speakers.

A keyboard is used for entering data and commands.

The screen shows what the computer is doing. Messages on the screen can tell you what to do next or warn you of problems.

When the mouse is moved, a ball underneath rotates. This movement, changed into electronic signals, makes a marker move over the screen.

The graphics/sound card changes data into images that can be seen on the screen and sounds that can be heard.

Modem means modulator-demodulator. Modems change computer signals so that they can be sent along telephone wires between computers.

When a stylus is drawn over a graphics tablet, the movements are changed into electric signals. These make the computer draw matching lines on the screen.

INPUT DEVICES

General-purpose computers have a keyboard. This has all the letters and numbers of a typewriter, plus a few extra keys. The keyboard is used to feed words and numbers into the computer. It is also used to type in commands and to move objects around the screen when playing games. But other input devices are sometimes more useful. A joystick is better for controlling moving objects when playing games. A mouse may be moved around the desk to make a marker move on the screen. A mouse can also be used to draw a picture, but a graphics tablet is easier to use for this. Musical notes may be fed in from the "typewriter" keyboard, but it is easier to use a specially designed music keyboard.

This mouse detects where it is by bouncing a red light off your desk mouse pad.

STORAGE

The large amounts of information and instructions that computers handle have to be stored. The instructions that make up programs are usually stored as pulses on magnetic tapes or disks. These instructions are fed into the computer and stored there temporarily in memory chips. Other chips in the computer are used to store information permanently. Work done on the computer is often stored on magnetic tapes or disks.

One DVD (digital video/versatile disk) can store a lot of information, such as a movie or thousands of books.

Chips store programs and information as electronic signals.

Flash memory drives are used to save and transfer information.

Many printers form letters and pictures using jets of ink.

OUTPUT DEVICES

You can usually see what a computer is doing by looking at its monitor (screen). And you can usually obtain a permanent record, called a printout or hard copy, by sending the information in the computer to a printer. Sometimes the output of a computer is fed via a telephone line to another computer using a device called a modem. Computers can also interpret our instructions to make robots move as we want.

Continued on next page

HARDWARE AND SOFTWARE

To make a computer do useful work, you need the equipment (hardware) and a set of instructions (called a program or software). Computers also need system software, which tells them how to operate. Computers work with information and instructions in the form of electronic signals representing the 1s and 0s of the binary code. Writing programs in this form would take a long time. So they are instead written in special programming languages that partly resemble English. These are automatically changed into the form that the computer understands.

COMPUTER

A personal computer is usually a box containing the main electronic units and equipped with sockets for connecting the power supply, keyboard, monitor, printer, and other equipment. Disk units, called drives, are usually fitted inside this box, but sockets are usually provided for connecting other disk drives.

These red switches are under the keys on a keyboard.

KEYBOARD

The keyboard is simply lots of push-button switches marked with letters and other characters. What happens when you press a particular key depends on how the computer is programmed. For example, pressing the key may make a letter of the alphabet appear on the screen or a character in an adventure game may move around.

COMPUTERS

1642 Blaise Pascal (1623–62) builds a mechanical calculating machine.

1805 Joseph Jacquard (1752–1834) builds an automatic loom. The patterns are controlled by punched cards. Cards are later used in computers.

1833 Charles Babbage designs the first general-purpose programmable computer, the Analytical Engine.

1890 Herman Hollerith (1860–1929) uses a punched-card system to make the United States census calculations hundreds of times faster.

1946 Engineers in the United States build the first electronic digital computer.

1951 The same team builds the first mass-produced computer, UNIVAC I.

Micrograph of an integrated circuit

MONITOR

The monitor, also called a VDU (visual display unit), is often a separate unit with a cable to connect it to the computer. Computer monitors are designed to give a high-quality picture so that words can be read from the screen without causing eyestrain. Some computers have a monitor permanently attached.

Router connected to the internet

Wi-Fi

WIRELESS NETWORKS

Wireless networks do away with cables by using invisible radio waves to send signals back and forth. If you have a wireless modem, you can connect your computer to the internet anywhere in your house without using any wires. Many public buildings have wireless networks like this so passing travelers can use the internet. They are called Wi-Fi hotspots.

Many computers have a built-in hard (rigid) magnetic disk drive to store programs and data. Most hard disks cannot be removed from the machine.

Chip

Microprocessor

Flash memory disk

Output on screen or printer

RAM chip

CPU

Input via keyboard

ROM chip

CPU

The central processing unit (CPU) is the computer's center of operations. It consists of large numbers of electronic circuits, all contained in a single chip called a microprocessor. The CPU takes in data from the keyboard, the ROM, and the RAM. It can also send data to be stored in the RAM, and send data to the monitor (and other output devices).

MEMORIES

Chips called the ROM (read-only memory) store information permanently needed by the computer. Other chips make up the RAM (random-access memory). The ROM is like a book: the computer gets information from it, but does not add to it. The RAM is like a notebook: the computer puts information in it and can use the information and alter it. But information in RAM is lost when the machine is switched off. Flash disks are similar to both RAM and ROM. Like ROM, they keep their information when the power is switched off. Like RAM, the information they store can be changed many times.

Find out more

HOW SCIENTISTS WORK P. 14
MAGNETISM P. 154
TELEVISION P. 166
INTEGRATED CIRCUITS P. 170
CALCULATORS P. 172
USING COMPUTERS P. 175
FACT FINDER P. 410

USING COMPUTERS

MOST HOME COMPUTERS have several programs so they can be used in different ways—for games as well as word processing, for example. But many computers are dedicated machines. They do just one thing and look very different. For example, a bank's automated teller machine uses computer technology to check people's accounts and allows them to withdraw money. The machine at the bank is a computer terminal that is connected to the bank's central computer, where details of all accounts are stored. Dedicated computers are also used to control industrial processes and transportation systems, and simulate real-life situations (like flying a plane) for research and training.

SIMULATION
Pilots can become experts at flying complex modern airplanes before ever getting into a real one. The trainee pilots are trained on computer-controlled machines called simulators. The computer makes the simulator react just like an airplane would: the simulator moves around, and the controls even give realistic readings of things like height and how much fuel is left in each tank.

This car design is being tested for wind resistance using a CRAY supercomputer.

When the packets arrive at the correct address they are reassembled into a readable message.

THE INTERNET
The internet is an international network of computers, modems, and telephone lines. Computers connected through the internet can send messages to, access information from, and run programs on other computers in the network. Most traffic on the internet is electronic mail (email). This is a cheap and speedy way to send messages across the world.

To be transmitted, the email message is divided into tiny packets of data.

CAD
Computer-aided design (CAD) is a way of designing things using computer graphics. Information is fed into the computer, which "constructs" the object on the screen. Different operating conditions are fed in too, and the design is tested. This helps to identify parts of the design that are not good enough so they can then be improved.

VIRTUAL REALITY
Virtual reality is a way of going into a world completely created by a computer. The computer creates 3-D images and stereo sound in a special helmet connected to a handheld unit. Any move you make with the hand unit is transmitted to the headset, so that you appear to be interacting with the events happening on the screen.

ALAN TURING
The British mathematician Alan Turing (1912–54) was a major contributor to theories used in modern computing. He helped to develop the electronic device and the ideas used to decode German secret messages during World War II (1939–45). He was the first to suggest that computers could be "intelligent."

Find out more
HOW SCIENTISTS WORK P. 14
COMPUTERS P. 173
ROBOTS P. 176
ELECTRONIC SOUNDS P. 189

ROBOTS

MOST ROBOTS YOU SEE in movies look a little like humans. They can walk and talk and, like humans, will tackle almost any problem that occurs. In real life, most robots work in factories, but they don't look at all like us. The most common type of robot has one arm and no legs, and does just one job. Robots used in industry are controlled by computers and obey instructions stored in an electronic memory. One way of recording the required movement is for a skilled human worker to perform a task first. The movements involved are stored as electronic signals so that the computer can make the robot copy them precisely. Different kinds of robot do other jobs, such as moving goods around factories, and exploring other planets.

ROBOTS IN FICTION
The robots from the film *Star Wars* are humanlike: C3PO can communicate in three million ways, and R2D2 can repair spaceships. Real robots will never need to be so versatile, but some can already do simple translations and others can do repairs.

Gripper — Signal to gripper — Control circuit — Signal from sensor

FEEDBACK
The grippers on a robot arm could crush fragile objects when picking them up. So pressure sensors are provided to detect when the grippers have a firm hold. The sensors feed an electric signal back to a control circuit, which then stops any further pressure being applied.

Closed-circuit television camera

Arm

Grab

Case under investigation

BOMB DISPOSAL
Bomb disposal experts can check safely for bombs, thanks to this mobile robot. Closed-circuit television cameras on the robot send back pictures to the controller. He or she uses the pictures to check objects suspected of being bombs. The robot also has floodlights for getting clear pictures at night. The remote-controlled grab on the end of the arm is used to pick up a suspicious object.

Antenna for communication with controller

Tracks for moving over rough ground

Floodlight

The Mars Rovers are among the most complex robots to have been sent into space.

Space robots must be able to work independently because radio instructions could take minutes or even hours to travel from Earth.

MARS MISSION
In 2003, American scientists sent two unmanned exploration rovers, named *Spirit* and *Opportunity*, to Mars. They touched down in January 2004 and went on to explore and photograph the surface of the planet. They analyzed rocks and soil and sent back important data suggesting liquid water had once flowed there. Robot space probes such as these are designed to obey instructions from controllers on Earth, but decide for themselves how to carry them out.

INDUSTRIAL ROBOTS
Robots like this weld together metal parts to make cars. Other robots spray the car bodies with paint. Unlike humans, robots never get fed up with doing the same work every day. They can also work for much longer without stopping.

Find out more
CARBON P. 40
COMPUTERS P. 173
MARS P. 289
SPACE PROBES P. 301

SOUND AND LIGHT

THE SOUNDS AND SIGHTS of the world are carried to us by energy in the form of sound and light. In some ways, sound and light are very similar. The energy of both is carried from one place to another by waves. The energy of sunlight warms the Earth, tans fair skin, and makes plants grow. The energy of the sonic boom—the bang made by a jet breaking the sound barrier—can shake buildings and shatter windows. In other ways, sound and light are different. Sound can only travel through matter—through gases such as the air, through liquids, and through solids. Light can travel through a vacuum. We see light from the stars that has been traveling for thousands of years before reaching our eyes.

Image is artificially colored.

SOUND PICTURES
Cameras collect light to create images on film and on television screens. Sound can produce images too. This image of a fetus inside the womb was made with sound echoes. The echoes are made when very high-pitched sound waves—ultrasonic waves—travel through the mother's body. These are recorded and used to build up a computer image of the unborn baby.

SILENT JAR
The Ancient Greek philosopher Aristotle believed that both sound and light traveled through the air like waves in the sea. He also believed that neither could travel through a vacuum. But it was not until the 17th century that scientists were able to create a vacuum to test Aristotle's theory. One experiment was by the Irish scientist Robert Boyle in 1658. He slowly pumped air out of a glass jar containing a ticking watch. The sound of the ticking disappeared completely as the jar was emptied. Boyle concluded that sounds are carried by air to our ears. Aristotle had been right about sound.

Robert Boyle

The sound of the ticking watch became fainter as air was pumped out of the jar.

THUNDER AND LIGHTNING
A lightning strike releases huge amounts of sound and light energy. The crash and flash of the storm can be heard and seen from a great distance. We see the lightning before we hear the thunder because light travels nearly a million times faster than sound. We see the flash within millionths of a second of it happening, but may not hear the thunder until several seconds later.

This spray of optical fibers is made up of 2,000 individual strands.

COMMUNICATIONS
Both sound and light enable us to communicate. We use our voices to talk, and need light to see each other. Telephone systems convert the sounds of voices into electrical signals that are transmitted by cable and satellite to every part of the world. Modern communications networks use optical fibers to carry information. Pulses of light carry telephone calls, television pictures, and computer data along cables made from fine glass fibers.

QUIET SPACE
There is no air in space, so there are no sounds there. Astronauts talk to each other using radios because, unlike sound waves, radio waves can travel through space. Astronauts are able to see each other because light, like radio waves, can travel through a vacuum.

SOUND

WE LIVE IN A WORLD full of sounds. Some occur naturally: thunder, ocean waves breaking on the shore, the wind in the trees. Others are made for a purpose: birds sing to attract a mate, bats squeak to locate their prey, people speak to communicate. Some sounds are just noise—annoying sounds that pollute the environment: the roar of traffic, aircraft, and factory machines. All sounds are caused by vibrations—the rapid motion of particles of matter colliding with each other and passing on energy as a traveling pulse or wave. You can feel sound vibrations. Place your fingertips against your throat when you speak or gently touch a bicycle bell as it rings.

Direction of wave

Pull end of spring in and out to send a longitudinal wave along the spring.

VIBRATIONS
A gong vibrates when it is struck—it flexes backward and forward rapidly. The vibrating gong pushes to and fro on the air molecules around it, making the air pressure rise and fall. These pressure changes are passed on by collisions between air molecules and a sound wave travels away from the gong. The parts of the wave where the air pressure is increased (air molecules are bunched up) are called compressions. The parts where the pressure is decreased (air molecules are spaced out) are called rarefactions.

Compression

Rarefaction

Move end of spring up and down to send a transverse wave along the spring.

Direction of wave

TRANSVERSE AND LONGITUDINAL
When you throw a stone into water, waves spread out from the splash and move across the water. The surface seems to vibrate up and down at right angles to the wave direction. This kind of wave is called a longitudinal wave. You can send both longitudinal and transverse waves along a coiled spring.

Direction of wave *Buoy*

WATERY SOUNDS
Sound travels faster in water and loses its energy less rapidly than in air, so underwater sounds travel farther before dying away. Whales and dolphins use underwater sounds to communicate and to navigate. Some whales "sing" songs that carry for hundreds of miles through the oceans.

WAVES OF ENERGY
A traveling wave carries energy from one place to another. For example, a water wave passing a buoy makes it bob up and down energetically. But the vibrating particles do not actually travel along the wave. They just move to and fro about the same spot—like the buoy on the water's surface.

Motion of wave lifts buoy up.

Buoy falls as the wave of energy passes on.

SEISMIC WAVES
Earthquakes and explosions generate seismic waves—sound waves that travel through the ground. The vibrations made by these waves are recorded on a seismograph. By studying these waves, seismologists can sometimes predict earthquakes and can also learn about the interior of the Earth.

Vibrations produced by the quake or explosion are recorded on the seismometer screen.

The speed of sound in air changes with the temperature. At 32°F (0°C), it is 1,086 ft (331 m) per second. At 104°F (40°C), it is 1,161 ft (354 m) per second.

SPEED OF SOUND

In 1708, William Derham (1657–1735) became one of the first people to establish the speed of sound accurately. He stood on top of Upminster Church in Essex, England, and watched as a cannon was fired 12 miles (19 km) away. He timed the interval between the cannon flash and the boom, taking an average of several measurements to allow for changes in wind direction. His result was close to the modern value of 1,130 ft (343 m) per second at a temperature of 68°F (20°C).

TAPPING MESSAGES
Workers building the Channel Tunnel linking the United Kingdom to continental Europe sent messages by tapping on pipes. Sound travels farther and faster in metal than in air.

Sound travels at 1,130 ft (343 m) per second through air at 68°F (20°C).

Sound travels through water at 5,000 ft (1,500 m) per second.

DIFFERENT SPEEDS
Sound travels more quickly through solids and liquids than through gases. Solids and liquids are "stiffer" than gases because the molecules are closer together. They spring back into shape more readily when they are compressed, passing on sound pulses more quickly. Sound travels nearly five times faster in water than in air and almost 20 times faster in steel.

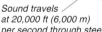

Sound travels at 20,000 ft (6,000 m) per second through steel.

SHOCK WAVES
Supersonic jets fly faster than the speed of sound, so you cannot hear them coming toward you—the jet passes you before the sound arrives. But when the sound catches up, it arrives suddenly as a shock wave that produces a sonic boom.

Sound waves spread ahead of a jet flying at less than the speed of sound so you hear it approaching.

Sound waves pile up in front of a jet traveling at the speed of sound. They form a large shock wave.

Shock wave

When the jet breaks the sound barrier, it leaves a shock wave behind it. This shock wave produces a sonic boom as it passes over the ground.

ERNST MACH
More than 50 years before the first supersonic flights, Austrian physicist Ernst Mach (1838–1916) described how shock waves are formed. Today, Mach numbers are used to give aircraft speeds in terms of the speed of sound. An aircraft flying at the speed of sound is flying at Mach 1. Mach 2 is twice the speed of sound. All passenger aircraft, except the Concorde, are subsonic; they fly below Mach 1. The Concorde was supersonic; it flew at Mach 2.

WHIP CRACK
The loud crack a whip makes may well be because the tip of the whip moves faster than the speed of sound, generating a shock wave.

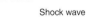

Find out more
STATES OF MATTER P. 18
PROPERTIES OF MATTER P. 22
BONDING P. 28
VIBRATIONS P. 126
EARTHQUAKES P. 220

MEASURING SOUND

The microphone, which is connected to the oscilloscope, converts the flute's sound into an electrical signal.

SOUNDS CAN BE LOUD OR QUIET, high-pitched like a whistle or low-pitched like a car engine. Some sounds are pleasant, others are annoying or even painful. But what makes one sound different from another? It has nothing to do with speed. All sounds travel at the same speed. If sounds did travel at different speeds, the sounds of instruments in an orchestra would reach your ears at different times and the music would be mixed up. The answer is that different sounds have differently shaped waves. The feature of a sound wave that makes it quiet or loud is called its amplitude. The feature that makes the sound high-pitched or low-pitched is called the frequency. The wavelength—the distance between two wave compressions (crests)—also affects the sound.

AMPLITUDE

An oscilloscope displays the pattern of a sound wave on a screen. The pattern traced on the screen shows how the air pressure rises and falls as the sound wave passes the microphone. If the sound is made louder, the pressure changes are greater and the amplitude of the wave is increased.

High amplitude—a loud sound

Low amplitude—a quiet sound

HEINRICH HERTZ

The German physicist Heinrich Hertz (1857–94) was the first to produce and detect radio waves. The unit of frequency used for all kinds of waves and vibrations—including sound waves, radio waves, and light waves—is named after him. One Hertz (1 Hz) is equal to one vibration per second.

Siren of approaching car produces short, high-frequency waves.

As the car drives past, sound waves become longer, and sound lower.

THE DOPPLER EFFECT

The pitch of sound you hear as a police car speeds by depends on whether the car is moving toward or away from you. As the car approaches, the sound waves ahead of it are bunched up. These short waves have a high frequency, so the siren sounds high. Behind the car, the waves are stretched out. These longer waves have a lower frequency, so the siren sounds lower as the car drives past.

High-frequency wave—a high-pitched sound

in one second

Low-frequency wave—a low-pitched sound

in one second

Peaks of a high-frequency sound wave on the screen are closer together than lower frequency wave peaks because they arrive at the microphone more frequently.

Compression   Rarefaction

FREQUENCY

The frequency of a wave is the number of vibrations it makes in one second. This is measured by counting the number of wave crests that pass in that time. A wave with a low frequency has a long wavelength. A wave with a high frequency has a short wavelength. High-frequency, short wavelengths make high-pitched sounds. Low-frequency, long wavelengths make low-pitched sounds.

SOUND WAVES

Sound waves actually travel through air like a wave along a coiled spring. A compression (where the air molecules are bunched up) corresponds to the crest of a water wave. A rarefaction (where the air is more spaced out), corresponds to the trough of a water wave.

WAVELENGTH

Short and long waves are easy to see in water. The wavelength of a water wave is the distance between two neighboring crests. The wavelength of a sound wave is the distance between two neighboring compressions. In a short wavelength sound, the waves are close together. If the waves are farther apart, the wavelength is longer.

Trough   Crest

Long wavelengths

Short wavelengths

Find out more

SOUND P. 178
MAKING AND HEARING SOUNDS P. 182
LOUDNESS P. 181
MUSICAL SOUNDS P. 186
FACT FINDER P. 412

LOUDNESS

THE LOUDNESS OF A SOUND depends on the intensity (amount of energy) the sound waves carry. Big vibrations have a lot of energy and produce intense sound waves with a large amplitude. Very loud sounds, such as sonic booms and shock waves from explosions, can be painful and sometimes cause a lot of damage—the sound waves bang into structures and cause them to vibrate. A special scale called the decibel scale, named after Alexander Graham Bell, is used to measure the loudness of sound.

HIDDEN DANGER
A personal stereo does not produce much power, but because nearly all the sound goes directly into the ears, the sound levels inside the ear can be very high. Playing personal stereos too loud for too long can cause hearing loss.

THE DECIBEL SCALE
The difference in amplitude between the quietest sounds and sounds so loud they hurt is almost too great to write down in numbers. The decibel scale is an example of a logarithmic scale. Every time another 10 decibels (dB) are *added* to the sound level, the loudness of the sound is *multiplied* by 10. Increasing the amount of sound by 20 dB multiplies the loudness by $10 \times 10 = 100$ times.

120 dB

100 dB

80 dB

40 dB

20 dB

The sound of a rock group is a 100 million times louder than the sound of falling leaves!

It is not uncommon for rock musicians to suffer hearing losses. Sounds over 120 dB can cause intense pain and deafness.

Special padding absorbs sound.

Ear protectors

EAR PROTECTION
People who have to work surrounded by loud sounds must protect their ears. They wear ear protectors to muffle the noise. Prolonged exposure to high sound levels causes hearing loss at certain frequencies.

MEASURING SOUND
Sound levels inside factories can be monitored with sound level meters to make sure the levels are not dangerous. The level should not exceed 110 dB at any time. For a full working day, the level should not exceed 90 dB.

People should spend only short periods working in sound levels over 100 dB.

ANTINOISE
It is possible for two sounds to add together to make silence! This is unlikely to happen by chance, but if a sound wave is measured, a computer can produce its mirror image. The peaks of the original sound wave correspond exactly to the troughs in the new sound wave. When the two sounds overlap, they cancel each other out. This method is called "antinoise." In hospitals, some body scanners are equipped with antinoise systems to make them quieter for the patient. Future refrigerators and washing machines equipped with antinoise systems may be completely silent.

Sound is canceled out.

Peak

Trough

Find out more

VIBRATIONS P. 126
TELECOMMUNICATIONS P. 162
SOUND P. 178
MUSICAL SOUNDS P. 186

MAKING AND HEARING SOUND

IF YOU HAVE EVER LOST YOUR VOICE, you know how difficult it is to make people understand you without it. Speech is our main form of communication. When we speak, we produce vibrations that travel through the air as sound waves. These sound waves are changed into sounds we can recognize with our ears. Although our ears can detect sounds in the range of 20–20,000 Hz, they are most sensitive to sounds with frequencies of around 1,000 Hz. This is the frequency range of voices in normal conversation, although our voices may contain sounds as low-pitched as 50 Hz and as high-pitched as 10,000 Hz. Just as we use our voices to talk to other people, animals use the sounds they make to communicate with each other.

MAKING SOUND

We produce our voices by forcing air from our lungs past the vocal cords in our throats. The rushing air makes the cords vibrate. When we speak and sing, we make constant adjustments to the tension of our vocal cords, the shape of our mouths, and the speed of the projected air. In this way, we control the pitch, quality, and loudness of our voices.

If a sound comes from the right, sound waves reach the right ear a split second before they reach the left ear. This is why you can tell which direction the sound is coming from.

RESONANCE

Most objects can vibrate. The frequency at which an object vibrates naturally is called its resonant frequency. If a sound of exactly that frequency is played near the object, it picks up energy from the sound wave and vibrates in sympathy. This is resonance. You can often hear resonances when you play loud music in a room. A particular note will cause a door panel or an object near the speakers to resonate. If a singer sings with a frequency equal to the natural frequency of a wine glass, the glass may resonate so strongly that it shatters.

HEARING SOUND

Sound waves collected by the outer ear force the eardrum to vibrate. These vibrations are carried on to the inner ear through a series of tiny bones. Fluid inside a narrow tube, the cochlea, vibrates. These vibrations stimulate tiny hairs on nerves. These nerves send electrical impulses to the brain, which enables us to recognize the sound.

The aid can be adjusted to amplify particular sound frequencies.

AIR IN BOTTLES

You can see and hear how different amounts of air vibrate to give different sounds by blowing across the tops of bottles. If you blow across the top of an empty bottle, the air inside vibrates at its resonant frequency. Pouring water into the bottle changes the volume of the air and alters the pitch of the note. Short columns of air vibrate more quickly and give a higher pitch than long air columns.

Volume control

Microphone

Hearing aid is shaped to fit around the ear.

Earhook

DEAFNESS

People who have some hearing loss, but who are not completely deaf, can be helped by wearing a hearing aid. This consists of a miniature microphone, amplifier, and loudspeaker. Sounds arriving at the microphone are amplified and fed into the earpiece.

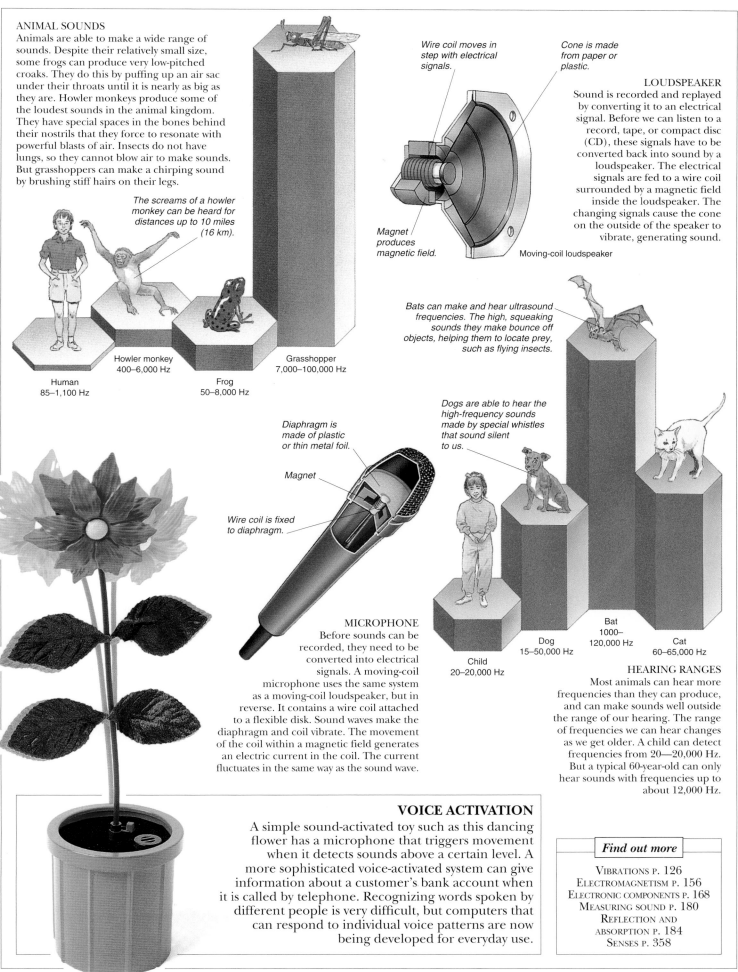

ANIMAL SOUNDS

Animals are able to make a wide range of sounds. Despite their relatively small size, some frogs can produce very low-pitched croaks. They do this by puffing up an air sac under their throats until it is nearly as big as they are. Howler monkeys produce some of the loudest sounds in the animal kingdom. They have special spaces in the bones behind their nostrils that they force to resonate with powerful blasts of air. Insects do not have lungs, so they cannot blow air to make sounds. But grasshoppers can make a chirping sound by brushing stiff hairs on their legs.

The screams of a howler monkey can be heard for distances up to 10 miles (16 km).

Human
85–1,100 Hz

Howler monkey
400–6,000 Hz

Frog
50–8,000 Hz

Grasshopper
7,000–100,000 Hz

Wire coil moves in step with electrical signals.

Cone is made from paper or plastic.

LOUDSPEAKER

Sound is recorded and replayed by converting it to an electrical signal. Before we can listen to a record, tape, or compact disc (CD), these signals have to be converted back into sound by a loudspeaker. The electrical signals are fed to a wire coil surrounded by a magnetic field inside the loudspeaker. The changing signals cause the cone on the outside of the speaker to vibrate, generating sound.

Magnet produces magnetic field.

Moving-coil loudspeaker

Bats can make and hear ultrasound frequencies. The high, squeaking sounds they make bounce off objects, helping them to locate prey, such as flying insects.

Dogs are able to hear the high-frequency sounds made by special whistles that sound silent to us.

Diaphragm is made of plastic or thin metal foil.

Magnet

Wire coil is fixed to diaphragm.

MICROPHONE

Before sounds can be recorded, they need to be converted into electrical signals. A moving-coil microphone uses the same system as a moving-coil loudspeaker, but in reverse. It contains a wire coil attached to a flexible disk. Sound waves make the diaphragm and coil vibrate. The movement of the coil within a magnetic field generates an electric current in the coil. The current fluctuates in the same way as the sound wave.

Child
20–20,000 Hz

Dog
15–50,000 Hz

Bat
1000–120,000 Hz

Cat
60–65,000 Hz

HEARING RANGES

Most animals can hear more frequencies than they can produce, and can make sounds well outside the range of our hearing. The range of frequencies we can hear changes as we get older. A child can detect frequencies from 20—20,000 Hz. But a typical 60-year-old can only hear sounds with frequencies up to about 12,000 Hz.

VOICE ACTIVATION

A simple sound-activated toy such as this dancing flower has a microphone that triggers movement when it detects sounds above a certain level. A more sophisticated voice-activated system can give information about a customer's bank account when it is called by telephone. Recognizing words spoken by different people is very difficult, but computers that can respond to individual voice patterns are now being developed for everyday use.

Find out more

VIBRATIONS P. 126
ELECTROMAGNETISM P. 156
ELECTRONIC COMPONENTS P. 168
MEASURING SOUND P. 180
REFLECTION AND
ABSORPTION P. 184
SENSES P. 358

REFLECTION AND ABSORPTION

HAVE YOU EVER WONDERED why your voice sounds fuller and more powerful than usual when you sing in the shower? It is because sound waves are reflected by smooth, hard surfaces such as the bathroom walls. They bounce off like a rubber ball bounces off the walls in a squash court. Although the direction of the sound waves changes, their pitch is not altered. In addition to being fun, echoes (sound reflections) can be useful. Before the days of radar, sailors caught in fog could tell how far they were from dangerous cliffs by sounding the ship's fog horn and timing the interval before the reflection was heard. But sounds are not always reflected. If they meet a soft surface, such as a cushion, they will be absorbed and will not bounce back.

ECHOES

If you stand some distance away from a wall and make a sound, it will be reflected back to you shortly after. The time it takes depends on how far away the wall is. If you are standing 200 ft (60 m) away, the sound has to travel there and back—a distance of 400 ft (120 m). Dividing 400 feet by the time taken between making the sound and hearing the echo will give you the speed at which the sound is traveling.

Sound-absorbing panels

Carefully positioned panels reflect sounds from the stage toward the audience.

Curtains and the bodies of people in the audience absorb sound, reducing reverberation.

Reflecting panels

ANECHOIC CHAMBER

The sound-absorbing panels in the walls and ceiling of an anechoic wind tunnel reduce reverberation. This enables scientists to measure accurately the noise generated by an aircraft propellor.

ACOUSTICS

The way sound echoes around a building is called acoustics. Large buildings can seem full of echoes, especially if they have many bare surfaces. Reverberation occurs when sounds echo around for several seconds. In a concert hall it is important to control the echoes. If there is not enough reverberation, the music sounds thin with no sparkle. Too much reverberation, and the sounds are jumbled. Special panels direct sound reflections toward the audience. Others, along with curtains, absorb excess reverberation.

SOUND DISHES

Parabolic dishes are used to collect and concentrate sound. Their special shape reflects and concentrates any sound coming from directly in front of the dish toward the microphone at the center. In this way, the microphone receives more sound energy than it would without the dish. Parabolic dishes make it possible to record low-level sounds such as bird song.

SOUND ABSORPTION

Soft surfaces absorb sound energy in the same way as sand absorbs energy from a ball thrown onto it. In this room, the rug, curtains, sofa, and plant all absorb sound energy so that it does not bounce back.

SOUND REFLECTION

Smooth, hard surfaces reflect sound energy in the same way as a ball bounces off concrete. In this room, the sound from the stereo speakers bounces off the floor, walls, and wooden chair.

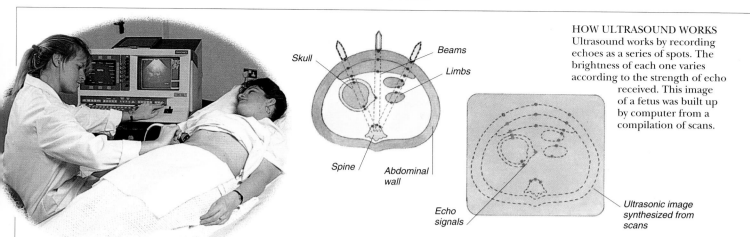

HOW ULTRASOUND WORKS
Ultrasound works by recording echoes as a series of spots. The brightness of each one varies according to the strength of echo received. This image of a fetus was built up by computer from a compilation of scans.

Skull
Beams
Limbs
Spine
Abdominal wall
Echo signals
Ultrasonic image synthesized from scans

ULTRASOUND

Sound waves with frequencies above 20,000 Hz are beyond the range of human hearing. Sound with a frequency greater than this is described as ultrasound, or ultrasonic. Ultrasound is often used in medicine because, unlike X-rays, ultrasonic waves do not damage human tissue. A scanner transmits ultrasound waves into the body, where they are reflected by different organs. The scanner receives these reflections back and displays them as an image on a screen.

ECHOLOCATION

Dolphins use ultrasound frequencies to communicate with each other and also to locate fish and underwater obstacles. The loud clicking sounds the dolphins produce bounce off objects and make echoes. These echoes enable dolphins to tell the size and distance of objects in the water around them. This system is invaluable when it comes to detecting predators such as sharks.

Clicking sounds are produced by a special organ on the dolphin's head.

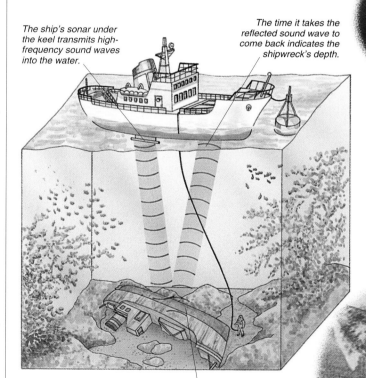

The ship's sonar under the keel transmits high-frequency sound waves into the water.

The time it takes the reflected sound wave to come back indicates the shipwreck's depth.

The shipwreck reflects the sound back.

NONDESTRUCTIVE TESTING
Important components in aircraft must not contain hidden flaws. Tiny internal cracks could grow and cause a component to fail when an aircraft is in flight. Nondestructive testing (NDT) uses ultrasound as a means of spotting such flaws without damaging the component. Pulses of ultrasound are reflected by any cracks, which show up in ultrasonic images on a screen.

Metal component is immersed in water, which acts as a conducting medium for the sound.

ECHO-SOUNDING

As a result of the *Titanic* disaster in 1912, when the ship collided with an iceberg on her maiden voyage, French scientist Paul Langevin led research projects to develop sonar. Sonar uses reflected ultrasound waves to locate icebergs, shoals of fish, wrecks, submarines, and to measure the depth of water under a ship. Pulses of sound are transmitted into the ocean. Any echoes bouncing back from an object are monitored. The time delay between transmitting a pulse and receiving its echo indicates how far away the object is.

SCREEN IMAGE

This image of a shipwreck was produced by scanning the direction of the outgoing sound. The patterns of echoes were then gradually built up on a computer screen.

Find out more

SOUND AND LIGHT P. 177
MEASURING SOUND P. 180
MAKING AND HEARING SOUND P. 182
MAMMALS P. 334

MUSICAL SOUNDS

ALL MUSICAL INSTRUMENTS work by making air vibrate. Players control the frequency and amplitude of the vibrations to play tunes and make rhythms. The distinctive timber (quality of sound) of an instrument depends on the way the air vibrates. Musicians blow air into wind instruments either across a hole or past a flexible reed. The air inside a flute, which does not have a reed, vibrates simply to make a pure, sweet sound. Air blown past the reeds inside bagpipe tubes vibrates in a complex way to produce a rich, rasping sound. All acoustic (nonelectric) string, wind, and percussion instruments are played by plucking or bowing, blowing, and striking.

Long, thick strings make low-pitched notes. Short, thin strings make high-pitched notes.

Soundboard resonates and amplifies the sound of the piano.

Hammers

Keys

Pianists can use all their fingers to play up to 10 notes at the same time.

STRING HARMONICS

Harmonics are the different frequencies at which something can vibrate. A string stretched between two supports can vibrate so that varying numbers of wavelengths fit along the string. The wave with the longest wavelength is called the fundamental. Other vibrations have shorter wavelengths and higher frequencies. This progressive series of frequencies is known as harmonics. The proportion of different harmonics gives an instrument its individual sound.

Node   Antinode   Node

Fundamental harmonic

Second harmonic

Third harmonic

PIANO

Piano keys are connected to hammers that strike strings when the keys are pressed. The pianist can press several keys at once to play chords. Some combinations of notes are pleasing to the ear, but others are not. The effect of combining notes to make chords is called musical harmony.

Short pipes make high-pitched notes.

Antinodes at either end of an open pipe are where the air moves most.

Air does not move at a node.

PIPES

The column of air inside a pipe vibrates by stretching and compressing. There is a point in the middle of the column where the air does not move. This is called the node. The air vibrates most at the ends of the column. These areas are called antinodes.

Long pipes make low-pitched notes.

Turning the keys changes the tension of the string.

Pressing the strings onto frets shortens the length.

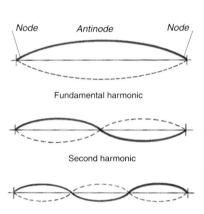

TRUMPET

A trumpeter vibrates his or her lips to make the air inside the tube resonate. Trumpeters can play different notes by changing lip tension and by opening and closing valves that alter the length of the tube. Long columns of air vibrate more slowly and make lower-pitched notes than shorter columns. Blowing harder makes the sound louder.

SITAR

Each string of a stringed instrument vibrates at its own natural frequency. The frequency of a string can be increased by shortening the length, increasing the tension, and by using a lighter string. In many stringed instruments, vibrations are passed to the body of the instrument, which resonates to amplify the sound.

ORCHESTRA

The combination of differently pitched string, wind, and percussion instruments in an orchestra produces a huge variety of harmony and timber. It is a combination that has been carefully planned—each group of instruments has its own special part to play in the performance of a piece of music. An orchestra can play so softly that it can only just be heard, but when everyone plays together loudly, the sound level can reach 100 dB.

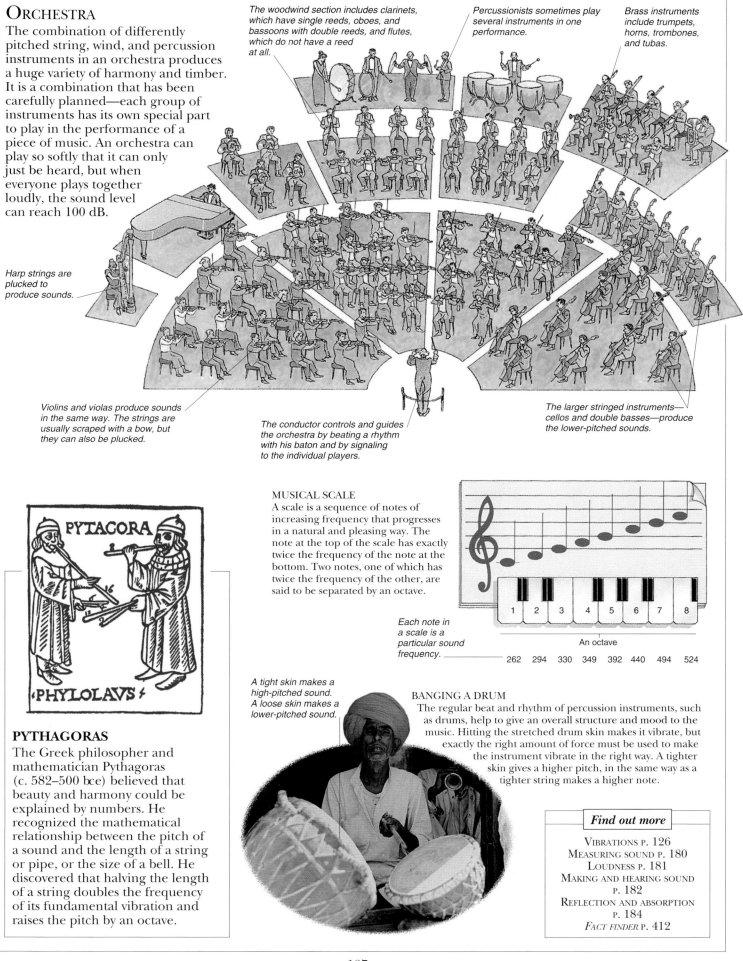

The woodwind section includes clarinets, which have single reeds, oboes, and bassoons with double reeds, and flutes, which do not have a reed at all.

Percussionists sometimes play several instruments in one performance.

Brass instruments include trumpets, horns, trombones, and tubas.

Harp strings are plucked to produce sounds.

Violins and violas produce sounds in the same way. The strings are usually scraped with a bow, but they can also be plucked.

The conductor controls and guides the orchestra by beating a rhythm with his baton and by signaling to the individual players.

The larger stringed instruments—cellos and double basses—produce the lower-pitched sounds.

PYTHAGORAS

The Greek philosopher and mathematician Pythagoras (c. 582–500 bce) believed that beauty and harmony could be explained by numbers. He recognized the mathematical relationship between the pitch of a sound and the length of a string or pipe, or the size of a bell. He discovered that halving the length of a string doubles the frequency of its fundamental vibration and raises the pitch by an octave.

MUSICAL SCALE

A scale is a sequence of notes of increasing frequency that progresses in a natural and pleasing way. The note at the top of the scale has exactly twice the frequency of the note at the bottom. Two notes, one of which has twice the frequency of the other, are said to be separated by an octave.

Each note in a scale is a particular sound frequency.

An octave

1	2	3	4	5	6	7	8
262	294	330	349	392	440	494	524

A tight skin makes a high-pitched sound. A loose skin makes a lower-pitched sound.

BANGING A DRUM

The regular beat and rhythm of percussion instruments, such as drums, help to give an overall structure and mood to the music. Hitting the stretched drum skin makes it vibrate, but exactly the right amount of force must be used to make the instrument vibrate in the right way. A tighter skin gives a higher pitch, in the same way as a tighter string makes a higher note.

Find out more

VIBRATIONS P. 126
MEASURING SOUND P. 180
LOUDNESS P. 181
MAKING AND HEARING SOUND
P. 182
REFLECTION AND ABSORPTION
P. 184
FACT FINDER P. 412

SOUND RECORDING

JUST AS WORDS written on paper can be read again and again, sounds can be recorded and replayed. All sound recordings store sounds by making a copy of the sound waves. There are two types of sound recording: analog and digital. Analog recordings store sound wave patterns as a wavy line cut in a record or as magnetic patterns on a strip of tape. Digital recordings convert sound wave patterns into numbers that map the positions of all the points on a sound wave before being recorded. These numbers are stored as tiny pits on a compact disc (CD) or as magnetic patterns on digital audio tape (DAT), and then converted back into sound by a microprocessor chip.

Sounds are recorded on a CD as tiny pits that are detected by a laser.

The pits are digits in binary numbers.

Electrical signals from the microphone are fed to the record head. Its magnetic field arranges the particles into a pattern.

Digital recordings do not suffer from hiss like tapes, or from scratches like records.

DIGITAL RECORDING

Sound is recorded on a CD as tiny pits pressed into the surface of the flat disc. The pits are digits in binary numbers. Each number is a measure of the height of the sound wave at a given moment. As the disc spins, the CD player's beam scans the surface. When the beam hits a flat part of the disc, it is reflected to a photo-detector that changes the light into electrical pulses. When the beam strikes a pit, it is reflected away.

Sound waves can be recorded as a series of numbers. Each number gives the height of the sound wave at a particular instant.

TAPE RECORDING

The tape inside a cassette is coated with a layer of oxide containing magnetic metals. On a blank tape, the magnetic particles point in random directions, but when a sound is recorded on the tape, the particles are arranged in a pattern that changes in step with the sound.

RECORDING STUDIO

Recordings are made by mixing sounds from different instruments and vocalists. There is no need to record everything at once—the sound engineer can add sounds one on top of the other. The engineer mixes the sounds using sliders on the mixing desks.

RECORDS

As the stylus in the pickup head of the record player runs in the groove, it vibrates, following the pattern of the sound waves. This sets up electrical signals in the pickup head. On a stereo record, the patterns on opposite sides of the groove are slightly different, so different sounds come from right- and left-hand speakers.

Stylus in pickup head runs in the groove.

Groove is more than 1,300 ft (400 m) long!

THOMAS EDISON

The first sound recording in 1877 was of the words "Mary had a little lamb..." spoken by Thomas Edison (1847–1931) into his phonograph. This recorded sound by scratching a groove in a wax cylinder. It had no electrical parts, and relied on the mechanical vibrations of a needle to record and reproduce sounds.

Find out more

SEMIMETALS P. 39
MAGNETISM P. 154
ELECTROMAGNETISM P. 156
ELECTRONIC SOUNDS P. 189

ELECTRONIC SOUNDS

EVERY SINGLE SOUND we know, including the sounds of the human voice, can be produced electronically by digital sound technology. Electronic instruments can also create completely new sounds. Acoustic instruments can be replaced by synthesized sounds or by sound samples—recordings that can be played forward, backward, at a different pitch, or processed in various ways by computer. Echoes and reverberation can also be added to sounds electronically. In fact, it is possible for one person working in a small room with a keyboard and computer to produce the sound of a whole orchestra.

Machine head alters the tension in the strings so that they can be tuned.

Pickups produce a small electrical signal when the strings vibrate.

The guitarist controls the signal processing with a foot pedal.

The amplifier amplifies the signal from the guitar to drive a loudspeaker.

The effects processor can add echo, fuzz, or distortion to the sound of the guitar.

SPECIAL EFFECTS

Electronic music and special effects are composed for radio and television in a radiophonic workshop. In the early days of broadcasting, the sounds of thunder were made by shaking a large metal sheet; and the sounds of horses' hooves by tapping coconut shells. Now these sounds can be synthesized.

ELECTRIC GUITAR

An electric guitar actually makes little sound of its own—the sound it produces is made possible by electricity. Plucking the metal strings makes them vibrate. These vibrations are changed into tiny electrical signals in the pickups beneath the strings. These signals are amplified and processed to make the guitar sound clear or fuzzy, harsh or sweet.

Words are entered into the computer through the keyboard and spoken by a synthesized voice.

SYNTHESIZED SOUNDS

A synthesizer is a musical instrument used to make sounds electronically. The Moog synthesizer, which was designed and developed by the American engineer Robert Moog in the 1950s, played one note at a time. Today's digital synthesizers can produce very complex arrangements of sounds. Professor Stephen Hawking cannot speak, but is able to communicate using a computer that synthesizes speech.

Computer

With a MIDI link, a computer can be programmed to control the sounds produced by electronic instruments.

Sound is picked up by a microphone.

SAMPLING

A sampler records natural sounds and stores them digitally. When the sound is played back, the numbers can be altered to change the frequencies, and therefore the pitch, of the original sound. A sampler can even make a musical scale from the sound of a dog barking.

Drum machine

Keyboard

Sounds are stored digitally in the sampler.

Sound is played back on a keyboard.

MIDI SYSTEM

A Musical Instrument Digital Interface (MIDI) system makes it possible for a computer to trigger instruments such as keyboards and drum machines to make sounds together or in sequence. This means that composers using a MIDI system can write film scores, music for television, and pop songs—without having to use a band or an orchestra.

Find out more

COMPUTERS p. 173
MEASURING SOUND p. 180
REFLECTION AND
ABSORPTION p. 184
MUSICAL SOUNDS p. 186
SOUND RECORDING p. 188

LIGHT

WHAT IS LIGHT? It is something we see and use every day, but do not often think about. Light is a form of energy. The energy from the Sun powers all of life on Earth. Light travels very fast. When we switch on a lightbulb, light floods the room almost instantly. Almost, but not quite; it is actually traveling at about 186,000 miles (300,000 km) per second. In fact, the speed of light is the universal speed limit. Nothing can travel faster. Light sometimes seems to act as a wave, but unlike sound waves or water waves, it can travel through a vacuum. At other times, light seems to act as if it were a stream of particles. Light usually comes from hot objects—such as the Sun or flames—but it can be made in other ways too. Electricity can give off light, and some chemical reactions can too—such as those in a firefly which cause it to glow in the dark.

LIGHT ENERGY

Just by standing in sunlight, you can feel the energy that light carries. It heats your body and causes chemical reactions that tan and burn skin. The light falling on each square yard of the Earth's surface could power 10 electric lightbulbs. Solar power plants harness this energy by using mirrors to focus sunlight on to a central receiver. This creates steam that can then generate electricity.

Mirror

When the laser beam meets a mirror, it is reflected, just like a pool ball bouncing off the side of the table.

Hot objects, such as the hot filament of this lightbulb, give out light.

Light sometimes behaves as though it were made up of a stream of particles.

Light sometimes behaves as though it is traveling in transverse waves.

In empty space, the light of a laser beam travels in a straight line.

REFLECTION AND REFRACTION

Light travels in a straight line through empty space, but when it meets an object, it changes direction. Some surfaces, such as mirrors, reflect light like a ball bouncing off a hard surface. Other materials, such as glass and water, refract light. This means they slow down the light beam, and deflect its path (slightly change its direction).

When the laser beam meets glass, it is refracted. Its path is deflected as it travels into the glass from the air.

PARTICLES OR WAVES?

Isaac Newton (1642–1727) thought that light was made of microscopic particles resembling tiny pool balls. Dutch mathematician Christiaan Huygens (1629–95) suggested that light is a wave motion, like sound or water waves. Modern quantum theory describes how light behaves in some ways like waves, but in other ways like particles.

PHOTOELECTRIC EFFECT

If light is shone on to a metal, it can knock electrons out of metal atoms. This principle, called the photoelectric effect, is used in the photocells of a solar-powered calculator, which can generate electricity from light. But increasing the intensity of the light does not increase the speed of the ejected electrons, it just increases their number. This can only be explained by thinking of light as little packets of light energy called photons. When a photon strikes an atom it gives its energy to an electron, which flies out of the atom. More photons knock out more electrons.

Photons of light

Transparent film

Silicon

Solar-powered calculator

A photon gives its energy to an electron in a silicon atom. The electron flies out and can join with others to make an electric current to show the numbers.

DIFFRACTION AND INTERFERENCE

When a light beam passes through a narrow slit, it spreads out. The narrower the slit, the wider the spread. This is called diffraction. You can see this effect if you squint at street lamps through your eyelashes. If two diffracted light beams overlap, the pattern they make can only be explained if light is a wave made up of peaks and troughs. In some places, two peaks or two troughs will meet to form very bright spots. In other places, a trough will meet a peak; these cancel each other out, leaving darkness. This is called interference.

QUANTUM THEORY

The German physicist Max Planck (1858–1947) was the first to suggest that light is neither purely a wave nor purely a particle, but has a combination of both properties. This theory was later expanded by Albert Einstein. To understand how light is reflected, refracted, and diffracted, we need to think of light as being like sound waves, with both a wavelength and a frequency. But to understand how atoms emit and absorb light, we must think of light as a stream of particles called photons, each carrying a certain amount of energy. This theory is called quantum theory.

An atom is given energy that can "excite" an electron, causing it to jump into a higher energy level.

When this excited electron falls back down into its original energy level, a photon of light is emitted.

SPEED OF LIGHT

Light travels much too fast to be measured with an ordinary clock. French physicist Hippolyte Fizeau (1819–96) made an experimental measurement of the speed of light in 1849. He shone a light through a toothed wheel toward a mirror 5.5 miles (9 km) away. He speeded up the wheel until the reflected light beam could be seen through the gaps between teeth. Fizeau then knew that the light had traveled to the mirror and back in the time the wheel had turned by just one tooth.

The light from the source is reflected straight back by a mirror 5.5 miles (9 km) away.

Source of light

The observer speeds up the wheel until a continuous beam of light can be seen.

A toothed wheel is rotated very fast so that the light beam passes through one gap on its outward journey, and can return through the next gap.

Find out more

ENERGY SOURCES P. 134
SOUND P. 178
ELECTROMAGNETIC SPECTRUM P. 192
SOURCES OF LIGHT P. 193
REFLECTION P. 194
REFRACTION P. 196
LIGHT AND MATTER P. 200

ELECTROMAGNETIC SPECTRUM

JUST AS LIGHT TRAVELS IN WAVES, so do other forms of energy, including radio waves, microwaves, and ultraviolet waves. These are all electromagnetic waves. The total range of electromagnetic waves is called the electromagnetic spectrum. The colors of the rainbow form the only part of this spectrum that we can see. All the other waves are invisible. Although all these waves travel at the speed of light, each group of waves has a different wavelength and carries a different amount of energy. Infrared, microwave, and radio waves have a longer wavelength and carry less energy than visible light. Ultraviolet, X-ray, and gamma rays have a shorter wavelength and carry more energy.

The Sun is a source of electromagnetic waves.

GAMMA RAYS
Gamma rays are very penetrating. They carry lots of energy and damage living cells as they pass through. Gamma rays are given out by the nuclei of radioactive atoms in nuclear reactions and explosions.

RADIO WAVES
The electromagnetic waves used to broadcast radio and television have wavelengths ranging from hundreds of feet down to fractions of an inch. The size of the antenna needed to detect a radio signal is closely related to the wavelength.

Visible light is the only part of the electromagnetic spectrum we can see.

X-RAYS
X-rays have enough energy to travel through a considerable thickness of material—including the human body. On an X-ray photograph the denser parts of the body show up as shadows.

MICROWAVES
Microwaves are the shortest of the radio waves and are used to transmit radar signals. Some microwaves have the same frequency as water molecules, and can be used to cook moist food. The energy of the microwaves is converted into heat as the water molecules vibrate.

ULTRAVIOLET WAVES
Sunlight contains ultraviolet (UV) rays. Small amounts of UV rays are good for us, but large amounts can be bad for our eyes and cause skin cancer. It is these waves that tan and burn fair skins.

JAMES CLERK MAXWELL
It was the Scottish physicist James Clerk Maxwell (1831–79) who formulated the equations of electricity and magnetism that predicted the existence of electromagnetic waves. Approximately 15 years after Maxwell published his equations, Heinrich Hertz first produced and detected radio waves.

INFRARED WAVES
All warm objects give off infrared rays. Special photographs taken with infrared rays are called thermographs. Each color represents a different skin temperature, ranging from yellow (hottest) through to blue (coldest).

Find out more

SOURCES OF LIGHT

EVERY OBJECT IN THE UNIVERSE gives off electromagnetic waves—stars, trees, and even our bodies. Most of the time these are invisible because their frequency is below that of visible light. But if an object is heated, the frequency of the radiation increases and visible light is produced. Objects start to glow dull red at about 900°F (500°C). At 3,500°F (2,000°C) they are bright orange, while at 9,000°F (5,000°C) they glow white hot, emitting all the colors of the visible spectrum. But it is not only hot objects that produce light. An electric current passed through a gas excites electrons which then lose their extra energy as light. Chemicals can also release light. The glowing patterns along the bodies of some deep-sea fish are produced by chemical reactions.

SOLAR SPECTRUM

The surface temperature of the Sun is 10,000°F (5,500°C). At this temperature all the colors of the visible spectrum are produced. But atoms in the cooler outer layers of the Sun's atmosphere absorb certain frequencies of the sunlight as it passes through. This causes dark lines on the solar spectrum, which are known as the Fraunhofer lines.

EDISON'S LIGHTBULB
American inventor Thomas Edison (1847–1931) made the first practical electric lightbulb in 1879. He passed an electric current through a carbon filament to heat it so that it glowed brightly. Modern bulbs have a tungsten filament that heats up to about 5,500°F (3,000°C).

Different gases produce different colored lights. Neon, for example, always gives out a red light.

NEON LIGHTS
A glass tube filled with gas produces light when an electric current flows through it. This is not because the gas is hot, but because the electrons of the gas are given energy that they lose by emitting it as light.

Positions of the Fraunhofer lines indicate which elements are present in the Sun's atmosphere.

SPECTROMETER
A glass prism changes the direction of different colors of light by varying amounts. In this way it can split a light mixture into a spectrum. An instrument called a spectrometer uses a prism to split the light from a light source into a spectrum. The wavelengths of light in the spectrum show which elements are present in the source.

LEDs can produce red, orange, yellow, and green light.

GUSTAV KIRCHOFF

German physicist Gustav Kirchoff (1824–87) studied light spectra using the spectrometer he developed with the chemist Robert Bunsen. He observed that individual atoms and molecules emit certain colors only when heated. Kirchoff realized that each element produces a distinct spectrum of colored lines that can be used to identify the element.

LIGHT-EMITTING DIODES
Many modern appliances have a light-emitting diode (LED) display. LEDs change electrical energy into light energy—they give out light when a current flows through them. LEDs are small, need only a small current, and last longer than filament lamps.

LEDs are sometimes used in displays in calculators, cash registers, and digital clocks.

Find out more

NOBLE GASES P. 48
CHEMICAL REACTIONS P. 52
ELECTRICITY SUPPLY P. 160
COLOR P. 202

REFLECTION

The image in a plane mirror is laterally inverted. This means that the right side of the object appears as the left side of the image.

WE SEE SOME OBJECTS because they make their own light—like the Sun or a lightbulb. But we can also see objects that do not give off their own light. They reflect light—light rays bounce off them. We see the Moon because it reflects the Sun's light. Gases are generally invisible because they are too thin to scatter enough light to be seen. But liquids and solids are clearly visible. The appearance of an object depends both on the amount of light it reflects and on the texture of its surface. A smooth white surface, for example, reflects more light than a rough dark one does. If a surface does not reflect any light at all, it looks black.

MIRROR IMAGE

Have you ever noticed that the mirror image of an object appears to be as far behind a plane (flat) mirror as the object is in front? But it is not a real image; there is no light coming from behind the mirror—the reflected light just travels to our eyes as if it had come from an object where the image is. This type of image is called a virtual image.

Virtual image is the same size as the object.

Light source

SPECULAR REFLECTION

Light is reflected from a smooth surface at a definite angle. Specular reflection of a laser beam produces a bright spot on a screen.

Specular reflection

Reflected image

Light source

Diffuse reflection

DIFFUSE REFLECTION

Rough surfaces reflect light diffusely—scattering it in all directions. Diffuse reflection of a laser beam produces a fuzzy patch of light on a screen.

TWO-WAY MIRRORS

A glass sheet reflects about 5 percent of the light falling on it. The other 95 percent passes through. If the light is equally bright on both sides, the reflections look weak. But if it is dark on one side and bright on the other, the bright side looks like a mirror because there is no transmitted light swamping the reflection. People on the bright side can see themselves reflected. People on the dark side can see through the glass to the other side.

Angled glass

Audience

Hidden actor

Mirror

Stage

Light

GHOSTLY APPARITION

A two-way mirror was used in 19th-century theaters to produce a ghostly image. Light shining on a hidden actor was reflected from a mirror onto a large sheet of angled glass, and then onto the stage. If the stage was dark, the audience could not see the glass. All they could see was the phantom appearing and disappearing!

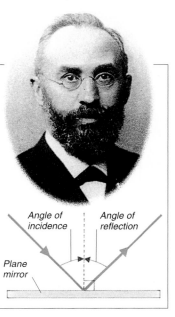

HENDRIK LORENTZ

The Dutch physicist Hendrik Lorentz (1853–1928) used James Clerk Maxwell's theory of electromagnetic waves to explain how light is reflected. Light energy is absorbed by electrons, which then reemit it at a new angle. Lorentz's theory confirms the law of reflection, which states that the angle of reflection is equal to the angle of incidence.

Angle of incidence

Angle of reflection

Plane mirror

TELESCOPE MIRRORS

The world's largest optical telescopes use a large concave (dish-shaped) mirror to collect the light from distant stars. This curved mirror catches parallel light rays in such a way that they are concentrated on one point.

The large main mirror is a concave mirror several yards in diameter.

Light reflected from the concave mirror is sent to a smaller mirror. This smaller mirror reflects the light to a camera that produces either a photographic image or a television image.

Image is upside-down, real, and reduced.

REAL IMAGE IN A CONCAVE MIRROR

A concave mirror can focus light from a distant object to project an upside-down image onto a screen. The size of the image depends on the distance between the object and the mirror. The nearer the object is to the mirror, the larger the image becomes.

Reflected waves seem to come from a point behind the barrier.

Barrier

Reflected wave

REARVIEW MIRROR

Rearview mirrors are convex. They are curved outward like the back of a spoon. Convex mirrors reflect light to produce an image that is always upright and reduced (smaller). This is useful if you want a wide field of view, such as in the rearview mirror. The driver can see farther out of the sides than with a flat mirror.

VIRTUAL WAVES

The way in which a plane mirror produces an image can be demonstrated with water waves. Think of the barrier as a plane mirror. When the circular waves meet the barrier, they are reflected. These reflected waves appear to come from a point behind the barrier. As the waves do not really come from this point, it is called a virtual image.

NOVELTY MIRRORS

A curved fairground mirror produces distorted images that can be both scary and amusing. In reality, it is the mirrors themselves that are distorted. Their concave and convex surfaces make the mirrors hollow in some places and bumpy in others. A bumpy convex surface makes things look smaller. A hollow concave surface magnifies. You may appear to have a long thin body and short fat legs. Other parts of you may be upside-down.

Image is upright and virtual, as well as magnified.

SHAVING MIRROR

If you put your face close to a concave mirror, the light is reflected, producing a magnified image of your face. But if you move farther away from the mirror, the image becomes confused and then reappears upside-down and reduced. You can see the same effects by looking into the curved surface of a shiny spoon.

Find out more

ELECTROMAGNETIC SPECTRUM P. 192
LENSES P. 197
OPTICAL INSTRUMENTS P. 198
LIGHT AND MATTER P. 200

REFRACTION

LIGHT TRAVELS in straight lines. But when it passes from one transparent material to another, the light rays bend. This is called refraction, and is why a straw standing in a glass of water looks bent at the point where it enters the water. Refraction occurs because light travels at different speeds in different materials. Refraction was first investigated by a Dutch mathematician called Willebrord Snell in 1621. A number called the refractive index measures the amount a light beam bends when it travels from one substance to another. Relative to air, air has a refractive index of 1, water 1.3, and most glass 1.5. Light is not bent as much when it enters water as when it enters glass because it is not slowed down as much.

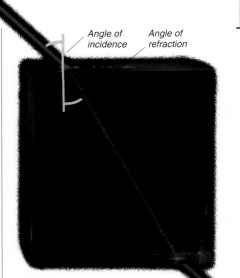

Angle of incidence   Angle of refraction

REFRACTIVE INDEX

A laser beam entering a glass block at an angle (the angle of incidence) is refracted because light travels more slowly in glass than in air. A number called the refractive index of a material gives the relationship between the two speeds. In this case, the speed of light in air divided by the speed of light in glass gives the refractive index of glass as compared with air.

Fast truck

Truck slows down

ALL CHANGE
When a truck's wheels move at an angle from a hard surface onto grass, the grass slows down the wheels of the truck on one side, causing the truck's path to bend. Light is refracted in the same way when it travels from air into glass.

Each fiber is a fine strand of glass. Internal reflection channels light along the fiber even if it is bent or twisted.

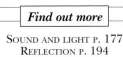

ENDOSCOPE
The principle of internal reflection is put to good use in medicine. An endoscope is an optical device for inspecting the inside of the body without having to operate. It consists of a bundle of flexible optical fibers. Light is channeled along the fibers by internal reflections. A doctor can insert an endoscope down a patient's throat to examine the inside of the stomach.

Angle of incidence

Incident beam

Angle of incidence equals critical angle.

The light beam is internally reflected.

INTERNAL REFLECTION
The glass block above shows how light is refracted as it emerges from glass into air and its speed increases. When the angle of incidence is small, the beam emerges at a larger angle. But as the angle of incidence increases (right), the light beam becomes more and more refracted until, at a certain angle of incidence called the critical angle, the light is bent so much that it does not emerge from the glass at all—it is reflected inside. This is called internal reflection.

Angle of refraction

Light rays from the button are refracted as they leave the water. You see the button as though the light rays were traveling in a straight line.

Bent light rays

Light from distant object

Cool air

Warm air

DIFFERENT DEPTHS
Have you ever noticed that pools and ponds are always deeper than they look? This is because light is refracted as it leaves the water, making the bottom of the pool appear closer than it really is. You can see this effect in this glass of water. Light rays are refracted in such a way as to make the button look closer than it really is.

MIRAGE
When light bends, it tricks us into seeing things in the wrong place. A mirage is caused by light refraction in the atmosphere. Light travels more quickly through the warmer air near the ground than it does through the cooler air above. Light is refracted in a curved path, producing a false image of a distant object. Mirages are common in deserts where the air is very hot.

Image appears here

Find out more
SOUND AND LIGHT P. 177
REFLECTION P. 194
COLOR P. 202
VISION P. 204
FACT FINDER P. 412

LENSES

Light source

Concave lens

Convex lens

Light rays diverge

THE FACT THAT LIGHT BENDS when it passes from air to glass can be made to work to our advantage. Lenses are specially shaped pieces of glass or transparent plastic that focus light, produce images, and magnify or reduce a scene by bending the light traveling through them. A lens becomes steadily more angled toward the edge and may be either thicker or thinner at the center than at the edge. The shape of the lens means that light is bent either toward or away from a single focus (point). Each of our eyes has a natural lens. You are using yours now to focus on these words.

Light rays converge to a focus

THICK AND THIN

A lens that is thicker in the middle than at the edge is called a convex lens. A convex lens converges (brings together) parallel light rays to a focus after they have passed through the lens. A lens that is thinner in the middle is called a concave lens. This kind of lens diverges (spreads out) parallel light rays so that they appear to come from a focal point on the other side of the lens.

FRESNEL LENS
French physicist Augustin Fresnel (1788–1827) invented a lens made from a series of glass rings. Fresnel lenses are not suitable for producing images because they distort too much, but they are good for concentrating light beams. They are often used in lighthouses, car headlights, and projectors.

Convex lens magnifies image on the slide

Object

Magnified virtual image

SLIDE PROJECTOR
The convex lens in a projector produces a magnified real image of the slide. The image is real because light passes through it and the image can be projected on a screen. The image is inverted (upside-down), so the slide must be put in upside-down to appear the right way up on the screen.

Magnified virtual image

Object

Lens

ANTONI VAN LEEUWENHOEK
Dutchman Antoni van Leeuwenhoek's (1632–1723) microscope made it possible to study bacteria and blood cells for the first time. This simple device was basically a powerful lens made from a glass bead mounted on a metal plate.

MAGNIFYING GLASS
Objects look much bigger when seen through the convex lens of a magnifying glass. Tracing the path of light beams through the lens shows how it produces a magnified virtual image of an object. The extent of the magnification depends on the focal length of the lens. The thicker the lens, the shorter the focal length. Lenses with shorter focal lengths are more powerful.

Find out more

POLYMERS P. 100
GLASS P. 110
OPTICAL INSTRUMENTS P. 198
VISION P. 204
PHOTOGRAPHY P. 206

OPTICAL INSTRUMENTS

MANY FASCINATING DISCOVERIES have been made through the lens of an optical instrument. Even a simple magnifying glass reveals many times more detail than we can see with the naked eye. The more sophisticated instruments—made with a combination of mirrors and lenses—make it possible to study everything from the tiniest living organisms to the most distant objects in the universe. Microscopes using light can magnify up to 2,000 times. Telescopes can capture and analyze light from objects a million times more distant than any star we can see in the night sky.

Eyepiece lens

Different strength objective lenses can be swung into position when needed.

Specimen table

Mirror reflects light on to specimen above.

BINOCULARS
Binoculars consist of two refracting telescopes. Each contains an objective lens and eyepiece to form an image that appears much larger than the object being viewed.

COMPOUND MICROSCOPE
A compound microscope magnifies in two stages. Light from a mirror is reflected up through the specimen into the powerful objective lens, which produces the first magnification. The image produced by the objective lens is then magnified again by the eye lens, which acts as a simple magnifying glass.

Scales

Wasp at actual size

Veins

MICROSCOPE IMAGE
When a wasp's wing is magnified to 50 times its original size, details of the scales and veins are clearly visible. This photograph was taken through the lenses of a compound microscope.

Light source

REFLECTING TELESCOPES
Most modern astronomical telescopes are reflectors, with a large concave mirror that collects and concentrates light. A second mirror reflects the light to the eye lens or camera.

Second mirror

A camera or electronic light detector is often attached to the eyepiece.

Concave mirror

Light source

Objective convex lens

REFRACTING TELESCOPE
A refracting telescope has a large convex lens that refracts the light to form an upside-down image of a distant object.

Eye lens magnifies image.

IMPORTANT TELESCOPES

1789 William Herschel telescope, England, 4 ft (1.23 m) diameter.

1845 Lord Rosse telescope, Ireland, 6 ft (1.83 m) diameter.

1917 Mount Wilson telescope, California, 8 ft (2.54 m) diameter.

1948 Hale Reflector, Palomar, California, 16 ft (5 m) diameter.

1976 Mount Semirodriki telescope, Russian Federtion, 19.5 ft (6 m) diameter.

1992 Keck telescope, Hawaii, 33 ft (10 m) diameter.

HERSCHEL TELESCOPE
This 13 ft- (4.2 meter-) diameter reflecting telescope, named after William Herschel, has electronic cameras and computers to record and analyze starlight. It is situated in the clear atmosphere of the mountains of La Palma, one of the Canary Islands off Africa's northwest coast.

Find out more

REFLECTION P. 194
REFRACTION P. 196
LENSES P. 197
STUDY OF ASTRONOMY P. 296
TELESCOPES ON EARTH P. 297
TELESCOPES IN SPACE P. 298

LASERS

PENCIL BEAMS OF LASER LIGHT are now familiar sights at rock concerts. But in addition to being used for entertainment, laser light is used in many practical ways, including eye surgery, surveying, cutting steel, carrying television and computer signals along optical fibers, and for reading information from bar codes and compact discs. The property of laser light that makes it so useful is its coherence (regularity). Ordinary light waves are jumbled and irregular, but laser light waves are all in step with each other—like a marching band. They can be directed in powerful beams that are both much brighter and more parallel than light from any other source.

Laser beam is both powerful and delicate.

LASER SURGERY
Surgeons can control laser beams with great precision to make delicate cuts in the surface of a damaged eye or to burn cancer cells from a tumor.

Photon

Laser light can be produced by feeding energy into solids, liquids, or gases. The color of laser light depends on the elements present in the material.

Helium-neon laser emits red light.

Partially silvered mirror reflects most light but lets some light escape.

Power supply

LASER

Laser stands for Light Amplification by the Stimulated Emission of Radiation. That is quite a mouthful! But what happens inside a laser is easily understood. Energy from a flash tube or an electric current excites atoms in the laser material. Some of the atoms emit photons, which then stimulate more atoms to emit photons traveling in the same direction. Photons bounce up and down between the mirrors at each end of the tube.

SUPERMARKET CHECKOUT
The computerized information contained in the bar code of your shopping items is read by reflected laser light. The lasers in bar code readers are now made with semiconductors. Semiconductor lasers use much less power than the helium-neon gas lasers which were used in earlier machines.

A hologram is a 3-D picture taken with laser light. You can look around the image to view it from the side.

INDUSTRIAL LASERS
High-power lasers cut through thick steel sheets as easily as a hot knife cuts through butter. Lasers are also valuable for surveying, because a laser beam travels in such a precise straight line. The course of the Channel Tunnel between France and England was plotted by laser.

THEODORE MAIMAN
The idea for the laser, which was based on Albert Einstein's theories of light, was developed by Gordon Gould in 1957. The first working laser was built by Theodore Maiman (born 1927) in 1960. Maiman's laser generated laser light by energizing a ruby crystal with light from a flash tube. Although only an inch or so long, it worked very well.

THREE-DIMENSIONAL IMAGES
An ordinary photograph is made by one set of light waves being reflected from the object on to film. But because laser light is so regular, it can be split into two to produce a three-dimensional (3-D) image. One set of waves is reflected by the object. The other set of waves arrives at the film from a different direction without meeting the object. Where the two sets of waves meet, an interference pattern is produced which is recorded on film. When the hologram is lit in the right way, a 3-D image is reproduced.

LIGHT AND MATTER

HAVE YOU EVER FELT THE HEAT given off by a asphalt road on a sunny day? The dark asphalt absorbs the light energy falling on it, and its temperature gradually rises. While black surfaces absorb light, white surfaces reflect light and heat up more slowly in the Sun. This is why light-colored clothes are cooler than dark clothes in hot weather. In addition to being absorbed or reflected, light can also be transmitted; it passes straight through transparent materials such as glass. The way that an object (matter) absorbs, reflects, or transmits light affects the way it looks.

Photochromic spectacle lenses darken when they are exposed to bright sunshine.

PHOTOCHROMIC GLASS

In dull light, photochromic glass is almost transparent. But when it is exposed to brighter light, it darkens. The light energy changes the structure of some glass molecules so that they absorb more light. This process is reversible—away from bright light, the glass clears.

A transparent material transmits most of the light falling on it. A little is reflected, which is why we can see the surface of the glass.

A translucent material transmits light, but the light is scattered inside the material. This gives the material a milky appearance.

OPAQUE, TRANSPARENT, AND TRANSLUCENT

Everyday materials respond to light in different ways. Transparent materials transmit nearly all the light that falls on them. Other materials are translucent. Although they transmit light, the light is scattered in all directions by tiny particles inside the material. Opaque materials do not transmit any light. They either reflect it or absorb it.

Most materials are opaque. They do not transmit any light and cast dark shadows.

FLUORESCENCE

Some chemicals absorb ultraviolet light and then release the energy as visible light. This is called fluorescence. These chemicals can be used to create "glowing" clothes, paints, crayons, and even makeup. Detergent manufacturers put fluorescent chemicals in detergents to help white clothes appear even whiter in sunlight.

Light is reflected off the shiny spoon at the same angle as it arrives.

BLUE SKIES

Have you ever wondered why the sky appears blue? It looks blue because tiny particles of dust and water vapor in the atmosphere scatter the short wavelength blue light from the Sun more strongly than the longer wavelength red light. But when we look toward the setting Sun, we see the unscattered red light.

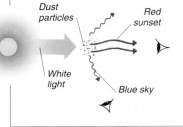

Dust particles
Red sunset
White light
Blue sky

Vertically polarized light

Horizontally polarized light

Transmitted light

Light is not transmitted

POLARIZATION

Light waves are transverse. This means that they vibrate at right angles to the direction in which they are traveling. Polarizing sunglasses only transmit light that is vibrating vertically. By absorbing horizontally polarized light, they help to reduce glare.

Find out more

SOUND P. 178
ELECTROMAGNETIC SPECTRUM P. 192
REFLECTION P. 194
REFRACTION P. 196

SHADOWS

SHADOWS ARE FORMED because light rays travel in straight lines and cannot bend around opaque objects in their path. The sharpness of a shadow depends on the light source. A point (small, concentrated) source casts sharp shadows. An extended (large) source casts fuzzy shadows. The Sun is almost a point source because it is so far away; the shadows it casts are very sharp at the edges. A more extended light source, such as a fluorescent tube, casts less distinct shadows. Perhaps the most spectacular shadows of all are eclipses—the shadows cast by the Earth and the Moon on each other when they block the light from the Sun.

SUNDIAL
The shadow cast by a sundial moves as the Sun appears to move through the sky. The motion of the shadow can be used to tell the time. The first sundials, which consisted of simple vertical poles, were used more than 4,000 years ago in China.

SHADOWS
When the Sun is directly overhead, it does not cast a shadow. But when it is lower in the sky, shadows lengthen and are much longer than the objects producing them. There are two parts to the shadow cast by the Sun—the umbra and the penumbra. The umbra is the region where the object blocks all of the Sun's light. The penumbra is where the object blocks light coming from some parts of the Sun but not from others.

Penumbra: Sun is partially hidden.

Sun

Moon

Earth

Umbra: Sun is fully hidden.

SOLAR ECLIPSE
During an eclipse of the Sun, the Moon passes between the Sun and the Earth, casting its shadow on the Earth's surface. At points lying in the penumbra, the eclipse is partial, and the Sun is only partly hidden. But in the umbra, day becomes night for a few minutes as the Sun disappears.

Penumbra

Umbra

Umbra   Penumbra

Sun

Earth   Moon

LUNAR ECLIPSE
Sometimes the Earth passes between the Sun and the Moon. This is called a lunar eclipse. When this happens, we see the Earth's shadow as it moves across the face of the Moon. At the center of the eclipse, the Moon is blocked from view for more than an hour.

SOLAR CORONA
During a total eclipse, the Sun's atmosphere, called the solar corona, is visible. Scientists are able to study the activity of the gases in the corona. Prominences, which are normally invisible because they are swamped by sunlight, can be seen hanging above the Sun's surface.

ECLIPSES AND MYTHS
Before the scientific explanation was found, an eclipse was a frightening event. It seemed to early civilizations that a monster was swallowing the Sun. But as science developed, and astronomical records were kept, it became clear that the eclipses were regular events that could be predicted.

> ### Find out more
> LIGHT P. 190
> LIGHT AND MATTER P. 200
> SUN P. 284
> MOON P. 288
> STUDY OF ASTRONOMY P. 296

COLOR

IMAGINE A WORLD in which everything was the "color" of daylight—white. Life would be very drab. Luckily, our world is colorful. Our eyes are able to distinguish the different wavelengths of visible light as different colors. Each wavelength of light, or combination of wavelengths, is a particular color. The longest wavelength that we can see is red light, and the shortest wavelengths are blue and violet. If equal amounts of all the wavelengths of light are mixed together, the result is white light. Many animals cannot distinguish between different wavelengths, so they live in a world in which everything is colorless.

White light is a mixture of wavelengths from different parts of the spectrum.

Light from the Sun is a mixture of all wavelengths from long wavelength red light to short wavelength violet light.

RAINBOW COLORS
The different colors that make up white light can be seen when a beam of light is split by a prism. The prism refracts the different wavelengths by different amounts and disperses them (spreads them out) into a spectrum so that they can be seen. Red light is refracted least, violet light the most.

Prism splits white light into its component colors.

INTERFERENCE COLORS
The brilliant colors you sometimes see on bubbles are caused by light interference. White light rays reflected from the inside of the soap film travel slightly farther than those reflected from the outside. The waves in each ray interfere with each other where they meet. Some colors cancel each other out, while others combine to form bands of colors on the surface of the bubble.

Bar is emitting waves just within the red end of the visible spectrum.

White light contains all the colors of the spectrum.

Magenta filter transmits red and blue light but absorbs green.

Green filter transmits only the green region. It absorbs red and blue regions.

As the bar is heated more, the hottest part of it turns yellow.

The bar is now emitting most colors of the visible spectrum, which add together to give white.

COLOR TEMPERATURE
All objects give out electromagnetic waves. But they are often invisible to the eye. Heating an object gives the waves more energy, and they become shorter—short enough for us to see. At first, the heated steel bar above glows dull red. As it gets hotter, it turns to yellow. At the highest temperature, the bar gives out most colors of the visible spectrum, which mix together to give white.

Magenta

Yellow

Cyan

White light can be made by adding together just red, green, and blue light.

FILTERS
A filter is a plastic sheet that absorbs some colors but lets others pass through. For example, a green filter absorbs the red and blue parts of the spectrum but transmits the green region. A magenta filter absorbs green light and transmits red and blue.

COLORED LIGHTS
Red, green, and blue are known as the primary colors: you can mix these colored lights together to make almost any other color. If red, green, and blue lights are mixed together, we see them as white light. Where two primary colors overlap, they produce a secondary color. Red and blue make magenta. Red and green make yellow. Green and blue make cyan.

Find out more

LIGHT P. 190
ELECTROMAGNETIC SPECTRUM
P. 192
SOURCES OF LIGHT P. 193
SPECIAL EFFECTS P. 269

COLOR SUBTRACTION

OBJECTS THAT DO NOT PRODUCE light themselves are colored by a process called "color subtraction." They subtract (absorb) light from some parts of the visible spectrum but not others. For example, a leaf looks green because it absorbs nearly all the colors in sunlight except one—green, which it reflects. Pigments and dyes are natural or artificial substances added to paints and inks to give them color. A red pigment absorbs green and blue and reflects only red light. A blue pigment absorbs red and green light and reflects blue. By taking away color, these substances actually add color to our world!

Chameleon

NATURAL PIGMENTATION
The chameleon has pigmented skin cells that change size and shape to blend in with the color of the background. In this way, it is excellently camouflaged when danger threatens. Cuttlefish have evolved a "language" based on patterns of color change that ripple across their bodies.

When the color images are printed on top of each other, a full-color picture is reproduced.

Yellow

Magenta

Cyan

Black is treated as a separate color so that text and outlines are reproduced sharply.

Yellow absorbs blue light, so reflects a mixture of red and green.

Magenta absorbs green light, so reflects a mixture of red and blue.

Cyan absorbs red light, so it reflects a mixture of blue and green.

FOUR-COLOR PRINTING
All color photographs and illustrations are reproduced from just four colored inks—magenta, cyan, yellow, and black. Mixing these colors in different proportions produces all the different colors you can see. When a book or magazine is prepared for printing, the color images are scanned to separate the four colors photographically. The films are used to prepare a printing plate for each color.

MIXING PAINT
Color mixing with paint works by subtraction. Magenta, cyan, and yellow ink absorb just one primary color each from white light. Mixing any two of these colors produces a bright, primary-colored paint. Mixing all three colors together produces black.

MUNSELL COLOR TREE
If you have ever tried to match a color exactly, you know how difficult it can be. Our eyes are incredibly sensitive to very slight color differences. In fact, we can probably distinguish more than 10,000,000 various shades! The Munsell color tree is a system of grading colors. The hue (basic color), chroma (amount of color), and value (lightness or darkness) are measured. Each color is then put in position on the tree. Hue is shown by its place on the circumference; chroma by its distance from the trunk, and value by its position on the trunk.

In daylight, sneakers reflect only red light and absorb all the other colors.

In blue light, the red pigment absorbs the blue light.

RED OR BLACK SHOES?
The sneakers above appear red in daylight or when lit by red light because they reflect only red light and absorb all the others. But what happens when they are lit by blue light? They look black (above right). This is because the red pigment in the sneakers absorbs all the blue light and there is no red light in the light source to be reflected.

Find out more
DYES AND PIGMENTS P. 102
ELECTROMAGNETIC SPECTRUM P. 192
REFLECTION P. 194
COLOR P. 202

VISION

THE WAY THAT OUR EYES AND BRAIN work together to produce images is incredibly sophisticated. Imagine building a robot that could track a tiny baseball, hit at 100 miles (160 km) per hour, into the air and run across a field to make a one-handed catch. The robot would need *at least* two eyes to see in three dimensions to judge the distance to the ball. But most important of all would be the robot's brain—the computer that interprets the images that the eyes create. When it comes to recognizing images, the human brain is still far more powerful than even the most powerful computers.

Contact lens

CONTACT LENSES

As an alternative to glasses, many people wear contact lenses— thin lenses that fit over the cornea. These correct vision defects in the same way as conventional glasses, but are virtually invisible. Modern lenses are made from a soft, almost jellylike, material that floats on the surface of the eye.

Retina

Iris

Cornea

Lens

Pupil

Light rays from image travel to the eye.

Optic nerve

A concave lens spreads out light rays to correct near-sightedness

Image is upside-down because light rays cross each other in the eye. The brain interprets the image so that we see it the right way up.

THE EYE

The human eye is a tough ball filled with fluid that sits in a bony socket. The cornea is the transparent, protective surface of the eye. It also focuses light. The iris controls the amount of light passing through the pupil. It closes up the pupil in bright light and opens it wide in dim light. The lens helps to focus light on the retina, which contains a layer of light-sensitive cells. These send signals via the optic nerve to the brain, where they are interpreted to build up our view of the world.

A convex lens concentrates light rays to correct far-sightedness.

NEAR AND FAR SIGHT

Muscles change the shape of the lens to focus light onto the retina. In farsighted people, the muscles are unable to make the lens strong enough; light rays are focused *behind* the retina. In nearsighted people, the muscles cannot relax the lens enough; light rays are focused *in front* of the retina. Lenses can correct both these conditions.

Chess board seen through left eye

OPTICAL ILLUSIONS

Much of the information we gather from an image is based on our knowledge of how things *should* look. We judge the distance to an object because we are familiar with its size and know how big it should be at a certain distance. But we can be fooled! An optical illusion misleads us about the relative size or distance of an object by placing it in an unexpected situation. The two balls here look the same size, but the one behind is a soccer ball, the one in front, a golf ball.

Chess board seen through right eye

STEREO VISION

Having two eyes helps you to judge the distance to an object by giving you two viewpoints. If you look at your finger, first through one eye and then through the other, it seems to move. The movement gets bigger as you move the finger closer to your eyes. Our brains combine our right- and left-eye views into a single 3-D image.

Balls are about 9 ft (2.7 meters) apart

Retina contains a layer of light-sensitive cells called rods and cones.

Nerve cells

Cone-shaped cells detect different colors

In bright sunlight, both rods and cones are fully activated and color differences are clear.

Only the rods are stimulated in moonlight, so we cannot see colors.

RODS AND CONES

The retina contains two kinds of light-sensitive cells—rods and cones. You have about 6,000,000 cone cells and 120,000,000 rod cells in each eye. The cone-shaped cells respond to bright light and different light wavelengths, so they enable us to see colors. The rod-shaped cells are sensitive to dim light, but not to color.

Rod-shaped cells detect low light levels

NIGHT AND DAY

Color differences are clear in bright sunlight because both the rods and cones are fully activated. In moonlight, only the rods are stimulated, so color differences are much less distinct.

Loop of green dots

HOW MANY COLORS?

If your color vision is normal, you will be able to see the loop of green dots concealed in this network of red and yellow dots. About one in 15 males cannot see this pattern because they are red-green color blind; they are not as sensitive to differences between red and green as people with normal sight. Far fewer females are color blind—only one in 1,000 have difficulty in seeing the pattern.

Yellow dot

Red dot

A fly can see you coming from any direction!

Conical lens

Lens

Facet

COMPOUND EYES

The reason it is so difficult to swat a fly is because it has hundreds of eyes! Each of its compound eyes is made up of hundreds of individual facets (eyes) facing in all directions. Each facet consists of a lens at the surface with a second conical lens inside. These focus and direct the light to the optic nerve and brain.

Optic nerve fibers

Guidelines visible in ultraviolet light.

INSECT'S-EYE VIEW

Insect eyes are sensitive to a different part of the electromagnetic spectrum from the human eye. Insects can see ultraviolet radiation that we cannot detect. Some flowers have evolved with pigments that are visible only in ultraviolet light. These form guidelines that direct bees to the center of a flower to find nectar.

SIMPLE EYE

Clams have a row of simple eyes that are little more than pinhole cameras. But they are sensitive to light. They are able to detect the motion of predators so that the clam can snap shut until the danger has passed.

Find out more

ELECTROMAGNETIC SPECTRUM P. 192
LENSES P. 197
COLOR P. 202
PHOTOGRAPHY P. 206
SENSES P. 358

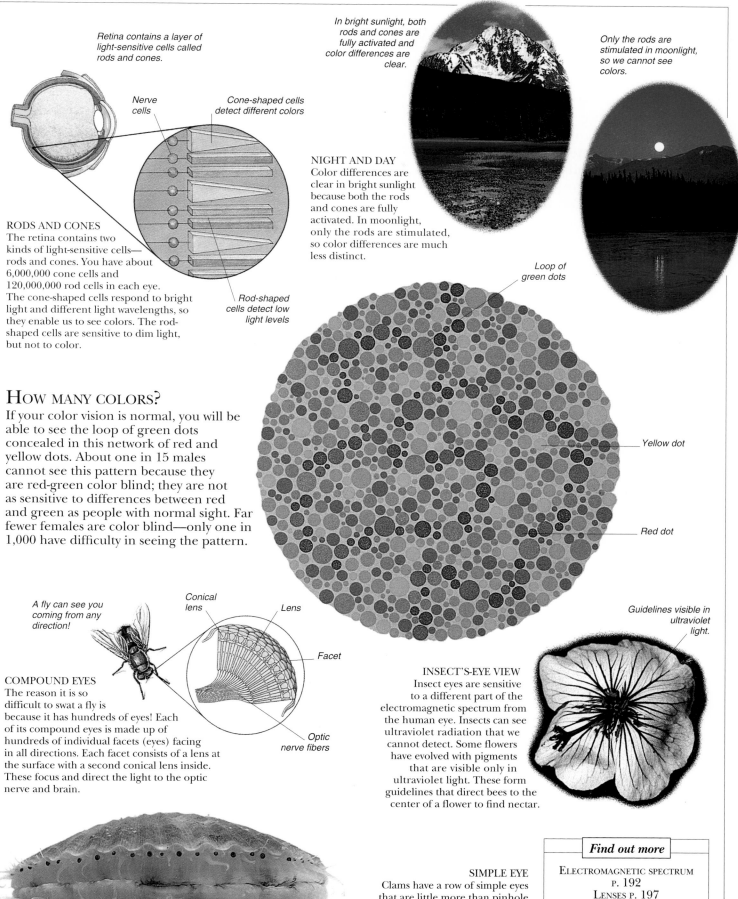

PHOTOGRAPHY

DRAMATIC NEWS PICTURES, vacation snapshots, and advertising and fashion photographs are so much a part of our lives that we take them for granted. But until the 19th century, the only way of recording a scene was to draw or paint it. The discovery that the chemical compound silver nitrate darkens when exposed to light was made by a German doctor called Johann Schulze in 1727. However, it was not until 1822 that Frenchman Joseph Nicéphore Niepce took the first photograph. Early photographs appeared in shades of dull, silvery gray, and could be seen only from certain angles. But as with most scientific discoveries, the principle was worked on and improved by others. Today, we can store electronic photographs in computers using digital cameras. "Painting with light" has come a long way!

Pop-up flash unit

Sensors read metal strips on the film cassette to detect which type of film is being used

Grip sensors shut down LCD displays to conserve power when camera is not being held

Autofocus zoom lens

Motordrives advance film and reset shutter after each shot

While the shutter is closed, a mirror and a prism send the light from the lens into the viewfinder

Light enters camera

CAMERA OBSCURA
The first cameras were based on camera obscuras. These were darkened rooms into which an image of the surrounding landscape was projected through a lens. Although entertaining, images formed by camera obscuras could not be recorded.

CAMERA
Ordinary (nondigital) cameras work by focusing the correct amount of light onto a film to form an image. The amount of light can be changed by adjusting the aperture—a hole through which the light passes, and by altering the exposure time—the time the shutter stays open to let light through. Many cameras, such as this modern Single Lens Reflex (SLR) camera, have built-in photoelectric light meters that set the correct combination of exposure time and aperture automatically.

FILM FORMATS
Early photographs were recorded on metal or glass plates. Today's flexible plastic film is far more versatile. It comes in a wide range of sizes and speeds to suit different purposes. The speed of a film is a measure of the amount of light that must fall on it for correct exposure. Fast films work with short exposure times, which means there is less danger of blurring the image with camera shake. Slower films, however, record more detail because they develop finer silver grains when exposed.

Studio photographers use large format film plates. These record very sharp images.

35 mm roll film is the most popular film format.

Pinhole

Light rays from object travel in a straight line through the pinhole and onto the screen

PINHOLE CAMERA
The simplest possible camera is a closed box with a small hole instead of a lens. This lets light through onto a screen at the back of the box. The image can be very fuzzy and long exposure times are needed.

Image is upside-down

DARKROOM

A film is coated with chemicals that are sensitive to light, which is why film developing and printing has to be done in a darkroom. Producing a black-and-white photograph is a two-stage process—each stage consisting of several steps. When print film is developed, the result is a negative image. This then has to be turned into a positive image by printing it on photographic paper.

DEVELOPING

The exposed film is taken out of its case and wound on a reel. It is then immersed in a tank containing chemicals that develop the image. The film is rinsed, after which more chemicals that fix the image are added.

Chemicals

Timer

POLAROID FILM

A Polaroid film produces almost instant pictures. When the exposed film is pulled from the pack, rollers squeeze chemicals onto the surface of the film and the image develops in about a minute. The film itself has nine separate layers, including three light-sensitive layers. Cyan, yellow, and magenta dyes spread through the image as it develops.

Shutter
Lens
Film pack
Rollers
Developer

JOSEPH NICÉPHORE NIEPCE

The first photographic image was produced by Joseph Nicéphore Niepce (1765–1833). He focused the view from his window onto a pewter sheet coated with light-sensitive bitumen and left it for eight hours. Niepce's partner, Louis Daguerre (1787–1851) later developed a more sensitive process (the Daguerreotype), requiring less than a minute's exposure.

ENLARGING AND PRINTING

After the negative has been rinsed and dried, it can be printed. The negative is placed in an enlarger. Light is shone through the negative, and a lens produces an enlarged image on light-sensitive paper. The print is then developed and fixed in the same way as the film.

Dark areas on negative let less light through than lighter areas.

COLOR PROCESSING

Color film works in a similar way to black-and-white film, but the film has three layers, each of which is sensitive to either blue, green, or red light. When the film is processed, yellow, magenta, and cyan dyes are added to the layers. The result is a full-color image.

Laptop computer

Screen

Connection cable

Mini tripod

DIGITAL PHOTOGRAPHY

A digital camera does not use film at all. Instead, it contains a light-sensitive image sensor—a chip made up of millions of tiny silicon photo diodes, each of which records the brightness and color of the light falling on it when the picture is taken. The picture information is translated into digital data and stored on the camera's memory card from where it can be printed or downloaded to a computer.

> ### Find out more
> TRANSITION METALS P. 36
> HALOGENS P. 46
> LENSES P. 197
> COLOR P. 202
> VISION P. 204
> *FACT FINDER P. 412*

CINEMA

THE NOVELTY of being able to record images on film was so exciting that people soon began looking for a way to record *moving* images. The very first "movies" were made by Thomas Edison in 1893. But these 15-second films could only be seen by one person at a time through a machine called a kinetoscope. Two French brothers, Auguste and Louis Lumière, were the first to show a moving picture to an audience in 1895. Early films were flickery, black-and-white, and silent. The first Hollywood movie with a sound track was not shown until 1927; color movie film became available in the 1930s. Today's filmakers not only have the creative ability to tell a story, but they also understand the science of sound and light.

Housing for carbon arc lamp

CINE PROJECTOR
Intense white light is generated when an electric current flows across a small gap between two carbon rods. A carbon arc lamp in this 1950s cine projector produced enough light to project a bright image onto a large screen.

CINE FILM
Cinema film, or "cine" film, is actually a series of still photographs taken rapidly one after the other. A modern cine camera takes 24 frames (photographs) each second. When the images are projected at the same rate onto a screen, the illusion of movement is created.

Image is focused by moving the lens toward or away from the film.

Light is reflected from the closed shutter and then deflected by the prism into the viewfinder so that the camera operator can see the image.

CINE CAMERA
When the camera is running, the shutter rotates—opening and shutting 24 times a second to expose each frame of the film in turn. When the shutter is closed, a special mechanism called a claw hooks into the slots at the edge of the film and drags the next frame down into the gate to be exposed. The jerky motion of the claw and film makes the whirring noise you hear when a film camera or projector is working.

Claw

Gate

FILM EDITING
Many more minutes of film are shot than are used in the final movie—and they are never shot in sequence! The film editor has to assemble the individual shots and link them together in the right order so that the film tells a story. This involves editing the film on a computer. The computer stores each image in digital form as a series of numbers.

Image is made up of red, green, and blue strips.

TV AND VIDEO
Movement on the television and video screen is created in just the same way as cinema film. Most televisions show a complete picture 25 times every second. If you look at a television screen with a magnifying glass, you can see it is made up of tiny red, green, and blue dots.

Dots combine to form strips.

Zoetropes were popular in the 19th century.

ZOETROPE
The zoetrope was a slotted drum lined with images. As it spun around, each picture was seen for a fraction of a second through a slot. If the drum spun fast enough, the pictures merged together and appeared to move.

Find out more
TELEVISION P. 166
SOUND RECORDING P. 188
LIGHT P. 190
PHOTOGRAPHY P. 206

EARTH

OF ALL THE PLANETS that have been discovered so far, Earth is the only one that contains life. From above, the Earth is seen as a mass of land, sea, and air. Each of these is changeable depending on the movement within Earth, and the energy from the Sun. The study of the Earth is ongoing, and scientists are constantly making new discoveries. The study of geology was once known as the observation of the rocks. However, during the late 20th century, geology began to broaden to the study of Earth and of all the sciences that deal with the Earth, known as "Earth sciences." This incorporates parts of modern technology, chemistry, physics, biology, and the applied sciences. Together, these teach us about the Earth.

A close look at minerals reveals the chemistry of the Earth and the different substances that are produced by geological processes. This is important in mining. The study of minerals is known as mineralogy.

Different types of minerals form different rocks. We use different kinds of rocks for buildings, for road surfacing, or as raw materials for chemicals. The study of rocks is known as petrology.

Skyscrapers are built of stone removed from the rocks, around frameworks of steel obtained from iron ore, and windows of glass made from sand. Oil is used to power the construction workers' machines. The use of geological principles to find usable materials is known as economic geology.

EARTH SCIENCE

Earth science includes the chemistry, physics, and biology of all the events that formed the Earth and that control its past, present, and future processes. In this century, a vast range of information about the Earth has been collected by geographers, geologists, oceanographers, climatologists, astronomers, and so on. We are gradually relating all these new facts to one another, building a clear picture of the structure of the Earth and its evolution through time.

We must understand the structure of the rocks to discover how safe the foundations are before sinking our buildings into them, or tunneling through mountains. The study of how rocks move and change shape is known as structural geology.

The location of farmland or towns depends on the geography and landforms of an area. The study of landforms produced by the rocks and their structures is known as geomorphology.

This map of the world is dated Antwerp, 1598.

We can compare the geology of our home planet with that of our nearest neighbors, and contrast their histories. The study of the planets, including the Earth, is known as planetology.

OLD IDEAS OF THE EARTH

About 1,500 years ago, some Hindus believed that the world was supported by four elephants standing on a giant turtle. Myths such as these of how the Earth was created are part of the tradition and early scientific thought of any civilization. As technology advances, so does our knowledge of how the Earth formed. Every new investigation and analysis brings us closer to understanding our planet and everything it contains.

EARLY MAP

The 15th and 16th centuries were a time of exploration. Sailors set out from Europe to find new lands, to expand trading empires, and to circumnavigate (sail around) the globe. The observations that they made, the specimens they collected, and the tales that they brought back provided the foundations of the earliest understanding of the Earth.

FORMATION OF THE EARTH

AROUND 5,000 MILLION YEARS AGO, the Earth was no more than a spinning cloud of gas and dust in space, part of a much, much bigger cloud. Most of the material in this big cloud clumped together at the center to form the Sun. Across the rest of the cloud, rings of material started to clump together to form planets, one of which was the Earth. Like all planets, the Earth has a layered structure, with lighter material on the outside and heavier material at the core. The original spin of the whole cloud is seen in the way the Earth moves.

The new Sun

The solar system starts as a rotating disk of gas and dust.

Heavy particles of iron and nickel sink to the center of the cloud. Lighter particles remain on the outside.

Particles of all sizes are drawn together by gravity to form balls that will eventually become planets.

THE EARLY EARTH
The solar system is thought to have formed as a rotating disk of dust and gas. Denser materials separated toward the center of the disk (eventually forming rocky planets such as Mercury, Venus, Earth, and Mars) while lighter material occupied the edge of the disk (becoming the gas planets Jupiter, Saturn, Uranus, and Neptune). Scientists believe that when the individual planets formed, material of all types was brought together by the force of gravity and then separated out into different layers. The Earth formed as ball of iron and silica-rich material. The iron and nickel sank to the center to form the core, leaving lighter material on the surface to form the crust.

A flat shield area called a continental platform is formed because an area becomes covered by undisturbed sediments.

Continental crust

Some new mountains form as oceanic crust is pulled down under a continent.

In many places the continental crust continues under the sea for some distance, forming a continental shelf.

Flat areas of continental crust are formed when deformed ancient rocks are worn smooth and covered with sediments.

Where a continent is beginning to split apart, it creates a rift valley, as in Eastern Africa.

A series of mountains forms where two continents collide.

Mountains such as the Andes of South America are formed by volcanic activity.

Ocean crust drawn down under a continent melts to produce volcanoes.

OCEANIC CRUST
The outermost layer of the Earth that lies beneath the oceans is called the oceanic crust. The oldest parts of the crust are no more than 200 million years old. This crust is continually being produced at ridges under the ocean by volcanoes that push out molten rock. Oceanic crust is destroyed as it is pulled into deep trenches. The ocean crust is made up mainly of silica and magnesium (or SIMA for short).

Oceanic crust

Ocean ridge

Volcanoes at ocean ridges push out molten rock.

The molten rock solidifies to form a layer of dense rock.

The oceanic crust is oldest and deepest away from the ocean ridge.

CONTINENTAL CRUST
The outside layer of the Earth that forms the land masses is called the continental crust. It is older and thicker than oceanic crust. Some of it has been submerged and uplifted. Each continent's complicated history is shown by its structure and the different kinds of rock it contains. Continental crust is made up of mainly silica and aluminum (or SIAL for short).

Summer in the Northern Hemisphere is when the North Pole tilts toward the Sun. There is constant daylight at the North Pole. Meanwhile, the Southern Hemisphere experiences winter.

At springtime in the Northern Hemisphere, the North and South poles receive the same amount of sunshine, so their days are the same length.

TILTED SPIN
The Earth spins on an imaginary line called its axis, running between its North and South poles. However, this axis is not a vertical line. It is tilted, so that the Earth orbits the Sun at an angle.

SEASONS
The Earth's tilted spin has a big effect on our lives; at certain times of the year, the North Pole points away from the Sun; at other times, it points toward the Sun. This produces changes in the climate that we call the seasons. Areas near the equator are not so affected by this tilt, so they have a more constant climate.

When it is fall in the Northern Hemisphere, it is spring in the Southern Hemisphere. Their days are the same length.

Winter in the Northern Hemisphere is when the North Pole is pointing away from the Sun and is in constant darkness. At the same time, the Southern Hemisphere experiences summer.

SPINNING EARTH
You might think you are standing still, but the Earth you are standing on is continually spinning in space; it is not only circling the Sun, but it is spinning on its own axis as well. A year is the time the Earth takes to make one complete circuit around the Sun. A day is the time the Earth takes to make one complete turn on its axis. When the part of Earth you are on is facing the Sun, it is day; when it is facing away from the Sun, it is night.

It takes the Earth approximately 365 days to orbit the Sun.

The Earth spins around its axis, which passes through the North and South geographic poles.

A planet's equator is at 90° to its axis.

BULGING BELLY
The Earth is not a perfect sphere shape. It bulges slightly in the middle. As the Earth spins, places on the equator move much faster than places near the poles. The faster the rotation, the stronger the force, called the centrifugal effect, which pushes material out from the center of rotation. This is what happens when you spin around, and your hair is thrown outward. This means the Earth is pushed out most around its middle.

LONGER YEARS
The spin of Earth on its axis is very, very gradually slowing down. This is because of the friction of the tides dragging water back and forth around the surface. From growth lines on coral, scientists have worked out that 400 million years ago, a year was about 400 days long. This was because the Earth was spinning faster then, and so produced shorter days.

The diameter of the Earth from pole to pole is 7,900 miles (12,714 km). The diameter through the equator is just 27 miles (43 km) longer. At the poles, the circumference (distance around the Earth) is 24,860 miles (40,008 km); the circumference at the equator is 42 miles (67 km) longer.

The bulge around the middle of Earth will decrease as the Earth's spin slows over the next few billion years.

The angle of the Earth's tilt is about 23°.

Find out more

MAGNETISM P. 154
STRUCTURE OF
THE EARTH P. 212
ROCKS AND MINERALS P. 221
ORIGIN OF THE UNIVERSE P. 275
EARTH P. 287

STRUCTURE OF THE EARTH

The Earth's layers

The upper mantle is solid and contains a soft layer called the lithosphere. It differs from the mantle below in the type of minerals it contains.

The outer layer of the Earth is made up of the crust and part of the upper mantle; together, these form the lithosphere.

The mantle is about 1,800 miles (2,900 km) thick.

This lower part of the mantle makes up the greatest part of the Earth. It consists of stony materials formed from silicate minerals.

The solid inner core is about 850 miles (1,370 km) from the Earth's surface. It is made of iron and nickel.

The Earth's only liquid layer, the outer core, is about 1,200 miles (2,000 km) thick. It is made of iron, nickel, and possibly other substances.

WHEN YOU PEEL AN APPLE, you remove only a thin, outer covering. Similarly, the surface of the Earth is only a thin layer compared to what is below. Because of the Earth's immense size, drilling does not reveal much of exactly what lies beneath. Instead, other methods have been used to discover what is inside the Earth. Most of what we know has come from the study of earthquake vibrations that run through the Earth. Over the years this has enabled geologists to build up a picture of a multilayered Earth with a solid metal center surrounded by lighter materials. The more that is known about the structure of the Earth, the more we are able to understand about the way it works.

The Earth's crust is about 4 miles (6 km) thick under the oceans, and about 22 miles (35 km) thick under the continents.

P waves detected in this area have been refracted (bent) by the different thickness of the mantle and the core.

Earthquake vibrations

Focus of an earthquake

S (secondary, shaking) waves

P (primary, pressure) waves

Neither S nor P waves are detected here as they have all been refracted (bent) by the sudden change in density between the Earth's mantle and core.

An area where no waves can be detected is known as a shadow zone.

S waves cannot pass through the liquid core and are held back in this region: only P waves manage to get through.

LAYER UPON LAYER

The Earth is made up of three main layers—the crust, the mantle, and the core. The outer layer, the crust, is a thin hard layer of rock. Heat from within the Earth causes some of the rock in the mantle to melt, whereas greater internal pressure in layers below compresses the rock into a solid state. The center of the Earth, the core, has a liquid metal outer layer, and a solid metal interior.

SEISMIC WAVES

Vibrations caused by an earthquake are known as seismic waves and can be recorded by sensitive equipment. Two types run though the Earth's interior: fast-moving primary (P) waves and slower-moving secondary (S) waves. The time delay between them can provide geologists with valuable information about where the waves originate. The waves refract (bend) when they pass through different substances, revealing changes within the Earth's interior.

The deepest hole in the world, when compared to the layers of the Earth, gives an idea of how thick each layer is.

THE DEEPEST HOLE

In 1990 the deepest hole ever drilled was in the Kola peninsula, in the former USSR. It reached a depth of 7 miles (12 km) and is planned to go down to 9 miles (15 km). But drilling would have to continue for a farther 3,947 miles (6,355 km) before the center of the Earth could be reached!

MOHO

The boundary between the crust and the mantle is known as the Mohorovicic discontinuity, or Moho for short. It is named after Andrija Mohorovicic (1857–1936), who discovered it in 1909. Mohorovicic was born in Croatia, and was a professor at Zagreb University. He noticed that earthquake waves moved at different velocities in the two layers.

EARTH'S MAGNETIC FIELD

The Earth acts in the same way as a huge magnet. A magnet attracts certain materials toward it (such as iron) in an area known as the magnetic field. Each magnet has two magnetic poles. These are places around which magnetic materials tend to concentrate. The Earth's magnetic poles are situated near the geographical North and South poles. The Earth's magnetic field is known as the magnetosphere. This reaches far out into space and protects our planet's life from harmful solar radiation. The magnetosphere is pulled into a teardrop shape by the continuous stream of electrically charged particles from the Sun, known as the solar wind.

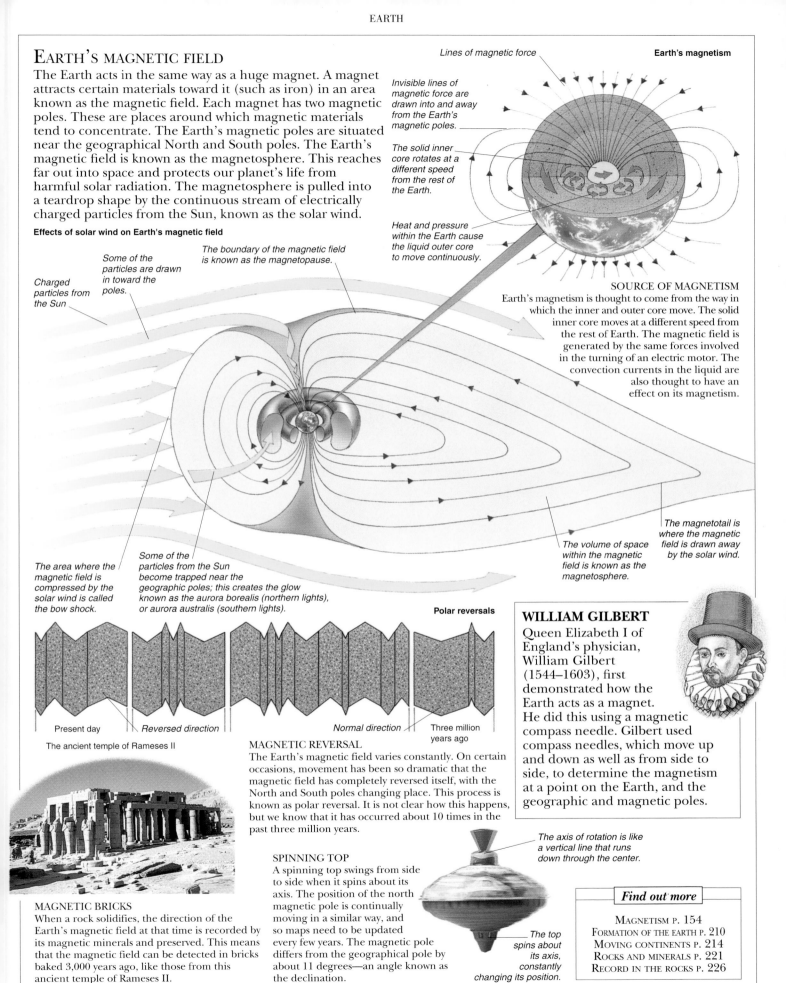

Earth's magnetism

Lines of magnetic force

Invisible lines of magnetic force are drawn into and away from the Earth's magnetic poles.

The solid inner core rotates at a different speed from the rest of the Earth.

Heat and pressure within the Earth cause the liquid outer core to move continuously.

Effects of solar wind on Earth's magnetic field

Some of the particles are drawn in toward the poles.

The boundary of the magnetic field is known as the magnetopause.

Charged particles from the Sun

The area where the magnetic field is compressed by the solar wind is called the bow shock.

Some of the particles from the Sun become trapped near the geographic poles; this creates the glow known as the aurora borealis (northern lights), or aurora australis (southern lights).

The volume of space within the magnetic field is known as the magnetosphere.

The magnetotail is where the magnetic field is drawn away by the solar wind.

SOURCE OF MAGNETISM
Earth's magnetism is thought to come from the way in which the inner and outer core move. The solid inner core moves at a different speed from the rest of Earth. The magnetic field is generated by the same forces involved in the turning of an electric motor. The convection currents in the liquid are also thought to have an effect on its magnetism.

Polar reversals

Present day | Reversed direction | Normal direction | Three million years ago

The ancient temple of Rameses II

MAGNETIC REVERSAL
The Earth's magnetic field varies constantly. On certain occasions, movement has been so dramatic that the magnetic field has completely reversed itself, with the North and South poles changing place. This process is known as polar reversal. It is not clear how this happens, but we know that it has occurred about 10 times in the past three million years.

WILLIAM GILBERT
Queen Elizabeth I of England's physician, William Gilbert (1544–1603), first demonstrated how the Earth acts as a magnet. He did this using a magnetic compass needle. Gilbert used compass needles, which move up and down as well as from side to side, to determine the magnetism at a point on the Earth, and the geographic and magnetic poles.

MAGNETIC BRICKS
When a rock solidifies, the direction of the Earth's magnetic field at that time is recorded by its magnetic minerals and preserved. This means that the magnetic field can be detected in bricks baked 3,000 years ago, like those from this ancient temple of Rameses II.

SPINNING TOP
A spinning top swings from side to side when it spins about its axis. The position of the north magnetic pole is continually moving in a similar way, and so maps need to be updated every few years. The magnetic pole differs from the geographical pole by about 11 degrees—an angle known as the declination.

The axis of rotation is like a vertical line that runs down through the center.

The top spins about its axis, constantly changing its position.

Find out more
MAGNETISM P. 154
FORMATION OF THE EARTH P. 210
MOVING CONTINENTS P. 214
ROCKS AND MINERALS P. 221
RECORD IN THE ROCKS P. 226

MOVING CONTINENTS

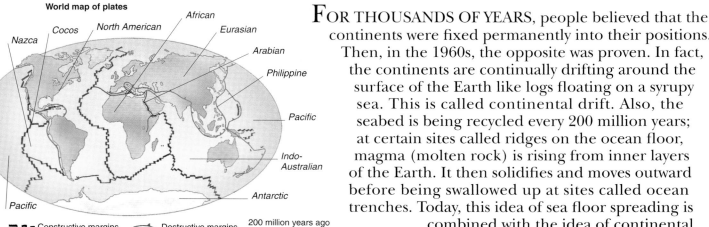

World map of plates

Nazca
Cocos
North American
African
Eurasian
Arabian
Philippine
Pacific
Indo-Australian
Antarctic
Pacific

🔵〰️ Constructive margins   ⌇ Destructive margins

FOR THOUSANDS OF YEARS, people believed that the continents were fixed permanently into their positions. Then, in the 1960s, the opposite was proven. In fact, the continents are continually drifting around the surface of the Earth like logs floating on a syrupy sea. This is called continental drift. Also, the seabed is being recycled every 200 million years; at certain sites called ridges on the ocean floor, magma (molten rock) is rising from inner layers of the Earth. It then solidifies and moves outward before being swallowed up at sites called ocean trenches. Today, this idea of sea floor spreading is combined with the idea of continental drift in a theory called plate tectonics.

EARTH'S PLATES

The Earth's surface is divided into a number of plates, like the panels of a soccer ball. Each plate is growing at one of its edges, moving along, and then being destroyed at another. The edge of a plate where it is growing is called a constructive plate margin, and these lie along the ocean ridges. The edge of a plate where it is being destroyed is called a destructive plate margin, and these lie along the ocean trenches. The continents are embedded in these plates and are carried around by their movement.

If two continents collide and neither can be subducted, they just wrinkle up to form mountain ranges.

200 million years ago

Geologists call the large landmass that existed millions of years ago Pangaea.

50 million years ago

Present day

Plates collide, pushing up land to form mountains.

INTERLOCKING CONTINENTS

Perhaps the most obvious sign that the continents are moving is given by their shapes. The west coast of Africa and the east coast of South America look like pieces of a jigsaw puzzle that, if brought together, would fit snugly. This suggests that they were once part of a larger continent that has broken up. This was noticed as early as the 17th century, when mapmaking was becoming a more accurate science.

A moving plate consists of the ocean crust and the topmost solid layer of the mantle.

Asthenosphere

An ocean ridge, where new plate material pushes up.

An ocean trench, where two plates meet. Old plate material descends into the mantle and is melted. The molten remains form volcanoes on the plate above.

LITHOSPHERE

The Earth's plates consist of the crust and the topmost layer of the mantle. This layer is called the lithosphere. Below this is a layer of mantle called the asthenosphere, which is very soft, lubricating the movement of the solid plates above. At the ocean ridges, new crust is formed by magma welling up through volcanic action as the plates are pulled apart. The ocean trenches are where two plates meet and one is swallowed up (subducted) beneath the other and destroyed.

F. Vine   D. Matthews

FREDERICK VINE AND DRUMMOND MATTHEWS

Evidence for the movement of continents is easy to find. But finding tell-tale signs of sea floor spreading is very difficult. In 1963, two British geophysicists, Fred Vine and Drummond Matthews, were the first to recognize the importance of one clue. They showed that the pattern of magnetic stripes in the rocks of the ocean floor was convincing evidence for sea floor spreading.

The movement of continents

EVIDENCE FOR PANGAEA

How do we know that at one time the Earth held just one continent? Because there is lots of evidence to prove it. For example, geologists have found parts of the same ancient mountain range on different continents. Also, the same fossils have been found scattered over the globe, showing that the same animals existed over one big supercontinent.

Fossils of a freshwater swimming reptile, Mesosaurus braziliensis, have been found in South Africa and Brazil.

PRE-PANGAEA

Before Pangaea existed, the landmasses of the world were in separate continents. These continents were scattered across the globe, but were very different from those of today. Very slowly, they were moving toward one another.

PANGAEA

About 300 million years ago, all the continents came together to form a single vast supercontinent that geologists call Pangaea. This supercontinent existed for about 100 million years. It then began to split into two parts—a northern section called Laurasia, and a southern section called Gondwanaland.

FOSSIL EVIDENCE

Fossils of an animal called *Mesosaurus* found in Brazil are identical to fossils found in South Africa. But such an animal could not have crossed the Atlantic. This indicates that the animal lived when the Americas and Africa were joined together. The continents moved apart and the fossils were separated by the Atlantic Ocean. Also, fossils of the same plant and of the same age have been found in South America, Africa, India, Australia, and Antarctica.

FUTURE OF THE CONTINENTS

About 200 million years ago, Pangaea began to break up, and today's continents split away. Ever since, they have been moving at the rate of an inch or more per year (about the same rate as your fingernails grow). The position in which the continents are today is just a temporary one. A map of the world of the future would be as strange to us as a map of the world of the past.

The way in which the continents are moving today has been "fast-forwarded" to create a map of Earth in the far future.

In this "new world," Australia has moved much farther to the north, and North America has split away from South America.

This image shows magnetic stripes in each layer of the ocean ridge.

When rock wells up from the ridge, it is magnetized toward the magnetic north of the time.

Every few million years, the Earth's magnetic field reverses; north becomes south. Rocks formed during this period will have a reversed magnetic alignment.

COLUMBUS

In 1492, Italian-born explorer Christopher Columbus sailed across the Atlantic. The voyage took him 70 days. The same voyage today would take him a little longer. For today, North America and Europe are farther apart—the Atlantic ocean is 66 ft (20 m) wider now than it was 500 years ago!

Columbus's ship

Ocean ridge

MAGNETIC STRIPES

The rocks of the seabed are magnetized in stripes; a strip of rock magnetized toward today's magnetic north lies parallel to a strip magnetized in the opposite direction. This pattern of stripes is exactly the same on each side of the ocean ridge. This is evidence of seafloor spreading.

OCEAN FLOOR

The rocks close to the ocean ridge are very clean, because they have had little time to collect sediment. But farther away from the ocean ridge, the rocks are piled with thick layers of sediment, showing the ocean floor is older there. This is more evidence of seafloor spreading.

Find out more

FORCES P. 114
STRUCTURE OF THE EARTH P. 212
MOUNTAIN BUILDING P. 218
SEAS AND OCEANS P. 234
EARTH P. 287

VOLCANOES

IMAGINE SHAKING AND OPENING a can of soda. The pressure that forces the liquid to spray out of the can is similar to the pressure that causes a volcano to erupt. This violent explosion forms thick clouds of ash and red-hot lava that spray out of the volcano and flow down its sides. The eruption occurs when slabs of rock forming the Earth's surface, called plates, begin to move. When old plates collide, and one plunges down beneath the next, the plates melt and produce very violent volcanoes. Other types of volcanoes also exist, such as those that form as new plates grow. The runny molten material wells from the mantle, creating nonexplosive volcanoes. Some volcanoes lie away from the plate edges, above a very active spot in the Earth's mantle.

POMPEII
In CE 79, Mount Vesuvius erupted and engulfed the Roman city of Pompeii in hot ash. This covered the bodies of victims and their pets. When the bodies decayed, they left hollows in the ground. These hollows are filled with plaster to make models of the victims.

Cauliflower-shaped clouds of ash and dust are blasted into the atmosphere and cover the surrounding landscape.

ANDESITIC VOLCANO
An andesitic volcano is a steep-sided cone. This forms as the melted plate material comes exploding out of the ground. The volcano gradually builds up from the slow-moving lava flows and ash layers. The thick lava it produces is called andesite.

Nuée ardente flowing down the side of a mountain in New Zealand, August 1968.

NUÉE ARDENTE
When the pressure in andesitic lava is suddenly released at the surface, it produces a *nuée ardente*. This is a glowing cloud which causes an avalanche containing a mixture of gases, fragments of rock, and white-hot ash. It crashes down the hill slopes and valleys at speeds up to 60 mph (100 km/h), smothering everything in its path.

World map of volcanoes

The side of the mountain collapses, releasing a nuée ardente *that rapidly covers the countryside.*

Andesitic lava often becomes solid in the volcanic vent. This causes it to block the vent. As the pressure builds up, the volcano may suddenly explode.

The volcanic vent is shaped like a funnel, partly filled with ash from previous eruptions.

Mount Saint Helens

Yellowstone

▲ Andesitic volcano

Vesuvius, Italy

ANDESITIC ERUPTION
An active andesitic volcano is extremely violent. The eruptions can happen at any time and the explosions cause considerable damage. This type of eruption can also send clouds of hot ash and dust over great distances. The image opposite is of an andesitic volcano after the eruption.

In 1980, Mount Saint Helens, an andesitic volcano, erupted, destroying miles of forest.

DISTRIBUTION
Andesitic volcanoes are named after the Andes mountains where they were first noticed. They are found in areas where each of the Earth's plates is swallowed up beneath the next.

MUD POOL

Water seeping through the ground in a volcanic area may be heated by the hot rocks beneath. The rocks absorb volcanic gases, making them acidic. The hot acid absorbed by the rocks produces a sludge that comes to the surface as a boiling mud pool. The mud pools of Yellowstone National Park are popular tourist attractions.

HOT SPRINGS

Water from the ground heated by volcanic rocks may come to the surface as steaming hot springs. Often a network of underground chambers forms and if water turns to steam in one of these, the expansion pushes water up and out at the surface. The reduced pressure allows even more steam to form, and the water is blasted upward, gushing out of the ground as a boiling fountain called a geyser.

HOT SPOTS

Deep within the Earth's mantle are areas of great heat and turbulence. These are known as hot spots. They create the right conditions for basaltic volcanoes to form on the crust above. Continuous plate movement produces a string of volcanoes.

An exploding hot spot island in Hawaii

Plate moves over hot spots.

Volcano forms on the surface as rising material breaks through.

Chain of extinct volcanoes stretches away across the ocean.

The great flow of lava from basaltic eruptions solidifies and builds up as flood basalts.

BASALTIC VOLCANO

Over areas such as hot spots, molten material rises up from the mantle. If it breaks through to the surface, it forms a dark runny lava called basalt. Unlike andesitic lava, basaltic lava usually flows for long distances before solidifying. The resulting volcano is broad and low, known as a shield volcano. Most basaltic volcanoes lie deep below the sea and the lava that erupts into the water cools quickly into blobs called pillow lavas. On land, molten basalt sprays into the air as a fire fountain. The drops may solidify in flight, forming volcanic bombs.

Hawaii

Mount Fuji, Japan

New Zealand

▲ Basaltic volcano

Beneath a volcano is a magma chamber, a reservoir of molten material, that feeds the eruption.

Fissure eruptions, in which lava rises through the long cracks, are common in basaltic volcanoes.

Molten lava flowing over rocks in Hawaii

DISTRIBUTION

Basaltic volcanoes are found where the mantle material rises up to form new plates. They rarely appear above the sea surface. Hot spot volcanoes, such as those in Hawaii, may form a long way from the edge of the plate.

LAVA SURFACES

Basaltic lava flows freely. Its cooling surface forms a skin, which wrinkles and puckers with the movement beneath. This ropy lava is known by its Hawaiian name *pahoehoe*. If this surface breaks up, it forms blocks of lava with rough surfaces, also known as *aa*.

MOUNTAIN BUILDING

LIKE YOU, MOUNTAINS ALSO GROW OLD, but not so quickly. The vast Himalayan mountain range in Asia began to grow 50 million years ago, but it is so young that it is still being formed. Mountains are formed by the forces of plate tectonics, movements that take place in the Earth's crust, pressing and squeezing against the edges of continents. These forces thrust mountains out of the Earth. Some ancient mountain ranges, such as the Urals in Russia and the Scottish Highlands, mark where continents collided at some time in the past. Great stresses are involved in mountain building: look for the twists and breaks of the rocks in mountainous areas.

World map of mountains

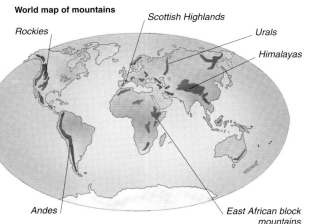

Rockies

Scottish Highlands

Urals

Himalayas

Andes

East African block mountains

MOUNTAIN DISTRIBUTION

The major mountain ranges of the Earth are fold mountains. These are formed by compression at the edges of continents, or where continental plates have collided. Block mountains, caused by stretching, are less noticeable on the world scale. Volcanoes can be formed among either fold or block mountains.

Fold mountains: in theory

Continental rocks squeeze, crumple, and twist into deep folds.

Molten material rises from the descending plate.

The pressure breaks and crumples the rocks well into the continent.

An ocean plate slides beneath a continent. The friction splits the continental edge into wedges, forcing each one back beneath the next.

Erosion carves the rounded fold surfaces into a jagged mess.

Fold mountains: in practice

The broken continental wedges produce islands and rugged coastal ranges. They consist of a complex mixture of oceanic sediments and continental material.

FOLD MOUNTAIN FORMATION

Fold mountains are formed at the edge of a continent. The continental plate crumples as it crashes into an oceanic plate, which is forced beneath it. Islands and sediments brought along by the oceanic plate become plastered to the continent's edge. These fold and force their way up to become part of the mountain range. The descending plate melts, and the liquid rises into the base of the mountains, raising them farther and sending volcanoes to the surface.

Molten rock pushes through openings to form andesitic volcanoes.

Granite is left exposed at the surface.

Old mountains formed on the coast, now far from sea.

The gentle inland folds wear down (erode) into steep slopes, known as scarps and vales.

FLOATING MOUNTAINS

In 1855, G.B. Airy, the British Astronomer Royal, suggested that mountains behave like blocks of wood floating in water. The higher they are above the surface, the deeper they must be below it. Modern research shows that the continental crust is far thicker in mountainous areas than in flat regions and that mountains have deep roots stretching down into the mantle.

Mountain roots model

Block mountains

Without erosion

With erosion

BLOCK MOUNTAIN FORMATION

The formation of new constructive plates puts the Earth's crust under tension. This causes the crust to split into blocks, separated by cracks called faults. Some of these blocks may subside, producing rift valleys, leaving the upstanding blocks between them as block mountains, such as those found in East Africa.

Under tension, a continent will split into blocks that move in relation to each other.

Surface erosion rounds off the edges of the blocks and covers the faults. This can make it difficult to identify them.

FORMATION OF A FOLD

When beds of rock are subjected to such pressures that they bend, the result is called a fold. A fold that sags downward is a syncline, while one that arches upward is an anticline. These two are usually found together. The line along which the rock bends is called the axis.

Features of a typical fold

Thick beds of coarse rock, like sandstone, crack as they fold, forming joints. These fan out from the fold axis.

Beds of thin layers, like shale, crumple up when they fold.

Thick beds of rock, like limestone, may be split by joints parallel to the axis.

Competent beds crack when they are folded, but incompetent beds deform and crumple.

TYPES OF FOLD

Rocks deform in different ways producing different types of fold. Those shown above are symmetrical, which means that the plane that the fold bends around is vertical. In asymmetrical folds, the fold appears to be tipping over because of the pressure applied to it. The pressures may become so great that the whole bed cracks and becomes a thrust.

Asymmetrical fold

Recumbent fold

An asymmetrical fold appears to lean. The fold axes of each bed are not directly above one another.

A recumbent fold is one that appears to have fallen over itself.

FOLD
This folded rock strata found in Newfoundland, New Jersey, shows the shapes formed by folds. A fold is recognizable in an outcrop by the rounded shape it produces in the rock strata.

Thrust

When under continuous pressure, the fold becomes a thrust. This can be seen as either a fold or a fault.

This rock found in Nikshahr, Iran, shows both normal and reversed faults.

FAULT
A fault can be seen as a crack, with the rocks at each side displaced in relation to each other.

Normal fault

A normal fault forms by tension. Rocks crack, and one slides down against the next.

The block below is separated from the block above by the fault plane.

The overhanging block at the surface soon disappears by erosion.

Thrust

The edges of the beds are curled against the fault. This is known as a drag.

Thrusts are very shallow reverse faults that can be found in mountainous areas.

Reverse fault

A reverse fault is formed by compression. One block moves up in relation to the other.

SAN ANDREAS FAULT
The spectacular San Andreas fault crosses the Carrizo Plain. It stretches across 300 miles (450 km) south of San Francisco and 100 miles (160 km) north of Los Angeles. It is an example of a seismic fault and is responsible for some major earthquakes in the United States.

Dextral strike slip fault

Right-handed (dextral) strike slip fault.

In a strike slip fault, the blocks move sideways rather than vertically.

TYPES OF FAULT

Sometimes, usually under tension rather than pressure, the rocks do not bend and fold. Instead, they crack into blocks that are moving in relation to each other or that have moved in the past. This is called faulting. The surface area on which the blocks slide past each other is known as the fault plane.

Sinistral strike slip fault

In a sinistral, or left-handed, strike slip fault, the opposite block has moved to the left.

> ### *Find out more*
> PRESSURE P. 127
> STRUCTURE OF THE
> EARTH P. 212
> MOVING CONTINENTS P. 214
> WEATHERING AND EROSION P. 230
> *FACT FINDER P. 414*

EARTHQUAKES

IMAGINE THE FORCE used by two people to crack open a coconut. Now imagine the much greater force needed to snap open the layers of rock that make up the Earth's surface. Rocks do not bend or break easily. Tension, caused by movement of Earth's plates, builds up over the years until the rocks can take the strain no longer. Suddenly they crack and shift, sending out shock waves and reducing anything built on the surface to rubble. This is what we call an earthquake. The shock of the initial earthquake may be followed by a series of aftershocks over the next few days. These fade as the rocks settle down into their new positions.

World map of earthquake zones

Deep earthquake zones   Shallow earthquake zones

EARTHQUAKE ZONES

Earthquakes, like volcanoes, are found along the edges of the Earth's plates. Shallow earthquakes happen where the plates actually meet on the surface, while deeper earthquakes occur where one plate is sliding down beneath another.

MERCALLI SCALE

An earthquake's intensity, or the amount it shakes, is measured on the Modified Mercalli Intensity Scale. This scale is based on what is seen and felt during an earthquake. It runs from the very gentle tremor of point I, to point XII, which can cause total destruction. The point within the Earth where the earthquake takes place is called the focus. The greatest intensity is felt at the epicenter, the point on the Earth's surface just above the focus.

At point II on the Mercalli scale, the earthquake shock is slight. You would notice it only if you were standing upstairs.

At point VI on the Mercalli scale, windows break, heavy furniture is moved and chimneys and plaster come tumbling down.

Mercalli scale

The greatest rock movement takes place at the focus.

Lines called isoseisms connect the points at which earthquake shocks are of equal intensity.

Before an earthquake

After an earthquake

In earthquake zones, buildings are designed to reduce the dangers. High buildings should swing without breaking. Low ones are made of lightweight materials.

Even the best-designed buildings will collapse in a severe earthquake. Taller buildings may survive better than low ones, and fire and disease are constant dangers afterward.

Vertical reading

The spring supports the weight of the seismometer.

The movement of the rest of the room is magnified.

The revolving drum records the magnified movement.

Horizontal reading

The room shakes while the weight remains still.

The shaking is magnified by the leverage.

The movement is recorded on a rotating drum.

SEISMOMETER

The seismometer is an instrument that records earthquakes. It contains a weight that is so heavy that it remains still while everything else shakes around it. The shaking is magnified by levers and recorded on rotating drums.

RICHTER SCALE

The size, as opposed to the intensity, of an earthquake is measured on the Richter scale using a seismometer. The scale was designed in 1935 by American seismologist C. F. Richter. Severe earthquakes reach a reading of 6 or more, but some have reached 8.9. Each figure means a force 10 times that of the number below it.

TOTAL DESTRUCTION

At point XII on the Mercalli scale, destruction is widespread. The ground moves in ripples like waves in the sea. Objects are thrown into the air. Buildings are completely destroyed. The geography of an area is changed permanently, but, luckily, few earthquakes are this severe.

Find out more

FORCES AND MOTION P. 120
VIBRATIONS P. 126
STRUCTURE OF THE EARTH P. 212
MOVING CONTINENTS P. 214
MOUNTAIN BUILDING P. 218
FACT FINDER P. 414

ROCKS AND MINERALS

THE GROUND WE WALK ON, build on, and grow gardens on is made of rock. All the rocks in the world are made up of chemicals called minerals. Through a microscope, a rock shows that it is made of crystals of different minerals all growing together like a mosaic. Each mineral has its own chemical composition, and there are usually no more than half a dozen types in each rock. Three types of rock make up the Earth's crust: igneous, sedimentary, and metamorphic rocks. Igneous rocks form when molten magma from inside the Earth cools and hardens. Sedimentary rocks form when rock fragments and other debris are deposited under water and chemically cemented together. Metamorphic rocks form when igneous or sedimentary rocks are metamorphosed (changed) by great heat and pressure.

Gray quartz crystals

Biotite granite

Graphic granite

Pink granite

DIFFERENT GRANITE
In some rocks, such as granite, the crystals of mineral are big enough to be seen with the naked eye. Granite consists of the minerals quartz, feldspar, and mica. The rock can be pink or gray, depending on what type of feldspar it contains.

CROSSED POLARIZED VIEW
When the same slice of rock is viewed through two polarized filters, the minerals show up in a spectacular range of colors. These colors change if the rock is turned under a microscope. The individual minerals can be identified by their appearance and by their color changes.

POLARIZED LIGHT
When a slice of rock is viewed through a microscope equipped with a single polarized filter (a special filter that only lets through certain light waves), the individual minerals are mostly transparent. Some may show a slight color, and a few, such as iron, show up as completely opaque.

Hematite, iron ore

HEMATITE
The ore minerals contain a metal that can be removed very easily. Hematite is an iron ore. Iron is both durable and flexible and can combine with other metals to form an alloy. Its uses range from being made into pairs of scissors to industrial construction work.

JEWELRY
Some minerals are very beautiful, and are used to make jewelry. Their value depends on how popular and rare they are.

Amethyst crystals forming a rim in the geode

GEODE
Minerals may dissolve out of the rock by water or by volcanic fluids passing through it. The minerals are then carried elsewhere. Those that build up along the sides of a hollow in the rock can produce a geode (a group of crystals that grow inside a cavity in a rock).

MOHS' SCALE
Minerals can be identified by their hardness. A mineral that can scratch another mineral must be harder than the mineral it scratches. Mohs' scale of hardness ranges from 1 to 10. Talc (the softest) is 1, gypsum 2, calcite 3, fluorite 4, apatite 5, orthoclase 6, quartz 7, topaz 8, corundum 9, and diamond 10 (the hardest).

Diamond

Talc

Find out more
BONDING P. 28
CRYSTALS P. 30
ELEMENTS P. 31
CERAMICS P. 108
STRUCTURE OF THE EARTH P. 212
FACT FINDER P. 415

IGNEOUS ROCKS

BASALT
A typical extrusive igneous rock is basalt, formed from lava. It is dense and dark, because of the minerals it contains, and fine-grained because of its quick cooling.

Basalt is formed when lava from a volcano cools on the Earth's surface.

Granite crystals are large enough to see without a microscope.

GRANITE
Granite is an intrusive igneous rock. There are several types of granite, but all are light-colored because of the light-colored minerals within them. Granite takes much longer to cool than basalt, forming larger crystals that are easier to see.

FORMATION
Molten material from the Earth's mantle forms an igneous rock low in silica, such as basalt. The molten material from the Earth's plates forms an igneous rock that is high in silica, such as granite. Igneous rock solidifies in huge masses called batholiths, and in dome-shaped laccoliths. Or it forms in cracks, making vertical dykes or horizontal sills. It can also burst through the surface. The rock is only seen when overlying rocks are worn away.

VOLCANIC DYKE
When molten material squeezes its way into a crack and solidifies, it produces a medium-grained intrusive rock. It is usually harder than the surrounding rocks, so after erosion, this intrusion stands out as a prominent landscape feature.

WHEN A CANDLE BURNS, a runny wax is formed that trickles down its side and solidifies. Igneous rocks are formed in a similar way. The rocks solidify from a mass of molten rock, such as when a lava flow cools and hardens. Because of the heat needed to form igneous rocks, they are sometimes called "rocks of fire." There are two main types of igneous rock: extrusive and intrusive. Extrusive types form when molten rock comes to the surface and cools quickly, as with lava. This gives a very fine-grained rock. Intrusive rocks are those that have solidified underground, cooling slowly to produce coarse-grained rocks.

Igneous rock structures

Magma reaches the Earth's surface through cracks in the bedding plane, eventually forming dykes.

A volcano is formed when magma forces its way through a weak point in the Earth's surface, usually via a dyke.

Magma flows along bedding plane to form sills.

After erosion

Sills appear as cliffs.

Batholith

Molten material pushes upward, or "domes," to form a laccolith.

Cedar-tree laccolith

Ring dyke

Multiple dyke

A structure called a neck stands proud once the surrounding volcano has been eroded.

ROAD SURFACING
Igneous rocks tend to be very hard. When broken up, they make a good, strong road-surfacing material, especially when coated with tar. This prevents their silicate minerals (feldspars) from breaking down in the atmosphere.

A road surface is often made by adding granite chippings to hot tar.

Find out more
CARBON P. 40
STRUCTURE OF THE EARTH P. 212
VOLCANOES P. 216
ROCKS AND MINERALS P. 221
FACT FINDER P. 415

SEDIMENTARY ROCKS

CONGLOMERATE

Shingle from the beach becomes the coarse clastic sedimentary rock called conglomerate. Other clastic sedimentary rocks include sandstone—made from layers of sand in deserts or in sea beaches—and shale, made from layers of mud.

Conglomerate

Clastic sedimentary rock

Rain and weather break down the rocks exposed on the land into rubble.

The rocky debris is washed down to the sea by rivers and deposited there.

Shingle pebble beaches

Sandy and muddy beds

Chemical sedimentary rock

A lake or an isolated arm of the sea evaporates. The dissolved salts gradually become more concentrated and are eventually deposited.

Biogenic sedimentary rock

Different layers of rock contain minerals with different solubilities.

Coral reef debris

Rock salt

YOU NEVER KNOW what you might find in a sedimentary rock. Many rocks of this type are made up of lots of other rocks, or even animal remains, all stuck together. Sedimentary rocks are built up from particles laid down as layers, or beds, of sediment and later buried, compressed, and cemented into a solid mass. There are three types of sedimentary rock. Clastic sedimentary rock is made of broken bits of preexisting rocks. Chemical sedimentary rock forms when salt and other substances dissolved in water are separated from the solution. And biogenic sedimentary rock is built up from the remains of living things.

Shelly limestone

A coral reef is, itself, a biogenic sedimentary rock. Pieces broken from it and spread over the surrounding seafloor can produce another reef.

Millions of years ago

SHELLY LIMESTONE

Biogenic rocks are made up of once-living material. The shelly limestone above is made up of broken seashells. Other examples of biogenic sedimentary rocks are chalk and coal.

ROCK SALT

Seawater contains dissolved minerals. When an area of sea dries out, these minerals are deposited as a layer on the bottom. Rock salt and certain kinds of limestone are typical chemical sedimentary rocks.

LAYERS OF SEDIMENT

Sediments that eventually become sedimentary rocks may cover whole seafloors or small areas. Where two environments meet, as when a river delta runs into the sea, there is a mixture of sediment types.

FORMATION

The process that turns the loose sediments lying on the bottom of the sea or on a riverbed into hard sedimentary rocks is known as lithification. There are two stages: first, the layers that continually build up on top of the bed compress it, squeezing out the air pockets, and interlocking the particles. Later, underground water seeping through the rocks deposits minerals—usually calcite or silica—as it goes. These minerals build up on the sediment particles, cementing them together into a solid mass.

Deep-water mud and clays are deposited on the sea bottom.

Today

Sand and silt from the mouth of a river

Hard bed of limestone produces a prominent ridge.

Sandstone beds are more resistant than the shale beds.

BUILDING STONE

Bedding planes—the boundaries between the individual beds of rock—tend to make sedimentary rocks easy to split and to work. The harder, more thickly bedded sedimentary rocks, such as sandstone and limestone, are commonly used as building materials.

Brownstone house, New York City.

TODAY

Once the sediments are turned to sedimentary rock, they may be lifted by Earth movements and exposed at the surface. Harder rocks, like sandstone or limestone, may be resistant to erosion while softer rocks, like shale, may be quickly worn away. This will form a steplike landscape. This process is continually happening today.

Find out more

CRYSTALS P. 30
MOUNTAIN BUILDING P. 218
ROCKS AND MINERALS P. 221
WEATHERING
AND EROSION P. 230
RIVERS P. 233

METAMORPHIC ROCKS

MARBLE

Marble is a type of thermal metamorphic rock, formed when heat is applied to limestone. Its smooth texture and haphazard structure make it an attractive building and sculpting material. Its color can vary from white to white streaked with brown, red, green, or gray.

Marble

The composition of the rock changes; this is known as metasomatis. This kind of metamorphism is produced by hot fluids moving from an igneous intrusion.

The metamorphic rock mylonite forms from the movement of a fault.

WHEN YOU BAKE BREAD, you mix flour, yeast, and water together and bake it in a hot oven. In a similar way, heat and pressure from the overlying rocks may change the nature of the rocks below. This process is called metamorphosis, which means "change." There are two main types of metamorphic rock. The most common is known as regional (dynamic) metamorphic rock. This type involves vast volumes and lies at the heart of mountain ranges and deep within the Earth's crust. The second kind of metamorphic rock is known as thermal (contact) rock. It is produced by heat from nearby igneous rock when the rocks come into contact with each other, and the volume involved may be no more than an inch or so.

Slate

Slight metamorphism gives only partial crystallization of some minerals.

Metamorphic minerals aligned according to the direction of pressure.

Deep metamorphic rocks show signs of compression, rather than directed stress.

SLATE

Slate is dark gray, shiny, and splits easily into thin slices, because of the flat crystals of mica produced in it by metamorphism. A low-grade regional metamorphic rock, it is formed from a fine-grained rock such as shale.

Igneous intrusion provides heat for thermal metamorphism.

Thin layer (auriole) of thermal metamorphic rock around the intrusion.

Area of greatest pressure and temperature in mountain roots.

FORMATION

Pressure and heat deep underground crush and bake existing sedimentary and igneous rocks, to form metamorphic rocks. These forces change the mineral content of the rock, sometimes completely, as in the case of gneiss, a high-grade metamorphic rock. The importance of this change is the change in the mineral composition that takes place in the solid state. If the rocks just melt and solidify again, the result is still an igneous rock. Regional metamorphic rock is only exposed after millions of years of erosion.

The lower continental crust is made up of high-grade regional metamorphic rocks.

SCHIST

There are many varieties of schist, a high-grade regional metamorphic rock. None of the rock's original minerals are left unchanged.

Schist

Gneiss

SLATE IN USE

New materials have largely replaced slate as a roofing material and as a chalkboard surface. However, one important property of slate is that its flat mica crystals enable it to be split easily.

Slate roof of a house in Britain

GNEISS

Pronounced "nice," this is the highest grade of regional metamorphic rock. The minerals within it separate into distinct bands. The rock breaks in all directions, but not along the bands, as in the case of schist and slate.

Find out more
CHANGES OF STATE P. 20
MOUNTAIN BUILDING P. 218
IGNEOUS ROCKS P. 222
SEDIMENTARY ROCKS P. 223
WEATHERING AND EROSION P. 230
FACT FINDER P. 415

FOSSILS

FOOTPRINTS
A trace fossil is one that does not contain parts of the original creature, just the marks that it made. These include dinosaur footprints, such as those opposite found in sandstone in Connecticut. Ancient dung is sometimes preserved as fossils that geologists call coprolites.

A FLOWER PRESSED between heavy books, or in a flower press, can be preserved for many years. Rocks also do this by preserving plants and animals as fossils. A fossil is any evidence of a once-living thing preserved in a rock. It may be an entire body, a single bone, or just a set of footprints. Fossils tell us about life in the past and help us to date rocks and past environments. They show how mammoths walked the cold tundra wastes of the Ice Age thousands of years ago. Tens of millions of years before that, dinosaurs ruled, and before then all life was in the sea. Many of these animals have left their remains in the Earth as fossils.

An insect trapped in tree resin becomes preserved when the resin turns to amber. The amber preserves the entire insect.

TYPES OF FOSSILS
There are many types of fossil preservation. Only rarely is the whole plant or animal present. Usually it is just part of the hard skeleton, and even then the original material is often replaced by minerals. If the organic material rots away completely, there may be only a hole left in the shape of the original.

Sharks' teeth are hard and durable, so they can be preserved unaltered, unlike the rest of the skeleton.

Leaves in shale may decay, leaving just a thin film of the original carbon in the leaf's shape. When this happens to entire forests, it produces coal.

If the original remains decay completely, they may leave a hole in the rock called a mould. If the mould later fills with minerals, it produces a fossil called a cast.

Mould

Cast

MARY ANNING
Fossil enthusiast Mary Anning (1799–1847) came from Dorset, in southern England. She became one of the most famous early professional fossil collectors. As children, she and her brother Joseph found the first complete skeleton of the swimming reptile *Ichthyosaurus*.

Fossilized animals that evolved quickly, and lived over a wide area, are the most useful for dating rocks. Ammonites, octopus-like animals that lived in coiled shells, are a good example of such creatures.

Fossils are rarely found on their own. More often, many are preserved together as assemblages. Fossil assemblages are useful in giving us an insight into ancient environments and how animals lived and survived under such conditions.

SABRE-TOOTHED TIGER
When an entire skeleton is preserved, a museum may mount it and put it on public display. One example is this fossilized skeleton of a saber-toothed tiger found in the tar pits in Los Angeles, California.

Ammonites in red chalk

Ammonites help to date rocks.

FOSSIL DATING
Fossils can tell us how old a rock is. If the rock contains a fossil of an animal that we know only lived during a certain period of time, the rock can be dated from that period. When several datable fossils are present in the rock, the dating becomes more accurate. This is because the rock would have formed when all the age ranges overlapped.

89 million years ago

97 mya

112 mya

125 mya

132 mya

| Deshayesites forbesi | Douvilleiceras mammillatum | Hoplites dentatus | Scaphites equalis | Hamites maximus |

Find out more

CARBON p. 40
ROCKS AND MINERALS p. 221
SEDIMENTARY ROCKS p. 223
RECORD IN THE ROCKS p. 226
WEATHERING AND EROSION p. 230
FACT FINDER p. 415

RECORD IN THE ROCKS

THE ROCKS YOU SEE around you today are filled with clues from the past. Like pages in a book, they record much of the history of the Earth. Since layers of sedimentary rock are laid down one on top of the other, those at the bottom must be the oldest. A geologist, working like a detective, can make a study through these layers; each layer reveals the conditions under which it must have been laid down. The composition of a rock, its structure, and the fossils it contains all paint a picture of a certain environment from the far past. This study of rock layers is called stratigraphy.

Unconformity between rocks in the Grand Canyon, Arizona.

UNCONFORMITY
A break in a sequence of rocks is called an unconformity. It happens when a layer of rock is lifted into a mountain chain and erosion wears it down to a flat surface. This is covered by sea, and upper beds of rock are laid on top of it. A gap in the record of the Earth's history has been created.

ROCK SEQUENCE
A sequence of rocks can be used to figure out the history of an area. If the column of rocks has been undisturbed, the beds of rock at the bottom will always be the oldest, and those at the top will be the youngest—this is the principle of superposition. The layers of rock then represent periods of time that follow on from one another. This example tells the story of a shallow sea that was laden with sand by a delta and eventually became a desert.

DISCOVERIES

1669 Danish mineralogist Nicolaus Steno notes that sedimentary rocks were laid down in the sea and so the sea level must always be changing.

1788 Scottish geologist James Hutton realizes that sedimentary rocks are formed by erosion and deposition.

1830–33 British geologist Sir Charles Lyell publishes *Principles of Geology*, which says that factors influencing landscape today have operated throughout Earth's history.

1915 German meteorologist Alfred Wegener puts forward the theory of continental drift.

CROSS BEDDING
S-shaped bedding (called cross bedding) in a layer of sandstone, show that the sand was laid down in a river. The changing current in a river creates sandy "tongues" that are preserved.

Large scale current marks in Wealden sandstones, Sussex, England.

Rounded sand grains show that they have been polished by wind. Their red color is due to iron oxide, created by dry desert air.

The youngest rock is a thick layer of red sandstone. This indicates a desert environment.

The sandstone is cross-bedded. This happens when sand dunes moved over one another.

DESERT ENVIRONMENT
In a desert, the sand is carried around and set down by the wind to form sand dunes. The corners of the grains of sand are worn off. The iron they contain combines with oxygen to form a red color.

Shale is formed from mud, sandstone from sand banks, and coal from the plants that grew on the sand.

At the bottom is the oldest rock— a thick layer of limestone (calcium carbonate), crammed full of fossils of shells. This indicates that the area used to be covered by sea.

Above the limestone are alternating thin layers of soft shale and hard gray limestone, with some beds of coal.

DELTA ENVIRONMENT
In a delta, the river channels bring sand down to the sea, covering up muddy sea deposits to form islands on which plants grow. These islands are only temporary since the sea often sweeps back again.

SEA FLOOR ENVIRONMENT
If the sea is warm and shallow, and the currents are gentle, the chemicals in seawater may form a deposit on the seabed. This will be mixed with the remains of animals that live there.

When the shelly animals that live in the sea die, their shells collect on the sea floor (if there are no strong currents to wash them away).

Calcium carbonate, dissolved in the water, precipitates out to give a deposit of fine white crystals on the seabed.

Dinosaur bones found in Utah.

FOSSILS IN ROCK
Some animals may only live in very specific environmental conditions—for example, in mud that is very low in oxygen. Their presence as fossils in a rock layer tell geologists about the conditions under which that rock formed.

QUATERNARY PERIOD
The time from 1.6 million years ago to the present day is called the Quaternary period, shown left. During this time, the Ice Age occurred and human beings evolved.

JAMES HUTTON
Scotsman James Hutton (1726–97) was a great historian of geology. In 1795, he published *Theory of the Earth* in which he explained that the Earth's features have developed over many years from changes that are still taking place today. He thought that there was no sign of Earth's beginning, nor an outlook for its end.

TERTIARY PERIOD
The time stretching from 65 million to 1.6 million years ago is called the Tertiary period. This was the time when mammals and birds took the place of the dinosaurs and other great reptiles that had just become extinct. Forests gave way to grasslands and the climate became cooler.

GEOLOGICAL TIME
The timing of events in Earth's history can be done in two ways. The most useful way is comparative dating, in which one event is placed either earlier or later than another. The other way is absolute dating, in which actual dates are given to events. Absolute dating is very difficult; any timescale produced in this way tends to change with every new piece of evidence.

GEOLOGICAL COLUMN
Just as we date human history by naming periods after famous events, such as the Pre-Columbian age, so geological time is divided into periods depending on the kind of life that existed at that time. These periods are grouped together into eras.

Quaternary
Tertiary
Cretaceous
Jurassic
Triassic
Permian
Carboniferous
Devonian
Silurian
Ordovician
Cambrian
Precambrian

CRETACEOUS PERIOD
The Cretaceous period lasted from 135 million to 65 million years ago. The Earth was home to the great reptiles. Most of the modern continents had split away from the large land mass Pangaea; many were flooded by shallow chalk seas.

TRIASSIC AND JURASSIC PERIODS
The Triassic and Jurassic periods stretched from 250 million to 135 million years ago. Reptiles were beginning to evolve on Earth. Pangaea started to break up, and deserts gave way to forests and swamps.

CARBONIFEROUS AND PERMIAN PERIODS
These periods spanned from 355 million to 250 million years ago. This was the time when continents came together to form one big landmass, Pangaea. Forests (which form today's coal) grew on deltas around the new mountains, and deserts formed.

RADIOACTIVE DATING

Radioactive mass remaining

When a rock forms, it may contain some radioactive elements.

After a time, known as the half-life, half of the amount of the radioactive element has decayed.

After a further half-life, half of the remainder has decayed.

This continues until less and less of the radioactive element remains in the rock. By measuring this amount, the age of the rock can be calculated.

1/1
1/2
1/4
1/8
1/16

0   1   2   3   4   5
Time (half lives)

In most rocks, there are tiny amounts of radioactive elements. Over the years, these break down into more stable elements. As scientists know the precise rate at which they do this, the age of a rock can be calculated from the proportion of radioactive elements it contains. The less it contains, the older it is. This is a type of absolute dating.

DEVONIAN PERIOD
The Devonian period lasted from 410 million to 355 million years ago. Continents started moving toward each other. At this time, the very first land animals, such as insects and amphibians, existed, and many fish swam in the seas.

ORDOVICIAN AND SILURIAN PERIODS
These periods spanned from 510 million to 410 million years ago. Sea life flourished at this time, and the very first fish evolved. The earliest land plants began to grow around shorelines and estuaries.

CAMBRIAN PERIOD
The Cambrian period stretched from 570 million to 510 million years ago. At this time, there was no life on land, but all kinds of sea animals existed. The animals with hard shells formed many of today's fossils.

PRECAMBRIAN PERIOD
This is the largest length of geological time, covering seven-eighths of Earth's history right up to 570 million years ago. It is divided into the earlier Archean period, when there was no life, and the later Proterozoic period, when life of some sort existed.

Find out more
RADIOACTIVITY P. 26
STRUCTURE OF THE EARTH P. 212
ROCKS AND MINERALS P. 221
FOSSILS P. 225
WEATHERING AND EROSION P. 230

ICE AND GLACIERS

HAVE YOU EVER SQUEEZED some snow in your hands? It holds together because the pressure of your hands has turned the snow particles into ice crystals. The same thing happens when great masses of snow build up on top of each other, compressing the layers beneath. This may happen in a shady valley of a mountain range, where the snow does not melt from one year to the next. Snow compressed in a hollow forms a mass of ice, which moves slowly downhill toward the lower slopes of the valley. This is known as a glacier. On cold continents, the same thing happens, and the ice builds up into an ice cap.

Glacier-cut valley in Zermatt, Switzerland

AFTER THE GLACIER
A valley glacier exerts such pressure on its base and sides that it wears them away. When the ice eventually melts, the valley is seen to be worn into a U-shape. This has vertical sides and a flat bottom.

VALLEY GLACIER
Glacier ice may start off smooth, clean, and snow-covered, but it soon breaks as it begins to move. It becomes stained by the rock fragments worn away from the valley sides. At its lower end (its snout), the glacier appears dirtier as once-buried rocks appear on the surface. Gullies and tunnels carved into the ice by the meltwater (ice melting into water) also make the ice look unclean.

Valley glacier

Lateral moraine along the sides

Medial moraine along the middle, where two moraines merge

Arête: a narrow ridge between two glaciers

Bergschrund: a big crevasse formed as the glacier pulls away from the headwall

Area of compacted snow, known as firn

Transverse crevasse: a crack in the ice as a glacier moves over an obstacle

A glacier's structure breaks while coming down a steep slope. This is called an icefall.

Subglacial moraine on the bottom

Serac: a pinnacle where the crevasses meet

Englacial moraine embedded in the ice

Ice cave, worn out by meltwater

Ablation moraine left on the surface as ice melts

A hanging valley is the side valley left as the U-shaped valley deepens.

Terminal moraine left at the end as a glacier retreats

Kame: a delta formed by meltwater

Glacier flowing into the sea

Movement of waves and tides exerts pressure on the snout of the glacier.

Glacier calves an iceberg

The rock was dropped in East Greenland by a glacier.

GLACIAL DEBRIS
The rocky material picked up, carried along, and dropped by a glacier is called a moraine. This may consist of mounds of clay, or gigantic boulders that have been carried for many miles. Much of the Northern Hemisphere landscape is formed by moraine left behind after the Ice Age.

NORTHERN HEMISPHERE ICEBERG
When a glacier reaches the sea, particularly along the Greenland coast, tides and waves heave it up and down. The strains exerted on it cause pieces to break off and float away, forming icebergs. This process of producing icebergs is known as calving.

ICE AGES

At certain times in the Earth's history, the climate becomes so cold that extensive ice sheets are formed. Such periods are called ice ages. The most recent began about 1.6 million years ago, and after warmer interludes, ended around 10,000 years ago. Others took place in the distant past. There were four in Precambrian times, one in the Ordovician period, and one in the Carboniferous and early Permian periods.

LOUIS AGASSIZ

The Swiss Louis Agassiz was the first to recognize that an ice age had taken place. He noted that some landscape features in Switzerland had been produced by glaciers. He also saw similar features in Scotland, where there are no glaciers. He deduced that at one time Scotland had been covered in ice.

Louis Agassiz (1807–1873)

Ice age time line

Permo-Carboniferous Ice Age; glaciers covering much of the Southern Hemisphere

Pennsylvanian
Mississippian
Devonian
Silurian

Permian
Triassic

Jurassic; middle of the age of dinosaurs, warm stable climates

Cretaceous

Palaeocene; tropical forests
Eocene
Oligocene
Miocene; dry grasslands
Pliocene; climates cooling
Pleistocene Ice Age; the most recent

Ordovician Ice Age; affecting what is now the Sahara desert

Cambrian; a mild phase

Carboniferous

Precambrian

Verangian; final phase of late Precambrian Ice Age

Sturtian; middle phase of late Precambrian Ice Age

Gnejso; earliest phase of Precambrian Ice Age

Huronian; earliest known Precambrian ice age, known from evidence found in Canada, southern Africa, and India

Quaternary period

Modern times

Pleistocene Ice Age world

North Pole

The world today

North Pole

LAST ICE AGE

The Pleistocene Ice Age was very irregular. The glaciers advanced and, a few thousand years later, retreated again, giving an interglacial spell with warmer climates than now. This cycle took place about 20 times in the 1.6 million years of the Ice Age. It may not be over. We may just be living in another interglacial era.

ICE SHEET

In the far north and the far south, glaciers build up over continental areas, forming ice sheets or ice caps. These move outward rather than downhill as valley glaciers do. The two main ice sheets are the Antarctic ice cap and the Greenland ice cap. These make up about 90 percent of the Earth's freshwater. Snow in the center of a land mass will eventually find its way to the edge as ice.

Ice cap

Valley glaciers formed as ice cap moves between nunataks

Meltwater streams

Prevailing wind direction

Lake of water formed by pressure

Elevation of the ground without the glacier

Elevation of the ground with the glacier

Mountain sticking through, called a nunatak

Tabular icebergs

Bare rock kept free of ice by prevailing wind

Piedmont glaciers form as the valley glaciers reunite

Ice shelf forms, as ice caps float out to sea

Rock material carried vast distances by icebergs and dropped on sea floor

The weight of ice moved by the tides absorbs a significant fraction of the world's tidal energy.

Broad, flat-topped icebergs

Broad stable ice sheet creeping slowly out to sea

SOUTHERN HEMISPHERE ICEBERG

The icebergs that form in the southern ocean, broken off the ice shelves of Antarctica, are broad and tabular (flat). They may be many hundreds of miles long and exist for years before melting. Often these are tracked by satellite to help build up a picture of the world's ocean currents.

ICE CAP

The windswept surface of the ice cap may be nearly a mile above the bedrock. Because of global warming, the Antarctic ice cap has begun to melt in recent years, and some European glaciers are smaller.

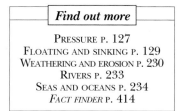

Edge of the ice cap in Iceland

Find out more

PRESSURE P. 127
FLOATING AND SINKING P. 129
WEATHERING AND EROSION P. 230
RIVERS P. 233
SEAS AND OCEANS P. 234
FACT FINDER P. 414

WEATHERING AND EROSION

Effects of weathering and erosion on rocks

THE SURFACE OF THE EARTH is constantly changing. The movement of the Earth's plates pushes up mountains and builds up continents. At the same time, these new surfaces are worn back down again and ground to dust, in a process called erosion. It can be caused by many agents, but the most powerful one is that of the weather. There are two types of weathering—physical and chemical. Physical weathering is the buffeting of the wind, the washing of the rain, and the pull of gravity. An example of chemical weathering is when the acids in rainwater dissolve away rocks.

The rock falls away layer by layer. This is called onion skin weathering.

INSELBERGS
Rounded hills in dry regions, such as Uluru (Ayers Rock) in Australia, have been eroded by a combination of physical and chemical weathering. These are known as inselbergs. Infrequent rain eats into the surface layers of the rock. The hot days and cool nights cause daily expansion and contraction, which eventually splits the surface.

Pancake rocks, known as zeugens, found in Punakaiki, South Island, New Zealand

DEFLATION EFFECT
Desert soil is a mixture of fine dust, sand, and coarse pebbles. Wind blows away the fine material—a process called deflation—leaving the heavier pebbles, which eventually form a continuous crust. The erosion then stops.

ZEUGENS
Sand flung around by the wind causes erosion. Exposed rocks are sandblasted into unusual shapes and polished smooth. Most erosion takes place near the ground, producing overhanging cliffs and top-heavy rock structures called zeugens.

The arrows show the direction in which the wind is blowing.

DESERT WINDS
Sand flung around by the wind is the most powerful erosional force in a desert. There are few plants in desert areas, so the soil is not held together by roots—nor is there much moisture to stick the particles to one another. The wind therefore easily picks up the loose sand and hurls it around in sandstorms. Rocks blasted by the sand are worn down to sand themselves; this is used by the wind for further erosion.

These arrows show how high the wind blows the sand and the direction it travels.

Formation of a mushroom rock by saltation

A pebble is blasted on one side by a strong wind.

When one side is worn flat, the pebble overbalances.

Rolling over, the pebble exposes a new face.

The resulting pebble has several flat, polished faces.

DREIKANTER
Pebbles lying on the ground receive an intense blasting by sand. This wears away one side quickly, causing the pebble to overbalance. This exposes another pebble face. The result is a pebble that is polished flat on several sides— called a dreikanter. The larger pebbles that are found on beaches or dry riverbeds show this effect.

SALTATION
Because of their weight, sand particles are usually bounced along close to the ground. This process is called saltation, which means "leaping." As a result, most erosion occurs within about 3 ft (1 m) of the ground. Tall pinnacles of rock are worn away at the base, producing the mushroom-shaped zeugens.

SAND DUNES

The sand that is blown from loose desert soil usually builds up into heaps called dunes. Sand dunes are moved along gradually by the wind. Only about one-fifth of the world's desert areas consist of sand; in these areas the dunes can form in many different ways.

BARCHAN DUNES

The most familiar type of dune is the crescent dune or the barchan. These dunes are shaped like a crescent. They form because the sand on the two ends is blown faster than that in the middle. Many of these barchans together form the typical sand and sealike landscape seen in big deserts, such as the Sahara.

The wind blows up and around an exposed outcrop.

Head and tail sand dune

The head of the dune forms as the sand builds up against the obstacle.

Rocky outcrops are common in deserts, posing obstacles to the wind.

The tail of the dune fills in the sheltered area behind the obstacle.

Barchan dune

The low sides of the dune move faster than the high center of the dune.

Coastal sand dunes showing typical sand dune structures in England

Sand is deposited by the eddy on the sheltered side of the dune.

Decomposed granite in Cornwall, England

ROTTING GRANITE

Minerals such as feldspars, one of the constituents of granite, are vulnerable to chemical weathering. Once the feldspars react to the acid in rainwater, the other minerals become loose and the granite crumbles.

Ridges of sand build up parallel to the wind direction.

Seif dunes

The sand is carried along the sides of the ridges by the wind.

The wind is slowed at the ridges by friction, producing a series of eddies.

HEAD AND TAIL DUNES

Head and tail dunes grow near an obstacle, such as a shrub. Sand builds up in front of the obstacle and forms a tail behind it. However, there are different types; an advanced dune, for example, may be deposited some distance before the obstacle, and wake dunes may line up at each side.

The wind is fastest and strongest where it is channeled along the troughs.

SEIF DUNES

Dunes called longitudinal, or seif, dunes form as long ridges parallel to the direction of the wind. They are most obvious in places where the sand is being blown across bare rock.

Sand ridges build up from the sand deposited in the eddies and shifted by the wind.

FROST WEDGING

In cold climates, a type of physical weathering called frost wedging is common. Water seeps into cracks in the rock; as this water freezes, it expands and enlarges the cracks. Eventually, chunks of rock fall away and pile against the mountainside as scree slopes, such as the one opposite in Camp Pont, in the Antarctic peninsular.

Clints and grikes in The Yorkshire Dales, England

CLINTS AND GRIKES

Calcite suffers from chemical weathering. Where limestone is exposed to rain, the calcite decays on the surface and along cracks. This process erodes the rock into blocks called clints separated by enlarged cracks called grikes.

ACID RAIN

The natural acids in rainwater come from dissolved carbon dioxide. In built-up areas, the rain also contains acids from dissolved industrial gases, such as sulfur dioxide, causing acid rain. This increases the rate of chemical weathering, damaging buildings and statues such as this stone lion in Leeds, England.

Find out more
ACIDS P. 68
FROST, DEW, AND ICE P. 268
WEATHER WATCHING P. 272
CYCLES IN THE BIOSPHERE P. 372
DESERTS P. 390

SOILS

WHEN WE LOOK at a landscape, we usually see grass, plants, and trees. Without soil, these would not exist. Soil is a complex mixture of fresh and eroded rocky material, dissolved and redeposited minerals, and the remains of once living things. These components are mixed together by the burrowing of animals, the pressure of plant roots, and the movement of water underground. The type of soil, its chemical composition, and the nature of its organic origin are all important to agriculture, and therefore to all our lives. Many different types of soil exist. Soils vary from one place to another, depending mainly on the underlying rock.

Different layers of soil

Horizon 0, humus layer: deposits of plant material

Horizon A, the topsoil: this is organically rich, but some minerals are taken out by groundwater.

Horizon B, the subsoil: this is less organic, but is rich in minerals brought down from the topsoil.

Horizon C, the parent rock: this is broken and weathered into loose chunks, and contains no organic material.

Horizon D, the underlying bedrock: the mineral content of the soil comes from this.

A sandy soil is light, and water drains through it easily. It only contains a small amount of organic matter, and so it is not very fertile.

Peat is a dark colored soil containing a large proportion of humus that comes from the partial decay of bog plants. This soil tends to retain water.

Clay is a heavy soil and water cannot drain through it. It is sticky and plastic when wet, and can contain many nutrients.

Chalky soil is thin and stony, and drains water quickly. The organic material it contains decays quickly, and so it contains only a small amount of humus.

SOIL PROFILE

Soil is formed in a number of layers. Their sequence is called the soil profile. The layers, also called horizons, show the different things that go into making a soil—from the decay of rocks to the addition of material from living things. Not all soils have the same horizons, and their sizes vary from soil to soil.

A cloud forest in Venezuela

Arctic landscape

Hot climates can weather the bedrock to form thick soils rich in vegetable material.

Cold climates produce little weathering, so Arctic soils tend to be very thin.

SOIL THICKNESS

The depth of soil depends on a number of factors, such as the presence of a slope, where any soil formed may be washed away, and the nature of the bedrock. Limestone, for example, erodes more easily than sandstone, so it produces more decay products. But the most important factor is the climate and the erosional effect of the weather.

Small landslide in the Pindus Mountains, Greece

SLOPES

Slopes are unstable because gravity pulls anything on them downward. Any change in the soil adds to this downhill movement; the first frost pushes the soil downhill; raindrops dislodge particles downhill, and soil expansion caused by soaking takes soil downhill. As a result, artificial structures on a slope tend to lean, and growing trees are distorted.

Soil creep on slope

Weathered blocks move downhill.

The soil creep pulls over the exposed ends of rock strata.

Trees are tilted but try to grow vertically, causing the trunks to curve upward.

Walls, telephone poles, and other artificial structures begin to lean and eventually collapse.

Roads crack as the underlying soil moves.

SOIL CREEP

Soil on a slope moves gradually downhill, particle by particle—a process called soil creep. Usually, the particles of soil are bound together by grass roots, forming rigid slabs. These move downhill as a series of steplike structures called terracettes. They are often used as trackways by grazing animals, such as sheep and cows, increasing the rate of erosion.

Soil creep on the Chiltern Hills, England

Find out more

ORGANIC CHEMISTRY P. 41
ROCKS AND MINERALS P. 221
FOSSILS P. 225
WEATHERING
AND EROSION P. 230
CLIMATES P. 244

RIVERS

FLOOD
Rivers are important to people as a form of transportation, as supplies of drinking and industrial waters, and as a source of irrigation. But they can also be a menace. A sudden increase in rainfall can produce floods that destroy the towns and cities that are built alongside the rivers.

A flood in Bangladesh. The river carries particles of sediment which give it its color.

RAINWATER FALLS to form pools of water, or sinks into the soil and reemerges as springs. This water is channeled into valleys and hollows, eventually forming the streams and rivers that flow down to the sea. Flowing water helps shape the landscape. It wears away the rocks of the mountains, redepositing the debris on the plains and lowlands, and eventually the floor of the sea. Many of the world's greatest rivers lie in tropical areas, where there is usually a constant supply of water because of heavy tropical rainfall.

River formation—first stage

Spring

Tributary

A V-shaped gorge is caused by the vigorous erosion action of the river cutting downward.

Waterfalls and rapids are caused by the river passing over harder beds of rock.

Deep pools are eroded from the riverbed by the swirling water and stones bounced along the floor.

Second stage

A floodplain is formed by the deposition of sediments brought down from the first stage. Most deposition takes place at times of flood.

RIVER STAGES
A river has three stages. In its first stage, it moves rapidly, cutting deep into its bed, picking up rocky debris and carrying it along. In its second stage, it slows down, depositing sediments as well as continuing the erosion. In its third stage, all its strength has gone, and all the transported debris is dropped.

The meander is the temporary river loop. Its position changes by erosion on the outside and deposition on the inside.

The river meanders back and forth, wearing back the surrounding hills.

River terraces are the remains of old floodplains formed when the land was higher.

Erosion by a waterfall

Eventually the ledge will be eroded down and the waterfall will become a rapid (a fast-flowing and turbulent section of the river).

Ledge of harder rock

Positions of waterfall before erosion

The deposition of sediment is carried beyond the plunge pool.

Plunge pool

WATERFALL
A waterfall occurs when a river pours over a ledge of hard rock. The drop causes the erosion of a plunge pool at the bottom, undermining the ledge. The ledge collapses, and the new waterfall forms over the newly exposed outcrop.

Third stage

An oxbow lake is a cutoff meander.

Irrigation on Playa Del Ingles, Grand Canaria, Canary Islands

A delta is formed when a river sheds a large amount of its sediment at the mouth of the river.

A levée is a bank of sediment deposited along the sides of a river when it floods.

IRRIGATION
Crops need water to grow. Often the water from rivers is channeled to feed crops—a system known as irrigation. The early civilizations of Ancient Egypt produced complex irrigation systems fed from rivers such as the Nile.

HYDROELECTRIC POWER
The energy in moving water has been harnessed throughout history. Waterwheels once turned machinery that ground corn or worked looms. Today, water from dams can turn turbines that generate electricity for whole communities.

Sashta Dam, a hydroelectric power plant in Redding, California

Find out more
WATER INDUSTRY P. 83
GENERATORS P. 159
WEATHERING
AND EROSION P. 230
SHORELINE P. 236
RAIN P. 264

SEAS AND OCEANS

World map of ocean ridges and trenches

East Pacific Rise

Mid-Atlantic Ridge

Mariana Trench

Philippine Trench

Java Trench

Tonga Trench

Southeast Indian Ridge

Atlantic Indian Ridge

Peru-Chile Trench

DEEP BENEATH THE OCEAN waves, on the seabed, lies hidden land. There are mountain ranges, deep trenches, and vast open plains covering as much as two-thirds of the Earth's surface. The only way we can see them is by using complicated scientific equipment. The pattern of the land on the ocean bed is caused by the great movements of the Earth, called plate tectonics. The vast ocean ridges build up where new material is added to the Earth's plates. The deep underwater trenches are where one plate is sucked down under another and disappears.

SEABED MAP
A few decades ago, the ocean floor was a mystery. Then, in the 1960s, scientists invented instruments that could detect shapes in the land from a distance. Today's maps of the seabed are made using these remote sensing images.

A coelacanth (*Latimeria chalumnae*) found near the Comoros Islands

COELACANTH
Strange creatures lurk in the hidden depths of the oceans. The coelacanth is a fish that scientists thought had been extinct for 200 million years. In 1938, one was caught in the ocean waters off Madagascar and they have been caught there ever since. It is easier for ancient animals to survive in the ocean depths because living conditions do not change much.

Island arc—volcanoes along an ocean trench

Continental rise—piles of sediment at the foot of the continental slope

Ocean ridge—undersea mountains

Abyssal plain—huge expanse of flat seabed

Continental slope—the edge of the continental shelf

Ocean trench—deep troughs in the sea floor

Continental shelf—underwater edges of the continents

The lower part of the diagram shows the heights and depths in their true scale.

OCEAN FLOOR FEATURES
Most of the ocean bed is an enormous flat plain which lies 1–3 miles (3–4 km) below the sea's surface. From this, the tall mountainous peaks of ocean ridges rise up to within 1 mile (2 km) of the waves. Right down in the depths, dark ocean trenches fall to 6 miles (10 km) and more. Around the coast, where the land rises up to form continents, the water is shallowest.

An atoll in the Maldives

A coral reef begins to grow in the shallow water around a tropical island.

If the island sinks, the coral keeps growing and forms a barrier reef separated from the island.

When the island disappears under the waves, it leaves a ring, or atoll, of coral with a lagoon in the center.

SMOKER COMMUNITY
Hot volcanic waters full of chemicals bubble up along the ocean ridges, forming dark plumes called "black smokers." The chemicals support bacteria. Animals that eat the bacteria have evolved there, and so have other animals that eat them. Creatures that have never seen sunlight, such as these crustacea and mussels, live in these waters.

CORAL REEFS
Coral will only grow where the water is clear, warm, and shallow. The shores of small, tropical islands are ideal. Each coral organism makes a limy shell that joins with others to form a firm foundation on which still more corals can grow. In this way, vast shelves, called reefs, build up to just below the water surface.

Find out more
CHEMISTRY OF WATER P. 75
STRUCTURE OF THE EARTH P. 212
ROCKS AND MINERALS P. 221
WAVES, TIDES, AND CURRENTS P. 235

WAVES, TIDES, AND CURRENTS

World map of currents

South Pacific Gyre

Peruvian Current

Gulf Stream

North Atlantic Gyre

North Pacific Gyre

South Indian Gyre

South Atlantic Gyre

⇒ Warm currents ⇒ Cool currents

THE OCEANS NEVER STAND STILL. Local winds push the surface of the sea into waves that pound onto the shore. The tides wash in and out of harbors twice a day, following the pull of the Sun and the Moon. Winds sweep the surface of the sea into great ocean currents. As the Earth spins, the currents twist and flow in huge circles called gyres. Generally, warm water travels away from the equator, and cold water moves in to replace it. Winds that blow over the sea carry warm or cool temperatures to nearby land. Warm water from the Gulf Stream helps keep western Europe warm in winter. Many cold currents flow deep under the warm ones, sometimes in the opposite direction.

OCEAN CURRENTS
The huge swirling currents in the oceans are caused by prevailing winds. The Trade Winds in the South Pacific Ocean sweep the cold Peruvian current up the west coast of South America.

Wind blowing over the water surface pulls each water particle over.

TSUNAMI
This giant wave is caused by an undersea earthquake. Vibrations rush through the ocean at hundreds of miles an hour. When they reach shallow waters they slow down and build up into vast waves, at times 250 ft (75 m) tall. The tsunami crashes onto the shore, sweeping away anything in its way.

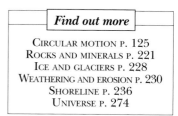

Banda Aceh, Sumatra, after the Indian Ocean tsunami in 2004

At the beach, the movement slows down. The top part of the circle falls down and the wave breaks.

The circles spread below the surface but die out farther down.

The water particles close to the surface continue to turn over and over.

HOW DO WAVES MOVE?
When the wind brushes the surface of the sea, it sends ripples through the water. Although the waves travel vast distances across the ocean, each water particle only goes around in a circle.

Moon pulls out a high tide on the Earth just beneath it.

Another high tide forms on the far side because of the Earth's spin.

When the Sun and Moon line up, the high tides are very high and the low tides very low.

When the Sun and the Moon pull in different directions, the tides are not as high and low.

Child swings around in big circle like the Moon circling the Earth.

Mother swings in a smaller circle, like the rotation of the Earth.

Highest high tides | Lowest high tides

HOW THE TIDES WORK
Imagine a mother swinging her child around in circles. As they twirl, the mother's skirt flies out behind her. The child is like the Moon circling the Earth. The mother is like the Earth, and her skirt is like the high tide on the side of the Earth facing away from the Moon.

Skirt flies out behind like water flung away from the Moon.

SUN, MOON, AND TIDES
The pull of the Moon makes the water bulge into a high tide on both sides of the Earth. As the Earth spins, each place has a high tide twice a day. The Sun pulls up the water too, but not so strongly. At one time of the month it adds to the Moon's pull. At another, it fights against it.

Find out more

CIRCULAR MOTION P. 125
ROCKS AND MINERALS P. 221
ICE AND GLACIERS P. 228
WEATHERING AND EROSION P. 230
SHORELINE P. 236
UNIVERSE P. 274

SHORELINE

WHENEVER YOU GO PADDLING on a beach, you are standing on the edge of the sea, but on the beginning of the shore. Every piece of land has a shore, and each shore is unique. The features of a shore are determined by many factors, such as the strong winds, crashing waves, the temperature, climate, and the types of rocks that exist there. Shores can change from being sandy to rocky, or vice versa. The shoreline is shaped as the wind blows across the ocean surface, transferring some of its energy to the water, making waves. The energy in waves can travel over long distances before hitting the shoreline, where the energy can wear away headlands and cliffs.

COASTLINE
The tremendous power of the sea is demonstrated here on this rocky coast at Kiwanda, Oregon. Rocks form the basis of our landscape, but these are broken down and worn away by the continuous pounding of waves.

Air compressed in a sea cave may burst through the roof, forming a blowhole. In storm conditions, water and air is released from the blowhole.

Waves erode any cracks in the headland, enlarging them into sea caves.

Sea caves on both sides of a headland may enlarge and join, to form a natural arch.

With continued erosion, the roof of the arch collapses, leaving one side on its own as a stack.

HEADLAND EROSION
Headlands are made up of hard rocks, but even these are eventually worn away. Waves approaching a headland curve around it, attacking it from the sides. This creates caves and arches, which are then eroded further. Erosion occurs in two main ways. Rock is damaged by stones flung up by the waves (a process known as corrasion or attrition), or cavitation may take place. In this process, cracks in the rock are enlarged, as air compressed by incoming water expands when the water retreats.

The headland is eventually worn down, first into caves, then into arches and stacks (sides of arches that become separated by water from the seashore).

Geiringerfjord, Norway

Gairloch, Scotland

Sylt Island, Germany

Oregon

Galicia, Spain

RIAS
If land subsides (sinks) or the sea level rises, coastal regions become flooded. At the end of the last ice age, ice caps melted in oceans worldwide and raised the sea level. Hills became islands and river valleys flooded, creating indented coastlines with branching inlets called rias.

Rias and estuaries in Galicia, Spain

Geiringerfjord in Norway

World map of coastlines

FJORDS
When glaciers melt, they often leave U-shaped valleys. On the coast, rising sea levels flood these valleys, producing long narrow inlets with vertical sides. Deposits of rocks and other materials at the mouths of the valleys give the inlets very shallow entrances. Such inlets have the Norwegian name fjords or fiords, meaning a narrow strip of sea between steep cliffs.

CHANGING COASTLINES
The coastlines of the world do not always stay the same. They can change dramatically in a relatively short time as waves wear away the land and changing sea levels submerge or expose coastal areas.

BEACH FORMATION

Rocks worn away from headlands do not stay as rubble for long. They are ground down by waves into shingle (fragments of rock) and sand, dragged along the seafloor and eventually deposited in a fairly sheltered place to form a beach. Even there, rock particles do not stop moving. They are constantly picked up and moved farther by storm-generated waves and the lightest pieces are shifted around by wind. Because of this continual movement, a winter beach may consist of coarse pebbles, while the same beach in the summer may be sandy. Today, special fences called groynes help stop this process.

Longshore drift carries sand across a bay or river mouth, dropping it to form a spit.

Sand spit

Waves slow down around the end of a spit, creating a "hook."

Beach material is drawn away from the sheltered side (lee) of the groyne.

Beaches are made up of sand and shingle and continually change; shingle is deposited by big waves, and sand is deposited in quieter times.

Beach material builds up against a groyne (fence).

Longshore drift is the movement of sand and shingle along the shoreline. A saw-toothed coastline results when sand builds up against groynes.

Longshore drift

3. The next wave washes the stone diagonally up the beach again. In this way, the stone follows a zigzag path parallel to the coast. This movement is called longshore drift.

2. The wave withdraws, and the stone rolls directly down the sloping beach with the water.

Storms wash shingle up the beach and deposit it as a berm (ledge), which remains until the next storm.

Fences called groynes, bolted to beams sunk 6 ft (2 m) down, are built out into the sea to prevent longshore drift.

1. A wave striking a beach at an angle washes a stone diagonally up the beach.

A tombolo in Cha Bahar Makran, Iran

MOVING BEACHES

Beach particles are continually moved by the ebb and flow of waves in a process called longshore drift. As they reach the shore, waves wash stones and sand grains backward and forward and may cause them to drift along the beach to a new place.

Cha Bahar Makran, Iran

This map shows a few examples of the different types of coastlines found around the world. The color coding helps identify each type.

SAND SPITS
A sand spit forming outward from the land across a bay may go right across to form a bar. If a spit forms between an island and the shore, it is given the name tombolo.

SALT MARSHES
Areas of sand built up by waves can be moved about by wind to form dunes. The dunes may cut off areas of fresh or slightly salty (brackish) water, which then collect mud and develop into salt marshes.

A lowland beach in Sylt Island, Germany

A raised beach in Gairloch, Scotland

MAKING NEW LAND
The sea has the power to build up as well as destroy land. Eroded material deposited on beaches increases the land area, while lowering sea levels expose land that was once submerged.

RAISED BEACH
When land rises or the sea level falls, the shoreline is left high and dry. This is known as a raised beach. Many raised beaches formed in northern Europe at the end of the last Ice Age. As ice melted, the land slowly began to rise up.

Find out more

ROCKS AND MINERALS P. 221
WEATHERING
AND EROSION P. 230
WAVES, TIDES,
AND CURRENTS P. 235
WEATHER P. 241

COAL

THE SUN'S ENERGY from millions of years ago has been preserved in a rock called coal. The Sun makes plants grow. If these plants are preserved under pressure for millions of years, they form a solid—coal. When coal is burned today, this ancient energy is released as heat. Coal contains the element carbon—wood contains about 50 percent carbon; coal can contain up to 90 percent carbon. Most coal in Europe and North America began to form about 350 million years ago, during the Carboniferous period. The huge swampy forests that grew then are preserved today as the world's main coal deposits.

World distribution of coal

COAL MAP
Most of the world's coal comes from deposits laid down in the Carboniferous and Permian periods, when the Earth's vegetation was most lush. However, some important coal seams (deposits of coal) of northern Europe are much younger, made of plants from the early Tertiary period, about 40 million years ago.

COAL FORMATION
As coal is a rock formed from the remains of living things, it is called a biogenic sedimentary rock. Millions of years ago, forests died and were buried in swamps before the trees and plants had time to decay. As the mud and sand of the swamps slowly turned to stone, the makeup of the wood changed. Its components were carbon, hydrogen, and oxygen; the hydrogen and oxygen were removed, leaving a concentrated deposit of carbon.

MINING COAL
Coal is extracted from the ground by mining. If a coal seam emerges at the ground surface, miners can tunnel in horizontally. This is a drift mine. More often, a vertical tunnel is needed to reach coal deep underground. This is a shaft mine. If the coal occurs near the surface, the covering layers of ground are stripped off to reach the coal. This is a strip mine. Here extracted coal is being stacked in Australia.

Forests grow well in swampy conditions.

The trees eventually die, covered with swamp material. This is compressed into a layer.

A peat cutting site in the Falkland Islands

PEAT
Before coal is formed, a fibrous material called peat develops. In fact, at this very minute, peat is developing in all the bogs of the world. It is sometimes used for fuel and as a rich plant food.

Peat

As it loses its oxygen, the buried plant material is compressed into the fibrous material called peat.

Lignite

Sediments continue to be deposited that compress the peat into rock. More oxygen is removed from the peat, turning it into soft brown coal, called lignite.

DANGEROUS MINES
The Industrial Revolution in Europe during the 18th century depended on coal—it was vital as an energy source. But mining coal was very dangerous. Even children had to work down in the mines in appalling conditions. One safety device was invented by a scientist named Humphry Davy. The Davy safety lamp detected when gases in a mine reached a dangerous level.

Davy lamp

Bituminous coal

Eventually the lignite is compressed so much that it becomes the compact black glossy coal called bituminous coal. This is the most common type of coal used by industry.

Find out more

CARBON P. 40
ORGANIC CHEMISTRY P. 41
COAL PRODUCTS P. 96
STRUCTURE OF THE EARTH P. 212
SEDIMENTARY ROCKS P. 223
FACT FINDER P. 414

OIL AND GAS

WHAT HAPPENED to all the tiny plants and animals that died millions of years ago in the sea? Many formed oil—the oil that drives cars, runs factories, and is used to make many useful chemicals. The animal matter that gathers on a seabed is broken down slowly by bacteria. This process gives off a gas called methane, or natural gas. If the material left heats up, it breaks down into light molecules called hydrocarbons that move through the rocks and gather as oil. Although natural gas is a by-product, the natural gas that is extracted from the rocks in places such as the North Sea is actually a breakdown product of coal.

OIL MAP
The oil in the main oilfields of the world comes out of rocks that date from two periods in time: the Ordovician-Devonian period (400 to 350 million years ago) and the Jurassic-Cretaceous period (200 to 65 million years ago).

Gas collects in porous rocks above the oil.

OIL RESERVOIR
Animal matter collected in the rocks decays into oil droplets that float in the groundwater below. Because they are lighter than the groundwater, the droplets float upward through pores in the rock until they are trapped by a layer that will not let them pass—a cap rock. Here they collect to form an oil reservoir.

Impermeable rock that the oil cannot travel through. Oil is trapped beneath it.

Fault

Porous rock that the oil can travel through.

Oil collects in a porous rock called a reservoir rock, where it is trapped. Usually it is trapped by impermeable rock that will not let the oil pass.

One oil trap occurs when the reservoir rock is faulted against another rock.

In a stratigraphic trap, isolated beds of porous rock are embedded in impermeable rock. If these beds are tilted, the oil collects at one end.

ALTERNATIVE THEORY
Although most scientists agree that oil has been made from living things, there is a theory that it is actually formed from metamorphic rocks. This may be proved or disproved by a borehole that is currently being drilled into metamorphic rocks in Sweden.

Siljan ring experiment

Beds of salt may bend under pressure and rise through the rocks above, pushing them into a dome. Oil can gather in this dome.

EXPLORATION RIGS
Possible oil reservoirs are found by studying the surface land and by a method called seismic exploration—sound waves are sent into the Earth and their reflections are recorded. However, the presence of oil can only be proved by drilling a hole into this ground. This work is done with a structure called an exploration rig.

Workers on an exploration rig in the North Sea

The oil rig floats low in the water, so that it is not affected by waves.

PRODUCTION PLATFORM
Once it has been proved that a good amount of oil is present, it is extracted by means of a production platform. This sends down boreholes to the reservoir rocks, pumps up the oil, and channels it into pipelines or into tankers that transport it to a refinery.

A jack-up rig is used in fairly shallow waters. It has legs that extend to the seafloor.

A tension-leg rig is used in deeper water. It floats but is secured to the seabed by tethers.

In very deep water, ships are used. The oil drill is put out through a hole in the hull.

Find out more
ORGANIC CHEMISTRY P. 41
CHEMICAL INDUSTRY P. 82
GAS PRODUCTS P. 97
OIL PRODUCTS P. 98
SEAS AND OCEANS P. 234
FACT FINDER P. 414

MAPPING THE EARTH

IMAGINE TRYING TO SEE the whole world at a glance. This is what a map enables us to do. Without a map, it would be very difficult to get an idea of what the Earth looks like. For thousands of years, people have been creating maps to help them discover their surroundings. As maps have become more sophisticated, large-scale maps have been drawn that show geographical features, such as mountains and rivers, using symbols. Mapping the whole Earth, however, involves laying out the curved surface of the globe on a flat piece of paper. But any map that is created to do this will be distorted in some way.

Landsat image of Peloponnesus in southern Greece

SATELLITE MAP
Modern space technology has revolutionized cartography (mapmaking). Maps are drawn from satellite photographs, which show how the Earth looks from space. Satellites are very sensitive and can pick out details such as types of crops grown in certain parts of the world, and the heat given off by factories.

MAP
A map is a picture designed to show an area of the Earth's surface. There are many different types of map available. The appearance and detail of each map depends on what it will be used for. Those used for route finding, for example, may emphasize the roads, showing different types of road represented by different symbols. Political maps will concentrate on boundaries and legal divisions.

Key to symbols

- 🏨 Hotel
- ✝ Church
- 〰 Land contours
- 🛣 Road
- River
- ▦ Building

Gmünd in Austria

AERIAL PHOTOGRAPH
A photograph of an area taken from an airplane gives an accurate representation of what an area looks like. However, this photograph will not show the conventional symbols that make a map usable.

Cylindrical projection

In the cylindrical projection, the imaginary sheet of paper is rolled around the Earth, touching it at the equator. A map designed in this way distorts the polar regions the most, but North is usually at the top.

Conical projection

In the conical projection, the imaginary paper forms a cone, touching the Earth along a particular line of latitude. The map drawn in this way shows the least distortion to areas.

In the zenithal or azimuthal projection, the paper touches the globe at one point. If this point is the pole, then the lines of longitude show their correct angles.

Zenithal projection

PROJECTIONS
To display the curved surface of the Earth accurately on a flat sheet of paper, a technique called projection is used. Imagine that the Earth is transparent and that there is a light at the center. This light throws shadows of the Earth's surface features on a flat sheet of paper positioned nearby. The shadow image that falls on the sheet of paper is the basis of the map.

PETERS' MAP
The Peters' map was designed in 1977 by Arnos Peters. This map shows the true sizes of continents. But, for Peters to achieve this, the shapes of the continents have had to be stretched.

MERCATOR
The Mercator projection, first published in 1569, is based on the cylindrical projection. As directions are not distorted, it is useful for navigation and meteorological maps in which wind directions are important. However, the distortion of areas is so great that Greenland appears bigger than Africa, when in fact it has only about one-twelfth of its area.

Mercator's projection

Flemish geographer Gerardus Mercator, born Gerhard Kremer (1512–94)

Peters' projection

Find out more

TELESCOPES ON EARTH P. 297
TELESCOPES IN SPACE P. 298
SATELLITES P. 300
SPACE PROBES P. 301
SPACE STATIONS P. 304
FACT FINDER P. 414

WEATHER

THE LIVES OF US ALL are affected by the weather—what we eat and drink, what we wear, how we behave, and what our homes are like. Weather has even shaped the landscape. Wind and rain, snow and ice all wear away the rocks and grind down the mountains. Weather is with us all the time. It is the state of the air at any particular place and time. It can be hot, cold, windy, still, wet, or dry. In some places it changes from day to day; in others it stays much the same all year round. The usual weather of a place from year to year is called its climate. Climate depends mainly on how far north or south of the equator a place is and therefore how much sun it gets.

RAIN
People who have a lot of rainy weather will know that a sky full of dark gray-black clouds means it's going to rain. Rain clouds are deep and filled with water droplets. They stop the Sun's rays from shining through to the ground. The deeper and darker the clouds, the more rain is likely to fall.

Swirl of clouds in a depression

Heavy clouds over Asia

Clouds and rain over the tropics

Clear skies over the Sahara Desert

Clear skies over Antarctica

SUN
The places with the hottest weather in the world are the dry deserts, a little way away from the equator. Here, there are rarely any clouds to stop the sun from getting through. The Sahara Desert in Africa has cloudless skies nearly every day.

SUN GOD
Many ancient civilizations worshiped special gods who they thought were responsible for the weather. The Aztecs of Mexico worshiped the Sun god Tonatuich to ask for sunshine to ripen their crops. Without enough sunshine, the crops failed and there was famine. Tonatuich and all that he represented was so important to the Aztecs that they built temples and even sacrificed humans in their eagerness to please him.

CROP DAMAGE
Strong winds, rain, and hail are all bad news for farmers, since crops can be severely damaged by them. Forecasters try to give farmers warning of bad weather so that they can take precautions. All the oranges in this pile from California have been spoiled and are unfit for sale.

SUNSHINE

IF THE SUN were surrounded by a shell of ice about 1 mile (1.5 km) thick, the heat from the Sun would melt all the ice in just over two hours. All this heat comes from nuclear reactions inside the Sun. The surface of the Sun has a temperature of more than 9,900°F (5,500°C). The Sun pours out energy in all directions and our weather and climate depend on this energy. The Sun is so big that one million planets the size of the Earth could fit inside it. It looks so small because it is 93 million miles (150 million km) away. But even at this distance, the Sun is so bright that you must never look directly at it: it could damage your eyes.

SUNSPOTS
Sometimes there are dark spots on the Sun. They are cooler than the rest of the Sun, but still as hot as 7,000°F (4,000°C). The number of these sunspots increases and decreases in an 11-year cycle. This photograph was taken on September 1, 1989, a few months before maximum sunspot activity.

DROUGHT CYCLE
Some scientists think that sunspots affect the weather. In some parts of the world, the rains have failed roughly every 22 years—every two sunspot cycles—causing severe drought. This was significantly notable in North America in the 1930s, the 1950s, and the 1970s. Drought can cause rivers to dry up completely.

MAKING WEATHER
All weather conditions happen because the heat from the Sun keeps the air moving constantly. As the surface of the Earth heats up, it heats the air. Hot air rises and cooler air moves in to take its place, stirring up winds. Heat from the Sun makes water evaporate from the seas and form clouds. When the clouds cool down, their moisture falls as rain.

EDWARD MAUNDER
The British astronomer Edward Maunder (1851–1928) was surprised to find that historical records of the Sun's activity showed there were no sunspots at all between 1645 and 1715. This is now called "the Maunder Minimum." At the same time, Europe was so cold that the period is known as the "Little Ice Age." Maunder married his assistant, Annie Russell, and worked closely with her. She was one of the world's first women astronomers and became famous in her own right.

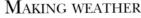

The diameter of the Sun is 108 times bigger than the diameter of the Earth. But the Earth is a solid ball of rock, and the Sun is a ball of hot gas.

MAGNIFYING THE SUN
The power of the Sun's rays can be focused by an ordinary magnifying glass to burn holes in a piece of paper. Do not try this without an adult to help you. In hot, dry countries, special curved mirrors can be used to focus the Sun's rays to heat up a "hotplate" for cooking.

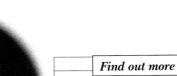

Find out more

CHANGING CLIMATES P. 246
WINDS P. 254
FORMATION OF CLOUDS P. 262
RAIN P. 264
SUN P. 284
EARTH P. 287

SEASONS

THE EARTH IS LIKE a spinning top moving in an orbit around the Sun. The spinning Earth leans over in its orbit, always tilting the same way. It takes 365.26 days to orbit the Sun completely. When the Earth is on one side of the Sun, the tilt leans the Northern Hemisphere toward the Sun. Six months later, when the Earth is on the other side of the Sun, the Southern Hemisphere leans toward the Sun. In the hemisphere leaning toward the Sun, the Sun rises high in the sky and the days are long and hot; it is summer. In the hemisphere leaning away from the Sun, the Sun rises lower in the sky and days are short; it is winter.

MIDNIGHT SUN
In regions near the North and South poles, the Sun does not set for several months during the summer. In countries such as Finland it is daylight for 24 hours. This happens because of the tilt of the Earth. These areas are called the land of the midnight Sun. While one pole has constant daylight, the other is shrouded in a dark midwinter where the Sun never rises.

WHITE CHRISTMAS
At Christmas, in December, it is winter in the Northern Hemisphere. Countries such as Norway and Canada are cold and usually have snow. People have to wear warm clothes when they go outside.

The poles have only two seasons: six months of winter and six months of summer.

The Northern Hemisphere is tilted away from the Sun and has winter.

AT AN ANGLE
The Earth leans at an angle of 23.5° and spins around an imaginary line joining the North and South poles. Depending on the time of year, one hemisphere gets more sunlight than the other, and therefore more heat. The change in temperature throughout the year causes the seasons.

The Northern Hemisphere is tilted toward the Sun and has summer.

CHRISTMAS ON THE BEACH
In the Southern Hemisphere, countries such as Australia have Christmas during the summer. The weather is just right for a dip in the sea.

Summer in the Southern Hemisphere

Places between the poles and the tropics have four seasons. They gradually change from spring to summer to fall to winter.

Winter in the Southern Hemisphere

Places near the equator always get the full heat of the Sun.

In midwinter when the hemisphere is the farthest it gets from the Sun, the pole is in darkness all day.

CASTING SHADOWS
The Sun was worshiped by some Ancient civilizations. They knew the Sun's path changes. This stone in the Inca city of Machu Pichu in Peru is the *Intihuatana*—the seat of Inti, the Sun Lord. The Incas noted how the length of the shadow the stone cast at noon changed during the year.

Find out more
FORMATION OF THE EARTH P. 210
SUNSHINE P. 242
SNOW P. 266
SOLAR SYSTEM P. 283
POLAR AND TUNDRA LANDS P. 382

CLIMATES

THE CLIMATE OF ANY AREA depends on its position on the Earth's surface. Land near the equator has a hot climate because it gets sunshine from almost directly overhead. Far away from the equator the climate is always cold. But climate does not depend only on how near to the equator a place is. Ocean currents carry warmth around the world and affect land climate. Distance from the sea affects the climate of a place, as does its height above sea level. The higher a place is, the colder the climate it is likely to have. Climates are classified into eight main types, with variations within each one.

Places with a warm temperate climate have mild, wet winters and hot, dry summers.

Mountain climates depend on the latitude and height.

North America

South America

Typical annual temperature change in an inner continental climate

Typical annual temperature change in a maritime climate

TEMPERATE
Places with a temperate climate (above) can have rain any time of year. Their summers are usually not very hot, and winters are not very cold. But they can suffer short hot spells in summer and severe snowfall in winter. The prairies in Wyoming are in a temperate region.

BY THE SEA
Countries surrounded by sea and with a relatively small landmass such as Great Britain or New Zealand have an even-tempered climate: the winters are mild and the summers are cool. Nowhere is very far from the sea. These countries have a maritime climate. They do not experience very great temperature changes because the sea heats up and cools down more slowly than the land does. The sea soaks up heat in summer and releases it in winter.

MICROCLIMATE
Small areas can have their own particular climate, called a microclimate. Most cities are covered by a warm air mass called a "heat island" that may be 11°F (6°C) warmer than the air outside the city. This special satellite picture of Paris, France, shows the hottest areas in blue and the coolest areas in green.

TROPICAL
Land that has a tropical climate lies in a band between 10° north and 10° south of the equator. It always has hot weather; the temperature is usually between 75°F and 81°F (24°C and 27°C). There are bouts of heavy rainfall throughout the year with an annual total of at least 59 in (150 cm) of rain. These are ideal conditions for rain forests (above).

KEY TO MAP
- Polar
- Tundra
- Mountain
- Cool temperate
- Warm temperate
- Desert
- Monsoon
- Tropical

POLAR
Alaska has a polar climate. The Sun is always low on the horizon, even at noon. A polar climate is very cold and dry with strong winds. Summer temperatures only rise to about 50°F (10°C) near coasts, and it is much colder inland.

Places with a tundra climate are cold with a low rainfall and short summers.

Europe

Asia

Africa

MONSOON
In areas that have a monsoon climate, seasons change very suddenly from wet to dry. In northwest India, a dry wind blows steadily off the land from the northeast for half the year. Then, for the other half of the year, a wind blows from the southwest, bringing torrential rain from the sea.

Indonesia

Australia

New Zealand

Places with a cool temperate climate have rainfall throughout the year, with warm summers and cold winters.

DESERT
Regions which have a desert climate have less than 9 in (25 cm) of rain a year. There are no clouds to block the Sun's heat by day, or to hold in the warmth at night. This means the days are very hot with temperatures up to 126°F (52°C), but nights are very cold. This is the Pinnacles Desert in Western Australia.

BUILDING FOR THE WEATHER
People build their homes to suit the climate. In the far north, where it is always icy, people used to build temporary homes, called igloos, from slabs of snow and ice. In hot climates, houses have few inside walls so that air can circulate. In monsoon areas, houses are often built on stilts to prevent flooding. In desert climates, buildings are painted white to reflect the Sun's heat. In places with lots of snow in winter, houses have steeply sloping roofs so that the snow can slide off easily.

Igloo from Alaska, North America

House on stilts from India, Asia

White-painted house from Egypt, Africa

House with a sloping roof from Switzerland, Europe

Find out more
HEAT TRANSFER P. 142
SEASONS P. 243
CHANGING CLIMATES P. 246
TEMPERATURE P. 251
DESERTS P. 390
POLAR AND TUNDRA LANDS P. 382
MOUNTAINS P. 384
FACT FINDER P. 416

CHANGING CLIMATES

THE WORLD'S CLIMATES are always changing. In the past, the world has sometimes been hotter than it is now, and sometimes cooler than it is now. More than 65 million years ago, when dinosaurs roamed the planet, there were no polar ice caps and tropical vegetation grew where it is temperate today. More recently, in the past million years, there have been times when great glaciers and ice sheets stretched out from the polar regions. In the future, there may be a new Ice Age or a new Tropical Age. The climates are changing naturally but they are also being changed by human activities.

1956 1300 800 900 BCE

STUDYING TREE RINGS
Scientists can study the growth rings in ancient wood to discover how climates have changed. This is called dendroclimatology. Californian bristlecone pine trees can reveal the climate of up to 9,000 years ago. A wide ring means that the weather was good for tree growth that year; a narrow ring means the weather was too cold or dry for much growth.

GREAT ICE AGE

We are living in a period of warmth between glacial periods. During glacial periods, huge ice sheets developed over North America, northwest Europe, and Russia. There were probably ice sheets over Greenland and Antarctica for most of the time, but varying in size. There may have been warm periods separating at least 11 glacial periods in a Great Ice Age that started about 3 million years ago.

MAXIMUM ICE
The latest Ice Age was greatest about 18,000 years ago. Ice stretched from the North Pole as far south as The Great Lakes in North America and over most of Britain and Scandinavia. There were smaller ice masses in the Southern Hemisphere.

ICE TODAY
The amount of ice cover today is normal to us. It may seem quite a small area, but in the long history of the Earth it has been rare to have so much.

LITTLE ICE AGE
The world was noticeably colder than it is now for most of the past thousand years. There was a period called the Little Ice Age between about 1550 and 1800. In the worst cold winters of the 17th and 18th centuries, even the Thames River in London, England, froze hard. Frost fairs were held on the river. Even as recently as 1895, the Thames was partly frozen, as shown by this photograph of Tower Bridge. Since then, the world has warmed by almost a degree Fahrenheit.

JAMES CROLL
British scientist James Croll (1821–90) was born near Perth in Scotland. He left school at the age of 13, but continued to study in his own time. After having many jobs, he was made keeper of the Andersonian Museum in Glasgow, Scotland, in 1859. In 1864, he published a theory that the ice ages were caused by changes in the tilt of the Earth's axis and in its orbit around the Sun. Croll observed that these changes, which happened in cycles lasting thousands of years, caused a change in the balance of seasons. This in turn caused the Earth to warm or cool.

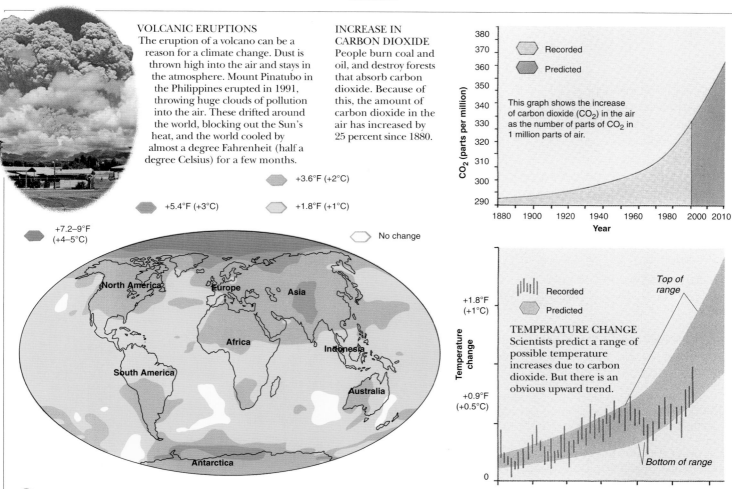

VOLCANIC ERUPTIONS

The eruption of a volcano can be a reason for a climate change. Dust is thrown high into the air and stays in the atmosphere. Mount Pinatubo in the Philippines erupted in 1991, throwing huge clouds of pollution into the air. These drifted around the world, blocking out the Sun's heat, and the world cooled by almost a degree Fahrenheit (half a degree Celsius) for a few months.

INCREASE IN CARBON DIOXIDE

People burn coal and oil, and destroy forests that absorb carbon dioxide. Because of this, the amount of carbon dioxide in the air has increased by 25 percent since 1880.

This graph shows the increase of carbon dioxide (CO_2) in the air as the number of parts of CO_2 in 1 million parts of air.

Recorded
Predicted

+3.6°F (+2°C)
+5.4°F (+3°C)
+1.8°F (+1°C)
+7.2–9°F (+4–5°C)
No change

TEMPERATURE CHANGE

Scientists predict a range of possible temperature increases due to carbon dioxide. But there is an obvious upward trend.

Recorded
Predicted
Top of range
Bottom of range

GLOBAL WARMING

There are natural reasons for the Earth warming up, but people are contributing to global warming by producing too much carbon dioxide and other gases, known as greenhouse gases. These gases trap heat that would otherwise escape into space, strengthening "the greenhouse effect." If carbon dioxide and other greenhouse gases continue to pour into the atmosphere unchecked, the world will warm rapidly. This computer forecast shows how much temperatures will increase by 2010, compared with the temperatures in 1950.

This graph shows the changes in sea level, compared with the average for the 1970s.

Recorded
Predicted

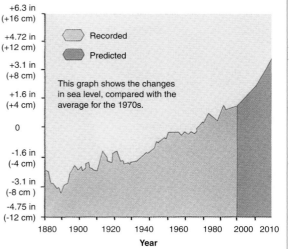

Florida coastline today

Sea level rise of 3 m (10 ft)

CHANGES IN SEA LEVEL

The overall rise in sea level since 1880 corresponds to the rise in temperature. It exactly matches the amount by which the upper layer of the ocean would be expected to expand if warmed by one degree Fahrenheit (half a degree Celsius).

EVIDENCE OF PAST CLIMATE

Past climate is revealed by this ancient cave painting that shows cattle grazing on the Algerian plateau in Africa. The cave is now in the desert. The desertification is due to natural climate change at the end of the last Ice Age.

FLOODED LAND

Low-lying regions of the world will be devastated if global warming and sea level rise continue. This computer forecast shows the effect of a 10-ft (3-m) rise in sea level on Florida. This could happen within 100 years.

Find out more

FORMATION OF THE EARTH P. 210
VOLCANOES P. 216
ICE AND GLACIERS P. 228
GROWTH AND DEVELOPMENT P. 362
CYCLES IN THE BIOSPHERE P. 372

ATMOSPHERE

LIFE ON EARTH EXISTS only because of the atmosphere. It is like a blanket around the Earth, protecting it from the Sun and providing the necessary conditions in which animals and plants can live. Other planets have atmospheres, but these are very different. On Venus, the air is thick. It contains many more gas molecules than Earth's atmosphere and the pressure is 100 times greater than on Earth. The Sun's heat is trapped and temperatures reach 900°F (480°C). It is too hot for liquid water to exist. The atmosphere on Mars is thin. The Sun's heat bounces away and temperatures can fall to -180°F (-120°C). Liquid water cannot exist here either. Conditions on Earth are in between those on Mars and Venus. Earth is sometimes called the Goldilocks planet because the conditions are like Baby Bear's porridge—just right!

EARTH FROM SPACE
Satellites can take photos of the Earth at three different wavelengths at the same time. Infrared pictures show temperature changes—black, blue, green, red, and white showing hot to cold. Normal photos show the land and sea. Other pictures show how much water vapor is in the air.

LAYERS OF THE ATMOSPHERE
The atmosphere is made up of five main layers: the troposphere, stratosphere, mesosphere, thermosphere, and exosphere. The air gets thinner as you go higher, which is why climbers usually take oxygen with them when climbing high mountains. The troposphere is the only layer in which living things can breathe normally.

Exosphere

EXOSPHERE
The top layer of the atmosphere sits about 560 miles (900 km) above Earth. The air is very thin and gas molecules are constantly "exiting" into space. This is why it is called the exosphere.

THERMOSPHERE
The top of the thermosphere is about 280 miles (450 km) above the Earth. It is the hottest layer, as the few air molecules absorb radiation coming from the Sun. Temperatures reach as high as 3,600°F (2,000°C) at the top.

BELT AROUND THE EARTH
This photograph, taken from space as the Sun sets, shows bands of air of different heights (and different densities). The photo reveals how narrow the belt of atmosphere around the Earth is.

MESOSPHERE
The top of the mesosphere is about 50 miles (80 km) above the ground. It is very cold here, with temperatures less than -150°F (-100°C). The lower part is warmer because it picks up heat from the stratosphere just below.

Thermosphere

Mesosphere

Stratosphere

Ozone layer

Troposphere

STRATOSPHERE
Up to about 30 miles (50 km) above the ground lies the stratosphere. The temperature in this layer warms from about -76°F (-60°C) at the bottom to just above freezing at the top. The stratosphere contains ozone, a gas that absorbs harmful ultraviolet rays from the Sun. Today, pollution is making holes in the ozone layer.

TROPOSPHERE
Weather conditions happen in the bottom layer of the atmosphere, called the troposphere. This layer stretches up 12 miles (20 km) from the ground at the equator, and about 6 miles (10 km) at the poles.

600 miles (1,000 km)

HOW FAR UP?
The atmosphere above your head stretches up about 600 miles (1,000 km). It sounds like a lot but compare it with distances on the surface of the Earth. If you could drive a car straight up at 30 mph (50 km/h), you would be in space in less than a day! You could even walk 9 miles (15 km) to the top of the troposphere in a few hours.

600 miles (1,000 km)

WEATHER LAYER

The lowest layer of the atmosphere, the troposphere, is sometimes called the weather layer. It is the layer in which convection happens—warm air rises and cold air sinks to take its place. Clouds form in this layer too, bringing rain and snow. The clouds are trapped in the troposphere because the next layer up, the stratosphere, is warmer and acts like a lid. The troposphere cools from an average of 59°F (15°C) at the Earth's surface to -76°F (-60°C) at the tropopause (the top of the troposphere).

JAMES GLAISHER

A balloonist, Englishman James Glaisher (1809–1903), was also interested in the atmosphere. He and Henry Coxwell went up into the troposphere in a balloon and discovered that the air got cooler the higher they went. On one flight, Glaisher fainted because he had no oxygen equipment or protective clothes. In 1848, Glaisher started the first newspaper weather report in Europe for the *London Daily News.* He also made some of the first daily charts.

18 miles (30 km)

15 miles (25 km)

12 miles (20 km)

Stratosphere

Ozone layer

9 miles (15 km)

6 miles (10 km)

Troposphere

Storm clouds can reach up to 49,000 ft (15,000 m) high.

Cirrus clouds are the highest clouds. They form at the top of the troposphere.

Air has to rise to go over mountains. The weather on each side can be very different.

Flying though the troposphere can be bumpy because of the moving air.

Small, puffy, white clouds form when bubbles of warm air rise and cool.

Lightning is caused by the build-up of static electricity in storm clouds.

The air is full of water vapor, which turns to water droplets in some clouds and falls as rain.

Almost all clouds form in the bottom 6–7 miles (10–12 km) of the atmosphere.

ATMOSPHERIC POLLUTION

The rays of sunshine shining through this window in St. Peter's Cathedral in Rome, Italy, show that the air is full of particles of dust and dirt that you cannot see most of the time. Try hanging a clean, white handkerchief outside your window on a dry, calm, cloudy day and look at it several hours later. You may find that your handkerchief has become dirtier just by being outside, especially if you live in a city. Smoke from factories and fumes from cars pollute the atmosphere. Some pollutants get trapped just above the ground and this causes people to have breathing problems and eye irritations.

AIR PRESSURE

WE CANNOT SEE AIR, but it is all around us. Gravity pulls the atmosphere down on to the Earth. This is air pressure. You do not normally feel this pressure because there is an equal pressure inside your body pushing outward. At ground level, the pressure is greatest because there is a large weight of air overhead pushing down. The higher you go, the less air there is so the less pressure it exerts. You have to boil an egg for longer to cook it at high altitudes because the lower air pressure allows water to boil at a lower temperature. Airplanes flying high in the sky have pressurized cabins so that there is enough air to breathe.

MAPPING PRESSURE
Pressure is measured in millibars (mb). On weather maps, all the areas of equal pressure are joined to make a curving line called an isobar. Areas of high and low pressure can then be easily identified.

HIGH AND LOW PRESSURE
Pressure is not the same everywhere. If the air is cold, it sinks, pushing down to create a higher pressure on Earth. As the air is squashed together, it warms up and so brings good weather. If the air is warm, it rises and so there is a lower pressure on Earth. The warm air may also evaporate water from the sea and take it up to form clouds. This is why low pressure can bring rain.

In a high (an area of high pressure), air sinks to the ground and spreads. It absorbs moisture and usually brings good weather.

In a low (an area of low pressure), air rises and condenses into cloud.

Pressure scale
32 in (81.3 cm)
30 in (76.2 cm)
28 in (71.1 cm)
26 in (66 cm)
24 in (61 cm)
22 in (55.9 cm)
20 in (50.8 cm)
18 in (45.7 cm)
16 in (40.6 cm)
14 in (35.6 cm)
12 in (30.5 cm)
10 in (25.4 cm)
8 in (20.3 cm)

1 in (2.54 cm) = 33.87 millibars

Air presses down on the mercury and forces it up the tube.

Mercury is poisonous.

In La Paz, at 12,000 ft (3,658 m) high, the standard pressure is 690 mb.

In Concepción at 1,600 ft (490 m) high, the standard pressure is 1,013 mb.

BAROMETERS
Air pressure is measured with barometers. An aneroid barometer looks a little like a clock. It contains a sealed metal box with no air inside. The pointer is joined to the box. When air pressure rises, the box is squashed inward and the pointer shows the change on a dial. Changing air pressure is a good indicator of weather to come.

Pressure is shown in millibars and pounds per square inch.

CHANGING PRESSURE
A glass tube standing in an open dish of mercury is a simple way of seeing how air pressure changes. As air pressure rises and falls, the level of mercury in the tube also rises and falls.

PRESSURE AND ALTITUDE
As you go up a mountain, the air pressure gets lower and lower. This is shown by the standard pressure of two cities in the Andes mountains in Bolivia—Concepción and La Paz.

TEMPERATURE

DEPENDING ON WHERE YOU ARE, the Earth may be hot or cold. The average temperature at Dallol, Ethiopia, is 93°F (34°C). The average temperature at the Plateau research station, Antarctica, is -70°F (-56°C). Temperatures are always highest near the equator and where there is no cloud so that heat from the Sun can easily reach the ground. They are lowest far from the equator and where there is no cloud, so that heat can escape easily into space. The temperature also depends on how shiny the Earth's surface is—this is called its albedo. Areas of snow and ice have a high albedo so they reflect solar radiation back into space: temperatures remain low. Bare soil and forests absorb more radiation and keep warm.

HIGHEST TEMPERATURE
The highest temperature ever recorded was taken at al'Aziziyah, near Tripoli, in Libya. It was 136°F (58°C) in the shade.

TEMPERATURE VARIATIONS
The temperature varies over the 24 hours of the day. It is colder at night and warmer in the daytime. In areas midway between the equator and the poles, the diurnal (daily) variation in temperature may be about 18°F (10°C).

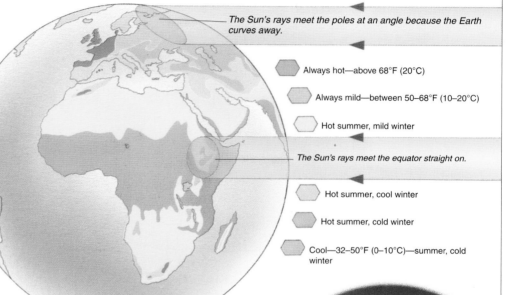

The Sun's rays meet the poles at an angle because the Earth curves away.

Always hot—above 68°F (20°C)

Always mild—between 50–68°F (10–20°C)

Hot summer, mild winter

The Sun's rays meet the equator straight on.

Hot summer, cool winter

Hot summer, cold winter

Cool—32–50°F (0–10°C)—summer, cold winter

Always cold—below 32°F (0°C)

Mild summer, cool winter

The liquid in each tube moves an indicator that stays at the highest or the lowest temperature reached.

THERMOMETERS
Temperature should always be measured in the shade. The temperature change in a day can be measured with a maximum and minimum thermometer. This thermometer shows the highest and lowest temperature of the day.

HEAT FROM THE SUN
Temperature is different around the world because of the way the Sun's rays strike the surface. At the equator, the Sun's rays hit the Earth straight on and so these areas are usually hot. At the poles, the Sun's rays hit the Earth at a shallow angle so their heat is spread out.

In La Paz, at 12,000 ft (3,658 m) high, the temperature in June is 62°F (17°C).

In Concepción at 1,600 ft (490 m) high, the temperature in June is 80°F (27°C).

AIR TEMPERATURES
The ground is warmed up by sunlight falling on it. But the air is warmed by heat rising from the ground. This is why it is always colder at the top of a mountain than at the bottom, as shown by the average maximum June temperatures in La Paz and Concepción in Bolivia.

COLDEST PLACE
The coldest temperature ever recorded was taken at Vostock Station, Antarctica, in July 1983. It was -129°F (-89°C)—four times colder than a freezer at home.

Find out more

HEAT TRANSFER P. 142
SEASONS P. 243
CLIMATES P. 244
WEATHER WATCHING P. 272
POLAR AND TUNDRA LANDS P. 382
DESERTS P. 390
FACT FINDER P. 416

HUMIDITY

WHEN THE AIR CONTAINS lots of water vapor, the weather is described as humid. The warmer the air is, the more moisture it can hold. If the air cannot carry any more water vapor, the humidity is 100 percent. At this point the vapor condenses back into water and forms clouds, fog, or rain. Plants grow well in high humidity but it is uncomfortable for us. It is difficult for the body to cool down because sweat cannot evaporate into the air. Low humidity is better for us but it is hard to grow crops. Scientists often talk about relative humidity. This is the amount of water vapor in the air relative (compared) to the maximum it can hold at that temperature.

A twisted hair inside the house stretches when it is wet and shrinks when it is dry. As it stretches and shrinks, it turns a turntable.

A model of a man and a woman stand on the turntable. In humid conditions, the stretched hair allows the turntable to turn, and the man appears. In dry conditions, the hair shrinks, pulling the turntable so that the woman appears.

The woman is outside the house when the humidity is low.

ADAPTING TO HUMIDITY
Hard physical work in humid air is exhausting if you are not used to it because your body finds it hard to keep cool. But with practice, the body gets more efficient. The British athlete Yvonne Murray trained in a greenhouse to become used to high humidity. She was going to compete in the World Championships in Tokyo, Japan, where it would be much more humid than in Great Britain.

MEASURING HUMIDITY
The amount of water vapor in the air can be measured with a hygrometer. This measures absorption or condensation of water from the air. There are different kinds of hygrometer. The earliest one was a sponge. When the air was humid, the sponge absorbed water and became heavier. A weather house is a simple hygrometer that indicates wet weather by the stretching of a hair.

FERDINAND II
Ferdinando de Medici, Duke of Tuscany (1610–70) was an Italian experimenter who worked with Galileo. In 1655, he invented a condensation hygrometer. This instrument calculated the humidity of the air by measuring the amount of dew that appeared on a cool surface. He also invented the modern thermometer. A specially sealed glass tube made sure the results were not confused by the effect of air pressure.

Farming is difficult in deserts such as this one in Saudi Arabia. There is very little water for people, livestock, or crops.

Farming is successful in areas of medium humidity, such as Great Britain.

EFFECTS OF HUMIDITY
Water vapor in the air is important for life to survive. Deserts occur where humidity is low—less than 10 percent. If the normal rains fail to fall in an area, the people living there may starve. At the opposite extreme, where humidity is high, rain forests may grow.

Where humidity is very high, rainfall is heavy. This creates ideal conditions for plants. This rain forest is on the island of Grenada.

FRONTS

THE WORLD'S WEATHER is carried around the Earth by huge swirling weather systems called highs and lows—areas of high and low pressure. Areas of high pressure, called anticyclones, are made by falling air. They move slowly, leading to settled weather. The air is dry, bringing hot, dry weather in summer and cold, clear weather in winter. Areas of low pressure are called cyclones (depressions). They are caused by rising air. The air is moist, bringing cloud, rain, or maybe snow. A depression is formed where a belt of warm and cool air collide. The two do not mix, but push into each other. Fronts form at the boundaries of the air masses and the weather becomes unsettled. A depression can be hundreds of miles across but usually passes overhead in less than 24 hours. A warm front is usually the first to arrive. When it has passed, a cold front follows close behind.

UNDER A WARM FRONT
When a warm front arrives, at first there is no change in the weather. The first sign is wispy clouds high in the sky, then some light drizzle.

The anticyclone is traveling from right to left

Wispy clouds

Warm front

Warm air

Thick rain clouds

Cold air

WARM FRONTS
A warm front has warm, moist air behind it. This warm air rises up over the cold air and forms cloud along the front. When the warm front has passed, there will be dry weather before the cold front arrives.

Rain falls behind the front

Heavy rain along the front

UNDER A COLD FRONT
A cold front brings clouds and rain immediately. There may be strong gusts of wind, called squalls, or violent storms.

This depression is traveling from right to left.

Cold front

Cold air

Warm air

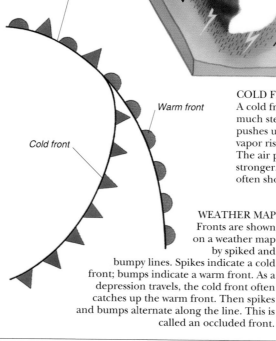

Showers

COLD FRONTS
A cold front has cold air behind it. The front is much steeper than a warm front. The cold air pushes underneath the warm air, and water vapor rises and condenses into cloud and rain. The air pressure drops and the wind gets stronger. As the front moves on, there are often showers from rain clouds trailing behind.

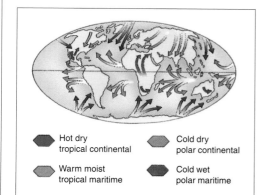

Hot dry tropical continental	Cold dry polar continental
Warm moist tropical maritime	Cold wet polar maritime

AIR MASSES

There are four main air masses that form over different parts of the Earth. These air masses affect the weather of the area over which they lie. They are blown by the winds and, where they meet and compete, the weather can be very changeable.

Occluded front

Warm front

Cold front

WEATHER MAP
Fronts are shown on a weather map by spiked and bumpy lines. Spikes indicate a cold front; bumps indicate a warm front. As a depression travels, the cold front often catches up the warm front. Then spikes and bumps alternate along the line. This is called an occluded front.

Find out more

CLIMATES P. 244
AIR PRESSURE P. 250
HUMIDITY P. 252
CLOUDS P. 260
FORMATION OF CLOUDS P. 262
FORECASTING P. 270

WINDS

THE AIR NEVER STOPS MOVING. As it moves, it carries heat and water around the globe, giving us our weather. World winds blow because there is a difference in air pressure and temperature between one place and another. Winds blow from an area of high pressure to an area of low pressure. You can show this with a balloon. When you blow up a balloon you squeeze in more and more air until the balloon is under high pressure. If you let the air escape, it rushes out like a wind to where the pressure is lower. When air is warm, it is less dense than cold air and rises up into the sky causing an area of low pressure. Cold air sinks down to the Earth and moves in to fill the gap left by the warm air. It is this circulation of air that forms the winds.

WIND DIRECTION

Wind socks are used at small airports to show pilots the strength and direction of the wind. A floppy wind sock means that the wind is only light. When strong winds blow, the sock is filled with moving air and billows in the direction the wind is blowing. A wind is described by the direction from which it is coming. For example, a west wind comes from the west; a north wind comes from the north.

JET STREAMS

At about 6 miles (10 km) above the ground, strong winds called the jet streams circle the Earth—one in each hemisphere. This photograph from space shows jet stream clouds over Egypt. The jet streams are only a few hundred miles wide but sometimes stretch halfway around the Earth. They usually blow at about 125 mph (200 km/h), but can go twice as fast. The jet streams play a large part in moving the major air masses and therefore affect the weather considerably.

Winds are turned to the right in the Northern Hemisphere.

Doldrums

Polar Easterlies

Westerlies

Trade winds blow from the northeast and the southeast, on each side of the equator.

Warm air rises and spreads out.

Cool air sinks and rushes in to replace the warm air.

Winds are turned to the left in the Southern Hemisphere.

Westerlies

Polar Easterlies are caused by cold polar air sinking and spreading out to warmer areas.

Cold polar air

Warm air rises over polar air.

MAIN WINDS

Winds that blow all the time in the same area of the world are called prevailing winds. They determine the weather patterns around the globe. They move because the equator gets more heat from the Sun than the poles. Hot air moves north and south from the equator, where it cools. The direction of the winds is also affected by the Earth's spin.

DOLDRUMS

Along the equator there is an area of low pressure where the trade winds meet. In this area, called the doldrums, there is very little wind. When ships were powered only by sail they sometimes got stuck in the doldrums. Food and water began to run out and all they could do was wait until they drifted toward the trade winds.

LOCAL WINDS

All over the world there are regular local winds that have their own names. For example, the Föhn is a dry wind that blows from the Alps in Europe. This storm is blowing up over the Matterhorn in the Alps. Other local winds include the Chinook, a dry wind which blows down the east of the Rockies in North America. It creates rapid changes in temperature and humidity. The Doctor is a refreshing sea breeze that develops around midday in Fremantle, Australia. The Pampero is a cold, southwesterly wind blowing from the Andes in South America.

SEA BREEZES

Land and sea breezes happen only in hot, sunny weather. They are convection currents caused by the land and the sea heating up and cooling down at different rates. During the day, the land heats up more quickly than the sea. Warm air rises from the land and forms an area of low pressure. Air moves in from the sea to replace this rising air, causing a sea breeze. If there are no hills to act as a wind break, the breeze can blow up to 18 miles (30 km) inland.

Warm air

Sea breeze

Cold air

Land

Sea

Cold air

Land breeze

Cold air

Land

Warm air

Sea

LAND BREEZES

At night, the land cools down more quickly than the sea. Cold air sinks over the land and pushes out to sea. The air over the sea is still warm so it rises. The colder air moves in to replace it causing a land breeze.

WIND RECORD
The windiest place in the world is George V Coast in Antarctica—shown here. The winds regularly blow at 200 mph (320 km/h). The strongest wind ever recorded on the surface of the Earth was 231 mph (371 km/h) at Mount Washington, in New Hampshire, on April 12, 1934. Strong winds, however, are difficult to record since they can sometimes break the weather-measuring instruments.

TOWER OF WINDS
In the 1st century BCE the Greek astronomer Andronicus built a Tower of Winds called a horologium. It had eight sides and on each one was carved a wind god. Each god showed off the style of his own wind. The god of the cold north wind was Boreus who was carved as an old man wearing warm clothes and playing a conch shell. The god of the warm east wind was in light clothes carrying fruit and grain.

WIND POWER
The wind can be captured to create electricity. In an experimental station in the United States, rows and rows of windmills are driven naturally by the forceful local winds. The windmills drive turbines that are connected to an electricity generator. They can collect enough energy to light and heat a small town. Unlike coal and nuclear power plants, wind turbines do not create any pollution.

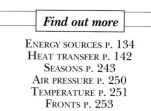

Find out more

ENERGY SOURCES P. 134
HEAT TRANSFER P. 142
SEASONS P. 243
AIR PRESSURE P. 250
TEMPERATURE P. 251
FRONTS P. 253

WIND STRENGTH

0. Calm. Chimney smoke rises straight up.

1. Light air—average wind speed 2 mph (3 km/h). Smoke drifts gently.

2. Light breeze—wind speed 5.5 mph (9 km/h). Leaves rustle. Wind felt on your face.

3. Gentle breeze—wind speed 9 mph (15 km/h). Leaves and twigs on trees move. Flags flutter.

19th-century anemometer

ANEMOMETER
An anemometer is an instrument for measuring wind speed. The first anemometers had a ball that was blown up a curved scale. Anemometers today have three or more cups mounted on the end of arms that spin around a vertical pole. As the cups catch the wind, the arms spin around and the speed is recorded.

BEAUFORT SCALE
This scale of wind strength was originally based on the effect that wind speed had on a full-rigged sailing ship and stated the amount of sail the ship should carry at different levels of wind. The scale is still in use today and has been adapted for use on land. There are 13 levels of wind strength on the scale, ranging from dead calm to hurricane.

FRIEND AND FOE, the wind has a large effect on our lives. Sometimes it blows gently giving a refreshing breeze. At other times it blows strongly, creating storms, gales, tornadoes, and hurricanes in which widespread damage is caused and people are killed. The first attempt to standardize the reporting of winds was made by Admiral Sir Francis Beaufort in 1805. He devised a scale to help sailors estimate wind strength. In the past, the energy of the wind was used to drive windmills to grind corn. And even now, with all our modern technology, the wind's energy is still used. But now it drives wind turbines to generate electricity.

4. Moderate wind—wind speed 16 mph (25 km/h). Small branches move. Paper blows around.

5. Fresh wind—wind speed 22 mph (35 km/h). Small trees start to sway.

6. Strong wind—wind speed 28 mph (45 km/h). Difficult to control umbrella. Large branches move.

7. Near gale—wind speed 35 mph (56 km/h). Whole trees sway.

8. Gale—wind speed 42 mph (68 km/h). Difficult to walk into wind. Twigs broken off trees.

9. Severe gale—wind speed 50 mph (81 km/h). Small branches, slates, and chimney pots blown off.

10. Storm—wind speed 58 mph (94 km/h). Houses damaged. Trees blown down.

11. Severe storm—wind speed 68 mph (110 km/h). Serious damage.

12. Hurricane—wind speed more than 73 mph (118 km/h). Widespread damage.

SIR FRANCIS BEAUFORT
Born in Ireland, Sir Francis Beaufort (1774–1857) was only 12 years old when he joined the British Royal Navy as a midshipman. He devised his wind scale after many years of observation of ships at sea.

Calm

Windy

KITE FESTIVAL
The Chinese flew kites 2,500 years ago. Today, people all over the world fly kites for fun. In Japan, traditional kites are decorated with legendary characters or animals that symbolize different things.

Find out more
ENERGY SOURCES P. 134
WINDS P. 254
HURRICANES P. 258
TORNADOES P. 259

THUNDER AND LIGHTNING

DARK THUNDERCLOUDS form on hot, humid days. A storm cloud is usually about 3 miles (5 km) across and 5 miles (8 km) high. Often, an individual thunderstorm is just one "cell" in a group of storms that may be nearly 20 miles (30 km) across and can last for five hours or more. Sometimes a single cell can become a "superstorm," more than 30 miles (50 km) across. This can produce large hailstones as well as thunder and lightning. If the storm is overhead, you can hear thunder at the same time as you see lightning. If it is not overhead, you can see the lightning first because light travels much faster than sound. If you count the seconds between the lightning and the thunder and divide by five, that gives you a rough idea of how far away the storm is in miles; for kilometers, divide by three.

SHEET LIGHTNING
When a flash of lightning lights up the sky, it is sheet lightning. This is a stroke of lightning that occurs within the storm cloud and doesn't come down to Earth.

THUNDERSTORM
Thunderclouds form when warm, wet air surges upward into the sky and cools dramatically. Inside these clouds, some of the water freezes and strong air currents make the ice and water droplets bump together. This knocks tiny charged particles called electrons from the ice and there is a buildup of electrical charge. This charge is released by a stroke of lightning. The lightning heats the air around it to an incredible 54,000°F (30,000°C)—five times hotter than the surface of the Sun. This heat causes the air to expand very fast—in fact, faster than the speed of sound. It is this which causes the crash of thunder.

ELECTRICAL CHARGES

Inside a storm cloud, the bumping of water and ice particles creates a buildup of static electricity. Positive charge piles up at the top of the cloud; negative charge piles up at the bottom and tries to escape to the ground. When the difference between the charges is large enough, a lightning stroke flashes either from the bottom to the top of a cloud or from the bottom of the cloud to the ground.

FORKED LIGHTNING
Forked lightning begins when a "leader stroke" zigzags toward the ground at 60 mps (100 km/second), taking the easiest path. It creates a path of electrically charged air for a return, or main, stroke to shoot back immediately. It is this return stroke that we see.

GOD OF THUNDER
Thor was the Norse god of thunder, depicted here in a 10th-century bronze from Iceland. He was said to be a huge man with red hair and beard. He was a symbol of tremendous strength and power and was believed to make thunderbolts that fell from the clouds.

SAFE PLACE
If you are caught out in a storm, do not take shelter under an isolated tall tree. Lightning looks for the quickest path to the ground and could strike the tree. One of the safest places to be is inside a car. If the car is struck by lightning, the steel frame conducts the electricity over the surface of the car to the ground.

Find out more
STATIC ELECTRICITY P. 146
CURRENT ELECTRICITY P. 148
SOUND P. 178
LIGHT P. 190
HAIL P. 267
SUN P. 284

HURRICANES

SOMETIMES CALLED TROPICAL CYCLONES, typhoons, or willy-willies, hurricanes can rip up trees, destroy crops, and flatten buildings. Torrential rain causes flooding and coastal regions may be swamped by huge waves whipped up by winds that blow as fast as 185 mph (300 km/h). Hurricanes start to form when the Sun's heat stirs up moist air over the oceans, where the temperature is more than 80°F (27°C). At first, the ring of low pressure at the center of the storm, called the eye, can be more than 185 miles (300 km) across and the winds only gale force. But as the eye narrows to about 30 miles (50 km) across, the winds begin to swirl around it at hurricane force.

HURRICANE KATRINA
In 2005, hurricane Katrina swept across the southern United States, devastating the coasts of Louisiana, Mississippi, and Alabama. More than 1,500 people lost their lives and many thousands more were left homeless.

A huge circle of clouds is formed by air spreading out from the top of the storm.

Scientists are trying to make a second eye in a hurricane by "seeding" it with salt, ice, or silver iodine crystals. If this eye joins the first, to make one large eye, wind speed could be reduced.

Air spirals counterclockwise in storms in the Northern Hemisphere, and clockwise in the Southern Hemisphere.

1. At the beginning of a hurricane, air is sucked in toward the center of the area of low pressure, creating fierce surface winds.

Eye

2. If the eye of the storm is very wide, the surrounding winds will be weak. As the eye becomes narrower, the wind speed increases violently.

WHAT HAPPENS IN A HURRICANE?

At the eye in the center of a hurricane, it is calm. A huge column of rising hot, moist air develops around the eye. As this humid air spirals up and cools, the water in it condenses into rain. Although the heaviest rain and strongest winds occur right next to the eye of the hurricane, lesser effects can be felt up to 250 miles (400 km) away.

3. As the hurricane progresses, the air moves even faster and swirls upward in an enormous spiral.

STORM OR HURRICANE?
Meteorologists are always on the look out for possible hurricanes. Satellites are used to take pictures of developing hurricanes. Supercomputers can predict the path of a hurricane, using thousands of atmospheric measurements to produce pictures showing how the weather will develop over the next few hours. In the pictures on the left, the colors show wind speed, with red being the fastest.

CLEMENT WRAGGE
Australian Clement Wragge (1852–1922) introduced the idea of naming hurricanes. He decided to give them women's names. It is said he used the names of people he disliked! Since 1970, an alphabetical list of alternating male and female names has been drawn up every year. Each time a hurricane is detected, it is given the next name on the list.

4. At full strength, the winds spin round at over 75 mph (120 km/h). The hurricane only runs out of steam when it passes over land or over cooler water—below 80°F (27°C).

TORNADOES

THE HIGHEST WINDSPEEDS on Earth occur in tornadoes. Winds whip round in a twisting funnel of air at maybe 300 mph (500 km/h), far higher than the windspeed inside a hurricane, although we cannot know exactly, since meteorological instruments do not survive in the strongest tornadoes. Tornadoes are small, extremely powerful whirlwinds that form very suddenly and often occur in groups. They are most common and most violent in the United States, where more than 500 spring up every year. A tornado may measure anything from just a few yards across to nearly 350 feet (100 meters) across and can travel for more than 125 miles (200 km). As it goes, it can suck up anything in its path, including buildings, trees, and trains, and then drop them when its force fades.

TORNADO IN A BOTTLE

Spiral forms in the water of the upper bottle.

To see how a tornado works, take two plastic bottles with screw tops and glue the tops together. Make a small hole through both tops with a nail. Fill one bottle about three-quarters full with water, and screw the double top on. Screw the empty bottle on to the top of the full bottle. Turn the two bottles upside-down, and give the water a slight swirl to set it off. It will form a spiral in the middle, just like a tornado.

TORNADO FORMATION

Tornadoes form when a long funnel of quickly rising warm air stretches up from the ground, often to a thundercloud. They may happen when the ground gets very hot and a bubble of air starts rising. In North America, they form when cold, dry air from the Rocky Mountains flows east on top of warm, wet air moving north from the Gulf of Mexico. If the updraft of air is set spinning by strong winds, the updraft can become a tornado.

Whirling funnel of air stretches to the ground like a huge vacuum cleaner.

Pressure in the center of the tornado is hundreds of millibars lower than normal atmosphere. Buildings can explode as air inside bursts out toward the area of low pressure.

SEA MONSTERS
If a tornado forms over sea, it is known as a waterspout. When it touches the surface of the ocean, water is sucked up inside the spinning wind. Waterspouts seem to rise up out of the sea like enormous dark gray serpents. They are probably the basis of legends about sea monsters.

TORRO SCALE

Tornadoes develop so suddenly that it is impossible to forecast the exact time and location of a tornado strike. When weather conditions that encourage tornadoes develop, general warnings are broadcast and then updated with more specific alerts as storms are identified. The Torro tornado intensity scale classifies the speed and destructive power of a moving tornado on a scale from 0 to 12. For example, Torro force 1 is described as mild: small trees will be uprooted and chimneys removed. Torro force 12 is described as a super tornado: even steel-reinforced buildings will be seriously damaged.

STRANGE RAIN
As a tornado loses energy and disintegrates, things that it has picked up come crashing down. This could be the cause of strange "rain," such as frogs, falling. When a tornado passes over water, it can suck up small fish and frogs as well as the water. These can be carried a long way before being dropped.

Find out more

AIR PRESSURE P. 250
WIND STRENGTH P. 256
HURRICANES P. 258
CLOUDS P. 260
RAIN P. 264

CLOUDS

CIRRUS

Cirrus clouds form high up in the sky—so high, that the water inside them is frozen to crystals of ice. Sometimes, cirrus clouds create a complete layer of white cloud.

WEATHER WITH CIRRUS
Cirrus clouds are often the first sign of good weather coming to an end. The Sun and Moon can look as if they are surrounded by a halo when they shine through a layer of cirrus clouds. This is a strong indication that rain is on the way.

CLOUDS ARE RESPONSIBLE for many aspects of weather. They therefore give some of the best clues as to what the weather will be like in the next few hours or days. If you look up and see a sky full of dark, menacing clouds, you know that it is likely to rain heavily. Fluffy, white clouds form on a warm sunny day and mean the weather will probably stay warm and dry. There are three basic types of cloud: cumulus, meaning heaped, stratus, meaning layered, and cirrus, meaning feathery. All the other many shapes and shades of cloud are a mixture or variation of these three.

CUMULUS

Cumulus are puffy, white clouds with a flat base. They look a little like balls of cotton drifting around in the sky. They are sometimes called cauliflower clouds because of their shape. Cumulus clouds are produced by rising bubbles of warm air called thermals.

WEATHER WITH CUMULUS
Small, puffy, cumulus clouds are often seen on hot summer days. They disappear at night when the air is no longer heated by the ground, and warm air does not rise to form them.

STRATUS

Stratus clouds form in layers that build up and can reach across the whole sky. In hilly regions, a layer of stratus cloud often covers the ground as a wet mist.

LUKE HOWARD

In 1803, Luke Howard (1772–1864) devised a program for the classification of cloud types. He was a pharmacist and an avid amateur meteorologist. He tried, but failed, to find a link between the Moon's phases and the weather. Howard used Latin names to identify each type of cloud, since Latin names were being used in the classification systems for animals and plants. Howard's classification is based upon the shape of clouds and their height above the ground.

WEATHER WITH STRATUS
Stratus clouds form perhaps the most depressing types of cloud. They bring persistent drizzling rain or light falls of snow.

Cirrocumulus are a heaped-up form of cirrus. They are clouds of icy particles that often make a pattern like fish scales, called a mackerel sky. They bring unsettled weather.

Cirrostratus is a layer of cirrus clouds. They look like a transparent, white veil high in the sky and often mean that wet weather is on the way.

Sometimes called mares' tails, cirrus are the highest clouds. They form in the top of the troposphere where it is coldest.

Altostratus clouds form a thin, watery sheet of cloud across the sky. It is thin enough for the Sun to shine weakly through. Altostratus often indicate that rain is on its way.

The engines of high-flying aircraft release water vapor into the cold air. The water vapor condenses and freezes making thin cloud trails in the sky. These are called contrails, from the word condensation.

Altocumulus clouds are a mixture of ice and supercooled water. They are flattened globules of white and gray cloud and sometimes signal a thunderstorm at the end of a long hot spell.

Stratocumulus are probably the most common clouds. They form a low sheet of gray or white, rounded clouds. The clouds can form a regular pattern and look joined together, but these often break up, letting the Sun shine through.

Puffy cumulus clouds occur in the middle of the cloud layer. They are usually gray at the bottom but brilliant white at the top.

Cumulonimbus clouds are sometimes called anvil clouds. They are massive, flat-topped storm clouds that stretch in a vertical column from about 6,500 ft (2,000 m) up to 50,000 ft (15,000 m) above the ground.

Stratus are the lowest clouds. They form at about 1,600 ft (500 m) above the ground. Sometimes they are much lower and form fog over the ground.

Nimbostratus clouds can cover the sky and blot out the Sun completely, making daytime very dark. They always bring rain or snow. (Nimbus is Latin for rain).

Altitude scale (right margin):
- 40,000 ft (12,000 m)
- 36,000 ft (11,000 m)
- 33,000 ft (10,000 m)
- 30,000 ft (9,000 m)
- 26,500 ft (8,000 m)
- 23,000 ft (7,000 m)
- 20,000 ft (6,000 m)
- 16,500 ft (5,000 m)
- 13,000 ft (4,000 m)
- 10,000 ft (3,000 m)
- 6,500 ft (2,000 m)
- 3,000 ft (1,000 m)
- Sea level

CLASSIFIED CLOUDS

There is a huge variety of clouds but only 10 kinds are officially classified. Different clouds form at different levels in the sky—from sea level up to about 33,000 ft (10,000 m). Low-altitude clouds have a base below 6,600 ft (2,000 m), medium-altitude clouds form between 6,600–16,500 ft (2,000–5,000 m), and high-altitude clouds form above 16,500 ft (5,000 m).

Find out more

FORMATION OF CLOUDS P. 262
FOG, MIST, AND SMOG P. 263
RAIN P. 264
SPECIAL EFFECTS P. 269
MOON P. 288
CLASSIFYING LIVING THINGS P. 310

FORMATION OF CLOUDS

THE AIR SOAKS UP WATER from rivers, lakes, and seas like a sponge. The water is in the form of an invisible gas called water vapor. It is this water vapor that forms the clouds, since clouds are made chiefly of water droplets. When the air near the ground rises into the sky, it cools and some of its water vapor condenses (turns into drops of liquid water). These gather together to form clouds. Air rises for several reasons. It may rise because it has been heated up by the warm ground. It may rise because cold air has pushed under warm air, lifting it higher. Or it may rise to pass over hills and mountains.

Ice cube

Cloud forms

Hot water

CLOUD IN A BOTTLE
You can create a cloud in a plastic bottle. Fill up the bottle with hot water (don't use boiling water because the bottle could melt). Leave it to stand for five minutes and then pour away three-quarters of the water. Lay an ice cube over the open top of the bottle and watch a cloud form. How does it work? Some of the water turns to water vapor in the warm air. When it meets the cold area by the ice cube, the water vapor turns into droplets to make a cloud.

Warm air expands and spreads out.

As clouds get bigger, cool air may circulate inside.

The Sun heats the ground. This warms the air nearby and the warm air rises into the sky.

As the air rises, it becomes cooler and the water vapor it contains condenses into droplets of water. These join together to form a cloud.

As the day goes on, more and more warm air rises and more water vapor condenses to form a bigger and bigger cloud.

CLOUDS AND DEW
Clouds form when the water vapor in the air is lifted high enough up into the sky for it to cool down and condense. The temperature at which this happens is called the dew point. Water vapor will turn to droplets only if the air contains small particles, such as dust or smoke, for it to condense on. If the air was clean, no clouds would form.

THERMALS
Cloud-forming is a useful sign to glider pilots of where warm air is rising. The pilots use pockets of rising air, called thermals, to give them lift. Birds of prey use thermals to help them stay up in the air while they circle around searching the ground for food.

On the okta scale, a vertical line across a circle represents 1 okta. This means there is a very fine cloud covering.

When the sky has 4 oktas of cloud, it means that about half the sky is covered by cloud. The circle is half shaded in.

8 oktas is the highest point on the okta scale. It means that the sky is completely covered by cloud. All of the circle is shaded in.

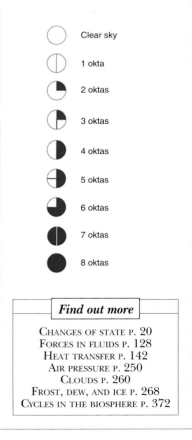

◯	Clear sky
◓	1 okta
◔	2 oktas
◔	3 oktas
◑	4 oktas
⊕	5 oktas
◕	6 oktas
◕	7 oktas
⬤	8 oktas

MEASURING CLOUD
Meteorologists measure the amount of clouds covering the sky in a unit called an okta. One okta represents one-eighth of cloud cover. The number of oktas of cloud cover are represented on a weather map by a partly shaded circle.

Find out more
CHANGES OF STATE P. 20
FORCES IN FLUIDS P. 128
HEAT TRANSFER P. 142
AIR PRESSURE P. 250
CLOUDS P. 260
FROST, DEW, AND ICE P. 268
CYCLES IN THE BIOSPHERE P. 372

FOG, MIST, AND SMOG

CLOUDS THAT FORM near the ground are called fog or mist. Like other clouds, they are made when the air is full of water vapor. When the air comes into contact with cold ground, the water vapor condenses. If the distance we can see through the cloud is between a half mile and 1.25 miles (1 and 2 km), it is called mist. If the distance we can see is less than a half mile (1 km), the cloud is called fog. A dense fog is the most dangerous cloud. It is a hazard to all types of vehicle—cars, ships, and airplanes.

The light from dipped headlights does not reflect straight back to the driver off droplets in the fog.

DRIVING IN FOG
Drivers in fog have to be very careful. Cars must use dipped headlights. If their lights are on full beam (directed straight ahead), the light reflects off the water droplets in the fog and the driver cannot see properly.

ICEBERG FOG
Icebergs are often shrouded in fog. This is because the air around them is cold but the water in which they float may be warmer. The water evaporates into water vapor, which condenses in the cold air to form fog. A ship called the *Titanic* collided with an iceberg in 1912. The crash may have been caused because the crew did not see the iceberg in the surrounding heavy fog.

RADIATION FOG
The most common kind of fog is radiation fog. On a night when there are no clouds in the sky to trap heat, the ground radiates heat so that it cools quickly. The air near the ground then cools too. If it cools to a low enough temperature, water vapor in the air will condense to form fog near the ground.

SMOG
Smog is smoky fog. In cities, the air contains many extra particles because of the smoke released by some industries. Water vapor condenses on these to form smog. This is worsened by an effect called an inversion—a layer of warm air prevents the surface air, and the pollutants it contains, from rising. This can happen in regions, such as Los Angeles, where air is trapped by surrounding mountains.

PEA SOUPERS
At one time, London, England, had heavy yellow smogs, nicknamed "pea soupers." This photograph was taken in 1952. These smogs were caused by smoke from the burning of coal in industry and in homes. The smog was no joke. It seeped into buildings, causing throat, eye, and breathing problems, and many people died because of it. Clean Air Acts passed during the 1950s have made such smogs a thing of the past.

Warm air above stops fog form escaping.

Fog forms over the sea.

Sea

Wind direction

High land stops fog from blowing inland.

ADVECTION FOG
Fog and mist often form over rivers or seas. Water evaporates from the river or sea and early on a cold morning, it condenses into mist over the water. When warm air blows over a cold sea, a type of fog called advection fog is produced. A layer of fog forms just above the water, sandwiched between the sea and the warm air above. Advection fog will only push inland if the land around is low.

Find out more
CHANGES OF STATE P. 20
HEAT TRANSFER P. 142
REFLECTION P. 194
FORMATION OF CLOUDS P. 262
CYCLES IN THE BIOSPHERE P. 372

RAIN

Snowflakes melt to form rain.

A raindrop is shaped like a flattened ball. It is not perfectly round, nor is it shaped like a teardrop.

Each raindrop is made up of millions of specks of water vapor—each one only a fraction of a millimeter in diameter.

LIFE ON LAND DEPENDS on rain. Rain fills the rivers and lakes, it lets seeds germinate and grow, and provides us with drinking water. In some areas, if the rains fail for just one season many thousands of people can die of starvation because crops fail. Too much rain is also a problem. Floods can destroy homes, farmland, and wildlife. Rain never falls from a clear, blue sky. It can only form in a cloud, usually either a nimbostratus or a cumulonimbus. Water that falls from a cloud is called precipitation. The temperature of the air, both inside and outside the cloud, determines whether precipitation is rain, snow, sleet, or hail.

HOW RAIN FORMS

Most rain outside the tropics starts off as snow, even in summer. High up in the clouds, the temperature is below freezing, and ice crystals form. The crystals grow bigger, form snowflakes, and fall from the cloud. If the temperature of the air nearer the ground is above freezing, the snow melts and turns into rain as it falls. In the tropics, where the clouds are warm, rain is formed when microscopic drops of water in the clouds collide and join together. When the drops are too heavy to stay up, they fall as rain. In thin clouds, fewer drops collide so the falling raindrops are smaller. Very small drops are known as drizzle.

FLOODING
When there is a heavy downfall of rain, floods may happen if the water cannot drain away quickly. The Indian monsoon brings some of the heaviest rain in the world and floods the land every year, usually in September.

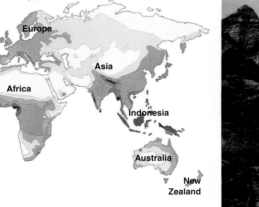

Rivers burst their banks and the surrounding flat land can be covered with several feet of water.

After a long, dry spell the soil is baked hard and water cannot drain away properly.

Key to map of annual rainfall

- More than 118 in (3,000 mm)
- 78–118 in (2,000–3,000 mm)
- 39–78 in (1,000–2,000 mm)
- 20–39 in (500–1,000 mm)
- 10–20 in (250–500 mm)
- Less than 10 in (250 mm)

North America

Europe

Hawaii

Asia

Central America

Africa

South America

Indonesia

Australia

New Zealand

Measuring rule

MEASURING RAINFALL
Rainfall is measured in inches or millimeters. It can be measured with a rain gauge. A funnel catches the rain and directs it down into a cylinder. The height of water in the cylinder is the amount of rain that has fallen.

ANNUAL RAINFALL AROUND THE WORLD
Different regions of the world get different amounts of rain. There are several reasons for this variation. For example, in the tropics, there is a lot of rain because a considerable amount of water evaporates from the warm sea and makes clouds. Land near the sea usually gets more rainfall than land far from the sea. Mountain ranges can block off the winds that bring rain clouds making it wet on one side and dry on the other. And there are dry deserts where air masses get hot and dry as they descend toward the ground.

RECORD RAINFALL
On the top of Mount Wai-ale-ali, on the island of Kauai in Hawaii, it rains on 350 days a year. The average annual rainfall is about 460 in (11,680 mm). The moist southeast trade wind rises and cools as it passes over the mountain and this causes the rain.

DROUGHT

If, over about two weeks, there is less than 1/100 in (0.2 mm) of precipitation, there is said to be a drought. Without reservoirs, there is not enough water for people and crops. Some places have extreme drought that lasts for many years. It is said that Calama in the Atacama Desert in Chile did not have any rain for 400 years until 1972. In temperate Europe and North America, periods of drought are unexpected. But in Australia and parts of Africa, Central America, and Asia, drought happens regularly.

MAKING RAIN
Clouds are sometimes "seeded" to make them rain. Aircraft drop dry ice (frozen carbon dioxide) or silver iodide crystals on to them. The chemicals provide "seeds" for snowflakes to grow on. The snowflakes turn into rain as they fall down to the ground. The effect on the clouds where the aircraft has just sprayed can clearly be seen in this photograph.

Weather in the area under the blocking high is dry and settled.

Lows have to go around the outside of the high.

Weather in the area away from the high is unsettled.

BLOCKING HIGH
A drought can be caused by an area of high pressure blocking the passage of moving low pressure systems. If the high pressure sticks in one place for a long time, it can prevent any change in the weather for weeks. Blocking highs are always dry. They bring clear, cold weather in winter and hot, dry weather in summer.

THE DUST BOWL
During the 1930s, there was a long period of prevailing Westerlies over North America. This meant that the Great Plains were in the "rain shadow" of the Rocky Mountains and had no rain. The drought was made worse because the farmers had plowed up all the natural grasslands, letting the topsoil get dry and dusty. The worst-affected area was in the Southern part of the Great Plains, and became known as the Dust Bowl. Crops could not grow and farming families were forced off the land.

SURVIVING A DROUGHT
Flowers are blooming in this normally dry area in Australia, forming a pink carpet for a few days. Most plants cannot survive in the desert because it is so dry. But some seeds can survive for years in the soil. As soon as the rains come the seeds spring into life, flower, and quickly set new seeds before the ground dries up again.

BUSH FIRES
In hot, dry regions, bush fires often start. They clear the land, making room for new plants to grow, and the heat is necessary to make certain seeds germinate. Where people prevent bush fires, some kinds of plants die out. Today, bush fires are often left to burn, provided that they do not threaten people's lives.

Water does not reach the top branches, so they die and go brown.

There is only enough water to keep the lower branches alive.

THIRSTY PLANTS
Most plants need a constant supply of water to survive. If there is a drought, many plants will die, even established trees. You can tell when trees are not getting enough rain because their topmost branches will die.

Find out more

CLOUDS P. 260
SNOW P. 266
HAIL P. 267
CYCLES IN THE BIOSPHERE P. 372
DESERTS P. 390
FACT FINDER P. 416

SNOW

NO TWO SNOWFLAKES are exactly the same. Each one is a collection of ice crystals, made of frozen water vapor, frozen together. Ice crystal shapes are divided into about 80 categories. They can be shaped like needles, prisms, plates, hexagons, and columns. The shape depends on the temperature, height, and water content of the cloud in which they form. Snow can be "wet" or "dry." Wet snow is made of large snowflakes and forms when the temperature is just about freezing. It is perfect for making snowballs but difficult to clear away. Dry snow is powdery and easy to clear. It forms when the temperature is well below freezing. Sleet is usually half-melted snow, but it can be half-frozen rain formed when raindrops evaporate and cool as they fall.

AVALANCHES
If a mountain slope is steeper than 22°, avalanches can happen. The snow piles up until a small amount starts to slip, collecting more and more snow as it goes down the slope. Avalanches may be set off by a heavy fall of snow on ice, a rise in temperature, a skier, or even by a loud noise.

All snowflakes form in a six-sided symmetrical pattern.

Ice caps have a shiny, white surface that reflects the Sun's heat. This helps to keep them cold even during the summer.

PERMANENT SNOW
Glaciers and ice caps are made from snow that has never melted. Instead, all the crystals and snowflakes have been squeezed together by the weight of more snow falling on top. Ice caps and glaciers form on mountain tops and near the poles.

HOW SNOW FORMS

Ice crystals form in clouds where the temperature is between -4°F and -40°F (-20°C and -40°C). To form snowflakes, the crystals join together as they fall and become wet, and then refreeze. When they fall out of the cloud, they will reach the ground as snow only if the temperature of the air is freezing all the way down. If it is too warm, the crystals may evaporate back into water vapor or melt and fall as sleet or rain. Sometimes, it can be snowing on the top of a tall skyscraper, while it is raining in the street below.

SNOW DRIFTS
When snow builds up in drifts, people can get stuck in cars or even inside their homes. If animals or people get buried in snow, they can survive for a long time. This is because freshly fallen snow contains air in the gaps between the ice crystals that the animals can breathe.

PINK SNOW
Snow is not always white! It can be pink, brown, or even red. This pink snow is in Greenland. The color is caused by algae living in the snow. The pigment that makes the algae red also protects them in the extremely cold conditions.

Find out more

HEAT TRANSFER P. 142
ICE AND GLACIERS P. 228
TEMPERATURE P. 251
CLOUDS P. 260
POLAR AND TUNDRA LANDS P. 382

HAIL

New layer of ice freezes around the hailstone.

HAILSTONES ARE FROZEN drops of rain. They form inside tall cumulonimbus clouds, which are much warmer at the bottom than at the top, where it is freezing. The temperature difference causes strong currents inside the cloud. These currents toss the raindrops up to the freezing top of the cloud and down again. In order for a hailstone to stay up in a cloud long enough to become even pea-sized, it needs to be swept up and down at speeds of about 100 ft (30 m) per second. As hailstones rise and fall inside a cloud, they crash into each other often causing electric charges to separate out and make lightning. Even when the hail is not falling to the ground, it can still make lightning inside the clouds.

32°F

(0°C)

Current of air takes the hailstone back up to the top of the cloud.

The hailstone eventually becomes too heavy to be held up in the cloud and it falls to the ground.

HOW HAIL FORMS

Hailstones develop inside cumulonimbus clouds which have grown to a height of about 6 miles (10 km). Strong, uprising air currents within a cloud can lift raindrops up into the frozen cloud top. The first time this happens the raindrop freezes and falls. When it is tossed upward again a further layer of ice builds around it. The ice builds up, layer upon layer, until the hailstone finally falls to the ground.

LAYERS OF ICE
This cross-section of a hailstone clearly shows that a hailstone is made in layers, like the layers of an onion. Each layer represents one journey up to the top of a storm cloud and back down to the bottom.

HAIL DAMAGE
Hailstones can cause severe damage. They ruin crops, such as these apples, making them unfit to sell. Large hailstones can break windows and dent cars. Small birds, caught in a storm with no cover, have been killed by hailstones.

RECORD HAILSTONES

Hailstones are often as big as marbles, and sometimes as big as tennis balls. Less common are those that fell in Bangladesh in 1986. They weighed 2 lb 4 oz (1.02 kg). Shown here is a giant hailstone that fell in Kansas in 1970. It measured 17.25 in (43.6 cm) in circumference and weighed 1 lb 11 oz (765 g).

HAIL PREVENTION
Many attempts to prevent hail damage have been made, including firing guns into the clouds, as shown by this French magazine of 1910. More recently, silver iodide crystals have been sprayed across clouds by airplanes. It is hoped that this will turn the hailstones into rain.

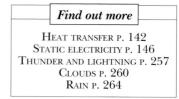

Find out more

HEAT TRANSFER P. 142
STATIC ELECTRICITY P. 146
THUNDER AND LIGHTNING P. 257
CLOUDS P. 260
RAIN P. 264

FROST, DEW, AND ICE

WHEN THE SUN HAS SET at night, the ground begins to lose its heat. The air does not lose heat so fast so the ground becomes colder than the air above it. On a clear, still night, water vapor in the air condenses on the ground as dew drops. The temperature at which dew starts to form is called the dew point. If the temperature of the air falls below freezing, the water vapor turns into ice crystals and coats everything with frost. Sometimes, a layer of transparent ice forms on the ground making roads slippery. It happens when rain falls through very cold air on to ground that is below 32°F (0°C), where it freezes into "black" ice. It is called black because the road can be seen through it.

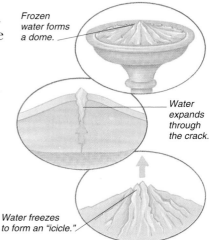

Frozen water forms a dome.

Water expands through the crack.

Water freezes to form an "icicle."

"UPSIDE-DOWN" ICICLES
Sometimes "icicles" form in shallow puddles or birdbaths—sticking up. This happens because water expands when it freezes and pushes up a little dome of ice. If this cracks, water from underneath the dome pushes up through the crack and freezes. When this happens several times, the result is a spike of ice.

HOAR FROST
Frost usually occurs on a cold night when there is no blanket of cloud to stop warmth from escaping from the ground. The most usual kind of frost is hoar frost. This coats the ground, leaves, branches, and even spiders' webs with a thin layer of tiny ice crystals. Sometimes hoar frost is so white and so deep on the ground that it looks like snow.

It is unusual for the ice on a river or lake to be thick enough to skate on.

DEW POND
Dew that forms at night covers the ground in the early morning. When the Sun comes up and it begins to get warmer, the dew evaporates into the air. Some farmers make dew ponds—hollows in the ground in low-lying parts of a field. Dew runs down and collects in the dew ponds for animals to drink first thing in the morning. Sometimes dew ponds occur naturally.

FROZEN WATER
If it is very cold, a layer of ice can form over rivers and lakes. This ice may seem strong and thick at the edges, but there will be weak spots where the ice is thinner. That is why it is dangerous to walk on water that is covered with ice. Fish survive because the ice acts like a lid, stopping the water underneath from freezing.

FROZEN SEA
Seas do not often freeze because saltwater freezes at a lower temperature than freshwater. But if it is cold enough, ice can cover the sea, especially near the coast.

ICEFISH OF ANTARCTICA
The waters around Antarctica are so cold that they would freeze the blood of ordinary fish. Fish that live in these waters have evolved chemicals in their blood that act as a natural "antifreeze"—just like the antifreeze put in a car to stop the water from freezing in the winter.

Find out more
CHANGES OF STATE p. 20
HEAT TRANSFER p. 142
ICE AND GLACIERS p. 228
SNOW p. 266
POLAR AND TUNDRA LANDS p. 382

SPECIAL EFFECTS

THE COLORED PATTERNS of a rainbow or a glorious sunset are familiar to everybody. But the changing patterns of weather can play other strange tricks on us. They produce pillars of light in the sky, rings around the Sun and Moon, and strange distortions of the shape of the Sun as it sets. The way stars twinkle in the sky has nothing to do with the stars themselves, but is caused by the effect of the air on light passing through it. And the atmosphere can even bend light, to bring you an image of a far-distant object.

Ray of light

Raindrop

HOW SUNLIGHT IS SPLIT
A ray of light passing through a raindrop is bent on its way in and on its way out. It is also reflected off the inside of the raindrop.

If there is a second rainbow, the colors are reversed.

ST. ELMO'S FIRE
In stormy conditions, an electric discharge, like lightning, may form a bluish-green ball of light on pointed objects. One of these on a ship's mast was known to sailors as St. Elmo's Fire. It is sometimes seen today on the wingtips of aircraft, or lightning conductors.

The colors of a rainbow are, from the outside inward, red, orange, yellow, green, blue, indigo, and violet.

RAINBOWS
You can see a rainbow only when the Sun is shining behind you and it is raining in front of you. Rainbows form when sunlight shines through millions of raindrops. Sunlight is a mixture of colors. When it passes through a raindrop, it is refracted (bent) and the light splits and spreads out into seven colors. All rainbows are part of a circle, but you can usually see only part of it, since the Earth is in the way. If you are lucky, you may see a complete circle from an aircraft.

MIRAGES
Mirages are associated with hot deserts, but you may see one on a hot road. Light bends from warmer air toward colder air. When air near the ground is hotter than air above, light rays are bent up so that they come to the eye from a different place to where they started. It can look as if there is a lake ahead, but this is really an image of the sky. You see light rays from the sky coming from near the ground.

HALOES AROUND THE MOON
When light from the Moon passes through ice crystals high in the sky, haloes sometimes form around the Moon. Light reflecting off the ice crystals is bent at angles of either 22° or 46° to make two separate haloes. The haloes are often incomplete, and usually only the smaller one can be seen.

Haloes around the Moon

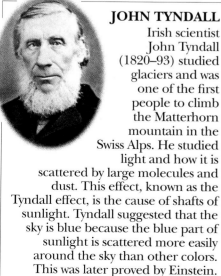

JOHN TYNDALL
Irish scientist John Tyndall (1820–93) studied glaciers and was one of the first people to climb the Matterhorn mountain in the Swiss Alps. He studied light and how it is scattered by large molecules and dust. This effect, known as the Tyndall effect, is the cause of shafts of sunlight. Tyndall suggested that the sky is blue because the blue part of sunlight is scattered more easily around the sky than other colors. This was later proved by Einstein.

BROCKEN SPECTER
An unusual effect can be seen, especially in mountains, when the Sun is low in the sky. The Sun casts a large shadow of objects or people on to low-lying mist or clouds. The shadow is called the Brocken specter after the Brocken mountain in Germany.

Find out more

STATIC ELECTRICITY P. 146
REFRACTION P. 196
LIGHT AND MATTER P. 200
SHADOWS P. 201
COLOR P. 202
ATMOSPHERE P. 248

FORECASTING

WHAT IS THE WEATHER going to be like today? To forecast the weather accurately, information must be gathered from all around the world. There are two types of forecast—long-range forecasts predict the weather for up to five days ahead; short-range forecasts predict the weather for the next 24 hours. The biggest nonmilitary customers for weather forecasts are civil aviation organizations, such as airlines and airports, which need to know conditions at different altitudes. Sea couriers needs to be warned of storms; power plants need to know if it is going to be cold, so that they can estimate the demand for energy. Farmers need forecasts so they can plan harvesting and protect crops. And you want to know what clothes to wear, or whether to take an umbrella out with you, even if the Sun is shining!

A weather sign for thunder marks the battle site.

Depression moving slowly east, bringing heavy rain to the Waterloo area

WEATHER IN HISTORY
Using old records, experts can draw up weather maps, or charts, for days in history. This map is of the night before the Battle of Waterloo, June 17, 1815. The battle was between the armies of the French emperor Napoleon and the Allied army commander the Duke of Wellington. Heavy rain made the ground muddy and delayed the French attack. This gave time for more troops to reach and support Wellington's army, which won the battle.

Circle indicates cloud cover

Depression

Star indicates snow

Isobar joining areas of equal pressure

No arrow indicates calm

Warm front

Occluded front

White upside-down triangle indicates showers

Black dot indicates rain

Cold front

"Arrow" indicates direction of wind; "feathers" indicate the strength

Thick cloud in the depression, bringing rain and snow

High pressure brings clear air with no precipitation.

CHART FOR JAPAN
Forecasters draw up weather charts to show the picture of what conditions such as temperature, wind, pressure, and rainfall are like. They use internationally agreed upon weather symbols. This chart for December 16, 1992, shows a developing low pressure system, or depression, over Japan. Strong winds sweep counterclockwise around the low, swinging warm and cold fronts around with it. Japan has wet windy weather, while, to the west, high pressure means that the weather over China is cold and dry.

VIEW FROM SPACE
Photographs of clouds are taken from space by weather satellites. They show at a glance what the weather is like. This satellite picture shows the cloud patterns associated with the weather chart above. The cloud forms a dense knot near the center of the depression, with more cloud spreading out along the line of the front.

SATELLITES
Information from Earth is collected by satellites and sent down to weather stations every 30 minutes, with photos of cloud patterns.

COLLECTING INFORMATION
The World Meteorological Organization (WMO) has 150 member countries that share information in the World Weather Watch. Data from nearly 10,000 land stations, 7,000 ships, hundreds of aircraft and balloons, and several satellites are gathered each day at centers in Moscow in Russia, Washington, D.C., and Melbourne in Australia. Regional and worldwide forecasts are made and sent to members of the WMO. These send the data to national weather offices, which make the forecasts for their own countries.

SHIPS
Weather ships take measurements of pressure and temperature at sea level, and they measure the temperature of the sea itself. They launch weather balloons that send back information about the atmosphere at different heights.

AUTOMATIC BUOYS
Weather buoys are used in place of crewed ships. They record information about the local weather at sea level. The information is collected by satellites.

COMPUTERS
Information from around the world is fed into computer "models." The computers help make forecasts of future weather.

RADIOSONDES
Helium-filled balloons carry packages of instruments, known as radiosondes, into the atmosphere. In addition to sending back temperature and pressure data, the radiosondes are tracked to show wind speeds.

AIRCRAFT
Specially adapted aircraft carry instruments up into the atmosphere. The measurements are sometimes immediately beamed back to the ground, and sometimes recorded and brought back.

SMALL STATIONS
Individuals with a few simple instruments play an important part in weather forecasting. They send their information about local conditions to a main weather station.

Radiosondes are released at least twice a day.

USING FORECASTS
Airports need forecasts of bad weather so that equipment can be made ready to keep the runways open. Snow and ice are the worst hazards, but warnings of strong winds are also important.

LEWIS FRY RICHARDSON
British mathematician L.F. Richardson (1881–1953) worked out how to use mathematical techniques to forecast the weather. He worked on his theory while serving in the ambulance corps during World War I. His manuscript was lost during a battle in 1917, but it showed up several months later under a heap of coal. Richardson's work was published in 1922, but his ideas could not be used until the electronic computer was developed years later.

AUTOMATED STATIONS
Weather information in remote regions is collected at unstaffed stations. The information is sent automatically via satellite to the forecasting centers. Similar stations are set up on some offshore oil rigs.

WEATHER WATCHING

FOR THOUSANDS OF YEARS, before weather-recording instruments were invented in the 16th century, people had to study natural signs to know what weather was coming. In addition to the sky and clouds, animals, plants, the Sun, and the Moon all had their part to play. Many sayings arose from the signs and are now part of folklore. There are, of course, different signs and sayings in different parts of the world. Many of these are more than folklore—they work. Careful weather watching, combined with simple measurements of temperature and pressure, makes do-it-yourself local forecasting very reliable.

RED SKY
The sky is red every dawn and dusk. But when it is cloudy the sky's color is hidden. In Europe and North America, winds usually bring weather from the west. If plenty of red sky is seen when the Sun is setting in the west, it means clear weather is on its way. Red sky in the morning means the good weather is on its way out.

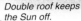
Double roof keeps the Sun off.

The screen shades instruments from the Sun's direct heat. But louvered sides allow air to circulate through the box.

Wet- and dry-bulb thermometers

The bulb of one thermometer is kept wet in distilled water. As the water evaporates, heat is taken from the thermometer.

All Stevenson screens stand at 4 ft (1.2 m) high, so records from them all can be compared accurately.

JAPANESE CHERRY
In Japan, the dates on which the cherry trees blossom have been recorded for centuries. The records help weather watchers to know what the weather was like hundreds of years ago, and whether there was a harsh winter or an early spring in any year.

STEVENSON SCREEN
Most weather stations and many schools have a Stevenson screen. This may contain a wet- and a dry-bulb thermometer to record humidity. The wet and dry thermometers show different temperatures according to the humidity. The humidity is worked out from a scale. There may also be a maximum and minimum thermometer and chart recorders of humidity and temperature.

COWS
It is popularly thought that if cows lie down it means that rain is coming. The cows are supposed to be making sure they have somewhere dry to lie. Unfortunately, even if this is true, cows lie down at all sorts of times. So a field full of cows lying down doesn't always indicate rain!

Human knee

Animals suffer rheumatism in their joints.

BONES
During spells of mild weather, people who suffer from rheumatism can be free of pain. But when cold, damp weather is on its way they can "feel it in their bones."

The seaweed feels damp when rain threatens.

SEAWEED
A piece of seaweed brought back from the beach, such as this kelp, can help you to observe changes in the weather. When the weather is dry, the moisture in the seaweed evaporates, leaving it brittle and hard. In humid weather, the seaweed absorbs moisture from the air and it becomes plump and soft again. Seaweed changes tell us about the weather that we are having now, rather than what is coming.

SPACE

LOOK UP INTO THE SKY and you are looking out into space. You can see stars and planets, as well as vast expanses of virtually empty space in between. From the earliest times, people have tried to understand how we on Earth fit into our local part of space, and into the rest of the universe that lies beyond. Early civilizations used the movements of objects in the sky (celestial objects) as a calendar, as a means of navigation, or to predict events in their lives. Early astronomers (people who study objects in space) tried to explain the movements of the celestial objects. Since the 19th century, they have tried to explain what the objects actually are. Today, astronomers have the most sophisticated technology available, which they use on Earth and in space, to pursue their quest.

In 1609, the Italian astronomer Galileo Galilei was the first person to make a study of the skies with a telescope.

When Galileo studied the Moon with his telescope, he saw craters and mountains that were invisible to the naked eye.

TELESCOPES
Technology has had a big effect on astronomy. In the early 17th century, the newly invented telescope was first used to look at the sky. It revealed spots on the Sun's surface, four of the planet Jupiter's moons, and countless more stars. Since then, the telescope has become more powerful and sophisticated. Modern telescopes are used to measure star positions, make digital images, and to analyze star light.

Galileo's telescope

The regions of red are where most X-rays are being given out.

X-ray image of Cassiopeia A (supernova remnant)

IMAGES OF SPACE
For centuries, the only way to learn about the universe was to collect and study the light waves given out by objects in space. Today, astronomers are able to collect and examine other types of radiation that are given out, such as X-rays, to build up a more complete picture of the universe. This X-ray photograph of the leftovers of a supernova (exploding star) reveals clear, bright details. An image that captured only light waves would have shown just a dimly glowing gas.

LONELY SPACE
The universe is full of billions of stars and galaxies, but it is still a very empty place. The universe is so vast that even the light from all the billions of stars doesn't illuminate it. In between the stars are billions of miles of virtually empty, cold, and dark space. The only known intelligent life form in the universe is human. For humans, space is a very lonely place.

Between them, two space probes called Voyager 1 *and* 2 *visited the planets Jupiter, Saturn, Uranus, and Neptune over the period 1979–89. They confirmed some scientific theories, but also made some unexpected discoveries.*

MODERN EQUIPMENT
Astronomers not only use equipment on Earth, they also send it into space to get a better look at our surroundings. Telescopes in orbit around Earth can see objects in space more clearly and can pick up radiation that cannot penetrate Earth's atmosphere. Robots called space probes are sent on lonely journeys to fly around and land on other planets, sending their discoveries back to Earth. Most telescopes and space probes are controlled from Earth by computers.

UNIVERSE

Universe
In all, there are at least 100,000 million galaxies in the universe.

THE UNIVERSE IS EVERYTHING you can think of, and more. It includes all the stars, planets, moons, animals, plants, books such as this one, and you—it even includes all the space in between. Early people thought that the universe only contained what they could see with their eyes from Earth. They thought of Earth as the central and most important part of the universe. Today, we know just how vast the universe is and what a tiny part of it the Earth makes. Our present understanding of the universe has been developed by astronomers and cosmologists working in the past 100 years. Astronomers study specific parts of the universe; cosmologists strive to explain the universe's origin and development.

CHANGING UNIVERSE

Everything in the universe is changing. On Earth, humans or plants change as they live out their lives; stars in space have lives too, so they are also continually changing. Even the universe as a whole does not stay the same. It too has a life of its own. Early in the 20th century, astronomers discovered that all galaxies (enormous collections of stars) are rushing away from each other. The universe is getting bigger.

Cluster of galaxies
The Milky Way lives in a cluster of about 30 galaxies. Such clusters of galaxies are loosely grouped into superclusters.

LIGHT-YEAR

Distances in the universe are so vast that a light-year is used to measure them. This is the distance a ray of light travels in one year. As light travels at 186,000 miles (300,000 km) per second, it covers 5,870,000 million miles (9,460,000 million km) in one year.

Humans
Humans make up a tiny fraction of the universe.

Earth
Humans live on a planet called Earth.

Solar System
Earth is one of nine planets that travel around a star called Sun.

Milky Way
The Sun is just one of at least 500,000 million stars in a galaxy called the Milky Way.

The speed of light is the universal speed limit. Nothing can travel faster. Even so, the light from the nearest star to us (aside from the Sun) takes 4.3 years to reach us. It is 4.3 light-years away. We see this star as it was 4.3 years ago.

Astronomers believe there are millions of stars in the universe with their own planets. The first such planet was discovered in 1995; over 150 are now known.

EDWIN HUBBLE

In 1924, an American astronomer, Edwin Hubble (1889–1953), showed that nebulae (fuzzy light patches in the sky) were distant galaxies. In 1929, he found the speed a galaxy moves away from Earth depends on its distance from Earth. If a galaxy is five times as far away as another, it is moving five times as fast. This is Hubble's law.

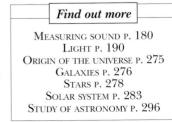

RED SHIFT

Light travels as a wave. A squashed-up light wave is blue. A stretched-out light wave is red. In between are all the other colors of the spectrum. The light from a galaxy moving away from us will be stretched toward the red end of the spectrum. This is called a red shift. It will be more red-shifted if the galaxy is moving faster. From Hubble's law, astronomers know that the more distant galaxies move away faster than closer ones. The red-shift therefore shows how far away the galaxy is.

The orange-red light from this galaxy shows it is moving away from us.

The light from this galaxy is shifted farther toward the red end of the spectrum. This shows us that the galaxy is moving faster and is farther away than the galaxy above.

ORIGIN OF THE UNIVERSE

MOST SCIENTISTS THINK THAT the universe was born in a colossal explosion called the Big Bang. In this explosion, around 13,000 million years ago, all matter, energy, space, and time were created. Of course, no one was there to tell us what happened. But discoveries in physics and astronomy have enabled scientists to trace the universe's history to its first fraction of a second. They believe at that time, the universe was squashed into a tiny volume, and it has been expanding ever since. The Big Bang Theory was put forward in 1933. Another idea, called the Steady State Theory, was suggested in 1948. This said that new material was continuously being created, so overall the universe would not change. The Steady State Theory has now been discounted. More recently, scientists have been looking into the future of the universe. What happens next?

BIG BANG

Around 13,000 million years ago, the universe was very small and very hot. An explosion, the Big Bang, started off the process of expansion and change which still continues today. Within minutes of the explosion, atomic particles came together to make the gases helium and hydrogen, which over millions of years produced the galaxies, the stars, and the universe as we know it today.

The universe started to expand as a result of the Big Bang.

The universe may come together again in a "Big Crunch."

Another explosion may start the process off again.

BOUNCING UNIVERSE

What will happen to the universe? Scientists have different views about this. Some think it will have no definite end, but will gradually run down. This is the open universe theory. Others think that it will stop expanding and start to contract until it is compressed and hot once more. This is the closed universe theory.

The Cosmic Background Explorer (COBE) satellite investigated the radiation from the early universe. In 1992, it detected unevenness in this radiation—the first signs of galaxy-birth.

BACKGROUND RADIATION

From the 1940s, scientists studied what the very young universe was like. They realized it must have been full of radiation. As the universe grew and cooled, the radiation would have cooled too. Russian-American scientist George Gamow even worked out the temperature that it should now be. In 1965, two American scientists, Arno Penzias and Robert Wilson, detected exactly this type of radiation (called the background radiation). It provided evidence for a Big Bang.

The Sun was born about 5,000 million years after the Big Bang. The Earth and planets evolved from the debris.

Our Galaxy, the Milky Way, formed into a disc shape 5,000 million years after the Big Bang.

2–3,000 million years after the Big Bang, quasars (forerunners of galaxies) evolved.

TIMELINE

When the universe was born, it was more or less the same throughout. As it expanded, material inside it clumped together. Gravity drew more and more material together, leaving regions of virtually empty space in between. The regions of material eventually gave birth to stars and galaxies.

In minutes, the universe was made of 75% hydrogen and 25% helium.

The temperature was over 10,000 million degrees.

Birth of universe— Big Bang

The first life forms appeared on Earth about 3,000 million years ago.

Dinosaurs lived 190 million years ago. Humans have been around for just 2 million years—a tiny fraction of the universe's life.

The present time is around 13,000 million years after the Big Bang.

3 billion years after the Big Bang, galaxies started to take shape.

1 billion years after the Big Bang, material started to come together.

GALAXIES

OTHER GALAXIES
In 1924, the American astronomer Edwin Hubble proved the existence of other galaxies. He showed that stars within the Andromeda Nebula (later called the Andromeda Galaxy) were too distant to be members of the Milky Way.

STARS LIVE TOGETHER in "star cities" called galaxies. These enormous collections of stars started off as huge clouds of gas soon after the birth of the universe. Gravity eventually pulled the gas into separate stars. Galaxies are so vast that it takes starlight hundreds of thousands of years to travel from one side to the other. The way the stars are arranged within a galaxy gives it a distinctive shape. Our star, the Sun, lives in a spiral-shaped galaxy called the Milky Way. Up until this century, astronomers thought that the Milky Way Galaxy was the only galaxy in the universe. Today, we know it is just one of more than 100,000 million galaxies that exist.

DISTANT WORLDS

By the start of the 20th century, astronomers had listed large numbers of dim, fuzzy patches in the sky that they called nebulae. Many of these had been seen for centuries. Some people thought they were just clouds of gas in the Milky Way. Others thought they might be distant galaxies. And indeed this is what many turned out to be. American astronomer Edwin Hubble studied them and classified them according to their shape. There are four main types of galaxies—spirals, barred spirals (like the Milky Way), ellipticals, and irregulars.

Spiral galaxy
NGC 5194

SPIRAL
Spiral galaxies contain young and old stars. They are disk-shaped with spiral arms. In a barred spiral, the arms come out from the ends of a bar across the center of the galaxy.

Galaxies start their lives as giant clouds of gas. The cloud spins, stars start to form, and the galaxy takes shape. The faster the spin, the flatter the galaxy.

Radio image of quasar 3C 273. Its core (top left) and its tail (bottom right) are powerful emitters of radio waves.

Part of the Virgo cluster of galaxies, the nearest major cluster to our Local Group.

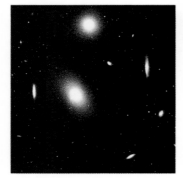

ELLIPTICAL
Elliptical galaxies are flattened ball-shaped collections of old stars (stars at the end of their lives). They are the most common type of galaxy in the universe.

M49 elliptical galaxy. It has a diameter of 50,000 light-years.

IRREGULAR
Irregular galaxies are those that have not formed into a specific shape. They are the rarest type of galaxy in the universe.

CLUSTERS
Galaxies tend to stick together. They are spread throughout the universe in clusters. The Milky Way is in a cluster of about 30 galaxies called the Local Group. Other clusters can contain thousands of galaxies. Clusters group together loosely into superclusters.

Irregular galaxy M82

QUASARS
In 1963, a new category of object—the quasar—was identified. We know these are very luminous, distant objects, moving away from us at great speed. However, many questions about them remain unanswered. At present, they are thought to be the bright cores of very distant galaxies.

MILKY WAY

The Milky Way is a barred spiral galaxy with a concentration of stars at its center. This gives the Galaxy a central bulge from which arms of stars radiate out. We live in one of these arms. This means that from the Southern Hemisphere of Earth, we look in toward the center of the Galaxy; from the Northern Hemisphere, we look out to its edge. Like all galaxies, the Milky Way is moving. Not only is the whole galaxy traveling through space, but the stars within it are continuously moving around the galactic center.

Photograph of Milky Way taken from New Zealand

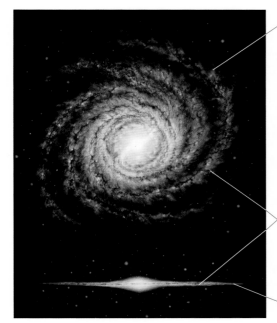

Milky Way—view from above

All the stars you can see in the night sky belong to the Milky Way. Sometimes, you can see a milky path made from the light of the Galaxy's millions of stars.

Stars don't stay in the same position within the Galaxy. Over long periods of time, they move in and out of the spiral arms.

It would take a ray of light 100,000 years to travel from one side of the Galaxy to the other.

Position of Sun

The Sun takes around 220 million years to make one journey around the galactic center.

Milky Way—side-on view

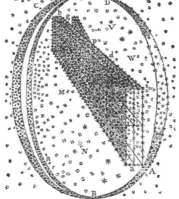

Origin of the Milky Way by Tintoretto

MYTHICAL ORIGIN

The Milky Way is so-called because it looks like a splash of milk in the night sky. In Ancient Greece, long before people understood the nature of the Milky Way, they explained that the Milky Way originated from milk spilled as young Hercules drank from the goddess Juno's breast.

SUN'S POSITION

Our Sun lives in one of the Milky Way's spiral arms, about two-thirds from the center. It is just one of the estimated 500,000 million or so stars that make up the Galaxy. There are stars that live in between the spiral arms, but because the stars in the arms are younger and brighter, it is these that give the Galaxy its distinctive shape.

William Herschel's model of stars in the Milky Way

HERSCHEL'S MODEL

In the 18th century, the British astronomer William Herschel (1738–1822) surveyed the stars in the Milky Way. With the naked eye, you can see around 6,000 stars; with a telescope, you can see many millions—far too many to count. Herschel decided to count certain areas of stars and then average out the results. In this way, he made a fairly accurate model of the Milky Way. He also proposed that some nebulae might be star systems outside our own Galaxy. It was more than a century later before he was shown to be correct.

Photograph of light released from the Andromeda (M31) Galaxy. This is the closest major galaxy to our own.

Infrared image of the Andromeda Galaxy. These infrared rays have travelled for 2.2 million years before they reach Earth.

VIEWING GALAXIES

To build up a more complete picture of our universe, we can gather other types of radiation from it as well as light. For example, X-ray views will show up very hot regions of energetic activity. Gamma-ray views reveal regions in which energy is released from nuclear reactions. Other wavelengths can pick out concentrated areas of hydrogen gas between stars and areas of cold dust.

An X-ray image of the Andromeda Galaxy. The bright region in the center is the core of the galaxy (the part that releases the most X-rays).

STARS

EVERY ONE OF THE STARS you can see in the night sky is actually a violent, spinning ball of hot, luminous gas. The gases of a star are held together by gravity. Stars get their energy by "burning" their gases. This is not like burning coal, but it is a more efficient reaction called nuclear fusion. A star's mass—the amount of gas it is made of—is very important because it influences the gravity, temperature, pressure, density, and size of the star. Stars live in galaxies and each galaxy contains many different types of star. Astronomers came to understand the true nature of stars during the course of the 20th century. Until then, they were more concerned with the positions of stars.

Gravity pulls the gases inward; light and pressure push them outward.

A star's temperature and density increase toward the center.

Instruments such as spectrometers contain prisms that split the light from a star into a spectrum that can be analyzed.

A star is made of gas throughout.

Core of star where nuclear reactions occur

Energy is released at the surface as light and heat.

STAR SPECTRA

Astronomers use special equipment to collect and then separate a star's light into its spectrum. On the spectrum are dark lines called absorption lines. These show which elements the star contains. Every star gives a different spectrum. An American astronomer called Annie Jump Cannon sorted the spectra of thousands of stars into different types. Each type is given a letter of the alphabet. The main types are O, B, A, F, G, K, M, where each star type is cooler than the previous one.

The gaps, or absorption lines, in a spectrum show which types of light the star has "used" or absorbed. This is an indication of which elements the star contains.

INSIDE A STAR

Most stars, such as our Sun, are made almost entirely of two gases, hydrogen and helium, with very small amounts of other elements. The gases are compressed in the center of a star, which becomes very dense and hot—so dense and hot that nuclear fusion reactions occur here: hydrogen atoms combine to form helium, mass is lost, and energy is released. This energy travels from the core to the surface of the star, where it is let loose as light and heat.

Energy released from the core is carried through the star by convection and radiation.

The nearby star moves against the background of more distant stars. The more it moves, the closer it must be to Earth.

Background stars. Because they are so far away from Earth, they appear not to move.

Nearby star

CECILIA PAYNE-GAPOSCHKIN

In the 19th century, the English astronomer William Huggins showed that stars are made of the same elements that exist on Earth. In the 1920s, a British astronomer named Cecilia Payne-Gaposchkin (1900–79) proved that stars are made mostly of hydrogen. She also found that the makeup of most stars is the same. These were great discoveries that made her a pioneer of stellar astrophysics (the study of the physical and chemical processes in stars).

A measurement is taken of the star's position when the Earth is here.

Sun

Another measurement is taken of the star's position when the Earth is here.

PARALLAX

If you hold your finger in front of you and look at it first with just your left eye and then with just your right eye, your finger shifts position against the background. The closer your finger is, the bigger the shift. The shift is a measure of the distance between finger and eye. This effect is known as parallax and, on a much grander scale, it can be used to calculate the distances of nearby stars. As the Earth orbits around the Sun, a star will appear to move slightly against the background of more distant stars. This produces a parallax angle that can be used to measure the distance of the star from Earth.

Main sequence stars

Stars at the top of the main sequence have 60 times the Sun's mass. Those at the bottom have just one-twelfth the Sun's mass.

This blue-white star is a B-type, with a temperature of about 36,000°F (20,000°C).

White stars are classified as A-types, with a temperature of about 18,000°F (10,000°C).

This yellow-white star is an F-type star, with a temperature of about 13,500°F (7,500°C).

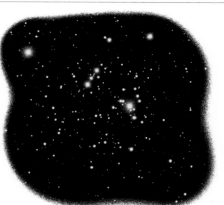

Blue giants are very bright and very hot stars. They are O-type stars with a temperature of around 63,000°F (35,000°C).

The spectral types of stars, O, B, A, F, G, K, and M, relate to the star's color and temperature. O-type stars are blue and hot; M-type stars are red and cooler.

JEWEL BOX
Most stars look like silver pinpoints of light in Earth's sky. But we can see the true color of some stars. This colorful group of brilliant stars is called the Jewel Box Cluster.

This yellow star is like our Sun—a G-type star, with a temperature of about 10,800°F (6,000°C).

MAIN SEQUENCE STARS

The color of a star gives us an idea of its surface temperature. Blue stars are hot; red stars are cooler. If the temperature is plotted on a graph against the star's absolute magnitude (how much light it releases), most stars fall within a band called the main sequence—the hotter the star, the brighter it shines. All stars on the main sequence are in a stable time of their lives—they are shining steadily because they are fusing hydrogen in their cores. When the hydrogen fuel has been used up, the star will move off the main sequence. More massive stars will move off more quickly than less massive stars.

This orange star is a K-type star, with a temperature of about 8,460°F (4,700°C).

Main Sequence

Bright stars

Absolute magnitude

Dim stars

Hot, blue stars   Surface temperature   Cool, red stars

The graph is called a Hertzsprung-Russell diagram, after two astronomers: Ejnar Hertzsprung from Denmark and Henry Norris Russell from America. It has been used since 1913.

This tiny star is a red dwarf. It is a dim and fairly cool star. It is classified as an M-type, with a temperature of about 5,400°F (3,000°C).

Brighter star

Dimmer star

Absolute magnitude

At this point, the binary system would appear dim from Earth because the dimmer star is blocking the brighter one.

From Earth, this binary system would appear bright, because the brighter star is in front of the dimmer star.

ECLIPSING BINARIES

About half the stars in the universe belong to a double or binary system in which two stars orbit around each other. The two stars can be close enough to almost touch or they can be millions of miles apart. We can detect binary systems in different ways. If we have a side-on view of a binary system from Earth, we can detect the changes in brightness as the two stars take it in turns to pass in front of each other. They are called eclipsing binaries.

Time ➡

This diagram shows how the brightness of a Cepheid star varies with time.

VARIABLE STARS

Some stars vary in brightness. There are different types of these variable stars. Some, called RR Lyrae stars, change in less than a day. Others, called Cepheid stars, take one to 100 days to change. Still more, called Mira variables, can take up to two years to complete one cycle of change. Cepheid stars change in brightness because they change physically in size and temperature. They give off more light when they are expanding and less when they are contracting. The star won't always be like this—it is just a normal star going through an unstable period in its life.

<table>
<tr><td>Find out more</td></tr>
<tr><td>NUCLEAR ENERGY P. 136
SOURCES OF LIGHT P. 193
REFRACTION P. 196
GALAXIES P. 276
LIFE CYCLE OF STARS P. 280
SUN P. 284
FACT FINDER P. 418</td></tr>
</table>

LIFE CYCLE OF STARS

NOTHING IN THE UNIVERSE stays the same forever, and stars are no exception. However, we cannot see a star changing because it lives for billions and billions of years. The birthplaces of all stars are clouds of gas and dust that have slowly formed from the sparsely scattered atoms in space. Stars are born in groups, most of which break up, but others are kept together by gravity. The rest of a star's life depends on how massive it is. The more massive a star, the quicker it uses its hydrogen fuel, and the shorter and stormier its life is. Some are simply so massive they explode. But most, like our Sun, have a stable period in their lives when they shine steadily.

Nebula

New stars are being born all the time from clouds of gas and dust.

Parts of the cloud collapse under gravity. Each becomes most dense at the center, where heat is trapped, to form a protostar.

When the protostar is hot enough, nuclear fusion reactions start and energy is released. It is now called a T.Tauri type star. The rest of the cloud is blown away.

Protostar

T.Tauri type star

STAGES IN A STAR'S LIFE

The Sun started its life in a group of stars, but now it is on its own. The pictures here represent its life cycle from a young star called a protostar, through its present life as a stable, shining star, to its future death as a white dwarf. Stars more massive than the Sun are hotter and use up their fuel much more rapidly, so they only spend a fraction of their lives as a stable shining star.

Gravity pulls hydrogen atoms in the Sun toward the center, where they smash and fuse to form helium and energy. The pressure at the center keeps the star expanded. This is a stable period in the star's life. It is known as a main sequence star.

Main sequence star

A star like the Sun spends 10,000,000,000 years as a main sequence star. The Sun is now in the middle of its main sequence life.

The star's luminosity (amount of light it gives out) increases as its core becomes denser and hotter.

• Open clusters of young stars
○ Clusters of middle-aged stars
○ Globular clusters of old stars

STAR CLUSTERS

Within the Milky Way Galaxy are concentrated groups of stars called star clusters. All the stars in a cluster were born from the same cloud, are the same age, and initially had the same composition. There are two types of cluster—open and globular. Open clusters contain up to a few hundred randomly arranged stars. They are found in the flat disk of our Galaxy. Globular clusters contain hundreds of thousands of very old stars arranged in ball shapes. They are found throughout a huge sphere around the center of our Galaxy.

Pleiades cluster of stars

47 Tucanae cluster of stars

GLOBULAR CLUSTER

Globular clusters contain very old stars. It is thought they were formed around the same time as the galaxies that they live in. This is why globular clusters can provide information on the early life of the Milky Way. This globular cluster, 47 Tucanae, is visible to the naked eye if you are in the Southern Hemisphere.

OPEN CLUSTER

The Pleiades is an open cluster of young stars that spreads across 30 light-years in space (in star terms, "young" means around 60 million years old). To the naked eye, the Pleiades looks like a fuzzy patch of light with seven prominent stars. Through powerful telescopes, we can see many more of its bluish stars, as well as gas and dust that the stars have plowed into.

NEUTRON STARS

When a star several times heavier than the Sun dies, its core collapses to become a tiny neutron star, with a mass between 1.4 and 3 times the Sun's mass. The collapse is so violent that the electrons and protons within atoms are forced together to form neutrons. All the material is squashed into an incredibly dense sphere around 6 miles (10 km) across. A pulsar is a fast-spinning neutron star that flashes a signal Earthward as it spins (like a lighthouse). Pulsars were first detected in 1967 by British astronomers Jocelyn Bell and Antony Hewish.

In 1054, the Chinese recorded a star bright enough to be seen in daylight. It was a supernova. Today, we see its remains in the Crab Nebula. The core of the exploding star is now a pulsar, rotating 30 times every second.

White dwarf star

The outer layers of the star become unstable and puff away into space as a cosmic smoke ring called a planetary nebula. The inner layers do not have enough energy to keep them expanded, and they collapse to form a very small and dense white dwarf. This will slowly fade to become a black dwarf.

ALTERNATIVE DEATHS

Not all stars end their lives as white dwarfs. Massive stars end their lives in spectacular fashion—they collapse so quickly that they explode. This explosion is called a supernova. The core may remain as a neutron star or a black hole. The star's far-flung ashes will provide material for new stars to be born.

Cepheid star

Red giant star

The helium left begins to fuse with itself to form carbon. The star is now called a Cepheid, and it continually shrinks and expands, losing its outer layers of material.

From Earth, a supernova looks like a bright new star in the sky—hence its name (nova means "new").

The hydrogen is used up. The center is so hot by now that the star expands. The surface cools and turns red. Such a star is called a red giant.

The enormous gravity of a black hole can drag in material from a nearby star. This is how a black hole is discovered. As the material swirls into the black hole, it becomes very hot and gives off X-rays. These X-rays can be detected.

BLACK HOLES

Strange things happen to the most massive stars at the end of their lives. If the core has a mass of more than three times the mass of the Sun, it will collapse, becoming more and more compact until the star becomes so dense that nothing, not even light, can escape from its gravity. It has become a black hole, with a singularity (a point of infinite density) at its center.

According to General Relativity, bodies of matter curve space. If the body of matter is very dense (a large amount of matter squashed into a small space), it would stretch space into an infinitely deep chasm—a black hole.

GENERAL RELATIVITY

In 1915, Albert Einstein published his startling but now famous theory called General Relativity. It gave a totally different view of gravity, proposing that it was a property of space and not a force between bodies. Bodies of matter curve space, rather like a weight curves a trampoline, and so bodies "fall" toward other bodies. Even light "falls" into the curved space around a body and so its path is bent. This strange idea was put to the test during an eclipse of the Sun in 1919. The light from a distant star was indeed seen to be bent by the gravity of the Sun. Einstein was proved right.

The star appears to be in a different position from where it actually is because its light is bent by the Sun.

Actual position of star

Apparent position of star

Around a black hole, light is bent so much that it cannot escape.

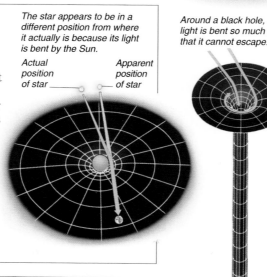

> ### Find out more
>
> ATOMIC STRUCTURE P. 24
> GRAVITY P. 122
> NUCLEAR ENERGY P. 136
> ORIGIN OF THE UNIVERSE P. 275
> GALAXIES P. 276
> STARS P. 278
> SUN P. 284

CONSTELLATIONS

THE TWINKLING PINPOINTS of light in the night sky can all look the same at first. Thousands of years ago, early astronomers divided the stars into groups and drew imaginary pictures around them so they were easy to remember—pictures such as a scorpion or a bear. This is how our present-day system of constellations was born. The stars in a constellation are actually unrelated; they only appear to make these groups when viewed from Earth. The stars are all so far away that they appear to be at the same distance and to move together as if stuck on the inside of an enormous bowl—the celestial sphere.

STAR TRAILS
From Earth, the stars appear to spin around two imaginary points in the sky—the north and south celestial poles. This photograph has captured the movements of the stars as trails in the night sky.

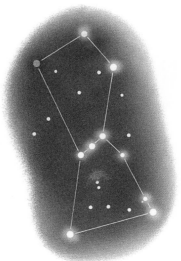

ORION
Orion, the hunter, is an easy constellation to see. Four bright stars mark his shoulders and knees. Three more mark his belt, and the Orion Nebula, a star-forming region, marks his sword.

Earth inside the "celestial sphere"

From Earth, the Sun appears to move against a background of stars. The star groups it moves in front of are known as the Zodiac.

Star patterns can be used to navigate (Polaris, the North Star, lies above Earth's North Pole) or as a calendar (from Earth we see different star patterns over the year as the Earth orbits the Sun).

Some of the early star maps were more artistic than scientific.

GROUPING STARS

An internationally recognized system of 88 constellations is used by astronomers today. Twelve of the constellations are together known as the Zodiac. These form the backdrop against which the planets, the Moon, and the Sun move. Individual stars are identified within a constellation by a letter of the Greek alphabet. The brightest star is alpha, the next is beta, and so on.

Modern star map

MAGNITUDES
Astronomers use numbers to describe a star's brightness. The scale of apparent magnitude is so called because it doesn't describe how bright the star actually is, just how bright it is as seen from Earth. The larger the number given to the star, the fainter the star is. Stars classified 1–6 are visible with the naked eye.

1
2
3
4
5
6

STAR MAPS
Early star maps filled the northern sky with animals and mythical figures. As navigators voyaged south, more and more of the sky could be charted. Positions of the stars were pinpointed with increasing accuracy as the telescope and observing techniques improved; fewer charts with artistic representations of the constellations were produced. Celestial charts started to be made photographically and then with the aid of computers. Today, satellites plot positions of the stars with even greater accuracy and speed.

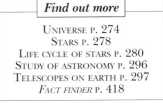

Find out more

UNIVERSE P. 274
STARS P. 278
LIFE CYCLE OF STARS P. 280
STUDY OF ASTRONOMY P. 296
TELESCOPES ON EARTH P. 297
FACT FINDER P. 418

SOLAR SYSTEM

MILLIONS OF YEARS AGO, a family was born around the Sun: balls of matter that we call the planets. The Sun and this system of planets that orbit around it make up the solar system. Asteroids, comets, moons, Kuiper Belt objects, and interplanetary dust also form part of this large family, which extends out to about 9 trillion miles (15 trillion km) from the Sun. The dominant body is the Sun which accounts for more than 99 percent of the mass of the solar system. Our solar system was once regarded as the largest and central part of the universe. Today, we know it is just a tiny speck compared with the rest of the universe.

Planets and planet-forming disks have been found around other stars. This enhanced infrared image shows what scientists believe may be a planet orbiting a brown dwarf star.

FORMATION
The planets and other bodies were formed 4,600 million years ago from material left over from the Sun's birth. The Sun was surrounded by a rotating disk of gas (hydrogen and helium) and dust (iron, rock, and snow) called the solar nebula. The dust came together to form planetesimals (rocks hundreds of miles across), which then joined to create four planets—Mercury, Venus, Earth, and Mars. Farther out, dust and snow combined with the gases to produce Jupiter, Saturn, Uranus, and Neptune. Pluto is a leftover planetesimal.

Orbit of Pluto

Orbit of Neptune

Orbit of Uranus

Orbit of Mars

Orbit of Earth

Orbit of Jupiter

Asteroid belt

Orbit of Saturn

Orbit of Mercury

Orbit of Venus

All but two planets, Mercury and Pluto, have orbits in the same plane.

Mercury
Venus
Earth
Mars
Jupiter
Saturn
Uranus
Neptune
Pluto

PLANET SIZES
Astronomers are more interested in the mass of a body (the amount of material it contains) than its diameter (its size). Of all the planets, Jupiter has the largest mass as well as the biggest diameter.

Gravity keeps the planets orbiting the Sun, and the moons orbiting the planets. The effect of gravity decreases with distance; the farther a planet is from the Sun, the slower it moves.

ORBITS
The solar system is disklike in shape. The Sun is at the center and the planets follow individual paths called orbits around it. They all travel in the same direction, but move at different speeds and take different times to complete an orbit.

GRAVITY IN THE SOLAR SYSTEM
What keeps the solar system together? A force called gravity, which is an attraction between any two bodies that have mass. Its strength depends on how massive the bodies are and how far apart they are. Gravity keeps the material in a body together; if it is strong enough, it will pull gases toward a planet or moon to form an atmosphere. In the 17th century, the English scientist Isaac Newton investigated the motion of the Moon and the planets, and outlined a universal law of gravitation. It is one of the fundamental laws by which the universe operates.

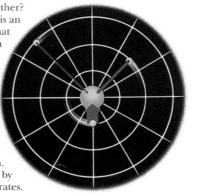

Find out more
GRAVITY P. 122
SUN P. 284
MERCURY AND VENUS P. 286
EARTH P. 287
MARS P. 289
JUPITER P. 290
SATURN P. 291
URANUS P. 292
NEPTUNE AND PLUTO P. 293
FACT FINDER P. 418

SUN

THE NEAREST STAR TO US is the Sun. By studying it, we can learn about the other stars in the universe. Like all stars, the Sun is a huge, luminous ball of hot gas—mostly hydrogen, but some helium, with tiny amounts of other elements. Within the Sun, a process called nuclear fusion continuously generates energy such as light and heat; at its center, the temperature is around 25,000,000°F (14,000,000°C). The Sun was born from a cloud of gas and dust about 5,000 million years ago. It was created in a group of stars that slowly broke up so that now the Sun is alone. A family of nine planets and billions of smaller bodies orbit around it. To one of these planets, the Earth, the Sun is not just any old star; it is a provider of energy for life.

Prominences are only visible during a total solar eclipse or by using special equipment.

PROMINENCES
Huge, flamelike clouds of hot gas sometimes explode from the photosphere. These are called solar flares and prominences, and they are associated with sunspots. Flares are short-lived bursts of light. A large prominence may reach heights of 60,000 miles (100,000 km) and may last for months.

LAYERS OF SUN
The Sun is made of different layers of gas. The surface layer we see is called the photosphere. Here, gas swirls and bubbles about, giving the Sun a mottled look. Surrounding the photosphere is a faint layer of gas called the chromosphere. Above this is a layer of gas called the corona (which means "crown").

Different parts of the Sun take different times to rotate. Its middle takes around 25 days, while its top and bottom take around 30. This was discovered by observing the movement of sunspots.

This ultraviolet picture of the Sun reveals a hole in the corona.

ULTRAVIOLET SUN
Today it is not only the visible light given out by the Sun that can be recorded. Astronomers have special equipment that can make images at other wavelengths, such as ultraviolet or infrared. These show up details that optical images cannot reveal.

NEVER look at the Sun directly with your eyes, through binoculars, or through a telescope.

SUNSPOTS
On close inspection, the Sun's photosphere is at times riddled with dark patches. These are sunspots—patches of gas that look darker because they are cooler. Sunspots are caused by magnetic fields that slow down the flow of heat from the Sun's center. They have a dark central region called the umbra, surrounded by a lighter region called a penumbra. They generally occur in pairs or groups.

Group of sunspots

SOLAR TELESCOPE
Astronomers use special instruments based on Earth, and others up in space, to study the Sun. The Sun's light is collected and then an instrument called a spectroscope is used to split it into its spectrum (the different wavelengths of light it emits). Astronomers have gained most of their knowledge about the Sun by studying its spectrum.

Rays from Sun

The Sun's light is reflected down to a mirror in an underground tunnel. The Sun's image is formed in an observation room where astronomers can study its light.

Year 1	Year 4	Year 7	Year 10	Year 12

Sunspots go through a cycle lasting 11 years. At the beginning, the Sun is free of spots. A few then appear near the Sun's north and south poles. These then disappear and new ones form nearer and nearer toward the equator (middle).

One solar telescope is at the Kitt Peak National Observatory in Arizona.

ARTHUR EDDINGTON

The English astronomer Sir Arthur Eddington (1882–1944) was the first to work out what the inside of a star was like. He discovered that the luminosity of a star (amount of light it gives out) depends on how massive it is. In 1919, he was the first person to find proof of Einstein's theory of relativity; during a total solar eclipse, he recorded the displacement (bending) of light from a distant star.

LIFE OF THE SUN

In star terms, our Sun is middle-aged and will die one day. But don't worry; it has another 5 billion years of shining to do until it uses up its hydrogen fuel. It will then start using its helium; as it does so, it will turn into a red giant star, shining 1,000 times brighter than now, and it will be around 100 times larger in size. Next, it will shrink to become a white dwarf star, the size of the Earth. Billions of years later, it will cool down and end its life as a cold dark body called a black dwarf.

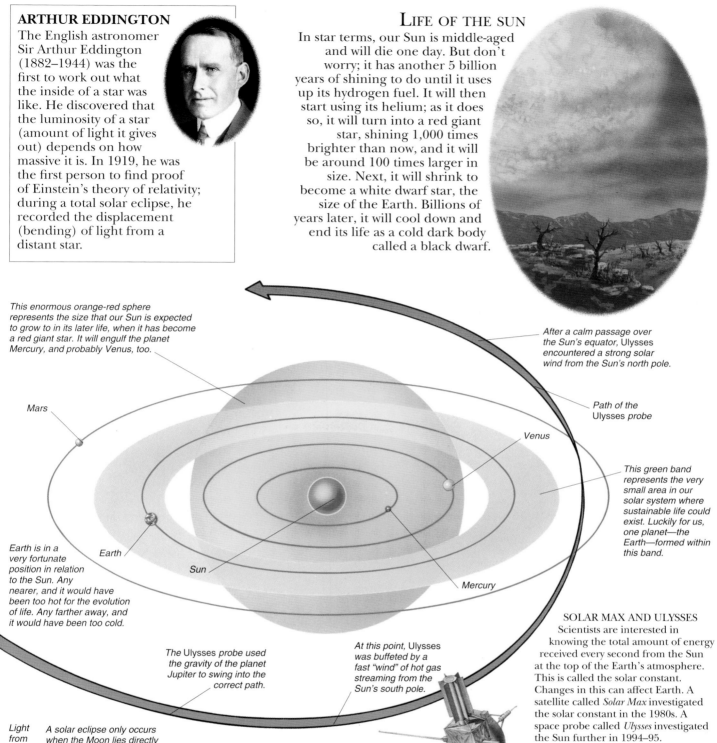

This enormous orange-red sphere represents the size that our Sun is expected to grow to in its later life, when it has become a red giant star. It will engulf the planet Mercury, and probably Venus, too.

Mars

After a calm passage over the Sun's equator, Ulysses encountered a strong solar wind from the Sun's north pole.

Path of the Ulysses probe

Venus

This green band represents the very small area in our solar system where sustainable life could exist. Luckily for us, one planet—the Earth—formed within this band.

Earth is in a very fortunate position in relation to the Sun. Any nearer, and it would have been too hot for the evolution of life. Any farther away, and it would have been too cold.

Earth

Sun

Mercury

The Ulysses probe used the gravity of the planet Jupiter to swing into the correct path.

At this point, Ulysses was buffeted by a fast "wind" of hot gas streaming from the Sun's south pole.

SOLAR MAX AND ULYSSES
Scientists are interested in knowing the total amount of energy received every second from the Sun at the top of the Earth's atmosphere. This is called the solar constant. Changes in this can affect Earth. A satellite called *Solar Max* investigated the solar constant in the 1980s. A space probe called *Ulysses* investigated the Sun further in 1994–95.

The Ulysses probe was launched in 1990 to investigate the poles of the Sun (which are invisible from Earth).

Light from Sun

A solar eclipse only occurs when the Moon lies directly between the Earth and the Sun.

Penumbra

Umbra

Earth

Eclipses occur because the Sun and the Moon appear to be the same size in Earth's sky. In fact, the Sun is 400 times larger, but because it is also 400 times farther away, it appears Moon-sized.

Variation of Moon's orbit

SOLAR ECLIPSE
Occasionally, the Earth, Moon, and Sun happen to line up so that the Moon blocks the Sun's light from Earth. This is called a solar eclipse. The Moon's shadow or umbra only covers a small area of Earth's surface. Anyone standing in this umbra sees the Sun totally eclipsed by the Moon. Surrounding the umbra is an area of partial shadow called the penumbra. From this area, the Sun is partially eclipsed.

MERCURY AND VENUS

THE CLOSEST PLANETS to the Sun, Mercury and Venus were known and observed even by early people. Mercury is the most difficult to see because the Sun's glare usually blinds us to it. By contrast, Venus is easy to see. It is the brightest object in the sky after the Sun and the Moon. Like the Moon, it goes through a cycle of phases, from a slim crescent to a full disk. Galileo Galilei was the first person to observe this cycle in 1610. But it was only in the 20th century, when probes were sent into space for the first time, that astronomers built up our present-day picture of barren and lifeless Mercury, and of the hostile world that lies behind Venus' serene face.

Mercury
Venus
Rocky mantle and crust
Metallic core

MERCURY STRUCTURE
The weak magnetic field and high density of Mercury point to an enormous iron core. Above this is a layer of compressed molten rocks—the mantle. A solid, rocky crust floats on top of the mantle.

Crust
Mantle
Core

VENUS STRUCTURE
Like Earth, Venus underwent a molten period when denser material sank to the center, leaving a lighter crust. Its semisolid iron-nickel core is surrounded by a rock mantle, which supports the rock crust.

MERCURY
The space probe *Mariner 10* flew by Mercury three times in 1974–75, and revealed Mercury's surface. Only one hemisphere was mapped. A second probe, *Messenger*, set off for Mercury in 2004. It should reveal much more.

MERCURY CRATERS
Like our Moon, Mercury is small and scarred by craters that were formed soon after the birth of the solar system. It also has cliffs, or scarps, which formed when the young, cooling Mercury shrunk like a shriveling apple, wrinkling its surface.

VENUS
Venus is completely choked by a thick, dense atmosphere. Upper cloud layers rotate every four days—much faster than the 243 days it takes the rocky planet to complete one rotation around its axis. It is the Sun's reflection on these heavy clouds that we see from Earth.

SURFACE IMAGE
Over 20 spacecraft have investigated Venus. They have revealed a surface dominated by volcanoes and extensive plains of volcanic lava.

FORMING CRATERS
The many craters on Mercury's surface were formed when rocks smashed into the planet. The material blasted away from the surface left saucer-shaped hollows.

Image of Venus' surface taken by Magellan space probe

MERCURY LANDSCAPE
The surface gravity of Mercury is under half that of Earth. This is too weak to hold gas to the planet and so Mercury has almost no atmosphere. Without air, sound cannot travel, and so it is also a silent world. Without an atmosphere to keep in heat, Mercury has the biggest day and night temperature variations of any of the planets: burning hot days of 752°F (400°C), and freezing cold nights of -328°F (-200°C).

VENUS LANDSCAPE
Anyone thinking of landing on Venus has to travel through its atmosphere first. This consists of thick, yellow-white clouds of sulfuric acid gas. On the surface, the heat is an intense 895°F (480°C) because the atmosphere works like a greenhouse, trapping the Sun's energy. Finally, the surface pressure, 100 times that of Earth, would crush any human in seconds.

Find out more
SOLAR SYSTEM P. 283
SUN P. 284
EARTH P. 287
MOON P. 288
SPACE PROBES P. 301
FACT FINDER P. 418

EARTH

EARTH STRUCTURE
Crust *Mantle* *Outer core* *Inner core* *Earth*

The young Earth was formed with the other solar system planets 4.6 billion years ago. At first it was cold, but radioactivity heated it until it melted. The heavy iron sank to the center and the lighter rocks floated to the top. Today, Earth's iron core is surrounded by a fluid mantle of rock. The rocky surface crust we live on is only a few miles thick.

WHAT IS THE MOST thoroughly investigated planet in the solar system? Earth, of course—more is known about it than about any other planet. Like all the others, it is unique. It has features that are not found anywhere else in the solar system. An obvious one is that it is the only planet supporting life. But the presence of liquid water is equally unique. These two factors shaped its evolution from a molten planet with a hydrogen-rich atmosphere to today's world. Life started in Earth's oceans 3,000 million years ago. The development of life forms helped produce today's atmosphere of nitrogen and oxygen which in turn helps provide the conditions to maintain life. Earth is the third nearest planet to the Sun. It has one natural satellite—the Moon.

ACTIVE EARTH
The surface of Earth is constantly changing. Its crust is made of enormous moving slabs or plates. Volcanoes and earthquakes occur as these plates collide and rub together or slip beneath each other. Molten rock forces its way to the surface. In this way, the Earth's crust renews itself.

PLANET EARTH
Earth shines brightly in space. It reflects about one-third of the sunlight that falls on it. Earth's atmosphere scatters the light and creates a predominantly blue-colored planet. Brown land masses are visible, as are the oceans that cover around two-thirds of the Earth's surface. The Pacific Ocean alone covers half the globe. Many clouds can be seen in the atmosphere.

EARTH ATMOSPHERE
Compared to its neighbor Venus, Earth has a thin atmosphere—thin, but very useful. It is thin enough to let sunlight through, but thick enough to bar the way of other forms of harmful radiation from the Sun; ultraviolet rays, dangerous to human life, are mostly filtered out. The atmosphere also slows down and vaporizes tiny space rocks known as meteoroids. It also provides the air we breathe.

ARISTARCHUS
The fact that Earth travels around the Sun has been accepted for only about 400 years. Copernicus, the 16th-century Polish astronomer, is usually credited with disproving that the universe is Earth-centered. But a Greek astronomer, Aristarchus, (310–230 BCE) working centuries earlier, had the idea first. Using geometry, he worked out the relative sizes and distances of the Sun and Moon. He concluded that as the Sun is by far the largest, the Earth must travel around the Sun.

The conditions on Earth are just right for life forms such as us!

EARTH LANDSCAPE
Millions of years ago, an atmosphere of carbon dioxide, water vapor, and nitrogen formed around Earth. The water vapor formed rain which made the oceans. Today, both of these features are very important. Water is exchanged between the atmosphere and the oceans, while the atmosphere acts like a blanket to keep an almost even emperature.

Find out more
FORMATION OF THE EARTH P. 210
STRUCTURE OF THE EARTH P. 212
SOLAR SYSTEM P. 283
FACT FINDER P. 418

MOON

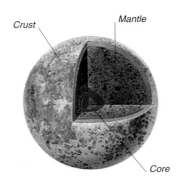

Crust | Mantle | Core

MOON STRUCTURE
Scientists are divided over whether the Moon is entirely made of rock or has a solid iron core at its center. The lower mantle rock is partially molten, above this is the solid mantle rock. A crust of calcium-rich, granitelike rock surrounds the Moon.

THE NEXT-DOOR NEIGHBOR of Earth in space is the Moon—a ball of rock that spins on its own axis as well as orbiting the Earth and traveling with the Earth as it orbits the Sun. It is one of the best studied objects in the solar system. Detailed maps of the side that faces Earth were drawn soon after the invention of the telescope. In the 1960s, space probes were sent crashing into its surface, and orbiting around it. In 1969, people even walked on the Moon, and brought back rocks from its surface. All the solar system planets except Mercury and Venus have moons. They range a great deal in size, but Earth's moon is one of the largest—around one-quarter of the size of Earth.

LUNAR LANDINGS
The six Apollo landing missions of the 1960s and 1970s are still regarded as the high point of space exploration. These missions set 12 astronauts on the Moon and returned them safely back to Earth. The results from surface experiments, orbital flights, and many photographs are used to produce our picture of the Moon's surface.

BIG SPLASH
It is not certain where the Moon came from. It may have broken off from Earth, been captured by Earth, or formed from material around the young Earth. Most astronomers favor the big splash theory, where a Mars-sized body collided with the young Earth. Debris from this collision formed the Moon.

The surface of the Moon has changed little for millions of years; with no atmosphere there is no weathering effect.

MOON WATCHING
The Moon is a good object for novice astronomers to observe because its surface features are easily visible to the naked eye. The dark patches that can be seen are flat areas of land called "maria." The lighter areas are mountains. Binoculars can even reveal some of the craters that cover much of the Moon's surface.

Nobody would hear you shout on the Moon!

MOON LANDSCAPE
If you landed on the Moon, you would find a very quiet world. It has no atmosphere surrounding it and so sound cannot travel (and you wouldn't be able to breathe either!). Craters up to hundreds of miles wide cover its surface. Many of them were formed around 4 billion years ago when giant meteorites collided with the Moon.

PHASES OF THE MOON

Crescent Moon

Gibbous Moon. The Moon has started to wane ("shrink") in Earth's sky.

Full Moon. The Moon is behind Earth (but not in Earth's shadow). We see the whole of the Moon's sunlit face.

Sunlight

Earth

New Moon. The Moon lies between the Sun and Earth. The side facing Earth is in darkness.

Crescent Moon. The Moon has started to wax ("grow") in Earth's sky.

Gibbous Moon. The Sun lights up most of the side of the Moon that faces Earth.

PHASES OF THE MOON
Even though it has no light of its own, the Moon is the brightest object in the night sky because it reflects sunlight well. As the Moon travels around Earth we see different amounts of its sunlit face—ranging from a thin crescent to a full face. When the side of the Moon facing us has no sunlight on it, we cannot see it at all. We call this a New Moon. The lunar month, which lasts 29.5 days, is measured from one New Moon to the next.

MOON ROCK
Around 2,000 samples of moon rock, weighing almost 880 lb (400 kg), have been brought back to Earth. By studying these rocks, scientists have built up a picture of the composition and history of the Moon. Some rocks, for example, were formed from molten lava.

Find out more

WAVES, TIDES, AND CURRENTS P. 235
SOLAR SYSTEM P. 283
EARTH P. 287
HUMANS IN SPACE P. 302
FACT FINDER P. 418

MARS

MARS STRUCTURE

Crust
Mantle
Core

The young Mars was only fully molten for a short time. This meant that some of the heavier material was prevented from sinking to the center. This made Mars's core smaller than those of the other rock planets.

WATERY PAST

The surface of Mars is covered with dramatic features such as deserts, high mountains, deep craters, and enormous volcanoes. Dry riverbeds and ancient floodplains indicate that water flowed over its surface more than 300,000 million years ago. Some of that water is in today's frozen polar ice caps. These grow and shrink with the Martian seasons.

The BRIGHTEST RED "STAR" in Earth's sky is actually the planet Mars. This red color, the most distinctive feature of Mars, comes from rock and dust covering its surface. When two Viking spacecraft landed on Mars in the summer of 1976, they analyzed the soil and found it to be iron-rich; Mars is just rusty! Spacecraft have revealed several gigantic volcanoes and a set of canyons, called the Valles Marineris—this is 10 times longer and four times deeper than the Grand Canyon. There are also dried-up riverbeds, showing Mars was warmer and wetter long ago. Simple life may have started then. The Viking landers searched unsuccessfully for life, but some scientists believe they have found fossils of Martian cells in a meteorite.

Drawing of Mars by Percival Lowell

Lowell observed Mars and interpreted surface markings as water-carrying canals built by an advanced Martian civilization.

PERCIVAL LOWELL

Percival Lowell (1855–1916), a rich amateur astronomer, was fascinated by Mars. Looking at it from his observatory in Arizona, he believed he could see canals on the planet. He thought it was inhabited and the canals took water from the polar caps to dry farmland. They turned out to be an optical illusion.

The planet's deep red color led to its being named after the God of War, Mars.

MARS LANDSCAPE

If you were transported to Mars, you would find a lonely and cold place. Its gravity is about half as strong as Earth's and so the planet can only hold on to a thin atmosphere. Even so, at certain times wind speeds increase to over 60 mph (100 km/h), blowing up a dusty storm that lasts for months. The dust makes the sky appear pink.

MARTIAN BACTERIA?

This meteorite, which fell in Antarctica, almost certainly came from Mars. In 1996, American scientists found that it contains many tiny worm-shaped structures, each one-thousandth the thickness of a human hair. These may be the fossils of early Martian cells, similar to bacteria on Earth.

Phobos (meaning "terror") was named after a mythical servant of the God Mars.

PHOBOS

Two tiny moons, Deimos and Phobos, orbit around Mars. From Earth, they look like specks of light, even through our most powerful telescopes. Spacecraft have shown they are dark, strangely shaped bodies. Both have craters, but Phobos is also covered in grooves. In many ways, the moons of Mars are like asteroids—they are widely believed to be members of the asteroid belt that have been captured by Mars.

OLYMPUS MONS

The giant volcano Olympus Mons is not only the largest mountain on Mars, but in the whole solar system. At 435 miles (700 km) across and 17 miles (27 km) high, it is around three times as high as Mount Everest on Earth.

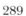

Find out more

ROBOTS P. 176
VOLCANOES P. 216
SOLAR SYSTEM P. 283
EARTH P. 287
MOON P. 288
ASTEROIDS P. 294
FACT FINDER P. 418

JUPITER

THE GIANT PLANET in the solar system is Jupiter—it contains three times more mass than the other eight planets put together. It is mostly made of gases and liquids, with a fairly small rocky core. The thick clouds at the top of its atmosphere reflect sunlight well and so the planet shines brightly in Earth's night sky. Much of our knowledge of Jupiter has been learned through space probe missions. Four craft flew by in the 1970s, and the *Galileo* space probe arrived at Jupiter in December 1995 to make an in-depth study. It spent eight years studying the planet and flying by each of its four major moons.

Jupiter

Atmosphere

Liquid hydrogen

Metallic hydrogen. At very high pressures, hydrogen behaves like a metal.

Core

JUPITER STRUCTURE
Jupiter's small, rocky core is surrounded by an ocean of hydrogen in metallic and liquid form. Above this is the vast atmosphere of hydrogen and helium, eight times thicker than Earth's. The temperature drops toward the cloud tops; the core is at 63,000°F (35,000°C), while the upper cloud layers are at -220°F (-140°C).

PROBE
The *Galileo* probe carried a smaller probe (shown here) that plunged into Jupiter's atmosphere. For 58 minutes it transmitted information on the atmospheric temperature, pressure and composition, and winds and lightning.

JUPITER ATMOSPHERE
If you were landing on Jupiter, you wouldn't "land" at all but would sink through its atmosphere—a 795 mile- (1,280 km-) thick layer that contains methane and ammonia, as well as hydrogen and helium. The *Galileo* probe found less water than expected and very strong winds deep in the atmosphere.

Hydrogen, helium, and ammonia ice crystals form the clouds in the upper layers of the atmosphere.

STORMS
Jupiter takes just under 10 hours to rotate on its axis. This fast spin causes high winds. As the gases in the atmosphere circle the planet, they produce colorful belts and zones in the cloud tops. Giant storms are created. The Great Red Spot, more than twice the size of Earth, is the biggest hurricane in the solar system.

GALILEO GALILEI
The Italian astronomer and physicist Galileo (1564–1642) discovered four of Jupiter's moons in 1610; Io, Europa, Ganymede, and Callisto are known as the Galilean moons. Galileo used the discovery to try to convince people that the Earth was not the center of the universe, but that the Earth and planets move around the Sun.

COMET IMPACT
In 1993, American astronomers Gene and Carolyn Shoemaker and David Levy discovered a remarkable comet that looked like beads on a string. Comet Shoemaker-Levy 9 had been broken up by Jupiter's powerful gravity. The following year, the comet fragments crashed into the giant planet. The impacts created huge hot spots, bigger than the Earth, and long-lasting dark clouds.

IO

Just a little bigger than Earth's Moon, Io is one of the most remarkable bodies in the solar system. It is among the largest of Jupiter's family of 16 moons. Jupiter's strong tidal force helps heat Io's core, leading to the formation of active volcanoes.

Find out more

ATMOSPHERE P. 248
SOLAR SYSTEM P. 283
MOON P. 288
SPACE PROBES P. 301
FACT FINDER P. 418

SATURN

Saturn

A PLANET that just looks like a bright star from Earth has turned out to be the jewel of the solar system. Saturn is the sixth planet from the Sun and is almost twice as far away as its neighbor Jupiter. It is a gas giant and is well known for its amazing system of colored rings. Since 1610, astronomers have gazed through telescopes at Saturn. But explaining what they saw was a major problem. The extent and complexity of the Saturnian system has been revealed by space probes: *Voyagers 1* and *2* in the 1980s, and *Cassini* since 1994.

Atmosphere · Liquid hydrogen · Metallic hydrogen · Core

SATURN STRUCTURE
There are three distinct layers inside Saturn. It has a central rock-ice core that is surrounded by metallic hydrogen. The outer layer is made up of hydrogen and helium—liquid near the center but turning to a gas farther out.

EARLY OBSERVATIONS
When Galileo observed Saturn in 1610, he saw three bodies. Was it possible that Saturn was a triple planet? A few years later, astronomers were surprised to find that the two small globes had moved and changed shape. In 1659, Christiaan Huygens, a Dutch astronomer, correctly explained that they were observing Saturn's rings whose appearance changed as the planet orbited the Sun.

BULGING EQUATOR
Saturn spins very quickly on its axis; its day is only 10.5 hours. Combined with the planet's low density, this creates Saturn's bulging equator. In fact, Saturn's belly bulges more than any other in the solar system.

Saturn would actually float like an iceberg—7/10 of it would be hidden under water.

FLOATING PLANET
Although Saturn has 95 times the mass of the Earth, its average density is so low that it is the only planet lighter than the same volume of water. This means that if we could put Saturn in an enormous bucket of water, it would float.

CLOUD BANDS
The colored clouds on the surface of Saturn's atmosphere form bands around the planet. These clouds are made from ammonia and other chemicals. Oval spots can sometimes be seen in the bands; these are storms. On a blustery day on Saturn, winds up to 1,100 mph (1,800 km/h) blow in the upper air.

SATURN MOONS
Saturn has at least 34 moons and it is believed to have more. Most are small and irregularly shaped. Round Titan is the largest and was the first to be discovered, in 1655. It is unique because it is the only solar system moon with a substantial atmosphere. The space probe *Huygens*, carried to Saturn by *Cassini*, descended through its atmosphere in January 2005 and landed on Titan's surface.

Titan

RINGS
Jupiter, Saturn, Uranus, and Neptune all have rings. But Saturn's are by far the most spectacular. From Earth, astronomers worked out that the rings were not solid because they could see stars through them. Spacecraft have revealed that the rings are made of countless pieces of icy rock—some pieces are as small as dust, others as big as huge boulders. Saturn has not always had rings. It is thought they were created when a comet collided with one of Saturn's moons.

Find out more
FLOATING AND SINKING P. 129
SOLAR SYSTEM P. 283
MOON P. 288
SPACE PROBES P. 301
FACT FINDER P. 418

URANUS

Uranus

ASTRONOMERS WERE DUMBSTRUCK by the discovery of Uranus in 1781. Until then, it was thought that the solar system consisted of the planets as far out as Saturn but no more. Its discovery doubled the size of the solar system in one stroke—Uranus is twice as far from the Sun as Saturn. At such a distance, little was learned about Uranus until a space probe called *Voyager 2* flew by in 1986. It found a cold gas giant with a large family of moons and 11 thin, black rings surrounding it.

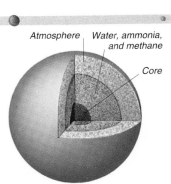

Atmosphere   Water, ammonia, and methane

Core

URANUS STRUCTURE
The rocky core of Uranus makes up about one-quarter of the planet's mass. Above this is a layer of water, ammonia, and methane, in ice and liquid form. The outer layer is made up of hydrogen and helium gases.

BLUE-GREEN PLANET
Even through Earth's best telescopes, Uranus appears as a fuzzy blue-green ball of gas; methane in its atmosphere reflects blue and green sunlight. Through the cameras on *Voyager 2*, Uranus still appears as a featureless globe. But computer processing and images taken at nonoptical wavelengths have revealed ammonia and water clouds carried around the planet by winds.

URANUS MOONS
Uranus has 27 moons; most of which are small. Its five major moons were discovered before the start of the space age. Others were discovered in *Voyager 2* data and by using present improved observing techniques. More small moons are expected to be found.

Uranus' moons and rings circle around the middle of the globe.

URANUS LANDSCAPE
It doesn't get any warmer than -344°F (-209°C) on Uranus. The planet receives about 370 times less sunlight than Earth, although its atmosphere carries what heat there is around the planet. If you found yourself on Uranus, as well as being very cold, you would sink into the choking atmosphere of hydrogen, helium, and methane.

TITANIA
The moons of Uranus are dark bodies of rock and ice. Titania is the largest. Craters and valleys cover its surface.

Page from Herschel's diary

DISCOVERIES

1781 Uranus discovered
German-born astronomer William Herschel was not looking for a planet; but during routine observations on March 13 he found Uranus. This led astronomers to believe other planets may lay beyond undetected.

1846 Neptune discovered
Neptune's position had been calculated and a search was carried out. Johann Galle from Germany located it on September 23, 1846.

1930 Pluto discovered
The American Clyde Tombaugh found Pluto when he was comparing photographic plates in January 1930.

SIDEWAYS PLANET
Uranus appears to lie on its side. It is thought that the planet was tipped up after a collision with a planet-sized body when it was young.

One of Uranus' moons, Miranda, is a hodge-podge of deep craters, high cliffs, and smooth plains. Most are ancient structures, but, surprisingly, some have been formed more recently.

Find out more

SOLAR SYSTEM P. 283
SATURN P. 291
NEPTUNE AND PLUTO P. 293
SPACE PROBES P. 301
FACT FINDER P. 418

NEPTUNE AND PLUTO

Neptune   Pluto

Atmosphere   Water, ammonia, and methane

Core

NEPTUNE STRUCTURE
Neptune has a small rocky core, surrounded by an ocean of water, ammonia, and methane. Its atmosphere is made of hydrogen, helium, and methane. The methane gives Neptune its intense blue color.

THE TWO MOST DISTANT PLANETS are worlds of contrast. Neptune is the most distant gas giant. Pluto is a frozen world, the smallest of all the planets. Their existence was not known until fairly recently. Both were predicted and then discovered within the last 160 years. The two planets are so distant that very powerful telescopes are needed to see them. Details of Neptune were revealed when *Voyager 2* flew by in 1989. Its images showed that Neptune had a thin, dim ring system. Pluto is, to date, the only planet unexplored by spacecraft. But this will change in about 10 years time when the *New Horizons* spacecraft reaches Pluto.

Water and methane ice   Water-ice

Core

PLUTO STRUCTURE
The makeup of Pluto is very different from that of the other outer planets. Its density suggests that it has a rocky core. Its methane frost surface probably covers a water-ice layer below.

PLUTO
The planet Pluto is the smallest in the solar system. It has one moon called Charon, which is fairly close to Pluto, and is about half its size. This makes it difficult to separate the two bodies when viewed from Earth.

NEPTUNE
Voyager 2 images of Neptune show a blue planet, flecked with white clouds of methane ice crystals. A region known as the Great Dark Spot in the Southern Hemisphere is in fact a huge storm. When the Hubble Space Telescope looked for it in 1996, it had disappeared.

PLUTO LANDSCAPE
If you were unlucky enough to land on Pluto, you would find a frozen, lonely, and very dark world. Because Pluto is nearly forty times farther from the Sun than the Earth, the Sun would probably just look like a very bright star.

NEPTUNE LANDSCAPE
Being on Neptune would be a very windy experience. The *Voyager 2* spacecraft recorded winds of up to an incredible 1,340 mph (2,160 km/h).

Triton, a moon of Neptune

Some of Neptune's moons were discovered from Earth. Others were first seen in Voyager 2 data.

Pluto's orbit

Much about Pluto, such as its orbit, leads astronomers to question whether it is a planet at all.

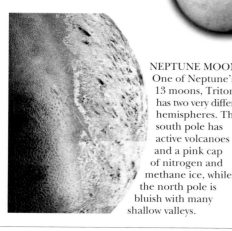

NEPTUNE MOONS
One of Neptune's 13 moons, Triton, has two very different hemispheres. The south pole has active volcanoes and a pink cap of nitrogen and methane ice, while the north pole is bluish with many shallow valleys.

BEYOND PLUTO
Since the discovery of Pluto in 1930, some scientists believed the gravity of a more distant planet was pulling on Uranus and Neptune. New measurements show no such pull. In 1992, the first of a flat belt of icy rocky bodies was discovered. The Kuiper Belt stretches beyond Neptune and past Pluto. By 2002, more than 600 Kuiper Belt objects had been found. The largest— 2003 UB313—was discovered in 2005.

Some consider UB313 to be the tenth planet in the solar system. This image shows that it is orbited by at least one moon.

ORBITS
Pluto moves in strange ways. Its orbit is tilted farther and is more elongated than that of any other planet. In fact, for part of its orbit, Pluto moves closer to the Sun than Neptune, so that for a time, Neptune is the most distant planet in the solar system.

| **Find out more** |
| SOLAR SYSTEM P. 283 |
| URANUS P. 292 |
| SPACE PROBES P. 301 |
| *FACT FINDER P.* 418 |

ASTEROIDS

DID YOU KNOW that there are really millions of planets orbiting the Sun? Aside from nine "regular" planets, there are a few million minor ones, called asteroids. These are different-sized chunks of rock, ranging from specks of dust to some which are a few hundred miless across. Most of them travel in an orbit between Mars and Jupiter called the asteroid belt. Others follow different orbits. In the 18th century, astronomers were convinced that a missing world existed between Mars and Jupiter. A search was mounted and the first asteroid, Ceres, was found by chance in 1801. Today, more than 200,000 have been discovered.

If all the asteroids were put together, they would still only make up a tiny fraction of Earth's mass.

ASTEROID BELT
Although the main planets formed from a disk of material surrounding the young Sun, the material in the region of the asteroid belt did not form a planet. It was prevented from clumping together by the enormous gravity of nearby Jupiter.

The smallest asteroid seen so far from Earth is around 245 ft (75 m) across. Space probes traveling through the belt have detected some only millimeters in diameter.

ASTEROID ORBITS
Most asteroids travel around the Sun in the asteroid belt. Others are in smaller groups with different orbits. A group named the Trojans travels along Jupiter's path: some in front of the planet, and some behind. A group called the Apollo family has orbits that cross the path of Earth. One remote asteroid called Chiron orbits between Saturn and Uranus. At this distance from the Sun, it is made of ice, not rock.

ELEANOR HELIN
American astronomer Eleanor Helin has spent many years discovering and charting asteroids, particularly those that come close to Earth. She works in California, where she makes detailed studies of photographic plates, searching through the stars for new asteroids. The relatively fast movement of an asteroid against the background of distant stars is captured on photographic plates mounted on special telescopes.

FIRST PHOTOGRAPH
Until 1991, asteroids had mainly been studied from Earth-based telescopes. In October of that year, the Galileo space probe, on the way to Jupiter, observed an asteroid called Gaspra that lies on the edge of the asteroid belt. The probe took the first close-up photographs of an asteroid. Gaspra is a small, irregular-shaped asteroid, 8 miles (12 km) across, which rotates once every seven hours.

Most asteroids are irregular in shape.

ASTEROID SIZES
Astronomers can calculate an asteroid's size by studying its brightness (how much of the Sun's light it reflects), by timing it as it crosses a background star, or by direct measurement if it comes close to Earth. The largest asteroid, Ceres, is 580 miles (933 km) in diameter, but most are under 60 miles (100 km). Many would dwarf the Empire State Building in New York City.

NAMING ASTEROIDS
New asteroids are numbered and later named from suggestions that can be made by their discoverers.

1801 The first asteroid is discovered. It is numbered 1 and named Ceres.

1891 Asteroid number 323 is the first to be discovered by photography. It is named Brucia.

1977 Asteroid number 2060 is discovered and named Chiron. It has the most distant orbit of an asteroid.

1983 Asteroid number 3200 is the first to be discovered by a spacecraft. It is named Phaethon.

Find out more

SOLAR SYSTEM P. 283
MARS P. 289
JUPITER P. 290
COMETS AND METEORS P. 295
SPACE PROBES P. 301

COMETS AND METEORS

IMAGINE A GIANT, DIRTY SNOWBALL streaking around the very edge of the solar system. This is a comet. Far beyond Pluto's orbit are the leftovers of the cloud that formed the solar system. It contains billions of icy lumps called comets, and now and then, one may be knocked off course and onto a path toward the Sun. Here, the ice boils away to form an enormous head and a long two-part tail. As a comet travels, it sheds bits of itself; from Earth, these are seen as showers of light called meteors. The first comet sample was brought back to Earth in January 2006—the *Stardust* space probe had collected it from Comet Wild 2. It has given astronomers their first chance to study material from the birth of the solar system.

Comet West on March 13, 1976

HAIRY STARS
Comets have been observed and recorded for thousands of years but they have not always been understood. They were once called "hairy stars" and their sudden appearances made superstitious people regard them as bad omens.

NUCLEUS OF A COMET
People could only guess what a comet's nucleus was like until a space probe called *Giotto* flew past the nucleus of Comet Halley in 1986. *Giotto* provided the first confirmation that comets are giant, dirty snowballs (predicted by an American, Fred Whipple, in 1949). In 2004, the *Stardust* spacecraft flew past Comet Wild 2 and became the first mission to collect dust from a comet for analysis on Earth. It sent back images, such as the one on the left, that show the comet's nucleus in amazing detail.

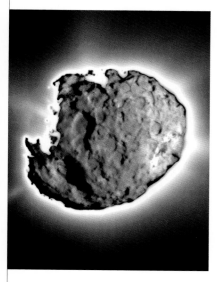

As a comet travels away from the Sun, its tail gets smaller until the comet is once again just a dirty snowball.

A comet's tail always points away from the Sun. So if a comet is traveling away from the Sun, it travels tail first.

Once a comet is near the Sun, the comet starts to shed material. Comet Halley will make around 2,300 more trips around the Sun before it decays completely.

— Sun

— Dust tail

— Gas tail

For most of a comet's life, it is a dirty snowball. When it travels close to the Sun, the surface snow is turned to a head of gas called a coma. The Sun's radiation sweeps this into a gas tail. Dust particles are also swept back to form a dust tail.

EDMOND HALLEY

The English scientist Edmond Halley (1656–1742) worked in many areas of astronomical research, but he is best known for his work on comets. He showed that comets observed in 1531 and 1607, and one he saw himself in 1682, were in fact the same comet. He predicted that it would return in late 1759. It did. And again in 1835, 1910, and 1986. It is known as Comet Halley. He was the first to show that some comets follow orbits that keep returning them to the vicinity of the Sun.

METEORITES
Meteorites are any old lumps of interplanetary rock (from asteroids or the surface of planets, for example), large enough to survive the journey through Earth's atmosphere. Most are fist-sized. But larger ones have smashed into Earth. The Barringer meteorite landed in Arizona, producing a crater over three-quarters of a mile (1.3 km) across.

Meteorite crater in Arizona

Every August, Earth travels through a band of dust which is material from a comet called Swift-Tuttle. This results in a meteor shower called the Perseids.

METEOR SHOWER
Comets shed enormous amounts of gas and dust. After about 1,000 years, this dust forms a ring. If the Earth passes through this, the dust burns up in the atmosphere. From Earth, this is seen as a meteor shower or shooting stars.

> ### *Find out more*
> SOLAR SYSTEM P. 283
> ASTEROIDS P. 294
> *FACT FINDER* P. 418

STUDY OF ASTRONOMY

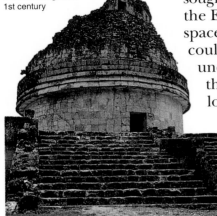

Mayan observatory in Mexico dating from 1st century

ASTRONOMY IS THE oldest science. For thousands of years, people have sought to understand space and Earth's position in it. As long ago as 4000 BCE, the Egyptians developed a calendar, based on the movement of objects in space. Observation of the skies continued, and soon events such as eclipses could be predicted. Since the 17th century, the pace of discovery and understanding has quickened. We have learned more about space in the past 100 years than at any other time. Today, the astronomer is no longer a person working in many fields of science, but is a specialist who concentrates on one specific aspect of astronomical research.

ANCIENT ASTRONOMY
Ancient civilizations around the world relied on the movements of the bodies in space. The positions of the Sun and Moon were used to measure time—in days, months, seasons, and years. The Sun, Moon, and stars were also used to navigate on land and sea. As the bodies were not fully understood, some astronomical happenings were believed to be ill omens.

Tycho Brahe's observatory

CHANGE OF DIRECTION
During the 19th century, the focus of astronomy changed. Rather than cataloging and trying to understand the movement of stars, astronomers thought about what stars actually were (the study of astrophysics). In the 1860s, a British astronomer, William Huggins, analyzed the light from stars (their spectra). Others took up this work, and soon the stars were able to be classified by their spectra.

USING TECHNOLOGY
Early astronomers had to work with their eyes alone. In the 16th century, Tycho Brahe made the most accurate measurements of the stars possible with the naked eye from his observatory. The telescope was first used in the 17th century, and over the years, it has remained the astronomer's fundamental tool. Today, powerful telescopes, satellites, and space probes are all used to collect information from space. Scientists then use sophisticated equipment to study the data.

JOHANNES KEPLER
Danish astronomer Tycho Brahe (1546–1601) spent years cataloging the stars and planets with great accuracy. His assistant Johannes Kepler (1571–1630) put his observations to good use. He developed three important laws of astronomy. His first law describes the shapes of planetary orbits. His second law describes the speed at which the planets travel along their orbits. His third law relates the different planetary orbits to one another.

Astronomers use computers to analyze images, to calculate orbits, and to control instruments such as telescopes, satellites, and space probes.

PRESENT-DAY ASTRONOMY
As astronomers answer questions that puzzle them, new problems take their place. For example, it is now accepted that the universe started with the Big Bang. But how did the material from the Big Bang come together to form galaxies? Today's scientists can work faster on such problems with the help of computers. These can solve mathematical problems in hours rather than the weeks it would have taken a hundred years ago. Computers also enable astronomers around the world to link up so they can work together on our understanding of the universe.

TELESCOPES ON EARTH

BEFORE THE TELESCOPE was invented, the only way people could observe the universe was to look at it with just their eyes. From 1609, when Galileo first used the telescope to look into the sky, astronomers have been able to peer farther and farther into space. They can see surface details on planets and can look at galaxies that were once invisible to them. The first telescopes used lenses to gather the light from stars. These are called refracting telescopes. Telescopes that use mirrors rather than lenses are called reflecting telescopes. Today's telescopes take measurements, analyze starlight, and record the data on computer. The telescope is an astronomer's best friend.

Halley's Comet, 1910

TELESCOPE IMAGES

Images from space (comets, for example) have been recorded photographically from the earliest days of photography. Today, astronomers use electronic chips to record telescopic images. These are then processed using computer software, which can bring out detail on a particular aspect of an image.

The Keck Telescope is on the 14,000 ft (4,200 m) summit of Mauna Kea on the island of Hawaii. This peak is home to an international collection of telescopes.

The success of the multifaceted Keck has led to the construction of an identical twin, Keck II, right next door.

OBSERVATORIES

Telescopes need homes. Usually they are kept in observatories, special buildings that are always built high on mountain tops. This is so the telescope can obtain the very best view of space—away from city lights, and high enough so that Earth's atmosphere doesn't get in the way too much.

Radio image of the Crab Nebula, taken by the Very Large Array (VLA) telescope

GIANT EYE IN THE SKY

The world's biggest telescope collects light with a jagged-looking mirror 33 ft (10 m) across. It would be impossible to make a single mirror this big, so the Keck telescope actually uses 36 hexagonal mirrors, fitted together with extreme accuracy. The Very Large Telescope in Chile consists of four 26 ft (8 m) telescopes looking at the same object to gather the maximum amount of light. Such instruments can see distant galaxies up to 10,000 million light-years away. Because light takes time to travel this immense distance, they reveal the universe soon after it was born.

Dawn over the enormous reflecting dish of the Arecibo radio telescope

TELESCOPES WORKING TOGETHER

Lots of small radio telescopes can be used to work like one enormous one. A computer combines the information received by each dish. This technique is called interferometry and it was first used in the 1960s. The biggest radio telescope of this type uses dishes positioned on different continents!

RADIO TELESCOPES

To collect radio waves from space, an astronomer uses a radio telescope. These work like optical telescopes (that collect light)—a dish faces the sky to collect and focus the waves. However, as radio waves have a larger wavelength than that of light waves, a radio telescope has to be much bigger than an optical one to collect the same amount of information. The largest single dish telescope in the world is in Arecibo, Puerto Rico. Its 1,000 ft- (305 m-) dish is built into a natural hollow in the jungle. As the Earth moves, the dish points to a different part of the sky.

RADIO IMAGE

Radio waves from space (sometimes called radio noise) were first detected in 1931. However, it wasn't until the end of the next decade that radio telescopes were built and used. The radio waves are changed into electrical signals that can be used to make radio images or pictures.

In New Mexico, the VLA radio telescope uses 27 dishes, each 82 ft (25 m) across.

Find out more

REFLECTION P. 194
LENSES P. 197
OPTICAL INSTRUMENTS P. 198
TELESCOPES IN SPACE P. 298

TELESCOPES IN SPACE

JUST AS SUNGLASSES protect our eyes, Earth's atmosphere prevents a lot of radiation from reaching Earth. It lets light through, but even this is affected—images are blurred and stars twinkle, when in reality they shine steadily. For this reason, from the middle of the 20th century, astronomers have been sending telescopes into space to get a better look at our surroundings. These telescopes can see views of the universe that are invisible from Earth. They work day and night, recording data and transmitting it to Earth to be analyzed. Telescopes enable us to look into space with X-ray, ultraviolet, and infrared eyes.

An X-ray image of the Crab Nebula

UV image of the Crab Nebula

IR image of the Orion Nebula

EARLY ATTEMPTS
During the 1930s and 1940s, balloons were used to carry scientific instruments above most of the Earth's atmosphere. Rockets were another option. Once high enough, they had a few minutes in which to record a view, such as the Sun in X-rays, before plunging back down to Earth.

Earth's atmosphere is divided into different layers—the troposphere, the stratosphere, the mesosphere, and the thermosphere. Different types of radiation get stopped by different layers.

Gamma rays have the shortest wavelengths.

X-rays

Ultraviolet rays

INFRARED PICTURES
Although some infrared (IR) rays reach Earth from space, they get mixed up with the infrared rays that Earth itself produces. Therefore, astronomers like to have infrared telescopes out in space. These can detect heat sources that light-detecting telescopes would not show up.

ULTRAVIOLET PICTURES
Most ultraviolet (UV) light is absorbed by Earth's atmosphere (although some gets through to give us a suntan). Satellites for collecting UV waves were first launched in the 1960s. The International Ultraviolet Explorer (IUE), used from 1978 to 1996, is the longest working telescope in space so far.

X-RAY PICTURES
From 1948, when the first X-rays from space were detected, astronomers have been looking at the X-ray universe. X-rays can reveal "hot spots" or areas of energetic activity in space. They can also help us to see otherwise dim objects such as pulsars.

The Hubble telescope uses mirrors to collect and focus light and ultraviolet rays from space.

A computer on board controls the telescope and transmits data to and from Earth.

HUBBLE TELESCOPE
The Hubble Space Telescope was launched in April 1990. It orbits Earth 300 miles (500 km) up in the sky. From its position, the Hubble collects images from millions of years ago, giving astronomers a chance to see the young universe forming after the Big Bang. A new satellite—the James Webb Space Telescope—is being prepared to replace it.

Thermosphere

RADIATION
Light waves are just one of the many types of radiation that objects in space give out. Other forms have different wavelengths. Radio waves, for example, have a longer wavelength than light waves; X-rays have a shorter wavelength. Not all this radiation gets through Earth's atmosphere to reach the surface—most light does, some infrared does, but no gamma rays are able to get through. If astronomers want to collect such radiation, they must send their instruments into space.

Longwave radio waves are collected in space.

Top of mesosphere

Shortwave radio waves reach Earth.

Ozone layer

Infrared waves get stopped by a low part of the atmosphere called the troposphere. A few penetrate to Earth, where large telescopes are ready to collect them.

Light waves reach Earth, but they are blurred by traveling through the atmosphere.

Earth's surface

Top of stratosphere

Top of troposphere

Find out more

ELECTROMAGNETIC SPECTRUM P. 192
OPTICAL INSTRUMENTS P. 198
ATMOSPHERE P. 248
TELESCOPES ON EARTH P. 297
ROCKETS P. 299
SATELLITES P. 300

ROCKETS

ANYTHING THAT WANTS TO GET AWAY from Earth must travel in a rocket. Rockets are used to propel satellites and astronauts into space. Without them, we would know little about Earth's surroundings, and we would not have all the benefits that satellites give our lives. Rockets burn fuel to make a thrust that pushes them upward. In fact, most of a rocket is made up of fuel—its cargo or "payload" takes up a fairly small amount of room in comparison. In 1903, a Russian schoolmaster, Konstantin Tsiolkovskii, put forward the first scientific ideas on rocket propulsion. However, it wasn't until 1926, when an American engineer, Robert Goddard, launched the first liquid fuel rocket, that space travel was really born.

Apollo command module. This was the space capsule that the astronauts eventually returned to Earth in.

Inside is the Apollo lunar module that landed on the Moon.

LAUNCH SITE
Rockets are launched from space centers. There are more than 20 of these around the world. Each space center has technical and control areas as well as the launch pad itself. Once everything is prepared, the rocket is mounted on the launch pad ready for liftoff. The nearer a launch site is to the equator, the more help it gets in lifting off from Earth's spin (which is faster there).

VOSKHOD
The Russian Voskhod rocket was designed to send more than one astronaut into space at a time. In 1964, three Russians were launched into space. On the second Voskhod flight in 1965, Russian cosmonaut Aleksei Leonov became the first to venture outside the capsule.

Rocket's nose is shaped to cut through the air.

Third stage containing fuel

Stage 3 engine

Second stage containing fuel

Stage 2 engines

First stage containing fuel

Payload

Second stage containing liquid fuel

First stage containing liquid fuel

Solid fuel booster

Ariane 5

Saturn V weighed nearly 3,000 tons and needed an enormous thrust to lift off from Earth. This was provided by five engines in its first, lower stage. Within minutes, this stage stopped burning and fell back to Earth.

SATURN V
The massive Saturn V rocket was designed to send people to the Moon. On board was the Apollo craft that would reach the Moon, land safely, and then return the astronauts to Earth. Such a mission requires a lot of fuel. Rockets do not carry their fuel in one tank, however, but in several separate containers called stages. Once one stage is empty, it drops off to lessen the load. The fuel from the next stage is then used.

Rocket fuel usually consists of two liquids— when mixed, these burn and throw exhaust gases out of the back of the rocket. This pushes the rocket forward.

ARIANE
The European Space Agency uses a series of rockets called Ariane to launch its satellites. As with all space rockets, the payload—in this case, a satellite—is carried at the nose end. The larger the Ariane, the bigger and heavier its payload can be. The extra thrust needed to get into space is provided by the large boosters strapped to the first stage.

ESCAPE VELOCITY
If you throw a ball into the air, Earth's gravity will slow it down until it eventually falls back. If you could throw it as fast as 25,000 mph (40,000 km/h), it would be slowed down, but its speed would still be great enough to carry it out of the reach of Earth's gravity and into space. This speed is called the escape velocity. Rockets must reach this speed if they are to escape from Earth.

The force with which a rocket moves away from Earth must be greater than the force of gravity pulling it toward Earth.

SpaceShipOne is an experimental spaceplane. It is launched from the air by a carrier craft called White Knight.

SPACEPLANE
The problem with multistage rockets is that they can only be used once. When the stages fall back to Earth, they burn up in the atmosphere and are destroyed. This is why scientists in several countries are trying to develop a reusable "spaceplane" that takes off horizontally. While in Earth's atmosphere, it would take in air to burn fuel (like a normal airplane). When in space, where there is no air, it would burn liquid hydrogen and oxygen (like a rocket).

Find out more
GRAVITY P. 122
MOON P. 288
TELESCOPES IN SPACE P. 298
SATELLITES P. 300
SPACE PROBES P. 301
HUMANS IN SPACE P. 302

SATELLITES

IMAGINE SOMETHING LOOKING down on Earth that could tell us about the weather or point out areas such as mineral deposits. Such things exist. They are called satellites. There are many different types of satellite orbiting the Earth, all performing different tasks. Navigation satellites help ships or airplanes pinpoint their positions. Astronomers use satellites to look out into the universe. Some satellites provide us with instant phone calls or television broadcasts.

The antenna measures the exact position relative to navigation satellites.

The high-gain antenna sends data back to Earth.

The solar array turns sunlight into electricity.

A radar altimeter measures the precise distance down to the ocean surface below.

Topex/Poseidon satellite

TOPEX/POSEIDON
From an orbit 820 miles (1,320 km) above the Earth's surface, this US-French satellite is investigating ocean currents and wind speeds over the seas. It has found "sea level" is not the same everywhere: the western Atlantic Ocean is 27 in (70 cm) higher than the eastern side!

SPACE TELESCOPE
The Spitzer telescope is the largest infrared telescope ever put into orbit. It was launched in 2003 to observe the distant universe by detecting infrared (heat) radiation emanating from objects in space. Infrared signals can pass through the clouds of gas and dust that lie between Earth and distant objects. So the pictures Spitzer has sent back have allowed scientists to study details of star-forming regions that had never been seen before.

Eccentric orbit: a satellite measuring Earth's magnetic and electric fields will use this orbit, because it can take measurements at different distances from Earth.

Low-Earth orbit: the easiest orbit to reach. It is where the Hubble Space Telescope and the International Space Station orbit.

ORBITS
The path that a satellite takes around Earth depends on the job it has to do. For example, the geostationary orbit is 22,280 miles (35,880 km) above the equator. Satellites in this orbit will complete one orbit in the same time that Earth completes its daily spin. So the satellite will always be above the same point on Earth. This is useful for television satellites.

Polar orbit: circles around Earth's poles. Weather satellites often travel in this orbit because it enables them to scan the entire Earth as the planet spins.

Geostationary orbit: holds communication satellites such as the European satellite Olympus.

Sputnik 1 was an aluminum sphere measuring only 23 in (58 cm) across.

SPUTNIK
The USSR put the first ever artificial satellite into orbit in October 1957. During its short time in space, it investigated Earth's atmosphere. Just a month later, *Sputnik 2* was launched. On board was the first living thing in space—a dog called Laika.

SATELLITE DISH
Once an astronomical satellite is in orbit, it can start its work. Ground stations track the satellite. They monitor its condition and redirect it if necessary. They also receive and process the data from the satellite ready to pass on to scientists. Signals from the satellite are collected by dishes on the ground. These are similar to satellite television dishes, but are much larger.

Find out more
TELECOMMUNICATIONS P. 162
REFLECTION P. 194
WEATHER WATCHING P. 272
TELESCOPES IN SPACE P. 298
ROCKETS P. 299
SPACE PROBES P. 301

SPACE PROBES

MOVING THROUGH SPACE like roving reporters, space probes are unstaffed spacecraft that are sent to investigate and report back on our solar system. They have made many discoveries that would be impossible from Earth. Space probes are highly sophisticated robots. Once launched, they follow a prearranged route to a target, such as a planet. As they fly near or orbit around the planet, instruments on board set to work. Results are sent back to Earth by radio. Some of this data is made into pictures to give close-up views of distant worlds. The Sun, comets, asteroids, and all the major planets and moons have been visited by different space probes.

After discarding its protective heatshield, Huygens parachutes down through Titan's lower atmosphere.

The Huygens probe has a tough exterior protecting its six delicate scientific instruments. Huygens' batteries will last for an hour on Titan's surface.

These instruments test Titan's 'air'.

Two rocket engines slow down Cassini on arrival, so it swings into orbit around Saturn.

PROBE VISITS

1959 First successful probe, *Luna 2*, reaches the Moon.

1962 First successful planetary probe, *Mariner 2*, flies by Venus.

1973 Launch of *Mariner 10*; first probe to visit two planets, Venus and Mercury.

1976 *Viking 1* and *Viking 2* probes land on Mars.

1977 *Voyager 1* and *Voyager 2* sent to Jupiter, Saturn, Uranus, and Neptune.

1985 Five probes sent to investigate Comet Halley.

1995 *Galileo* probe enters atmosphere of Jupiter.

2004 *Cassini* arrives at Saturn to start its four-year study.

A boom 34.5 ft (10.5 m) long carries magnetometers, which measure the strength of Saturn's immense magnetic field.

On its way to Saturn, Cassini carries Huygens piggyback under its turtlelike heatshield.

This image of Europa, a moon of Jupiter, was sent to Earth by Voyager.

Cassini carries 12 different scientific instruments, and is controlled by 44 onboard computers.

CASSINI/HUYGENS

The international *Cassini/ Huygens* probe, launched in October 1997, arrived at Saturn in 2004. The larger part of the craft, the American orbiter *Cassini*, toured around the ringed planet. The small European probe, *Huygens*, was sent into the dense atmosphere of Saturn's largest moon, Titan and landed on its frozen surface.

The dish-shaped aerial sends pictures and other information back to Earth.

IMAGES
Space probes provide so much data that scientists have to analyze it for years after a craft has finished its job. Moons of all four of the giant planets have been discovered by space probes. Scientists are sure that more smaller moons are still waiting to be found.

The orbiter continues to travel around the planet.

The Viking orbiter and lander separate.

A parachute slows the fall of the lander.

VIKING PROBE
Not only can space probes orbit around a planet, but they can also place craft—a lander—on its surface. During the 1960s and 1970s, both the Americans and the Soviets sent off space probes that orbited and landed on Mars. The *Viking 1* and *Viking 2* probes successfully placed landers on Mars in July and September 1976. Between them they sent back almost 3,000 images, studied the Martian soil, took meteorological measurements, and searched for evidence of life.

The lander is released from the parachute.

The lander touches down on the surface of Mars.

VOYAGER PROBES
The twin *Voyager* space probes, *Voyager 1* and *Voyager 2*, were launched in 1977. Their task was to find out more about the four gas giants. They both flew by Jupiter and Saturn. Then *Voyager 2* alone traveled on to Uranus and Neptune. Each spacecraft had 11 instruments on board, including two television cameras.

Scientists can use the gravity of planets to swing a probe toward its target.

Voyager 1 at Saturn in November 1980

Voyager 1 at Jupiter in March 1979; Voyager 2 in July 1979

Voyager 2 at Saturn in August 1981

Voyager 2 at Uranus in January 1986

Voyager 2 at Neptune in August 1989

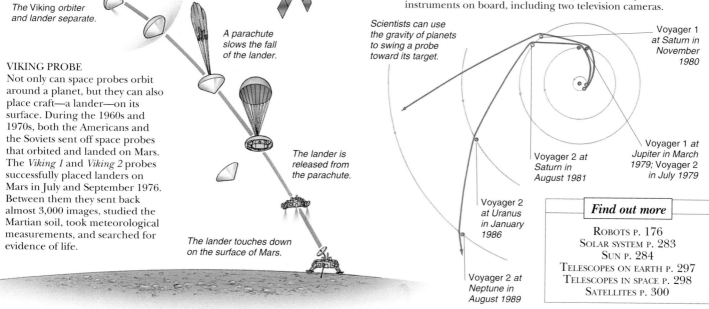

Find out more

ROBOTS P. 176
SOLAR SYSTEM P. 283
SUN P. 284
TELESCOPES ON EARTH P. 297
TELESCOPES IN SPACE P. 298
SATELLITES P. 300

HUMANS IN SPACE

FOR CENTURIES, humans have dreamed of traveling in space. But the dream only became a reality in 1961 when a Russian astronaut called Yuri Gagarin rocketed into space and orbited around the Earth. Today, many men and women travel into space; most go just for a few days, but others go for months at a time. Even so, space remains a hostile environment for humans. Spacesuits are needed for protection and to provide air to breathe. If humans are to live and work more permanently in space, and to land on Mars in the decades ahead, we must learn all we can about the long-term effects of space travel.

TRAINING FOR SPACE
For journeying into space, astronauts need to be physically and mentally fit. They undergo very long and hard periods of training in conditions that are similar to those in space. For example, astronauts may train in large swimming pools so that they have some idea of what feeling weightless is like. They wear special suits and practice the jobs they will do in space.

WOMEN IN SPACE
The United States and the Soviet Union dominated the first two decades of space exploration. In 1963, the Russian astronaut Valentina Tereshkova became the first woman to travel into space.

SPACE WEAR
The first astronauts had just one spacesuit per journey. But today, astronauts wear different clothes for the different jobs they do. One suit is for traveling to and from space. Then, in orbit, they wear specially designed casual clothes. If they are working outside their spacecraft, they wear a suit called an extravehicular mobility unit (EMU). On top of this is a strap-on motor called a manned maneuvering unit (MMU) that can fly the astronaut around.

There are lights on the helmet so that the astronaut can see.

Under the helmet is a cap with headphones and microphones for communication with Earth and with astronauts in the craft.

SPACEWALK
Sometimes astronauts must carry out repairs to the outside of a spacecraft while it is in orbit. This is known as a spacewalk or EVA (Extra-Vehicular Activity). The astronaut is usually tethered to the craft by a mechanical arm, to prevent him or her from drifting off into space.

A camera on the astronaut's shoulder takes pictures as he or she moves around.

The upper half of the suit is a hard shell of fiberglass.

Aluminum-coated fabric deflects the Sun's heat

Innermost layer, known as the bladder, is pressurized and airtight

To keep cool, astronauts wear an undergarment equipped with water cooling tubes.

Layer of rubberized nylon helps protect against damage from space debris

A type of plastic prevents the pressurized inner layer from blowing up like a balloon

Underneath the suit is a urine-collection device that is emptied on return to the spacecraft.

SALLY RIDE
Until 1983, all the American astronauts were male. When the Space Shuttle program was introduced in the 1970s, both men and women could apply to be astronauts. In 1983, Sally Ride became the first American woman in space, and in 1991 Helen Sharman became the first British astronaut.

On July 20, 1969, Neil Armstrong became the first human to step on anything other than the Earth. His colleague Buzz Aldrin joined him 19 minutes later.

MOON MISSIONS
During the late 1950s, there was a race to conquer space by sending up the first satellites and then humans: the space age had begun. In 1961, the Americans promised to land a man on the Moon by the end of the decade. They did. In 1969, Neil Armstrong became the first person to walk on the Moon. Between 1969 and 1972 astronauts spent nearly 80 hours on the Moon's surface.

LIVING IN SPACE

Space travel has changed since Yuri Gagarin's day. In orbit, astronauts move about their craft in casual clothes and eat their favorite meals. When they are not working, they relax with taped music and a good book. They even take it in turns doing "housework." But all of this is done in a state of weightlessness. Since bodies are not working against gravity, bones and muscles may weaken (which is why astronauts must exercise every day). So far, the effects of weightlessness on the human body have reversed once the astronaut is back on Earth. But scientists are monitoring the effects as astronauts spend longer and longer in space.

MONITORING ASTRONAUTS

In March 1992, Russian astronaut Sergei Krikalev returned to Earth after spending 313 days in space. On his return, his physical health was closely examined. In space, astronauts can expect their heartbeat to slow and to suffer from space sickness.

Sergei Krikalev

In space, astronauts may feel dizzy and sick as their bodies move around.

Astronauts suck drinks through straws but eat snacks such as chocolate or nuts in the usual way. Meals are oven warmed before being placed in a special tray to stop them from floating away as they are eaten.

Most foods are dehydrated— the astronauts just add water before eating. Other foods are sealed in cans or pouches just as on Earth. Fresh food may be available for the first part of a trip.

In space, liquids are very difficult to control. This water has formed into a floating ball.

WEIGHTLESSNESS

The gravity of Earth continually pulls on our bodies to give us weight. But if you are in an elevator that is speeding downward, you feel lighter. This effect is exaggerated in a spacecraft; as it is falling in a gravitational field, the astronauts inside it are falling at the same rate and become weightless. Experiments on animals and plants are conducted in space to learn of the effects of weightlessness. Certain experiments, impossible on Earth, can also be performed.

SPACE SHUTTLE

The first astronauts were sent into space in small capsules that sat on top of rockets. They returned by splashing into the sea. These missions were expensive since the rockets could only be used once. Since 1981, American astronauts have been transported into space by the Space Shuttle. The main parts—the orbiter spacecraft, and the rocket boosters—are reusable. The orbiter returns to Earth like a plane and can be used over and over again.

The orbiter leaves its orbit tail first.

A thermal protection system enables the orbiter to survive the high temperatures it encounters as it reenters Earth's atmosphere.

SHUTTLE JOBS

The Space Shuttle has proved very versatile. It has been used for launching satellites, for servicing them, and for retrieving them for return to Earth. Not only this, but it has been used as a laboratory in space, and to transport International Space Station parts into space for assembly, as well as crew to the completed station. A shuttle mission lasts around seven days, and has a crew of up to eight people.

After landing, new fuel tanks are fitted for the next launch.

A braking system brings the orbiter to a halt.

The unpowered orbiter glides back to Earth and lands on a runway like a plane.

Find out more

GRAVITY P. 122
SOLAR SYSTEM P. 283
ROCKETS P. 299
SATELLITES P. 300
SPACE PROBES P. 301
SPACE STATIONS P. 304

SPACE STATIONS

TRIPS INTO SPACE need no longer be short stays. Astronauts can now stay in a space station. This is a large satellite orbiting around Earth with room on board for people both to live and work for weeks or months at a time. In the future, it will also be used as a hotel where astronauts can stay before traveling farther into the solar system, or before coming back to Earth. Space stations are important because experiments in microgravity (conditions of very low gravity) can be conducted there by a person rather than a machine. The astronauts also perform experiments on themselves to see how humans cope in space.

SKYLAB
For five years in the 1970s, Skylab, the first American space station, became a "drop-in" center for visiting astronauts. Skylab was the size of an average house. It offered astronauts the first chance of comfortable surroundings in space.

The photovoltaic array converts sunlight into electrical power. For safety reasons, the huge solar panels are positioned far from the docking ports.

The large concertinaed panels keep the International Space Station cool.

The module from the Japanese space agency (NASDA) ends in an exposed pallet, for the experiments that need to be exposed to space.

In the main American laboratory, astronauts perform experiments in microgravity. They will make a wide range of new materials here.

The US Space Shuttle will transport crew members to and from the space station.

European module

The habitation module is where astronauts relax, eat, and sleep.

INTERNATIONAL SPACE STATION
The world's first multinational base in space was launched in segments from 1997 through to 2002. It was built by the American space agency NASA, the Russians, the Japanese, and the European Space Agency. End to end it stretches 290 ft (88 m), with a "wingspan" across its solar panels of 361 ft (110 m). The International Space Station flies 220 miles (407 km) above the Earth and is home to six crew.

The Russian section: these modules were the first to be launched and have their own power supply and crew quarters.

Russian Soyuz capsules act as "lifeboats," allowing the crew to return to Earth immediately in case of emergency.

EXPERIMENTS
Chemists, biologists, and physicists will all benefit from having a laboratory in space. They will be able to work in conditions of microgravity, where they can process and produce materials (such as drugs or electrical components) to a level of purity that is not possible on Earth.

SPACE STATIONS

1971 First Russian space station is launched. It is called Salyut.

1973 First American space station is launched. It is called Skylab.

1980 Skylab reenters Earth's atmosphere and disintegrates.

1983 First specially designed space laboratory is launched. It is called Spacelab.

1986 The largest space station, Mir, is launched from Baïkonur in Russia.

1988 Russian cosmonauts Musa Manarov and Vladimir Titov return from 366 days in space.

Photograph of solar prominence taken from space station Skylab

Towering solar panels supplied Mir with electricity.

The crew lived in the main module.

In the laboratory module, the crew experimented in microgravity conditions.

The manned Soyuz capsule carried crew to and from Mir. The unmanned craft, Progress, brought supplies.

Handrails helped the crew working outside Mir, as they repositioned the solar arrays and exposed some experiments to space conditions.

MIR
The Russian space station, Mir, was launched in February 1986 and boarded by astronauts three months later. Spacecraft take astronauts to the station by docking (connecting) with one of its six ports. At present, the station has room for up to six crew, but the station's size can be changed by adding new modules to the basic structure.

Find out more
GRAVITY P. 122
SATELLITES P. 300
SPACE PROBES P. 301
HUMANS IN SPACE P. 302

LIVING THINGS

YOU WILL FIND living things almost everywhere you look. A single crumb of bread can support a tiny mold. A spoonful of river water may be home to many different microscopic forms of life. Living things are spread across vast land masses and throughout the oceans between them. Even where conditions seem extremely hostile—in scorching dry deserts, or on freezing mountain tops, for example—some forms of life survive and multiply. Biology is the study of all living things, from those that can be seen only with a microscope to those that are much bigger than we are. Biologists study living things to find out how they work and how they are linked together in the complex pattern of life on Earth.

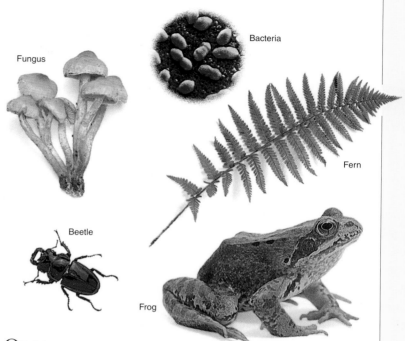

Fungus

Bacteria

Fern

Beetle

Frog

Moths from the *Arctiidae* family

HOW BIOLOGISTS WORK
During the 19th century, scientists often studied animals by killing and collecting them. These moths are part of a typical museum collection that contains thousands of specimens. Collecting can provide useful information, but it can also harm rare species. Because today's biologists are more aware of the need for conservation, they spend more time studying animals in the wild. In this way, they can learn about an animal without harming it or changing its natural behavior.

ORGANISMS AND SPECIES
To biologists, the word "organism" means anything that is alive. A bacterium (singular of bacteria) is an organism, and so too is a plant, an insect, or a human being. Another word that is often used in biology is "species." A species is a group of organisms that are able to breed with each other, such as lions or ostriches. The organisms above belong to different species. They can breed with members of their own species, but not with members of any other species. Organisms usually live separately, but sometimes members of the same species live together very closely in a colony (large group).

FRIEDRICH WÖHLER
All living things contain carbon compounds. Until the 19th century, most scientists believed that carbon compounds in living things were quite separate from those in nonliving things. But in 1828, the German chemist Friedrich Wöhler (1800–82) disproved this idea, which was known as "vitalism." He made urea, a carbon compound formed by animals, from a compound that is found only in nonliving matter.

HIDDEN LIFE
Although this plant looks quite lifeless, it is actually very much alive. *Lithops* (*Lithops aucampiae*), known as the "living stone" plant, grows in dry parts of southern Africa. For most of the year, the *Lithops* plant is well camouflaged. But it has to reproduce. To do this, it grows brightly colored flowers. These flowers attract insects that transfer pollen from one plant to another. After the plant has been pollinated, it produces seeds.

EXPLORING NATURE
The English naturalist Henry Bates (1825–92) was one of the first European people to investigate the wildlife of the Amazon rain forest in South America. He collected many new species and studied the ways in which they compete for survival. Today, scientists are still discovering new species. At the same time, many species are becoming extinct because of the damage we are doing to the natural world.

WHAT IS LIFE?

LIVING THINGS EXIST in many different shapes and sizes. They range from trees that are higher than a 20-story building to bacteria that are far too small to see. Plants spend their lives in the same place, but many animals travel huge distances through the air, over land, or in the sea. Despite these differences, all forms of life share some important characteristics. They all take in raw materials, either in the form of food or in the form of simpler substances. They all use chemical reactions to get energy from these raw materials, and they all make waste products from this process. The energy they obtain enables them to grow, to reproduce, and to respond to the world around them.

PLANT LIFE
Plants cannot move around, but they are just as alive as we are. An oak tree collects energy from sunlight and builds it into food. It uses this food to grow and to reproduce. Although the tree does not have any special sense organs, it can detect and respond to light.

Chemical reactions inside a mouse's body enable it to move and stay warm.

A female mouse uses the energy and nutrients (raw materials) from food to make milk for her young.

When it breathes, a mouse takes in oxygen and gives out carbon dioxide as a waste product.

Young mice use energy and nutrients from food to grow.

PLANKTONIC LIFE
Most forms of life are far smaller than we are. These tiny planktonic organisms drift with the currents in the open sea. Each member of the plankton is very small, but together they weigh millions of tons.

CHARACTERISTICS OF LIFE
The most important daily task for these mice is to find food to fuel their bodies. They use their senses to track down anything they can eat and to check for danger. A mouse obtains energy by combining its food with oxygen. When it does this, carbon dioxide is formed as a waste product. It also uses the nutrients in food to build new body parts. Within six weeks of being born, a mouse is ready to reproduce.

LIFELESS MACHINE
Robots may seem to be alive, but they are really just complicated, nonliving machines. It is true that a robot can use energy to move. But it cannot get this energy on its own—it depends on people. Not only this, it cannot grow or reproduce. Without regular maintenance, a robot will eventually break down and fall apart.

A robot's shape is fixed—it cannot grow or develop without human help.

This shell was once home to a nautilus—a mollusk that lives in the sea. As the mollusk grew, it made sure the shell grew too by secreting calcium, which gradually crystallized to form a new shell.

ORDER FROM CHAOS
A wind-up toy will gradually lose its energy if you do not turn its key. After a few years, it may also rust and break. It is typical of nonliving things. Living things work the other way around. They take in energy and use it to build structures such as cells or shells. This ability to create order from chaotic matter is unique. Only living things can do this. When they die, this ability is lost.

Find out more
PHOTOSYNTHESIS P. 340
NUTRITION P. 342
CELLULAR RESPIRATION P. 346
INTERNAL ENVIRONMENT P. 350
GROWTH AND DEVELOPMENT P. 362
ASEXUAL REPRODUCTION P. 366
SEXUAL REPRODUCTION P. 367

HOW LIFE BEGAN

OUR PLANET has been around for about 4.6 billion years. In its early years, it was far too hot and dangerous to support life. It was bombarded by meteors and torn apart by volcanic explosions. But as the Earth cooled, its surface became calmer. Steamy water vapor from the constant eruptions formed clouds and rain fell. In this water, life appeared over 3.5 billion years ago. Some people believe that living things were specially created, but most scientists think life came about through a series of chemical reactions that happened by chance. Over millions of years, these reactions slowly built living things from simple chemical substances.

OLDEST LIFE FORMS
These cyanobacteria are simple forms of life that live like plants. They usually live in shallow water and make their food by photosynthesis. Geologists have found fossilized mats of cyanobacteria that date from 3.5 billion years ago. These life forms must have been among the earliest on Earth.

Ammonia

Hydrogen

Methane

Water

Urea, a common waste product of living things

Glutamic acid, an amino acid used by living things to build proteins.

RAW INGREDIENTS
The ocean and atmosphere of the early Earth contained simple chemicals, such as water, methane, ammonia, and hydrogen. In their famous experiment, Urey and Miller sealed a mixture of these chemicals in a container. They wanted to see what would happen when the chemicals were allowed to react.

Energy produced by electrical sparks caused chemicals in the container to react with each other.

Water, methane, ammonia, and hydrogen chemicals were sealed in a container.

RESULTS
After running the experiment for a week, Urey and Miller found that several new and complex substances had formed. Among them were amino acids. These are important chemicals that link together to form proteins, the building blocks of life.

LIFE FROM LIFE

At one time, people thought that living things could suddenly appear from lifeless substances. They thought, for example, that maggots developed from decaying meat. Experiments by Italian scientist Lazzaro Spallanzani (1729–99) and French scientist Louis Pasteur (1822–95) showed that this idea was wrong. Living things are always formed by reproduction.

By laying her eggs on meat, this female bluebottle fly (Calliphora vomitoria) ensures a plentiful supply of food for the maggot larvae when they hatch.

CRADLE OF LIFE

Imagine a young Earth covered with oceans that contained simple chemicals. Energy from sunlight and from strikes of lightning would have made these chemicals react with each other. Eventually, some of these reactions may have created chemicals that could copy themselves, or membranes (coatings) that would shield them from the outside world. In 1953, American chemists Harold Urey and Stanley Miller tested this idea. They found that complex substances could be built up from simpler ones.

LIFE BEYOND EARTH?
If life arose on Earth by chemical reactions, it is possible that it also evolved elsewhere. In 1996, American scientists announced that they had found fossils of microorganisms in a meteorite from Mars. Not all scientists are convinced that the structures are fossils, or that they formed before the meteorite reached Earth. Many believe that the "fossils" were etched by chemical processes and are not the remains of life forms.

Original chemical attracts other chemicals and reacts with them.

After several reactions, a copy of the original chemical is formed.

CHEMICAL REPRODUCTION
Life may have started in a simple way. By chance, a chemical may have entered into a series of reactions that resulted in it making a copy of itself. This copy, through the same reactions, could then make a copy of itself. The chemical was able to reproduce.

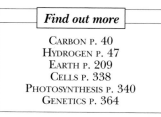

EVOLUTION

These colors are imaginary. Nobody knows what colors Archaeopteryx was.

Archaeopteryx had peg-shaped teeth, just like those of reptiles.

Chicken-size body

Feathered, long front legs

Long, reptilelike tail

IMAGINE BEING ABLE to go back in time to see what living things looked like millions of years ago. Sadly, this is impossible, but we can find out a lot about the past by looking at fossils. A fossil is created when something that was once alive becomes buried by mud or sand. The soft parts of the plant or animal often rot away without trace, but the harder parts, such as stems, bones, teeth, and shells, very slowly turn to stone. Fossils from all over the world show that living things have gradually changed over many millions of years. Some kinds have become extinct (ceased to exist), and new kinds have developed from older ones. This process of slow change is called evolution.

REPTILE OR BIRD?

Very occasionally, a fossil is found that shows how one major group of living thing may have evolved from another. One such fossil is that of *Archaeopteryx*, which means "ancient wing." The fossil shows an animal that had scales and teeth like a reptile, but which also had feathers like a bird. From this evidence, biologists can be almost certain that birds evolved from reptiles.

FOSSIL RECORD
This *Archaeopteryx* fossil was found in Germany in 1861. It is thought that *Archaeopteryx* evolved from small dinosaurs (a type of reptile) that ran on two legs.

EVOLUTION OF THE HORSE
Fossil evidence shows that the modern horse has evolved from smaller ancestors, which lived quite differently. The earliest horse, *Hyracotherium*, was about the size of a small dog. It had four-toed hooves on its front feet and browsed on the leaves of bushes. Over millions of years, its descendants became bigger and their diet changed from leaves to grass. They developed longer legs with fewer toes, enabling them to run away from their enemies on open grassland.

Hyracotherium lived over 50 million years ago. It probably hid from its enemies because it was small and could not run fast.

Mesohippus, which lived about 30 million years ago, had longer legs and just three toes on its front feet.

Merychippus appeared about 20 million years ago. It was the first horse to eat grass. It also had three toes, but one of the toes formed a large hoof.

Equus, the modern horse, evolved about 2 million years ago. It lives on grass and it has just a single toe on each foot, forming a hoof.

A SHARED PATTERN
Evolution works by adapting things that already exist. One species may evolve into others that look very different, but they all share the same basic pattern. Mammals are a good example. They have front limbs of many different shapes and sizes, and they carry out many different functions—from swimming to flying. But each one is built on the same basic pattern. This suggests that mammals have evolved from a common ancestor.

A human arm contains two sets of long bones. The hand is made up of five sets of finger bones.

A porpoise's front flipper contains two sets of short "arm" bones and five sets of "finger" bones.

A bat's wing contains two sets of "arm" bones, and is stretched out by five sets of long "finger" bones.

GEORGES-LOUIS BUFFON

In the 17th century, most people believed that living things had been specially created. They thought that each kind of plant or animal had fixed characteristics, a view still held by some people today. Count Georges-Louis Buffon (1707–88) was a wealthy French naturalist who gradually came to doubt this idea. During research for his 44-volume work *Natural History*, he decided that some species of plants or animals must have given rise to others. He was one of the first people to write about the idea of evolution.

Find out more

FOSSILS P. 225
HOW EVOLUTION WORKS P. 309
CLASSIFYING LIVING THINGS P. 310
REPTILES P. 330
BIRDS P. 332
GENETICS P. 364
FACT FINDER P. 420

HOW EVOLUTION WORKS

Tool-using finch holds a cactus spine in its beak to pick out insects from bark crevices.

Warbler finch has a sharply pointed beak. It feeds entirely on insects.

Large ground finch eats mainly big seeds. It cracks them open with its heavy beak.

Small tree finch eats insects. It uses its fine beak to snap them up.

Cactus ground finch has a sharp beak. It eats mainly seeds, but also some insects.

Vegetarian tree finch has a curved beak. It eats buds and leaves.

WHY SHOULD PLANTS or animals slowly change as one generation follows another? Two 19th-century biologists, Charles Darwin and Alfred Russel Wallace, separately hit upon the answer. They knew that members of a species vary from each other slightly and that these differences can be passed on to the next generation. They also knew that all living things have to compete for resources, such as food. Darwin and Wallace realized that the young born with the most useful differences would produce the most offspring. As a result, the species would evolve, or become better adapted to its way of life. This process is called natural selection.

CHARLES DARWIN AND ALFRED RUSSEL WALLACE

The theory of natural selection, also called "survival of the fittest," was conceived by Darwin (1809–82) and Wallace (1823–1913). Before they published their work in 1858, many people thought that plants or animals evolved by changing *during* their lives. It was thought that these changes were passed on to offspring by their parents, causing evolution. Darwin and Wallace put forward evidence to support the theory of natural selection. In 1859, Darwin outlined this idea in his best-selling book, *The Origin of Species.*

Wallace

Darwin

GALAPAGOS FINCHES

During an around-the-world voyage on board *HMS Beagle*, Charles Darwin landed in 1832 on the remote Galapagos Islands, off the west coast of South America. Here he saw many unique animals, including 13 species of finch. Darwin studied the finches carefully, noting their similarities and differences. It became clear to him that they must all have descended from one species of finch that had arrived from the mainland. The original finch ate seeds and lived on the ground, but its offspring had gradually evolved different beak shapes and different ways of life. Seed-eating finches usually have big, powerful beaks, while insect-eating finches have thinner, pointed beaks.

STRUGGLE FOR SURVIVAL
This female spider laid hundreds of eggs. Not all of the baby spiders have survived and more will die before they can reproduce. If these spiderlings did not have to compete for food and shelter the world would soon be overrun by spiders!

Adult spider carries her offspring around on her back.

ARTIFICIAL SELECTION
Variations within a species do not always happen naturally. The stripes on these flowers are artificial—they were brought about by exposing a plant to X-rays. The X-rays changed the plant's own chemical "blueprint" (genetic makeup), so that the stripes were passed on to the next generation. The striped characteristic can be made more common by deliberately breeding these plants. This way of spreading changes in plants and animals is called artificial selection.

Rabbit flea (Spilopsyllus cuniculi) *feeding on a rabbit.*

Stripes on petunia are a result of artificial selection.

EVOLUTION OF THE FLEA
Natural selection does not always make things bigger or more complicated. It often "doubles back" on itself. Long ago, the ancestors of fleas evolved wings. But wings are not particularly useful to fleas. As a result of natural selection, fleas have lost their wings. Instead, they have developed powerful back legs so that they can leap aboard their hosts.

Find out more

CLASSIFYING LIVING THINGS

KINGDOM ANIMALIA
The animal kingdom is one of five major groups of living things. The kingdom is divided into about 30 groups. Each group is called a phylum. Some of these groups contain many species, while others contain just a few. The Roman snail belongs to the mollusk phylum, or Phylum Mollusca.

This chart shows some of the animal kingdom phyla.

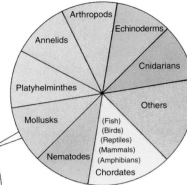

LONG BEFORE BIOLOGY became a science, people used ordinary names for common plants and animals. These names usually described what something looked like, where it was found, or how it was used. But these names do not work for scientists because they vary between languages. Even in one language, some things have several names, while others have none. The 18th-century Swedish botanist Linnaeus devised a way of naming living things and classifying them into groups. In his binomial (two-part) system of classification, every species has its own name. As well as identifying the species, it also shows where it fits into the world of living organisms.

Heb.Reem, Rhinoceros, *Neushoorn*

NAMES TO REMEMBER
Even before Linnaeus devised his binomial system, educated people were using Latin to name plants and animals. This engraving of a rhinoceros appeared in a medieval "book of beasts."

PHYLUM MOLLUSCA
The mollusk phylum contains about 90,000 species, making it one of the largest phyla (plural of phylum) in the animal kingdom. A mollusk has a special body layer, called a mantle, that can produce a shell. The mollusk phylum is divided into seven groups called classes. The Roman snail belongs to the Class Gastropoda, which means "stomach-foot."

CLASS GASTROPODA
Gastropods have a single, suckerlike foot, and most move by creeping along on it. The majority have well-developed heads, and eyes on tentacles. The Class Gastropoda consists of three subclasses. The Roman snail has a lung, and so is a member of the Subclass Pulmonata, which means "with lung."

CHANGING NAMES
Scientific names often change as biologists find out more about how living things are related. The bluebell was originally named by Linnaeus, who included it in the genus *Hyacinthus*. It has been renamed many times as a result of scientific studies, and it is now classified as belonging to another genus, *Scilla*.

SUBCLASS PULMONATA
The Subclass Pulmonata is split into two groups, called orders. The Roman snail lives on land. It has eyes at the tips of its tentacles, and so is included in the Order Stylommatophora.

CLASSIFICATION
Here you can see how one species, the Roman snail, is classified. As you work down the page, you will notice that the classification starts with the animal kingdom, and then narrows down until it picks out just one species—according to various characteristics. These categories have been devised by biologists and work like divisions in a vast filing system. Biologists often use additional divisions, such as subphylum and superorder, that are not shown here.

ORDER STYLOMMATOPHORA
This order contains many kinds of air-breathing mollusks that live on land and that have eyes on tentacles. It is divided into several groups, called families. These include families of both snails and slugs, which are similar, although most slugs do not have a shell. The Roman snail belongs to a family of snails called the Helicidae.

FAMILY HELICIDAE
In biological classification, a family means a collection of species. Within a family, there are groups of species called genera (plural of genus). The Roman snail belongs to the genus *Helix* because of its shell's *helical* (coiled) shape.

SPECIES *Helix pomatia*

GENUS HELIX
The genus *Helix* contains many species that are very similar. Each one has a binomial scientific name. The first part of the name identifies the genus that all the species belong to—in this case, *Helix*. The second part identifies the species itself. The species name of the Roman snail is *pomatia*, meaning "apple-shaped." The Roman snail's full scientific name is therefore *Helix pomatia*.

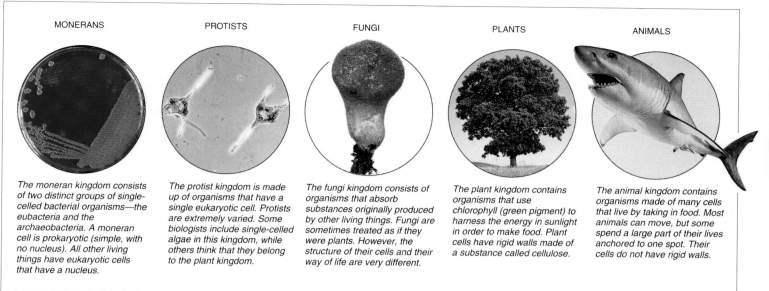

MONERANS

The moneran kingdom consists of two distinct groups of single-celled bacterial organisms—the eubacteria and the archaeobacteria. A moneran cell is prokaryotic (simple, with no nucleus). All other living things have eukaryotic cells that have a nucleus.

PROTISTS

The protist kingdom is made up of organisms that have a single eukaryotic cell. Protists are extremely varied. Some biologists include single-celled algae in this kingdom, while others think that they belong to the plant kingdom.

FUNGI

The fungi kingdom consists of organisms that absorb substances originally produced by other living things. Fungi are sometimes treated as if they were plants. However, the structure of their cells and their way of life are very different.

PLANTS

The plant kingdom contains organisms that use chlorophyll (green pigment) to harness the energy in sunlight in order to make food. Plant cells have rigid walls made of a substance called cellulose.

ANIMALS

The animal kingdom contains organisms made of many cells that live by taking in food. Most animals can move, but some spend a large part of their lives anchored to one spot. Their cells do not have rigid walls.

FIVE KINGDOMS OF LIVING THINGS

At one time, biologists divided the living world into just two groups: the plant kingdom and the animal kingdom. Telling the difference between a plant and an animal seemed easy. Plants were green, rooted in one place, and needed light to live. Animals usually moved around and fed by eating other things. However, biologists have since discovered that the living world is not that simple. In any handful of soil or bucket of water there are vast numbers of tiny living things that do not belong to either kingdom. Today, the living world is usually divided into five kingdoms. As ideas change about how living things are related, the way that they are classified changes too.

HOW MANY SPECIES?

Biologists still have no real idea how many species of living things exist on Earth. Almost two million have been discovered and described, but there may be 10 times that number. We know of about 550 species of conifers and nearly 400,000 species of beetles.

These are just five of the thousands of beetle species.

Tachelophorus giraffa

Eupholus beccarii

Julodis klugi

Helaeus subserratus

Heterorrhina macleayi

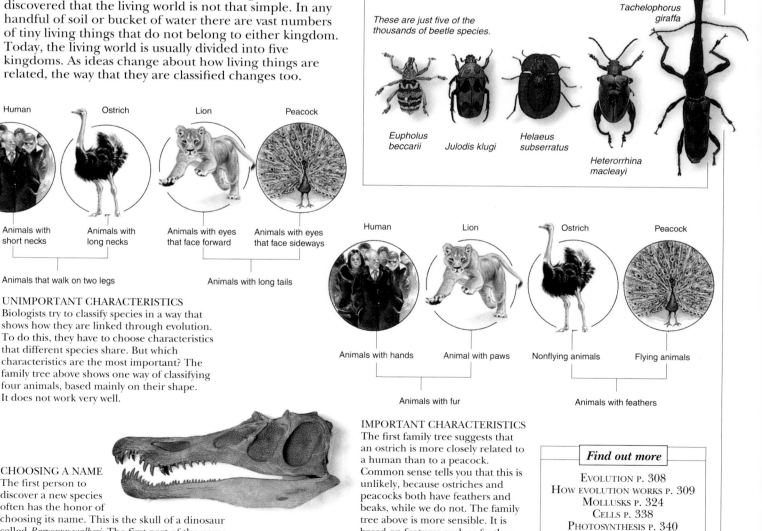

Human — Ostrich — Lion — Peacock

Animals with short necks — Animals with long necks — Animals with eyes that face forward — Animals with eyes that face sideways

Animals that walk on two legs — Animals with long tails

UNIMPORTANT CHARACTERISTICS

Biologists try to classify species in a way that shows how they are linked through evolution. To do this, they have to choose characteristics that different species share. But which characteristics are the most important? The family tree above shows one way of classifying four animals, based mainly on their shape. It does not work very well.

Human — Lion — Ostrich — Peacock

Animals with hands — Animal with paws — Nonflying animals — Flying animals

Animals with fur — Animals with feathers

CHOOSING A NAME

The first person to discover a new species often has the honor of choosing its name. This is the skull of a dinosaur called *Baryonyx walkeri*. The first part of the name refers to the dinosaur's heavy claws. The second part commemorates the discoverer—Bill Walker.

IMPORTANT CHARACTERISTICS

The first family tree suggests that an ostrich is more closely related to a human than to a peacock. Common sense tells you that this is unlikely, because ostriches and peacocks both have feathers and beaks, while we do not. The family tree above is more sensible. It is based on features such as feathers and bone structure, which give a much better guide to classification.

VIRUSES

A RUNNY NOSE AND SORE THROAT are unpleasant symptoms of a cold virus. A virus is a tiny package of chemicals coated by protein that breaks into living animal or plant cells. Once inside, it "hijacks" the cell's chemical processes, so that instead of working normally, the cell makes copies of the virus. Scientists do not consider viruses to be fully alive because they cannot reproduce on their own—they need the help of living cells. In addition to the common cold, viruses cause many other diseases. These include chicken pox, mumps and measles, and also AIDS (Acquired Immune Deficiency Syndrome), which is now known to be caused by HIV (Human Immunodeficiency Virus). This virus puts the body's natural defenses out of action, so that other viruses or bacteria can attack.

Empty viruses attached to outside of cell.

BACTERIOPHAGES
Some viruses, called bacteriophages, attack bacteria in order to reproduce. This bacterium has been attacked by T4 bacteriophages. Empty viruses, which have injected their DNA (deoxyribonucleic acid) into the bacterium, are attached to the outside of the cell.

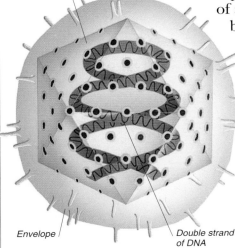

Protein case

Envelope

Double strand of DNA

HOW VIRUSES ARE COPIED
The T4 bacteriophage virus looks like a miniature spaceship. It forms copies of itself by injecting its DNA into a bacterium. The DNA makes the bacterium build all the parts needed to assemble new viruses. The parts are then put together, and the new viruses break out of the bacterial cell.

Head

DNA

Collar

Tail

Copied viruses are released as bacterium bursts open.

Virus lands on bacterium cell wall.

Bacterium makes copies of the virus's DNA.

New heads and tails form.

Tail contracts, and DNA is injected into the bacterium.

HERPES VIRUS
Chicken pox, shingles, and cold sores are caused by herpes viruses. Inside each virus is a double strand of the genetic chemical DNA. This contains all the "instructions" needed to make a living cell produce copies of the virus. The DNA is protected by a case made of protein, which has 20 identical sides. Around the case is a coating called an envelope. When the virus encounters a suitable cell, its envelope links up with the cell's membrane—sort of like two bubbles joining together. The rest of the virus then enters the cell, where it is copied. Herpes viruses sometimes live in the human body for many years without causing any harm.

SMALLER AND SMALLER
Viruses are not the only chemical particles that can infect living cells. Viroids are similar to viruses, but they are even smaller. A viroid is made of a short length of the genetic chemical RNA (ribonucleic acid), without a protein coat. Prions are smaller still. Unlike viruses or viroids, they are thought to be made of proteins. Viroids cause several diseases of plants, while prions cause scrapie, a disease of sheep and cattle.

Part of a bacterium

T4 bacteriophage virus

Viroid

Prion

Streaky tulip petals

Vase of Flowers by Jan van Huysum (1682–1749).

TREASURED VIRUS
Tulip mosaic virus creates beautiful streaks in the petals of tulips. In 17th-century Holland, tulips infected with this virus were highly prized. People traded tulips like stocks and shares, and the price of a single tulip bulb was often more than an ordinary person's yearly income.

RUNNY NOSES
Cold viruses give you a "runny nose." When you sneeze, droplets of moisture containing millions of viruses are sprayed into the air. If someone close breathes in some of these droplets, they may catch the cold as well.

Find out more
BACTERIA P. 313
CELLS P. 338
INTERNAL ENVIRONMENT P. 350
GROWTH AND DEVELOPMENT P. 362
GENETICS P. 364

BACTERIA

IF YOU HAVE EVER LEFT MILK OUT in warm weather, you will know how quickly it turns sour. This change is caused by the rapid growth of microscopic moneran organisms called bacteria. Bacteria are the most widespread living things on Earth. They are found in the air, in the ground, and all over plants and animals, including humans. A few kinds even live in hot springs and ice. There are many different bacteria—some harmful, some very beneficial. Harmful bacteria include those that cause dangerous diseases, such as tetanus and septicemia (blood poisoning). Beneficial bacteria include those that break down waste and those that live in plant roots, gathering nitrogen from the air.

BUBONIC PLAGUE
Before antibiotics were invented, bacterial diseases sometimes swept vast areas in terrifying epidemics. During the 14th and 17th centuries, the bubonic plague, known as the Black Death, killed millions of people in Europe. Bubonic plague is caused by a bacterium that lives in rats, and which is spread to humans by fleas.

BACTERIAL CELLS
A typical bacterium is about 1,000 times smaller than an animal cell and can only be seen in detail with an electron microscope. It has a thick cell wall, but does not have a nucleus. Bacteria live either by using energy from chemicals or sunlight, or by absorbing food substances. Bacteria can absorb food from dead matter, such as plant and animal remains, or from living cells.

A bacillus is a rod-shaped bacterium. Bacilli live singly or in chains.

A coccus has a round cell. Some cocci live in clusters or in long chains.

A spirillum has a corkscrew shape. Some form chains.

BACTERIAL REPRODUCTION
Bacteria reproduce mainly by dividing in two. With good conditions—warmth, moisture, and food—they do this every 20 minutes. This means that three generations of bacteria can be produced within just one hour. In 24 hours, repeated divisions would produce nearly 5,000 billion billion offspring!

MAKING WASTE SAFE
Bacteria play an important part in processing our body waste and in preventing it from causing pollution. In a sewage farm, liquid waste is slowly trickled through beds of clinker (lumps of solid ash) or fine gravel. Bacteria living on the surface of the clinker digest the waste, breaking it down into simpler substances. These can be released into streams and rivers without harming wildlife.

ROBERT KOCH
A German doctor named Robert Koch (1843–1910) helped to establish the study of bacteria as a medical science. In 1876, he discovered that the bacterium that produced anthrax, a disease of cattle and humans, could be cultured (grown) in a laboratory. He also identified the bacteria that cause tuberculosis and cholera.

TOOTH DECAY
We all have many kinds of bacteria living on and in our bodies. Your mouth contains bacteria that digest traces of leftover food. If you do not brush your teeth regularly, these bacteria build up, forming a white coating called plaque. Acids produced by the bacteria attack the hard outer covering of teeth. If the acid gets through to the soft layer underneath, the teeth decay more.

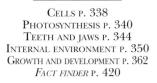

Bacteria on surface of tooth

SINGLE-CELLED ORGANISMS

WET PLACES such as the sea, ponds, and damp ground are alive with tiny single-celled organisms called protists. Although protists are bigger than bacteria, most are still far too small to see with the naked eye. Each protist cell is very different from those of bacteria. It contains a nucleus and also has special structures called organelles that carry out various tasks to keep the cell alive. Protists feed in two ways. Some make their food like plants—by using the energy in sunlight. Others, called protozoa ("first animals"), catch and eat prey. But protists cannot always be separated neatly into plantlike or animal-like forms. Some can do both: they can make food using sunlight *and* eat other organisms.

Liquid cytoplasm flows through the pseudopods, carrying organelles with it.

An amoeba's top speed is just under 1 inch (2 cm) in an hour.

The amoeba sends out pseudopods in the direction of motion.

HOW AN AMOEBA MOVES
An amoeba can change parts of its cytoplasm (cell fluid) into a jellylike solid and back to a fluid again. It does this to make temporary "feet," called pseudopods. As the amoeba moves, the sides of the pseudopods become solid and stay still, while the front and inside flow forward.

AMOEBA

An amoeba is a special kind of protist that does not have a fixed shape. Its single baglike cell moves by flowing in any direction. Amoebas live in water and feed by engulfing their prey. Their food becomes locked up in bubbles called food vacuoles, where it is eventually digested. To reproduce, an amoeba simply divides itself in two.

The nucleus controls how the cell works. When the amoeba reproduces, both nucleus and cell divide in two.

Pseudopod

Liquid cytoplasm

Jellylike cytoplasm

Food vacuoles digest things that the amoeba has engulfed. Any remains are then ejected from the cell.

The contractile vacuole is like a pump. It collects surplus water and then squirts it out of the cell.

A Didinium swims around looking for food.

The Didinium has bumped into a Paramecium. The Didinium stretches wide to take in its enormous meal. Within two or three hours, it will be ready to feed again.

PROTIST BATTLE
Protists may be small, but their world includes some ferocious predators. Here, a protist called *Didinium* is attacking another called *Paramecium*. The battle begins when *Didinium* fires poisonous threads at its prey. Although much smaller than its meal, the *Didinium* then swallows the *Paramecium*. Both these protists are ciliates—organisms that "row" through water by beating tiny hairs called cilia.

MOSQUITOES AND MALARIA

Malaria is a dangerous disease that is particularly widespread in the tropics. It is caused by a protist called *Plasmodium*. People catch malaria when they are bitten by a mosquito carrying this protist. Once inside a human, *Plasmodium* lives and reproduces inside liver and red blood cells. Every few days, the new protist cells break out of the red blood cells, producing bouts of fever.

An infected mosquito has Plasmodium cells in its salivary glands. These can enter a human when the mosquito bites.

The blood cell is destroyed as its invaders reproduce.

Mosquito (*Anopheles arabiensis*)

Human red blood cell infected with *Plasmodium*.

ROCK-MAKING PROTISTS
Foraminiferans ("hole-bearers") are protists that live in microscopic shells rich in calcium. Each shell is covered with tiny holes through which special "feet" project to gather food. Foraminiferans live in huge numbers in the sea. When they die, their shells pile up on the seabed. Eventually, they turn into rocks such as the chalk seen in these white cliffs.

Find out more

BACTERIA P. 313
CELLS P. 338
PHOTOSYNTHESIS P. 340
ASEXUAL REPRODUCTION P. 366
FACT FINDER PP. 420, 422

FUNGI

FOR MANY PEOPLE, a fungus is a mushroom or a toadstool. But mushrooms and toadstools are just the visible parts of fungi. The rest of a fungus is made up of a mass of tiny threads called hyphae, which are usually hidden in the ground or in organic matter such as dead wood. Unlike green plants, fungi cannot make food by capturing sunlight energy. Instead, they use their threads to absorb chemicals that have already been made by other living things that have died. Together with bacteria, fungi are important decomposers. They break down the remains of dead plants and animals, releasing chemicals that can be recycled. Fungi do not only feed on dead matter. Some attack living plants and animals and often cause diseases.

FLAVOR FROM FUNGI
Although some fungi are poisonous, many harmless species are used to flavor food. These cheeses have been infected with *Penicillium* fungus. It grows through the cheese, giving it a special taste.

FLY AGARIC
The fly agaric (*Amanita muscaria*) is a poisonous fungus that reproduces by forming toadstools. The toadstool has flaps called gills that hang from its cap. The gills make spores, which are like tiny seeds. These spores are shed into the air and if one lands in a suitable place it produces a new mass of fungal threads.

SINGLE-CELLED FUNGI
Yeasts are microscopic single-celled fungi that reproduce mainly by budding. They feed on sugars, turning them into alcohol or other substances through a process called fermentation. Yeasts are used to produce alcoholic drinks and to make bread rise.

Yeast cells (*Saccharomyces cerevisiae*)

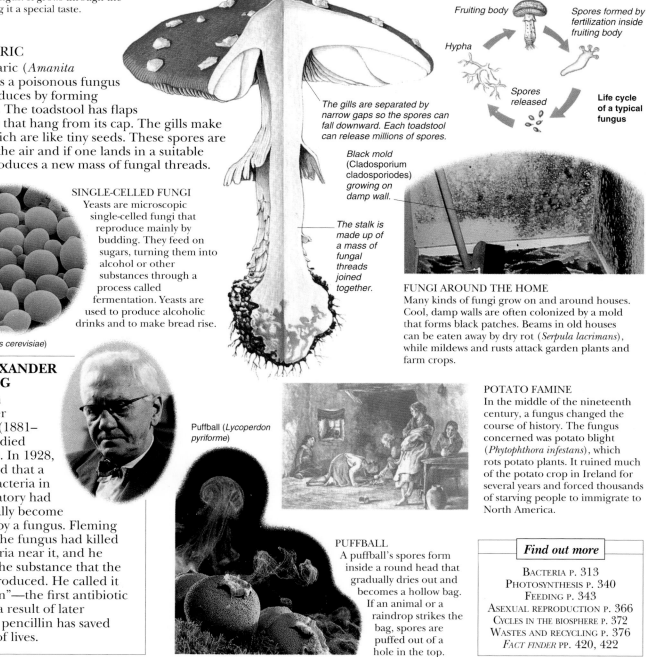

The gills are separated by narrow gaps so the spores can fall downward. Each toadstool can release millions of spores.

The stalk is made up of a mass of fungal threads joined together.

Fruiting body

Hypha

Spores formed by fertilization inside fruiting body

Spores released

Life cycle of a typical fungus

Black mold (*Cladosporium cladosporiodes*) growing on damp wall.

FUNGI AROUND THE HOME
Many kinds of fungi grow on and around houses. Cool, damp walls are often colonized by a mold that forms black patches. Beams in old houses can be eaten away by dry rot (*Serpula lacrimans*), while mildews and rusts attack garden plants and farm crops.

SIR ALEXANDER FLEMING

Scotsman Alexander Fleming (1881–1955) studied medicine. In 1928, he noticed that a dish of bacteria in his laboratory had accidentally become infected by a fungus. Fleming saw that the fungus had killed the bacteria near it, and he isolated the substance that the fungus produced. He called it "penicillin"—the first antibiotic drug. As a result of later research, pencillin has saved millions of lives.

Puffball (*Lycoperdon pyriforme*)

POTATO FAMINE
In the middle of the nineteenth century, a fungus changed the course of history. The fungus concerned was potato blight (*Phytophthora infestans*), which rots potato plants. It ruined much of the potato crop in Ireland for several years and forced thousands of starving people to immigrate to North America.

PUFFBALL
A puffball's spores form inside a round head that gradually dries out and becomes a hollow bag. If an animal or a raindrop strikes the bag, spores are puffed out of a hole in the top.

Find out more

BACTERIA P. 313
PHOTOSYNTHESIS P. 340
FEEDING P. 343
ASEXUAL REPRODUCTION P. 366
CYCLES IN THE BIOSPHERE P. 372
WASTES AND RECYCLING P. 376
FACT FINDER PP. 420, 422

PLANTS WITHOUT FLOWERS

PLANTS ARE DIFFERENT from fungi because they can make their own food using chlorophyll, a green pigment in their leaves. Plants evolved from organisms called algae, and fall into two main groups: plants without flowers, and plants with flowers. Plants without flowers appeared more than 300 million years ago. They included liverworts, mosses, and ferns, and some of them reached great sizes. Today, plants without flowers still exist, but those on land are often quite small, and are usually tucked away in shady places. Plants without flowers spread by shedding spores. Many of them, such as ferns, exist as two different kinds of plant. One kind, the sporophyte, makes the spores. These then germinate to make a second kind of plant, the prothallus, which produces gametes (sex cells).

A kelp does not have true leaves. It has pointed fronds.

PLANT LOOKALIKE

Giant kelp (*Macrocystis pyrifera*) is a huge seaweed that grows in the cool waters off California. It can be 650 ft (200 m) long, and forms underwater "forests" that provide a home for many animals, including fish and sea otters. Although they look like plants, seaweeds are usually classified as protists. Unlike other protists, seaweeds consist of many cells that live and work together. They do not have flowers, and they reproduce by spores instead of seeds.

Life cycle of a typical plant without flowers

Fern plant (Sporophyte)
Spores
Zygote beneath gametophyte
Fertilization
Egg cell
Sperm cell
Prothallus (gametophyte)

Ferns have special tissues that carry water through the plant.

WEALTH OF ALGAE

Plants almost certainly evolved from protists called algae, which live by photosynthesis. This photograph shows green alga called *Volvox*, which is made of a ball of cells set in jelly. There are over 20,000 species of algae. They include microscopic forms, but also seaweeds such as the giant kelp.

Colony ruptures to release daughter colonies.

Instead of a stem, kelp has a tough rubbery stipe.

TREEFERNS

Treeferns are the tallest nonflowering plants on land. They grow mainly in the tropics, although some are found in cooler places such as New Zealand.

Liverworts either have flat ribbons, or ribbons made of pieces that look like leaves.

LIVERWORTS

Liverworts are closely related to mosses. They are low-growing plants that look like pieces of green ribbon. As the plant grows forward, the ribbon keeps dividing in two. Liverworts like places that are very damp, such as rocky hollows and the banks of streams.

USES OF SEAWEED

You probably encounter seaweeds every day without knowing it. Extracts from seaweeds are often used to thicken ice cream. They are also used in soft drinks, glue, toothpastes—and even explosives. Seaweeds contain large amounts of useful minerals. They are sometimes harvested and used to make fertilizer.

Giant kelp is clamped to the sea bottom by a rootlike anchor called a holdfast.

Carrageenan and alginate from seaweeds are used as thickeners in foods.

Mosses are anchored with rootlike hairs called rhizoids.

MOSSES

A clump of moss is made up of a number of plants growing closely together. Mosses release their spores from capsules held on little stalks. You can sometimes see these capsules if you look closely.

Find out more

CELLS P. 338
PHOTOSYNTHESIS P. 340
TRANSPORT IN PLANTS P. 341
CELLULAR RESPIRATION P. 346
ASEXUAL REPRODUCTION P. 366
SEXUAL REPRODUCTION P. 367
FACT FINDER P. 420

CONIFERS

YOU WILL NEVER SEE a conifer with flowers, and it does not grow from spores. So how does a conifer reproduce? The answer is that it forms cones. Each cone makes either male or female cells, and the male cells are carried to the female ones to produce seeds. Conifers were among the first plants to make seeds. Unlike spores, these seeds are complete with their own food supply. There are about 550 species of conifer, and nearly all of them are trees, such as firs and pines. Most have narrow, tough leaves known as scales or needles, and many are good at coping with severe cold. In parts of the world that have hard winters, conifers can form forests that stretch from one horizon to another.

MONKEY PUZZLE
The Chile pine (*Araucaria auracana*), also known as the monkey puzzle, is an unusual conifer that comes from South America. It has sharp, leathery leaves, and the male and female cones grow on separate trees.

CONES AND SEEDS
Mature seed-bearing cones grow in many shapes and sizes. Most are woody, but some are soft and look like berries. The cones of pines and spruces usually fall to the ground in one piece, but the cones of cedars and firs slowly break up while still on the tree.

Scales close in damp weather.

Pine cone scales open in dry weather to release the seeds.

Each scale protects a pair of winged seeds.

AMBER TRAP
This spider is millions of years old. It has been preserved in amber—the fossilized remains of a sap called resin. Resin is extremely sticky, and conifers use it to stop small animals from eating their wood. If a conifer's bark is wounded, resin oozes out, trapping any insects or spiders that it touches.

*Yew (*Taxus baccata*) has flat needles that grow on opposite sides of the stems.*

ANCIENT PINES
The North American bristlecone pines (*Pinus longaeva*) are the world's oldest living trees. Some surviving examples took root more than 6,000 years ago! Scientists study the width of growth rings in their wood to see how the world's climate has changed.

Each soft male cone sheds millions of pollen grains (male cells) into the air.

Young female cones sit upright on the branches. Their female cells are fertilized by male pollen grains that fall on them from the air.

Mature female cones hang from the branches. When the winged seeds are released, they flutter away.

Life cycle of a typical conifer

Adult tree

Seed inside cone

Cone

Ovule

Pollen

Fertilization

SITKA SPRUCE
The Sitka spruce (*Picea sitchensis*) is a North American conifer that is now grown in plantations all over the world—both for lumber and for making paper. The male and female cones grow on the same tree. Spruces are easy to recognize because their stiff needles are attached to small pegs on the branches. You can feel these pegs on an old branch that has shed its leaves.

CONIFER LEAVES
Most conifers have small, leathery leaves that stay on the tree for a year or more. Not all these leaves are needle-shaped. Many are short and flat, and are known as scales. A few conifers shed their leaves in the fall. These include the larches (*Larix species*) and also the swamp cypress (*Taxodium distichum*).

Scots pine (Pinus sylvestris) has narrow needles that grow in pairs.

The needles of the larch (Larix decidua) grow in bunches. They fall in autumn.

Giant sequoia (Sequoiadendron giganteum) has tiny, scalelike leaves that lie almost flat against the stems.

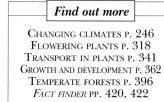

Find out more

CHANGING CLIMATES P. 246
FLOWERING PLANTS P. 318
TRANSPORT IN PLANTS P. 341
GROWTH AND DEVELOPMENT P. 362
TEMPERATE FORESTS P. 396
FACT FINDER PP. 420, 422

FLOWERING PLANTS

WE ALL LOVE the beautiful shapes, colors, and scents of flowers. But flowers have not evolved for our pleasure. They have developed as a way of spreading pollen (male cells) to other flowers of their own kind. Flowers receive pollen so that their own ovules (female egg cells) can be fertilized. There are more than 250,000 species of flowering plant on Earth, and these are divided into two main groups: monocotyledons and dicotyledons. Monocotyledons have one cotyledon (a special leaf packed inside the seed), and long adult leaves with parallel veins. Dicotyledons have two cotyledons and adult leaves with a branching network of veins.

Pollen from other flowers is collected by the stigma. A poppy flower cannot fertilize itself with its own pollen.

Pollen is produced by the anthers. Insect visitors eat some of the pollen, and carry the rest to other flowers.

Bright petals attract bees, beetles, and flies to the poppy flower.

Flower buds are protected by two scales called sepals. These fall off as the flower opens. Each common poppy flower lasts for one day.

Cucumber plant

Male flower

WIND POLLINATION
Grasses are pollinated by the wind. Their anthers dangle in the air so that the pollen is blown away. Grasses make up one of the largest families of monocotyledon plants.

Female flower with long ovary

SEPARATE SEXES
Unlike the poppy flower, which contains both male and female parts, the cucumber plant (*Cucumis sativus*) has separate male and female flowers. Kiwi fruit plants (*Actinidia chinensis*) are either male or female.

TREES AND FLOWERS
A tree is a plant with a single tall, woody stem. Some trees are conifers. Hundreds of others are broadleaved (flowering) plants. Cherry trees belong to the rose family of flowering plants.

Flowering cherry tree (*Prunus serrulata*)

The poppy is a dicotyledon, and has net-veined leaves. Like many dicotyledons, it also has four petals.

PARASITIC PLANTS
Some plants get all or part of their food by stealing it from others. The roots of mistletoe (*Viscum album*) penetrate the wood on trees, and take water and mineral salts from the tree. But because mistletoe has green leaves, it can also make its own food from sunlight. The *Rafflesia* plant, the giant flower of which is shown on the opposite page, is completely parasitic.

Yellow, disk florets produce pollen and egg cells.

Ray florets

MANY FLOWERS IN ONE
A daisy (*Bellis perennis*) is not a single flower. The flowerhead is made of many tiny flowers called florets, packed together. It is a composite flower. The disk florets in the middle are yellow and tubular. The ray florets around the edge have a single white petal each.

COMMON POPPY
The common poppy (*Papaver rhoeas*) is a typical annual flowering plant. It flowers, sets seed, and dies in a single season. Annual plants grow rapidly, and are quick to make use of any patch of bare ground. Once the seeds are scattered, they remain dormant (inactive) until conditions are right for germination. This can sometimes take several years. Perennial plants live for more than one season. They have well-developed roots, and often store food underground in bulbs or tubers. Some perennials flower just once, but most flower every year.

INSECT POLLINATION

Compared to a poppy, a foxglove (*Digitalis purpurea*) has very complicated flowers. The petals are joined together to form a tube, and the male and female parts of the flower lie under the tube's roof. This shape has evolved so that one kind of insect, a bumblebee, can pollinate the flower. The anthers and stigma in each flower mature at different times, so a foxglove cannot pollinate itself. When a bumblebee enters the flower, it either collects pollen off the ripe male anther, or brushes pollen from another flower onto the ripe female stigma. When the bee visits another flower, the process is repeated.

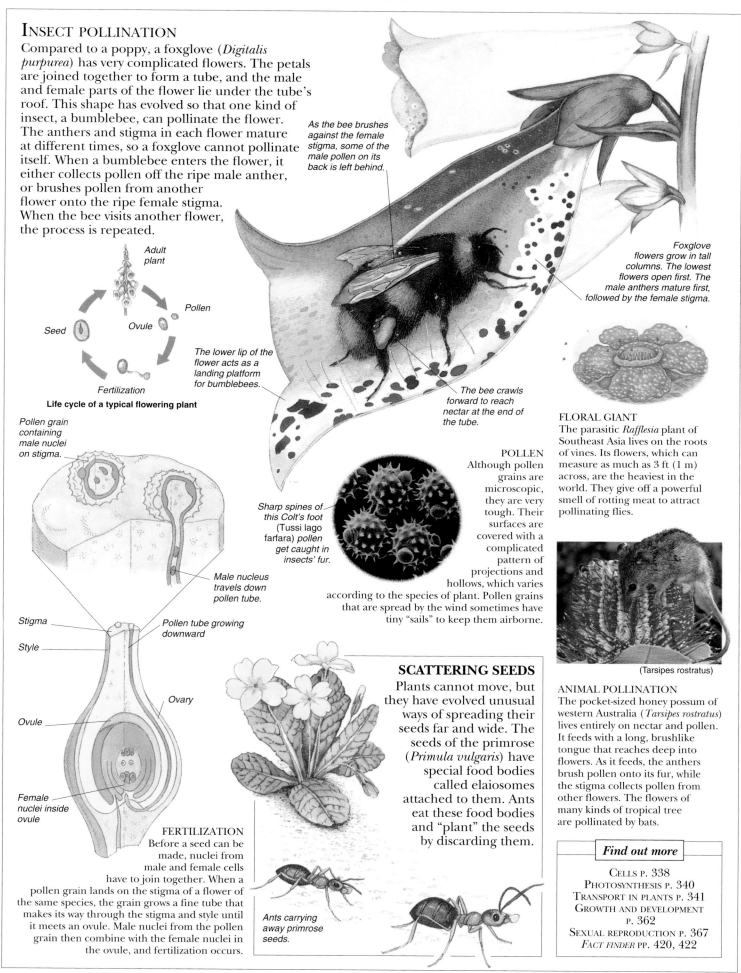

As the bee brushes against the female stigma, some of the male pollen on its back is left behind.

Foxglove flowers grow in tall columns. The lowest flowers open first. The male anthers mature first, followed by the female stigma.

The lower lip of the flower acts as a landing platform for bumblebees.

The bee crawls forward to reach nectar at the end of the tube.

Adult plant

Pollen

Ovule

Seed

Fertilization

Life cycle of a typical flowering plant

Pollen grain containing male nuclei on stigma.

Male nucleus travels down pollen tube.

Stigma

Style

Pollen tube growing downward

Ovary

Ovule

Female nuclei inside ovule

Sharp spines of this Colt's foot (*Tussi lago farfara*) pollen get caught in insects' fur.

POLLEN

Although pollen grains are microscopic, they are very tough. Their surfaces are covered with a complicated pattern of projections and hollows, which varies according to the species of plant. Pollen grains that are spread by the wind sometimes have tiny "sails" to keep them airborne.

FLORAL GIANT

The parasitic *Rafflesia* plant of Southeast Asia lives on the roots of vines. Its flowers, which can measure as much as 3 ft (1 m) across, are the heaviest in the world. They give off a powerful smell of rotting meat to attract pollinating flies.

(Tarsipes rostratus)

ANIMAL POLLINATION

The pocket-sized honey possum of western Australia (*Tarsipes rostratus*) lives entirely on nectar and pollen. It feeds with a long, brushlike tongue that reaches deep into flowers. As it feeds, the anthers brush pollen onto its fur, while the stigma collects pollen from other flowers. The flowers of many kinds of tropical tree are pollinated by bats.

SCATTERING SEEDS

Plants cannot move, but they have evolved unusual ways of spreading their seeds far and wide. The seeds of the primrose (*Primula vulgaris*) have special food bodies called elaiosomes attached to them. Ants eat these food bodies and "plant" the seeds by discarding them.

FERTILIZATION

Before a seed can be made, nuclei from male and female cells have to join together. When a pollen grain lands on the stigma of a flower of the same species, the grain grows a fine tube that makes its way through the stigma and style until it meets an ovule. Male nuclei from the pollen grain then combine with the female nuclei in the ovule, and fertilization occurs.

Ants carrying away primrose seeds.

Find out more

CELLS P. 338
PHOTOSYNTHESIS P. 340
TRANSPORT IN PLANTS P. 341
GROWTH AND DEVELOPMENT P. 362
SEXUAL REPRODUCTION P. 367
FACT FINDER PP. 420, 422

JELLYFISH, ANEMONES, AND CORALS

JELLYFISH, SEA ANEMONES, AND SPONGES are all invertebrates (without a backbone). Invertebrates make up about 97 percent of the animal species on Earth. They have evolved a great range of body forms and many different ways of feeding and reproducing. Many invertebrates live in water. Some spend their adult lives swimming or drifting with the current, while others stay anchored to one spot. Bryozoans (mosslike animals) and sponges filter food from the water. Jellyfish, sea anemones, and corals—which belong to a group of animals called the cnidarians—attack their food with tiny stinging threads. They all have circular bodies without a head or a tail, and a digestive cavity with only one opening.

BRYOZOAN COLONY
Without a microscope, a bryozoan colony looks like a plant. It is actually a collection of thousands of tiny animals. Each one lives in a hard case and traps food with a ring of tentacles. If disturbed, a bryozoan pulls in its tentacles and shuts the case.

Float is a single, gas-filled polyp that acts like a sail.

SPONGES
Do you realize that some bath sponges were once living animals in the sea? A living sponge is lined with special cells that work like pumps. Water flows in through the holes in the sponge and out through a vent. Any food in the water is trapped by tiny sieves and then absorbed.

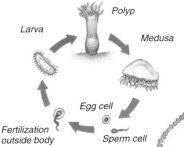

Polyp

Larva

Medusa

Egg cell

Fertilization outside body

Sperm cell

Life cycle of a typical cnidarian

The man-o'-war's tentacles reach up to 65 ft (20 m) when they are fully extended. If a tentacle catches a fish, it contracts and pulls the food upward.

The man-o'-war (*Physalia physalia*) is a typical cnidarian.

CNIDARIANS
The blue, baglike float of the man-o'-war spells danger for sea animals, and for any swimmer who ventures too close. A true jellyfish is a single animal that moves through the water with a pulsating motion. But a man-o'-war is a floating colony of many animals called polyps, which live and work together. Some of these polyps form long tentacles that sting prey and haul it in. Some specialize in digesting food, while other polyps take care of reproduction.

HOW A JELLYFISH STINGS
The tentacles of a jellyfish are covered with special cells that contain tightly coiled stinging threads called nematocysts. If a passing animal brushes one of these cells, the nematocysts explode outward. Within a fraction of a second, the threads turn inside out and stab the victim with their sharp tips. Most nematocysts inject a poison, but some wrap themselves around the prey to prevent it from escaping.

Sea anemones live singly or in small groups.

Out of water

Under water

SEA ANEMONES
If you explore a rocky shore at low tide, you may sometimes find small, jellylike blobs attached to rocks. These are probably sea anemones. A sea anemone grips the rock with a suckerlike disk. When it is under water, it spreads out its ring of tentacles to catch passing animals, which it attacks with nematocysts (stinging threads). As the tide goes out, the anemone withdraws its tentacles to prevent them from drying out.

Nematocyst explodes outward.

Nematocyst coiled inside cell.

CORALS
Some corals live on their own. Others grow in large colonies and very slowly build up, layer upon layer, to make coral reefs. A coral usually feeds at night. It catches food particles with its tentacles and pulls them into its digestive cavity.

WORKS

IF YOU WALK on a beach at low tide, you may notice coils of muddy sand that look like toothpaste squirted out of a tube. These are the feeding remains of lugworms, which are hidden beneath the surface. Lugworms are animals that have a long body divided into many sections. Like earthworms and leeches, they are members of a group of animals called the annelids (segmented worms). Annelids make up a small fraction of the animals we call worms, all of which are invertebrates. Two other large groups of worms, the platyhelminths (flatworms) and nematodes (roundworms), do not have segmented bodies. Many of these worms live as parasites, feeding inside other animals. Parasitic worms are common in wild animals, but they also infest farm animals and pets. Some cause diseases in humans, such as river blindness and elephantiasis.

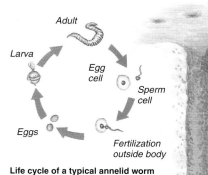

Adult
Larva
Egg cell
Sperm cell
Eggs
Fertilization outside body

Life cycle of a typical annelid worm

Annelids that live on land usually develop inside the egg and hatch as fully formed worms.

ANNELIDS

A lugworm (*Arenicola maritima*) is a segmented worm that spends most of its life in a U-shaped burrow that it digs in muddy sand. It lines this with mucus to prevent it from collapsing and feeds by pumping water through the burrow. The worm swallows particles that are carried in by the water, and digests any organic matter that they contain. From time to time, it reverses up the burrow until its tail meets the surface, where it ejects waste sand and mud. It is this waste matter that forms a cast on the surface.

Waste sand and mud

Detail of tapeworm's head
Hooks
Suckers

PLATYHELMINTHS
The flat body of a tapeworm is like a long egg-making machine. The worm lives in the intestines of animals called hosts, such as cats and dogs, and hangs on by the suckers and hooks on its head. The tapeworm absorbs food from its host and releases eggs in packets that break off from its body.

Earthworms help to keep soil fertile. As they burrow, they mix the soil layers and allow air and water to soak in.

GIANT EARTHWORM
Australia is the home of the giant earthworm (*Megascolides australis*), which can reach a length of over 10 ft (3 m). These worms live in the same way as their smaller relatives—by swallowing soil and digesting the organic matter it contains.

SEA MOUSE
The segmented sea mouse (*Aphrodite aculeata*) is a very unwormlike worm. It is about the size of an adult's hand and has a broad, flat body fringed with bristles. Sea mice burrow through mud and sand on the seabed, eating any small animals they find on the way.

LEECH TREATMENT
A leech has a segmented body with a sucker at each end. Many species of leech feed on blood. When a leech bites, it produces a chemical that stops blood from clotting. Leeches were once used by doctors to drain blood from patients.

A leech can rapidly take in three or four times its own weight in blood.

RIFTIA WORMS
Giant riftia worms like these were only seen for the first time in 1977. They live around vents on the seabed, where volcanically heated water gushes out of the Earth's crust. The worms contain bacteria that obtain energy from chemicals in the water.

*Human roundworms (*Ascaris lumbricoides*)*

NEMATODES
Roundworms live either as parasites or as independent animals. They are often hidden away and exist in vast numbers in soil and in plants. Biologists often say that if all the trees in a forest were taken away, but the roundworms from the trees left behind, you would still be able to see the outline of the forest.

Find out more
SKELETONS P. 352
NERVES P. 360
GROWTH AND DEVELOPMENT P. 363
SEXUAL REPRODUCTION P. 367
OCEANS P. 386
FACT FINDER P. 420

ARTHROPODS

THE LARGEST GROUP of invertebrates is made up of arthropods—animals that have a segmented body and an exoskeleton (hard case on the outside). This case has special hinges that bend so that its owner can move. As an arthropod grows, it molts (sheds its case) from time to time so that its body can expand. Well over a million species of arthropods are known to biologists, making this the largest group of animal species on Earth. Of these species, nearly 90 percent are insects. The remainder of arthropods are either arachnids (mainly spiders), crustaceans—such as crabs and lobsters—or diplopods (millipedes) and chilopods (centipedes).

Giant spider crabs live on the seabed. Their body cases are reinforced with calcium, making them hard and very strong.

Arthropods do not have internal skeletons.

Life cycle of a typical crustacean

Adult

Larva

Egg cell

Sperm cell

Eggs

Fertilization outside body

CRUSTACEANS

Most crustaceans live in the sea. Sea-dwelling crustaceans can grow bigger than arthropods that live on land because their big body cases are supported by the water. The largest crustaceans of all are spider crabs (*Macrocheira kaempferi*), which can measure up to 11 ft (3.5 m) with their legs stretched out. But not all crustaceans are as big as this. The water fleas that live in freshwater are also crustaceans, but they are about the size of the period at the end of this sentence. A few crustaceans, including woodlice, live on land and breathe air, but they usually need damp conditions.

The centipede's first pair of legs are modified to act as a pair of poisonous fangs.

A millipede's body is made up of many ring-shaped segments. Each segment has two pairs of legs.

DIPLOPODS AND CHILOPODS

From a distance, centipedes and millipedes look very similar. But if you look more closely, it is easy to tell them apart. A centipede has just one pair of legs on each body segment, while a millipede has two. Centipedes are hunters. They paralyze their prey with poisonous fangs. Millipedes live on decaying plants. Both animals prefer dark, moist areas.

SCORPIONS

Some arachnids look after their young until they can fend for themselves. A female scorpion gives birth to fully formed young. The tiny scorpions climb onto their mother's back, where they are protected by the poisonous sting in her tail. After they have shed their skin for the first time, the young scorpions climb down from their perch.

The bolas spider hunts with a glue-tipped thread instead of a web.

ARACHNIDS

Spiders, scorpions, ticks, and mites make up a group of arthropods called the arachnids. Nearly all arachnids live on land and most of them are hunters. Bolas spiders hunt by whirling a silk thread tipped with glue around in the air. If the glue sticks to a passing insect, the spider pulls it in.

A spider begins its web by stretching strands of silk between solid supports. It climbs along the silk using the hooks and bristles on its feet.

The spider spins around and around in a spiral until the web is finished. The web is covered with blobs of glue that trap insects.

SPINNING A WEB

A spider builds its web out of silk, which is rich in protein. The silk is formed by special glands in the spider's abdomen and is squeezed out through tiny nozzles called spinnerets. The liquid silk solidifies when it meets the air. An orb (round) web like this one can take up to an hour to make.

INSECTS

Insects have been very successful on land, mainly because they have evolved the ability to fly. Insects with wings can travel larger distances than wingless insects, and so can find more food. A wasp is a typical flying insect. Its body is divided into three sections—the head, thorax, and abdomen. It also has two pairs of wings. Like beetles and butterflies, a wasp undergoes a complete metamorphosis (change in shape). Young wasps are raised in a nest by adults, but the young of most insects must fend for themselves. Insect parents and young often live in different habitats. An adult dragonfly lives in air, but a young dragonfly lives in water. Some insects spend their whole lives in water.

The head has a pair of large compound eyes and a pair of antennae (feelers). The mouthparts cut up food and chew wood into pulp for making the nest.

Head

Thorax

Abdomen

Each nest contains a single queen wasp who lays eggs. The other wasps are her offspring. They collect food and look after the eggs and young.

Hind wings of wasps and bees are attached to the forewings by tiny hooks.

Adult

Pupa

Egg cell

Sperm cell

Larva

Fertilization inside body

Eggs

This life cycle is typical of insects that undergo complete metamorphosis.

Life cycle of a typical insect

INSECTICIDES
Some insects are very useful because they pollinate flowering plants. But others are voracious plant-eaters that cause tremendous damage to crops. Farmers often spray fields with insecticides to prevent insect damage. Unfortunately, these chemicals often kill helpful insects as well as the harmful ones.

WINGLESS INSECTS
Despite its name, the silverfish is not a fish at all, but a small, wingless insect. There are about 300 species of silverfish. Like other wingless insects, silverfish feed mainly on dead plants. They sometimes live indoors, where they eat leftover food.

BOMBARDIER BEETLE
The insect world is full of animals that have unusual ways of repelling attackers. If a bombardier beetle is threatened, it tucks up its abdomen and mixes together a brew of special chemicals. These react with each other and explode out of the beetle, giving the attacker a hot, poisonous shower.

Wings of praying mantis look like leaves.

Legs look like stems

Sharp spines on the legs grip the trapped insect.

MANTIS ATTACK
A praying mantis relies on stealth and camouflage. A hunting mantis flutters onto a plant and folds up its wings. It then waits. If another insect comes within striking range, the mantis stabs it with its front legs. The legs have sharp spines that grip the insect so that it cannot escape the jaws of its predator.

JEAN-HENRI FABRE
Fabre (1823–1915) was a French entomologist (scientist who studies insects). He researched insect life extensively and described his work in a series of books. Fabre's observations, and his gift for writing and painting, helped to create great interest in the insect world.

Find out more
VISION P. 204
FLOWERING PLANTS P. 318
BLOOD P. 348
GROWTH AND DEVELOPMENT P. 362
SKELETONS P. 352
MOVEMENT P. 356
SEXUAL REPRODUCTION P. 367
FACT FINDER PP. 420, 422

MOLLUSKS

MOLLUSKS MAKE UP the second-largest group of invertebrates. There are more than 90,000 species of mollusk, most of which live in water, although some live on land and breathe air. All mollusks have a soft body, which is often protected by a hard shell. There are three main groups of mollusk. Gastropods, which include limpets, snails, and whelks, usually have a coiled or pyramid-shaped shell. Bivalves, such as clams and mussels, have a shell that is made of two parts joined by a hinge. Slugs are gastropod mollusks, but they usually do not have shells. The third group, cephalopods, which includes octopuses and squids, have a small shell that is hidden inside their bodies.

MATING SLUGS
These two slugs are mating as they hang from a thread of mucus. Each slug is hermaphrodite (both male and female). When slugs mate, they exchange sperm through special organs, and each slug then lays eggs. Being hermaphrodite is not unusual in the mollusk world. Some mollusks even start life as one sex and then change to another.

Great slug (*Limax maximus*)

Shell coils in clockwise direction.

Siphon

Tentacles

Large, muscular foot

Adult

Larva

Egg cell

Sperm cell

Fertilization outside body

Eggs

Life cycle of a typical mollusk

Land snails have internal fertilization. Their young develop inside the egg and hatch as miniature snails.

GASTROPODS

The common whelk (*Buccinium undatum*) is a typical gastropod ("stomach-foot") mollusk. It has a large, muscular foot and a shell that coils in a clockwise direction. Only a few gastropod shells coil in the other direction. The whelk's shell is made by a special body layer called the mantle. The whelk lives under water and breathes using gills. The siphon on top of its head funnels water into the chamber that contains the gills.

KILLER CONE
Cone shells are gastropods that attack their prey with a deadly poison. If an animal comes within range, the cone flicks out its proboscis (tubular mouthpart). This stabs the victim like a harpoon and injects a paralyzing poison. The poison of some cones is powerful enough to kill humans.

CEPHALOPODS

Giant squids are the largest cephalopod mollusks. They are also the largest invertebrate animals. Giant squids live in the depths of the sea, where they catch their prey with sucker-covered tentacles. There are many stories about giant squids, but little is really known about them. The largest specimens found measure over 50 ft (15 m).

Common octopus (*Octopus vulgaris*)

INTELLIGENT MOLLUSK

Octopuses have good eyesight and large brains. They are probably the most intelligent of all invertebrate animals. They can remember shapes and colors and are able to figure out quickly how to reach food. Like squids, octopuses can move fast by squirting a jet of water backward through a funnel.

Common mussel (*Mytilus edulis*)

BIVALVES

Mussels spend most of their lives anchored to rocks by very tough silklike threads. Like most bivalves, they pump water through their gills and feed on the small food particles that become trapped as the water flows past. Some bivalves can burrow and move around. A few—like the scallop—can even swim.

Find out more

SKELETONS P. 352
MOVEMENT P. 356
BRAINS P. 361
GROWTH AND DEVELOPMENT P. 362
SEXUAL REPRODUCTION P. 367
FACT FINDER P. 420

STARFISH AND SEA SQUIRTS

STARFISH AND THEIR RELATIVES, which include sea urchins and sea cucumbers, make up a group of invertebrate creatures called echinoderms ("spiny skins"). Echinoderms have a skelton made of chalky plates and are easy to recognize because their bodies are divided into five similar body parts. A starfish, for example, usually has five arms. It also has five sets of reproductive organs and a digestive system made up of five branches. Sea squirts belong to a different group of animals, the tunicates. They have soft, baglike bodies and tadpole-shaped larvae.

Adult

Egg cell

Larva

Sperm cell

Eggs

Fertilization outside the body

Life cycle of a typical echinoderm

If a starfish loses an arm, it regenerates (grows back).

Tips of tentacles are sensitive to light. This helps the starfish to find shady crevices in which to shelter.

Anus

TUBE FEET
The underside of a starfish's arms carry two rows of water-filled tube feet connected by a system of internal canals. Each tube foot ends in a sucker and can be moved independently. The starfish uses its tube feet to move and to hold its prey.

Shallow water starfish

ECHINODERMS
Like all echinoderms, starfish have a skeleton made of chalky plates covered by a thin layer of cells. The plates have small bumps and spines, as well as tiny pincers that stop animals from settling on the starfish's body. The plates are hinged to allow the starfish to bend. A starfish's mouth is on the underside of its body. When it feeds, the starfish pushes its stomach out through its mouth, turning it inside out.

Water expelled here

Water sucked in here

Larvae have a notochord—a structure that is related to the backbones of vertebrate animals.

Brittle star

Crown-of-thorns starfish

Feather star

STARFISH SHAPES
There are about 2,000 species of ordinary starfish. Like all echinoderms, they live only in seawater. The starfish of shores and shallow water feed mainly on living animals. They use their tube feet to prise open the shells of bivalve mollusks and feed by pushing their stomachs between the shell halves. Brittle stars and feather stars live in deeper water. They use their long tube feet to collect tiny particles of food, which they then push to their central mouth.

Cushion star

TUNICATES
Adult sea squirts are small animals that filter food from seawater. They live either singly or in groups, usually attached to rocks. Their larvae are free-swimming and look very different. They are shaped like tadpoles.

Tube feet project through holes.

Sand dollars live on the seabed in shallow water and feed by collecting small edible particles.

Test (skeleton)

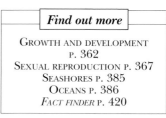

SAND DOLLARS
A sand dollar is a sea urchin that has short spines and a very flattened skeleton (test), making it look like a cookie or a large coin. When the spines have rubbed off after death, you can see an intricate pattern of holes where the tube feet once poked out.

SEA URCHINS
Sea urchins look very different from starfish, but underneath their spines they also have a body divided into five similar parts. A sea urchin has a rounded test (skeleton), with a mouth on the underside. It feeds by creeping over rocks and scraping off small plants and animals with its five teeth.

| **Find out more** |
| GROWTH AND DEVELOPMENT P. 362 |
| SEXUAL REPRODUCTION P. 367 |
| SEASHORES P. 385 |
| OCEANS P. 386 |
| FACT FINDER P. 420 |

FISH

STRANGE ARMORED ANIMALS called ostracoderms swam in the world's seas more than 400 million years ago. They did not have jaws or fins, but they did have backbones, making them the first vertebrates (animals with a backbone) on Earth. Today, their aquatic descendants—fish—live throughout the world's seas, lakes, and rivers. Fish are ectothermic (cold-blooded)— their body temperature changes according to their surroundings. The colder the surroundings, the less active they are. There are more than 21,000 species of fish. Most have jaws. Their bodies are streamlined and are usually covered with scales. Fish absorb dissolved oxygen from water through gills.

SHARK'S TEETH
A shark's teeth are larger, sharper versions of the scales that cover its body. The teeth grow on a nonstop production line that starts at the back of the jaw. Each tooth gradually swings forward until it reaches the front of the mouth. If it breaks off, it is soon replaced by the tooth behind it.

CARTILAGINOUS FISH
Sharks, rays, and skates have skeletons that are made of cartilage (gristle) instead of bone. There are about 700 species of cartilaginous fish and nearly all of them are predators that live in saltwater. Cartilaginous fish have a streamlined shape and paired fins. Their skin is covered in placoid (toothlike) scales that gives them a rough texture.

Paired pectoral fins used for steering.

Overlapping placoid scales

Eggcase hooked around seaweed

DOGFISH
Dogfish are small sharks that live in shallow water. The male mates with the female, fertilizing her eggs while they are inside her body. The female then lays her eggs in leathery cases that hook around seaweed. The parent dogfish do not guard the eggs.

Asymmetric (irregular) caudal (tail) fin shape is a characteristic feature of sharks.

Single dorsal fin

Gill arch. As the shark moves forward, the gills absorb oxygen from the water.

Good sense of smell helps the shark to find its food.

Spiral valve gives intestine large surface area for absorbing food.

Intestine

Stomach

Heart

Large, oil-filled liver acts as a float.

Wide jaws armed with many rows of teeth.

INSIDE A SHARK
Most of a shark's body is made up of the muscles that it uses to swim. As in all vertebrates, these are arranged in blocks called myotomes. Part of a shark's intestine is coiled into a spiral, which gives the short intestine a large surface area for absorbing food. The shark's large liver helps to keep it afloat.

JAWLESS FISH
This group, which includes lampreys and hagfish, has some features in common with the very first fish. They do not have jaws or paired fins, and their gills have openings like portholes, rather than slits. There are only about 70 species of jawless fish. Adult lampreys live parasitically on other fish, while young lampreys filter particles of food from water.

An adult lamprey has a mouth that is ringed with hooks. It clamps itself to another fish and sucks its blood.

FISH SPEEDS
Generally, the more streamlined a fish is, the faster it swims. Most fish swim faster than humans, who have an average speed of 4 mph (6 km/h) over a short distance.

Human 4 mph (6 km/h)

Salmon 10 mph (17 km/h)

Blue shark 40 mph (64 km/h)

Marlin 50 mph (80 km/h)

BONY FISH

This trout, and all the other fish shown on this page, belong to a group called the bony fish—the largest of the three groups of fish. These fish have bony skeletons, and a special gas-filled bag, called a swim bladder, which works like an inbuilt float. Their bodies are usually covered with cycloid (slippery, flat) scales, and their gills are tucked away behind a flap called an operculum. During the last 250 million years, bony fish have evolved an amazing variety of shapes and sizes.

Adult

Egg cell

Sperm cell

Fertilization outside body

Eggs

Life cycle of a typical bony fish

Most cartilaginious fish have internal fertilization. They lay eggs, or give birth to live young.

Head covered by bony plates

Slippery overlapping scales reduce the friction between the moving fish and the water.

The trout's mouth can shoot open suddenly to suck in small animals.

The gills are covered by an operculum. This can open and close to help pump water over the gills.

Pectoral fins for steering.

Dorsal fin gives the fish stability.

Fins are reinforced by stiff rays. These can be moved independently, allowing the fish to change direction.

Heart

Liver

Stomach

Bony fish have long intestines without a spiral valve.

Bony fish have regular caudal fins. The caudal fin pushes the fish forward.

Anal fin gives the fish stability.

The swim bladder is a gas-filled bag. It adjusts to give the fish neutral buoyancy, so that it does not rise or sink.

Special sensors in the lateral line (fluid-filled tube on each side of the body under the skin) detect movement in the water caused by currents and other animals.

FISH THAT FLY

A flying fish (*Cypselurus heterurus*) escapes its enemies by launching itself into the air. It bursts through the surface of the sea and glides as far as 330 ft (100 m) before splashing back into the sea. A flying fish's "wings" are very enlarged fins. Some species glide using one pair of fins, while others, like this one, use two.

PORCUPINE FISH

The greatest danger for most fish is from other predator fish around them. When threatened, the porcupine fish (*Diodon hystrix*) protects itself by gulping water. This makes it swell up like a balloon, and its spines stand up on end. Although it can hardly swim when it is inflated, its spines make it almost impossible to attack.

SEAHORSES

Many bony fish lay vast numbers of eggs, but take no part in looking after their young. Seahorses are different. The female lays a small number of eggs in a special pouch on the male's abdomen. The male seahorse looks after the eggs until they hatch and continues to look after the young seahorses. Although seahorses lay fewer eggs, each one has a better chance of survival.

Eels have paired pectoral fins, but no pelvic fins.

White's seahorse (Hippocampus whitei)

Red batfish (*Halieutaea stellata*)

DEEP-SEA FISH

There is no light or plant life at the bottom of the sea. Everything that lives here has to feed either on "leftovers" that fall from above, or on other animals. The batfishes are among the strangest fish of the seabed. They eat invertebrates and small fish, and shuffle foward using their fins.

EELS

Some eels look like snakes, but their fins and gills show that they are fish. The green moray (*Gymnothorax prasinus*) is a typical eel. It lurks in rocky hideouts and attacks passing animals with its sharp teeth. Eels start life as tiny larvae that look very different from adults. It can take several years for a larva to develop into an adult.

Find out more

BREATHING P. 347
CIRCULATION P. 349
INTERNAL ENVIRONMENT P. 350
SKIN P. 354
MOVEMENT P. 356
SENSES P. 358
FACT FINDER PP. 420, 422

AMPHIBIANS

AMPHIBIANS HAVE A SPECIAL PLACE in the evolution of life on Earth. Their ancestors were the first vertebrates to emerge from water and spend some of their time on land. Most of today's 4,000 species of amphibian still divide their time between water and land, but in different ways. A few amphibians, such as the axolotl, spend nearly all their lives in water, but most spend their adult lives on land and return to water only to breed. Amphibians do not usually have scales, and their skin is generally loose-fitting and moist. All amphibians are ectothermic (cold-blooded) and are divided into three groups: the anurans (frogs and toads), the urodeles (newts and salamanders), and a small third group without legs, the caecilians, or apoda.

FLYING FROGS
The flying frog (*Rhacophorus nigropalmatus*) hunts for small animals on trees in Southeast Asia. To move from one tree to another, it launches itself into the air. The frog spreads out its webbed feet—which work like small parachutes—and angles them to steer as it glides.

Thin, moist skin absorbs oxygen.

Eyes and nostrils are above water when rest of the body is submerged.

Large mouth without teeth

Strong back legs for jumping

Back legs have five toes.

Front legs have four toes.

Adult

Tadpole larva

Egg cell

Sperm cell

Eggs (spawn)

Fertilization outside body

Life cycle of a typical amphibian

ANURANS
Amphibians in this group have short bodies, strong legs, and no tails. This South African bullfrog (*Pyxicephalus adspersus*) is a powerful predator. It feeds on small mammals and reptiles and also on smaller frogs. Like all frogs, it has a thin skin that has to be kept moist. Toads usually have drier skins and are usually covered with warts. On land, frogs usually move by hopping, while toads often walk. Frogs and toads both have simple, internal lungs.

Poison is secreted by glands on the frog's skin.

WATER-HOLDING FROG
Some frogs and toads survive drought by burrowing underground and sealing themselves in a waterproof membrane. The Australian water-holding frog (*Cyclorana* species) spends most of its adult life underground. As soon as it rains, the frog breaks out of the membrane and digs its way to the surface.

POISON-ARROW FROGS
The thumb-sized poison-arrow frog (*Phyllobates terribilis*) that lives in the forests of Central and South America is one of the most dangerous of all amphibians. The frog's bright colors warn other animals that its skin produces a deadly poison. Forest Indians use this to make poison-tipped arrows that kill other animals.

EARLIEST AMPHIBIAN
The oldest amphibian fossils that have been discovered belong to a creature called *Ichthyostega*, which lived about 375 million years ago. This animal was about 3 ft (1 m) long. It had a streamlined, fishlike body, but strong legs that supported its weight on land.

Sturdy ribs supported the weight of internal organs.

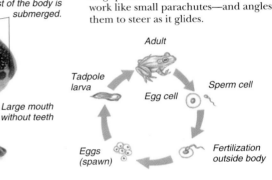

LOOKING AFTER EGGS
Most frogs and toads lay hundreds or thousands of eggs and then abandon them. Other species lay fewer eggs, but look after them more carefully. The male midwife toad (*Alytes obstetricans*) wraps the female's eggs around his legs. When the tadpoles are ready to hatch, he carries the eggs to water.

URODELES

These amphibians have longer bodies and smaller legs than anurans. Some have flattened tails that they use for swimming. The fire salamander (*Salamandra salamandra*) has bright colors for the same reason as the poison-arrow frog—to warn that its skin is poisonous. Newts and salamanders are found mainly in the Northern Hemisphere and they live in water or in damp places, such as the woodland floor. Fire salamanders mate on land. The eggs develop and hatch inside the mother's body.

Fire salamander's skin secretes a toxic chemical.

Unlike frogs and toads, newts and salamanders do not lose their tails as they grow up.

Salamanders have small toes and their feet are not webbed.

3. After a series of moves, the male settles in front of the female. When the female touches his tail, he deposits his sperm packet. The female drops down onto it so that the sperm are taken into her body.

2. The male then swims in front of the female and settles at right angles so that he is blocking her way. The male waves his tail, pumping his scent toward the female.

1. The smooth newt's underwater dance begins when the male approaches the female and touches her side-on. He is able to smell "scent" chemicals that she releases into the water.

COURTSHIP DANCE

When newts or salamanders mate, the male deposits a packet of sperm and the female picks it up. In the case of the fire salamander, the male carries the female and then lowers her onto his sperm packet so that the sperm are taken up into her body. The smooth newt (*Triturus vulgaris*), shown here, mates under water. The male dances in front of his partner before mating occurs.

Female

Male

CAECILIANS

Caecilians are aquatic or burrowing animals that live in the tropics. They have no legs, and their cylindrical shape makes them look more like worms or small, rubbery snakes than amphibians. But some caecilians lay eggs that develop into tadpoles with gills, linking them directly to salamanders and other amphibians.

Olm belongs to the urodeles group.

Most caecilians have a covering of keratin plates.

Although caecilians have eyes, they are nearly blind.

AXOLOTL

The axolotl (*Ambystoma mexicanum*) is sometimes called the "Peter Pan" of the amphibian world because it never grows up. Axolotls are salamanders that come from one particular lake in Mexico. Like many salamanders, they begin life as tadpoles with feathery gills. But instead of losing their gills and taking up life on land, axolotls usually stay in water and breed without changing shape.

LIFE IN THE DARK

The deep limestone caves of southern Europe are home to the olm (*Proteus anguinus*). This aquatic relative of salamanders has a pencil-thin body with tiny legs and is almost completely blind. Olms live in underground pools and rivers, where they feed on small water animals. A similar cave-dwelling salamander lives in the caves of southern Texas.

> ### Find out more
>
> CIRCULATION P. 349
> INTERNAL ENVIRONMENT P. 350
> SKIN P. 354
> MUSCLES P. 355
> BRAINS P. 361
> SEXUAL REPRODUCTION P. 367
> *FACT FINDER* PP. 420, 422

REPTILES

THERE ARE ABOUT 6,500 SPECIES of reptile alive today. Further back in time, there were many more. For about 200 million years, prehistoric reptiles dominated life on Earth, and they included the largest plant-eaters and predators ever to live on land—the dinosaurs. Reptiles were the first vertebrates to become fully adapted to life on land. They do not need moist conditions in which to live. Their dry, scaly skin stops them from losing too much body water and their eggs, which they lay on land, have thick, leathery shells that stop them from drying out. Because reptiles are ectothermic (cold-blooded), they usually live in warm parts of the world, where the Sun warms their bodies and makes them active.

The cobra's hollow fangs are positioned at the front of its mouth. It can squirt venom through the air toward an attacker.

Flexible ligaments and joints allow the two parts of the lower jaw to move apart during swallowing.

When threatened, the cobra spreads out the ribs behind its head.

Snakes sometimes have over 400 pairs of ribs, but usually just one working lung. A snake's kidneys lie one behind the other, so that they fit into the narrow body.

Like all reptiles, the boa is ectothermic. When cold, it basks in the sun. If it gets too hot, it retreats into the shade.

SQUAMATES

Today's reptiles are split into three major groups. By far the largest group is the squamates (snakes and lizards). Although snakes look very different from lizards, they probably evolved from lizardlike ancestors by gradually losing their legs. The Indian cobra (*Naja naja*) is a typical front-fanged snake. It kills its prey by injecting a poison and swallows its food whole. Cobras lay about 20 leathery eggs, and the female guards the eggs until they hatch.

Small, overlapping scales

BOA CONSTRICTOR
A boa constrictor (*Constrictor constrictor*) kills its prey by suffocating it. The snake coils its body around the victim, preventing it from breathing. The snake waits until its prey is completely dead before swallowing it head-first. Boas produce eggs, but the mother snake keeps them in her body until they are ready to hatch.

GIANT LIZARDS
The Komodo dragon (*Varanus komodensis*) is the world's largest lizard. An adult can measure nearly 10 ft (3 m) from head to tail and can weigh more than a person. Komodo dragons live on islands in Indonesia and feed on animals as large as deer.

Geckos have large eyes, like many nocturnal hunters.

SHEDDING SKIN

Lizards and snakes shed the outermost layer of their skin from time to time so that they can grow. This process often takes several days to complete. The skin starts to split around the head and then begins to peel away along the rest of the body. Snakes often shed their skin in a single piece.

This slow worm (Anguis fragilis) is shedding its skin in very large pieces.

DIVING LIZARD
The Galapagos Islands in the eastern Pacific are the home of the marine iguana (*Amblyrhynchus cristatus*), the only lizard that feeds in the sea. When a marine iguana dives, its heartbeat slows down. This helps it to save oxygen and also prevents too much of the iguana's blood from being chilled by the cold water outside.

Marine iguana feeds on algae growing on submerged rocks.

CLIMBING LIZARDS
Geckos are nocturnal lizards that hunt small insects. They can run up walls, and can even walk upside-down on ceilings. Geckos are able to do this because they have special pads on their toes. These are covered with tiny bristles that hook into small cracks on the surface they are climbing.

The crocodile swims by holding its legs close to its body and waving its flattened tail.

Although the estuarine crocodile is a fearsome predator, it is a careful and gentle parent.

CROCODILIANS

Crocodiles, together with their relatives the alligators, caimans, and gavials, belong to a group of reptiles called the crocodilians. Crocodiles look like giant lizards, but the arrangement of bones in their skulls shows that they are more closely related to dinosaurs than to any living reptile. There are about 21 species of crocodilian, and all live partly in water. The largest species, the estuarine or saltwater crocodile (*Crocodylus porosus*), can reach a length of nearly 20 ft (6 m), making it the biggest reptile in the world.

A crocodile's body is covered with large scales. The scales on the back are reinforced with bone to form armor plating.

The crocodile's nostrils are at the tip of its snout. It can close them when it dives.

Simple, peg-shaped teeth for tearing flesh

A mother crocodile carries her young to water in her mouth. She guards them for several months until they can fend for themselves.

Short, powerful legs

Life cycle of a typical reptile

Adult

Shelled egg

Egg cell

Sperm cell

Fertilization inside the body

The eggs of some reptiles develop inside the body. The young are born after hatching.

REPTILE SKULLS

The estuarine crocodile's skull is broad and its jaw muscles are extremely powerful. It feeds on large animals, dragging its prey underwater and tearing off pieces, which it swallows whole. The smaller gavial (*Gavialis gangeticus*), which lives in rivers in the Indian subcontinent, eats fish. Its skull has very narrow jaws, and it catches its food by snapping like a bird.

Skull of estuarine crocodile

Skull of gavial

Broad snout

Long, narrow snout with small, sharp teeth.

TUATARA

Tuataras are the only living descendants of the sphenodonts—a group of reptiles that were common millions of years ago. Unlike other reptiles, tuataras can remain active in quite low temperatures. Wild tuataras (*Sphenodon punctatus*) live under special protection on small islands off New Zealand.

A fully grown tuatara is about 2 ft (60 cm) long. Tuataras live in burrows and feed on insects, eggs, frogs, and young seabirds.

CHELONIANS

Tortoises, turtles, and terrapins make up a group of reptiles called chelonians. These animals usually have a bony shell covered in scales made of horn. Chelonians feed on both plants and small animals and have horn-covered jaws instead of teeth. This Galapagos tortoise (*Geochelone elephantopus*) is a giant species that can weigh as much as three people.

RULING REPTILES

Reptiles were once the most successful vertebrates on land. Dinosaurs ranged from chicken-sized animals to the giant herbivore *Brachiosaurus*. The dinosaurs, together with many other forms of life, died out during a mass extinction. Some scientists think this was caused by the impact of a giant meteorite.

This dinosaur is called Deinonychus.

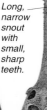

Find out more
BREATHING P. 347
INTERNAL ENVIRONMENT P. 350
SKELETONS P. 352
MOVEMENT P. 356
SENSES P. 358
SEXUAL REPRODUCTION P. 367
FACT FINDER PP. 420,422

BIRDS

FOSSIL EVIDENCE SHOWS that birds have evolved from reptiles. Like reptiles, birds are vertebrates that lay eggs with shells, but they have some features that reptiles do not have. Birds are the only animals that have feathers. They also have wings and beaks. Birds are endothermic (warm-blooded); the temperature of their body does not change with variations in external temperatures. Because a bird's body is warm, it is always ready to fly into action. In fact, birds are the most powerful fliers of all living things. There are about 9,000 species of bird. They live everywhere: in city centers, tropical rain forests, and ice floes.

Feathers have evolved from reptilian scales.

Wings have evolved from reptile forelimbs.

Feet are covered in scales.

Life cycle of a typical bird

Adult

Egg cell

Shelled egg

Sperm cell

Fertilization inside body

BIRD DESIGN
During the course of evolution, birds have developed bodies that are light, streamlined, and compact. This kingfisher (*Alcedo atthis*) is about 6 in (16 cm) long, but weighs just 1.5 oz (40 g). Like all birds, it has feathers. Its feet are covered in scales, and it has a hard but lightweight beak. Small birds like the kingfisher have the highest body temperatures of all animals. They need a constant supply of food to keep their bodies working.

Lungs are very efficient at extracting oxygen from the air.

Gullet

Kidney

Crop—temporary food store

Stomach

Gizzard

Heart

Liver

Intestine

INSIDE A BIRD
Birds do not have teeth, so they cannot chew their food. Instead, hard food is ground up in a special chamber called a gizzard. A bird's lungs are much more complicated than those of mammals or reptiles. When a bird breathes in, the air flows into special spaces called air sacs. It then travels through the lungs, and into more air sacs, before being breathed out.

Beak

Skull

Hollow wing bones

BIRD SKELETON
The delicate skeleton of a flying bird can make up as little as five percent of its total body weight. Although the wing bones are hollow, they are reinforced by struts to give them strength. The wing muscles are anchored by a bony flap, called a keel, which sticks out from the breastbone.

Keel

Ankle

Claws

BIRDS WITHOUT WINGS
The brown kiwi (*Apteryx australis*) from New Zealand is one of several birds that have lost the ability to fly. Its wings are tiny, and its feathers are hairlike. Unusually for a bird, the kiwi has a good sense of smell, which it uses to find food.

Courtship plumes from a wild turkey (Meleagris gallopavo). Each feather has two flexible shafts and short barbs.

Flight feather has strong shaft and tightly locking barbs and barbules.

Quill

Sail-shaped display feather from a mandarin duck (Aix galericulata) wing is used to attract females.

FEATHER CARE
Feathers need constant care to keep them in good condition. Birds use their beaks like combs to draw the barbs and barbules together and to remove lice and other parasites. Most birds molt (shed) their old feathers once or twice a year and grow a new set. This duck is spreading a special oil over its feathers that will keep them waterproof.

Down feathers insulate the body. The barbs do not hook together, but spread out to form a fluffy layer that traps air.

Body feathers streamline the body. The base of the feather is soft and fluffy, but the tip has a flatter surface.

FEATHERS
Feathers are made of keratin, the same substance that our hair and fingernails are made of. A quill that carries lots of side branches, called barbs, runs down the feather. The barbs have even smaller branches, called barbules, which hook together to form a single surface. A bird's plumage can contain over 10,000 feathers of several different types.

Brightly colored male chaffinch does not share the task of incubation. His colors would make it easier for a predator to spot the nest.

The female chaffinch incubates the eggs. She has a special area of bare skin, called a brood patch, on her front. This allows her body heat to warm the eggs.

The Gouldian finch (Chloebia gouldiae) has a typical seed-eater's beak— short, sharply pointed, and strong. The finch uses it for cracking open seed husks.

The beak of the greater flamingo (Phoenicopterus ruber) works like a sieve. The lower bill moves up and down to pump water against the top bill, where a fringe of slits traps the food.

NEST OF EGGS

A young bird develops outside its mother's body, inside an egg. It is protected by a hard shell that stops water from escaping, but that allows oxygen in. Small birds like this chaffinch (*Fringilla coelebs*) lay several eggs in a nest. The young birds do not develop unless the female warms them by incubating them (sitting on them).

Nest chamber

The avocet (Recurvirostra avosetta) is one of the few birds that has an upturned beak. It swings it from side to side to catch small animals in water.

African weaver birds (Ploceus species) are famous for their crafted nests. Each nest is made by the male, who weaves blades of grass with his beak and feet. When the nest is finished, he hangs below it and flutters his wings to attract a female.

Entrance

Entrance tube

The rufous ovenbird (Furnarius rufus) from South America builds a football-sized nest from mud, which hardens as it dries. The nest has a curved corridor that leads to an inner chamber.

Parrots (Psittacidae family) live almost entirely on fruit and seeds. A parrot cracks open the seeds with the base of its powerful beak and grasps fruit with the hook at the tip.

NESTS

All birds lay eggs, but not all make nests. Some seabirds lay their eggs directly onto cliff ledges, and many ground-dwelling birds lay eggs in a simple hollow, called a scrape, which they line with feathers. Birds that build complicated nests use many kinds of materials. These include leaves, sticks, mud, hair, spiderwebs, and even saliva. A bird does not have to learn how to make a nest—it does it by instinct.

The kestrel (Falco tinnunculus) eats insects and small mammals. Like other birds of prey, it tears up its food with its sharp, hooked beak.

The African palm swift (Cypsiurus parvus) glues feathers onto a palm leaf. It then glues its eggs onto this mat of feathers. The eggs stay attached even in strong winds.

BEAKS AND FOOD

A bird's beak is made of bone covered by a layer of horn. In an adult bird, the bone usually stays the same size, but the horn grows continuously to allow for wear. A beak is designed to suit the way its owner feeds. Birds with specialized feeding habits usually have distinctive-looking beaks.

BIRD MIGRATION

Birds often spend summer and winter in two different places. Many species of geese breed in the far north, where food is abundant during the brief summer. When it becomes colder, as winter begins, they fly south. Their long journeys are called migrations.

CUCKOOS

The female cuckoo (*Cuculus canorus*) does not make a nest. Instead, she lays an egg in another bird nest while its owners are away. When the young cuckoo hatches, it pushes the other eggs out of the nest. Its foster parents do not realize that it is a cuckoo and work nonstop to keep the imposter supplied with food.

Find out more

CIRCULATION P. 349
INTERNAL ENVIRONMENT P. 350
SKELETONS P. 352
MOVEMENT P. 356
BRAINS P. 361
SEXUAL REPRODUCTION P. 367
FACT FINDER PP. 420, 422

MAMMALS

A rabbit is a herbivore. It has front teeth that cut and rear teeth that grind.

Scissorlike carnassial teeth cut through meat.

A dog is a carnivore. Its long, pointed canine teeth grip its prey.

IF YOU ASK A FRIEND to name any animal, they will probably name a mammal. We are mammals, and so too are most of the large animals we see in daily life. But not all mammals are large—they range in size from tiny shrews and bats to elephants and whales. All mammals have three important features in common. They are endothermic (warm-blooded), they have hair or fur, and they suckle their young on milk produced by the mother's mammary glands. This milk is a complete food that nourishes a young mammal until it is able to find food for itself. On land, mammals—of which there are about 4,000 species—are the most widespread vertebrates.

TEETH AND DIET

A mammal's teeth are as varied as tools in a toolkit. Different adult mammals eat many different kinds of food, and their teeth are specially adapted to match their diets. Carnivores (meat-eaters) have teeth that grip or slice. Herbivores (plant-eaters) have some teeth that cut and some that grind. Omnivores, which live on all kinds of food, have teeth that can grip, slice, cut, and grind. Some mammals, including those that feed on ants, and whales that feed on krill, have lost their teeth altogether.

Fertilized egg develops inside body.

Adult

Egg cell

Sperm cell

Fertilization inside body

Life cycle of a typical mammal

ARMORED MAMMAL

The tree pangolin (*Manis tricuspis*) from tropical Africa is protected by hard, leaf-shaped scales that cover most of its body. It feeds on ants and termites, which it catches with its long tongue. Like the anteaters of South America, pangolins do not have any teeth.

AQUATIC MAMMALS

Dolphins are cetaceans—mammals that spend their whole lives in the sea. During the course of evolution, they have developed a streamlined, fishlike shape, but they still breathe air and suckle their young.

As soon as a young dolphin is born, adult dolphins push it to the surface so it can take its first breath.

Milk for the foal is produced by the mother's mammary glands.

Common or plains zebra (Equus burchelli)

Zebra's body is covered in hair.

PLACENTAL MAMMALS

The zebra, like all the mammals on this page, is a placental mammal. A zebra foal develops inside its mother in an organ called a uterus (womb). The foal gets nourishment from its mother through the placenta, a spongy tissue that passes food from the mother's blood to the baby's blood. The foal is well developed when it is born, and is soon able to run.

Common tree shrew (Tupaia glis)

Spinner dolphins (Stenella longirostis)

TREE SHREWS

The tree shrews of southern and eastern Asia may resemble the first mammals that evolved from reptilian ancestors. Tree shrews are nocturnal (active at night). They have large eyes and a well-developed sense of smell. Biologists believe that similar animals shared the Earth with the first dinosaurs, over 200 million years ago.

FLYING MAMMALS

Bats make up a quarter of all mammal species. Together with insects and birds, they are the only animals capable of powered flight. Most bats live on insects, which they pinpoint in midair by using pulses of sound. Larger species eat fruit.

MARSUPIAL MAMMALS

Marsupial young are born in an immature state. After birth, they crawl into their mother's marsupium (pouch) where they develop. In kangaroos, the marsupium is a roomy bag. In other marsupials, such as quolls, it is little more than a flap. The marsupium contains teats, and the young animal fastens itself onto a teat to feed. There are about 260 species of marsupials. Although people often associate them with Australia, many live in South America.

Fur or hair protects the skin from the Sun and injury. It also keeps body moisture out and heat in.

A female kangaroo can raise young on a production line system—with one forming inside her uterus, one in her pouch, and another one almost ready to live on its own.

Small front legs are used for digging, grooming, and fighting.

A young kangaroo, called a joey, jumps into the pouch if danger threatens. As it climbs aboard, it doubles up so its head and feet point in the same direction.

MONOTREMES

The duck-billed platypus (*Ornithorhynchus anatinus*) is a most bizarre mammal. It has webbed feet, a beak like a bird, and it lays eggs. When young platypuses hatch, they feed on their mother's milk, which is produced from teatless mammary glands. The young animals lap the milk from her fur.

Only two other species of mammal—the spiny anteaters—lay eggs. With the platypus, they make up a tiny group of mammals called the monotremes.

KOALA

The koala (*Phascolarctos cinereus*) is an Australian marsupial that has adapted to life in trees, and to a diet that consists mainly of eucalyptus leaves. Young koalas spend their early lives in their mothers' pouches. When they are large enough, they emerge from the pouch and cling to her back. Despite their shape, koalas are not close relatives of bears. Bears are placental mammals, not marsupials.

Long, sharp nails for shoveling sand

VIRGINIA OPOSSUM

The Virginia opossum (*Didelphis virginiana*) is a rare success story in the marsupial world. This tree-dwelling North American species has steadily increased its range and now lives as far north as Canada. It has managed to do this by adapting to life alongside humans. It wanders into yards and over rooftops and searches for food in household waste.

UNDERGROUND MAMMAL

Many marsupials have evolved shapes and ways of life that match those of placental mammals. The marsupial mole (*Notoryctes typhlops*) is shaped very much like a placental mole, with a blunt body and powerful digging legs. Like a placental mole, it also feeds on grubs and worms.

QUOLL

The beautifully spotted quoll (*Dasyurus viverrinus*) is Australia's marsupial equivalent of the cat. A nocturnal predator, it feeds on small animals such as insects and smaller marsupials. Unfortunately, the quoll is not such an efficient hunter as its placental equivalent. Since the domestic cat was introduced into Australia, quoll numbers have fallen. Many other marsupials have also declined because of competition with placental mammals.

Find out more

TEETH AND JAWS P. 344
BREATHING P. 347
CIRCULATION P. 349
INTERNAL ENVIRONMENT P. 350
SKELETONS P. 352
SEXUAL REPRODUCTION P. 367
FACT FINDER PP. 420, 422

PRIMATES

WE BELONG to a group of mammals called the primates. Primate means "the first," although there is really no top place in the evolution of living things. The primates are divided into two groups: the haplorhines (humans, apes, and monkeys) and the strepsirhines (which include lemurs, bushbabies, and aye-ayes). Humans are all members of one species, *Homo sapiens*. We live on the ground and walk on two legs, but most primates live in trees and use all four legs. Primates have forward-pointing eyes, which help in judging distances, and flexible fingers and toes that can grip branches. Haplorhines have large brains and are highly intelligent.

Arms are very long

Fingernails instead of claws

Orangutans grip branches with their hands and their feet. They can walk on two legs, but they mostly use all four.

Body is covered in hair.

Orangutans, and all other apes, have no tail.

Compared to an ape's skull, a human skull has a very large brain-case, short jaws, and small teeth.

ORIGIN OF *HOMO SAPIENS*
The shape of the human skull is important in deciding how the human species evolved, because it can be compared directly with the fossilized skulls of our distant relatives. Humans almost certainly evolved from apelike ancestors. Fossils show that several species of humanlike animals, called hominids, existed between one and five million years ago. Today, only our species survives.

ORANGUTAN
Most primates live in the tropics and subtropics. There are about 180 species altogether. The orangutan (*Pongo pygmaeus*) is a member of the ape family, which also includes gorillas and chimpanzees. Orangutans live in the rain forests of Southeast Asia. Like many primates, they are under threat because their forest home is being cleared for lumber and farmland.

STREPSIRHINE PRIMATE
The aye-aye (*Daubentonia madagascariensis*) is an endangered prosimian that is found only on the island of Madagascar in the Indian Ocean. It is a nocturnal tree-dweller and feeds on insect grubs and young leaves. The aye-aye's front hands have extralong third fingers, which it uses to pick out grubs from bark crevices.

Chimpanzee (Pan troglodytes) using tool to dig out insects from bark.

CHIMPANZEES
We often use tools to perform particular tasks. So, too, do some other primates. Chimpanzees, for example, use sharp sticks and blades of grass to probe for food. Baboons sometimes squash small animals with stones. Several other kinds of animal use tools, but they do this mainly by instinct. Primates can learn how to make tools by watching each other at work.

LOUIS AND MARY LEAKEY
The work of the Leakey family has helped to piece together the story of how our species has evolved. Louis Leakey (1903–72) discovered hominid fossils in East Africa and suggested that humans originated in this region. His wife, Mary (1913–96), discovered several fossils of human ancestors and human footprints that date back nearly 3 million years. Richard Leakey (born 1944), their son, has also made several important fossil finds.

HUMAN SUCCESS
Humans are by far the most numerous of all primates. In the last 300 years, the human population has grown from about 1 billion to nearly 6 billion. Never in the history of the world has a single species had such a wide-ranging effect on other living things.

Find out more

EVOLUTION P. 308
MAMMALS P. 334
SKELETONS P. 352
PEOPLE AND PLANET P. 374
FACT FINDER P. 422

HOW LIVING THINGS WORK

Each kind of living thing is adapted to the world around it. A gibbon's long arms enable it to swing through the treetops. Forward-pointing eyes make it good at judging distances as it swings from one branch to the next.

WHY ARE PLANTS GREEN? What is blood for? Is your skin dead or alive? In many cases, the answers to these questions lie in the makeup of living matter: living things contain different parts, which fit together amazingly well to make them work. In plants and animals, some of these parts are big enough to see, but others are so small that they can only be looked at through a microscope. In all living things, even the smallest parts can be very complicated. By finding out exactly how the small parts work, scientists have been able to see how whole organisms work.

ORGANISMS AND THEIR ENVIRONMENT

All living things, or organisms, need to fit in with their environment. They take in food from the world around them. They put the food to many uses, including producing energy for moving and raw materials for growing and reproducing. Through evolution, living things have developed different ways of getting their food. A gibbon is good at reaching leaves and fruit high in the treetops. Its body can break down this food to release the nutrients and energy that it contains.

THE BODY MACHINE

An animal's body is like a gigantic city of separate parts. The smallest of these parts are called cells. There are many types of cells in living things. Together they provide all the services that the body needs, from energy supply and communication to waste disposal. A single animal or plant may contain billions of cells arranged in a very precise way. Everything each cell does is controlled by its nucleus.

ORGANS

The gibbon's body contains a set of organs. They include its brain, heart, lungs, and liver. An organ is a structure that carries out particular tasks in the work of staying alive. Each one has a characteristic shape and is made up of several different kinds of cells.

CELLS

Cells are the smallest parts of a living thing that are fully alive. The cells in an organ are arranged in groups called tissues. Each tissue contains cells of one type, and it carries out a limited range of tasks.

GENETIC CODE

Almost every cell has a control center called the nucleus. Packed inside it are long molecules of a substance called deoxyribonucleic acid, usually referred to as DNA. Each DNA molecule is a double helix (spiral), and its two strands are linked by chemical "bridges." The exact sequence of these bridges makes up the cell's genetic code, which is like a recipe for what the cell does and how it works.

The liver is one of the gibbon's biggest organs. It processes digested food, performs many chemical reactions, and stores substances that are used to produce energy.

Hepatocytes are one kind of cells in the liver. They are arranged in sheets, and they make a fluid called bile, which helps in digestion.

Hepatocytes form one kind of tissue in the liver. There are other kinds of cells in the liver, which form other kinds of tissue, such as blood vessels.

Strands of DNA are found in the nucleus.

ANDREAS VESALIUS

Vesalius (1514–64) founded the modern science of anatomy, which looks at the structure of living things. He was Belgian, but he did his most important work in Italy. He became a professor of anatomy at the age of 23, and in 1543 he published a book called *The Structure of the Human Body*. It was based on careful observation, and was beautifully illustrated. This was the first book to show details of the body in an accurate way.

CELLS

EVERY LIVING THING is made up of cells. Each one is like a microscopic factory, where thousands of chemical reactions happen in a carefully controlled way. Cells use these reactions to perform all the tasks involved in being alive. Cells can divide in two over and over again. Some living things, such as amoebas, are just one cell. Others, such as ourselves, have millions of cells that all work together. Within an organism, the cells in different tissues are slightly different. Plant cells are different to animal cells in two ways. They have stiff cell walls and can make their own food.

ANIMAL CELLS

An animal cell is like a tiny, fluid-filled, squashy bag. The cell is held together by a thin, flexible layer called a plasma membrane. The membrane is semipermeable, meaning that it allows some chemicals to pass through it, but not others. At the heart of the cell is the nucleus, which controls everything that happens inside the cell. Around the nucleus is a jellylike fluid called cytoplasm. The cytoplasm contains tiny structures, called organelles. Each kind of organelle performs a different set of tasks.

Special proteins in the membrane carry complex substances in and out of the cell.

PLASMA MEMBRANE
The plasma membrane encloses the whole cell, but it has pores in it. These pores let some chemicals through, but not others. This means the membrane is semipermeable, which is very important, because then it can "choose" the chemicals it lets in and out of a cell.

The plasma membrane is made of a double layer of molecules.

Plasma membrane

Typical animal cell

Vacuoles are storage areas in the cell. They are used to store fats, for example.

The DNA in the nucleus stays inside it, but the instructions in it are copied and carried to different parts of the cell.

Smooth endoplasmic reticulum makes lipids (fat molecules).

Ribosomes are small organelles that make proteins. Ribosomes either float in the cytoplasm or are attached to the endoplasmic reticulum.

Rough endoplasmic reticulum

Cytoplasm is a jellylike fluid containing organelles. It often flows around inside the cell.

A mitochondrion is an organelle that produces energy for the cell. It breaks down substances to release energy. The folds inside a mitochondrion give a large surface area for these reactions to take place.

The pores in the membrane around the nucleus (called the nuclear membrane) allow copies of the DNA code to travel out of the nucleus.

NUCLEUS
The nucleus is the cell's command center. It contains chemical instructions in molecules of DNA (deoxyribonucleic acid) for everything that the cell does. Normally, the DNA is spread out in long strands. The nucleolus is a round "blob" inside the nucleus. It makes organelles called ribosomes.

An ostrich egg weighs up to 3 lb 5 oz (1.5 kg).

Ribosomes on the surface of rough endoplasmic reticulum (RER)

ENDOPLASMIC RETICULUM
The endoplasmic reticulum (ER) is the work surface of the cell. It is a system of double membranes on which chemical reactions take place. The membranes are folded up, and packed together like the layers in a sandwich. They link up with the membrane around the nucleus, and with the plasma membrane that encloses the cell.

Rod cells from a human eye measure 40 micrometers long, compared to ostrich eggs, which measure 250,000 micrometers across.

HOW BIG IS A CELL?
Most animal cells are between 10 and 20 micrometers (1/100th to 1/50th of a millimeter) across, while plant cells are slightly larger. But cells vary enormously in size. The smallest free-living cells are bacteria called mycoplasmas. Their cells are about 0.1 micrometers (1/10,000th of a millimeter) across. Eggs are giant cells. An ostrich egg cell can be up to 10 in (25 cm) long, which makes it the largest cell that we know of.

This false-color electron micrograph of rod cells from the eye shows four cells. The two round cells are nerve cells.

CELLS

1590 The Dutch optician Zacharias Janssen invents the compound microscope (a microscope with more than one lens). This makes tiny objects visible for the first time.

1665 The English scientist Robert Hooke (1635–1703) looks at thin slices of plants through his microscope. He sees boxlike shapes, and calls them "cells."

1838 Two German doctors, Theodor Schwann (1810–82) and Jakob Mathias Schleiden (1804–81), suggest that all living things are made of cells.

1937 Edouard Chatton, a French biologist, notices that some microorganisms (prokaryotes) have cells that are very different to those of all other living things.

Nerve cell

PLANT CELLS

A plant cell is different from an animal cell in two important ways. In addition to being surrounded by a plasma membrane, it also has a stiff cell wall. A plant cell also contains organelles called chloroplasts, which give it a green color. Chloroplasts catch the energy in sunlight for the cell to make its own food. Most plant cells also contain large vacuoles, which store cell sap. The sap presses against the walls of the cell, keeping it in shape. A plant wilts when it lacks water and the sap does not press against the cell wall.

Typical plant cell

The plasma membrane lies between the wall and the cytoplasm inside the cell.

Chloroplasts are scattered throughout the cytoplasm. They get their green color from a pigment called chlorophyll. Cells in roots and the inside of stems do not have chloroplasts.

Vacuole filled with cell sap

Mitochondrion

Cell wall

Endoplasmic reticulum

Nucleus

Cytoplasm

BUILDING A WALL
Plant cell walls are made of a tough material called cellulose. The cell makes tiny cellulose fibers and builds them up in crisscross layers on the outside of its plasma membrane. The cellulose layers make a strong, stiff box. Without their tough cell walls, most plants would collapse into a green sludge.

LOOKING AT CELLS
Most cells are far too small to see with eyes alone. To look at them, biologists have to use microscopes. A light microscope can magnify clearly up to about 2,000 times. Special stains or lighting are used to make different parts of the cell stand out. An electron microscope works in a different way. It can magnify over a million times, but normally it cannot be used with living specimens. A scanning electron microscope gives an almost three-dimensional image.

Light micrograph of Lactobacillus bulgaricus, a bacterium found in live yogurt. It is illuminated with green light and magnified 400 times.

Scanning electron micrograph of Lactobacillus bulgaricus magnified 1,000 times. Electron microscopes produce a black and white image. Here, the image has been artificially colored by a computer.

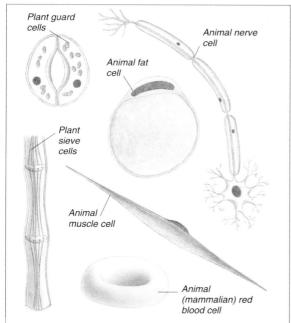

Plant guard cells

Animal nerve cell

Animal fat cell

Plant sieve cells

Animal muscle cell

Animal (mammalian) red blood cell

Light micrograph of hepatocytes (liver cells) magnified 56 times. The cells have been stained to make them easier to see. The nuclei absorb the dye, giving them a dark color.

Electron micrograph of liver cells, magnified 90 times and artificially colored. Electron microscopes can produce small magnifications as well as large ones.

Typical bacterium

Molecule of DNA loose in cytoplasm

Plasma membrane

Cytoplasm

Thick cell wall outside plasma membrane

Whiplike flagella that move the bacterium

DIFFERENT SHAPES FOR DIFFERENT WORK

The different cells in plants and animals are specialized, meaning that they can carry out only one kind of work. A fat cell is filled with fat either permanently or until it is needed for energy. A nerve cell carries messages from one part of the body to another, and a muscle cell contracts to make part of the body move. Red blood cells carry oxygen in animals, and sieve cells carry nutrients in plants. Unlike most cells, these two kinds do not have nuclei. Guard cells are found in plant leaves, controlling the pores that allow air into the leaf. They also have chloroplasts to harness the energy in sunlight.

Light micrograph of muscle fibers, magnified 140 times. Several nuclei can be seen, as well as the striations (stripes) that are typical of muscles that pull on bones.

Artificially colored electron micrograph of a single muscle fiber, magnified 1,940 times. The fiber is made up of many parallel fibrils. Each fibril is just 1/500th of a millimeter across.

SIMPLEST CELLS
The cells of bacteria and other microorganisms do not have nuclei or mitochondria. They are called prokaryotic. Other cells, such as plant and animal cells, do have nuclei and are called eukaryotic cells. They are more common.

Find out more
HOW SCIENTISTS WORK P. 14
VISION P. 204
SINGLE-CELLED ORGANISMS P. 314
BACTERIA P. 313
PHOTOSYNTHESIS P. 340
CELLULAR RESPIRATION P. 346

PHOTOSYNTHESIS

IMAGINE BEING ABLE TO MAKE FOOD just by standing in sunlight. This is what plants do when they carry out photosynthesis. The word photosynthesis means "putting together by light." During this process, plants collect energy from sunlight. They use this energy to turn water and carbon dioxide into a simple sugar called glucose. Plants then use glucose to fuel their cells and also to make other substances, such as starch and cellulose. Plants are not the only living things that carry out photosynthesis. Some protists and monerans also make food in this way.

WHY ARE MOST LEAVES GREEN?
Sunlight is made of many colors. Most plants contain a green pigment called chlorophyll, which reflects the green part of light. It captures the blue and red parts of sunlight and uses them to drive photosynthesis. Plants such as the copper beech in the woodland above and red and brown seaweeds also use other pigments as well as chlorophyll to capture different colors in light. That is why they are not green.

HOW PHOTOSYNTHESIS WORKS
Most plants carry out photosynthesis in their leaves. Many of the cells in a leaf contain tiny organelles called chloroplasts. Chlorophyll and other pigments in the chloroplasts trap the energy in sunlight. Once the energy has been trapped, it powers a complicated series of chemical reactions. During these reactions, water molecules are split apart into hydrogen and oxygen atoms. The hydrogen atoms combine with carbon dioxide molecules to make glucose, and oxygen is given off as a waste product.

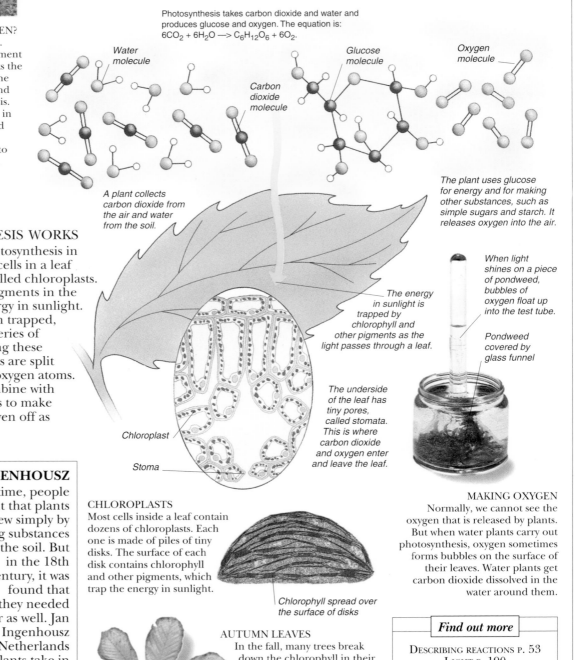

Photosynthesis takes carbon dioxide and water and produces glucose and oxygen. The equation is:
$6CO_2 + 6H_2O \longrightarrow C_6H_{12}O_6 + 6O_2.$

Water molecule

Carbon dioxide molecule

Glucose molecule

Oxygen molecule

A plant collects carbon dioxide from the air and water from the soil.

The plant uses glucose for energy and for making other substances, such as simple sugars and starch. It releases oxygen into the air.

The energy in sunlight is trapped by chlorophyll and other pigments as the light passes through a leaf.

When light shines on a piece of pondweed, bubbles of oxygen float up into the test tube.

Pondweed covered by glass funnel

The underside of the leaf has tiny pores, called stomata. This is where carbon dioxide and oxygen enter and leave the leaf.

Chloroplast

Stoma

JAN INGENHOUSZ
At one time, people thought that plants grew simply by absorbing substances from the soil. But in the 18th century, it was found that they needed air as well. Jan Ingenhousz (1730–99) of the Netherlands diskovered that plants take in carbon dioxide and release oxygen when sunlight shone on them. He found that the gases travel in the opposite direction when it is dark.

CHLOROPLASTS
Most cells inside a leaf contain dozens of chloroplasts. Each one is made of piles of tiny disks. The surface of each disk contains chlorophyll and other pigments, which trap the energy in sunlight.

Chlorophyll spread over the surface of disks

AUTUMN LEAVES
In the fall, many trees break down the chlorophyll in their leaves. The leaves are then colored by any pigments left behind. These include carotenoids, which make carrots orange, and anthocyanins, which make some apples red.

MAKING OXYGEN
Normally, we cannot see the oxygen that is released by plants. But when water plants carry out photosynthesis, oxygen sometimes forms bubbles on the surface of their leaves. Water plants get carbon dioxide dissolved in the water around them.

Find out more
DESCRIBING REACTIONS P. 53
LIGHT P. 190
COLOR P. 202
DIGESTION P. 345
CELLULAR RESPIRATION P. 346
GROWTH AND DEVELOPMENT P. 362

TRANSPORT IN PLANTS

When the water reaches a leaf, it evaporates through the pores on the underside. They are called stomata.

Phloem   Xylem

IF YOU FORGET TO WATER an indoor plant, it will eventually wilt and die. This happens because plants need water to survive. Water travels upward through a plant's roots and stems, and it evaporates into the air from its leaves and flowers. This movement is called transpiration. It keeps the plant's cells firm, and it also carries dissolved minerals up from the soil. Plants also have another transport system, called translocation, which often works in the other direction. It carries food substances away from the leaves into the buds, shoots, and roots.

Food substances made during photosynthesis move away from the leaves and down the plant through phloem cells.

TWO-WAY TRANSPORT
Water travels up a plant through xylem cells. These are cylindrical cells that link end to end. They eventually die, leaving tiny fluid-filled pipelines that stretch from the roots and up into every leaf. Dissolved food substances travel through a different system of pipelines made by phloem cells.

TRANSPIRATION
Every day, a large tree loses about 265 gallons (1,000 liters) of water from its leaves. But what makes the water move upward? It is both pushed and pulled. The roots often push the water upward a little way. The water that evaporates from the leaves draws up more water to take its place. This happens partly because water molecules attract each other, and partly through osmosis.

Phloem carries food   Vascular bundle

Xylem carries water

Water moving up plant from the roots

TUBES FOR TRANSPORT
Xylem and phloem cells are clustered together in groups called vascular bundles. The xylem is on the inside, and the phloem on the outside. Xylem cells are often strengthened, which keeps the tubes open so that liquids can pass up them easily.

FEEDING ON SAP
The sugary fluid in phloem cells makes an energy-rich food for sap-sucking insects. Aphids pierce the stem and phloem cells with their sharp mouthparts and then drink the fluid which oozes out. Sometimes there is too much sugar for an aphid to digest. The leftover sugar passes out of its body in drops of sticky liquid called honeydew.

Lady's mantle
(Alchemilla vulgaris)

Slice of celery stem, showing xylem cells stained by dye

Evaporation from leaves draws water and dye up through celery stem.

OSMOSIS
If you put a peeled potato in very salty water, water will be sucked out from its cells. If you put it in tap water, the cells will absorb water. This flow of water into and out of cells is called osmosis. During osmosis, water always flows through a semipermeable membrane. It always flows from the side that contains a bigger proportion of water molecules to the side that contains a lower proportion of water molecules and more dissolved substances.

A cube of potato was left in very salty water for a day and shrunk slightly because water was sucked out of it by osmosis.

A cube of potato of the same size was left in tap water for a day and it swelled slightly because water was absorbed by osmosis.

SEEING TRANSPIRATION
You can see transpiration at work by putting a stick of celery into some water containing a food dye. As water evaporates from the leaves, water travels up the celery and carries the dye with it. The dye shows that the water moves upward through narrow channels, which are the xylem cells.

GUTTATION
In low-growing plants, water is sometimes pumped upward by the roots faster than it is lost by the leaves. When this happens, water droplets form around the leaf edges because the water does not evaporate fast enough. This is guttation. It usually occurs after dark, and only when the air is still and humid.

Find out more
KINETIC THEORY P. 50
COLOR P. 202
FLOWERING PLANTS P. 318
CELLS P. 338
PHOTOSYNTHESIS P. 340
ASEXUAL REPRODUCTION P. 366

NUTRITION

EVERY LIVING THING needs nutrients (raw materials) to stay alive. Nutrition is the process by which they get these substances and put them to work. Like all animals, we get our nutrients by eating food. This is called being heterotrophic. Food contains three main kinds of nutrients: proteins, fats, and carbohydrates. We use proteins to build and repair our bodies, and fats and carbohydrates mainly for fuel. We need other nutrients, but in smaller amounts. These substances are minerals, used to build important molecules in the body, or vitamins, which enable particular chemical reactions to take place. Plants live in a very different way. They make their own food, which is called being autotrophic. They only need simple nutrients, such as carbon dioxide, water, and mineral salts from the soil.

KEEPING A BALANCE
Good nutrition means eating the right food in the right proportions. Here is a meal that has a range of different foods, which gives a balance of proteins, fats, and carbohydrates, as well as a range of minerals and vitamins. That's why it is important to eat a wide variety of food, rather than too much "junk" food, such as potato chips, which mainly provide fats and carbohydrates.

A hummingbird's beak makes a tube like a drinking straw.

Hummingbirds get the energy to hover in front of flowers from nectar, which is rich in sugars. But nectar contains very little protein, so hummingbirds also eat a few insects.

WHAT IS A DIET?
To a scientist, a diet has nothing to do with slimming. Instead, it means an animal's complete food intake. Some animals have a very varied diet. Others are much more choosy. An adult hummingbird lives mainly on nectar, a sugary liquid made by flowers. Nectar is packed with carbohydrates, which means that it is a good source of energy.

HERBIVORES
Many kinds of animal, from caterpillars to elephants, live entirely on plant food. They are called herbivores. Their food is often not very nutritious, and to get enough energy and nutrients to live, they have to spend a large part of their lives eating. Some herbivores, like camels, have bacteria in their digestive systems to help them release the nutrients from their food.

This swallowtail butterfly caterpillar (Papilio machaon) eats almost all the time it is awake.

MALNUTRITION
If an animal's diet is missing a particular kind of nutrient, it becomes malnourished. Its health declines, and it may suffer from a "deficiency disease." In some parts of the world, children suffer from kwashiorkor, which is a deficiency disease caused by a lack of protein. Plants, too, become unhealthy if important minerals are missing in the soil. These cherry leaves are suffering from magnesium deficiency.

CARNIVORES
A pike is a carnivore—an animal that feeds on other animals. Its food is rich in nutrients, so a single meal can last for a long time. However, its food is not always easy to obtain. Carnivores such as the pike often have to put a lot of energy and time into finding and catching a meal.

OMNIVORES
Raccoons, bears, and humans are omnivores, meaning that they can feed on both plant and animal food. Omnivorous animals are not very choosy, so they can usually find something to eat. Raccoons are particularly good at living on people's leftovers.

Find out more
CHEMISTRY OF FOOD P. 78
ARTHROPODS P. 322
FISH P. 326
FEEDING P. 343
TEETH AND JAWS P. 344
DIGESTION P. 345
FOOD CHAINS AND WEBS P. 377
FACT FINDER P. 422

FEEDING

LONG AGO, PEOPLE GOT THEIR FOOD by gathering seeds and fruit, and by hunting animals. Today, most of our food is produced by farming. Instead of gathering food ourselves, people who live in towns and cities buy it in stores. But in the natural world, things are very different. Wild animals spend a large part of their time either feeding or trying to find their next meal. The way that they do this depends on what they eat. Herbivores (animals that eat plants) do not usually have to look far for their food, because plants are rooted in one spot and cannot run away. Carnivores (animals that eat meat) usually have to track down their prey and overpower it. However, some animals, such as barnacles or sea anemones, stay in one place and wait for their food to come within reach.

SAFETY IN A HERD
Gazelles feed on grass, in the open country of the African plains. They have many enemies, and their only defense is to run away. Gazelles make themselves safer by living in herds. While some of the gazelles are eating, others keep a watchful eye for any signs of danger.

This jackal distracts the mother gazelle away from the baby.

WORKING IN A TEAM
Some hunting mammals catch their prey by working together. Here, one jackal attacks the mother gazelle, even though an adult gazelle is too big for it to kill. While the mother is distracted, the other jackal pounces on her youngster. By working as a team, the jackals get a meal that one jackal could not catch on its own.

PREDATOR AND PREY
The common shrew (*Sorex araneus*) is one of the smallest of all predatory mammals (mammals that hunt). It measures just 3 in (7.5 cm) from head to tail, and is about as heavy as a sugar cube. Despite its tiny size, it is a fierce hunter with a large appetite. It overpowers earthworms with its sharp teeth and quickly starts to feed. A shrew needs to eat its own body mass in food every day or it will die. Larger predatory mammals eat much less, because their bodies use energy at a much slower rate.

FEEDING ON LEFTOVERS
Several different fungi are living on food substances in this piece of bread. Instead of eating whole pieces of bread, they absorb food chemicals through a mass of tiny threads. Fungi and bacteria are important because they help to break down the dead remains of living organisms. Those that do this are called saprophytes, or saprobes. Other fungi live on things that are still alive.

FILTER FEEDING
This fanworm (*Trotula intestinum*) lives by filtering tiny particles of food from water. Its "fans" are rings of tentacles. The tentacles trap particles of food, and tiny hairs then push the food toward the worm's mouth. Many different animals live by filtering food. They include mollusks, such as oysters and mussels, and sponges and sea squirts. Small filter-feeding animals usually spend their adult lives in one place. The biggest filter-feeders of all, whales, filter food as they swim along.

UNDERWATER NET
The larvae of caddisflies live in streams. Most of them find their food by crawling around, but some have a different technique. They make nets from silk, and then sit inside the neck of the net. Small animals are swept into the net and then eaten.

Find out more
CHEMISTRY OF FOOD P. 78
FUNGI P. 315
JELLYFISH, ANEMONES, AND CORALS P. 320
MOLLUSKS P. 324
MAMMALS P. 334
TEETH AND JAWS P. 344
GROWTH AND DEVELOPMENT P. 362
FOOD CHAINS AND WEBS P. 377
FACT FINDER P. 422

TEETH AND JAWS

WHAT IS THE HARDEST PART of your body? It is the surface of your teeth. This surface is made of enamel, which protects teeth from wearing away, and helps to stop them from being attacked by chemicals in food. Teeth cut and grind your food so that it can be digested. Most mammals have specialized teeth that are shaped to carry out different tasks: some teeth cut and slice, others grip or crush. Our teeth grow in two separate sets, and once a tooth has appeared, it does not grow any bigger. Animals that feed by gnawing have chisel-shaped teeth that never stop growing.

TEETH FOR GNAWING
A coypu's chisel-shaped incisor teeth grow throughout its life. Each incisor has enamel only on the front face. The back of the tooth wears away fastest, leaving a front edge that is always sharp.

Self-sharpening incisor teeth

Diastema

HERBIVORE TEETH
The coypu is a typical herbivore—an animal that only eats plants. Its long incisor teeth cut through tough plant stems, while its molar teeth grind up its food. A gap called the diastema separates the two groups of teeth.

HUMAN TEETH
Humans are omnivores, meaning that we eat both plant and animal food. We use our front teeth (incisors) for biting into our food, and our cheek teeth (molars) for chewing it. We also have small canine teeth, which we use for gripping. The jaw is pulled upward by powerful muscles that connect it to the cheekbones and temples. When you chew, you can feel these muscles tightening.

Teeth fit into special sockets in the jaw.

CUTTING THROUGH FOOD
A dog's jaw muscles are strong enough to crack bones. When a dog feeds, its jaw moves up and down like a pair of scissors. Plant-eating animals have jaws that move from side to side as well as up and down.

Carnassial teeth

Incisors

Canine teeth

Flap of bone for anchoring jaw muscles

CARNIVORE TEETH
A dog is a typical carnivore—an animal that eats mostly meat. At the front of its jaw, it has long canine teeth that grip its food. Toward the back, it has sharp carnassial teeth that slice up food so that it can be swallowed.

Permanent teeth

Incisor

Canine

Premolar

Upper teeth

Molar

Third molar (wisdom tooth)

Lower teeth

HUMAN DENTITION
Your first set of teeth (your baby teeth) contains eight incisors, four canines, and eight molars. Most people have 32 teeth in their second set, known as the permanent teeth. The wisdom teeth are the last to appear, although not everybody has them.

SIMPLE TEETH
Not all animals have specialized teeth like those of mammals. Reptiles, such as this crocodile, have identical teeth that are shaped like pegs. A crocodile cannot chew its food. Instead, it wedges the food under something solid, tears it apart, and swallows it in chunks.

Enamel on crown

Dentine

Pulp cavity

Root

Blood vessel

A nerve runs alongside the blood vessels.

Cement holds the root in the jaw.

Jawbone

ANIMALS WITHOUT TEETH
Many animals have hard mouthparts instead of teeth. This dragonfly larva grabs its prey with a special hinged "mask." The mask shoots out to catch passing animals. Many plant-eating insects (such as grasshoppers) have a stomach chamber that grinds up their food after they have swallowed it.

INSIDE A TOOTH
The part of a tooth that you can see is the crown, which is only about half of it. The crown is covered with enamel, and underneath is a layer of hard dentine. The core of the tooth is filled with soft living pulp, which is supplied with blood. Long roots and a special cement keep the tooth anchored in the jaw.

Find out more

ARTHROPODS P. 322
REPTILES P. 330
MAMMALS P. 334
FEEDING P. 343
DIGESTION P. 345
SKELETONS P. 352

DIGESTION

DURING DIGESTION, all the complicated substances that food is made of (carbohydrates, proteins, and fats) are broken up into much simpler compounds that your body can absorb. Digestion starts almost as soon as you put food into your mouth. As the food travels through your stomach and into your small intestine, different enzymes (special proteins) digest carbohydrates, fats, and proteins. The products of digestion are absorbed through the intestinal wall, and anything you do not digest passes straight through your body. Digestion is the first step in getting energy from food.

SECONDHAND FOOD
Termites cannot digest the cellulose in plants themselves, so some get a fungus to do it for them. They pile up pieces of leaves underground and use this to grow a fungus. The fungus digests and takes in the plant food. The termites then eat pieces of the fungus, which they can easily digest.

EXTERNAL DIGESTION
Spiders have tiny mouths, and they digest their food before they swallow it. When a spider catches an insect, it injects it with a liquid that contains enzymes. The enzymes break down the soft parts of the insect's body, and the spider sucks up the nutritious liquid.

DIGESTION IN A MOUSE
When a mouse swallows, its food travels first to its stomach. Here, it is partly broken down by a strong acid. It passes on through the small and large intestines, which absorb all the products of digestion and water. The mouse's pancreas produces substances that neutralize the stomach acid. Its cecum is a dead-end chamber where plant food is digested.

Esophagus (gullet)
Small intestine
Stomach
Cecum
Appendix
Gall bladder
Pancreas
Liver
Large intestine

Normally a mouse's digestive system is packed into its abdomen. Here it has been spread out to make it easier to see.

Glucose is made by splitting starch molecules.

Digestive enzymes break the links between the sugar units.

Grains of wheat are full of starch.

DIGESTING STARCH
Wheat, rice, and potatoes all contain starch, a substance that plants make as a food store. Starch molecules contain hundreds of sugar units, linked to form long chains. During digestion, these chains are broken up by enzymes. The result is many molecules of glucose, a simple sugar that can be absorbed by the body.

Each starch molecule produces many molecules of glucose.

Starch molecules are too long to be absorbed so they must be digested.

HOW A COW DIGESTS GRASS
Cows digest grass with the help of microorganisms and a four-part stomach. First the food goes into the rumen and reticulum so that microorganisms can break down cellulose. The cow then brings up the food to chew it again. The food goes on to the other stomachs to be digested. We cannot digest the cellulose in plants, and it passes out of our bodies as roughage or fiber.

A protein molecule is made up of many amino acids.

Amino acid molecules

It takes several enzymes in the stomach and in the small intestine to digest proteins.

A fat molecule is made of glycerol and fatty acids.

Glycerol molecule

Fatty acid molecules

Fats are turned into droplets by bile, a fluid from the gall bladder. The droplets are digested by enzymes in the small intestine.

Rumen
Reticulum
Omasum
Abomasum

DIGESTING PROTEINS AND FATS
If you eat a piece of meat, the proteins and fats it contains are broken down into much smaller molecules, to be absorbed in your small intestine. Proteins are digested to produce chains called polypeptides, and these in turn are broken down to make amino acids. Fats are turned into tiny droplets and are then broken down to form glycerol and fatty acids.

Find out more

CATALYSTS P. 56
CHEMISTRY OF THE BODY P. 76
CHEMISTRY OF FOOD P. 78
CELLULAR RESPIRATION P. 346

CELLULAR RESPIRATION

ALL LIVING THINGS NEED ENERGY to survive. Your energy comes from food. After you digest a meal, food substances travel in your blood and then into your cells. Here, they are respired, which means that they are broken down so that their energy can be released and put to work. In anaerobic respiration, food substances (mainly glucose) are split apart without using oxygen, and a small amount of energy is released. In aerobic respiration, food substances are combined with oxygen, and carbon dioxide and water are produced as waste products. This kind of respiration takes place inside a cell's mitochondria, and releases a lot more energy. Aerobic respiration supplies most of the energy that your body needs.

Respiration works like a turnstile: it releases energy as and when it is needed.

MANAGEABLE ENERGY
Aerobic respiration is very like burning, because it combines food substances (the fuel) with oxygen to release energy. But there is an important difference. Burning happens very quickly, and it releases energy in a sudden rush. Aerobic respiration involves many chemical reactions, and it releases energy in a much more controlled and manageable way.

Chinese hibiscus (*Hibiscus rosa-sinensis*)

RESPIRATION IN PLANTS
During daylight hours, a plant builds up food (glucose and starch) by photosynthesis. It also breaks down some food by respiration. It makes more food than it breaks down, so its leaves take in carbon dioxide. At night, photosynthesis stops. Then the plant only breaks down food by respiration, so its leaves take in oxygen.

One glucose molecule

Six oxygen molecules

+

During respiration, one molecule of glucose is combined with six molecules of oxygen.

Respiration takes glucose and oxygen and produces energy, carbon dioxide, and water. The equation is:
$C_6H_{12}O_6 + 6O_2 \longrightarrow$ energy $+ 6CO_2 + 6H_2O$.

A lot of energy

+

Six molecules of carbon dioxide

+

Six molecules of water

A mitochondrion contains folded membranes that create large work surfaces on which reactions can take place.

Energy released during respiration has to be stored. The energy is used to turn ADP (adenosine diphosphate) into ATP (adenosine triphosphate). When energy is needed, ATP is broken down into ADP to release it.

HANS KREBS
The German biochemist Hans Krebs (1900–81) discovered exactly what happens when glucose is respired by cells. Krebs knew that a glucose molecule was split to make pyruvic acid, a simpler substance. However, no one knew what happened to the pyruvic acid. Krebs dicovered that it joins an endless cycle of chemical reactions, now known as the citric acid cycle or Krebs cycle. Energy is released at each turn of the cycle.

WHAT HAPPENS DURING RESPIRATION
The human body is powered mainly by glucose. This is a sugar that you get by digesting starch and other carbohydrates in your food. Before glucose can be respired, it has to be broken down into a simpler substance, pyruvic acid. This travels into the cell's mitochondria, where it is combined with oxygen to produce carbon dioxide and water. During this process, lots of energy is released. The energy can be used to make muscles work, for example. Aerobic respiration is exactly the opposite of photosynthesis, which uses energy to make glucose.

ANAEROBIC RESPIRATION
If you sprint very quickly, your muscles run out of oxygen. Without oxygen, your muscles cannot turn glucose into water and carbon dioxide. Instead, they turn glucose into a substance called lactic acid (too much of this gives you cramps). This is anaerobic respiration, because it does not use oxygen. Later, when you have stopped running, the lactic acid is broken down using oxygen. Some organisms, such as yeasts and bacteria, can live entirely by anaerobic respiration.

Find out more

PHOSPHORUS P. 43
OXYGEN P. 44
FERMENTATION P. 80
CELLS P. 338
PHOTOSYNTHESIS P. 340
DIGESTION P. 345
FACT FINDER P. 422

BREATHING

EVERY TIME YOU TAKE A BREATH, you suck air into your lungs. The oxygen in the air diffuses (spreads) through the thin lining of the lungs, until it reaches the blood in the tiny blood vessels in your lungs. It is then loaded on to red blood cells and carried to all parts of your body. At the same time, the waste gas carbon dioxide (from cellular respiration) moves in the other direction, so that your body can get rid of it. Mammals, birds, amphibians, and reptiles all have lungs. Fish breathe through thin flaps called gills, and insects have tiny air pipes running through their bodies.

You have two lungs, but they are not the same shape. Your right lung is broader, and has three lobes. The left lung has just two lobes.

The larynx is a passageway made of cartilage. It contains vocal cords. When these are vibrated by air, they make sounds.

The trachea, or windpipe, leads from the larynx to the lungs. It is held open with C-shaped rings of cartilage.

Your lungs are close together. They are illustrated apart here to show the airways clearly.

Hiccups happen when your diaphragm contracts suddenly.

BREATHING

Your lungs are surrounded by your ribs, and they sit on a dome of muscle called the diaphragm. When you breathe, your ribs and diaphragm change the shape of your lungs. Air is either sucked into the lungs, or squeezed out. The amount of air that moves depends on what you are doing. When you sit still, only a little air moves with each breath. When you exercise, you breathe faster and more deeply. Each deep breath moves up to six times more air as when you sit still.

Air moves out of lungs

Ribs move downward

Diaphragm moves upward

When you breathe out, your ribs move downward and your diaphragm springs upward. This reduces the space around the lungs, so that air is squeezed up through the trachea (windpipe).

INSIDE A LUNG

Your lungs are like a pair of large sponges. They have a very rich supply of tiny blood vessels called capillaries, and they are filled with a network of branching air passages. The smallest passages end in dead-end spaces, each called an alveolus, where the air and blood are brought close together. All the alveoli put together have a huge surface area—about 40 times that of your skin. This enables large amounts of oxygen and carbon dioxide to pass into or out of your body.

Alveolus

In an alveolus, blood and air are so close together that oxygen and carbon dioxide can easily move between them.

Tracheae lead from the abdomen to the thorax and head.

Spiracles allow air into the tracheal system. They can be opened and closed.

Bush cricket (Ephippiger species)

TRACHEAL SYSTEM

Insects breathe through a network of air-filled tubes, called tracheae. These lead deep into the insect's body, and divide into branches that are fine enough to reach right into its muscles. The tracheae are sometimes connected to air sacs, which can change shape just like our lungs. Each trachea opens to the outside through a small hole called a spiracle in the insect's body case.

Each filament carries tiny flaps, and oxygen goes into the flaps to reach the fish's blood.

Tracheae carry oxygen directly to an insect's cells.

A fish's gills are just behind its head.

Gills are made up of curved arches, which have feathery projections called filaments.

BREATHING WITH GILLS

Water contains oxygen, although much less than air does. Fish collect oxygen using their gills. A gill is a series of tiny flaps that have a rich blood supply, like our lungs. The fish takes in water through its mouth. As the water washes over the gills, the gills collect oxygen, and give up carbon dioxide. The water then flows out through one or more slits on the fish's body.

Find out more

MAKING AND HEARING
SOUND P. 182
CELLULAR RESPIRATION P. 346
BLOOD P. 348
CIRCULATION P. 349
INTERNAL ENVIRONMENT P. 350

BLOOD

BLOOD IS AN AMAZING SUBSTANCE. It is like a fluid conveyor belt that carries oxygen to every living cell in your body. It also transports food substances, hormones, waste products, and warmth, and it acts as your body's main defence against disease. If you look at a drop of blood, it seems to be just a red liquid. But under a microscope, the same drop turns out to be packed with millions of cells, floating in a watery fluid. The red blood cells carry oxygen, and the white cells attack anything that invades the body from outside. The plasma (the liquid part) carries most of the carbon dioxide. You have just over 8 pints (4 liters) of blood. Its cells are squashed, squeezed, and battered. Every day, millions of them are replaced.

In most people, the plasma makes up over half the blood's volume.

Thin layer of white blood cells and platelets

Red blood cells packed closely together

COMPOSITION OF BLOOD

If a sample of blood is spun around very quickly in a test tube, the cells settle to the bottom. At the top is a yellowish liquid, called the blood plasma. Plasma is 90 percent water. The rest of it is mainly dissolved food substances and salts, and also proteins such as fibrinogen, which forms blood clots. Cells make up just under half the blood's volume, and red blood cells usually outnumber white cells by 500 to 1.

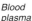

Blood plasma

Platelet

White blood cells can change shape. They squeeze through the walls of the smallest blood vessels to fight infections.

Red blood cell

HEMOGLOBIN

Hemoglobin is a pigment that gives red blood cells their color. It contains iron, and it is very special because it can make temporary bonds with gas molecules. Hemoglobin combines with oxygen when red blood cells travel through the lungs. It gives up the oxygen in other parts of the body, and collects some carbon dioxide. When it reaches the lungs once more, it releases the carbon dioxide, and the cycle starts again.

This computer-generated image shows a molecule of hemoglobin. The pink parts are the iron-containing groups that link with oxygen.

BLOOD IN CLOSE-UP

A single drop of blood contains millions of cells. Most of these are red blood cells, which contain a protein called hemoglobin. This boosts the amount of oxygen that the blood can carry by about 100 times. White blood cells are larger and fewer in number. They engulf foreign cells (such as bacteria) and attack intruders (such as viruses) by releasing antibodies. The blood also contains cell fragments, called platelets, which help it to form clots.

HOW BLOOD CLOTS

If you cut yourself, your blood eventually seals the wound. Blood platelets near the wound become sticky, and they join together to form a plug. While this is happening, a blood protein called fibrinogen changes into fibrin. It makes a dense network of threads, which contract and bind the red blood cells to form a clot.

BLUE-BLOODED LOBSTER

Crustaceans, such as crabs and lobsters, and some mollusks, use a pigment called hemocyanin instead of hemoglobin. This substance gives their blood a blue color. In crustaceans, hemocyanin is dissolved in the blood plasma, instead of being carried in blood cells.

Hemocyanin contains copper instead of iron and, as shown in this common lobster (Homarus vulgaris), makes blood blue not red.

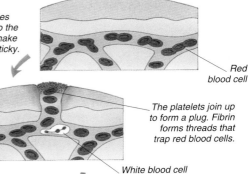

Cut skin releases substances into the blood. These make platelets turn sticky.

Red blood cell

The platelets join up to form a plug. Fibrin forms threads that trap red blood cells.

White blood cell

Fibrin threads

BLOOD GROUPS

Blood is slightly different from one person to another, because of special proteins on the surface of its red cells and in its plasma. People who have the same proteins share the same blood group. If blood from different groups is mixed, the proteins can make red blood cells stick together, which is dangerous. So if someone has to have blood replaced by a transfusion, the new blood must be of the right group.

The fibrin and red blood cells form a clot, which hardens to make a scab. When the skin has healed, the scab falls off.

Find out more

SEPARATING MIXTURES P. 61
ARTHROPODS P. 322
CELLULAR RESPIRATION P. 346
CIRCULATION P. 349
INTERNAL ENVIRONMENT P. 350

CIRCULATION

This artery takes oxygen-rich blood to the right side of the head and the right arm.

This artery supplies oxygen-rich blood to the left side of the head.

This vein carries deoxygenated blood from the head, neck, and arms.

This artery takes oxygen-rich blood to the left arm.

Aortic arch

This artery takes deoxygenated blood to the left lung.

This artery takes deoxygenated blood to the right lung.

These veins bring oxygen-rich blood to the heart.

Left atrium

Right atrium

Valves close as the ventricle contracts.

This vein brings de-oxygenated blood from the lower half of the body and the legs.

Left ventricle

The ventricles have thick, muscular walls.

Right ventricle

YOUR HEART BEATS 100,000 times every day. It squeezes your blood through a network of tubes that take it on a journey around your body. Humans have a "closed" circulation, which means that our blood travels in special vessels all the way around. When blood is pumped out of the heart, it surges forward under high pressure, which you can feel as a pulse. Blood circulates at an amazing speed: a single blood cell can take just one minute to travel from your heart to your knee and back to your heart. Simpler animals, such as snails, have "open" circulations. Their blood flows mainly through large body spaces, instead of through narrow vessels. It is not pumped with such pressure, so it moves quite slowly.

HUMAN HEART

Your heart is like two pumps working side by side. Each one is made of two muscular parts: an atrium at the top, and a ventricle at the bottom. During a heartbeat, the atrium contracts and forces blood into the ventricle. The ventricle contracts a split-second later, forcing blood out of the heart and into the arteries. The right side of the heart pumps blood from the body to the lungs. The left side takes oxygen-rich blood from the lungs and pumps it to the rest of the body.

FISH CIRCULATION

A fish has a heart with just two chambers, and its blood flows in a single loop. The blood travels through the gills, where it collects oxygen. It then flows around the body to deliver the oxygen and collect carbon dioxide, which it then takes back to the gills.

Body

Atrium

Heart

Gills

Ventricle

WILLIAM HARVEY

The Arab doctor Ibn An-Nafis (c. 1205–88) was the first person to describe how blood circulates through the lungs, but his work did not become known in Europe. It was not until 1628 that the English doctor William Harvey (1578–1657) published a full account of how the blood circulates around the body. He could not see capillaries, but he deduced that they must exist.

FROG CIRCULATION

A frog's heart has three chambers, two atria, and one ventricle. Its blood flows in two loops—one through the lungs to gain oxygen, and one around the body to give up oxygen. When blood from both loops returns to the heart, it becomes partly mixed.

Body

Lungs

Left atrium

Heart

Right atrium

Ventricle

Capillaries are the only vessels whose walls are thin enough to let substances, such as oxygen or hormones, pass out of blood to the cells.

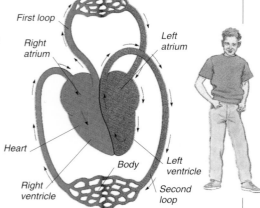

Lungs

First loop

Right atrium

Left atrium

Heart

Right ventricle

Body

Left ventricle

Second loop

HUMAN CIRCULATION

Like all mammals and birds, we have a double circulation. In the first loop of its journey, the blood travels from the right half of the heart through the lungs, gains oxygen, and is bright red. On the second loop, it travels from the left half of the heart, around the body to lose oxygen and gain carbon dioxide; it is now a darker red because it is deoxygenated.

BLOOD VESSELS

Your body contains about 60,000 miles (100,000 km) of blood vessels. Arteries take blood away from the heart, while veins carry it back. Arteries and veins are linked by a dense network of tiny capillaries, which can only be seen through a microscope. Capillaries form a network right through your body.

Arteries have muscular walls and a tough outer coating. This helps them to withstand high pressures.

Veins have thin walls, and valves that keep the blood flowing in one direction.

Find out more

BREATHING P. 347
BLOOD P. 348
INTERNAL ENVIRONMENT P. 350

INTERNAL ENVIRONMENT

THE WORLD AROUND US is always changing. The air can get warmer or colder, and it may pour with rain or stay sunny and dry. But inside your body, things stay much the same from one day to another. The temperature is always about the same, and a constant mixture of chemicals keeps your cells alive. This does not mean that your body never changes. Instead, it makes tiny adjustments to its internal environment all the time. Nerves and hormones (chemical messengers) work together to keep your body in a stable state. This process is called homeostasis, and it happens in all living things.

EXCRETION

All living things have to get rid of waste. This is called excretion. We excrete carbon dioxide and water through our lungs. We excrete nitrogen compounds, salts, and water in our urine, and some salt and water in sweat. We also get rid of the undigested parts of food—but this is not true excretion, because undigested food never passes through our cells. Excretion is important because waste can poison the body. In a healthy body, the nervous system and hormones make sure that waste products never build up.

Crystals of calcium oxalate in garlic (Allium sativum).

EXCRETION IN PLANTS

Plants have to get rid of waste, just like animals. During photosynthesis, plants release waste oxygen from their leaves. Some plants store solid waste in their cells. The cells shown here are from a clove of garlic. They have stored crystals of calcium oxalate as a waste product.

Lizard basking on a rock

"COLD-BLOODED" BODIES

Fish, amphibians, and reptiles are ectothermic ("cold-blooded") animals. But their bodies are not always cold. Instead, their temperature rises and falls with the temperature of their surroundings. Many ectothermic animals alter their body temperature through their behavior. A lizard will lie in the sun when it is cold, and it will hide in the shade to cool down when it is too hot.

"WARM-BLOODED" BODIES

Mammals and birds are endothermic ("warm-blooded") animals. They can keep their bodies at a set temperature, which is usually warmer than their surroundings. Endothermic animals can stay active even when it is very cold, but their bodies need lots of fuel to do this.

TEMPERATURE REGULATION

Unless you are sick, your body temperature stays at 98.6°F (37°C). Heat is produced by breaking down food during cellular respiration. At the same time heat is lost. If you lose more heat than you make, your brain signals your body to step up your heat production and prevents some heat from escaping by shutting off blood vessels near the skin and making your body hair stand on end. If you produce too much heat, you begin to sweat.

MONITORING THE BODY

Your brain is always monitoring the internal environment of your body. A part of the brain checks the amount of carbon dioxide in your blood, and increases your breathing rate if it is too high. Other parts of your brain check the water level in your blood and your body's temperature.

Every time you breathe out, your lungs give off carbon dioxide and water vapor (this vapor makes glass go misty if you breathe on it).

Your liver works like a filter and a chemical factory. It removes worn-out red blood cells and stores the iron that they contain. It also makes sure that your blood contains the right level of glucose, and it makes the proteins that make blood clot.

Your kidneys filter your blood. They drain off its fluid part as it passes through them and then make urine from the waste that it contains.

Sweat helps to cool you down. It contains salt, which is why your skin tastes salty if you have been sweating.

SHIVERING

If your body is too cold, your brain sends signals to some of your muscles to contract, or shiver. This produces heat, which warms up your body. At the same time, the blood vessels near your skin become narrow. This prevents too much of the body's heat from escaping through your skin.

This robin (Erithacus rubecula) has fluffed up its feathers to keep warm.

Hair   Sweat gland
Goose bump
Muscle lifts hair upright.
Nerve   Capillaries

GOOSE BUMPS

One of the first signs of feeling cold are goose bumps—tiny bumps on your skin. These appear when tiny muscles lift your body hairs upright.

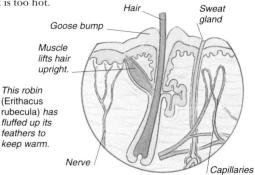

The pituitary is a small but important gland just under the floor of your brain. It produces many hormones that stimulate other glands to produce hormones of their own. The nearby hypothalamus links your endocrine (hormonal) system with your body's nervous system.

The thyroid gland produces thyroxine, a hormone that regulates growth, and the rate at which food is broken down to release energy.

The pancreas produces hormones that control blood sugar levels. The hormone insulin makes the cells use more glucose and the liver take glucose out of the blood. The hormone glucagon makes the liver put more glucose into the blood.

Throughout the body, a network of tubes called the lymphatic system drains fluid that seeps out of the capillaries. The fluid, called lymph, is filtered to remove foreign cells and particles. The filtered fluid then rejoins the blood through a duct near the heart.

Lymph nodes are spongy swellings in your lymphatic system, where white blood cells attack germs. If your body is infected by bacteria or poison, such as from a snake bite, the lymph nodes often swell up.

Your blood is one of the most important substances in keeping your internal environment stable. It takes oxygen to the cells, takes away waste products, kills harmful bacteria, and carries all the hormonal messages to and from the cells.

HORMONES

Hormones are substances that carry a message. In animals, they are made by glands. A gland releases a hormone into the bloodstream to travel around the body. When it reaches the target cells, its message is put into action. Your body produces more than 50 different hormones. Some regulate the levels of important substances in your blood, and others control the way that you grow and develop. They often work in pairs, with each hormone having an opposing effect.

Insulin decreases the blood glucose level, which triggers the release of more glucagon.

Glucagon increases the blood glucose level, which triggers the release of more insulin.

High blood glucose

Low blood glucose

FEEDBACK LOOPS

Insulin and glucagon are hormones that control the level of glucose in blood. Insulin decreases the blood glucose level, while glucagon increases it. The hormones form a feedback loop, because each hormone affects what the other one does.

CHEMICAL COMMUNICATION

Some animals release chemicals that send messages to others. These chemicals are called pheromones. Social insects, such as bees, ants, and termites, pass pheromones to each other through the air and by touching. A queen bee controls a hive by making a special substance containing pheromones.

HORMONES IN PLANTS

If you put some seedlings on a windowsill, they will bend toward the light. This happens because their growth is controlled by hormones. Hormones gather on the side of a stem that is away from the light, making it bend. Plant hormones mainly control growth and development. Some slow down a plant's growth, and others make leaves fall in the fall.

Honey bees (Apis mellifera)

Queen bee

MOBILE DEFENSES

The white cells in blood are the body's guards against invasion. One kind, called phagocytes, are shown here engulfing a string of *Streptococcus* bacteria. They move through the blood and body and engulf germs. Other white blood cells, called lymphocytes, make antibodies. These protein chemicals stick to invaders and kill them.

FIGHTING DISEASE

For microscopic organisms like bacteria, your body is an ideal place to live. It offers warmth and food. To stay in a stable state, your body uses its immune system to fight these germs. Your blood and lymphatic system are very important for doing this. Many of the germs that manage to get into your body are engulfed by white blood cells. Others are attacked by immune system proteins, called antibodies. Once you have been attacked by a certain bacterium, your immune system "remembers" its chemical makeup, so it can respond very quickly to a second attack. This is called immunity.

CLAUDE BERNARD

The French scientist Claude Bernard (1813–78) was one of the first people to study physiology, which is the study of how all the organs in the body work together and keep the internal environment stable. He discovered that glucose, the main source of energy for the body, is stored in the liver as glycogen and released as and when it is needed. He also studied digestion, how drugs change the way the body works, and the nervous system.

Find out more

BACTERIA P. 313
CELLULAR RESPIRATION P. 346
BLOOD P. 348
GROWTH AND DEVELOPMENT P. 362
FACT FINDER P. 422

SKELETONS

A SKELETON SUPPORTS an animal's body. It makes up a framework that protects and keeps the body in shape, and gives its muscles something to pull against. Most familiar animals have skeletons that are made of something hard, such as bone or shell. The larger an animal is, the stronger the support system has to be. Many small animals also have skeletons, but they are not always made from hard parts. An earthworm does not have a single bone in its body; instead, it supports itself by pressure from inside. Its body fluid presses against its skin like air inside a tire, making what is called a hydrostatic skeleton; that is what allows it to burrow through earth.

The horseshoe crab has a domed shield that covers its head. Its eyes are on top and its legs underneath. The crab has to molt in order to grow.

Spiny tail

Abdomen

A millipede's body is made of many segments. Each one hinges with its neighbors so the millipede can bend. Millipedes have to molt to grow.

Unlike an insect or a crustacean, a mussel does not have to molt. Its shell gets bigger with the rest of its body.

EXOSKELETONS

Many invertebrate animals have an exoskeleton, which is a hard case that supports their bodies from outside. In insects and other arthropods, the exoskeleton is made of stiff plates that meet at flexible joints. The plates cannot change size once they have formed. To grow, an insect has to shed its exoskeleton and make another one. In beetles, the forewings have evolved into a pair of hard plates, or elytra. These cover the wings underneath.

Leg joints

These horns are very hard because they are made of chitin.

LIVING IN A CASE
An exoskeleton has several advantages, and two important drawbacks. It protects its owner from injury, and it also makes it harder for disease-causing organisms to attack. In land animals, it also helps to stop the body from drying out. However, an exoskeleton can be heavy, particularly on land. Some exoskeletons also have to be molted (shed) as their owners grow. During molting, the exoskeleton splits and the animal wriggles out of it, exposing a new soft one underneath. Until this one enlarges and hardens, the animal has to hide because it is vulnerable to its predators.

Rhinoceros beetle

Claw joints

Layers of chitin laid on top of each other.

CHITIN
Insect exoskeletons are made from a substance called chitin. This is laid down in layers of parallel fibers. The fibers in the different layers often run in different directions, which makes the exoskeleton very strong.

The joints are made of flexible tissue so that the animal can move the different sections of its body easily.

A beetle's legs are covered with hard chitin plates, like the rest of its body. The muscles that move its legs are attached to the inside of the plates in the next segment.

Muscle

Flexible joint

Muscle

Young shell with few turns

Older shell with more turns

Spire of shell

SHELLS
Mollusks have hard exoskeletons— their shells— which are made from the mineral calcium carbonate. As a mollusk grows, it keeps laying down the mineral to the lip of its shell. This gradually adds extra turns, so that the space inside the shell gets bigger. By enlarging its shell, a mollusk can keep the same exoskeleton for the whole of its life. Unlike an insect or a crustacean, it does not have to molt.

Lip of shell

SUPPORT IN PLANTS AND SINGLE-CELLED ORGANISMS
All plant cells are supported by cellulose, but many of the cells in wood also have a tough substance called lignin. Trees stay upright because they have evolved this very strong support material. In the sea, single-celled diatoms make beautiful skeletons from silica, the same mineral that sand is made of. Each species of diatom makes a skeleton in a different shape.

Diatoms

Palm trees

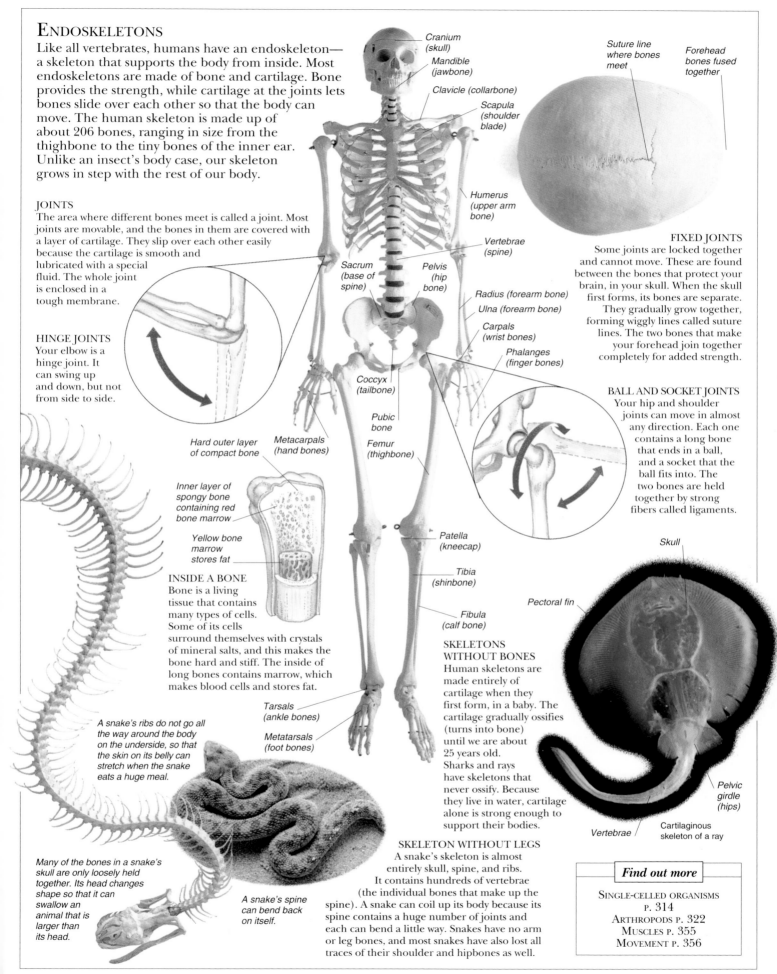

ENDOSKELETONS

Like all vertebrates, humans have an endoskeleton—a skeleton that supports the body from inside. Most endoskeletons are made of bone and cartilage. Bone provides the strength, while cartilage at the joints lets bones slide over each other so that the body can move. The human skeleton is made up of about 206 bones, ranging in size from the thighbone to the tiny bones of the inner ear. Unlike an insect's body case, our skeleton grows in step with the rest of our body.

JOINTS
The area where different bones meet is called a joint. Most joints are movable, and the bones in them are covered with a layer of cartilage. They slip over each other easily because the cartilage is smooth and lubricated with a special fluid. The whole joint is enclosed in a tough membrane.

HINGE JOINTS
Your elbow is a hinge joint. It can swing up and down, but not from side to side.

Cranium (skull)

Mandible (jawbone)

Clavicle (collarbone)

Scapula (shoulder blade)

Humerus (upper arm bone)

Vertebrae (spine)

Sacrum (base of spine)

Pelvis (hip bone)

Radius (forearm bone)

Ulna (forearm bone)

Carpals (wrist bones)

Phalanges (finger bones)

Coccyx (tailbone)

Pubic bone

Metacarpals (hand bones)

Femur (thighbone)

Hard outer layer of compact bone

Inner layer of spongy bone containing red bone marrow

Yellow bone marrow stores fat

INSIDE A BONE
Bone is a living tissue that contains many types of cells. Some of its cells surround themselves with crystals of mineral salts, and this makes the bone hard and stiff. The inside of long bones contains marrow, which makes blood cells and stores fat.

Suture line where bones meet

Forehead bones fused together

FIXED JOINTS
Some joints are locked together and cannot move. These are found between the bones that protect your brain, in your skull. When the skull first forms, its bones are separate. They gradually grow together, forming wiggly lines called suture lines. The two bones that make your forehead join together completely for added strength.

BALL AND SOCKET JOINTS
Your hip and shoulder joints can move in almost any direction. Each one contains a long bone that ends in a ball, and a socket that the ball fits into. The two bones are held together by strong fibers called ligaments.

Patella (kneecap)

Tibia (shinbone)

Fibula (calf bone)

SKELETONS WITHOUT BONES
Human skeletons are made entirely of cartilage when they first form, in a baby. The cartilage gradually ossifies (turns into bone) until we are about 25 years old. Sharks and rays have skeletons that never ossify. Because they live in water, cartilage alone is strong enough to support their bodies.

Tarsals (ankle bones)

Metatarsals (foot bones)

A snake's ribs do not go all the way around the body on the underside, so that the skin on its belly can stretch when the snake eats a huge meal.

Many of the bones in a snake's skull are only loosely held together. Its head changes shape so that it can swallow an animal that is larger than its head.

A snake's spine can bend back on itself.

Skull

Pectoral fin

Vertebrae

Pelvic girdle (hips)

Cartilaginous skeleton of a ray

SKELETON WITHOUT LEGS
A snake's skeleton is almost entirely skull, spine, and ribs. It contains hundreds of vertebrae (the individual bones that make up the spine). A snake can coil up its body because its spine contains a huge number of joints and each can bend a little way. Snakes have no arm or leg bones, and most snakes have also lost all traces of their shoulder and hipbones as well.

Find out more

SINGLE-CELLED ORGANISMS P. 314
ARTHROPODS P. 322
MUSCLES P. 355
MOVEMENT P. 356

SKIN

SKIN IS A TOUGH, FLEXIBLE COVERING that protects your body and helps to keep it at the right temperature. Although it feels alive, its outer surface is completely dead. Without this dead layer, your body would soon dry out or be invaded by bacteria. Your skin renews its outer surface all the time and quickly repairs itself when it gets cut or scratched. If part of your skin, such as the soles of your feet, gets more wear than normal, it gets thicker. Most of your skin is covered with hair, but most mammals have much more hair. Your skin is very good at cooling you down. If you are hot, the capillaries in your skin fill with blood so that heat is lost to the air, and you sweat, which cools you down when the sweat evaporates. Skin is your largest organ; in an adult it covers about 21 sq ft (2 sq m).

FEEDING ON SKIN
Every day, people shed millions of dead cells from the surface of their skin. These cells are found in house dust, and they provide food for tiny house dust mites. The mites are usually harmless, but some people can be allergic to their droppings.

INSIDE THE SKIN

Skin is made of two layers, the epidermis and the dermis. The epidermis is the outer layer. At its base is a single layer of cells that divide all the time. As the new cells are pushed upwards they die, forming a tough layer on the surface. The dermis is the lower layer and is much thicker. It contains elastic fibers that make the skin stretchy. It also has hair follicles, blood vessels, sensitive nerve endings, fat, and sweat glands. Sweat glands send sweat to the surface of your skin through little holes called pores.

Hair, nails, claws, hooves, and feathers are all made of the protein keratin.

Sebaceous (oil) gland

Muscle for making your hair stand on end

Pore

Surface cells gradually wear away, but are replaced by new cells from below. Each cell lasts about four weeks.

Dead layer about 25 cells deep

Epidermis

Single layer of dividing cells

Dermis

Section through human skin

Cells containing fat form a layer that helps to keep the body warm.

Nerves

Hair follicle

Sweat gland

Blood vessel

This capillary widens when you blush or do lots of exercise.

WRINKLES
If you pinch your skin and let go, it springs back into shape. This happens because skin contains proteins in the dermis that stretch like elastic. As people get older, their skin becomes less elastic, so it begins to form wrinkles.

SKIN COLOR
Some animals can change the color of their skin. For example, the cuttlefish changes its color by changing the size of special droplets in its skin. Humans get their skin color mainly from a pigment called melanin, which is made just beneath the skin's surface. Some people also have carotene in their dermis. So everyone's skin is the same except for the amount of pigment it contains.

Overlapping scales slide against each other, so the fish's skin is still flexible in spite of this hard covering.

SCALES
Most fish are covered in overlapping scales to protect their skin. They grow out from the dermis and are made from bone and other tissues. Most bony fish have round scales that make them shiny and smooth, while sharks have small pointed scales that give their skin a sandpapery texture.

FINGERPRINTS
The skin on the palms of your hands and the soles of your feet has tiny ridges. These give your skin a better grip for holding on to things. Every person has their own unique pattern of ridges. The pattern gets bigger as you grow, but it does not change shape.

Find out more

HEAT TRANSFER P. 142
MOLLUSKS P. 324
FISH P. 326
REPTILES P. 330
BIRDS P. 332
INTERNAL ENVIRONMENT P. 350

MUSCLES

ABOUT HALF THE WEIGHT of your body is taken up by muscles. They make your body move. Muscles can pull, but they cannot push. To make up for this, most of your muscles are arranged in pairs or groups, so that they pull in opposite directions. Vertebrates (animals with backbones) have three different types of muscles. Voluntary or skeletal muscles are attached to your bones by tough tendons, and when they contract, part of your body moves. These muscles are easy to feel, because you can make them move whenever you want to. You also have other muscles that work automatically. These are called involuntary or smooth muscles. They squeeze food through your digestive tract, for example. A third kind of muscle is found only in your heart. Cardiac or heart muscle contracts automatically and never gets tired.

HUMAN MUSCLES
The human body contains about 660 voluntary muscles (muscles you can move when you want to). They have a rich blood supply, which provides them with oxygen and glucose. Muscles get warm when they contract, and they supply about four-fifths of your body's heat.

Biceps

When you lower your arm, your biceps muscle relaxes. If you now try to make your arm as straight as possible, you can feel your triceps tighten up.

Triceps

Very few movements take just one pair of muscles. Most involve several muscles working together. For example, to swallow you use at least six muscles.

A human voluntary muscle

Myofibril

Muscle fiber

Biceps

When you raise your arm, your biceps contracts. The opposing muscle— the triceps—relaxes.

Triceps

Bundle of fibers

MUSCLE STRUCTURE
A muscle is made of lots of fibers arranged in bundles. Each fiber is a single cell. The cells are unusual because they have many nuclei, and can be more than ½ in (1 cm) long. The fibers (cells) are made of even smaller filaments, called myofibrils. These contain chemicals that slide past each other and make the muscle contract.

MAKING A MOVE
When a frog jumps, signals flash from its brain through its nerves to the muscles in its legs. The signals cross from the nerves to the muscle fibers and the fibers contract. Even when the frog is not moving, some of its muscle fibers contract while others relax. This makes each muscle firm (toned), which keeps the frog's body in shape. Muscle tone is important in our bodies as well and it is improved by regular exercise.

Muscles on the back of the frog's thigh make the leg extend.

Muscles on the back of the lower leg extend the frog's foot.

A tough membrane covers and protects the muscle.

Powerful muscles in the frog's hindlegs give it the power to jump.

LUIGI GALVANI
By accident, the Italian Professor of Anatomy Luigi Galvani (1737–98) discovered that a dead frog's legs contracted if they were pegged to an iron frame with brass pins. Galvani thought that frogs' muscles made electricity, which caused the contractions. Galvani was right to think that electricity made the muscles move, but in fact it was the two metals reacting together that made the electricity. We now know that in living animals, electrical signals from nerves make muscles contract.

Rough limpet (*Collisella seabla*)

LOCKING SHUT
If you lift a heavy weight, your arms will quickly get tired. But after the muscle in a limpet's foot contracts, it locks in position. Once locked, it does not need any more energy to stay contracted, although it does need energy to unlock. This is a special sort of voluntary muscle called catch muscle.

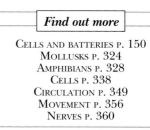

Myosin filament

Actin filament

Relaxed myofibril

Contracted myofibril

HOW A MUSCLE CONTRACTS
A myofibril contains bunches of two proteins, actin and myosin. Each one is made of separate filaments, and these are packed in overlapping layers. When the myofibril is relaxed, the actin and myosin filaments overlap slightly. If the myofibril is triggered by an electric signal from a nerve, the myosin filaments are attracted to the actin filaments, and they slide past each other. The myofibril shortens and the muscle contracts.

MOVEMENT

EVEN WHEN YOU SIT VERY STILL, parts of your body are moving. Your heart beats to send blood around your body, and food is moved through your digestive system. This is involuntary movement, because you do it without thinking about it. Like most animals, you use voluntary movement to move part of your body or carry your entire body from place to place. Moving your whole body from one place to another is called locomotion. The way an animal moves about depends on the shape of its body, its surroundings, and its size. Small animals generate more power in proportion to their weight, so in relative terms, they move faster than large ones. If a cockroach were as large as a human, and its speed was scaled up in proportion, it would race along at 85 mph (140 km/h).

MOVEMENT IN PLANTS
Some plants, such as daisies, open their flowers when the Sun rises and close them when it sets. This is known as sleep movement and happens because of pressure changes inside the plants' cells. Leaf-folding is another common form of sleep movement. It happens, for example, in clovers and other members of the pea family.

Daisies (Bellis perennis) *closing their flowers as the Sun goes down.*

PERISTALSIS
When you swallow, muscles at the back of your mouth contract to push food down your esophagus. This movement, called peristalsis, carries food through the whole of your digestive system. You decide when to swallow, but after that your food is moved by automatic peristalsis—an involuntary movement.

Muscles contract to tighten the esophagus and move the food.

Food

Peristalsis happens in reverse when the stomach rejects food. When this happens, you vomit.

Garden snail
(*Helix aspersa*)

A wink is a conscious movement that is relatively slow. Blinking is a very fast automatic movement that cleans your eyeballs.

FACIAL EXPRESSIONS
Facial expressions, such as looking shocked, or smiling, are tiny voluntary movements made by more than 30 different muscles. Although they are voluntary, you often make these movements with hardly any thought.

SNAIL TRAIL
Snails and slugs have a single suckerlike foot. The foot is made of muscle, which contracts in waves to allow the animal to creep forward. Mucus (slime) enables a snail to grip and move over rough surfaces.

ELASTIC POWER
A flea can leap over 100 times its own height because of tiny pads of resilin, a rubberlike protein that stores energy. The pads are in the joints between the flea's legs and its body. Before each leap, energy from the flea's contracted muscles is stored in the pads. As the flea jumps, this energy is instantly released, causing its legs to flick back suddenly, throwing the flea into the air.

MOVING ON LEGS
Animals with legs have to move them in a carefully coordinated way. We move our legs alternately. A walking cheetah moves its front right leg and back left leg together, then the opposite pair. When it is running at top speed, it moves its front legs together and then its back legs together.

The cheetah (Acinonyx jubatus) is the fastest land animal. It can reach a speed of about 70 mph (110 km/h) by taking enormous strides up to 23 ft (7 m) long.

The cheetah's fully extended legs spread out almost horizontally and its spine curves downward. Its skeleton is unusually flexible.

The cheetah's tail swings up and down to balance the movement of its legs.

The cheetah's spine curves upward so that its back legs can come as far forward as possible, ready for the next leap.

MOVING WITHOUT LEGS
Snakes move by four different methods. In the most common way, a snake curves its body. This is called serpentine motion. Each curve pushes against the ground so that the snake slides forward. In tight spaces, a snake anchors its tail and then stretches forward. Its tail then catches up in an accordion motion. Heavy snakes creep along in a straight line, by raising and lowering their belly scales. This is called rectilinear motion. Some snakes throw themselves forward in a special movement called sidewinding.

This common garter snake (Thamnophis sirtalis) is moving along using serpentine motion.

FLYING AND SWIMMING

Flying and swimming are ways of moving through two very different fluids. Animals fly and swim by pushing backward. A force called reaction acts in the opposite direction, so that they travel forward. The bodies of most swimming animals are as dense as the water around them, so they do not rise or sink. Flying animals have bodies that are far denser than air. They have to use their wings for staying up, as well as for moving along.

Albatross

Lift pushes upward

Gravity pulls downward

GLIDING FLIGHT

A bird's wing has an "aerofoil" shape, which means that it lifts upward when air flows over it. When a bird glides, gravity pulls it downward, but lift opposes the downward force. Birds use gliding flight to cover long distances with little effort, especially in warm rising air.

STEERING IN THE AIR

Many flying insects have two pairs of wings. Craneflies and house flies have just one pair. Their hindwings have evolved into tiny club-shaped organs called halteres. The halteres vibrate as the insect flies, and they produce nerve signals that keep the insect on course.

Halteres help this cranefly keep its balance as it flies along.

2. During the upstroke, the bird raises its wings so that they almost touch.

1. The woodpigeon's streamlined body reduces its friction with the air as it flies along.

Flapping flight

Swimming

1. A swimming dogfish contracts the muscles on each side of its body, one at a time. This makes its body curve from side to side.

FLAPPING FLIGHT

A bird flaps its wings to push itself through the air. As it moves forward, the air flowing over its wings creates lift, which holds the bird up. If the bird stops flapping, it slows down. The lift decreases, so it begins to drop. Birds use flapping flight to travel at speed or in a set direction.

5. The wings are ready to be pulled down again by powerful muscles in the bird's chest.

4. The wings begin to move up once again. Lift counteracts gravity, so the bird stays up as its flies along.

3. During the downstroke, the wings push down and backward against the air. Reaction makes the bird move up and forward.

A dogfish uses its pectoral (front) fins to alter the angle of its body as it swims.

Pelvic fin

Tail fin

2. The dogfish's tail and body push water backward. A reaction force pushes it forward.

SWIMMING

A fish swims by pushing against the water with its fins or with its whole body. Most cartilaginous fish, such as this dogfish, bend their bodies as they swim, but bony fish, such as a goldfish, often propel themselves just with their tail or pectoral fins. They use their other fins for steering. Fish such as tuna and mackerel have special groups of muscles that are used for bursts of speed.

JET PROPULSION

A squid's body contains a cavity that is normally filled with water. The squid can make the cavity contract very rapidly, so that the water squirts outward through a tube called a siphon. The force of the moving water pushes the squid in the opposite direction. The squid changes direction by altering the position of its siphon. Cuttlefish and octopuses also move by this kind of jet propulsion.

MOVING BY HAIRS

Sea gooseberries, also called comb jellies, do not have any legs or fins. Instead, they move by beating tiny hairs, called cilia. The cilia are arranged in clusters that work like paddles. A sea gooseberry uses its cilia to stay the right way up, and to keep near the sea's surface.

The cilia on a sea gooseberry's body are for locomotion. The cilia on its tentacles help it catch food particles.

STAYING IN ONE PLACE

Barnacles are marine animals that glue themselves to hard surfaces. They feed by beating their feathery legs and collecting any food that becomes trapped in them. Barnacles spend their entire adult lives in one place. Like all sessile animals (animals that are fixed in one place), their larvae can swim or drift from one place to another.

Find out more

SPEED P. 118
FORCES AND MOTION P. 120
MOLLUSKS P. 324
FISH P. 326
REPTILES P. 330
BIRDS P. 332
DIGESTION P. 345
MUSCLES P. 355

SENSES

IF YOU HAVE EVER TRIED to find a friend who is hiding, you will know how important your senses are. If your friend makes just one accidental sound, or moves something, it will be enough to let you know where she is. Senses keep us in touch with our surroundings, and also with our bodies. Sense organs like eyes and ears send a stream of information along nerves to the brain. The brain sorts out the signals, and then makes the body react to them. Different animals rely on different senses according to their way of life. Some, such as cats, have very good eyesight and hearing; others, such as dogs, have a strong sense of smell. Some animals find out about their surroundings by detecting pressure, heat, or even electricity.

ALL THE SENSES
People often refer to the five senses, but you have many more than this. Touch is actually several senses. Special nerve endings in your skin detect pressure, pain, heat, and cold. You can feel where your arms and legs are, and your sense of balance helps you stay upright.

Lateral line on the side of a rudd

LATERAL LINE
Many fish have a line of sensors along their sides, called a lateral line. These sensors detect waves of pressure traveling through the water. A fish's lateral line enables it to feel the movement of other animals around it.

WHISKERS
When there is no light to see by, you may walk with your arms out in front to feel your way. Other animals, such as this crested porcupine (*Hysterix africaeaustralis*), feel with their whiskers. These are long stiff hairs on an animal's head. They will brush against anything in the way before the animal bumps into it.

SENSING MOVEMENT AND PRESSURE
Many sense organs detect movement and pressure, which includes touch, sound, and vibrations. Most of a grasshopper's body is sensitive to touch. Its body also has cells that detect vibrations in the ground, and these warn it to hop out of the way when another animal approaches. Sound is another form of pressure, and the grasshopper detects this through its ears.

Antennae are sensitive to touch and chemicals in the air

SENSING LIGHT
A grasshopper has compound eyes. These are eyes which are divided up into many facets (simple eyes), each with its own lens. Each facet has a lens, and it forms a tiny image. The grasshopper combines these images to see the world around it. Our eyes work in a different way. They each have just one lens. The lens focuses light onto a curved screen of light-sensitive nerve cells, forming just one image.

A grasshopper's eardrums can be on the sides of its abdomen, or on the lower part of its legs.

Sensitive cells around joints between body plates

BODY SENSORS
The hard plates around a grasshopper's body are linked by flexible joints. Each joint has special cells on each side, which are either squashed or stretched, depending on the joint's position. The cells send signals to the grasshopper's brain, and from these signals the animal can sense the way the body is positioned. Like nearly all animals, a grasshopper also has other cells that detect the pull of gravity. This tells it which way is up.

SENSING SOUND
A grasshopper's ear is a flat drum on its body case, with an air-filled space behind it. Sound waves vibrate the drum. Cells attached to the drum sense the vibration, and send signals to the brain. Small insects, such as midges and mosquitoes, can detect sound with their antennae.

Your semicircular canals help you to keep your balance.

Cochlea

Middle ear

Outer ear

Ear bones

Eardrum

Inner ear

HUMAN EAR
Your outer ear channels sound waves into the eardrum, making it vibrate. Three tiny bones in the middle ear carry the movement to the cochlea. This contains a fluid and cells with special hairs. The vibrations travel through the fluid and make the hairs move. This triggers nerve cells, which send signals to your brain. The brain sorts the signals into sounds that you hear.

TASTE AND SMELL

Animals use the senses of taste and smell to detect chemicals. When you taste something, groups of cells on your tongue, called taste buds, detect chemicals dissolved in your saliva. When you smell something, cells at the top of your nose detect chemicals dissolved in the moist lining of your nose. Taste buds detect only what we describe as sweet, sour, salt, and bitter. Flavors are combinations of these four, so they are much more varied. Taste is linked to the sense of smell, which is why it is hard to tell different foods apart if your nose is blocked.

Adder
(*Vipera berus*)

JACOBSON'S ORGAN
A snake detects different smells in a pit in the roof of its mouth called a Jacobson's organ. The snake flicks out its tongue to collect chemicals from the air, then presses the forked tip into the Jacobson's organ. Special cells lining the pit detect the chemicals picked up from the air.

Jacobson's organ

SMELL
Some animals use scents to send and receive messages. For example, dogs leave their scent to mark their territory or to let other dogs know they are around. Dogs use their sense of smell to build up a "picture" of the world around them.

Most taste buds lie in tiny grooves in the surface of the tongue.

TASTE
Different taste buds on an animal's tongue detect different tastes, such as sweet or sour. An animal's sense of taste enables it to tell if something is good or bad to eat. Animals use this sense to choose food to eat and to avoid eating something poisonous.

JUDGING DISTANCES
Many animals, including humans, have "binocular vision," which allows them to judge distances. Binocular vision means having two eyes facing forward, which gives two slightly different views of the same object. The tiny jumping spider (*Lyssomanes viridis*) has four pairs of large eyes. Some of its eyes point sideways, but one pair looks directly forward. This pair of eyes enables the spider to judge how far away its prey is before it jumps on to it.

A male cockchafer's antennae unfold like fans.

FINDING A MATE
Female insects often let male insects know where they are by releasing tiny amounts of chemicals called pheromones that spread through the air. These are detected by a male of the same species, which then follows the pheromone trail to track down the female in order to mate. The male cockchafer (*Melolontha melolontha*) detects the female's pheromones with its feathery antennae.

PLANT SENSES
Plants do not have special sense organs, but they can respond to the world around them. All plants detect light and gravity, and some plants also sense nearby objects. The sensitive plant (*Mimosa pudica*) has very quick reactions. Its leaves go limp if they are touched. The tendrils of climbing plants can "feel" things that they touch. They respond by coiling up, to attach the plant to a support.

Tendrils of climbing plants, such as this pea plant, are modified leaves.

The folding leaves of the sensitive plant may help the plant escape being eaten.

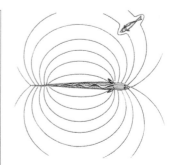

ELECTRIC FIELDS
In muddy water it is difficult to see. Some fish, such as this *Gymnarchus niloticus* use an electric field, produced by special muscles, to detect things nearby. If something disturbs the field, the fish can tell what it is by the size and position of the disturbance.

NERVES

1. Pain triggers the sensory neuron to produce a signal.

If you hurt yourself, the signals travel to your spinal cord and not your brain, for the quickest possible reaction.

WHEN YOU PICK UP this book, lots of things happen very quickly. Your arms adjust to the book's weight, so that they lift it with just the right force. Muscles in your back contract, so that you do not tip forward, and the lenses in your eyes change shape, so that your eyes focus on the pages. Thanks to your nerves, you are now ready to read. Nerves are bundles of long, thin cells called neurons which carry fast-moving electrical signals. The sensory neurons carry signals from different parts of your body to your brain or spinal cord. The motor neurons carry signals from your brain or spinal cord to your muscles to make them contract. Between them are different neurons: the association neurons, which pass signals to motor neurons, and send messages to your brain.

5. A motor neuron makes muscles contract, pulling your hand away from the source of the pain.

How NERVES WORK
You have three types of neuron (nerve cell) in your body. If you touch something that hurts, the pain is detected by a sensory neuron. This flashes a signal to an association neuron in your spinal cord. This neuron then passes the signal to one or more motor neurons, and these make you move. This kind of split-second reaction is called a reflex.

2. The signal races along the neuron's axon (fiber). Axons are much thinner than a hair, but they can be very long. Some run all the way along your arms or legs.

MYELIN
Some neurons are covered by a fatty substance called myelin. This helps to make the nerve signals travel faster. It also works like the plastic insulation around a wire, so that the neuron's electric signal does not leak away. The myelin is made by special cells that wrap themselves around the axon many times.

Myelin sheath

HUMAN NERVOUS SYSTEM
Your nervous system consists of the central nervous system (spinal cord and brain) and the peripheral nerves. Your brain coordinates almost everything that your body does. Some of your nervous system is under your control. The rest works automatically, so that your body runs smoothly without you telling it what to do.

Brain

Spinal cord

4. The association neuron passes the signal across a synapse to a motor neuron.

Cell body of sensory neuron

3. The signal is passed to an association neuron in the spinal cord.

The signal reaches the association neuron by jumping across a synapse.

NERVE NETS
A flatworm's nerves are scattered across its body in an interconnecting net. The nerves produce signals that make its body contract in waves, so that it swims.

Nervous system of flat worm

Brain

Ganglia

Cell body of association neuron

Candystripe flatworm (Prostheceraeus vittatus)

NERVES IN INSECTS
The nervous system of an insect is simpler than ours. It consists of a brain and clusters of neurons, known as ganglia. These are joined by rows of nerve fibers.

Cell body of motor neuron

Nervous system of a grasshopper

SYNAPSES
Neurons meet at tiny gaps, called synapses. Nerve signals jump across the gap in one direction. Some neurons pass on a signal as soon as they receive it. Others wait for a number of signals to arrive before sending one of their own.

Grasshopper

GIANT NERVES
An earthworm has special giant neurons that run from its tail to its head. These cells carry signals about 50 times faster than the rest of its nerves. If a bird pecks at a worm's tail, signals race along the giant nerves and make the worm contract almost instantly.

Find out more

WORMS P. 321
ARTHROPODS P. 322
INTERNAL ENVIRONMENT P. 350
MUSCLES P. 355
SENSES P. 358
BRAINS P. 361

BRAINS

YOUR BRAIN IS IN TOUCH with the rest of your body all the time. It contains billions of neurons (nerve cells) that link up with each other and with all of the nerves in your body. Scientists know a lot about individual neurons, but the way that the whole brain works is not fully understood. Experts are only just beginning to discover how we think or how we remember things. But it is known that our brains are divided up into separate areas. Some areas deal with the general running of the body. Others are involved in coordinating our movements, or understanding spoken words. While you are awake, you are conscious, or aware of what you are doing. When you fall asleep, your conscious brain shuts down, but other parts continue the essential work of keeping you alive.

View of the left half of the human brain, seen from inside

Area used to move body

Area used to control speech

White matter, made up of nerve fibers

Front

Gray matter, or cortex

Area used to interpret sensations

Back

Area used in vision

Cerebellum coordinates muscles and controls posture.

Spinal cord

Pituitary gland

Brain stem controls vital functions, including breathing and circulation.

Frontal lobe of cerebrum is involved in conscious thought.

HUMAN BRAIN
Your brain is divided into three main regions. Two of them, the brain stem and cerebellum, look after the running of your body. They control your breathing, your circulation, and your posture. The cerebrum, which is much larger, processes information. It is this part of your brain that you use to think. Your brain contains about a trillion nerve cells when you are born. This number slowly decreases as you get older, because neurons die and cannot be replaced.

Cerebrum (part of forebrain)

Optic lobe

Cerebellum

Brain stem

Forebrain

Pituitary gland

BIRD BRAIN
In a bird's brain, the cerebrum does not cover the cerebellum. The brain has a large optic lobe—the part that processes information from its eyes.

IVAN PAVLOV
Pavlov (1849–1936) was a Russian physiologist who investigated the way reflexes work. He knew that all animals have built-in reflexes, but he found that new reflexes could be conditioned (learned). Pavlov conditioned dogs to expect food after a bell was rung. He found that their new reflex made them salivate (drool) after the bell sounded, even if there was no food.

Cerebrum (part of forebrain)

Optic lobe

Cerebellum

Forebrain

Brain stem

FROG BRAIN
A frog's cerebrum is quite small, while its cerebellum is tiny. Its brain stem makes up about half of the brain's volume. Vision is important to a frog because it hunts by sight. Its optic lobes are not as large as a bird's, but they are still a major part of its brain.

Coordinating area of brain

Nerves to arms and head

These large lobes deal with nerve signals from the eyes.

Nerves to body

OCTOPUS BRAIN
An octopus has one of the largest brains of all invertebrates. It is built on a completely different plan from the brains of vertebrates and has many connected lobes. Octopuses have good eyesight and a large part of their brain deals with signals from their eyes. Experiments have found that octopuses are intelligent animals. They can work out how to reach food, even if this means taking the stopper out of a submerged bottle.

BRAIN CELLS
The nerve cells in the brain can have synapses with over 200,000 neighboring cells. Signals from their neighbors may either make a group of cells send a message (like making you swallow), or prevent them from doing so (like taking a breath while you are swallowing).

INSTINCT AND LEARNING
A male great bower bird (*Chlamydera nuchalis*) builds an extraordinary bower (an alleyway) out of sticks and decorates it with bright objects. If he is lucky, it will attract a mate for him. The male bower bird does not have to learn how to do this complicated work. Instead, he does it by instinct. Instinct is a kind of behavior that is inherited, rather than learned.

Find out more
MOLLUSKS P. 324
AMPHIBIANS P. 328
BIRDS P. 332
SENSES P. 358
NERVES P. 360

GROWTH AND DEVELOPMENT

MOST LIVING THINGS GET BIGGER as they get older. They do not do this by having bigger cells, but by making more of them. When a cell gets to a certain size, it makes a copy of itself to make two new cells. The two new cells can also divide, and so many cells build up. This is cell division. Some living things, such as plants, continue growing by cell division all their lives. But in most animals, including humans, cells divide more slowly once the adult body has taken shape.

1. For most of the time, in the periods between cell divisions, a cell's DNA (deoxyribonucleic acid) in the nucleus is spread out and too thin to see.

Nucleus

Spindle

Cell membrane

Chromosomes

2. The DNA copies itself and coils up into chromosomes. The chromosome and its copy are held together by a centromere. Tiny chemical threads, called the spindle, begin to take shape.

Spindle

3. The membrane around the nucleus disappears. The spindle is now fully formed, and the chromosomes start to line up in its center.

Half-chromosome

4. Each chromosome starts to separate into two identical halves, pulled apart by the spindle, which is attached to the centromere. The halves move toward opposite ends of the cell.

5. A membrane forms around each set of chromosomes, creating two new nuclei.

CELL DIVISION

Before a cell can divide, it must duplicate its chromosomes (the threadlike structures that contain DNA). The duplicated chromosomes are then pulled apart and two new nuclei are made. This is called mitosis. When mitosis is complete, the cell divides, so that two identical cells are made. This kind of cell division is used for growth. Another kind of division, called meiosis, occurs before sexual reproduction. It does not make identical cells.

DIVISION IN ACTION
In this thin layer of cells from an onion root, each cell is surrounded by a cell wall. The dividing cells have clearly visible chromosomes. In the other cells, the chromosomes are spread out in the nucleus. Plant and animal cells divide in a very similar way, although plant cells have to make a cellulose cell wall after they are formed.

GROWTH IN TREES
A tree grows in two different ways. Cells at the tips of its branches and roots divide so that the branches and roots grow longer. At the same time, cells just underneath the bark, called the cambium, divide to make the trunk and branches thicker.

6. A furrow starts to form around the cell. As the furrow deepens, the cytoplasm is pinched into two halves.

7. The two new cells are now complete. Each contains exactly the same DNA as its parent cell, and as each other. These cells can now duplicate themselves to produce four cells.

8. After division is complete, the DNA in the chromosomes spreads out again.

Growth rings are formed by a burst of growth every spring, slower growth in summer, and none in winter.

SEEDLINGS
Growth needs lots of energy. A seedling can grow quickly because it has a store of food in a tissue in the seed called the endosperm. Sometimes the seed leaves (cotyledons) also have a store of food. In many seedlings, the cotyledons quickly open up so that photosynthesis can begin.

Food stored in the seed gives it the energy to germinate.

As a sapling grows, its lowest branches drop off to leave a bare trunk. The trunk thickens but does not stretch upward—an old branch scar will always stay at the same height.

CELL CYCLE
Many of the cells in your body divide according to a fixed timetable. A cell inside your cheek, for example, divides about once every 24 hours. Not all cells divide this quickly. In some cells, division is "switched off" during a long gap period. In nerve cells, division stops altogether after the cell is formed in a baby in the womb.

4. Second gap period (4 hours)—cell grows and prepares to divide.

1. Mitosis and cell division (1 hour).

3. Synthesis period (9 hours) —chromosomes are duplicated.

2. First gap period (10 hours).

Division cycle of a cell from the inside of a cheek

GROWING UP

The cells in your body do not all divide at the same rate. As you grow up, many of your cells, particularly those in your arms and legs, divide faster than those in your head. As a result, your body slowly changes shape. This is development. Growth and development are controlled by hormones— chemical messengers that are carried by your blood to the different parts of your body. Some of these hormones make your body undergo a sudden burst of growth from the age of about 12 or 13 and make you stop growing altogether at around 21.

Human development

A newborn baby has a very large head and short arms and legs.

A two-year-old's legs and arms have grown a lot. Its legs are now strong enough for walking.

By the age of five, the arm and leg muscles have become much stronger. A five-year-old can walk and run.

A 10-year-old has longer limbs and has learned how to make precise movements, such as writing or catching a ball.

At the age of 13, many changes are taking place in the body. It is growing quickly and preparing for adulthood.

Most 20-year-olds are fully grown. The head is now a smaller part of the body. The wisdom teeth are one of the last parts to finish growing.

Southern white admiral (*Limenitis camilla*)

Inside a chrysalis, most of a caterpillar's cells are broken down. New cells then form the butterfly.

A caterpillar has powerful jaws but a butterfly has tubular mouthparts and can only drink its food.

TAKING TO THE AIR

By changing shape, the same animal can use different kinds of food and move in different ways. A caterpillar eats leaves and spends all its time on plants. But when it turns into a butterfly, it feeds on nectar. It can now fly far away to search for new food plants, on which it will lay its eggs if it is a female.

A mirid bug (leaf bug) in the second, fifth, and adult phases of incomplete metamorphosis.

A crab's zoea larva has a long tail and a curved spine on its back. It beats its legs to keep near the surface.

A megalopa larva has well developed legs, no spine, and a shorter tail. It lives partly on the seabed.

An adult crab has a short tail, which is folded up underneath its body. It has strong legs, but is not a good swimmer. This is a shore crab (Carcinus maenas).

COMPLETE METAMORPHOSIS

A crab changes shape completely as it grows up. It starts life as a tiny zoea larva, which floats in the upper waters of the sea. After molting its body case several times, the zoea turns into a megalopa larva, which can walk as well as swim. Finally, the megalopa molts and becomes a young crab.

INCOMPLETE METAMORPHOSIS

A bug gradually changes shape as it grows up. When it hatches, it has no wings or reproductive organs. As it grows up, it molts (sheds its case). After each molt, its body changes slightly, and after the fifth molt it becomes an adult. This slow change of body shape is called incomplete metamorphosis. Cockroaches and grasshoppers also develop in this way.

GROWING MISSING PARTS

If you cut yourself, cells in your skin start to divide until the cut has healed. This kind of growth is called regeneration. We can regenerate skin and bone, but some animals can regenerate entire parts of themselves, including legs and tails.

Starfish can grow a new leg if one breaks off.

Find out more

FLOWERING PLANTS P. 318
ARTHROPODS P. 322
STARFISH AND SEA SQUIRTS P. 325
CELLS P. 338
INTERNAL ENVIRONMENT P. 350
GENETICS P. 364

GENETICS

EVERY FORM OF LIFE, from an elephant to an alga, is put together and controlled by a chemical "recipe." Instead of being written down, this recipe is in the form of a chemical message. The message is contained in helical (spiral-shaped) molecules of deoxyribonucleic acid (DNA), which are packed away inside the cells of all living things. The chemical message is very complex. The message inside one human cell contains 25,000 separate instructions, called genes, and each one controls a different characteristic. Genetics is the study of the way that inherited characteristics are passed on.

Male and female sex cells have a single set of DNA molecules each, which means that they have half the amount of a normal cell.

A fertilized cell has a double set of DNA molecules. In other words, it has the usual double set of chromosomes.

Bases linked in pairs

HUMAN CHROMOSOMES
This photograph shows all the 46 chromosomes in a single human cell. They have been treated with a special dye and arranged in pairs. (The X and Y chromosomes are on the lower right.) Every species of plant and animal has a characteristic chromosome number. Some have fewer than 10, others over a thousand.

Each DNA molecule forms a threadlike structure, or chromosome. There are two copies of each chromosome—one from the father and one from the mother.

The DNA in a chromosome is coiled up on itself and wrapped around other chemicals.

The DNA molecule is in the shape of a double helix, linked by chemicals called bases, of which there are four kinds. The sequence of these bases makes up the cell's genetic message.

The message instructs the cell to assemble proteins.

DNA is "unzipped" while the message is copied.

Protein being assembled

CHROMOSOMES, GENES, AND DNA

In a cell's nucleus, there are several lengths of DNA. Each one is called a chromosome. A gene is one area of a chromosome that has the instructions to make one protein. DNA works by telling a cell how to make the many different proteins that your cells need to work. To do this, part of the DNA helix is temporarily "unzipped," so that its code can be copied. The copy moves out of the nucleus. Once outside, it instructs the cell to assemble a particular protein, which could be an enzyme, or collagen (a protein in your skin), for example.

These flowers are chamomile (Anthemis chia).

NATURAL VARIATIONS
These flowers may look the same, but each plant has its own unique DNA, because it was formed by sexual reproduction. This gives the plant a distinctive set of characteristics. It might have more flowers than others, or it might put slightly more energy into growing roots. Tiny variations like this are important, because they mean a species evolves (changes with time). Some DNA variations are more successful than others, so as one generation succeeds another, their more successful genes become more common.

ROSALIND FRANKLIN

The final breakthrough in the study of DNA's structure was made in 1953, by British bio-physicist Francis Crick (1916–2004) and American geneticist James Watson (born 1928). They suggested that DNA was a double helix—a conclusion they reached after studying X-ray photographs taken by British X-ray crystallographer Rosalind Franklin (1920–58). She used X-rays to look at DNA crystals. Crick, Watson, and Maurice Wilkins (1916–2004) got the Nobel Prize for Physiology or Medicine in 1962. Franklin died before her contribution was properly credited.

GENES AND PEOPLE
Unless you are an identical twin, you are unique, because nobody else has exactly your combination of genes. Genes control all the inherited characteristics of your body. Sometimes a single gene controls a characteristic that we can see, such as the color of your eyes, but usually several genes are involved. Many of the characteristics you inherit are modified by the way you live. For example, your height depends on what you eat, as well as on your genes.

MUTATIONS
DNA is an extremely long molecule, and it is frequently damaged. Normally, this damage is automatically repaired. But if the damage is extensive, it creates a permanent new piece of genetic code, called a mutation. Mutations normally have little effect if they occur in body cells. But if they occur in gametes (sex cells), they can be passed on from one generation to another. Mutations create new characteristics in living things.

Albino (white) color is a common type of mutation in animals and plants. This is an albino red squirrel.

MEIOSIS

Meiosis is a special kind of cell division that produces gametes (sex cells). During meiosis, a cell divides twice, so that it makes four new cells. The new cells have only half the amount of DNA in the original cell. Each of their chromosomes has a new and unique pattern, because the original cell's chromosomes swap pieces just before division begins. Unlike mitosis (ordinary cell division), meiosis makes cells that have new genetic instructions. A female gamete is usually called an egg cell, and the male gamete is a sperm cell.

The original male cell has a double set of chromosomes.

The original female cell also has a double set of chromosomes.

The female cell divides by meiosis. It produces four female sex cells, or eggs. Each has a single set of unique chromosomes.

The male cell divides by meiosis. It produces four male sex cells, or sperms. Each one has a single set of unique chromosomes.

In animals, the original female cell often divides unequally. It produces three small cells (polar bodies) and one large one.

During fertilization, one male gamete and one female gamete join together. They make a fertilized cell that has a double set of chromosomes once more.

The fertilized cell has a unique genetic blueprint. It divides by mitosis to produce a new organism. All the DNA in a new organism is a copy of the DNA in the egg and sperm.

Only the large cell can be fertilized

HAPLOID AND DIPLOID
A cell with a full (double) set of chromosomes is called diploid. Most of the cells in your body are diploid. A sex cell only has half the number of chromosomes, so it is called haploid. Sex cells are haploid so that they can join up with another sex cell to make a diploid cell. This cell can then grow into a new organism.

GREGOR MENDEL

Mendel (1822–84) was an Austrian monk and botanist who discovered how characteristics are inherited. He patiently carried out thousands of experiments on pea plants, cross-fertilizing particular parents and studying the results. He found out that inheritance does not work by blending characteristics together, as people then thought. Instead, they are inherited in pairs. In each pair, only one characteristic is usually expressed (shown). Mendel worked out the basic rules of genetics, but it was not until the 20th century that scientists rediscovered his work.

Reddish cats are usually male (XY). The gene for this color is carried on the X chromosome, but it is often masked if another X chromosome is present, as it is in a female (XX).

Tortoiseshell cats are always female, because this color can only be produced by two X chromosomes. Only females have the XX combination.

GENES AND SEX
In cats, humans, and many other animals, two differently shaped chromosomes decide what sex an individual will be. The chromosomes are known as X and Y. An animal can either have two X chromosomes, making it female, or it can have an X and Y chromosome, making it male. It cannot have two Y chromosomes, because it always receives one X chromosome from its mother. As well as sex, these chromosomes also determine some other characteristics. In cats, they include fur color, while in humans, they include color blindness.

HOW CHARACTERISTICS ARE INHERITED
Most cells contain two sets of chromosomes, one from each parent. This means they have two sets of genes. Normally one gene in every pair is dominant, meaning that it masks (hides) the effects of its recessive partner. Here, you can see how a pair of genes controls the color of pea flowers. The dominant gene (labeled R) makes flowers red. The recessive gene (labeled r) makes the flowers white. However, its effects are masked, unless there are two of them.

One parent plant has two dominant genes (RR), so its flowers are red. The other parent has two recessive genes (rr), so its flowers are white.

RR

rr

Recessive genes usually only show their effects if there are two of them.

Each offspring plant receives one flower color gene from each of its parents. In the first generation, there is only one possible combination of genes: Rr.

Rr   Rr   Rr   Rr

The first generation offspring all have red flowers. Although each has a recessive gene for white flowers, its effects are masked by the dominant gene.

In the second generation, there are four possible combinations of genes: RR, Rr, rR, and rr.

RR   Rr   Rr   rr

One-quarter of the plants have two recessive genes (rr). Only their flowers are white.

Find out more
HOW EVOLUTION WORKS P. 309
CELLS P. 338
GROWTH AND DEVELOPMENT P. 362
SEXUAL REPRODUCTION P. 367
HUMAN REPRODUCTION P. 368

ASEXUAL REPRODUCTION

ALL LIVING THINGS REPRODUCE. Reproduction and continuing the species is a basic feature of all living things. But living things reproduce in two very different ways. Here, you can find out about one way. It is called asexual reproduction, because it does not involve sex. In asexual reproduction, there is just one parent. Part of the parent buds off or splits away, and this becomes a new individual. Asexual reproduction is simple and quick, but it does have one result that can be a drawback under certain conditions. The parent and young share the same genetic material, so they have exactly the same characteristics. If the parent has a disadvantage, such as low resistance to a disease, its offspring will have it, too.

BUDDING YEAST
Yeasts are microscopic single-celled fungi. They reproduce asexually by budding off parts of their cells. A yeast cell can bud every two hours. The new cells sometimes start to bud before they have completely separated from their parent, so a branching chain is produced.

A young hydra polyp attached to its parent. The new polyp eventually breaks away to live by itself. This hydra is Hydra vulgaris.

ASEXUAL REPRODUCTION IN ANIMALS
Asexual reproduction is widespread in plants, but it is less common in animals. The first person to see an animal reproduce in this way was Antoni van Leeuwenhoek, one of the earliest users of the microscope. In 1701, he was watching a tiny animal called a hydra, which lives in ponds. He saw how parts of it bud off to become new animals.

PRODUCTION LINE BIRTH
In spring and summer, female aphids are often surrounded by dozens of young. The females produce babies by parthenogenesis (without mating), and they multiply very rapidly. This means that there are lots of aphids when there is plenty of food. Later, as the food supply starts to dwindle, their young reproduce sexually.

CLONES
Sea anemones usually reproduce sexually by releasing eggs into the water, but they can also multiply by breaking off parts of themselves, or by pulling themselves in two. Some species concentrate on this form of reproduction. They spread over rocks, forming a group of identical animals that share exactly the same genes. Groups like this are called clones.

An anemone gradually pulls itself apart as the two halves creep in different directions.

The two new animals are genetically identical to their "parent," which is the original anemone.

PROPAGATING CROPS
Bananas are never grown from seed. Instead, a farmer simply cuts off new shoots and plants them. With crops like this, the plants will all have the same characteristics. If one catches a disease, the rest may do so as well. This lack of variety is a major problem of asexual reproduction.

Parent strawberry plant

SPREADING BY RUNNERS
Many plants reproduce in two different ways at the same time. Strawberries have flowers, which make seeds by sexual reproduction. They also send out horizontal stems, called runners, which form new plants by asexual reproduction. Each runner develops several young plants, and these gradually take root. If a strawberry patch is left untended, new strawberry plants soon cover the ground.

New plant on runner

NEW BULBS
Bulbs contain food, which is stored in special leaves that are packed tightly together. As a bulb grows, it forms new small bulbs called bulbils around its base.

Daffodil bulb with bulbil

Find out more

SINGLE-CELLED ORGANISMS. P. 314
GROWTH AND DEVELOPMENT P. 362
FACT FINDER P. 422

SEXUAL REPRODUCTION

THERE ARE ALWAYS TWO PARENTS in sexual reproduction. Each parent makes gametes (sex cells) by a special kind of cell division called meiosis. The male gamete (the sperm) and the female gamete (the egg) are brought together and a new cell is formed. This is fertilization. From this fertilized cell, a whole new organism develops. Sexual reproduction is more complicated than asexual reproduction, but it has an important advantage. Instead of being the same as one of their parents, sexually produced offspring are unique. They have a unique combination of genes, so that they have a completely new mixture of characteristics. This means that some of them may be better equipped in the struggle to survive.

COURTSHIP AND MATING
Before grebes mate, they perform a series of complicated dances. This kind of behavior, called courtship, is common in many animals. It helps both partners to get used to each other and ensures that they choose a suitable and healthy mate. Courtship is then followed by mating.

Great crested grebes (*Podiceps cristatus*)

Californian mountain kingsnakes (*Lampropeltis zonata*) mating

INTERNAL FERTILIZATION

For sexual reproduction to work, the male and female sex cells have to be brought together. In some animals, this happens through mating. Snakes and many other land animals have internal fertilization: when two snakes mate, the male injects his sperm into the female so that fertilization of her eggs takes place inside her body. Animals that have internal fertilization produce fewer eggs and sperms since these are more likely to come together.

EXTERNAL FERTILIZATION
In some animals, the eggs and sperm join together outside the female's body, but the animals still have to come together. The male stickleback (*Gasterosteus aculeatus*) makes a nest in which the female lays her eggs. The male then adds his sperm to the eggs. Most animals with external fertilization have to produce lots of eggs so that enough will be fertilized.

Sporophyte stage

Spores produced by meiosis

A new sporophyte starts to grow.

Fertilization

Female gametophyte stage produces eggs.

Male gametophyte stage produces sperms.

ALTERNATING GENERATIONS
In some plant life cycles there are two different forms of the plant. In the brown algae *Laminaria*, the "adult" form (called the sporophyte) produces spores by meiosis. These develop into male and female plants called gametophytes. It is this stage that produces the gametes (sex cells). The eggs and sperm come together in the water to produce a fertilized cell. This grows into a sporophyte, and the cycle starts again.

SEX CELLS

Sex cells (gametes) have exactly half the amount of genetic material of ordinary cells. They are specially shaped so that they can join together. In some plants and animals, the sex cells are the same size. But more often, the female sex cell is much larger than the male. Female sex cells (eggs) stay in one place, while male sex cells (sperms) swim toward them.

The sea lettuce (Ulva lactuca) has identical male and female sex cells.

Flowering plants have several female sex cells in an embryo sac. The male cells are contained in pollen grains.

In most animals, the egg is far bigger than the sperm.

In "thrum" primrose flowers the stamens (which produce the pollen) are high up, and the stigma is short.

"Pin" primrose flowers have a long stigma (the female part). The stamens are low down.

ENSURING CROSS-FERTILIZATION
Many plants have both male and female parts in their flowers. They can often fertilize themselves, but they usually have features that encourage cross-fertilization (fertilization with sex cells from another plant). Cross-fertilization is useful, because it makes a plant's offspring more varied. Primroses (*Primula vulgaris*) have two types of flower, but only one type is found on a plant. Each flower type can only fertilize the other, so cross-pollination is guaranteed.

HUMAN REPRODUCTION

When a woman has a baby, her breasts make milk to feed it.

The ovaries store egg cells. They also release hormones that control a woman's reproductive cycle.

Sex hormones circulate in the blood and make a woman's body ready to look after a developing child.

LIKE EVERY PERSON ON EARTH, you started life as a tiny fertilized cell. This cell was formed when one of your father's sperms (sex cells) joined up with an egg cell in a tube that leads into your mother's womb (uterus) called the fallopian tube. Almost immediately, the fertilized cell began to change. It started to divide, and it then settled on the lining of the womb. Nourished by your mother's blood, it divided again and again, and slowly your body began to take shape. After nine months in the warmth and darkness of your mother's body, you were ready to be born.

From the start of puberty, sex hormones produce changes in the male body. The sex organs become fully developed and facial hair starts to grow.

Scrotal sac

A woman is born with all her egg cells, but a man makes new sperm cells all the time.

Bladder

Prostate gland

Testis

Testis

Penis

FEMALE SEX ORGANS
A woman's egg cells are stored inside two glands called ovaries. From the age of about 13, one egg cell is released every 28 days.

MALE SEX ORGANS
Male sex cells, or sperms, are made in two glands called testes. During lovemaking, the sperms are mixed with liquid from the prostate gland that makes the sperms swim. This means they can reach the egg in the woman's uterus.

The egg is now a hollow ball of cells. It lands on the lining of the uterus and gradually develops into an embryo, then a fetus.

The fertilized egg starts to divide rapidly by mitosis.

The egg is fertilized by a sperm swimming up the fallopian tube.

The egg is collected by a funnel and is carried along the fallopian tube.

Every 28 days or so, a ripe egg cell is released from a bubble on the ovary called a follicle.

The empty follicle produces a hormone that prepares the lining of the womb to receive the egg.

The ovaries take turns producing one egg each month.

The lining of the uterus builds up each month to receive the egg. If the egg has not been fertilized, the lining of the uterus breaks down. This is menstruation.

Sperms swim into the uterus through a tiny gap in the cervix.

The vagina holds the penis during lovemaking so that the sperms are ejaculated (pumped out) as near the egg as possible. The vagina is also the canal through which the baby is born.

Mother's cells which have been digested to provide nutrients

Lining of the mother's uterus

These cells will develop into the placenta and the umbilical cord.

These cells will develop into the baby.

This fluid-filled cavity will develop into the amniotic fluid, the "water" that the baby floats in.

THE UTERUS
The uterus is the organ that feeds and shelters a fetus (developing baby). The inside lining develops to feed a fertilized egg, then the embryo, and later the fetus. The uterus itself is very muscular—it has the strongest muscles in the human body. These push the baby out during labor, with help from the mother's other muscles in her abdomen and chest.

IMPLANTATION
When a fertilized egg lands on the wall of the uterus, it starts to break down some of the mother's cells. To begin with, it is nourished by these cells. Later, it gets oxygen and nutrients from its mother's blood through a spongy organ called the placenta. This is connected to the fetus by a long cord called the umbilical cord. These two organs take the fetus's waste products back to the mother. The placenta also produces hormones in pregnancy.

CHANGES IN PREGNANCY
To begin with, the fetus (developing baby) takes up little room, but by the ninth month it fills the whole of the uterus and this pushes up against the mother's stomach and diaphragm. The mother's body adapts to these changes. Her heart pumps more blood to nourish her growing child. She eats much more to feed it, and her breasts grow in preparation for breast-feeding after it is born. She also prepares herself mentally for the new baby.

Breasts produce milk very soon after birth.

The fetus usually lies upside-down, with arms and legs tucked close to its body.

The umbilical cord carries blood from the fetus to the placenta.

BREAST-FEEDING
Most baby mammals are fed with milk from their mother's breasts. Milk contains a perfectly balanced mixture of nutrients designed for the baby, and it is easily digested. Milk also has the advantage of being readily available.

Find out more
MAMMALS P. 334
PRIMATES P. 336
GROWTH AND DEVELOPMENT P. 362
GENETICS P. 364
SEXUAL REPRODUCTION P. 367

ECOLOGY

The weather is part of the rabbit's environment. The rabbit has to survive in different conditions. It needs clean air to breathe and water to drink.

THE STUDY OF LIVING THINGS in their natural surroundings is called ecology. And their surroundings are called their environment. Ecology is about seeing the whole picture as well as the pieces. By studying an animal's environment, ecologists can begin to understand why the animal behaves in a particular way. But ecology is still a "new" science, and the natural world is very complex. Ecologists know that problems exist but are not always sure how serious they are or how to solve them.

Animals that live in the rabbit's fur, such as fleas, or organisms inside its body, such as bacteria

Animals that eat rabbits, such as foxes and stoats

RABBIT'S ENVIRONMENT
The conditions in which an animal lives, and the other species of animals and plants that live in its area, all affect the animal's own life. This is why, when ecologists study the environment of an animal such as a rabbit, they study everything living and nonliving that is connected with it. This includes animals that hunt it, its food, other rabbits, the weather, air, and soil.

Plants that the rabbit eats such as grass, dandelions, and clover

Soil in which the rabbit digs burrows for shelter from the weather and predators, and to protect its young

Other animals, such as squirrels and mice, that eat the same food as the rabbit

Other rabbits that live together in the same warren (several burrows). Rabbits breed together to produce more rabbits and help each other to survive.

Animals that live in the same place, such as worms in the soil

HUMAN ENVIRONMENT
Unlike most other animals, humans can change their environment to suit their way of life. This does not always help plants and other animals. Human ecology is the study of how humans change the environment and how these changes affect humans themselves.

ERNST HAECKEL

German biologist Ernst Haeckel (1834–1919) was, in 1869, the first to use the word ecology. He defined it as "the study of the economy, of the household, of animal organisms." He took the word from the Greek *oikos*, meaning "house" or "place to live in." Haeckel supported Darwin's theory of evolution by natural selection. His idea of ecology was forgotten until about 1900 when biologists began to study it seriously.

GATHERING FACTS AND FIGURES
The information that ecologists need to collect involves a lot of counting, weighing, and measuring—on land and under water. Sometimes figures are fed into computers that work out the possible effects of certain changes to an area. Ecologists can then advise people about how to treat the environment.

THE BIOSPHERE

THE EARTH is a complicated system. The part in which life exists is called the biosphere. *Bios* is an Ancient Greek word meaning "life." The biosphere extends a little way above and below the surface of the planet. The habitat is made up of distinct areas, each with its own characteristic climate, soils, and living communities of plants and animals. These areas are called ecosystems. Each one consists of a number of parts that are related in such a way as to keep the whole system going. Although distinct, each ecosystem is not closed. Sunlight and rain enter it, water drains from it, nutrients enter and leave through the soil, and plant seeds and animals come and go.

NICHE
A niche is the position of a living thing within an ecosystem, including where it lives, what it absorbs or eats, how it behaves, and how it is related to other living things. The niche has been called the "profession" of a species.

LARGE AND SMALL
An ecosystem can be as small as a drop of rainwater on a leaf or as large as an ocean. Both have different characteristics from the surrounding area, and both contain groups of living things, which interact with each other. A single tree and a huge forest are also ecosystems. Human skin can even be studied as an ecosystem, since colonies of bacteria and mites live here.

HABITAT
A habitat is the natural home of a group of plants and animals. This group of living things is called a community. The habitat is sometimes called the "address" of a species. It contains several niches. Trees are an example of a habitat.

UNITS WITHIN THE BIOSPHERE

To make the biosphere easier to study, ecologists break it down into smaller units. Information about each unit can then be fitted together to give a more complete picture. One ecosystem can be studied as a whole, or the living things within it can be studied individually.

ECOSYSTEM
An ecosystem is a distinct area in the biosphere that contains living things. It includes the rocks and soil underneath the ground, the surface of the ground, and the air above it. It contains several habitats. A forest is an example of an ecosystem. The largest ecosystems, such as rain forests and deserts, are called biomes.

JAMES E. LOVELOCK
British scientist James Lovelock (born 1919) put forward his "Gaia hypothesis" in the 1970s. *Gaia* is an old Greek term for "Mother Earth," or "Earth goddess." After studying the atmosphere on Mars, Lovelock began to study Earth's atmosphere. He suggested that the atmosphere is regulated by the biosphere. All living things on Earth can be thought of as part of one being that can change its environment to suit its needs. Gaia will ensure conditions are right for its own survival, even if humans make the Earth unfit for themselves.

BIOSPHERE
The biosphere covers the whole surface of the Earth. It is the living part of the planet and includes the atmosphere. It contains many different ecosystems.

THE EARTH
The Earth is the only planet that we know for certain contains life. It has both water and an oxygen-rich atmosphere, which protects the planet from the Sun's more harmful rays. In 1996 scientists found signs indicating that Mars may once have had living things. Astronomers think that other stars may have planets similar to Earth.

THE WORLD'S ECOSYSTEMS

Ecosystems are distributed over the Earth mainly according to climate. There are zones of different climates ranging from cold and dry at the poles, to hot and wet at the equator. Plants and animals are adapted to the conditions and are associated with each other to form communities. They have particular roles within each ecosystem, competing for the resources to survive.

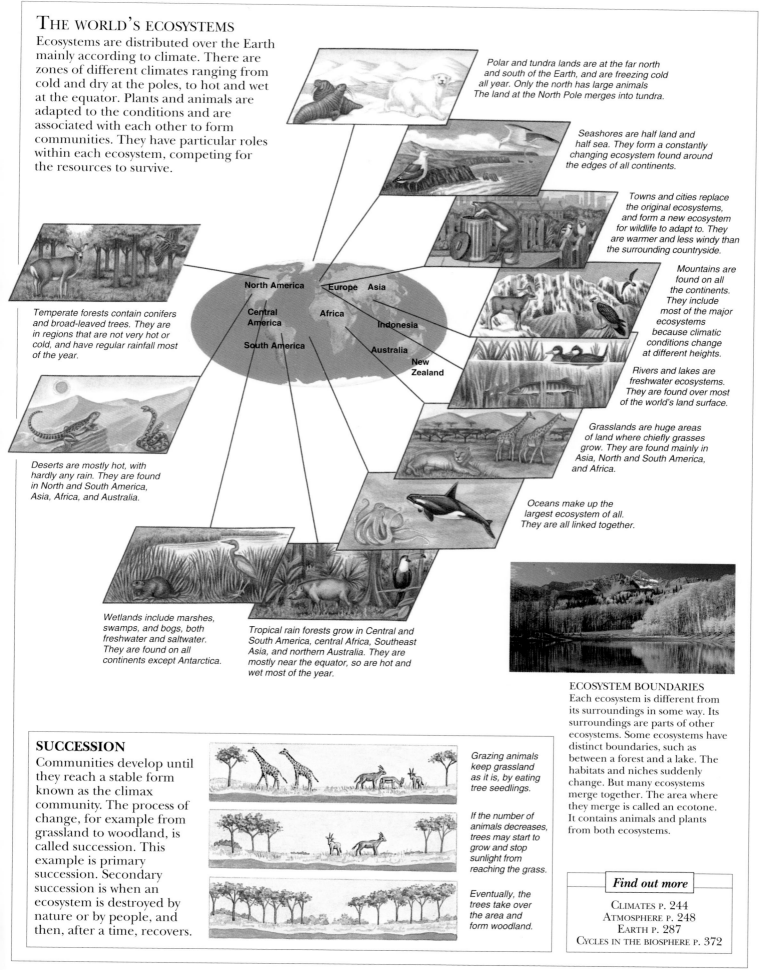

Polar and tundra lands are at the far north and south of the Earth, and are freezing cold all year. Only the north has large animals The land at the North Pole merges into tundra.

Seashores are half land and half sea. They form a constantly changing ecosystem found around the edges of all continents.

Towns and cities replace the original ecosystems, and form a new ecosystem for wildlife to adapt to. They are warmer and less windy than the surrounding countryside.

Mountains are found on all the continents. They include most of the major ecosystems because climatic conditions change at different heights.

Rivers and lakes are freshwater ecosystems. They are found over most of the world's land surface.

Grasslands are huge areas of land where chiefly grasses grow. They are found mainly in Asia, North and South America, and Africa.

Oceans make up the largest ecosystem of all. They are all linked together.

Temperate forests contain conifers and broad-leaved trees. They are in regions that are not very hot or cold, and have regular rainfall most of the year.

Deserts are mostly hot, with hardly any rain. They are found in North and South America, Asia, Africa, and Australia.

Wetlands include marshes, swamps, and bogs, both freshwater and saltwater. They are found on all continents except Antarctica.

Tropical rain forests grow in Central and South America, central Africa, Southeast Asia, and northern Australia. They are mostly near the equator, so are hot and wet most of the year.

North America
Central America
South America
Europe   Asia
Africa
Indonesia
Australia
New Zealand

ECOSYSTEM BOUNDARIES

Each ecosystem is different from its surroundings in some way. Its surroundings are parts of other ecosystems. Some ecosystems have distinct boundaries, such as between a forest and a lake. The habitats and niches suddenly change. But many ecosystems merge together. The area where they merge is called an ecotone. It contains animals and plants from both ecosystems.

SUCCESSION

Communities develop until they reach a stable form known as the climax community. The process of change, for example from grassland to woodland, is called succession. This example is primary succession. Secondary succession is when an ecosystem is destroyed by nature or by people, and then, after a time, recovers.

Grazing animals keep grassland as it is, by eating tree seedlings.

If the number of animals decreases, trees may start to grow and stop sunlight from reaching the grass.

Eventually, the trees take over the area and form woodland.

Find out more

CLIMATES P. 244
ATMOSPHERE P. 248
EARTH P. 287
CYCLES IN THE BIOSPHERE P. 372

CYCLES IN THE BIOSPHERE

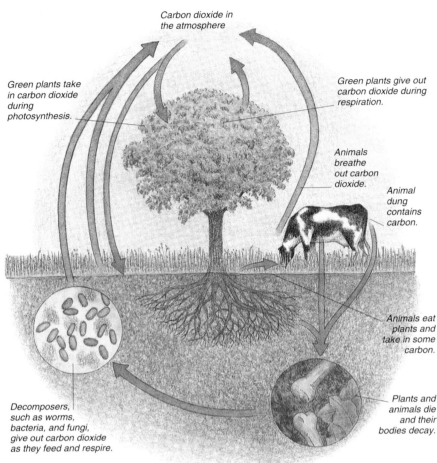

Carbon dioxide in the atmosphere

Green plants take in carbon dioxide during photosynthesis.

Green plants give out carbon dioxide during respiration.

Animals breathe out carbon dioxide.

Animal dung contains carbon.

Animals eat plants and take in some carbon.

Plants and animals die and their bodies decay.

Decomposers, such as worms, bacteria, and fungi, give out carbon dioxide as they feed and respire.

PART OF YOU might once have been part of a dinosaur. This is because the basic substances in your body have been recycled and used by other animals, and plants before you used them. Living things take in water, carbon, nitrogen, and oxygen and use them to live and grow. If these resources were used only once, they would run out. All animals and plants respire (breathe), grow, and eventually die and decompose. Decomposition releases the substances in their bodies back into the biosphere to be used again.

CARBON CYCLE
The bodies of all living things are based on the element carbon. The carbon comes originally from carbon dioxide gas in the atmosphere. Green plants and some bacteria take this in and use it to make food. When animals eat the plants, they take in some of the carbon. Carbon dioxide goes back into the atmosphere when living things breathe out, or when they produce waste, die, or decay.

LEAD POISONING
Fumes from traffic are responsible for releasing more than 225,000 tons of lead into the atmosphere every year. The lead is mixed into the air and absorbed by humans and other animals, poisoning their bodies. Children are especially at risk.

GLOBAL WARMING
When we burn oil, coal, and wood, we release carbon dioxide into the atmosphere. All this extra carbon dioxide is creating a "blanket" around the Earth. Most of the short-wave radiation from the Sun can get through the blanket. But most of the long-wave radiation from Earth cannot escape, causing the Earth to get hotter and hotter. This is called the "greenhouse effect" and causes global warming.

Long-wave radiation bounces back and forth between the surface of the Earth and the blanket.

Oxygen in the atmosphere

Plants take in oxygen and give out carbon dioxide at night.

Plants take in carbon dioxide and give out oxygen during photosynthesis in the daytime.

Animals breathe in oxygen and breathe out carbon dioxide.

Night   Day

OXYGEN CYCLE
Living things take in oxygen from the air. They use it to release energy from the food they eat. They may also use it, together with carbon, hydrogen, and nitrogen, to build new molecules in their bodies. Oxygen is released back into the atmosphere by green plants during photosynthesis and by plants and animals as part of carbon dioxide.

NITROGEN CYCLE

All living things need nitrogen to make proteins. Plants take up nitrogen in the form of nitrates from the soil. Animals obtain nitrogen compounds by eating plants. Animal waste and dead animals and plants are broken down in the soil by decomposing bacteria to release nitrogen compounds. These are converted by nitrifying bacteria into nitrates that are taken up by plants, thereby completing the cycle. In addition, nitrogen gas in the air is fixed, or combined with other elements, by special nitrogen-fixing bacteria and is then converted to nitrates by nitrifying bacteria. Nitrogen is released back to the atmosphere by denitrifying bacteria that converts nitrates to nitrogen gas.

Nitrogen gas in the atmosphere

Lightning makes nitrogen and oxygen combine and fall in the rain as weak nitric acid.

EUTROPHICATION

Farmers add nitrates to the soil, as fertilizers, to make better crop yields. These can get washed into waterways. Then too many plants and animals grow in the water, affecting the ecosystem there. This is called eutrophication.

Denitrifying bacteria take in nitrates and release nitrogen back into the atmosphere.

Nitrogen-fixing bacteria in plant roots convert nitrogen gas into nitrogen compounds.

Animals eat plants containing nitrogen.

Animal waste and dead plants and animals decay and release nitrogen compounds into the soil.

Nitrates in the soil

Nitrifying bacteria in the soil convert nitrogen compounds to nitrites.

Nitrifying bacteria in the soil convert nitrites to nitrates.

Plant roots take up nitrates from the soil.

Water vapor cools to form clouds.

Water falls back to Earth as rain.

Water flows back into the rivers and seas.

POLLUTION

Factory waste has polluted many rivers and lakes, killing the wildlife. And oil spilled at sea is very dangerous to wildlife. It clogs animals' feathers and fur, gets inside them, and stops them from finding food. They then die of cold and hunger.

Water evaporates from the Earth's surface.

WATER CYCLE

Water on the Earth's surface, such as seas and rivers, is heated by the Sun and evaporates as water vapor into the atmosphere. As it rises up into the air, it cools and condenses back into water again. Water droplets collect together to form clouds and then fall back to the surface as rain.

The gases mix with water in the air.

Poisoned water falls as acid rain.

ACID RAIN

Poisonous gases from power plants and vehicles mix with water in the air. This then falls as acid rain and becomes part of the water cycle. Acid in the rain can damage wildlife in all ecosystems where it falls. It also affects stone, causing statues and buildings to crumble away. Gases can be carried long distances by the wind, so pollution produced in one country can fall as acid rain in another.

Poisonous fumes are released into the atmosphere.

Acid rain damages plants, animals, and buildings and is mixed into rivers, lakes, and seas.

Find out more

CARBON P. 40
NITROGEN P. 42
OXYGEN P. 44
CHANGING CLIMATES P. 246
FORMATION OF CLOUDS P. 262
RAIN P. 264
PHOTOSYNTHESIS P. 340
TRANSPORT IN PLANTS P. 341
CELLULAR RESPIRATION P. 346

PEOPLE AND PLANET

THE EARTH IS ABOUT 4.6 BILLION YEARS OLD. If this time were fitted into one day, humans would have been around for less than a second. The United Nations estimates that world population (6.5 billion in mid-2005) will be over 7 billion by the year 2015. People need food and water, space in which to live, air to breathe, and energy to drive their machines. This leaves less and less space and food for other animals and plants. Many environmental problems have been caused by people. Global warming, acid rain, and holes in the ozone layer are three examples. There are no simple solutions to these problems. But we are becoming more aware of what harm we are doing.

DANGEROUS CHEMICALS
Some of the chemicals we spray on crops are poisonous to people as well as to the environment. Protective clothing should be worn but it is not always available in developing countries.

We put back:

Waste from homes, farms, and factories

Pesticides and fertilizers on crops

New trees in place of the ones cut down are a good thing to put back.

Poisonous fumes from power plants, factories, and vehicles

Nutrients from the soil to grow crops

Water for drinking, washing, irrigating fields, and for use in factory processes

We take out:

Energy resources such as coal

Wood for houses, furniture, and paper

Stone and clay for building, and minerals for factory processes

GIVE AND TAKE
People take many resources from the planet, but put back mainly harmful things, such as waste and pollution. Coal, gas, oil, and metals will run out. We need to find some renewable resources before the nonrenewable ones are all gone.

POPULATION EXPLOSION
It took thousands of years, until the 1830s, for the number of people in the world to reach 1 billion. But it took only 100 more years for there to be more than 2 billion. The world population has doubled in the last 40 years, but the rate of increase has slowed down, and the United Nations estimated in 2005 that world population would stabilize at 9 billion by 2050. This picture shows houses huddled together on a hillside in Rio de Janeiro, Brazil.

POLLUTION DISASTERS

1953–60 Mercury poisoning in shellfish in Minimata Bay, Japan, causes brain damage to people.

1976 Herbicide leak in Seveso, Italy, poisons hundreds of people. Domestic animals in the area have to be killed.

1984 Leak of chemicals from factory in Bhopal, India, kills 2,500 people.

1986 Nuclear reactor accident at Chernobyl, Ukraine, affects a wide area with radioactive poisoning.

1989 Tanker spills 40,000 tons of oil off the coast of Alaska, killing thousands of animals.

1993 Tanker spills 84,000 tons of oil into the sea off Shetland Islands, Scotland, polluting farms and beaches and killing wildlife.

CFCs produced by factories drift up into the atmosphere and destroy the ozone.

A complete ozone layer stops most of the Sun's ultraviolet radiation from getting through to Earth.

Too much ultraviolet radiation gets through holes in the ozone, harming all life below.

An ozone molecule consists of three oxygen atoms. When CFCs reach the ozone layer, the higher levels of ultraviolet radiation break up the CFCs and release chlorine atoms. These join up with one of the oxygen atoms from each ozone molecule, so destroying the ozone molecules.

HOLE OVER ANTARCTICA

In the 1980s, scientists discovered a hole as big as the United States in the ozone layer over Antarctica. This special photograph, taken from space, shows the hole clearly. A smaller hole has also been found over the Arctic and the ozone layer is becoming thinner over other parts of the planet too. Scientists blame mainly gases called chlorofluorocarbons (CFCs) for the destruction of the ozone. CFCs are used in some refrigerators, aerosols, air conditioners, fire extinguishers, and in the production of some kinds of polystyrene and cleaning substances.

Hole in ozone layer

OZONE LAYER

About 9–30 miles (15–50 km) above the Earth is a layer of ozone. This ozone layer shields the Earth from most of the Sun's harmful ultraviolet radiation. Too much ultraviolet can change the genetic structure of plants and animals and cause skin cancer in people. Holes have formed in the ozone layer, allowing more of the ultraviolet rays through to the Earth. In the Antarctic, high levels of ultraviolet are stopping plankton from photosynthesizing (making food using sunlight), which disrupts the food chains in the sea.

LIVING POLLUTION CLUES

By studying living things, we can tell how polluted the air or water is. Some living things can stand a lot of pollution, while others thrive only where the air is clean. Lichens are very sensitive to air pollution because they absorb minerals from rainwater all over their surface. Poisons in the rain soon build up in their tissues and kill them.

Crusty lichens such as Xanthoria species indicate the air is badly polluted.

Only a bright green, powdery alga called Pleurococcus can grow in very polluted air. There are no lichens.

Bushy Usnea lichens grow only in clean air.

Leafy lichens such as Parmelia species can stand a small amount of pollution.

Rat-tailed maggots, the larvae of hoverflies (Eristalis species), breathe oxygen directly from the air through a long tube so they can live in very polluted water.

Stone-fly nymphs such as Perla bipunctata live only in clean water.

Freshwater shrimps, such as Gammarus species, can put up with a small amount of pollution.

Bloodworms, which are really midge larvae of Chironomus species, can stand bad pollution.

Find out more

CATALYSTS P. 56
ENERGY SOURCES P. 134
ATMOSPHERE P. 248
PHOTOSYNTHESIS P. 340
CYCLES IN THE BIOSPHERE P. 372
WASTES AND RECYCLING P. 376
FACT FINDER P. 424

WASTES AND RECYCLING

IN THE NATURAL WORLD, nothing is wasted. Living things called decomposers eat dead and decaying material. The decomposers break everything down so it can be recycled and used again. The material is said to be biodegradable. But this natural recycling is upset by the huge amounts of waste produced by people. Most of this, such as tin, glass, and most plastic, is not biodegradable. When we throw it away, it stays for hundreds of years. Even if it rusts or breaks into tiny little pieces, it cannot be eaten by the decomposers. It pollutes the atmosphere, the land, and the water. We can recycle material by sending it back to be used again instead of throwing it away. And we can try to avoid using nonbiodegradable material and buy only items with biodegradable, or very little, packaging.

DECOMPOSERS

When an animal dies, it is recycled by nature. The larvae of the flies—maggots—will be the decomposers on this dead shrew. Decomposers help to clean up the environment and make material available for other plants and animals to use. When material has been broken down into small enough pieces, bacteria and fungi, the most important decomposers, can work on it.

GARBAGE DUMPS

Human garbage has to be put somewhere. Most methods of disposing, or getting rid of it, could harm the environment. A lot of our garbage is dumped into holes in the ground, called landfill sites. Heavy vehicles spread it out and squash it so it takes up less space. Soil is put on top of the garbage each day to stop birds and animals from feeding there and spreading disease. Although this hides the garbage, poisonous liquids can leak out, the garbage can get hot and catch fire, and gases are produced that can explode.

AVERAGE GARBAGE

In highly industrialized countries, where most people have a modern way of life, an average family throws away over 1 ton of garbage every year. Most of their garbage consists of paper from packaging and kitchen waste. A lot of this could be recycled and used again.

Garbage in an average family's trash can

Paper and cardboard 30%

Kitchen waste 23%

Glass 10%

Metals 9%

Plastics 5%

Cloth 3%

Dust 10%

Other garbage 10%

Keep the heat in by covering the heap with a piece of old carpet or sacking.

BUILDING A COMPOST HEAP

Dead leaves and other plant material are broken down in the soil into nutrients for plants to use. You could give plants in your garden extra nutrients by mixing compost into the soil. Instead of throwing away all your vegetable peelings, dead flowers, and leaves from the yard, make a compost heap. Collect layers of plant waste in a large container outside. Cover each layer with soil to keep in the heat caused by decomposers eating the dead plants. Keep the compost heap damp because decomposers like warm, wet conditions. It will take several months for the compost to form. Be careful because the heap can get very hot inside and even catch fire.

Find out more
BACTERIA P. 313
FUNGI P. 315
NUTRITION P. 342
CYCLES IN THE BIOSPHERE P. 372
PEOPLE AND PLANET P. 374
CONSERVATION P. 400

FOOD CHAINS AND WEBS

THE LIVING THINGS in a community are linked through their food. For example, a fox, a rabbit, and a plant are linked because the rabbit eats the plant and the fox then eats the rabbit. These links are called food chains. Animals and plants get the energy they need from their food. Plants use the Sun's energy to make their own food. They are called producers. Animals cannot make their own food, so they have to eat plants or other animals. They are called consumers. Animals often eat more than one kind of food so they are part of a number of food chains. Several food chains can be joined together into a food web.

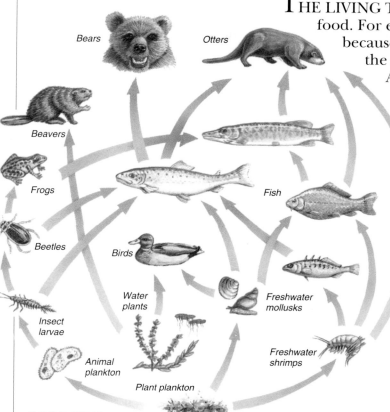

Bears
Otters
Beavers
Frogs
Beetles
Birds
Insect larvae
Animal plankton
Water plants
Plant plankton
Fish
Freshwater mollusks
Freshwater shrimps

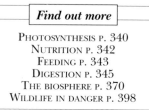

FOOD CHAIN

A food chain is a series of living things linked together because each one is food for the next, for example, plant to rabbit to fox. Most food chains have only three or four links. By the fourth link, all the energy has been used up.

FOOD WEB

A food web can include living things from several ecosystems. In this food web in a lake community, some animals and plants live in the water and some live on land. The producers are water plants and plant plankton. These are eaten by herbivores (plant-eaters), such as animal plankton, snails, insects, and some fish. The herbivores are eaten by carnivores (meat eaters), such as other insects, fish, and mammals. A change in the number of a species at one link will affect the plants and animals in the whole web.

The small amount of poison on each seed builds up into a larger amount of poison in the body of birds that eat the seeds.

Poison from several birds collects in one bird of prey.

POISON IN A FOOD CHAIN

Poisons build up as they are passed along a food chain. Chemicals sprayed on to a field of crops to kill insects are taken in by birds that eat seeds from the crops. If a bird of prey eats several of the smaller birds, it takes in a large amount of poison. This may be enough to kill it or cause it to lay eggs with thin shells. These break when the parent bird sits on them in the nest. The buildup of poisons is called bioamplification.

The steps get smaller as there is less energy at the top of the pyramid than at the bottom.

Trophic level 4 has fewer living things because there is less energy than on the levels below.

Trophic level 3
Trophic level 2
Trophic level 1

A pyramid of energy

JONATHON PORRITT

British lecturer and writer Jonathon Porritt (born 1950) is one of the leading activists in educating people about the importance of looking after the Earth and its wildlife. He became involved in "green politics," ran as a candidate for the British Green Party, and became Director of Friends of the Earth. In 1990, he resigned from his position in order to concentrate on lecturing, broadcasting, and writing on "green" (environmental) issues around the world.

TROPHIC LEVELS

One way of studying a community is to group the living things into feeding levels called trophic levels. *Trophe* is a Greek word meaning nourishment. Trophic levels are based on the numbers or mass (biomass) of living things at the same stage in a food web or on the amount of energy stored by a group of living things at one stage. They are drawn as steps, usually forming a pyramid, because the amount of energy in living things decreases as it is transferred to each successive level.

Find out more

PHOTOSYNTHESIS P. 340
NUTRITION P. 342
FEEDING P. 343
DIGESTION P. 345
THE BIOSPHERE P. 370
WILDLIFE IN DANGER P. 398

ANIMAL GROUPS

A PACK OF WOLVES, a herd of deer, a school of fish, and a flock of birds are all examples of animal groups. Animals may live in groups all the time or just come together to nest or feed in a particular area at a certain time of year. Members of a group are often related to each other. They may divide up the jobs, such as collecting food, caring for the young, and defending the group. Living as a group allows the young animals to learn skills and behavior from the adults. In this way they are more likely to survive and can pass on their knowledge to the next generation.

High-ranking wolves mark the edges of their territory with their scent. This tells wolves from other packs to keep out.

Wolves hunt in groups. This allows them to catch large animals such as moose.

Wolves howl to warn rival packs to keep away from their territory.

Young cubs learn by watching the adults and copying what they do.

High-ranking wolves hold their tails up in the air and prick their ears up.

Low-ranking wolves hold their tails low to show they are submissive.

A submissive wolf lies on its back to show the dominant wolf it will not fight.

WOLF PACK

Members of a pack of gray wolves (*Canis lupus*) help each other to survive by hunting together and defending the cubs. Within a pack, each wolf knows its own place. The high-ranking wolves tell the others that they are dominant, or superior, with special positions of the body, called body language. The low-ranking wolves also use body language to show that they are submissive—they know who's in charge. The top male and female wolf are both large and healthy. The top female is usually the only female to have cubs.

The straight line part of the dance represents the angle between the Sun and the food.

BIRD COLONIES

Many seabirds, such as gannets (*Sula bassana*), nest in large groups called colonies. They sit just out of pecking distance of each other. Nesting in numbers is safer because enemies are less likely to attack and birds warn each other of danger.

JANE GOODALL

English scientist Jane Goodall (born 1934) began to study chimpanzees at the Gombé Stream Game Reserve in Tanzania, Africa. After years of research, following chimp groups through the forest, Goodall began to piece together details of their family life. She could then work out the best way to protect the chimps. The Jane Goodall Institute focuses attention on the plight of chimpanzees. They are an endangered species due to destruction of their habitat, hunting, and illegal trade.

BEE DANCE

Honeybees (*Apis mellifera*) run in a figure-eight pattern to tell other bees in the hive where to find a good supply of food. The speed of the "dance" tells the other bees how far away the food is. The faster the dance, the nearer the food.

Find out more

BIRDS P. 332
PRIMATES P. 336
FEEDING P. 343
WILDLIFE IN DANGER P. 398
FACT FINDER P. 424

PARTNERSHIPS

DIFFERENT SPECIES OF PLANTS and animals can live together. In some cases, the partnership helps both species. This is called mutualism. In other cases, one of the partners is worse off. For example, a flea living on a dog does not help the dog. The dog is bitten and gets itchy skin. The flea is described as a parasite. In some partnerships, one of the species gains and the other is neutral—neither gaining nor losing. A partnership in which food is shared is called commensalism, which means "eating at the same table." Usually one partner benefits and the other is neutral. Animals that raid our trash bins, such as foxes and raccoons, have this kind of partnership with us.

MUTUAL PROTECTION

Acacia ants (*Pseudomyrmex* species) protect the bull's horn acacia tree (*Acacia cornigera*) in Costa Rica. They bite animals that try to eat parts of the tree. In return, the tree provides the ants with a safe place to nest inside its large thorns. It also produces parcels of a sweet substance that the ants eat.

Shell of a common whelk (Buccinum species)

The anemone filters food from the water. It can also pick up scraps of food dropped by the crab.

The hermit crab brings its head, antennae, front claws, and first two pairs of legs out of the shell when it is moving about.

A remora's suction disk has a series of plates.

PROTECTION IN EXCHANGE FOR FOOD

Hermit crabs do not have their own hard shells. They live in the empty shells of dead shellfish. As a crab grows, it moves on to a larger shell. Some sea anemones live on the shells inhabited by hermit crabs. The crab carries the anemone to new feeding grounds and provides it with leftover scraps of food. In return, the anemone's stinging tentacles protect the crab from attack.

The partnership between an oxpecker and a giraffe is an example of mutualism.

BOTH PARTNERS GAIN

The red-billed oxpecker (*Buphagus erythorhynchus*) climbs over the skin of large African animals, such as giraffes, searching for ticks and blood-sucking flies to eat. The giraffe (*Giraffa camelopardalis*) gains because the oxpecker takes away irritating pests.

Remora

Pink threads of dodder

ONE PARTNER GAINS, ONE LOSES

The dodder (*Cuscuta* species) is a parasitic plant. It lives on other plants, taking food from them. The other plant therefore does not get enough food. Dodders do not have any green coloring, necessary for photosynthesis, because they do not need to photosynthesize and make their own food.

The roots of the dodder penetrate into the other plant's tissue.

Close-up photograph of a cross-section through the stem of the host plant, showing the parasite

ONE PARTNER GAINS

The remora is a type of fish. It has a suction disk on top of its head with which it attaches itself to sharks. It is then protected by the shark and picks up scraps of food the shark drops in the water. The remora does not do much for the shark, although it may remove parasites from its body.

Stem of host plant

Find out more

FLOWERING PLANTS P. 318
JELLYFISH, ANEMONES, AND CORALS P. 320
FISH P. 326
TOWNS AND CITIES P. 397

COLOR AND CAMOUFLAGE

ANIMALS AND PLANTS look the way they do for a reason. Plants have bright colors that attract animals, which then carry the plant's pollen or seeds away to make new plants. Animals have bright colors that attract a mate or warn that the animal is poisonous. Dull colors camouflage, or hide, animals against their background. This helps hunting animals to creep up on their prey and the prey to hide from the hunters.

Hoverflies are harmless, but they look like bees or wasps, which makes predators think they can sting.

The wings of the common blue butterfly (Polyommatus icarus) are dull underneath for camouflage on some plants.

The bright flowers of foxgloves attract bumblebees, which feed on their nectar. The bees also collect pollen, some of which pollinates the next flower they visit.

The wings of the male common blue butterfly are bright blue on top, which attracts a mate.

The mottled brown and green colors of a grasshopper hide it among grasses.

The caterpillar of the privet hawk moth (Sphinx ligustri) is bright green with diagonal stripes. This helps it hide on the privet leaves on which it feeds.

SURVIVAL
Some animals and plants need to be noticed; others need to hide. All living things are a particular color, pattern, or shape to help them survive.

The bright colors of ladybugs warn predators that they have an awful taste.

CHANGE OF COLOR
Some animals change color with the seasons so that they are camouflaged all year round. The stoat (*Mustela erminea*) is brown and black for most of the year. In winter, in places where it snows, the stoat turns white, except for the black tip of its tail.

COLORFUL MALES
Male birds of many species are more colorful than the females. Females usually have to sit on the nest and look after the chicks, so bright colors would make it easy for predators to see them. The male frigate bird (*Fregata minor*) has a red throat pouch. During courtship, he puffs out his pouch to impress a female.

HENRY WALTER BATES
English naturalist and explorer Henry Bates (1825–92) studied camouflage in animals. He suggested that some harmless insects looked like unpleasant ones so that predators would not attack them. This is now known as Batesian mimicry. He suggested that mimicry was the result of evolution by natural selection.

SPOTS AND STRIPES
Patterns, such as spots and stripes, help to break up the outline of an animal's body. The leopard and bongo can be hard to see in the shadows of the forests where they live. Some young animals have spots or stripes when the adults do not. This camouflages them until they can defend themselves or run away from danger.

Clouded leopard (Neofelis nebulosa)

Bongo (Boocercus euryceros)

Find out more
EVOLUTION P. 308
FLOWERING PLANTS P. 318
ARTHROPODS P. 322
BIRDS P. 332
FEEDING P. 343
SENSES P. 358

MIGRATION and HIBERNATION

WHEN FOOD IS HARD TO FIND, in cold, hot, or dry seasons, many animals migrate, or move to another place, to find food and water. Other animals find a safe place, such as a burrow or cave, and go into a deep sleep for many months. This sleep is called hibernation. Before migrating or hibernating, animals eat as much as they can to build up extra reserves of fat in their bodies. In this way they can survive long periods without food. Migrating animals also feed when they can during the journey.

MIGRATION

Animals migrate to find food, warmth, water, space, or a safe place to raise their young. The champion long-distance migrators are birds, such as the Arctic tern, and butterflies. In the African dry season, thousands of wildebeest (*Connochaetes taurinus*) move to find fresh grass to eat. They follow their parents, but many animals have to make the first journey on their own. Then they remember landmarks or the position of the Sun or stars. Some sense the Earth's magnetic field. Fish and whales may recognize ocean currents.

Serengeti National Park, Kenya

Annual rainfall is greatest farther north.

Dry season

Direction of wildebeest journey

Wet season

WILDEBEEST JOURNEY

Migrating animals can cover thousands of miles. In the wet season, wildebeest graze on the southeastern plains in Kenya, but in the dry season they go west and then north to areas of greater rainfall. They return south again when the rains bring the dry grasslands there back to life. Predators of wildebeest, such as lions, have to follow them, otherwise they would go hungry too.

Temperature

Weight

Breathing rate

| Feeding before hibernation | Deep hibernation | Awake for a short time | Asleep again | After hibernation |

HIBERNATION

Body processes slow down in hibernation, so the animal is just alive. Body temperature falls to a few degrees above the air temperature, and there are fewer, weaker heartbeats. This chart shows a hibernating dormouse (*Muscardinus avellanarius*).

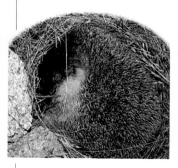

LENGTHS OF HIBERNATION

Marmots, such as this yellow-bellied marmot (*Marmota flaviventris*), are called true hibernators. They remain inactive during hibernation otherwise they would lose too much energy. Some animals, such as bears, are inactive for long periods. But their heartbeats hardly slow at all and, if there is a warm spell, they wake up and feed.

SURVIVING DROUGHT

Lungfish live in swamps where the water disappears during the dry season. They survive by burrowing in the mud and curling up inside a cocoon of wet, slimy mucus. This stops their bodies from losing too much water by evaporation. The lungfish breathes through a mud lid to its cocoon. When the rains return, the lungfish breaks out and swims off. This kind of hibernation, in hot, dry conditions, is called aestivation.

South American lungfish (*Lepidosiren paradoxus*)

Find out more

STRUCTURE OF THE EARTH P. 212
SEASONS P. 243
CLIMATES P. 244
NUTRITION P. 342
FACT FINDER P. 424

POLAR AND TUNDRA LANDS

Arctic
Fort Yukon
Antarctic
Tundra region
Polar region

World distribution of polar and tundra lands

AT THE TOP AND BOTTOM of the world are some of the harshest ecosystems on Earth. The region around the North Pole is called the Arctic, and the region around the South Pole is called the Antarctic. The Antarctic is the coldest region on Earth. Temperatures can be as low as -112°F (-80°C) and the wind can blow at 200 mph (320 km/h). There is not a large variety of life, so food webs are simple and can be easily upset. The wildlife is adapted for surviving the climate.

POLAR LANDS

A huge area around each pole is covered by ice. In the Arctic, the ice floats on top of the sea and is often only a few yards thick. In the Antarctic, the ice is on top of a rocky landmass and in places is about 2.5 miles (4 km) thick. Animals survive the cold because they have thick fur, dense feathers, or layers of fatty blubber under the skin. All these help to stop body warmth from escaping. Large numbers of birds, such as penguins and eider ducks, migrate to the polar regions in summer. There are few predators and plenty of food at this time of year.

WALRUS
Tough skin and thick layers of fat protect the walrus (*Odobenus rosmarus*) in the Arctic against the cold and from attacks by other walruses. The length of a walrus's tusks may indicate its status in the group. It uses its tusks to dig up shellfish from the seabed.

Shoreline

Ice floating on the water

Icebergs broken off the main ice pack

ARCTIC TERN
Arctic terns (*Sterna paradisaea*) raise their young in the Arctic summer, then migrate to the other end of the world for the Antarctic summer. They see more hours of daylight than any other living creature.

WHITE WHALE
The beluga, or white whale, (*Delphinapterus leucas*) may stay in Arctic waters all year round, although most whales only visit the Arctic in the summer. Belugas feed mainly on fish such as cod, halibut, and haddock.

POLAR BEAR

Thick fur and layers of blubber help to keep the polar bear (*Ursus maritimus*) warm in the Arctic. The blubber is a source of energy. Male polar bears may hunt seals all through the winter.

Monthly temperature and rainfall in Fort Yukon, Alaska

Temperature—°F (°C)   Rainfall—in (cm)

122 (50)	6 (16)
104 (40)	5.5 (14)
86 (30)	4.75 (12)
68 (20)	3.75 (10)
50 (10)	3 (8)
30 (2)	2.5 (6)
14 (-10)	1.5 (4)
-4 (-20)	.75 (2)
-22 (-30)	0

J F M A M J J A S O N D

CLIMATE
The polar and tundra regions are very cold. There is little rain or snow because the cold air cannot hold much moisture. Less snow falls around the poles than rain falls in the Sahara Desert. In winter, the polar regions are dark all the time; in summer, the Sun shines for 24 hours.

TUNDRA LANDS

The tundra is a barren landscape on the edge of the North Pole ecosystem. The ground is covered with lichens and small bushes that grow in low, dense cushions out of the wind. The plants have small leaves that stop them losing too much water. In summer, insects such as mosquitoes and blackflies hatch from eggs laid in the soil. The insects feed on the blood of large mammals, such as reindeer, and are themselves eaten by birds.

Reindeer moss (Cladonia species) absorbed radioactivity from the air.

Reindeer (Rangifer tarandus) ate the lichens, making their meat unfit for the Lapland people to eat.

POLLUTION CHAIN

In 1986, there was a serious nuclear accident at a power plant in Chernobyl in the Ukraine. The air was polluted with massive doses of dangerous radioactivity, which was absorbed by plants and passed on in the food chain. For example, radioactivity in a lichen called reindeer moss was passed on to reindeer and then to humans.

MUSK OXEN

Musk oxen (*Ovibos moschatus*) live in the Arctic tundra. They have a woolly coat and thick layers of fat. In winter, they grow a long overcoat of windproof hair. The oxen huddle together, with the young in the middle, for warmth and protection from predators.

EIDER DUCK

In the summer the eider duck (*Somateria mollisima*) migrates to the Arctic to nest. The female plucks feathers from her breast to line the nest and keep the eggs from losing heat.

Female

Male

STUDYING THE OZONE

Scientists go to the Arctic and Antarctic to study the ozone layer. They perform ground and balloon-based experiments to test the air for pollutants and for the amount of ozone. The ozone problem is bad over the poles because of the extreme weather conditions. High levels of ultraviolet rays are getting through to the Earth and harming plankton in the sea, so disrupting the start of many food chains.

A little way below the surface of the tundra is a frozen layer, called permafrost, which never thaws out. The soil above the permafrost thaws in summer but the water cannot drain away. It collects on the surface, forming marshy pools.

PENGUINS

Penguins live only in the Southern Hemisphere. They cannot fly, but are excellent swimmers, using their wings as flippers. They come ashore to lay eggs and to raise their young. Some, such as these Adelie penguins (*Pygoscelis adeliae*), march over 220 miles (350 km) from the sea to reach their nest site.

NORWAY LEMMING

Lemmings, such as the Norway lemming (*Lemmus lemmus*), spend most of their time sheltering among plants or in a burrow just under the soil. In winter, they tunnel beneath the snow, which acts like a blanket and keeps out extreme cold. The number of lemmings rises and falls, peaking about every four years.

▲ THREATS TO POLAR REGIONS

The Trans-Alaska oil pipeline stretches for 800 miles (1,300 km). It avoids the nesting places of rare birds and is raised in some places so that migrating animals can go underneath it. But the building of the pipeline damaged the environment and upset traditional migration routes. And roads near the pipeline opened up the area to poachers.

Find out more

NUCLEAR ENERGY P. 136
SEASONS P. 243
CLIMATES P. 244
TRANSPORT IN PLANTS P. 341
PEOPLE AND PLANET P. 374
FOOD CHAINS AND WEBS P. 377
MIGRATION AND HIBERNATION P. 381

MOUNTAINS

Rocky Mountains — Mt. Kenya — Alps — Himalayas — Mt. Everest — Andes

World distribution of major mountains

GOING UP A MOUNTAIN is like making a journey across the Earth from the equator to the poles. You go through all the main ecosystems, from forests on the lower slopes to grassland, tundra, and snow. The wildlife of the higher slopes has to cope with freezing temperatures, fierce winds, and thin air. Plants grow in dense cushions and have thick, hairy leaves that trap heat and reduce water loss. Wingless insects are common because the winds are too strong for insects to fly. Some mountain mammals have large hearts and lungs to help them get enough oxygen from the thin air. They may also have thick fur to keep out the cold. Some animals turn white in winter, for camouflage in the snow and ice.

The lammergeyer, or bearded vulture, (Gypaetus barbatus) soars on rising currents of hot air near the peaks.

Snow and rock where few living organisms survive

Snow leopards (Panthera uncia) have thick coats, which keep them warm.

Snow line

Tree line

TREE LINE
The height above which it is too cold and windy for trees to grow is called the tree line. The snow line is the lower edge of the part where snow stays all year round. The height of the snow and tree line depends on the weather and how near a mountain is to the equator.

| Mount Kenya on equator | Himalayas 30° north of equator | Alps 45° north of equator | Arctic 70° north of equator |

Tundra—bare rock and frozen soil

Takins (Budorcas taxicolor) have strong legs and large hoofs—used to climb the steep slopes.

Alpine grassland— rich in flowers and insects in summer

The wild ass, or onager (Equus hemionus) lives on the high grassland in summer but moves down to lower levels in winter.

THREATS TO MOUNTAINS
Mountain ecosystems are not as threatened as many others. Many mountains are the last refuge for rare species. But some mountain forests and scrublands are being destroyed by the construction of ski resorts. Unique alpine plants and fragile soils have to be cleared away to make ski runs, and new roads and vacation resorts can upset the natural mountain life.

Ski run

Low-growing shrubs— rhododendron, juniper, dwarf birch

The red panda (Ailurus fulgens) is a good climber.

Cool coniferous forest—cedar, pine, fir

MOUNTAIN ZONES
All mountains have broad bands, or zones, each with its own typical plants and animals. In the Himalayas, on the border of Nepal and India, the bottom zone is a warm deciduous forest. Above this is a band of cooler coniferous forest. The tree line is at about 11,200 ft (3,400 m). Higher than this, there are only low-growing bushes and shrubs, which merge into grassland and bare rock just below the snow-covered peaks.

Himalayan langurs (Presbytis entellus) move up and down the mountain as seasons change.

Temperate deciduous forest—oak, rhododendron

Subtropical deciduous forest— sal, arjun, teak trees

SEASHORES

WHERE THE LAND MEETS THE SEA there is an ecosystem rich in food. Some food is washed down by rivers; more is brought in from the sea by the tides. Animals and plants are adapted to survive these difficult conditions. The environment is constantly changing as waves and tides move water, sand, and pebbles up, down, and along the beach. When the tide goes out, the plants and animals are exposed to air, winds, strong sunlight, and rainwater. On tropical and polar shores, the animals and plants have to tolerate extreme temperatures.

ESTUARIES
The place where a river meets the sea is called an estuary. Birds known as waders, such as these redshank (*Tringa totanus*), walk through the shallow water searching for food in the mud with their long beaks. Estuaries are important to migrating birds in winter. Many birds break their journey to rest and feed there.

Seabirds such as shags (Phalacrocorax aristotelis) *and puffins* (Fratercula arctica), *far right, nest on cliffs where they are safe from enemies.*

Shag

Puffin

The roots of marram grass (Ammophila arenaria) *spread out under the sand in a thick network that holds the sand together.*

During the day, the masked crab (Corystes cassivelaunus) *stays under the sand. It breathes by taking in water through its tubelike antennae. Only the tips of these stick up into the water.*

SHIFTING SANDS
Beneath the surface of a sandy beach is a mass of worms and shellfish. There they are protected from pounding waves and drying air. Many sandy shore animals filter fragments of food from the sand and the seawater. Microscopic algae coat the surface of the sand or float in the water.

Thin tellins (Tellina tenuis) *burrow in the sand from the middle shore to shallow water. They suck in food from the seabed using a siphon like a vacuum cleaner.*

Lugworms (Arenicola marina) *live in a U-shaped burrow under the sand.*

THREATS TO SEASHORES
Beaches can be threatened by people building hotels and airports, dropping litter, and dumping oil and sewage into coastal seas. Birds and reptiles that nest on beaches are disturbed by the noise and bright lights in tourist areas. Loggerhead turtles (*Caretta caretta*) come ashore to lay their eggs on the beaches of the Greek island of Zakynthos. Their numbers have decreased but naturalists are now protecting their nesting sites.

Young loggerhead turtle

Upper shore

Channeled wrack (Pelvetia canaliculata)

Rough periwinkle (Littorina saxatilis)

Acorn barnacle (Balanus balanoides)

Middle shore

Beadlet anemone (Actinia equina)

Bladder wrack (Fucus vesiculosus)

Limpet (Patella intermedia)

Lower shore Oarweed (Laminaria digitata)

Common sea squirt (Ciona intestinalis)

Scarlet starfish (Henricia oculata)

ROCKY SHORE ZONES
Zones on a rocky shore are often clearly marked by the types of seaweed. Green seaweeds grow near the top of the shore, and brown ones grow near the lower shore. Different animals also live in each zone, according to the amount of time they can survive out of the water.

Find out more

SHORELINE P. 236
MIGRATION AND HIBERNATION P. 381
OCEANS P. 386
RIVERS AND LAKES P. 388
FACT FINDER P. 424

OCEANS

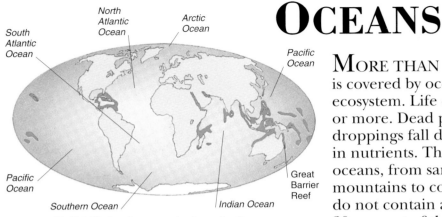

South Atlantic Ocean
North Atlantic Ocean
Arctic Ocean
Pacific Ocean
Pacific Ocean
Great Barrier Reef
Southern Ocean
Indian Ocean

World distribution of oceans and major coral reefs

MORE THAN 70 PERCENT of the Earth's surface is covered by ocean. This makes the oceans the largest ecosystem. Life exists at depths of 2.5 miles (4 km) or more. Dead plants and animals, food scraps, and droppings fall down on the ocean floor, making it rich in nutrients. There are many different habitats in the oceans, from sandy underwater deserts and huge mountains to coral reefs and open water. The oceans do not contain a great variety of species—only about 20 percent of the Earth's species live there, and nine out of 10 of these live on the ocean floor.

PLANKTON
Most ocean food chains start with the microscopic plankton in the euphotic zone. Tiny plants (phytoplankton), such as diatoms, are eaten by tiny animals (zooplankton). Zooplankton include a large number of larvae of animals such as shrimps and crabs. They provide food for a variety of fish, which are in turn eaten by other fish and marine mammals.

There are more phytoplankton in cooler oceans because there are more nutrients, such as phosphorus and nitrogen, which are needed for photosynthesis.

The oceans are linked and animals can move between them. One species may fill the same niche worldwide.

OCEAN ZONES
There are two main habitats in the ocean—the water itself, called the pelagic habitat, and the ocean floor, called the benthic habitat. The pelagic habitat is divided into several depth zones. Sunlight reaches down through only about 330 ft (100 m) and in very muddy waters it may reach down less than a yard. This thin zone, where plants can photosynthesize, is called the euphotic zone. Below this, down to about 6,500 ft (2,000 m), is the bathyal zone, where there is little or no light. The vast ocean deeps, or abyssal zone, go down to 20,000 ft (6,000 m) and more.

DEEP-SEA CHEMICALS
On the floor of the Pacific Ocean there are cracks in the Earth's crust where hot, sulfur-rich water gushes out of deep vents. Animals live nearby, absorbing chemicals dissolved in the water. Bacteria in their body tissues convert the chemicals into the energy that the animals need.

The food chain near the deep-sea vents begins with bacteria that do not need light for photosynthesis.

Giant worms (Riftia pachyptila), up to 10 ft (3 m) long, live near the deep-sea vents.

Sperm whales (Phyzeter catodon) feed mainly on squid and can dive to over 3,000 ft (1,000 m) in search of their prey. Their sonar system is very useful for finding food in the black ocean depths.

Deep ocean trenches are called the hadal zone. The deepest known trench is the Marianas Trench in the Pacific Ocean. It is 36,201 ft (11,034 m) deep. Mount Everest would fit inside it.

FINDING FOOD
Food is hard to find in the dark ocean depths. Deep-sea fish, such as this angler fish (*Melanocoetus johnsoni*), can have lights that attract prey, and large stomachs to hold as much food as possible.

JACQUES-YVES COUSTEAU

Frenchman Jacques Cousteau (1910–97) is famous for his underwater explorations. In the early 1940s, he developed the aqualung, a portable breathing apparatus for divers, with the French engineer Emile Gagnan. This encouraged more people to explore the oceans, which has greatly increased our knowledge of underwater life. Cousteau helped to develop an underwater camera and has made many films of life under the sea, including *The Silent World*. Cousteau has also campaigned to stop mining in Antarctica.

CORAL REEFS

The Great Barrier Reef of Australia is the largest coral reef in the world. Coral reefs contain a great variety of wildlife. The waters are not rich in nutrients, but the reef inhabitants recycle them very quickly so that nothing is wasted. Corals can live only in clean, warm, salty water less than 100 ft (30 m) deep, so that sunlight reaches them. Algae live in the bodies of the corals and they need sunlight to make food. Coral reefs are threatened by pollution, mining, and rising sea levels due to the greenhouse effect.

Corals are tiny animals that filter food from the water with waving tentacles. Skeletons of coral can build up to form a branched coral or a coral mound.

The shallow waters near continents are rich in nutrients because they are washed off the land and storms mix up the water, bringing nutrients to the surface.

Most of our fishing is done in shallow waters near the edges of continents.

A coral reef is built up over thousands of years from coral skeletons.

A narrow ledge of land called the continental shelf sticks out from continents under the oceans. The shallow water on the continental shelf is called the neritic (near shore) zone.

THREATS TO OCEANS

The biggest threat to ocean ecosystems is pollution from oil, sewage, and industrial waste. People also hunt fish, whales, and other wildlife. As the number of people in the world grows, more food is needed. In some places, there are no more fish left to catch. Strong nets stretch for nearly 40 miles (60 km) across the oceans. With these nets and new technology to find fish, they have little chance of escape. But some countries have set limits on how many fish can be caught. Others use nets with large holes so that young fish can escape and grow into the next generation.

Herring numbers have fallen dramatically in the last 20 years.

OCEAN MAMMALS

The largest animals on Earth, whales live in the oceans where the water supports their massive bodies. They are mammals so, although they can stay under water for a long time, they have to come to the surface to breathe air. They blow out the used air through nostrils on the tops of their heads, called spouting, then take in fresh air.

SHOALS OF FISH

Fish such as mackerel (*Scomber scombrus*) swim near the surface in shallow waters. They filter small pieces of food from the water with their brushlike gill rakes.

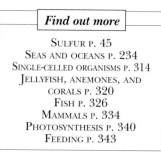

Find out more

SULFUR P. 45
SEAS AND OCEANS P. 234
SINGLE-CELLED ORGANISMS P. 314
JELLYFISH, ANEMONES, AND CORALS P. 320
FISH P. 326
MAMMALS P. 334
PHOTOSYNTHESIS P. 340
FEEDING P. 343

RIVERS AND LAKES

THE STILL WATERS OF TINY POOLS and great lakes and the flowing waters of mountain streams and wide rivers are all freshwater ecosystems. Some of these change with the seasons; others are changing all the time. The weather and natural processes, such as erosion, affect the amount of water in each area. Rivers change their course and new lakes form. They can also fill up with silt, material deposited by the water, and turn into dry land. Some pools and rivers appear only in a wet season, so only simple communities live there. But large rivers and lakes contain complex communities that have developed over hundreds of years.

The horse leech (Haemopis sanguisuga) clings on to stones with suckers. It eats insect larvae, snails, and worms.

Fast mountain stream

Brown trout (Salmo trutta) like cool water with plenty of oxygen. They are good swimmers and can move easily against the strong currents.

Adult dragonflies lay their eggs on plants, and the larvae, called nymphs, live in the water until they change into adults.

The Eurasian kingfisher (Alcedo atthis) nests in holes in the bank. It dives into the water up to 100 times a day to catch fish.

Young swift river

Water plantain (Alisma plantago-aquatica) provides shelter for birds. It grows to over 3 ft (1 m) tall.

Slow mature river

FROM SOURCE TO SEA

In fast-flowing water near the source (the start) of a river, there is plenty of oxygen but few plants for animals to eat. Most food chains start with dead material in the water. In the middle part of the river, the water flows more slowly. Plants take root and provide food and shelter for animals. The water in the lower part of the river, toward the sea, can be muddy. It flows slowly and contains less oxygen. Vertebrates, such as fish, are an important part of the community.

The otter (Lutra species) has webbed feet that help it to swim underwater. It can close its ears to stop water from getting in.

Greater reedmace (Typha latifolia) grows over 6 ft 8 in (2 m) tall. It can survive if the water level rises.

Dams are built across rivers to provide water, to generate electricity, or to stop flooding. Villages and farmland can be covered by lakes that are formed.

THREATS TO RIVERS

When dams are built across rivers, huge lakes are formed and the nature of the river is changed. The lakes provide a new habitat for fish, but make it difficult for some other animals and plants to survive. The Aswan High Dam, across the Nile in Egypt, also stops silt from flowing down the river. The silt used to flood over the land and enrich the soil.

RECORD-BREAKING LAKE
Lake Baikal, in Siberia, is the deepest and oldest freshwater lake in the world. It reaches a depth of 5,314 ft (1,620 m) and is at least 25 million years old. The lake contains more than 1,000 species of animals that are found nowhere else in the world. Sadly, this ecosystem is threatened by pollution from factories, towns, and agriculture around the lake.

TROPICAL RIVERS
The black caiman (*Melanosuchus niger*) lives in the Amazon in South America. It is related to crocodiles and alligators. It is the top carnivore in its ecosystem, eating everything from fish to wild pigs. Hunting by humans means it is now in danger of extinction.

Find out more
WEATHERING AND EROSION P. 230
RIVERS P. 233
WORMS P. 321
ARTHROPODS P. 322
FISH P. 326
REPTILES P. 330
FOOD CHAINS AND WEBS P. 377

WETLANDS

SIX PERCENT OF THE EARTH'S SURFACE is covered by wetlands. They can be fresh or saltwater and include wet grasslands, called marshes, wet peatlands, called bogs, and waterlogged forests called swamps. Wetlands are some of the world's richest ecosystems. They produce more plant material than most other ecosystems on Earth. A variety of small mammals, birds, insects, and other invertebrates live there. Birds flock to wetlands to nest because they do not have many enemies there. Large mammalian predators would sink into the wet ground. Water levels change with the seasons so the wildlife has to be able to survive in dry and wet conditions.

SITATUNGA
Long splayed-out hooves stop the sitatunga (*Limnotragus spekei*) from sinking into the swampy ground of Africa. The sitatunga can swim well and in times of danger hides under water with only the tip of its nose showing, so that it can breathe.

The manatee is a mammal so has to breathe air, but it can stay under water for up to 15 minutes.

The zebra butterfly (Heliconius charitonius) flies slowly on long, narrow wings. At night, large groups gather on bare twigs.

Stunted bald cypress (Taxodium distichum)

Sawgrass dotted with islands of trees

Slash pines (Pinus elliottii) and saw-palmetto (Serenoa repens) grow on higher ground.

The American darter (Anhinga anhinga) dives under water to catch fish. It then perches with its wings half-open to dry them in the sun.

Mangrove swamp on the coast

The water moccasin (Agkistrodon piscivorus) is a poisonous snake that hunts at night.

THE EVERGLADES

At the southern tip of Florida is a huge area of cypress swamp called the Everglades. It is home to rare species such as the manatee (*Tricheus manatus*) and the Florida panther (*Felis concolor coryi*). It is now a national park but is threatened by chemicals used in agriculture and by drainage, pollution, and tourism. Boats kill more than 100 manatees every year.

The American alligator (Alligator mississipiensis) is the largest and loudest reptile in North America. In the spring, the male bellows to attract females.

The garpike (Lepisosteus osseus) has gills for breathing under water, but can also breathe air if the water dries up.

1

2

Key

Water

Swamp peat

Lake clay

3

Lake mud

Peat

MANGROVES

The most common trees in tropical fresh and saltwater swamps are mangroves. They can survive in waterlogged mud because they have breathing pores in their roots. Some mangroves have roots that grow up into the air and get oxygen. The red mangrove (*Rhizophora mangle*) grows in coastal swamps and estuaries. It protects them from storms and tidal waves.

HOW A PEAT BOG FORMS
A peat bog may form where a lake fills in with mud and plants. (1) The water is clear, with mud on the bottom. (2) Mud collects around roots of plants. (3) Mosses grow and build up mounds of peat. (4) The lake disappears and is replaced by a dome of peat. Peat bog forming is an example of succession.

Find out more

PRESSURE P. 127
REPTILES P. 330
MAMMALS P. 334
THE BIOSPHERE P. 370
WILDLIFE IN DANGER P. 398

DESERTS

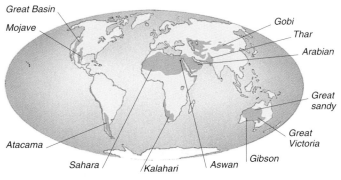

Great Basin
Mojave
Gobi
Thar
Arabian
Great sandy
Great Victoria
Atacama
Sahara
Kalahari
Aswan
Gibson

World distribution of major deserts

DESERTS ARE THE DRIEST PLACES on Earth. Most have less than 4 in (10 cm) of rain a year. Some may have no rain at all for several years. Most deserts are hot, so more water evaporates into the air than falls as rain. Desert plants have deep or wide-spreading roots, tough skins, small leaves or spines, and special ways of storing water. Many animals may never drink, getting all their water from their food. Only a few species of plants and animals can survive in the desert so there is little dead material to make the soil rich. The few nutrients that are present take a long time to cycle through the ecosystem.

DESERT BY DAY

Daytime temperatures in hot deserts may reach more than 120°F (50°C) and the surface of the sand can be as hot as 195°F (90°C). Most animals hide away in burrows or beneath rocks, where the air is cooler and more moist. Some desert plants have hairy leaves that reflect strong sunlight. The pores of most stay shut during the day so less water escapes.

Chuckwallas (Sauromalus obesus) bask in the morning sun until they are warm enough to crawl off in search of flowers, fruits, and seeds to eat.

The huge ears of the fennec fox (Fennecus zerda) help it to hear the faintest sound of prey moving nearby. The ears also help the fox to keep cool by giving off heat like a radiator.

CONVERGENT EVOLUTION

Animals living in similar habitats in different parts of the world often look similar, for example, the kit fox of North America and the fennec fox of Africa. This is because both foxes have adapted to survive in the same kind of ecosystem, where environmental conditions are similar. This is called convergent evolution.

The kit fox (Vulpes macrotis) comes out at night to hunt. It runs fast to catch small animals before they escape down a burrow.

On its powerful back legs, the black-tailed jack rabbit (Lepus californicus) can leap away from danger at speeds of up to 35 mph (56 km/h).

Kangaroo rats (Dipodomys deserti) get all the water they need from the seeds they eat. They carry seeds back to their burrow in cheek pouches.

STORAGE TANKS

Desert plants and animals have to survive long dry spells. Some animals can store fat in their bodies. The fat can be broken down to provide energy and water.

A camel, such as the one-humped Arabian camel (Camelus dromedarius), can go without water for weeks. A camel can drink up to 30 gallons (115 liters) of water at a time.

The gila monster (Heloderma suspectum) stores fat in its thick tail to help it survive hard times.

Because water is lost through leaves, cacti such as this Mammillaria elongata do not have any—just spines, which prevent them from being eaten. They store water in their thick stems.

SIDE-WINDING

Several snakes that live in sandy deserts, such as this sidewinder adder (*Bitis peringueyi*), move by throwing themselves over the sand in "S"-shaped curves. This is called sidewinding because the snakes travel sideways rather than forward. The advantage of this type of movement is that only two parts of the snake's body touch the hot surface of the sand at any one time. The snake also is less likely to sink into the soft sand.

The world's smallest owl, the elf owl (Micrathene whitneyi), hides away by day in holes made by woodpeckers in cactus stems.

The cactus wren (Campylorhynchus brunneicapillus) builds its nests in cacti, where its young are well protected from enemies by the sharp spines.

DESERT AT NIGHT

At night, the desert is much cooler and the air becomes more moist. Many animals come out to hunt and the desert comes to life. Food is still hard to find and many desert hunters, such as spiders and scorpions, are very poisonous. If a meal does come their way, they have to deal with it as quickly as possible and must not let it escape.

Monthly temperature and rainfall in Aswan, Egypt

CLIMATE

The largest deserts are near the equator. They are hot and dry all year round because the winds that blow across them contain very little moisture. Deserts in colder parts of the world, such as the Gobi Desert in central Asia, are hot in summer and cold in winter. Deserts also occur in the shelter of high mountains, such as the Atacama Desert in South America.

Saguaro cacti (Cereus giganteus) have thick rubbery "skin." They soak up water using a wide-spreading network of shallow roots.

The spotted skunk (Spilogale putorius) comes out mainly at night to hunt for small animals, eggs, insects, and fruit.

Creosote bushes (Larrea tridentata) grow evenly spaced out because the roots of each plant use up all the water and nutrients in the soil around it.

Western spadefoot toads (Scaphiopus hammondi) appear only at night. They use hard "spades" on their back feet to dig burrows.

The desert tarantula (Aphonoplema chalcodes) is a poisonous spider that spends the day hidden in a burrow.

By day, the kangaroo rat sleeps in a burrow, out of the heat of the Sun. At night, it travels long distances to find food.

Scorpions use the poisonous sting at the tip of the tail to defend themselves and kill their prey. This is an Arizona scorpion (Centruroides sculpturatus).

A chuckwalla spends the night sheltering under a rock and becomes active by day.

The water in an oasis comes from a rainy climate many miles away.

Oasis

Land surface

Water-filled rock

OASES

In a few places in a desert, water seeps through the ground to form a moist area called an oasis, where plants can grow. Oases are a vital lifeline for animals, including people traveling across the desert. The water in an oasis comes from water-filled rocks near the surface. It may have fallen as rain many miles away and drained down through the rocks under the desert. But oases do not last forever; the water may run dry or sand dunes may be blown over the oasis. People and animals then have to move on.

SPREADING DESERTS

The spread of deserts is a major threat. It is partly caused by people who live on the desert edges. The grazing of animals and the cutting down of wood for building can cause the land to turn to desert. This is called desertification. It is a particular problem in areas where several years have passed without any rain.

Oasis in Australia

Find out more

HEAT TRANSFER p. 142
CLIMATES p. 244
EVOLUTION p. 308
TRANSPORT IN PLANTS p. 341
MOVEMENT p. 356

GRASSLANDS

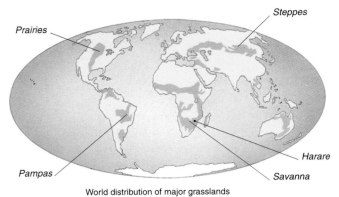

Prairies

Steppes

Pampas

Harare

Savanna

World distribution of major grasslands

WHERE THE CLIMATE IS TOO DRY, and the soils too poor for most trees, grasses grow. These areas are called grasslands. Grass is the start of many food chains. It is able to survive nibbling by animals because it sprouts from the bottom and not from the tips, as other plants do. The more the grass is bitten off, the more it grows. Grass also grows back well after fires, which are common in this ecosystem. In dry or cold seasons, animals have to migrate long distances to find enough food and water to survive.

FOOD FOR ALL

The tropical grasslands of East Africa are called the savanna. More than 40 species of grazing mammals live here and share out the food. There is usually enough to go around because the animals feed on different parts of the grasses, shrubs, and trees. For example, zebras eat the top of the grass stems, wildebeest eat the middle part, and Thomson's gazelles eat the bottom part. Dik-diks concentrate on small bushes near the ground, while giraffes feed high up in the trees.

Giraffes (Giraffa camelopardalis) feed on leaves up to 20 ft (6 m) above the ground.

Thomson's gazelles (Gazella thomsoni) feed on young grass shoots and high-protein seeds at ground level.

Wildebeest eat the leafy middle of grass plants. Up to 95 percent of their diet is grass.

Zebras feed on the coarse, tough tops of grasses and also dig for roots.

Dik-diks browse on young leaves of small bushes, especially acacia shoots.

Monthly temperature and rainfall in Harare, Zimbabwe

Temperature—°F (°C)   Rainfall—in (cm)

122 (50)	6 (16)
104 (40)	5.5 (14)
86 (30)	4.75 (12)
68 (20)	3.75 (10)
50 (10)	3 (8)
32 (0)	2.5 (6)
14 (-10)	1.5 (4)
-4 (-20)	.75 (2)
-30 (-22)	0

J F M A M J J A S O N D

CLIMATE
Tropical grasslands are warm all year round, but there is a long dry season in summer. Temperate grasslands have very cold winters, with hard frosts, and hot, dry summers. This graph shows the climate for a city in a tropical grassland area.

Cheetah (Acinonyx jubatus)

Thomson's gazelle (Gazella thomsoni)

Lion (Panthera leo)

Wildebeest (Connochaetes taurinus)

Hyena (Hyaena species)

Common zebra (Equus burchelli)

HUNTERS
The large number of herbivores on the African savanna are food for a whole range of predators. Each predator tends to have a favorite food because of the way it hunts. Cheetahs can chase gazelles at up to 60 mph (100 km/h), but for a short time only. Lions cannot run so fast. They have to get close to their prey. But they are strong and hunt in groups, so they can kill large animals such as wildebeest. Hyenas also hunt in groups, but usually kill animals only as large as a zebra.

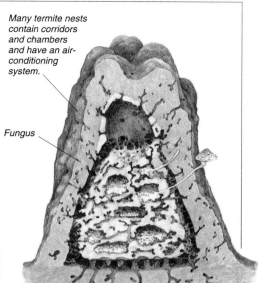

Many termite nests contain corridors and chambers and have an air-conditioning system.

Fungus

ASIAN STEPPES

Temperate grasslands called the Steppes stretch across central Asia from Europe to China. Large herds of grazing animals, such as bison (*Bison bonasus*) and saiga antelope (*Saiga tatarica*), used to graze here. As they moved around, the animals trod grass seeds into the ground, their grazing encouraged the grass to grow, and their droppings fertilized the soil. Hunting and farming have killed most of these animals, although saiga antelope are now increasing due to conservation measures.

Cavies (Cavia aperea) usually shelter under rocks or in burrows dug by other animals. They are wild relatives of the pet guinea pig.

The mara, or Patagonian hare (Dolichotis patagona) lives in burrows in groups of up to 40 animals. It can run swiftly away from danger, leaping over 6 ft (2 m) in the air on its long back legs.

BURROWING ANIMALS

On the pampas of South America, huge numbers of small mammals live underground, where they are safe from fires and predators. Their burrowing helps to mix up the soil layers and stops all the minerals from building up on the surface. This makes the soil rich and helps the grasses and other plants to grow. On the North American prairies, ground squirrels, called prairie dogs (*Cynomys* species) live in huge groups and have a whole "town" of interconnected burrows. They keep the ground grazed all around the burrow, so that they can see enemies coming.

Burrowing animals of the South American pampas

TERMITES

Insects called termites are a vital part of decomposition in grasslands. They eat dead material or take it inside their tall mud nests. They use it as compost for the fungus they grow for food. Termite nests can be up to 8 ft (2.5 m) high and contain up to 20 million individuals.

Viscachas (Lagostomus maximus) dig huge networks of tunnels with their strong front feet. They can close their nostrils while digging to keep soil from getting in. They come out at night to eat grasses and other plants.

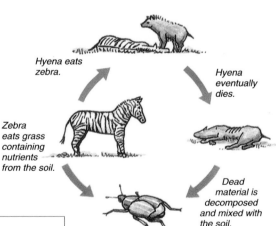

Hyena eats zebra.

Hyena eventually dies.

Zebra eats grass containing nutrients from the soil.

Dead material is decomposed and mixed with the soil.

Waste material is broken down into nutrients by decomposers such as beetles.

NUTRIENT CYCLE

Many grassland animals, bacteria, and fungi feed on dead plants or animals or on animal dung. Some of the nutrients become part of the decomposers' bodies and some eventually enrich the soil. This means that nothing is wasted, and the nutrients go around and around in an endless cycle.

THREATS TO GRASSLANDS

Hunting has drastically reduced the number of grazing animals and their predators on grasslands. Where hunting is banned, people still poach, or hunt illegally. At least 85 percent of the worlds's rhinoceroses have been killed by poachers during the past 30 years. Game wardens such as these in Kenya have to look out constantly for hunters. Sometimes they rescue animals that have been illegally trapped.

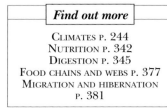

GEORGE AND JOY ADAMSON

British game warden George Adamson (1906–89) worked to protect and conserve wildlife in Kenya, Africa. He worked with his wife Joy (1910–80), who was especially interested in lions. She is famous for looking after the lioness Elsa as a cub, and the story of Elsa's return to the wild was made into the film *Born Free* in 1960. Both George and Joy Adamson were murdered in Kenya.

Find out more

CLIMATES P. 244
NUTRITION P. 342
DIGESTION P. 345
FOOD CHAINS AND WEBS P. 377
MIGRATION AND HIBERNATION
P. 381

TROPICAL RAIN FORESTS

MORE THAN HALF of all animal and plant species in the world live in tropical rain forest ecosystems. But these forests cover less than 10 percent of the Earth's land surface. Tropical rain forests grow in regions near the equator in South America, Africa, Asia, and Australia. They are so rich in life because they are wet and warm and have bright sunlight overhead—all conditions that encourage life. The trees grow fast and reach great heights as they compete with each other to get as much light as possible.

Malaysia
Borneo
Sumatra
Papua New Guinea
South America
Manaus
Africa

World distribution of major tropical rain forests

The harpy eagle (Harpia harpyja) is the biggest eagle in the world. It soars over the canopy hunting for monkeys and sloths to eat.

Toucans feed on fruit, leaves, and seeds.

LOOKING AFTER THE FORESTS
This family in the Brazilian rain forest is making baskets from natural materials. Over thousands of years, rain forest peoples have lived in harmony with their surroundings. They grow a mixture of crops in small areas to make the best use of nutrients. After a few years, the soil is left to rest and recover.

Sloths (Bradypus tridactylus) hang upside-down in the trees, using their long curved claws as hooks.

LAYERS OF LIFE
The wildlife in Amazonian rain forests lives at different levels. Most live near the top of the trees, in the canopy, where there is lots of sunlight, warmth, and food. Below the canopy, in the understory, it is darker and cooler, and wildlife is less varied. The largest animals live on the forest floor.

Army ants move through the forest in columns of up to 200,000 ants. They march to find food for their larvae.

Peccaries (Tayassu species) feed on plants at the forest edge.

Agouti (Dasyprocta species)

Temperature—°F (°C) | Rainfall—in (cm)

Temperature—°F (°C)	Rainfall—in (cm)
122 (50)	12.5 (32)
104 (40)	11 (28)
86 (30)	9 (24)
68 (20)	8 (20)
50 (10)	6 (16)
32 (0)	4.75 (12)
14 (-10)	3 (8)
-4 (-20)	1.5 (4)
-22 (-30)	0

J F M A M J J A S O N D

Monthly temperature and rainfall in Manaus, Brazil

CLIMATE
Rain forests are warm all year round, with temperatures between about 68°F and 82°F (20°C and 28°C). This is the wettest ecosystem, with rain nearly every day. Up to 160 in (4 m) of rain falls in a year.

Spider monkeys (Ateles species) use their tails to grip the branches.

Emerald tree boa (Corallus caninus)

Tree frogs are common because they can lay their eggs in pools of water that collect in the trees.

In the understory, climbing plants, such as lianas and vines, twine around the trees and bushes.

The spotted coat of the jaguar (Panthera onca) camouflages it as it preys on animals such as agoutis and peccaries.

Fungi can live on the forest floor because they do not need light to make their food.

MINI ECOSYSTEM
Plants called bromeliads live on the branches of trees. Pools of water collect in them, creating a mini-ecosystem. Rotting leaves and animal droppings provide food for bacteria and insects, which are in turn eaten by small animals.

MOVING THROUGH THE FOREST

Rain forest animals have special features that help them move through the trees. Birds have short, broad wings and can twist and turn between the branches. Some animals have flaps of skin that unfold like wings, enabling them to glide from branch to branch. Monkeys use their hands and feet to climb through the trees. Some can grasp branches with their tails, too, like an extra hand. This is called a prehensile tail.

BIRD OF PARADISE

The Raggiana bird of paradise (*Paradisea raggiana*) lives in the rain forests of Papua New Guinea. Its short wings enable it to fly through the trees and its strong feet enable it to grasp branches. The male, shown here, may hang upside-down on a branch while he tries to impress females with his brilliantly colored feathers.

ORANGUTAN

With their long arms and strong fingers, orangutans (*Pongo pygmaeus*) swing quickly, hand over hand, through the trees. They live in the rain forests of Borneo and Sumatra. The name orangutan is a Malaysian word meaning "man of the forests."

FLYING GECKO

The flying gecko (*Ptychozoon kuhli*) lives in the rain forests of Malaysia. Folds of skin along the sides of its body, tail, and legs allow it to glide from tree to tree. The folds also camouflage the gecko when it is resting on tree bark. The gecko has ridges of scales on its feet and sharp claws, which help it cling to the slippery tree trunks.

Rain drips down through the trees and is taken in through the leaves and roots. Water that the trees do not need is given out through the leaves.

RAIN FOREST CYCLES

Water, oxygen, minerals, and nutrients all pass through the trees. Due mainly to the warmth and moisture in a tropical rain forest, nutrients are recycled from the soil via the trees to the canopy quickly. This means that the soil is surprisingly poor, and attempts to farm on the land usually fail.

Oxygen is taken in during respiration and given out during photosynthesis. Carbon dioxide is given out during respiration and taken in during photosynthesis.

Dead leaves and animals fall to the ground.

Bacteria and fungi in the soil break down the dead material. The trees can then take up the nutrients through their roots and use them to grow.

THREATS TO RAIN FORESTS

Since 1945, more than half the world's rain forests have been destroyed. Hundreds of species of animals and plants are now extinct. An area of forest the size of a football field disappears every second. The main threats come from people cutting down the trees for lumber, to use the land for cattle ranches and farms, or to mine for oil and metals.

LUNGS OF THE PLANET

Rain forests are sometimes called the lungs of the planet. Large areas of rain forest, such as this one in Malaysia, take in huge amounts of carbon dioxide and give out lots of oxygen and water during photosynthesis. This influences the climate of the whole Earth.

STUDYING THE RAIN FOREST

There are thousands of species of animals and plants living in rain forests that scientists know nothing about. Ecologists are studying there all the time. They use mountaineering equipment to climb up to the canopy and build permanent walkways through the trees.

Find out more

CLIMATES P. 244
PHOTOSYNTHESIS P. 340
TRANSPORT IN PLANTS P. 341
CYCLES IN THE BIOSPHERE P. 372
COLOR AND CAMOUFLAGE P. 380
WILDLIFE IN DANGER P. 398

TEMPERATE FORESTS

CONIFERS AND BROAD-LEAVED TREES grow in temperate forests. The forests are found in north temperate regions, such as parts of Europe and North America, which have a mild climate. There are distinct seasons, with cold winters and warm summers, but nothing too extreme. Conifer forests tend to grow in the north, and broad-leaved forests farther south. Temperate forests provide food and shelter for a large number of plants and animals. More light reaches through the trees than it does in a rain forest because the trees are not as tightly packed. Small plants can survive without having to grow as creepers up trees to get sunlight. In colder areas, it can take years for dead material to be broken down, so the cycles of nutrients are slower.

The beak tips of the common crossbill (Loxia curvirostra) are crossed, enabling the bird to open pine cones to reach the seeds inside.

Acid rain damages conifers, making their needles drop off.

CONIFEROUS FORESTS

Conifers are more common where it is colder. Trees cannot take up water from the frozen soil in winter. But the needles of conifers lose less water than broad, flat leaves, so they can stay on the trees all year round. The pyramid shape of many conifers allows the snow to slide off their branches so the trees are not crushed by the weight of the snow.

Oak marble galls form when gall wasps (Andricus kollari) lay their eggs on the buds of the oak tree in spring. Larvae develop into adult wasps inside the galls and eat their way out in the fall.

Great spotted woodpeckers (Dendrocopus major) nest in holes in the tree and chisel into decaying trunks to search for insects to eat.

OAK TREE ECOSYSTEM

An oak tree is a broad-leaved tree. It is an ecosystem on its own. It makes its own food, and its leaves, flowers, fruit, bark, and wood are eaten by insects, birds, and small mammals. These creatures are in turn eaten by bigger animals. All the animals eventually die and rot back into the soil. The nutrients in their bodies are taken up by the tree again and used for growth. The ecosystem changes with the seasons as the tree sprouts leaves in spring and drops them in the fall. In winter the tree rests and the animals hibernate, migrate, or become less active.

THREATS TO FORESTS

Many temperate forests have been cut down to make way for farms and houses. Conifers from other countries are often planted in place of broad-leaved forests. These conifers grow faster and their straight trunks are easier to saw into planks for lumber. But the wildlife is often unable to live on the new trees.

Spruce and larch plantations in Scotland

Gray squirrels (Sciurus carolinensis) bury acorns to eat in winter. They do not find them all so some acorns sprout into new trees.

The fruiting bodies of honey fungus (Armillaria mellea) sprout from tree stumps and dead trees in the fall.

Woodlice (Porcellio scaber) live in damp, dark places under leaves, stones, bark, and logs. They feed on decaying leaves, bark, and fungi.

Centipedes (Lithobius forficatus) live in damp places such as leaf litter. They come out at night to hunt for food such as spiders, worms, and woodlice.

TOWNS AND CITIES

AS THE HUMAN POPULATION GROWS beyond 6.5 billion, more and more of the Earth's surface is taken over by towns and cities. The original wildlife of the areas now covered by buildings has been driven out, but some animals and plants have managed to take advantage of the new shelters. The edible garbage we throw away is a major source of food for animals, and city climates can protect animals and plants in cold parts of the world. Temperatures can be several degrees higher than they are in the surrounding countryside, and there is less wind, except around tall buildings.

LIFE IN AN URBAN ECOSYSTEM

A house and garden, such as this one in a British urban ecosystem, provide a variety of living spaces for plants and animals. Birds such as starlings roost and nest in the roof, together with bats and squirrels. Smaller creatures, such as cockroaches, ants, beetles, and moths, feed and shelter behind walls, under floors, and in cupboards. Mice and rats live in drains and sewers.

RED FOX
The intelligent red fox (*Vulpes vulpes*) has adapted well to living in a city. It has a varied diet and will eat almost anything it can find, often raiding trash cans for food thrown out by humans.

House martins (Delichon urbica) nest under the eaves of roofs.

The common pipistrelle bat (Pipistrellus pipistrellus) roosts in roofs.

Ivy (Hedera helix) climbs up walls. It clings on to the stone or bricks.

Spiders spin webs to trap insects for food.

Food left out on bird tables helps birds—and squirrels—to survive through the winter.

OPOSSUMS
The species of animals that live in towns and cities vary in different parts of the world because of the different conditions. The brush-tailed opossum (*Trichosurus vulpecula*) has adapted well to urban life in Australia. In the wild it shelters in burrows, caves, or tree hollows, but in towns it has learned to nest in the roofs of buildings. Colonies of opossums live in parks and they sometimes become tame enough to take food from people's hands.

Part of a yard can be made into a sanctuary for wildlife if left to grow wild. Long grass, weeds, compost heaps, and rotting logs will encourage wildlife to feed and shelter there.

Bees nest in holes in walls or in old flower pots.

Common toads (Bufo bufo) hide under stones during the day and come out at night to eat worms, snails, and woodlice.

Find out more

CLIMATES P. 244
PEOPLE AND PLANET P. 374
WASTES AND RECYCLING P. 376
PARTNERSHPS P. 379
FACT FINDER P. 424

WILDLIFE IN DANGER

Cause unknown

Hunting and collecting

Habitat destruction

Other causes, such as disease

Introduced animals

HUNDREDS OF MILLIONS OF SPECIES of plants and animals have become extinct (died out) since life began on Earth. Some of these have died out due to the natural process of evolution. But, in the past 300 years, people have speeded up the extinction process more than 1,000 times by destroying habitats, polluting the environment, and by hunting and collecting species. It is difficult to work out exactly how quickly species are becoming extinct, but one estimate suggests that about 100 species a day, or one species every quarter of an hour, disappear forever. There are probably one million species that are in danger of dying out within the next 20 years unless we act now to save unnecessary extinction.

REASONS FOR EXTINCTION
We do not know the exact reason for many animal extinctions. This pie chart shows that habitat destruction and animals introduced from one place to another are two major reasons. Hunting and collecting are also responsible for the disappearance of many animals.

Untouched wetlands, such as swamps and marshes, are a rich habitat for wildlife, especially insects, fish, and birds.

Scarlet ibis (*Eudocimus ruber*)

Reasons for wetland destruction include: drainage and filling in for farms, towns, ports, and factories; pollution; mining for peat, fuels, and minerals; cutting trees for lumber.

Puerto Rico: 34 species

Malaysia: 9 species

Trinidad and Tobago: 8 species

US: 5 species

Venezuela: 3 species

Seychelles: 2 species

BIRDS AT RISK
Mangrove swamps are a type of wetland on tropical coasts. Birds are especially at risk from the destruction of mangrove swamps. This chart shows the estimated number of bird species in danger of exinction in mangrove swamps around the world today.

DESTRUCTION OF WETLANDS
Wetlands are one of the world's most threatened ecosystems. More than half have already been destroyed. Some have disappeared due to natural causes, such as rises in sea level, drought, and violent storms. But many more have been destroyed by people. If they are drained, floods and insects can be controlled to make it safer for people to live nearby. But then the wildlife has nowhere to go.

PLANTS AT RISK
About a quarter of all the plant species in the world are thought to be threatened. They are in danger from habitat destruction, and many plants are taken from the wild to sell. The endangered silver sword (*Argyroxilphrum kauense*) from Hawaii, shown here, is threatened by introduced goats, which eat it, and by plant collectors.

RARE PANDA
The giant panda (*Ailuropoda melanoleuca*) lives in the bamboo forests of southwestern China. But most of the original bamboo has been cut down and replaced with villages and rice fields. It is thought that there are now only 1,600 giant pandas left. They live in small areas of bamboo forest separated by farmland.

Mice can be a pest to farmers, but they were not the intended prey for the cane toad.

The Australian sugar cane harvest is damaged by pests such as the cane beetle.

The cane toad eats small frogs.

Native frogs are not a pest to sugar-cane farmers.

The cane toad eats the cane beetle and other insects.

The cane beetle (Dermolepida albohirtum) eats the sugar cane.

The cane toad eats mice and other small rodents.

The cane toad eats geckos and other lizards.

Lizards and geckos help the farmers by eating insects.

The cane toad (Bufo marinus) was introduced into the food web.

There are not enough predators to eat the cane toad and control its population—only the occasional hungry snake or bird.

SPECIES INTRODUCTION

In 1935, a species of toad from Central and South America was introduced into Queensland, Australia. It was thought that the toads would eat beetles that were destroying the sugar cane. But the toads ate many other creatures as well. And because they had no natural predators, the toads multiplied into huge populations that are now destroying the native Australian wildlife.

GEORGE SCHALLER

The research done by American zoologist Dr. George Schaller (born 1933) has helped scientists to devise conservation methods. He studied the behavior of many animals in the wild, including pandas in China, gorillas and lions in Africa, orangutans in Sarawak, and tigers in India. His many books include *The Deer and the Tiger* and *The Year of the Gorilla*.

MONK SEAL

Monk seals (*Monachus* species) are some of the rarest seals in the world. There are less than 500 Mediterranean monk seals and 1,500 Hawaiian monk seals left, and the Caribbean monk seal is now extinct. Pollution of the sea, fishing, motorboats, and airplanes have disturbed the seals and caused them to stop breeding properly.

1983: 318,400 skins

1985: 109,500 skins

1987: 157,700 skins

1989: 68,800 skins

CATSKIN TRADE

Many animals are still hunted, often illegally, for their fur, horns, or tusks. Some people like to wear the skins of large cats, such as leopards and tigers, as coats. This chart shows the total world export of catskins. The amount decreased considerably during the 1980s, but many cats are still in danger of extinction.

ZOOS

For a long time, animals were taken from the wild to fill zoos. Many of these animals were rare and, by collecting them, zoos were driving them closer to extinction. Today, most zoos breed their animals. Some zoos have bred rare animals, such as the Arabian oryx, golden lion tamarin, and red wolf, and then released them into the wild.

CONSERVATION

Koala
(Phascolarctos
cinereus)—
hunting banned and
protected in wildlife parks

Hawaiian goose
(Branta sandvicensis)—
bred in captivity and
reintroduced into
the wild

Sea otter (Enhydra lutris)—
hunting banned and
protected in reserves

Heath fritillary (Mellicta athalia)—
special needs studied and
reintroduced into
the wild

Przewalski's horse
(Equus przewalskii)—bred in captivity
and reintroduced into the wild

By BANNING HUNTING, protecting habitats, setting up nature reserves, and reducing pollution, many rare species of animals and plants can be saved. People are starting to realize how important it is to save wildlife from extinction. Organizations, such as the Worldwide Fund for Nature (WWF), and the World Conservation Union (IUCN), make people aware of problems and raise money to protect species and habitats. The wildlife on this page shows some of the species being saved.

Red wolf (Canis rufus)—
bred in zoos and
reintroduced into the wild

Gray whale
(Eschrichtius glaucus)—
hunting banned

EARTH SUMMIT
In 1992, there was a conference on the environment in Rio de Janeiro, Brazil. Representatives from governments of most countries in the world discussed what should be done to save the planet. A special "Tree of Life" was created in Rio to which paper "leaves" were attached. Written on the leaves were things people promised to do and what they thought governments should do.

European bison
(Bison bonasus)—protected
in nature reserves in Poland

WILDLIFE RESERVES
The Yellowstone National Park in the United States was the world's first National Park. Today, there are areas of countryside all over the world that have been set aside as wildlife reserves. The plants and animals are protected, as much as possible, from human hunters, collectors, and developers who may want to build on the land. Some of these reserves cover thousands of square miles. Others are just a small wood or piece of undeveloped land in a city.

Polar bear
(Ursus maritimus)—habitat
protected and hunting controlled

Recycling
symbol

HOW YOU CAN HELP
Everyone can do something to help conserve wildlife. You can collect paper, cans, and bottles for recycling. This will help reduce the number of trees cut down and mines dug under rare habitats. You can stop buying things made from rare animals and plants, and try to avoid packaging that cannot be recycled.

Arabian oryx
(Oryx leucoryx)—
bred in zoos and
reintroduced into
the wild

New Zealand brush lily
(Xeronema callistemon)—
protected on island
reserves

Tiger (Panthera
tigris)—hunting
banned;
protected in
reserves

Pere David's deer
(Elaphurus davidiensis)—
reintroduced into the
wild in China from
reserves in the West

Find out more
THE BIOSPHERE P. 370
CYCLES IN THE BIOSPHERE P. 372
PEOPLE AND PLANET P. 374
WASTES AND RECYCLING P. 376
WILDLIFE IN DANGER P. 398
FACT FINDER P. 424

FACTFINDER SECTION

This section contains charts, tables, and maps full of important scientific information and statistics. The page numbers in this mini-index will help you look up the things you need to know.

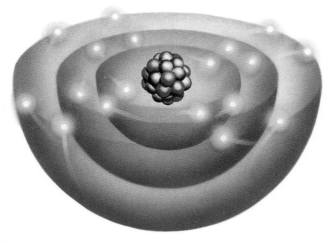

MATTER

PERIODIC CHART

In this chart, the elements are arranged in order of increasing atomic number, as they are in the traditional periodic table. The relative atomic mass shown here is for the most common isotope or, for radioactive elements, the most stable isotope. Where no data is shown, the element is so short-lived and has been made in such small amounts that it has not been possible to discover its properties. See pp. 22, 24, 31, 32.

Atomic number	Element	Symbol	Relative atomic mass	Melting point °C	Melting point °F	Boiling point °C	Boiling point °F	Valency	Date of discovery	Physical description
1	Hydrogen	H	1	-259	-434	-253	-423	1	1766	colorless gas
2	Helium	He	4	-272	-458	-269	-452	0	1868/1895	colorless gas
3	Lithium	Li	7	179	354	1340	2440	1	1817	silvery-white metal
4	Beryllium	Be	9	1283	2341	2990	5400	2	1798	gray metal
5	Boron	B	11	2300	4170	3660	6620	3	1808	dark brown powder
6	Carbon	C	12					2,4		
	graphite			none	none	3640	6580		ancient	black solid
	diamond			3500	6332	4827	8721		ancient	colorless solid
7	Nitrogen	N	14	-210	-346	-196	-321	3,5	1885	colorless gas
8	Oxygen	O	16	-219	-362	-183	-297	2	1772	colorless gas
9	Fluorine	F	19	-220	-364	-188	-306	1	1886	pale green-yellow gas
10	Neon	Ne	20	-249	-416	-246	-410	0	1898	colorless gas
11	Sodium	Na	23	98	208	890	1634	1	1807	silvery-white metal
12	Magnesium	Mg	24	650	1202	1105	2021	2	1808	silvery-white metal
13	Aluminum	Al	27	660	1220	2467	4473	3	1825	silvery metal
14	Silicon	Si	28	1420	2588	2355	4271	4	1824	dark gray solid
15	Phosphorus	P	31					3,5	1669	
	white			44	111	280	536			waxy solid
16	Sulfur	S	32					2,4,6	ancient	
	rhombic			113	235	445	833			yellow solid
17	Chlorine	Cl	35	-101	-150	-34	-29	1,3,5,7	1774	yellow-green gas
18	Argon	Ar	40	-189	-308	-186	-303	0	1894	colorless gas
19	Potassium	K	39	64	147	754	1389	1	1807	silvery-white metal
20	Calcium	Ca	40	848	1558	1487	2709	2	1808	silvery-white metal
21	Scandium	Sc	45	1541	2806	2831	5128	3	1879	metallic
22	Titanium	Ti	48	1677	3051	3277	5931	3,4	1795	silvery metal
23	Vanadium	V	51	1917	3483	3377	6111	2,3,4,5	1801	silvery-gray metal
24	Chromium	Cr	52	1903	3457	2642	4788	2,3,6	1797	silvery metal
25	Manganese	Mn	55	1244	2271	2041	3706	2,3,4,6,7	1774	red-white metal
26	Iron	Fe	56	1539	2802	2750	4980	2,3	ancient	silvery-white metal
27	Cobalt	Co	59	1495	2723	2877	5211	2,3	1735	red-white metal
28	Nickel	Ni	59	1455	2651	2730	4950	2,3	1751	silvery-white metal
29	Copper	Cu	64	1083	1981	2582	4680	1,2	ancient	pink metal
30	Zinc	Zn	65	420	788	907	1665	2	1746	blue-white metal
31	Gallium	Ga	70	30	86	2403	4357	2,3	1875	gray metal
32	Germanium	Ge	73	937	1719	2355	4271	4	1886	gray-white metal
33	Arsenic	As	75	none	none	613	1135	3,5	1250	steel-gray solid
34	Selenium	Se	80	217	423	685	1265	2,4,6	1817	gray solid
35	Bromine	Br	79	-7	19	59	138	1,3,5,7	1826	red-brown liquid
36	Krypton	Kr	84	-157	-251	-152	-242	0	1898	colorless gas
37	Rubidium	Rb	85	39	102	688	1270	1	1861	silvery-white metal
38	Strontium	Sr	88	769	1416	1384	2523	2	1808	silvery-white metal
39	Yttrium	Y	89	1522	2772	3338	6040	3	1794	steel-gray metal
40	Zirconium	Zr	91	1852	3366	4377	7911	4	1789	steel-white metal
41	Niobium	Nb	93	2467	4473	4742	8568	3,5	1801	gray metal
42	Molybdenum	Mo	96	2610	4730	5560	10040	2,3,4,5,6	1778	silvery metal
43	Technetium	Tc	97	2172	3942	4877	8811	2,3,4,6,7	1937	silvery-gray metal
44	Ruthenium	Ru	101	2310	4190	3900	7052	3,4,6,8	1844	blue-white metal
45	Rhodium	Rh	103	1966	3571	3727	6741	3,4	1803	steel-blue metal
46	Palladium	Pd	106	1554	2829	2970	5378	2,4	1803	silvery-white metal
47	Silver	Ag	108	962	1764	2212	4014	1	ancient	shiny white metal
48	Cadmium	Cd	112	321	610	767	1413	2	1817	blue-white metal
49	Indium	In	115	156	313	2028	3680	1,3	1863	blue-silvery metal
50	Tin	Sn	119	232	450	2270	4118	2,4	ancient	silvery-white metal
51	Antimony	Sb	121	631	1168	1635	2975	3,5	ancient	silvery metal
52	Tellurium	Te	128	450	842	990	1814	2,4,6	1782	silver-gray solid
53	Iodine	I	127	114	237	184	363	1,3,5,7	1811	purple-black solid
54	Xenon	Xe	132	-112	-170	-107	-161	0	1898	colorless gas

Atomic Number	Element	Symbol	Relative Atomic Mass	Melting Point °C	Melting Point °F	Boiling Point °C	Boiling Point °F	Valency	Date of Discovery	Physical description
55	Cesium	Cs	133	29	84	671	1240	1	1860	silvery-white metal
56	Barium	Ba	137	725	1337	1640	2984	2	1808	silvery-white metal
57	Lanthanum	La	139	921	1690	3457	6255	3	1839	metallic
58	Cerium	Ce	140	799	1470	3426	6199	3,4	1803	dark gray solid
59	Praseodymium	Pr	141	931	1708	3512	6354	3	1885	steel-gray metal
60	Neodymium	Nd	142	1021	1870	3068	5554	3	1885	yellow-white metal
61	Promethium	Pm	145	1168	2134	2700	4892	3	1947	metallic
62	Samarium	Sm	150	1077	1971	1791	3256	2,3	1879	light gray metal
63	Europium	Eu	152	822	1512	1597	2907	2,3	1896	steel-gray metal
64	Gadolinium	Gd	157	1313	2395	3266	5911	3	1880	silvery-white metal
65	Terbium	Tb	159	1356	2473	3123	5653	3	1843	silvery metal
66	Dysprosium	Dy	163	1412	2574	2562	4644	3	1886	metallic
67	Holmium	Ho	165	1474	2685	2695	4883	3	1878-9	silvery metal
68	Erbium	Er	167	1529	2784	2863	5185	3	1843	gray-silver metal
69	Thulium	Tm	169	1545	2813	1947	3537	2,3	1879	metallic
70	Ytterbium	Yb	173	819	1506	1194	2181	2,3	1878	silvery metal
71	Lutetium	Lu	175	1663	3025	3395	6143	3	1907	metallic
72	Hafnium	Hf	179	2227	4041	4602	8316	4	1923	steel-gray metal
73	Tantalum	Ta	181	2996	5425	5427	9801	3,5	1802	silvery metal
74	Tungsten	W	184	3410	6170	5660	10220	2,4,5,6	1783	gray metal
75	Rhenium	Re	186	3180	5756	5627	10161	1,4,7	1925	white-gray metal
76	Osmium	Os	190	3045	5510	5090	9190	2,3,4,6,8	1804	gray-blue metal
77	Iridium	Ir	193	2410	4370	4130	7466	3,4	1804	silvery-white metal
78	Platinum	Pt	195	1772	3222	3827	6921	2,4	1735	blue-white metal
79	Gold	Au	197	1064	1947	2807	5080	1,3	ancient	shiny yellow metal
80	Mercury	Hg	201	-39	-38	357	675	1,2	ancient	silvery metallic liquid
81	Thallium	Tl	204	303	577	1457	2655	1,3	1861	blue-gray metal
82	Lead	Pb	207	328	622	1744	3171	2,4	ancient	steel-blue metal
83	Bismuth	Bi	209	271	520	1560	2840	3,5	1450	red-silvery metal
84	Polonium	Po	210	254	489	962	1764	2,3,4	1898	metallic
85	Astatine	At	211	300	572	370	698	1,3,5,7	1940	metallic
86	Radon	Rn	222	-71	-96	-62	-80	0	1900	colorless gas
87	Francium	Fr	223	27	81	677	1251	1	1939	metallic
88	Radium	Ra	226	700	1292	1200	2190	2	1898	silvery metal
89	Actinium	Ac	227	1050	1922	3200	5792	3	1899	metallic
90	Thorium	Th	232	1750	3182	4787	8649	4	1828	gray metal
91	Protactinium	Pa	231	1597	2907	4027	7281	4,5	1917	silvery metal
92	Uranium	U	238	1132	2070	3818	6904	3,4,5,6	1789	blue-white metal
93	Neptunium	Np	237	637	1179	4090	7394	2,3,4,5,6	1940	silvery metal
94	Plutonium	Pu	242	640	1184	3230	5850	2,3,4,5,6	1940	silvery metal
95	Americium	Am	243	994	1821	2607	4724	2,3,4,5,6	1944	silvery-white metal
96	Curium	Cm	247	1340	2444	3190	5774	2,3,4	1944	silvery metal
97	Berkelium	Bk	247	1050	1922	710	1310	2,3,4	1949	silvery metal
98	Californium	Cf	251	900	1652	1470	2678	2,3,4	1950	silvery metal
99	Einsteinium	Es	254	860	1580	996	1825	2,3	1952	silvery metal
100	Fermium	Fm	253					2,3	1952	metallic
101	Mendelevium	Md	256					2,3	1955	metallic
102	Nobelium	No	254					2,3	1958	metallic
103	Lawrencium	Lr	257					3	1961	metallic
104	Unnilquadium	Unq	261						1964,1969	
105	Unnilpentium	Unp	262						1970	
106	Unnilhexium	Unh	263						1974	
107	Unnilseptium	Uns	262						1976	
108	Unniloctium	Uno	265						1984	
109	Unnilennium	Une	266						1982	
110	Ununilium	Uun	271						1994	
111	Unununium	Uuu	272						1994	
112	Ununbium	Uub	277						1996	

RADIOACTIVE HALF LIVES

Radioactive elements decay at different rates. A half-life is the time it takes for half of the original amount of radioactive element to decay. Different elements emit different types of radiation when they decay—alpha particles (α), beta particles (ß), and always gamma rays (γ).

Uranium-238 (α) 4,500 million years	Plutonium-239 (α) 24,400 years	Carbon-14 (ß) 5,700 years	Radium-226 (α) 1,600 years	Strontium-90 (ß) 28 years	Hydrogen-3 (ß) 12.3 years
Cobalt-60 (γ) 5.3 years (beta and gamma rays)	Phosphorus-32 (ß) 14.3 days	Iodine-131 (ß) 8.1 days	Radon-222 (α) 3.8 days	Lead-214 (ß) 26.8 minutes	Astatine-215 (α) 0.0001 seconds

REACTIONS

GAS LAWS

The gas laws predict how a gas will behave if you change its conditions—that is, its temperature (T) in degrees kelvin, its pressure (P), or its volume (V). In the equations below, the symbol K represents a constant number.

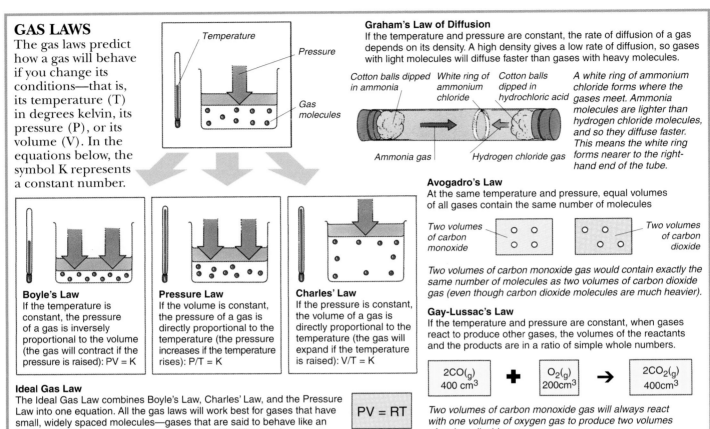

Temperature
Pressure
Gas molecules

Graham's Law of Diffusion

If the temperature and pressure are constant, the rate of diffusion of a gas depends on its density. A high density gives a low rate of diffusion, so gases with light molecules will diffuse faster than gases with heavy molecules.

Cotton balls dipped in ammonia
White ring of ammonium chloride
Cotton balls dipped in hydrochloric acid

Ammonia gas
Hydrogen chloride gas

A white ring of ammonium chloride forms where the gases meet. Ammonia molecules are lighter than hydrogen chloride molecules, and so they diffuse faster. This means the white ring forms nearer to the right-hand end of the tube.

Boyle's Law
If the temperature is constant, the pressure of a gas is inversely proportional to the volume (the gas will contract if the pressure is raised): $PV = K$

Pressure Law
If the volume is constant, the pressure of a gas is directly proportional to the temperature (the pressure increases if the temperature rises): $P/T = K$

Charles' Law
If the pressure is constant, the volume of a gas is directly proportional to the temperature (the gas will expand if the temperature is raised): $V/T = K$

Avogadro's Law
At the same temperature and pressure, equal volumes of all gases contain the same number of molecules

Two volumes of carbon monoxide
Two volumes of carbon dioxide

Two volumes of carbon monoxide gas would contain exactly the same number of molecules as two volumes of carbon dioxide gas (even though carbon dioxide molecules are much heavier).

Gay-Lussac's Law
If the temperature and pressure are constant, when gases react to produce other gases, the volumes of the reactants and the products are in a ratio of simple whole numbers.

$$2CO_{(g)} \quad 400\ cm^3 \quad + \quad O_{2(g)} \quad 200\ cm^3 \quad \rightarrow \quad 2CO_{2(g)} \quad 400\ cm^3$$

Two volumes of carbon monoxide gas will always react with one volume of oxygen gas to produce two volumes of carbon dioxide gas.

Ideal Gas Law
The Ideal Gas Law combines Boyle's Law, Charles' Law, and the Pressure Law into one equation. All the gas laws will work best for gases that have small, widely spaced molecules—gases that are said to behave like an ideal gas. (R is the gas constant. It is the same for all gases.)

$$PV = RT$$

COLLECTING A GAS

If a gas is a product of a reaction, it is not easy to collect it. The setup of the apparatus below shows how it can be done.

Bung
The gas given off by the reaction travels through the delivery tube.
Gas jar
Collected gas
Gas bubbles
Reactants
Round-bottomed flask
Trough of water
Bunsen burner
Beehive shelf

To make carbon dioxide gas, for example, the reacting chemicals would be marble chips (calcium carbonate) and dilute hydrochloric acid.

IDENTIFYING A GAS

Carbon dioxide
If you bubble a gas through limewater (calcium hydroxide solution) and the limewater turns cloudy, it proves the gas is carbon dioxide.

Hydrogen
If you put a lighted splint into a small sample of a gas and the gas ignites with a "pop," it proves the gas is hydrogen.

Oxygen
If you put a glowing splint into a small sample of a gas and the splint relights, it proves the gas is oxygen.

ENDINGS AND PREFIXES

A compound's chemical name can reveal what elements the compound is made up of. One way of obtaining this information is by looking at the endings and the prefixes in a name.

Compound ending in	Description	Example
-ide	Contains just the two elements in the name.	Iron sulfide FeS
-ite	Contains oxygen as well as the other elements in the name.	Iron sulfite $FeSO_3$
-ate	Contains oxygen as well as the other elements in the name. Contains more oxygen than is found in -ites.	Iron sulfate $FeSO_4$

Prefix	Number of atoms in prefix	Example
Mono-	1	Carbon monoxide CO
Di-	2	Dinitrogen oxide (Nitrous oxide) N_2O Nitrogen dioxide NO_2
Tri-	3	Boron trichloride BCl_3

REACTIVITY SERIES

This is a series that compares the reactivity of different metals. Those at the top are the most reactive; those at the bottom are the least reactive.

Increasing reactivity →

Increasing power of displacement →

Metal		Reaction when heated in air	Reaction with water	Reaction with dilute acid
Potassium	**K**	Burn vigorously to form oxides.	React with cold water to form hydrogen gas and alkaline hydroxide solution. React with decreasing vigor down the series.	Violent reaction to give hydrogen gas and salt solution.
Sodium	**Na**			
Calcium	**Ca**			
Magnesium	**Mg**	Burn with decreasing vigor down the series.		
Aluminum	**Al**		Do not react with cold water. React with steam to form hydrogen gas and oxide, with decreasing vigor down the series.	React to form hydrogen gas and salt solution with decreasing vigor down the series.
Zinc	**Zn**			
Iron	**Fe**			
Lead	**Pb**	React slowly to form oxide layer on surface.	No reaction.	No reaction.
Copper	**Cu**			
Silver	**Ag**	No reaction.		
Gold	**Au**			

APPARATUS

Here are some of the most common pieces of chemical equipment used in a laboratory.

Boiling tube: this tube is made of thick, heat-resistant glass and is used to hold liquids or solids for strong heating.

Evaporating dish: this is used to hold a solution that is being heated gently to drive off the solvent.

Separating funnel: this separates two liquids that do not mix. The denser liquid settles at the bottom and can be tapped off first.

Clamp: this stand holds apparatus in place.

Test tube: this is used for chemical reactions on a small scale. It is not suitable for strong heating.

Volumetric flask: this is used to make a solution with a very accurate concentration. The stopper allows solutions to be mixed thoroughly.

Flat-bottomed flask: this is used for liquid reactions when no heating is required.

Beaker: this is used to hold a liquid.

Measuring cylinder: this is used to give an approximate measure of the volume of a liquid.

Pipette: this is used to measure precise volumes of liquid.

Burette: this is used to add one solution to another. It accurately records the amount of solution used.

Watch glass: this is used to hold solids and to evaporate small amounts of liquid.

Conical flask: this is used to carry out reactions. Unlike the beaker, the flask can be stoppered.

Dropping pipette: this is used to add small, but not very accurate, amounts of one solution to another.

MATERIALS

ALKANES AND ALKENES

Alkanes and alkenes are chemical compounds of hydrogen and carbon. Although their hydrogen and carbon atoms are arranged in a similar way, alkanes have only a single bond between the carbon atoms, whereas alkenes have a double bond. This difference means that alkenes react with more substances than alkanes do (see Uses of Ethene, right). Alkanes are used mainly as fuels. The properties of alkanes and alkenes change according to the number of carbon atoms they contain.

ALKANES

Carbon atoms in chain	Name	Physical state at 77°F (22°C)	Molecular formula
1	methane	gas	CH_4
2	ethane	gas	C_2H_6
3	propane	gas	C_3H_8
4	butane	gas	C_4H_{10}
5	pentane	liquid	C_5H_{12}
6	hexane	liquid	C_6H_{14}
7	heptane	liquid	C_7H_{16}
8	octane	liquid	C_8H_{18}
9	nonane	liquid	C_9H_{20}
10	decane	liquid	$C_{10}H_{22}$

Ethane is an example of an alkane containing a single bond between its carbon atoms.

Ethene is a typical alkene containing a double bond between its carbon atoms.

ALKENES

Carbon atoms in chain	Name	Physical state at 77°F (22°C)	Molecular formula
2	ethene	gas	C_2H_4
3	propene	gas	C_3H_6
4	butene	gas	C_4H_8
5	pentene	liquid	C_5H_{10}
6	hexene	liquid	C_6H_{12}
7	heptene	liquid	C_7H_{14}
8	octene	liquid	C_8H_{16}
9	nonene	liquid	C_9H_{18}
10	decene	liquid	$C_{10}H_{20}$

USES OF ETHENE

The chemical ethene is obtained during the refining of petroleum, or crude oil, by a process known as cracking. This process is carried out in huge chemical plants, where heat is used to break, or crack, a mixture of hydrocarbons known as naphtha. By-products are then used for fuel, or as important raw materials for use in other chemical processes. Ethene is used on its own to ripen fruit artificially, but when reacted with the chemicals below, it forms new materials that have hundreds of uses in the manufacturing industry.

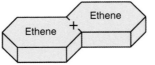

Polyethene
Packaging (plastic wrap, carrier bags, bottles); molded articles (buckets, cups, kitchenware); other (pipes, insulating cables, clothing, photographic film)

Ethanol
Solvent for after-shave lotions, perfumes, and cosmetics; methylated spirits; solvent for paints, resins, soaps, and dyes; other (plastics, drugs—such as anesthetics, textiles)

Polystirene
Ceiling tiles, cavity wall insulation, cups, bowls, packaging (yogurt cups); nylon (clothes, carpets, tennis racket strings, fishing nets); other (car tires, latex paints, computer disks, toys)

PVC
Insulating material and protective covering (gas and water pipes, hosepipes, insulating cables, roofing, window frames, floor tiles); wallpaper, curtains, furniture upholstery, car interior trim, rainwear, protective clothing, shoes, handbags; chemicals (fumigant, degreaser), refrigerant; other (toys, records, recording tape)

SODIUM CARBONATE

This important industrial chemical, also known as soda ash (Na_2CO_3), is made from limestone and salt. Its major use is in the production of glass. To make glass, soda ash is heated together with limestone and sand. Glass is not expensive to produce because there is an abundance of these raw materials.

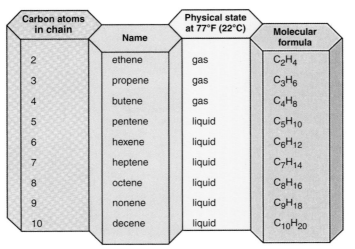

Glass
50%

Soda ash is mainly used for glass, chemicals, and detergents. A small amount is put to other uses.

Chemicals
25%

Detergents
15%

Other
10%

WORLD DISTRIBUTION OF RAW MATERIALS

This map shows the location of raw materials throughout the world. In 100 years or so a map bearing the same title may look very different, since many experts believe important minerals and energy sources, such as oil and natural gas, may have been exhausted by this time. Such resources take millions of years to form and once they are used up they cannot be renewed.

The symbols on this map correspond to the materials below.

LEADING PRODUCERS OF RAW MATERIALS IN 2006

	Material	Top producers	World total
	Bauxite (aluminum oxide)	Australia 58 million Brazil 18 million	165 million
	Coal	China 1,956 million US 933 million	4,629 million
	Copper	Chile 5.3 million US 1.2 million	14.9 million
	Natural Gas	Russian Federation 589,000 million m^3 US 543,000 million m^3	2,692,000 million m^3
	Iron ore	China 370 million Brazil 300 million	1,520 million
	Kaolin (clay)	US 7.8 million C.I.S. 6.2 million	44.5 million
	Oil	Saudi Arabia 505.9 million Russian Federation 458.7 million US 329.8 million	3,867.9 million
	Salt	US 45.9 million China 38 million	210 million
	Sulfur	US 9.6 million Canada 8.9 million	64 million
	Wood	US 541 million m^3 Brazil 290 million m^3	29,855 million m^3

All figures in metric tons
Except m^3 = cubic meters

USES OF RAW MATERIALS

Raw Materials	Uses
Bauxite (aluminum oxide)	Aluminum is extracted from bauxite and used for aircraft, foil wrapping, cars, paints, and kitchen utensils.
Coal	Coal is mainly made of carbon and is used as fuel. This fuel is used to heat homes and to generate electricity.
Copper	Copper is used to conduct electricity in wires and cables and to make a range of alloys such as brass.
Natural gas	This is used to make ammonia. It is also used in the home as a fuel for heating and cooking.
Iron ore	Engine parts for cars are made out of iron, as are magnets. Iron is also used to make steel. Steel is stronger than iron and is one of the main materials for building bridges.
Kaolin (clay)	This is used in the manufacture of bricks to build houses, ceramics to make pottery, and cement.
Oil	Oil is used to make plastics and as a fuel for airplanes and cars.
Salt	This is used as a food flavoring and to make sodium hydroxide (caustic soda) and sodium carbonate.
Sulfur	This is used to make sulfuric acid, which is used to make paints, detergents, plastics, and fibers.
Wood	Wood is used to make buildings, beams, doors, and furniture. It is also the raw material for making paper.

FORCES AND ENERGY

EQUATIONS

The following equations are commonly used in physics. Some of the units used to calculate these equations can be found in the metric and US measurement table opposite.

Average speed (m/s)	$\dfrac{\text{distance moved (m)}}{\text{time taken (s)}}$
Force (kgm/s^2 or N)	mass (kg) × acceleration (m/s^2)
Acceleration (m/s^2)	$\dfrac{\text{change in velocity (m/s)}}{\text{time taken for this change (s)}}$
Momentum (kgm/s)	mass (kg) × velocity (m/s)
Impulse (Ns)	force (N) × time (s)
Work done (Nm or J)	$\dfrac{\text{force (N) × distance moved in the}}{\text{direction of the force (m)}}$
Average power (J/s or W)	$\dfrac{\text{work done (Nm)}}{\text{time taken (s)}}$ or $\dfrac{\text{energy change (J)}}{\text{time taken (s)}}$
Efficiency (%)	$\dfrac{\text{work output (Nm) × 100\%}}{\text{work input (Nm)}}$
Pressure (N/m^2)	$\dfrac{\text{force (N)}}{\text{area (m}^2\text{)}}$
Density (kg/m^3)	$\dfrac{\text{mass (kg)}}{\text{volume (m}^3\text{)}}$

Key:
J - Joule   kg - kilogram   m - meter   N - Newton   s - second   W - Watt

TEMPERATURE SCALES

Temperature is measured using a thermometer. This measures how hot or cold an object or person is. The higher the reading on the scale, the hotter the object. Some objects measure below zero degrees Celsius, the freezing point of water, below which the Celsius reading becomes a minus figure.

Center of Sun 25 million°F (14 million°C)

Water boils 212°F (100°C)

Maximum temperature a naked body can stand 165°F (74°C)

Normal body temperature 98.6°F (37°C)

Minimum temperature a naked body can stand 50°F (10°C)

Water freezes 32°F (0°C)

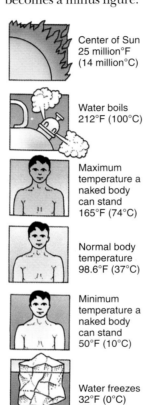

Celsius	Fahrenheit	Kelvin
100	212	373
90	194	363
80	176	353
70	158	343
60	140	333
50	122	323
40	104	313
30	86	303
20	68	293
10	50	283
0	32	273
-10	14	263
-20	-4	253

WORLD EXPORTERS OF ENERGY

Saudi Arabia 15.1%
Russia 9.8%
Norway 7.3%
Venezuela 5.7%
Mexico 5%
Iran 5%
Nigeria 4.8%
UK 4.5%
Canada 4.2%
United Arab Emirates 4.1%
Rest of the World 34.6%

ENERGY SOURCES

This graph shows that only 10 countries provide almost two-thirds the world's fossil fuels—oil, coal, and gas. Burning these fuels is the major cause of global warming, whereas hydroelectric power is a cheap and renewable energy source.

PLIMSOLL LINE

Ships float because their average density is less than that of water. But an overloaded ship will sink. Every merchant ship has a mark called the Plimsoll line painted on its hull. If this line sinks below sea level, the load is too heavy.

These lines indicate safe load levels in water of different temperatures and saltiness.

Tropical Fresh
Fresh
Tropical
Summer
Winter
Winter North Atlantic
L   R
The Plimsoll mark

METRIC AND US MEASUREMENT

UNITS OF MEASUREMENT

Metric unit	Equivalent
Length	
1 centimeter (cm)	10 millimeters (mm)
1 meter (m)	100 centimeters
1 kilometer (km)	1,000 meters
Area	
1 square centimeter (cm^2)	100 square millimeters (mm^2)
1 square meter (m^2)	10,000 square centimeters
1 hectare (ha)	1,000 square meters
1 square kilometer (km^2)	1 million square meters
Volume	
1 cubic centimeter (cc or cm^3)	1 milliliter (ml)
1 liter (l)	1,000 milliliters
1 cubic meter (m^3)	1,000 liters
Mass	
1 kilogram (kg)	1,000 grams (g)
1 metric ton (t)	1,000 kilograms

US unit	Equivalent
Length	
1 foot (ft)	12 inches (in)
1 yard (yd)	3 feet
1 mile	1,760 yards
Area	
1 square foot (ft^2)	144 square inches (in^2)
1 square yard (yd^2)	9 square feet
1 acre	4,840 square yards
1 square mile	640 acres
Volume	
1 pint	34.68 cubic inches (in^3)
1 quart	2 pints
1 gallon	4 quarts
Mass	
1 pound (lb)	16 ounces (oz)
1 ton	2,000 pounds

METRIC UNITS INTO US UNITS

To convert	Into	Multiply by
Length		
centimeters	inches	0.39
meters	feet	3.28
kilometers	miles	0.62
Area		
square cm	square inches	0.16
square meters	square feet	10.76
hectares	acres	2.47
square km	square miles	0.39
Volume		
cubic cm	cubic inches	0.061
liters	pints (US)	2.1
liters	gallons (US)	0.26
Mass		
grams	ounces	0.04
kilograms	pounds	2.20
metric tons	tons (US short)	1.10

US UNITS INTO METRIC UNITS

To convert	Into	Multiply by
Length		
inches	centimeters	2.54
feet	meters	0.30
miles	kilometers	1.61
Area		
square inches	square cm	6.45
square feet	square meters	0.09
acres	hectares	0.40
square miles	square km	2.59
Volume		
cubic inches	cubic cm	16.39
pints	liters	0.47
gallons	liters	3.78
Mass		
ounces	grams	28.35
pounds	kilograms	0.45
tons (US short)	metric tons	0.91

CHANGING ENERGY SUPPLIES

This diagram shows how the world's energy supply has changed since 1850. Using the key below, it becomes clear that the increasing sources of energy are oil, gas, and nuclear energy.

Power source
- Muscles
- Wood
- Coal
- Oil
- Gas
- Nuclear
- Hydro
- Geothermal

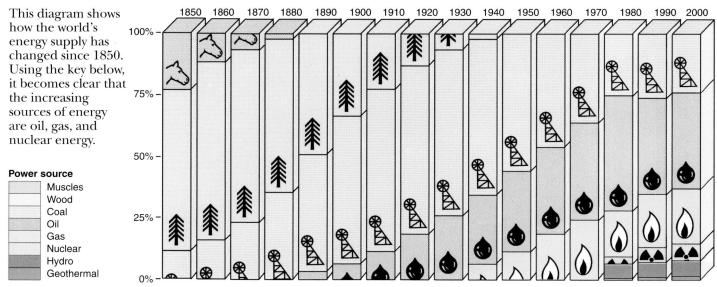

ELECTRICITY AND MAGNETISM

SI UNITS—TABLE OF SYMBOLS

SI units are an internationally recognized system of units used for scientific purposes. The full official name of this system is Système International d'Unités. Multipliers commonly used with some electrical units include: pico- (symbol p, × 1/1,000,000,000,000); micro- (symbol μ, × 1/1,000,000); milli- (symbol m, × 1/1,000); kilo- (symbol k, × 1,000); and mega- (symbol M, × 1,000,000).

Quantity	Symbol	Unit	Abbreviation	Explanation
voltage	V	volt	V	A battery or generator produces a voltage that makes current flow in a circuit. 1 volt will drive a current of 1 amp through a resistance of 1 ohm.
current	I	ampere (or amp)	A	A current is a flow of charged particles, usually electrons. A flow of 6 quintillion (18 zeros) electrons per second is equal to 1 amp.
resistance	R	ohm	Ω	Resistance is the degree to which a conductor opposes the flow of current. Resistance causes some electrical energy to change into heat.
energy	E	joule	J	One joule of electrical energy is used every second when a current of 1 amp flows through a resistance of 1 ohm.
power	P	watt	W	Power is the rate at which work is done or energy is used. A power of 1 watt is equal to a rate of 1 joule per second.
charge	Q	coulomb	C	A current is a flow of charged particles, usually electrons. A coulomb is the charge moved in 1 second by a current of 1 amp.

EQUATIONS

The expressions shown below are themselves meaningless, but each one will enable you to obtain three equations. Each equation will show you how to find one of the three quantities if the other two are known. All quantities must be expressed in units of the same system (such as SI) in order to obtain the correct answer.

$$\frac{a}{b\,c}$$

For all the following expressions, cover the quantity you want to find. This gives you:

$a = bc; \quad b = \dfrac{a}{c}; \quad c = \dfrac{a}{b}$

$$\frac{electric\ charge}{electric\ current \times time}$$

$$\frac{voltage}{current \times resistance}$$

$$\frac{power\ (dissipated\ in\ resistance)}{voltage \times current}$$

$$\frac{energy}{power \times time}$$

$$\frac{velocity\ of\ waves}{frequency \times wavelength}$$

RESISTORS

Resistors are used to control the flow of current in a circuit. Resistance is measured in ohms (Ω). The value of a resistor in ohms is usually shown by three colored bands on the resistor which are part of a special color code.

BANDS

Some resistors also have 4th and 5th bands:

4 Tolerance. This shows how close the resistance of a resistor is to the value marked on it. For example, a 100 Ω 2% resistor will have a resistance of between 98 Ω and 102 Ω.

5 Temperature coefficient in parts/million (ppm) per degree Celsius. This shows how much the resistance will change with temperature.

RESISTOR VALUES

The first three bands are parts of the color code (shown below). The first two stripes give you the first two numbers of the resistor's value in ohms. The third stripe indicates the amount by which the first two numbers must be multiplied (i.e: how many zeros to add after these numbers).

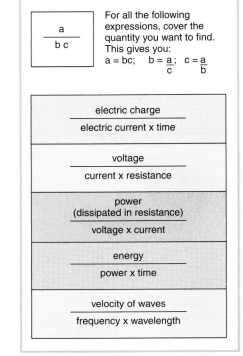

2,200,000 ohms (or 2.2 M Ω)

24,000 ohms (or 24 k Ω)

7,500 ohms (or 7.5 k Ω)

650 ohms

35 ohms

70 ohms

CODE	Black	Brown	Red	Orange	Yellow	Green	Blue	Violet	Gray	White	Gold	Silver
Band 1 1st fig.	0	1	2	3	4	5	6	7	8	9		
Band 2 2nd fig.	0	1	2	3	4	5	6	7	8	9		
Band 3 multiplier	1	10	100	1,000	10,000	100,000	1 million	10 million			0.1	0.01
Band 4 tolerance		1%	2%			0.5%	0.25%	0.1%			5%	10%
Band 5 temp. co-efficient	200 ppm/°C	100 ppm/°C	50 ppm/°C	25 ppm/°C	15 ppm/°C		10 ppm/°C	5 ppm/°C	1 ppm/°C			

ELECTRICAL AND ELECTRONIC SYMBOLS

Commonly used symbols for some components found in electrical and electronic circuits are shown below. Alternative symbols are sometimes used for many components, especially in books published in other countries.

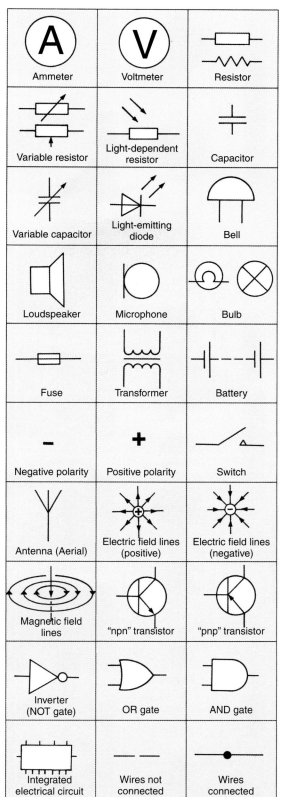

Ammeter	Voltmeter	Resistor
Variable resistor	Light-dependent resistor	Capacitor
Variable capacitor	Light-emitting diode	Bell
Loudspeaker	Microphone	Bulb
Fuse	Transformer	Battery
Negative polarity	Positive polarity	Switch
Antenna (Aerial)	Electric field lines (positive)	Electric field lines (negative)
Magnetic field lines	"npn" transistor	"pnp" transistor
Inverter (NOT gate)	OR gate	AND gate
Integrated electrical circuit	Wires not connected	Wires connected

MORSE CODE

Messages can be sent in Morse code as combinations of short and long signals called dots and dashes. These signals represent letters, numbers, and other characters.

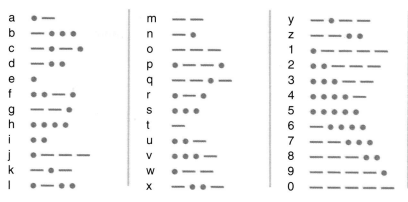

BINARY CODE

Electronic calculators use the binary system of numbers. This has just two digits, 0 and 1, unlike the decimal system, which has 10 digits, from 0 to 9. In the decimal system, long numbers represent (from right to left) units, tens, hundreds, thousands, and so on. In the binary system, long numbers represent units, twos, fours, eights, and so on.

Binary numbers   **Decimal numbers**

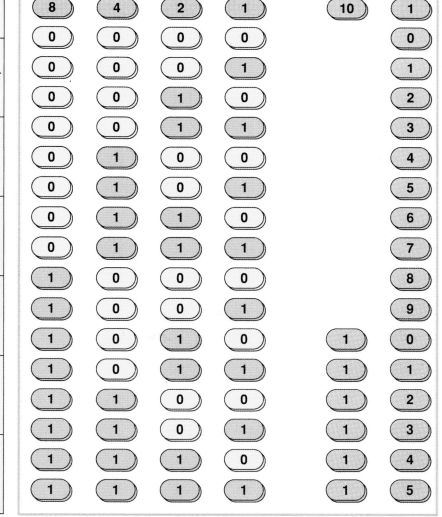

8	4	2	1	10	1
0	0	0	0		0
0	0	0	1		1
0	0	1	0		2
0	0	1	1		3
0	1	0	0		4
0	1	0	1		5
0	1	1	0		6
0	1	1	1		7
1	0	0	0		8
1	0	0	1		9
1	0	1	0	1	0
1	0	1	1	1	1
1	1	0	0	1	2
1	1	0	1	1	3
1	1	1	0	1	4
1	1	1	1	1	5

SOUND AND LIGHT

WAVE EQUATION

The amplitude of the wave (a) is the height of a crest (or trough) from the zero line. The distance between one crest and its neighboring crest is known as the wavelength (λ). The number of waves produced every second is called the frequency (f).

Low frequency   Long wavelength

High frequency   Short wavelength

The formula for any wave

$$\text{wave speed} = \text{frequency} \times \text{wavelength}$$
$$\text{(m/s)} \qquad \text{(Hz)} \qquad \text{(m)}$$

PHOTOGRAPHIC EXPOSURES

Exposure is a combination of shutter speed and aperture. This diagram shows how, by keeping a constant shutter speed of 1/250 with a 200ASA film, the aperture can be changed to achieve the correct exposure for the different lighting conditions shown.

Bright sunshine	f16 (small aperture)	Correct exposure
Part cloud	f8	Correct exposure
Subject in shade	f5.6	Correct exposure
Very cloudy	f4	Correct exposure

THE ELECTROMAGNETIC SPECTRUM

The light that we see is one type of electromagnetic radiation. There are many others as shown below. These waves all travel at the same speed but differ in their wavelength.

Wavelength (meters)

Type of radiation

Detectable objects

Source

Long wavelength

10^4

10^2

1

Radio waves — House — Radio transmitter

Cabbage — TV transmitter

Microwaves

10^{-2}

Fly — Microwave oven

10^{-4}

cell

Infrared — Visible spectrum — Infrared burner

10^{-6}

Ultraviolet — Protein — Ultraviolet lamp

10^{-8}

Molecule

X-rays

10^{-10}

Atom — X-ray machine

10^{-12}

Nucleus

Gamma rays — Proton — Nuclear explosion

10^{-14}

Short wavelength

Quarks

REFRACTIVE INDEX

The speed change when light travels from one transparent material to another causes it to change direction. The greater the change in speed, the more the light bends.

The refractive index is the ratio between the speed at which light travels in a vacuum and the speed it travels in another substance.

Refractive index of a substance	=	Speed of light in a vacuum
		Speed of light in substance

The refractive index of water (1.33) is less than that of glass (1.5). This means that the light is slowed down more and so is bent more when it passes through glass than when it passes through water.

Substance	Refractive index	Speed of light (m/s)
Air	1.0	300,000,000
Water	1.33	225,000,000
Perspex	1.5	200,000,000
Glass	1.5	200,000,000
Diamond	2.4	120,000,000

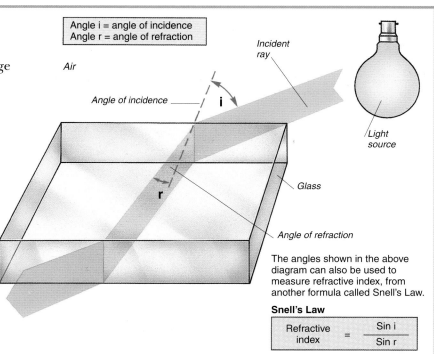

Angle i = angle of incidence
Angle r = angle of refraction

Air

Incident ray

Angle of incidence

i

Glass

r

Angle of refraction

Light source

The angles shown in the above diagram can also be used to measure refractive index, from another formula called Snell's Law.

Snell's Law

Refractive index	=	Sin i
		Sin r

FREQUENCY RANGE OF MUSICAL INSTRUMENTS

All instruments produce a sound by making something vibrate. The vibrations produce soundwaves in the air. These waves travel to our ears and produce rapid changes in air pressure at the same rate as the vibration of the instrument. The sound wave from each instrument has its own kind of pressure changes, which can be shown below by curved and jagged lines that are called waveforms.

Tuning fork
This produces a pure note of one frequency. Other instruments usually produce many frequencies at the same time to give a complicated waveform.

Flute
The pure fluid sound of the flute is reflected in the smooth curves of its regular waveform.

Oboe
The rich sounds made by reed instruments such as the oboe contain many more frequencies than the purer sounds of the flute.

Clarinet
The single reed of the clarinet produces a smooth, warm tone.

Violin
The bright sound of the violin contains many high frequency harmonics producing a very jagged waveform.

Cymbal
The crashing sound of the cymbal corresponds to a jagged irregular wave pattern that rises and falls in an almost random way.

EARTH

GEOLOGICAL TIMESCALE

The history of the Earth is outlined in the geological timescale and calculated by studying the ages of the various layers of sedimentary rock.

Era	Period	Epoch	Time began
Cenozoic	Quarternary	Holocene	0.01
		Pleistocene	1.6
	Tertiary	Pliocene	5.3
		Miocene	23
		Oligocene	34
		Eocene	53
		Paleocene	65
Mesozoic	Cretaceous		135
	Jurassic		205
	Triassic		250
Paleozoic	Permian		300
	Carboniferous (divided into Lower Mississippian and Upper Pennsylvanian in the United States)		355
	Devonian		410
	Silurian		435
	Ordovician		510
	Cambrian		570
Precambrian	Formation of the Earth		4,600

The figures of "Time began" given here are for millions of years.

LATITUDE AND LONGITUDE

At 0° latitude lies the line of the equator, 0° longitude runs through Greenwich, London, England. The positions of places are calculated by the degrees of latitude and longitude. Each degree is divided into 60 minutes.

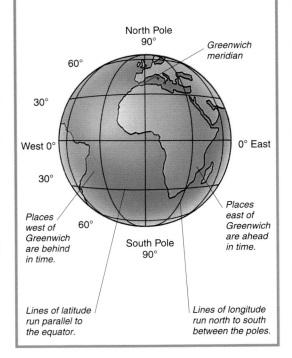

STRUCTURE OF THE EARTH

The Earth contains four layers. The outer layer, the crust, is made of different types of rocks such as basalt and granite. The mantle also contains rocks but these are heavier and darker than those found in the crust. The outer core is liquid and is thought to contain liquid iron, sulfur, and silicon. The inner core probably contains solid iron.

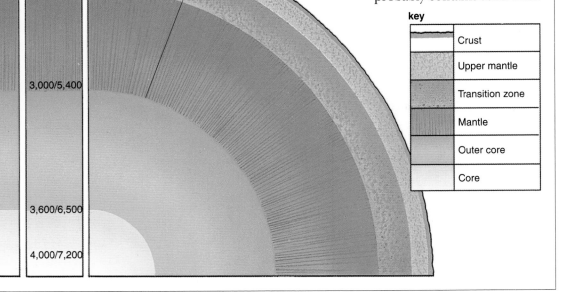

Depth (km/miles)	Pressure (k bar)	Density (kg/m³)	Temperature (°C/°F)
0	0	0	0
50/30 400/240	100 150	3,000 3,500	500/930 1,750/3,200
1,000/600	325	4,500	2,000/3,600
2,900/1,800	1,325	10,000	3,000/5,400
5,100/3,200	3,300	12,100	3,600/6,500
6,360/3,950	3,750	12,100	4,000/7,200

key

	Crust
	Upper mantle
	Transition zone
	Mantle
	Outer core
	Core

MOHS' SCALE OF HARDNESS

Friedrich Mohs, a German minerologist, created a table of 10 minerals to show their hardness. The higher the number, the harder the mineral. Each mineral can scratch those of a lower number.

1 Talc
6 Orthoclase

A fingernail has a hardness of about 2.5.

2 Gypsum
7 Quartz

A copper coin has a hardness of 5.5.

3 Calcite
8 Topaz

4 Fluorite
9 Corundum

5 Apatite
10 Diamond

A pocketknife has a hardness of 5.5 and can scratch apatite but not orthoclase.

THE MOST COMMON ROCKS

All the rocks that make up the Earth are igneous, sedimentary, or metamorphic rocks. Igneous rocks form when molten rock is cooled. Sedimentary rocks are fragments of rock, sand, and silt compressed to form a solid mass. Metamorphic rocks form when heat and pressure change the mineral content of a rock. Below are 10 common examples of each.

Igneous	Sedimentary	Metamorphic
Granite	Limestone	Slate
Syenite	Dolomite	Phyllite
Gabbro	Sandstone	Schist
Dolerite	Conglomerate	Gneiss
Basalt	Breccia	Hornfels
Andesite	Evaporite	Marble
Obsidian	Siltstone	Quartzite
Diorite	Mudstone	Migmatite
Porphyry	Shale	Amphibolite
Rhyolite	Clay	Tactite

THE ROCK CYCLE

The Earth's crust is made of recycled rocks. These are formed by external factors such as heat, pressure, and weathering. These factors are continually breaking up and rebuilding sedimentary, igneous, and metamorphic rocks in a process known as the rock cycle.

Key

Emplacement   Metamorphism

Solidification   Fusion

Erosion   Uplift

Deposition   Lithification (rock formation)

Extrusive igneous rock

Intrusive igneous rock

Sediment

Sedimentary rock

Metamorphic rock

Molten rock in the mantle

WEATHER

WORLD METEOROLOGICAL ORGANIZATION

The World Meteorological Organization consists of a network of about 10,000 national weather stations all over the world. Reports from these stations are sent by telephone every three hours to the 13 main weather centers shown on this world map. This information is then continually passed around the world to national weather stations, which put together their own weather forecasts.

EXTREMES IN WEATHER CONDITIONS

This chart shows the extreme weather conditions recorded around the world. In some places, extreme conditions are part of the normal seasonal weather pattern. In others, conditions such as floods and droughts can interrupt the usual pattern.

Greatest snowfall in a single snowstorm
189 in (480 cm). Mount Shasta, California. 02/13–19/1959.

Most intense rainfall
1.8 in (38.1 mm) in one minute. Basse Terre, Guadeloupe. 11/26/1970.

Driest place/longest drought
(Annual average) (Annual average) 0.5 mm, Quilagua, Atacama Desert, Chile.

Fastest surface wind speed at low altitude
207 mph (333 km/h). Thule, Greenland. 03/08/1972.

Maximum sunshine
(Annual average) 91%. 4,055 hours out of a possible 4,456 in a year. Yuma, Arizona.

Minimum sunshine
Nil, South Pole—for stretches of 182 days in winter.

Highest shade temperature
136°F (58°C). al' Aziz yah, Libya (alt. 367 ft/111 m). 9/13/1922.

Greatest temperature range
From -90.4°F to 98°F (-68°C to 37°C). Verhoyansk, Siberia.

Lowest temperature
-129°F (-89°C). Vostock, Antarctica. 07/21/1983.

Most rainy days
(Year) up to 350 per year, Mount Wai-ale-ali (alt. 5,148 ft/1,569 m) Kaunai, Hawaii.

Highest wind speed at high altitude
231 mph (371 km/h). Mount Washington (alt. 6,288 ft/1,916 m), New Hampshire. 04/12/1934.

READING WEATHER SYMBOLS

Air pressure: 1,018 mb
Temperature: 45°F (7°C)
Current weather: continuous heavy rain
Visibility: 1.5 miles (2.5 km)
Dew point: 43°F (6°C)
Stratus cloud
Cloud cover complete
Cloud base: 1,310 ft (400 m)
Rain in past hour

Wind arrows indicate the direction from which the wind is blowing—here, a moderate northeasterly wind. The marks ("feathers") on the arrows show the wind speed. Each whole mark equals a speed of 12 mph (19 km/h), each half mark 6 mph (9.5 km/h).

Pressure fallen by 2.7 mb in last 3 hours

This map shows the location of weather centers around the world. It also shows the major climatic regions and ocean currents of the world.

Greenland
North Atlantic Dri
North America
North Atlantic Dri
Gulf Stream
Alaska Current
California Current
North Equatorial Current
Equatorial Counter Current
South America
Equa
Cu
Peru Current

WEATHER MAP SYMBOLS

Meteorologists use a list of symbols to indicate weather and wind speed. The symbols shown are recognized internationally. Once plotted on weather maps they provide essential information used in making weather forecasts. Television weather forecasters use simplified versions of these symbols.

Mist	Fog	Drizzle
Rain	Rain and drizzle	Rain and snow
Snow	Rain shower	Rain and snow shower
Snow shower	Hail shower	Thunderstorm
Cold front	Warm front	Occluded front

Light to strong winds

Calm / Gale

WEATHER CENTERS

The location of the 13 main weather centers listed below is shown on the world map.

1 Washington, D.C.

2 Bracknell, UK

3 Paris, France

4 Offenbach, Germany

5 Prague, Czech Republic

6 Moscow, Russia

7 Cairo, Egypt

8 New Delhi, India

9 Beijing, China

10 Tokyo, Japan

11 Melbourne, Australia

12 Nairobi, Kenya

13 Brasilia, Brazil

Polar
Tundra
Temperate
Desert
Tropical
Mountain

CLIMATES OF MAJOR CITIES

These graphs show the average temperature and rainfall statistics for various cities around the world (the locations of these cities are shown on the world map above).

Ocean currents

① Adelaide, Australia

② London, England

③ Tokyo, Japan

④ Mumbai, India

⑤ Cape Town, South Africa

⑥ Moscow, Russia

⑦ San Diego, California

⑧ Arequipa, Peru

SPACE

THE SUN

By far the brightest star in our sky is the Sun because of its closeness to Earth. Even so, the light leaving it takes 8.3 minutes to reach us; the Sun we see is 8.3 minutes old.

Mass	1.99×10^{33}g
Surface temperature	6,000°C
Core temperature	14,000,000°C
Diameter	1,392,000 km

LARGEST METEORITES

Name	Country	Approximate tonnage
Hoba West	South West Africa	60
The Abnighito Tent	Greenland	30.4
Bacuberito	Mexico	27
Mbosi	Tanzania	26
Agpalik	West Greenland	20.1
Armanty	Outer Mongolia	20
Chupaderos	Mexico	14
Willamette	US	14
Campo del Cielo	Argentina	13
Mundrabilla	Australia	12

BRIGHTEST STARS

The brightness of a star is measured by its magnitude. The brighter the star, the lower the magnitude number. The apparent magnitude of a star is its brightness as seen from Earth. The absolute magnitude is how much light a star actually gives out.

Name	Magnitude Apparent	Magnitude Absolute	Distance from Sun (light-years)
Sirius	-1.46	+1.4	8.65
Canopus	-0.73	-4.6	1,200
Alpha Centauri	-0.1	+4.1	4.38
Arcturus	-0.06	-0.3	36
Vega	+0.04	+0.5	26
Capella	+0.08	-0.5	42
Rigel	+0.10	-7.0	900
Procyon	+0.35	+2.6	11.4
Betelgeuse	+0.49	-5.7v	310
Achernar	+0.51	-2.5	117
Hadar	+0.63	-4.6	490
Altair	+0.77	+2.3	16
Aldebaran	+0.85	-0.7	69
Acrux	+0.90	-3.7	370
Antares	+0.92	-4.5	430
Spica	+0.96	-3.6	260
Pollux	+1.15	+1.0	35
Fomalhaut	+1.16	+1.9	23
Deneb	+1.25	-7.1	1,800
Beta Crucis	+1.25	-5.1	489
Regulus	+1.35	-0.7	85
Adhara	+1.50	-4.4	681

THE PLANETS

There are nine planets in the solar system. They fall roughly into two groups. Closest to the Sun are four rocky planets. These are Mercury, Venus, Earth, and Mars.

Farther from the Sun are the gas giants. These are Jupiter, Saturn, Uranus, and Neptune. Pluto is the odd one out—it is the smallest planet and is made of rock and ice.

Planet	Mercury	Venus	Earth	Mars	Jupiter	Saturn	Uranus	Neptune	Pluto
Distance from Sun millions of miles (km)	36.0 (57.9)	67.2 (108.2)	93 (149.6)	141.5 (227.9)	483.3 (778.3)	886.1 (1,427)	1,782 (2,870)	2,774 (4,497)	3,672 (5,913)
Diameter at equator miles (km)	3,033 (4,879)	7,523 (12,104)	7,928 (12,756)	4,222 (6,786)	88,784 (142,984)	74,914 (120,536)	31,770 (51,118)	30,757 (49,528)	1,419 (2,284)
Mass (Earth = 1)	0.056	0.82	1	0.107	318	95	14.5	17	0.002
Volume (Earth = 1)	0.056	0.86	1	0.15	1,319	744	67	57	0.01
Surface temperature °F (°C)	-356 to +800 (-180 to +430)	+896 (+480)	-158 to +133 (-70 to +55)	-248 to +77 (-120 to +25)	-238 (-150)	-292 (-180)	-353 (-214)	-364 (-220)	-382 (-230)
Surface gravity (Earth = 1)	0.38	0.9	1	0.38	2.64	0.925	0.79	1.12	0.05
Time to orbit Sun ("year")	87.97 days	224.7 days	365.26 days	686.98 days	11.86 years	29.46 yrs	84.01 yrs	164.8 yrs	248.5 yrs
Time to turn 360° ("day")	58.65 days	243.01 days	23 h 56 m 4 s	24 h 37 m 23 s	9 h 55 m 30 s	10 h 39 m	17 h 14 m	16 h 7 m	6 days 9 h
Orbital velocity km/s (miles/s)	29.7 (47.9)	21.8 (35)	18.5 (29.8)	15 (24.1)	8.1 (13.1)	6 (9.6)	4.2 (6.8)	3.4 (5.4)	2.9 (4.7)
Number of moons	0	0	1	2	16	34	27	13	1

Northern Hemisphere

Pisces
Cetus
Aries
Pegasus
Delphinus
Andromeda
Triangulum
Taurus
Cygnus
Perseus
Sagitta
Cassiopeia
Orion
Aquila
Cepheus
Auriga
Lyra
Monoceros
Polaris (North Star)
Ophiuchus
Hercules
Draco
Ursa Minor
Gemini
Corona Borealis
Canis Minor
Ursa Major
Cancer
Serpens Caput
Böotes
Canes Venatici
Leo Minor
Hydra
Virgo
Leo

CONSTELLATIONS

Earth's sky contains around 6,000 stars that are visible to the naked eye. The stars that you see depend on where you are standing on Earth and what time of year it is. These star maps show the stars that are visible from the Northern and Southern hemispheres. As the Earth spins, the stars appear to move across the sky and so these maps will need to be rotated too. The stars in the center of the maps can be seen all year round; those at the edge may only be seen at certain times of the year.

Ursa Major
Also known as the Great Bear. Greek legend has it that a beautiful woman was turned into a bear by a jealous goddess.

Pegasus
This constellation takes the form of a winged horse. In Greek legend, the horse sprang from the blood of a monster called Medusa, after it was killed by Perseus.

Orion
This is one of the easiest constellations to find in the sky. In Greek legend, Orion was a successful but arrogant hunter.

Canis Major
This constellation represents one of the two dogs that are snapping at Orion's heels. One of the stars that makes up Canis Major is Sirius, the brightest star in the sky.

Centaurus
The constellation of Centaurus shows the centaur—half man and half horse. It contains the nearest star (aside from the Sun) to Earth—Proxima Centauri.

Scorpius
In Greek legend, this scorpion was sent to kill Orion. The characters are now at opposite ends of the sky. As Orion sets, the scorpion rises.

Southern Hemisphere

Cetus
Aquarius
Sculptor
Fornax
Piscis Austrinus
Phoenix
Capricornus
Eridanus
Grus
Tucana
Microscopium
Indus
Aquila
Horologium
Sagittarius
Lepus
Caelum
Reticulum
Hydrus
Columba
Mensa
Pavo
Corona Australis
Orion
Pictor
Ara
Canis Major
Carina
Volans
Apus
Triangulum Australe
Monoceros
Chameleon
Ophiuchus
Vela
Norma
Scorpius
Puppis
Crux
Pyxis
Lupus
Antlia
Centaurus
Libra
Hydra
Hydra
Sextans
Crater
Corvus
Virgo

LIVING THINGS

This chart shows how biologists classify the different forms of life on Earth. It is divided into five major groups, called kingdoms, and the kingdoms are themselves broken down into several smaller units. Each organism in the chart contains two pieces of information about it. First, you will be able to discover which group of the living world it belongs to. Second, you will be able to see what other living things are most closely related to it through the process of evolution.

HOW TO USE THE CHART
The chart is color-coded so that you can quickly tell the classification level of any group shown.

Kingdom — *The largest grouping in the classification of living things.*

Phylum — *A major group within a kingdom. This is sometimes called a division when used in the classification of plants.*

Subphylum — *Part of a phylum, or division, in the classification of plants.*

Class — *A major part of a phylum or subphylum.*

Subclass — *A large group within a class.*

Order — *Part of a class or subclass. Some classes are split into many orders.*

Family — *A large collection of species that have several features in common.*

Genus — *A small collection of species that have many features in common.*

Species — *A group of living things that can breed together in nature.*

Green algae
Chlorophyta — *Scientific name*
6,000 — *Number of species*
Nonvascular — *Further information*

MONERANS
This kingdom includes bacteria, which are the simplest forms of life on Earth. There are over 4,000 species.

Bacteria
2,000

FUNGI
Fungi absorb food made by plants or animals. There are over 100,000 species, classified into several phyla.

True fungi
100,000

PROTISTS
This kingdom contains simple organisms that mostly have a single cell. There are at least 65,000 species and most live in water. A selection of phyla are shown here.

Amoebas
10,000

Ciliates
8,000

Slime molds
10,000

Green algae
Chlorophyta
6,000
Nonvascular

Red algae
Rhodophyta
4,000
Nonvascular

Brown algae
Phaeophyta
2,000
Nonvascular

PLANTS
The plant kingdom contains organisms that produce their food using sunlight, together with some species that have since lost this ability. The kingdom contains more than 400,000 species. Plants cannot move, but they reproduce by making spores or seeds. These often spread far from the parent plant. The simplest plants reproduce by making spores. The most advanced plants, which include conifers and flowering plants, reproduce by making seeds.

NONFLOWERING PLANTS
This category includes simple, nonvascular plants, which do not have transport systems for water, salts, or food. It also includes some vascular plants, which transport these substances in special vessels. Unlike nonvascular plants, these can live in dry places. Some biologists classify algae as nonflowering plants, and not as protists.

Mosses and liverworts
Bryophyta
25,000
Nonvascular

Ferns
Pteridophyta
12,000
Vascular

Club mosses
Lycopodiophyta
400 Vascular

Horsetails
Sphenophyta
550
Vascular

Conifers
Coniferophyta
550
Vascular

FLOWERING PLANTS
There are more than 250,000 species of flowering plant. They are all vascular, and all produce seeds. Flowering plants such as buttercups have flowers made of many separate parts arranged symmetrically around the flower stem. Advanced flowering plants such as foxgloves have fewer parts. These are often fused together to form funnels or tubes, and the flower shape is often irregular.

Monocotyledons
Plants whose seeds have one cotyledon (seed-leaf), and leaves with parallel veins. Flower parts usually in threes, or multiples of three. Rarely woody.

Irises
Iridaceae 1,850

Grasses
Graminae
8,000

Orchids
Orchidaceae
17,500

Dicotyledons
Plants whose seeds have two cotyledons (seed-leaves), and leaves with a branching network of veins. Flower parts usually in fours or fives, or multiples of these numbers. Many species have woody stems. There are over 250 families of "dicots." Some of the most important are shown here.

Elms
Ulmaceae
140

Legumes
Leguminosae
18,400

Daisies
Compositae
21,000

Roses
Rosaceae
3,100

Cacti
Cactaceae
1,650

Foxgloves
Scrophulariaceae
4,500

Parsley and carrots
Umbelliferae
3,100

Cabbages
Cruciferae 3,000

Oaks
Fagaceae
1,050

Heathers
Ericaceae
3,350

ANIMALS
The animal kingdom contains organisms that feed on plants, on other animals, or on their remains. Most animals can move around, but some spend their adult lives in one place. There may be about 10 to 20 million species.

INVERTEBRATES
This informal category contains all animals that do not have a backbone, and it includes over nine-tenths of all animal species.

Many invertebrates are soft-bodied and live in water or in damp habitats. One phylum, the arthropods, has been outstandingly successful in water and on land.

Cnidarians
Cnidaria
9,500
Mainly marine

Corals
Jellyfish
Sea anemones
Hydras

Flatworms
Platyhelminthes
10,000

Free-living flatworms
Flukes
Tapeworms

Mollusks
Mollusca
90,000
Aquatic and terrestrial

Chitons
Slugs and snails
Clams, scallops
Tusks or tooth shells
Octopuses, squids, and cuttlefish

Annelid worms
Annelida
12,000
Aquatic and terrestrial

Earthworms and bloodworms
Leeches
Lungworms and other marine worms

Echinoderms
Echinodermata
6,000
Marine

Brittle stars
Sea urchins
Sea cucumbers
Starfish
Sea lilies and feather stars

Small phyla
Ctenopora, Rotifera, Nemertea
3,000+

Comb jellies
Rotifers
Nemertean worms

Sponges
Porifera
5,000
Mainly marine

Nematode worms
Nematoda
12,000

Bryozoans
Bryozoa
4,000
Mainly marine

Arthropods (Arthropoda)
This large phylum contains animals with a jointed body that is covered by an external skeleton and divided into a number of segments. The skeleton supports and protects the body; on land, it helps to prevent it from drying out.

Millipedes
Diplopoda
7,000

Crustaceans
Crustacea
40,000
Mainly marine

Water fleas
Wood lice
Crabs and lobsters
Fish lice
Barnacles

Centipedes
Chilopoda
1,700

Arachnids
Arachnida
70,000
Mainly terrestrial

Scorpions
Spiders
Mites
Daddy longlegs

Insects
Insecta 1,000,000+ Mainly terrestrial

Springtails
Silverfish and bristletails
Dragonflies and damselflies
Butterflies and moths
Grasshoppers and crickets
Earwigs
Stick insects
Cockroaches
Mantids
Termites

Lice
True bugs
Thrips
Lacewings
Beetles
Flies
Fleas
Bees, wasps, and ants

CHORDATES (Chordata)
This phylum contains animals that have a stiff cord that runs down their bodies. There are about 44,000 species, and almost all are vertebrates (animals with backbones). The lancelets and sea squirts, two subphyla, have a stiff cord but not a true backbone.

Jawless fish
Agnatha
70
Marine; skeleton made of cartilage

Cartilaginous fish
Chondrichthyes
700
Marine; skeleton made of cartilage

Amphibians
Amphibia
4,000
Freshwater or terrestrial

Frogs and toads
Newts and salamanders
Caecilians (Apodans)

Bony fish
Osteichthyes
21,000
Marine and freshwater; skeleton made of bone

Coelacanth
Lungfish
Birchirs
Sturgeons, paddlefish
Eels
Herrings, anchovies
Salmon, trout
Carp
Catfishes
Perches, marlins, swordfishes, tunas
Anglerfish
Cods
Flying fishes
Grunions
Sticklebacks
Seahorses

Reptiles
Reptilia 6,500 Mainly terrestrial; skin covered with scales

Snakes and lizards
Turtles and tortoises
Crocodiles, alligators
Tuatara

Birds
Aves 9,000 All breed on land; skin covered in feathers

Divers
Grebes
Albatrosses, petrels
Penguins
Pelicans, gannets, cormorants
Herons, storks
Ducks, geese, swans
Eagles, hawks, vultures
Pheasants, partridges
Gulls, plovers
Pigeons, doves
Parrots
Cuckoos, roadrunners
Owls
Hummingbirds
Kingfishers, bee-eaters, rollers
Perching birds (e.g., finches)

Mammals Mammalia 4,000 Suckle young on milk

Marsupials
Marsupialia
250
Mammals that raise their young in a pouch

Opossums
Koalas
Bandicoots
Kangaroos

Monotremes
Montremata
3
Egg-laying mammals

Duck-billed platypus
Echidnas

Placentals
Eutheria
3,810
Mammals that nourish their young through a placenta

Hedgehogs, shrews, moles
Bats
Rabbits, hares
Lemers, monkeys, apes, humans
Anteaters, armadillos
Rodents
Whales, dolphins
Dogs, cats, bears
Seals, sea lions, walruses
Elephants
Hyraxes
Manatees, dugongs
Horses, tapirs, rhinoceroses
Pigs, deer, sheep, antelope, cattle

HOW LIVING THINGS WORK

LIFE SPANS

Here you can see how long different kinds of organisms live. With most living things, life span is closely linked to reproduction. Most plants and animals do not survive for long after their reproductive life has ended. Bacteria and protists often reproduce by dividing in two, so their cells stay alive, even though they have split apart.

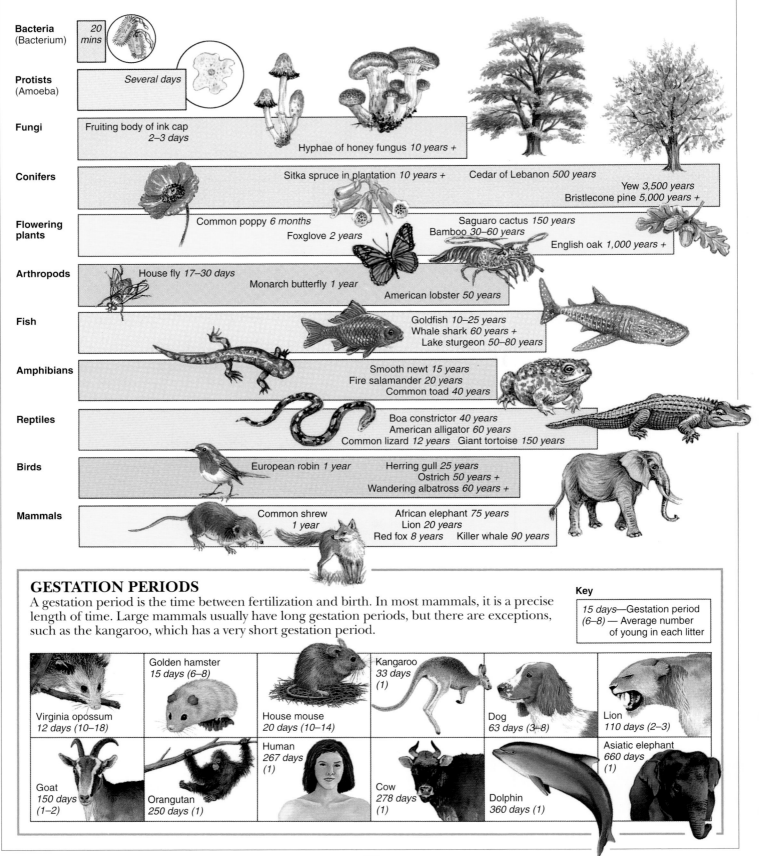

Bacteria (Bacterium)
20 mins

Protists (Amoeba)
Several days

Fungi
Fruiting body of ink cap *2–3 days*
Hyphae of honey fungus *10 years +*

Conifers
Sitka spruce in plantation *10 years +*   Cedar of Lebanon *500 years*
Yew *3,500 years*
Bristlecone pine *5,000 years +*

Flowering plants
Common poppy *6 months*
Foxglove *2 years*
Saguaro cactus *150 years*
Bamboo *30–60 years*
English oak *1,000 years +*

Arthropods
House fly *17–30 days*
Monarch butterfly *1 year*
American lobster *50 years*

Fish
Goldfish *10–25 years*
Whale shark *60 years +*
Lake sturgeon *50–80 years*

Amphibians
Smooth newt *15 years*
Fire salamander *20 years*
Common toad *40 years*

Reptiles
Boa constrictor *40 years*
American alligator *60 years*
Common lizard *12 years*   Giant tortoise *150 years*

Birds
European robin *1 year*
Herring gull *25 years*
Ostrich *50 years +*
Wandering albatross *60 years +*

Mammals
Common shrew *1 year*
African elephant *75 years*
Lion *20 years*
Red fox *8 years*   Killer whale *90 years*

GESTATION PERIODS

A gestation period is the time between fertilization and birth. In most mammals, it is a precise length of time. Large mammals usually have long gestation periods, but there are exceptions, such as the kangaroo, which has a very short gestation period.

Key

15 days—Gestation period
(6–8) — Average number
  of young in each litter

Virginia opossum *12 days (10–18)*

Golden hamster *15 days (6–8)*

House mouse *20 days (10–14)*

Kangaroo *33 days (1)*

Dog *63 days (3–8)*

Lion *110 days (2–3)*

Goat *150 days (1–2)*

Orangutan *250 days (1)*

Human *267 days (1)*

Cow *278 days (1)*

Dolphin *360 days (1)*

Asiatic elephant *660 days (1)*

BODY TEMPERATURE

"Warm-blooded" and "cold-blooded" are two terms that can be misleading. A desert pupfish is "cold-blooded," like all fish. However, it lives in hot springs, so its blood is actually warm. A "warm-blooded" hibernating bat has a much colder body temperature.

Ectothermic ("cold-blooded") animals

-5°C 0°C 5°C 10°C 15°C 20°C 25°C 30°C 35°C 40°C 45°C

Ice-fish
-2° 5°

Salmon
0°C   20°C

Frog
7°C   30°C

Lizard
18°C   45°C

Desert pupfish
34°C

Endothermic ("warm-blooded") animals

Bat
28°C

Spiny anteater
30°C

Hedgehog
35°C

Human
37°C

Bird
40°C

VITAMINS

Vitamins are essential nutrients that are needed in very small amounts. This list shows the daily vitamin requirements of an adult.

Vitamins that dissolve in fats

Vitamin A	1 milligram
Vitamin D	7.5 micrograms
Vitamin E	10 milligrams
Vitamin K	100 micrograms

Vitamins that dissolve in water

Vitamin B_1	1.5 milligrams
Vitamin B_2	1.7 milligrams
Niacin	19 milligrams
Vitamin B_6	2.2 milligrams
Vitamin B_{12}	3 micrograms
Pantothenic acid	6 milligrams
Folic acid	400 micrograms
Biotin	200 micrograms
Vitamin C	60 milligrams

METABOLIC RATE

An animal's metabolic rate is the rate at which it "burns" its food to release energy. Here you can see the metabolic rates of a range of different mammals, compared to that of humans. Small mammals have to burn their food at a high rate in relation to their volume; they have a high surface area of skin, through which their bodies quickly lose heat.

This chart shows how quickly animals burn their food for each unit of their body weight. The rate for humans is set at one.

Elephant *0.33*

Horse *0.52*

Human *1.00*

Sheep *1.05*

Dog *1.57*

Cat *3.24*

Rat *4.14*

Squirrel *4.90*

House mouse *7.86*

Harvest mouse *11.90*

Shrew *35.24*

ECOLOGY

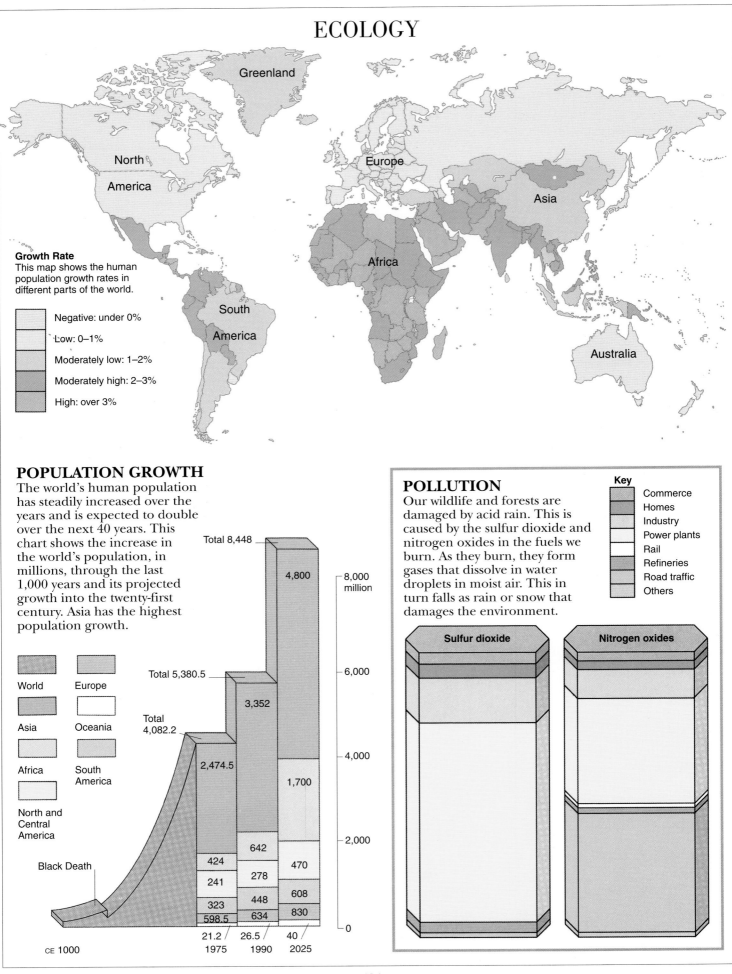

Growth Rate
This map shows the human population growth rates in different parts of the world.

- Negative: under 0%
- Low: 0–1%
- Moderately low: 1–2%
- Moderately high: 2–3%
- High: over 3%

POPULATION GROWTH

The world's human population has steadily increased over the years and is expected to double over the next 40 years. This chart shows the increase in the world's population, in millions, through the last 1,000 years and its projected growth into the twenty-first century. Asia has the highest population growth.

- World
- Europe
- Asia
- Oceania
- Africa
- South America
- North and Central America

Black Death

Total 8,448

Total 5,380.5

Total 4,082.2

4,800

3,352

2,474.5

1,700

642

424
470
241
278
323
448
608
598.5
634
830

8,000 million

6,000

4,000

2,000

0

CE 1000

21.2 / 1975

26.5 / 1990

40 / 2025

POLLUTION

Our wildlife and forests are damaged by acid rain. This is caused by the sulfur dioxide and nitrogen oxides in the fuels we burn. As they burn, they form gases that dissolve in water droplets in moist air. This in turn falls as rain or snow that damages the environment.

Key
- Commerce
- Homes
- Industry
- Power plants
- Rail
- Refineries
- Road traffic
- Others

Sulfur dioxide

Nitrogen oxides

THREATENED SPECIES

Many species of animal are threatened with extinction, such as those shown below, because of habitat destruction, pollution, hunting, and competition from introduced species.

Animal	Where found	Numbers remaining
Giant Panda	China	1,600
Iberian lynx	Spain	1,200
Indus river dolphin	Pakistan	1,100
Ethiopian wolf	Ethiopia	Under 1,000
Mountain gorilla	Central Africa	700
Golden-headed lion tamarin	Brazil	600
Mediterranean monk seal	Mediterranean	500
North Atlantic right whale	North Atlantic	300
Whooping crane	North America	200
Indonesian Javan rhino	Indonesia	60
Kakapo	New Zealand	50

RATE OF EXTINCTION

The rate of extinction traces how rapidly a species becomes extinct (dies out). A species is thought to be extinct if it has not been found in the wild for the past 50 years. The rate of extinction has increased over the past 300 years by human interference. Some species are becoming extinct 1,000 times faster than they did before people started to inhabit the Earth.

Number of species that became extinct in each year

Balinese tiger *1952*

Tasmanian wolf/tiger *1933*

Passenger pigeon *1914*

Tarpan *1900*

Great auk *1844*

Stellar's sea cow *1768*

Dodo *1690*

400
200
100
10
5
1

1700 1750 1800 1850 1900 1925 1950

MIGRATION ROUTES

At certain times of the year, some animals travel from one area to another. This is known as migration. The average distances traveled are shown in the box below.

Short-tailed shearwater
19,884 miles (32,000 km)
Golden plover
15,000 miles (24,140 km)
Arctic tern
24,856 miles (40,000 km)
Alaska fur seal
6,000 miles (9,600 km)
Monarch butterfly
3,500 miles (5,600 km)
Whitethroat
1,400 miles (2,250 km)
Wheatear
6,800 miles (11,000 km)
Caribou
1,400 miles (2,250 km)
Blue whale
12,500 miles (20,000 km)
European eel
3,500 miles (5,600 km)

GLOSSARY

Words in *italic* have their own entry in the glossary.

A

aa Volcanic lava with a rough surface.

absolute magnitude A measure of the actual *luminosity* of a star. (Compare to *apparent magnitude*.)

absolute scale A scale of temperature, also known as the Kelvin scale, that begins at *absolute zero*. Its unit of measurement is the kelvin.

absolute zero The lowest possible temperature—0°K or -459.67°F (-273.15°C).

acceleration The rate of change of *velocity*.

acid A *compound* containing hydrogen that splits up in water to give hydrogen *ions*.

acid rain Rain that has become *acid* due to water in the air reacting with acids from power plants and car exhausts. When acid rain falls it can damage plants and erode buildings.

acoustics 1. The study of sound. 2. How sound travels around a room—a concert hall, for example, must have good acoustics.

activation energy The energy needed to start a chemical *reaction*. A different amount is needed for every reaction.

adaptation The way in which a *plant* or animal changes over many generations to survive better in a particular *environment*.

additive Any substance added in small amounts, especially to food or drink, to improve it, e.g., to change color or taste.

adhesion The force of attraction between the *atoms* or *molecules* of two different substances.

adhesive A sticky substance, such as paste or glue, used to join two surfaces together.

ADP Adenosine diphosphate. A *compound* formed when *ATP* releases energy.

advection fog or **sea fog** A type of fog that forms where warm moist air moves over a colder surface.

aerobic respiration A type of *respiration* that needs oxygen.

aerofoil The special shape of an aircraft wing—more curved on the top than the bottom. It produces *lift* as it moves through the air.

aestivation The deep sleep or immobility that some animals go into when the weather is very hot and dry.

air resistance The force that resists the movement of an object through the air.

albedo How much an object, especially a *planet* or moon, reflects the light that hits it, i.e., its reflecting power.

alchemy A medieval science that tried, among other things, to find a way of changing metals such as lead into gold.

algae (singular **alga**) Simple *plants* found in water. They are nonflowering and do not have proper stems or roots.

aliphatic compound An organic compound made up of chains, not rings, of carbon *atoms*.

alkali A *base* that dissolves in water.

alkaline Describes a solution with a *pH* greater than 7.

allotropes Different forms of the same *element*, e.g., diamond and graphite are allotropes of carbon.

alloy A mixture of two or more metals, or of a metal and a nonmetal.

alternating current (AC) An electric current whose direction reverses at regular intervals. (Compare to *direct current*.)

alternator An electric *generator* that produces *alternating current*.

alveoli (singular **alveolus**) Tiny air sacs in the lungs.

AM Amplitude modulation. The transmission of a signal by changing the *amplitude* of the carrier wave.

amalgam An *alloy* of mercury and another metal, such as tin.

ammeter An instrument that measures *electric current*.

amp (**ampère**) The unit that measures *electric current*.

amplitude The size of a *vibration*, or the height of a wave, such as a sound wave.

anabolism A series of chemical *reactions* in living things that builds up large *molecules* from small ones.

anaerobic respiration A type of *respiration* that does not require oxygen. It produces less energy than *aerobic respiration*.

analog Representing a quantity by a varying electrical voltage. (Compare to *digital*.)

andesite Fine-grained brown or grayish volcanic rock.

angle of incidence The angle a light ray makes with the perpendicular to the surface it hits.

angle of reflection The angle a reflected light ray makes with the perpendicular to the reflecting surface.

anion A negatively charged *ion*.

anode A positive *electrode*.

anodizing The process of coating a metal object with a thin protective layer of oxide by *electrolysis*.

anthracite Hard coal that burns with hardly any flame or smoke.

antibodies Proteins in the blood that protect the body by fighting foreign bodies such as bacteria and viruses.

anticyclone An area of high pressure air which often produces fine weather.

antioxidant A compound added to foods and plastics, to prevent them from oxidizing and so going stale or breaking down.

antiseptic Able to kill bacteria.

apparent magnitude The brightness of a *star* as seen from Earth. (Compare to *absolute magnitude*.)

arteries Blood vessels that carry blood from the heart to other parts of the body.

artificial selection The process by which humans change the genetic makeup of a species. (Compare to *natural selection*.)

asexual reproduction Reproduction that involves only one parent.

asteroid or **minor planet** or **planetoid**. A rocky body that circles the Sun. Most asteroids are in the **asteroid belt**, between Mars and Jupiter.

asthenosphere A soft layer of the Earth's *mantle*.

astrology The study of how the movements of the stars and planets may affect our lives.

astronaut A person trained to be a crew member in a spacecraft.

astronomy The study of the *stars*, *planets*, and other bodies in space.

atmosphere The layer of gases that surrounds a *planet*.

atom The smallest part of an *element* that can exist. It consists of a *nucleus* of *protons* and *neutrons*, surrounded by orbiting *electrons*.

atomic number The number of *protons* in the *nucleus* of an *atom*.

ATP Adenosine triphosphate. A chemical in plant and animal *cells* that stores energy.

autoclave A strong, steam-heated container used for carrying out chemical *reactions* and *sterilization* at high temperature and pressure.

autotrophic A *plant* that makes its own food by *photosynthesis*.

axis 1. An imaginary line around which an object rotates. 2. The line along which rock bends in a *fold*.

B

background radiation 1. Low-intensity *radiation* emitted by *radioactive* substances in and around the Earth. 2. Radiation (in the form of *microwaves*) detected in space that may have come from the *Big Bang*.

bacteriophage A *parasitic* virus that lives on a *bacterium*.

bacterium (plural **bacteria**) A micro-*organism* that is a single *cell*.

barchan (say bar-can) A sand dune with a crest.

basalt A dark volcanic rock.

base A compound that reacts with an *acid* to give water and a *salt*.

batholith A dome of *igneous rock* that solidifies in a huge underground mass.

battery A series of two or more electrical *cells* that produce and store electricity.

Beaufort scale A scale used to measure wind speed, ranging from 0 to 12 (calm to *hurricane* force).

Big Bang The theory that the *universe* began with a massive explosion of matter. It is thought that everything in the universe is still moving apart because of the explosion.

binary system A number system with only two digits, 0 and 1.

binocular vision The ability of some animals to see objects in three dimensions and judge distance.

binomial system A system of giving an *organism* two names. The first is the genus and the second the species.

biodegradable A substance that can *decompose* and become harmless naturally.

biogas A gas made when *plant* or animal waste rots down without the presence of air.

biogenic Produced by *organisms*.

biology The study of living things.

biomass 1. The total number of living *organisms* in a given area. 2. Plant material used as a source of energy, e.g., wood that is burned to provide heat.

biome A large *ecosystem*, e.g., a tropical forest or a desert.

biosphere The region of the Earth and its *atmosphere* in which living things are found.

bituminous Containing bitumen, a tarlike substance produced from petroleum.

black dwarf The faded remains of a dead *star*. See also *white dwarf*.

black hole A highly dense object in space. Its gravity is so strong that it pulls in anything around it, even light, so that it looks black.

black ice Thin, hard, transparent ice, especially on the surface of a road.

blastocyst A hollow ball of *cells*.

boiling point The temperature at which a liquid becomes a gas.

bond The attraction between *atoms* or *ions* that holds them together in a *crystal* or *molecule*.

bone Hard tissue that is part of an animal's *skeleton*.

brine A strong *solution* of *salt* in water.

Brownian motion The random movement of tiny particles in a liquid or a gas, caused by *molecules* colliding with them.

buffer 1. A *solution* that is resistant to changes in *pH*. 2. An electric circuit used to join two other circuits.

C

CAD Computer-aided design.

calorie A unit of energy. The calorie used in food science is, in fact, a kilocalorie = 1,000 calories.

camouflage The color, markings, or body shape that helps to hide an animal or plant in its surroundings.

capacitance The ability to store electric charge.

capacitor A device used to store electric charge temporarily.

capillaries Tiny blood vessels which carry blood to and from *cells*.

capillary action The movement of a liquid up or down a tube due to attraction between its *molecules* and the molecules of the tube.

carbohydrate An energy-giving *c ompound* made up of carbon, hydrogen, and oxygen, found in foods such as potatoes.

carbon cycle The circulation of carbon (contained in carbon dioxide) from the *atmosphere*, through plants (by being trapped in *carbohydrates* by *photosynthesis*) and animals (which eat the plants), and back into the atmosphere (through *respiration* and *decomposition*).

carnivore A meat-eater.

cartilage Gristly connective tissue which makes up the soft parts of the *skeleton* and is present in some joints. The skeletons of some fish, e.g., sharks and rays, are made entirely of cartilage.

cartography The science of map-making.

cast A hollow in a rock, formed around a since decomposed animal or plant. The cast is a mold in which minerals collect and solidify to form a *fossil*.

catabolism A series of chemical *reactions* in living things that breaks down large *molecules* into small ones. This releases *energy*.

catalyst A chemical that speeds up a chemical *reaction* without being changed itself at the end of the reaction.

catalytic converter A device in a car that uses a *catalyst* to change toxic exhaust gases into less harmful gases.

cathode A negative *electrode*.

cation A positively charged *ion*.

cavitation The enlarging of cracks in rock by *compressed* air.

cecum (say ky-kum) A pouch in an animal's intestines where plant food is digested.

celestial body A natural object in space, such as a *planet* or *star*.

celestial pole One of two points in the *celestial sphere* about which *stars* appear to revolve when seen from Earth.

celestial sphere The imaginary sphere in which the *stars* seem to lie when seen from Earth.

cell 1. The smallest unit of an *organism* that can exist on its own. 2. (Voltaic) cell A device which produces electricity by chemical change.

cell division The process where one *cell* splits to produce two cells, called **daughter cells**.

cellulose A *carbohydrate* that forms the walls of plant *cells*.

centrifugal force (or **centrifugal effect**) The *force* that appears to push outward on a body moving in a circle.

centrifuge A device used to separate substances of different densities, by spinning them around at high speed.

centripetal force The force that pulls inward to keep an object moving in a circle.

Cepheid (say see-fee-id) **star** A type of *star* that has a cycle of varying brightness.

ceramics Objects made of clay or porcelain fired in a kiln.

cerebellum The part of the brain at the back of the skull that controls muscle movement and balance.

cerebrum The main part of the brain in the top of the skull that processes information.

cermet A material made from *ceramic* and *metal*. Cermets can withstand very high temperatures.

CERN Conseil Européen pour Recherches Nucléaires. The research center of the European Organization for Nuclear Research in Geneva.

CFC Chlorofluorocarbon. Gases, which if allowed to escape into the atmosphere, e.g., from refrigerators and aerosols, will cause holes in the *ozone* layer.

chain reaction A reaction which continues on its own, e.g., a *nuclear reaction* in which *neutrons* from the splitting of one *atom* go on to split other atoms.

chemical bond See *bond*.

chemical Any substance that can change when joined or mixed with another substance.

chemistry The study of *matter*.

chlorophyll The green *pigment* found in many *plants* which absorbs light to provide the energy for *photosynthesis*.

chloroplasts Tiny bodies in some plant cells which contain *chlorophyll*.

chromatography A method of separating a mixture by running it through a medium, e.g., filter paper. Different parts of the mixture move through the medium at different speeds.

chromosome A structure made up of *genes*, which carries the genetic information in a *cell*. Chromosomes are arranged in pairs in the *nucleus* of a cell.

chromosphere A layer of gases in the Sun's atmosphere that shines red.

cilia (singular **cilium**) Tiny "hairs" on the surface of many small *organisms*.

circuit A path around which an *electric current* can flow.

climate The normal weather conditions in an area over a long period of time.

clone Two or more identical *organisms* that share exactly the same *genes*.

cohesion The force of attraction between two particles of the same substance.

coke A fuel made by baking coal. It is mostly carbon and gives off much more heat than coal.

colloid A mixture made up of tiny particles of one substance dispersed in another in which it does not dissolve.

colony A large group of the same *species* of *organism* that live together.

coma A cloud of gas and dust that surrounds the center of a *comet*.

combustion (or **burning**) A chemical *reaction* in which a substance combines with oxygen, producing heat energy.

comet A ball of frozen gas and dust that travels around the Sun. Some of the dust streams out from the comet to make a "tail."

commensalism Where two or more *organisms* live together, and neither causes harm to the other.

community A group of people or animals who live in the same place.

commutator A device that reverses the direction of an *electric current*.

compound A substance containing *atoms* of two or more *elements*.

compression 1. Being pressed together or bunched up (e.g., the crest of a sound wave). 2. The increase in *density* of a *fluid*.

concave lens A lens that curves inward.

concentration A measure of the strength of a solution, i.e., the amount of *solute* dissolved in a certain amount of *solvent*.

condensation The change of a gas or vapor into a liquid.

conduction The movement of heat or electricity through a substance.

conductor A substance through which heat or electric current flows easily.

cones Light-sensitive *cells* in the retina of the eye that enable us to see colors.

constellation One of 88 regions of the night sky. Each constellation contains a grouping of stars joined by imaginary lines to represent a figure.

convection The transfer of heat through a *fluid* by currents within the fluid.

converging lens See *convex lens*.

convergent evolution The way in which different species *evolve* similar features because they are subjected to similar *environmental* conditions.

convex lens A lens that curves outward.

coprolites Fossilized dung.

corona The outer layer of hot gases surrounding the Sun.

corrasion The wearing away of a surface by the action of rocks carried in ice or water.

corrosion Chemical attack of the surface of a *metal*.

cosmology The study of the structure and origin of the *universe*.

cotyledon A simple leaf that forms part of a developing *plant*. Also called a seed-leaf.

covalent bond A chemical *bond* formed by *atoms* sharing one or more *electrons*.

CPU Central processing unit. The "brain" of a computer.

cracking The process of splitting larger *molecules* into smaller ones by heating under pressure.

cross-fertilization *Fertilization* of a plant with *gametes* from another species of plant.

crust The rocky outer surface of the Earth.

crystal A solid substance with a regular shape.

crystal lattice The repeating pattern of *atoms* or *ions* that forms a *crystal*.

crystallogram A pattern formed on a photographic plate by passing a beam of X-rays through a *crystal*.

cyclone Another name for a *hurricane* especially over the Indian Ocean.

cytoplasm The contents of a *cell*, except the *nucleus*.

D

decant To separate a mixture of a solid and a liquid by allowing the solid to settle and pouring off the liquid.

decibel A unit used to measure the loudness of a sound.

decomposer A tiny *organism*, such as a *bacterium*, which breaks down dead matter.

decomposition 1. *Organic* decay. 2. Breaking larger *molecules* into smaller ones.

density The *mass* per unit volume of a substance.

depression An area of low air pressure, which often brings bad weather.

dermis The thick layer of tissue in the skin below the *epidermis*.

desalination The removal of salt from sea water.

desertification The formation of a desert.

desiccate Dry out a substance by removing water from it.

desiccator A sealed container used to *desiccate* and keep substances dry.

detector The *circuit* in a radio receiver that separates a sound signal from a radio wave.

detergent A substance that, when added to water, helps the water to remove grease and oil.

dicotyledon A flowering *plant* with two *cotyledons*.

diffraction The spreading out of waves, e.g., light waves, when they pass through a narrow slit.

diffusion The mixing of two or more different substances because of the random movement of the *molecules*.

digestion The breaking down of food in the stomach into simple *molecules* that can pass into the bloodstream.

digital Representing a quantity by electrical signals that are either on or off. (Compare to *analog*.)

diode An electronic component that lets electricity flow in one direction only.

diploid cell A *cell* with two complete sets of *chromosomes*.

direct current (DC) An electric current that flows in one direction only. (Compare to *alternating current*.)

discharge The release or conversion of stored energy.

displacement A chemical *reaction* in which one kind of *atom* or *ion* in a *molecule* is replaced by another.

distillation A process in which a liquid is boiled and then *condensed*. It is used to separate mixtures of liquids or purify liquids.

DNA Deoxyribonucleic acid. The chemical that makes up *chromosomes* and is present in all *cells*. DNA can replicate itself to transmit genetic information from parent to offspring.

doldrums Area along the equator where the *trade winds* meet and form an area of very little wind.

drag The force that slows down an object as it travels through a liquid or gas.

drought A long period with no rain.

dye A substance that colors a material.

dynamo A *generator* that produces *direct current*.

E

Easterlies Major winds that blow from the east.

echo When a sound is heard again because it reflects off a solid object.

eclipse The shadow caused by a body blocking the light from another. See *lunar eclipse* and *solar eclipse*.

ecology The study of the relationships between *organisms* and their *environment*.

ecosystem A distinct area in the *biosphere* that contains living things, e.g., a lake or a forest.

effort A *force* applied to move a load.

elasticity The ability of a material to stretch and then return to its original shape.

electrode A piece of metal or carbon that collects or releases *electrons* in an electric circuit.

electric current The flow of *electrons* or *ions*.

electrolysis Chemical change in an *electrolyte* caused by an *electric current* flowing through it.

electrolyte A substance that conducts electricity when molten or in *solution*.

electromagnetic spectrum The complete range of electromagnetic radiation— *gamma rays*, *X-rays*, *ultraviolet radiation*, visible light, *infrared radiation*, *microwaves*, and radio waves.

electromotive force (e.m.f.) The *potential difference* of a *battery* or *cell*. It pushes an *electric current* around a *circuit*.

electron A particle with a negative electrical charge outside the *nucleus* in all *atoms*.

electron gun A device that produces a stream of *electrons*, called a cathode ray, for use in a television, for example.

electron micrograph A magnified image of an object made by an *electron microscope*.

electron microscope A *microscope* that uses a beam of *electrons* to produce a magnified image of an object.

electrophoresis The separation of charged particles in a mixture.

electroplating The coating of a metal object with a thin layer of another metal by *electrolysis*.

electroscope An instrument that detects electric charge.

electrostatic field The field of force surrounding an electrically charged object.

element A substance that cannot be broken down into more simple substances by chemical *reactions*.

emulsifier A substance used to make *immiscible* liquids blend.

emulsion Tiny particles of one liquid dispersed in another liquid.

endoplasmic reticulum (ER) A system of *membranes* in a *cell* on which chemical *reactions* take place.

endoscope An instrument used to examine the inside of the body.

endoskeleton The internal skeleton of *vertebrates*.

endosperm The tissue in a seed that stores food.

endothermic reaction A chemical *reaction* during which heat is absorbed from the surroundings.

energy The capacity to do *work*.

environment The surroundings of an animal or plant.

enzyme A *catalyst* in living things that increases the speed of *reaction* in natural chemical processes.

epidermis The outer layer of the skin.

equator An imaginary circle around the middle of the Earth, midway between the Noth and South poles.

equilibrium A state of physical or chemical balance.

erosion The wearing away of the Earth's surface due to the effects of weather, water, or ice.

erythrocytes Red blood *cells*.

escape velocity The minimum speed that a space rocket must reach to escape the Earth's *gravity*.

eukaryotic cell A *cell* with a *nucleus*. (Compare to *prokaryotic cell*.)

eutrophication Where an excess of nutrients, from fertilizers, for example, gets into water, causing the overgrowth of aquatic plants. This creates a shortage of oxygen in the water, killing animal life.

evaporation The changing of a liquid into a vapor by the escape of *molecules* from its surface.

evolution The gradual process by which life develops and changes.

evolve To undergo *evolution*.

excretion The elimination of waste by *organisms*.

exosphere The outermost part of the Earth's *atmosphere*, about 560 miles (900 km) above the surface of the Earth.

exoskeleton The hard outer "skin" of many *invertebrates*, such as insects.

exothermic A chemical *reaction* that produces heat.

extinction The death of all the members of a *species*.

F

fault A break in the Earth's *crust*.

fermentation The process in which yeast converts sugars in plant material to alcohol and carbon dioxide.

fertilization The joining of male and female *gametes*.

fiber An elongated, thick-walled plant *cell*.

filter A device that removes the solid material from a liquid.

fluid A substance that can flow, i.e., either a gas, a vapor, or a liquid.

fluorescence Light given off by certain *atoms* when they are hit by *ultraviolet radiation*.

FM Frequency modulation. The transmission of a signal by changing the *frequency* of the carrier wave, such as a radio wave.

fold A bend in rock layers.

food chain A series of *organisms*, each of which is eaten by the next.

food web The system of *food chains* in an *ecosystem*.

force Something that changes the movement or shape of an object.

force field The area in which a *force* can be felt.

formula (plural **formulae**) A set of chemical symbols that shows the makeup of a chemical.

fossil The remains of an animal or plant turned to stone.

fossil fuel A fuel that has been formed over millions of years from the remains of living things, e.g., coal and oil.

Fraunhofer lines Dark lines on the Sun's *spectrum* caused by elements in the Sun's gases absorbing certain wavelengths of light.

freezing point The temperature at which a substance turns from liquid to solid.

frequency The number of waves that pass a point every second.

friction A *force* that slows down or stops the movement of one surface against another.

front The first part of an advancing mass of cold or warm air.

fuse A safety device used in electrical circuits. It is a thin wire that melts if too much current passes through it.

G

Gaia (Say guy-a) **hypothesis** The theory that all the living things on the Earth form a huge "*organism*" that controls the *biosphere*.

galaxy A large group of *stars*, dust, and gas, all loosely held together by gravity. Our galaxy is called the Milky Way.

galvanize To coat iron with zinc to protect it from rust.

gamete A reproductive *cell*, such as a sperm or egg.

gamma rays A type of *electromagnetic radiation* with a very short *wavelength*.

ganglion (plural **ganglia**) A group of nerve *cells* enclosed in a casing of connective tissue.

Geiger counter An instrument used to detect and measure certain forms of *radiation*.

gene Part of the *chromosome* that controls a particular characteristic of an individual.

generator A device that converts mechanical energy into electricity.

geochemistry The study of the chemistry and composition of the Earth.

geomorphology The study of the physical features on the Earth's surface.

geothermal energy Energy harnessed from the hot rocks inside the Earth.

germination The early stages in the growth of a seed.

gland An organ or group of *cells* that produces substances used by the body.

global warming The heating of the Earth's *atmosphere* caused by the *greenhouse effect*.

gluons Particles within *protons* and *neutrons* that hold *quarks* together.

gravity The force of attraction between any two masses. It is what attracts all objects toward the Earth, giving them *weight*.

greenhouse effect The way in which certain gases in the Earth's *atmosphere*, especially carbon dioxide, trap heat. The build up of these gases leads to *global warming*.

grike An enlarged crack in limestone produced as the rock gradually dissolves in rainwater.

groynes Low walls or fences built along the seashore to prevent coastal *erosion*.

guttation The loss of water from the surface of a plant as liquid rather than vapor.

gyroscope A fast-spinning wheel whose axis stays pointing in the same direction once it is spinning. A gyrocompass is used in the navigation of ships and aircraft.

H

habitat The natural home of an animal or *plant*.

haploid cell A *cell* with a single set of *chromosomes*.

hard water Water that contains calcium and magnesium salts.

hardware The mechanical and electronic parts of a computer.

hemisphere One half of a sphere. The Earth is divided into the Northern and Southern Hemisphere by the *equator*.

hemoglobin A compound in red blood *cells* that carries oxygen around the body.

herbivore A plant-eating animal.

Hertz (Hz) The unit of *frequency*. One Hertz is one cycle per second.

hibernation The deep sleep or period of inactivity that some animals go into during the winter.

holography A method of producing a three-dimensional image of an object on a flat surface using a split beam of *laser* light.

homeostasis The way an animal keeps it internal environment (temperature, blood pressure, etc.) stable.

hominid Any member of the primate family Hominidae, including humans.

hormones Chemical "messengers" that move around in the blood stream and control the functions of the body.

humidity The amount of water vapor in the air.

hurricane A huge, circular tropical storm in which there are wind speeds of 75 mph (120 km/h) or more.

hydraulic Describes a machine that operates by transferring pressure through a liquid.

hydrocarbon A chemical *compound* made up of hydrogen and carbon only.

hydroelectricity The generation of electricity by harnessing the energy in flowing water.

hydrometer An instrument used to measure the *density* of a liquid.

hyphae (say hi-fee) (singular **hypha**) Tiny threads that form the main body of a fungus.

I

igneous rock Rock formed when molten *magma* cools and solidifies.

immiscible Describes two liquids that do not blend together, e.g., water and oil.

indicator A substance that shows the *pH* of a *solution* by its color.

induction The production of an *electric current* by a changing *magnetic field*.

industrial plant The land, buildings, and machinery used to carry out an industrial process.

inertia The tendency of an object to remain at rest or keep moving in a straight line until a *force* acts on it.

infrared radiation (IR) The type of electromagnetic *radiation* produced by hot objects.

inhibitor A substance that slows down a chemical *reaction*.

inorganic Not created by natural growth. (Compare to *organic*.)

inorganic chemistry The branch of chemistry that deals with chemicals except those that contain carbon. (Compare to *organic chemistry*.)

input Information fed into a computer.

insulator A material that reduces or stops the flow of heat, electricity, or sound.

integrated circuit A tiny electric circuit made of components built into the surface of a silicon chip.

interference The disturbance of signals caused where two or more waves meet.

interglacial The period of warmer weather between two ice ages.

internal reflection The reflection of some of the light in a ray that passes from a *dense* to a less dense medium, e.g., from glass to air.

invertebrate An animal with no backbone.

inverter A device used to convert *direct current* into *alternating current*.

ion An *atom* or group of atoms that has lost or gained one or more *electrons* to become electrically charged.

ionic bond A chemical *bond* made when one or more electrons are passed from one atom to another, forming two *ions* of opposite charge that attract each other.

ionosphere The part of the atmosphere, from 30–250 miles (50–400 km) above the Earth's surface, that reflects radio waves.

irradiation The use of *radiation* to preserve food.

isobar A line on a weather map that connects points with the same air pressure.

isomers *Compounds* that contain the same *atoms*, but in different arrangements.

isoseism A line on a map connecting places with equal strengths of earthquake shock.

isotopes *Atoms* of the same element that have the same number of *protons* but a different number of *neutrons*.

J

jet propulsion The pushing forward of a machine by a stream of *fluid*.

jet stream Strong winds that circle the Earth about 6 miles (10 km) above the surface.

joule (J) A unit of energy.

K

Kelvin scale See *absolute scale*.

keratin A *protein* that makes up hair, horns, hoofs, nails, and feathers.

kinetic energy The energy that an object has because of its movement.

L

laccolith A mass of *igneous rock* that pushes the rock above into a dome shape.

lactose A *sugar* that occurs in milk.

larva (plural **larvae**) The second stage in the life of an insect, between the egg and the adult (e.g., a caterpillar).

laser Light Amplification by the Stimulated Emission of Radiation. A device that emits an intense beam of light.

latent heat The heat needed to change a solid to a liquid or a liquid to a gas without a change of temperature.

latitude A measure of distance from the *equator* (the poles are at 90° latitude and the equator is at 0°). **Lines of latitude** are imaginary lines drawn around the Earth, parallel with the equator.

LDR Light-dependent resistor. A *resistor* whose *resistance* increases when the amount of light that hits it increases.

leaching The extraction of a soluble material from a mixture by passing a *solvent* through the mixture.

LED Light-emitting diode. A *diode* that emits light when a current flows through it.

leucocytes White blood *cells*.

lift The upward force produced by an aircraft's wings that keeps it in the air.

ligaments Short bands of flexible tissue that connect bones together in joints.

light-year The distance traveled by light in a year. It is equal to 5.9 million, million miles (9.5 million, million km).

lignin A *polymer* in the walls of the *cells* of trees and shrubs. It makes the plant woody.

lithosphere The layer of the Earth that includes the *crust* and the upper *mantle*.

longitude A measure of distance around the Earth, measured in degrees. **Lines of longitude** are imaginary lines drawn on the Earth's surface between the poles.

longitudinal wave A wave in which the particles of the medium vibrate in the direction in which the wave is traveling.

luminosity The amount of light given out by an object, such as a *star*.

lunar eclipse When the Moon moves into the Earth's shadow so that it cannot be seen from Earth.

lymphocytes White blood *cells* that fight disease.

lymphatic system A network of tubes and small *organs* that carries a fluid called **lymph** from the body's *cells* into the bloodstream.

M

magma Liquid molten rock in the Earth's *mantle* and *crust*. It cools to form *igneous rock*.

magnetic field The area around a magnet in which its effects are felt.

magnetic poles The two points on a magnet where magnetic effect is strongest.

magnetism The invisible force of attraction or repulsion between some substances, especially iron.

magnetosphere The *magnetic field* around a *star* or *planet*.

manned maneuvering unit (MMU) A backpack used by astronauts to move about in space.

mantle A thick, *dense* layer of rock under the Earth's *crust*.

mass The amount of *matter* in an object.

matter Anything that has *mass* and occupies space.

meiosis *Cell* division that produces four *gametes*, each of which has half the number of *chromosomes* as the original cell.

melanin A brown *pigment* found in the skin, hair, and eyes.

melting point The temperature at which a solid turns to a liquid.

membrane A thin skin.

meniscus The curved upper surface of a liquid in a thin tube.

Mercalli scale The scale used to measure an earthquake's intensity.

mesopause The part of the *atmosphere* about 50 miles (80 km) above the Earth's surface. It is the upper limit of the *mesosphere*.

mesosphere The part of the *atmosphere* from about 30–50 miles (50–80 km) above the Earth's surface.

metal Any of several elements that are usually shiny solids and good *conductors* of electricity and heat.

metallic bond A *bond* formed between metal *atoms*. The metal's *electrons* flow freely around the *atoms*.

metamorphic rock Rock that has been changed by great heat and pressure underground.

metamorphosis A change of form, e.g., from a caterpillar to a *pupa*.

meteor A tiny piece of dust from space that burns up as it enters the Earth's *atmosphere*, producing a streak of light.

meteorite A piece of rock or metal from space that enters the Earth's *atmosphere* and reaches the ground without burning up.

meteorology The study of the weather.

microclimate The particular climate of a small area, e.g., a valley.

micrograph A photograph taken using a *microscope*.

microorganism A tiny *organism* that can be seen only with the aid of a *microscope*.

microscope An instrument that enlarges the image of an object through a system of lenses.

microwave A type of electromagnetic *radiation*. Microwaves are very short radio waves.

migration The movement of some animals to find food, warmth, space, or a place to breed.

mimicry Where a *species* of *plant* or animal *evolves* to look like another.

mineral A naturally occurring substance not formed from plant or animal material, e.g., rock and metal.

mineralogy The study of minerals.

mirage An optical illusion produced by light bending through layers of air with different *densities*.

miscible Describes two or more liquids that can be blended together.

mitochondrion (plural **mitochondria**) An *organelle* that produces energy for a cell.

mitosis *Cell* division where the *nucleus* divides to produce two cells, each with the same number of *chromosomes* as the parent *cell*.

mixture A substance that contains two or more *elements* or *compounds* that are not combined chemically.

modulation The transmission of a signal by changing the characteristics of a radio wave (called the carrier wave).

mole The amount of a substance that contains the same number of *atoms* or *molecules* as there are in 0.4 oz (12 g) of carbon-12.

molecule The smallest unit of an *element* or *compound*. A molecule is made up of at least two *atoms*.

momentum The tendency of a moving object to keep on moving until a force stops it. See also *inertia*.

monocotyledon A flowering plant with a single *cotyledon*. See also *dicotyledon*.

monomer A *molecule* that is the building block of a *polymer*.

monsoon A strong wind that changes direction according to the season, bringing torrential rain from the sea to areas such as India and Bangladesh.

moon A small body that *orbits* a planet.

moraine Rocks and debris that have been deposited by a glacier.

mordant dyes *Dyes* that need another chemical to be added to fix them to a fabric.

mouse A handheld device that is used to control a cursor on a computer monitor.

mutation A random change in the *chromosomes* of a *cell*.

myelin A fatty material found around nerve fibers.

myofibril Stretchy threads found in muscle cells.

N

natural selection The process by which the characteristics that help a *species* to survive are passed on to the next generation.

nebula (plural **nebulae**) A cloud of dust and gas in space.

nectar A sugary liquid found in the flowers of some plants.

nematocyst A long, coiled thread that shoots out of a stinging *cell*, e.g., in a sea anemone.

nerve Part of a network of tiny "cables" that pass messages from the body to the brain and from the brain to the muscles.

neuron A nerve *cell*.

neutralize Make an *acid* or *alkali* into a neutral solution, i.e., make it neither acid nor *alkaline*.

neutron A particle in the *nucleus* of an atom that has no electrical charge.

newton (N) A unit of force.

niche (say neesh) The position that a living thing occupies in an *ecosystem*.

nocturnal An animal that is active at night and sleeps during the day.

nuclear fission A *nuclear reaction* in which the *nucleus* of an atom splits into two smaller nuclei, releasing energy.

nuclear fusion A *nuclear reaction* in which the *nuclei* of light *atoms* (e.g., hydrogen) fuse to form a heavier nucleus, releasing energy.

nuclear reaction A change in the *nucleus* of an *atom*.

nucleolus A small, dense, round body inside the *nucleus* of a *cell*.

nucleus 1. The central part of an *atom*, made up of *protons* and *neutrons*. 2. A body found in most plant and animal *cells* that contains the genetic material of the cell.

nutrients Substances in food that are used by plants and animals for growth.

O

observatory A building from which astronomers study space.

occlusion Where a cold *front* catches up with a warm front.

ohm (Ω) A unit of electrical *resistance*.

okta scale A scale for measuring cloud cover. One okta equals one-eighth cloud cover.

omnivore An animal that eats both plants and animals.

opaque Does not let light through.

optical fibers Thin glass fibers along which light travels. They are used in communications.

orbit The path of one body, such as a *planet* or *satellite*, around another body, such as a *star* or planet.

ore A naturally occurring rock from which metals can be extracted.

organ A self-contained part of an organism with a special function, e.g., the brain and the heart.

organelle Specialized structure that forms part of a plant or animal *cell*.

organic 1. A compound containing carbon. 2. Food production without the use of chemical fertilizers.

organism A living thing consisting of one or more *cells*.

oscillator An instrument that produces an *alternating* *current* of known *frequency*.

oscilloscope An instrument that shows electrical signals on a screen.

osmosis The movement of water through a semipermeable *membrane* from a weak *solution* to a strong one.

ossify Turn to bone.

output Information from a computer.

oxidation When a substance gains oxygen or loses hydrogen or an *atom* loses *electrons* in a chemical *reaction*.

oxide A *compound* formed between an *element* and oxygen.

oxidizing agent A substance that causes the *oxidation* of another substance.

ozone An *allotrope* of oxygen found in the Earth's upper *atmosphere*, where it forms the ozone layer. A *molecule* of ozone contains three oxygen *atoms*.

P

parabolic dish A specially shaped dish that collects and concentrates waves, such as sound or *electromagnetic* waves.

parallax The apparent movement of objects against each other as the observer moves, e.g., the movement of nearby trees against background hills.

parasite An *organism* that lives on and feeds off another organism, called the host, often until it destroys the host.

particle A tiny speck of *matter*.

parthenogenesis Reproduction without mating.

pasteurization The heating of food to destroy disease-carrying bacteria.

payload The equipment, e.g., a satellite, carried into space by a spacecraft.

penumbra A partial shadow, especially around the shadow of the moon or Earth in an *eclipse*.

periodic table A table of all the *elements* arranged in order of their *atomic numbers*.

pesticide A substance used to kill pests such as insects.

petrochemical Any chemical made from petroleum or natural gas.

petrology The study of rocks.

pH A measure of acidity or alkalinity of a *solution*.

phases 1. The changes in the apparent shape of a moon or *planet* caused by the reflection of sunlight. 2. The three states in which matter occurs—solid, liquid, and gas or vapor.

pheromones Chemical substances released by an animal to communicate with another by smell.

phloem Tissue that carries food in a *plant*.

photocell An electronic device that generates electricity when light falls on it, e.g., in a solar-powered calculator.

photochromic The ability of an object, e.g., a spectacle lens, to darken or change color when exposed to light and to return to its original color when the light is removed.

photoelectric effect The emission of *electrons* from the surfaces of some substances when light hits them.

photon The particle that makes up light and other *electromagnetic radiation*.

photosphere The visible surface of the Sun, which gives out almost all of its light.

photosynthesis The method by which plants make food from water and carbon dioxide using energy from the Sun.

physics The science of the properties and nature of *matter* and the interactions of energy and matter.

physiology The study of how *organisms* work.

phytoplankton Tiny plants that are part of *plankton*.

piezoelectric effect The production of electricity by applying stress to certain *crystals*, e.g., quartz.

pigment A substance that gives color to a material, but unlike a *dye*, does not dissolve in it.

pitch The property of a sound that makes it high or low.

placebo (say plas-see-bo) An inactive substance given to a patient to compare its effects with a real drug.

planet A large body that *orbits* a star.

plankton Tiny plants and animals that live near the surface of the seas and inland waters.

plant Any *organism* that contains *chlorophyll*.

plaque (say plack) A deposit on teeth where bacteria thrive.

plasma 1. The liquid part of the blood. 2. A hot, electrically charged gas, in which the *electrons* are free from their atoms.

platelet An irregular-shaped disk in the blood that releases chemicals to coagulate the blood.

plate tectonics The study of continental drift and the spreading of the seafloor.

polar reversal The reversal of the direction of the Earth's *magnetic field*.

pollution Substances, such as waste chemicals from factories, that dirty or poison the air, land, and water.

polymer An *organic* compound that has very long molecules made up from many *monomers*.

potential difference The difference in energy between two places in an electric field or circuit.

potential energy 1. *Energy* stored for use at a later time. 2. The stored energy that a body has because of its position or state.

power The rate of change of energy.

precipitate Tiny particles of solid in a liquid, made by a chemical *reaction*.

precipitation Rain, snow, sleet, or hail.

predator An animal that lives by hunting and eating other animals.

pressure The amount of *force* pushing on a given area.

prey An animal that is hunted or eaten by another animal.

prism A block of transparent material, e.g., glass with a triangular cross-section.

program A series of coded instructions to operate a computer.

prokaryotic cell A cell with no *nucleus*.

prominence A mass of glowing gas reaching out from the surface of the Sun.

protein A substance found in foods such as meat, fish, cheese, and beans, which the body needs for growth and repair.

proton A particle in the *nucleus* of an *atom* that has a positive electric charge.

protostar A gas cloud about to turn into a *star*.

pulsar A *dense* star that emits regular pulses of *radiation*, usually radio waves.

Q

qualitative analysis Finding out what a substance is made of.

quantitative analysis Finding out how much of each ingredient is in a substance.

quantum theory The theory that light and other electromagnetic *radiation* is made up of a stream of *photons*, each carrying a certain amount of energy.

quark (say kwark) One of a group of small particles that make up *protons* and *neutrons*.

quasar (say kway-zar) The brilliant core of a young *galaxy*, probably a disk of hot gas around a massive *black hole*.

R

radar Radio detection and ranging. A way of detecting objects by sending out radio waves and collecting the "echoes."

radiation 1. An electromagnetic wave. 2. A stream of particles from a source of *radioactivity*. See also *electromagnetic spectrum*.

radioactive dating A method of estimating the age of an object by measuring how much the radioactive *isotopes* in it have decayed.

radioactivity The disintegration of the *nuclei* in an *atom*, causing *radiation* to be given off.

radiosonde A package of instruments carried into Earth's upper *atmosphere* by a weather balloon to gather meteorological information.

RAM Random access memory. Computer memory chips where information can be stored and retrieved. The information is lost when the computer is turned off.

rarefaction Areas along a longitudinal wave, such as a sound wave, where the *pressure* and *density* of the *molecules* is decreased. (Compare to *compression*.)

reactants The substances that take part in a chemical *reaction*.

reaction 1. A *force* that is the same in magnitude, but opposite in direction to another force. Every force has a reaction. 2. (Chemical reaction) Any change that alters the chemical properties of a substance or that forms a new substance.

reactivity The ability of a substance to take part in a chemical *reaction*.

real image An image formed where light rays focus. It can be seen on a screen. (Compare to *virtual image*.)

recycling Using waste material again, thus saving resources and energy.

red giant A star near the end of its life that has swelled and cooled.

red shift The stretching out of light (moving it toward the red end of the *spectrum*) from a galaxy moving away from the Earth.

reducing agent A substance that causes the *reduction* of another substance.

reduction When a substance gains hydrogen or loses oxygen, or an *atom* gains *electrons* in a chemical *reaction*.

reflection The bouncing back of light, heat, or sound from a surface.

reflex An automatic reaction to something.

refraction The change of direction of a light beam as it passes from one medium to another of different *density*, e.g., from air to glass.

refractive index The ratio of the speed of light in one medium to the speed of light in a second medium when a light ray is *refracted*.

resistance A measure of how much an electrical component opposes the flow of an electric current.

resistor A component in an electric circuit that opposes the flow of electricity.

resonance When the *vibrations* of an object become large because it is being made to vibrate at its "natural" *frequency*.

resource A substance that can be used to make or do something useful. Oil and coal are natural resources.

respiration The process in which oxygen is taken in by living things and used to break down food. Carbon dioxide and energy are produced.

resultant The overall force that results from two or more *forces* acting on an object.

reverberation Where an echo reaches a listener before the original sound has finished. It makes a sound seem to last longer.

rheostat A *resistor* whose *resistance* can be changed.

ria (say ree-a) A long, narrow sea inlet caused by the flooding of a river valley.

ribosomes Tiny spherical bodies in the *cytoplasm* of *cells*, where *proteins* are made.

Richter (say rik-tur) **scale** A scale used to measure the strength of earthquakes.

robot A machine that performs jobs automatically.

ROM Read only memory. Computer memory in which information is stored permanently, so that it can be retrieved, but not altered.

S

salt 1. A compound formed from the *reaction* of an *acid* with a base. 2. The common name for sodium chloride.

sap The liquid that flows through a *plant*, carrying food and water.

saprophyte An organism, such as a fungus or bacterium, that lives on dead or decaying matter.

satellite An object that *orbits* a planet. There are natural satellites, e.g., a moon, and artificial satellites, e.g., a craft used for reflecting radio signals.

satellite dish A dish-shaped aerial that receives signals broadcast from *satellites*.

saturation When no more *solute* can be dissolved in a *solution*.

scalar quantity A quantity that has only magnitude, e.g., *mass* and time. (Compare to *vector quantity*.)

secretion The release of specific substances from plant and animal *cells*.

sedimentary rock Rock formed when fragments of material settle on the floor of a sea or lake in layers and are cemented together over time.

seismic wave A wave that travels through the ground, e.g., from an earthquake or explosion.

seismometer A device that records vibrations in the ground, such as those caused by earthquakes.

semiconductor A substance that has a *resistance* somewhere between that of a *conductor* and an *insulator*.

semipermeable membrane A *membrane* that lets small *molecules* through, but stops large molecules.

sessile 1. Describes animals that cannot move around, e.g., sea anemones. 2. Describes plants with no stalks, e.g., algae.

sex cell See **gamete**.

sexual reproduction Reproduction that involves the combination of male and female *gametes*.

sial The *silica*- and aluminum-rich upper layer of the Earth's *crust*.

silica A white or colorless *compound* of silicon that occurs naturally, e.g., quartz.

sima The *silica*- and magnesium-rich lower layer of the Earth's *crust*.

skeleton The frame of bone and cartilage in *vertebrates* that supports the body and protects its *organs*.

smog A poisonous mixture of smoke and fog.

soft water Water free of dissolved calcium and magnesium salts.

software The *programs* used by a computer.

solar constant The amount of heat energy from the Sun that hits a certain area of the Earth's surface.

solar eclipse An *eclipse* in which the moon passes between the Earth and the Sun so that the Sun, or part of it, cannot be seen from Earth.

solar flare A sudden burst of *radiation* from the Sun.

solar panel An object that collects energy from the Sun and uses it to heat water, for example, or to produce electricity.

solar system The Sun, the *planets* that orbit the Sun, their moons, and the other bodies in space whose movements are controlled by the Sun's gravity.

solder An *alloy* (often made of tin and lead) used to join metal surfaces together.

solenoid A coil of wire that produces a *magnetic field* when an electric current flows through it.

solubility The ability of a *solute* to be dissolved.

solute The substance that dissolves in a *solvent* to form a *solution*.

solution A mixture in which the molecules of a *solute* are mixed with the molecules of a *solvent*.

solvent The substance (usually a liquid) in which a *solute* dissolves to form a *solution*.

sonar Sound navigation and ranging. A way of detecting objects and of navigating underwater by sending out sound waves.

sonic boom The loud explosive noise made by the shockwave from an object traveling faster than the speed of sound.

space age The era of space travel.

space probe An unmanned spacecraft sent from Earth to investigate the *solar system*.

space station A spacecraft, big enough for people to live and work on, which *orbits* the Earth.

species A group of *organisms* that look alike and can breed with one another.

spectroscope An optical instrument that divides the light given off by an object into its *spectrum*.

spectrum (plural **spectra**) A particular distribution of *wavelengths* and *frequencies*, e.g., the *electromagnetic spectrum*.

specular reflection When light bounces off a surface at exactly the same angle as that at which it hits.

spinal cord A bundle of nerves running from the brain down through the spine.

star A *celestial body* that releases energy from the *nuclear reactions* in its core.

starch A *polymer* found in plants that is an important part of the human diet.

static electricity An electric charge held on an object, caused by the gain or loss of *electrons*.

sterilization The removal of bacteria from an object.

stoma (plural **stomata**) A tiny opening in a plant's leaf or stem through which gases and water vapor pass.

stratigraphy The study of rock layers.

stratopause The boundary between the *stratosphere* and the *mesosphere* in the Earth's *atmosphere*.

stratosphere The part of the Earth's atmosphere between the *troposphere* and the *mesosphere*.

subatomic particle A particle smaller than an *atom*, e.g., a *proton* or a *neutron*.

sublimation When a solid turns straight from a solid into a gas without becoming a liquid first.

substance Any kind of *matter*.

succession The process of change from one *ecosystem* to another, e.g., from grassland to woodland.

sugars A group of soluble, sweet-tasting *carbohydrates*.

sunspot A cooler patch on the Sun's surface that appears darker than its surroundings.

superconductor A substance that has no electrical *resistance* at very low temperatures.

supernova (plural **supernovae**) The explosion of a very large *star* at the end of its life.

supersonic Faster than the speed of sound.

surface tension An effect that makes a liquid seem as though it has an elastic "skin." It is caused by *cohesion* between the surface *molecules*.

suspension A mixture of tiny particles of solid matter in a liquid.

synapse A junction of two nerve *cells*.

synthesis The building of larger *molecules* from smaller molecules or *atoms*.

synthesizer A musical instrument that creates sound electronically.

T

temperate Describes a climate that has mild summers and cool winters.

temperature A measure of how hot or cold something is.

terminal A connecting point on an electrical component.

thermal A current of rising hot air in the *atmosphere*.

thermistor A *resistor* whose *resistance* changes with temperature.

thermoplastic A material that can be repeatedly softened by heating and hardened by cooling.

thermoset A soft material that sets hard when heated.

thermosphere A part of the Earth's atmosphere between the *mesosphere* and the *exosphere*.

timber The quality of a musical sound.

tissue A group of similar *cells* that carries out a function, e.g., muscle tissue.

titration A method of finding the *concentration* of a solution.

trace elements Substances, such as minerals, that are needed by living things in minute amounts.

trachea The main tube that carries air to and from the lungs.

trade winds Winds that blow steadily toward the *equator* from the northeast and southeast.

transformer A device that increases or decreases *voltage*.

translocation The movement of *fluids* through a *plant*.

translucent Allows some light through, but is not "see-through."

transparent Allows nearly all light through, so that it is "see-through."

transpiration The loss of water from a plant by *evaporation*.

transverse wave A wave in which the particles of the medium vibrate at right angles to the direction of travel of the wave.

trophic level The level at which an animal is in a *food chain*.

tropical Describes a climate that is hot with periods of heavy rainfall.

tropopause The boundary between the *troposphere* and the *stratosphere*.

troposphere The lowest layer of the Earth's *atmosphere*, between the surface and the *stratosphere*. It is about 8 miles (13 km) thick on average.

turbine A machine that is made to rotate by a *fluid* in order to drive a *generator*.

typhoon The name given to a *hurricane* in the Pacific Ocean.

U

UHF Ultrahigh-*frequency* radio waves.

ultrasound Sound with a *frequency* above which the human ear can detect.

ultraviolet (UV) A type of electromagnetic *radiation* with a wavelength shorter than visible light.

umbra The dark central part of a shadow, where no light falls.

universe The whole of space and everything it contains.

upthrust The upward push on an object in a *fluid*.

V

vacuole A small *fluid*-filled sac in the *cytoplasm* of a *cell*.

vacuum A space in which there is no *matter*.

valency The number of chemical *bonds* that an *atom* can make with another atom.

vector quantity A quantity that has both magnitude and direction, e.g., a force. (Compare to *scalar quantity*.)

veins Tubes that carry blood from all parts of the body back to the heart.

velocity Speed in a particular direction.

vertebrate An animal with a spine.

VHF Very-high-*frequency* radio waves.

vibration A quick back-and-forth movement. For example, an earthquake causes the Earth to vibrate; sound causes the air to vibrate.

virtual image An image formed where light rays appear to be focused, e.g., a reflection in a mirror. (Compare to *real image*.)

virus A microscopic particle that invades *cells* to reproduce and often cause disease.

viscosity A measure of how easily a substance flows.

vitamin An *organic* compound found in foods that is essential for good health.

volt The unit of *potential difference*.

voltaic cell See *cell*.

voltmeter or **voltammeter** A device used to measure *potential difference*.

volume 1. The space occupied by *matter*. 2. The loudness of a sound.

vulcanization The hardening of rubber by heating it with sulfur.

W

waterspout A column of water sucked up by a tornado moving over the sea.

watt (W) A unit of power (1 watt = 1 *joule* per second).

wavelength The distance between the crest of one wave and the crest of the next.

weight The force with which a *mass* is pulled toward the center of the Earth.

Westerlies Major winds blowing from the west.

whirlwind A column of air spinning rapidly in a funnel shape over land or water.

white dwarf The small, *dense* remains of a dead *star*.

WMO World Meteorological Organization.

work The energy transferred when a *force* moves an object or changes its shape.

X

X-ray A type of electromagnetic *radiation* with a *wavelength* shorter than *ultraviolet radiation*.

xylem (say zy-lem) The tissue that carries water through a plant.

Z

zeolite A natural or synthetic *compound* with an open structure that can act as a *catalyst* or a filter for individual *molecules*.

zeugen A ridge of hard rock formed by *erosion*.

zodiac The 12 *constellations* that are seen in the sky.

zooplankton The tiny, often microscopic, animals in the sea that form part of *plankton*.

INDEX

435

PICTURE SOURCES

The publisher would like to thank the following for their kind permission to reproduce their photographs:

(Key: a-above; b-below/bottom; c-centre; l-left; r-right; t-top)

Alamy Images/Judith Collins 162br; Comstock Images 173tr; Sami Sarkis 269bc; Stockbyte Platinum 14br; Hugh Threlfall 173bl
Albright & Wilson 43cl
Allsport 141bl/Gray Mortimer 116br, 346bc
Ardea 124tr, 127tl, 136bl/Anthony & Elizabeth Bomford 184bl
Art Directors & TRIP/Helene Rogers 173cr, 173crb, 174bl, 174br; Gerry Short 208c
Aspect Picture Library/Mike Wells 134tr
Associated Press 199bl
Aviation Photographers International/Jeremy Flack 128tr

BASF 90r
BBC Radiophonic Workshop/David Darby 189tr
Belkin.com 174tr
Biofotos/Heather Angel 341cr, 351tr, 357bl
Biofoto Associates 35cl, 198c & cr, 352bc
Biosphere Associates 348tr
BOC Ltd. 42br
Bodleian Library, Oxford 17bl
Bridgeman Art Library 14cl, 282bl, 312bc/Bodleian Library, Oxford, Ms Add.A.287.fol.78r, 31tl; British Museum, London 64tc; Christie's, London 64br; Louvre, Paris 63bc
British Alcan Aluminium plc. 87tl, 87bl
British Coal 96cl
Paul Brierley 37bc, 109tr, 191cl
British Museum/Peter Hayman 27bl, 81cl
Bruel & Kjaer 181br
Bubbles 105r/Jacqui Farrow 140br

Cambridge Botanic Gardens 140tl
Cambridge University Press, Star Atlas 2000.0 by Wil Tirion 282br
Casio UK Ltd 133tc
Ciba Geigy Plastics 106tc
Cleanair Transport 151br
Bruce Coleman 306tl, 316cl, 329cb, 336b/Bartlett 331cb; Stephen Bond 314crb; Jane Burton 324clb, 347bl, 356c, 363bl, 380cl; Neville Coleman 52cr; Eric Crichton clb; Gerald Cubitt 393cr, 395cl; Peter Davey 336clb; A.J.Deane 203tr; Jeff Foott 355bc, 373bl, 381bl, 387cr; CB & DW Frith 361bc; Francisco Futil 399br; J.S.Grove 331bc; Udo Hirsch 328bc; Carol Hughes 75br, 390br; Johnny Johnson 154cr; Steven C. Kaufman 397bl; Frans Lanting 399bl; Leonard Lee Rue 380cr; L.C.Marigo 334cb, 374bl; Norman Myers 374tr; C. Martin Pampaloni 373tr; Goetz D.Plage 106tl; Fritz Prenzel 335cl; Andrew Purcell 324cb; Timm Rautert 399cr; Marie Read 379tl; Hans Reinhard 342br, 381bc; Carl Roessler 325cb; Frieder Sauer 311tlc & tcr, 320tr, 257cr, 343bc, 363cl; Nancy Sefton 320cra; Kim Taylor 363c, 366tr, 366c, 367cr; Michel Viard 317c; Paul R.Wilkinson 42cl; Rod Williams 389tr; Conrad Wottle 336c; J.T.Wright 336cr
Colorific!/T.Spencer 86tr; Ann Purcell 153tr; Carl Purcell 195cb
Colorsport 118c, 120cl, 141bl
Copper Development Association 86cl
Corbis Kim Kyung-Hoon 235cl; Vincent Laforet 258t
Andy Crawford & Dave King 207br

Derby Museums & Art Gallery 60bl
Deutsches Museum, Munich 90tc & cl

E.T. Archive 65tl, 100br
Mary Evans Picture Library 25tl, 28bl, 30bl, 55tl, 61tl, 71b, 74bl, 81b, 86cr, 108t, 188bl, 193tr, 201bc & crb, 206cl, 295tl, 297tr, 305bl, 308cr, 324cr, 337bl, 380bl

Barry Finch Photography 89bl, 107bl & cl
Martyn Foote 130cl, 249bl, 260cl, 260br, 262cr, 262cr, 262br
Geoscience Features 30cl, 39c, 43c, 46tr, 178bc
Getty Images/Andreas Pollok 162c; Science Faction 48cla
Jane Goodall Institute 378bl
Dr. Julian Goodfellow, Birkbeck College 30bc
Greenpeace/Morgan 400cr
Derek Hall 364c
Robert Harding Picture Library 23tl, 35bl, 72cla & cl, 87br, 113t, 114br, 117bc, 122b, 179cr, 192tl, 201tl/Walter Rawlings 113cr
Courtesy of Harvard University Archives 278bl
Stuart Hildred 149br
Michael Holford 80r, 138tr
Holt Studios International/Nigel Cattlin 90b, 91bl; Primrose Peacock 71cr
Hulton-Deutsch Collection 32br, 47bl, 57tl, 104cr, 115tr, 121cr, 285tl, 351br, 369bl
Henry Huntington Library 276tl
Hutchison Library/Edward Parker 395cr; Philip Wolmoth 96bl

IBM Research Laboratory, Zurich 149bl
ICI Katalco 56cr
The Image Bank 48tr, 74c/Anthony A. Boccaccio 44br; Paolo Curto 52tr; Arthur D'Arazieu 43tr; Jon Davison/Stockphotos 88tr; Mel Digiacomo 199tr; Grant V. Faint 113bl, 193cl, 197; Nicholas Foster 46c; Gregory Heisler 93bl; Laurence Hughes 343tl; Don Landwehrle 177tr; David de Lossy 99bl; Leo Mason 43bl; Eric Meola 140c, 140cr; J.Ramey/Stockphotos 84tl; Co. Rentmeester 337t; Al Satterwhite 44tl; Erik Leigh Simmons 92cl; Paul Trummer 55bl; Pete Turner 103tr; Anne van der Vaeren 37c; Hans Wendler 52cl; Ernst Wrba 130br
Institute of Agricultural History & Museum of English Rural Life, University of Reading 96tr

Jet Propulsion Laboratory 294bl & crb

Kobal Collection 176tl

Frank Lane Picture Agency 322cr/David T. Grewc 367tl; Eric & David Hosking 343cr, 360bc; Steve McCutcheon 205tc, 205tr, 383bc; F.Polking 121bl; John Tinning 391bl; D.P.Wilson 386tl
London Transport Museum 124b
Lowell Observatory 289 tr & cra

Mansell Collection 290clb, 315crb, 323bc
John Marmaras/Du Pont 101bl
Memtek International 182c

NASA 56bc, 59tc, 70cl, 97bl, 177br, 258tr, cr, crb, & br; 277clb, 284c & tr, 286br & cl, 287cr, 288tr, c & crb, 289crb, 291c, crb, br & bc, 292cr, cb, bc & ca, 293c, & bl, 294cb, 298c, clb, crb & crb, 299tl, 301cl & cr, 302tl, cr, cl, bl, & br, 303cra, cl & bl, 304tl, bl & crb, /John Frassanito and associates 304c; MSFC 273bc/JPL 295cl
NASA/JPL/Caltech 37cl, 176bl, 293bc, 293br, 300tr

NHPA 321crb/ANT 321cr, 332clb, 333cb, 335crb br, 395tc; ANT Kelvin Aitkin 327bl; Anthony Bannister 314bc, 345tr; G.I.Bernard 21tr; Laurie Campbell 356tr; James Carmichael Jnr.325cb; Stephen Dalton 341cr, 342cl, 344bc, 356cr, 376tr; R.J.Erwin 400cl; Stephen Krasemann 398bl; Michael Leach 318bl; Tsueneo Nakamura 327cl; Peter Parks 306cr; Otto Rogge 391bc; Carl Roessler 325cb; Kevin Schafer 395bc; Philippa Scott 393tl, 341tl; John Shaw 332bl, 335bc; Karl Smith 332clb; Martin Wendler 323cl
National Gallery 277cra
National Medical Slide Bank 88bl, 192tr, 204tr
Nature Photographers 370tl/Christopher Grey-Wilson 354cr; Richard Mearns 396br; Paul Sterry 350bc, 378br, 381cl, 384br

Omega 118cl
Oxford Scientific Films 19cr, 132c, 134bl, 201cl, 201bl, 305cb, 326cl, 327tr, 341tl/Doug Allan 51t; Eyal Bartov 352br; Fred Bavendam 102tr; Stuart Bebb 340tl; G.I.Bernard 308crb, 323cr; Deni Brown 78bc; Cambridge Productions Ltd. 68cr; N.M.Collins 345tl; Jal Cooke 320crb; Gilbert S.Grant 385br; Rudi Kuiter 354bl; Leonard Lee 344tl; London Scientific Films 50bl; Sean Morris 323crb; Stan Osolinski 364br; Richard Packwood 315bc; Peter Parks 327tr; Ronald Toms 366cr; Babs & Bert Wells 319crb; Kim Westerskov 151cr; David Wright 70b

Panos Pictures/Ron Gining 87cl
Photolibrary/Phototake 15cr
Photos Horticultural 342cr
Pictor International 54tl
Planet Earth Pictures 328crb, 371cr, 389bl/Sean Avery 94b; Gary Bell 387tc; Richard Coomber 351cr; Walter Deas 363cr; J.Duncan 387cb; Wayne Harris 357cl; Robert Hessler 386bl; Chris Huxley 357cr; P.Losse 347br; Richard Matthews 388bcr; Christian Petron 369bc; Mike Potts 385tr; Flip Schulke 387tl; Jonathan Scott 381tl, 393bl; Peter Stephenson 61bl; James D.Watt 185cr; Norbert Wu 353br
Popperfoto 191c
Premaphotos Wildlife/K.G.Preston-Mafham 369br

QA Photos 179tl, 181c
Quadrant Picture Library 148bc

Redferns/David Redfern 188c
Rentokil 315cr
Rex Features 47bc, 55cl & br/P.Villard 42tr; 65br
Rockwell International 111r
Roger-Viollet 107b
Rolls Royce plc. 88r
Ann Ronan at Image Select 34tr, 74bc, 96tc, 96br, 145br, 187cl, 208bc, 277crb, 287clb, 310cr
Royal Astronomical Society Library 291tl, 292cr, 296cl

St.Paul's School 364bl
Santapod Dragways 119c
Peter Saunders 113cr
Scala/Biblioteca Nationale 273cl
Scaled Composites LLC 299br
Science Museum 194cl
Science Photo Library 37br, 48bl, 50br, 54cr, 63tl, 84tr, 102bl, 106br, 137br, 138br, 144cr, 179bl, 180tr, 192bl, 194cbr, 274crb, 282tl, 305tr, 312tr, 313c & bc, 321bc, 346bl, 349bl, 354tr, 355bl, 365cl, / Michael Abbey 339c; Doug Allan 18tr; Jodrell Bank crb; Alex Bartel 112bl; Biofoto Associates 61cr; Dr.Jeremy Burgess 29cra, 70tl, 71bc & cl, 75c,

446